The Enterprise of Living
Growth and Organization in Personality

Robert W. White
Harvard University

Holt, Rinehart and Winston, Inc.
New York Chicago San Francisco Atlanta
Dallas Montreal Toronto London Sydney

Excerpts from *Opinions and Personality* (1956) by M. B. Smith, J. S. Bruner, and R. W. White reprinted with permission of John Wiley & Sons, Inc.

Excerpts from *The Study of Lives* (1963), ed. R. W. White reprinted with permission of Atherton Press.

Figure 1 adapted from E. W. Schaefer, "A Circumplex Model for Maternal Behavior," *Journal of Abnormal and Social Psychology,* 1959, 59, 232. Used with permission of the author and the American Psychological Association.

Excerpt reprinted with permission of Coward-McCann, from *The Little Locksmith* by K. B. Hathaway. Copyright © 1943 by Coward-McCann, Inc. Renewed copyright 1971 by Warren H. Butler.

Excerpts from *The Widening World of Childhood* by L. B. Murphy reprinted with permission of the author and publisher. © 1962 by Basic Books, Inc., Publishers, New York.

Excerpts from *Explorations in Personality* (1938) by H. A. Murray. © 1938 by Oxford University Press. Renewed 1966 by H. A. Murray. Reprinted with permission of Oxford University Press.

Excerpts from "Identity and the Life Cycle," *Psychological Issues,* 1959, 1, 55–56, by E. Erikson reprinted with permission of the author and International Universities Press.

Excerpt from *Childhood and Society* by E. Erikson. By permission of the author and W. W. Norton & Co., Inc. Copyright © 1950 by W. W. Norton & Co., Inc.

Excerpt from "New Light on the Honeymoon," *Human Relations,* 1964, 17, 33–56, by R. Rapoport and R. N. Rapoport reprinted with permission of the authors and Plenum Publishing Corp.

Reprinted with permission of The Macmillan Company from *Makers of Modern England* by Giovanni Costigan. Copyright © 1967 by The Macmillan Company.

Preface

Prospective readers of a book on personality are entitled to know in advance what the author had in mind in choosing his way of writing about the subject. This book is intended primarily for readers who have not made a systematic study of personality, however much they may have picked up about it in the course of living. Their interests are best met, it seems to me, by a broad, live, comprehensive description that is as systematic as the subject matter permits.

The study of personality starts from the observation of individual lives. The initial object of curiosity is the whole person in all the complexity of his past learnings, present interactions, and future plans. However much the focus must be narrowed when specific investigations are undertaken, it is important not to lose the connection with the whole. Not all readers who are drawn to the study of personality will have the intention of going further and specializing in the subject. For this audience a broad descriptive treatment, rather than one that is highly theoretical or technical, seems most likely to be illuminating and valuable. It is my belief, however, that this is also the most appropriate first step for future specialists. Whether they are attracted by clinical work, social service, the development of theory, or the enlargement of knowledge through scientific investigation, the most important prerequisite is to have a mind well furnished with comprehensive impressions and ideas about personality in its wholeness and in its growth.

Because clinical work has been such an important source of information, we are currently more adept at explaining how personality comes to grief than at understanding its natural and often relatively successful growth. Dealing constantly with blockages in growth, clinicians

iii

naturally created a portrait that emphasized helplessness, inhibition, and the use of defense mechanisms that distorted further learning. Ideas were developed about the devastating consequences of events in early childhood and the crushing effects of parental training. But these ideas were then shaken by the discovery of apparently equal horrors in the lives of normal people. What is needed to account for such diverse outcomes is a conception of development that recognizes human versatility in dealing with the inevitable problems of living. Of especial relevance are the concepts of efficacy, sense of competence, cognitive organization, and strategies of adaptation, to which I have given a prominent place in this book. Clinical work itself stands to benefit by more explicit ideas about the normal course of growth.

What I have tried to do, then, is to lay a descriptive foundation for the study of personality. Anyone who has tried this will know that it entails great problems with respect to order of presentation. Personality cannot be conceptualized as anything less than a complex system with many simultaneous interactions both internal and external. This suggests, however, that we should properly talk about everything at once; there is something unavoidably arbitrary about separating topics to be taken up one at a time. It may be felt that by beginning with several chapters on the social background of personality, especially the family viewed as a social system, I have sacrificed the chance to organize the account around an orderly chronology. But it has been my experience as a teacher that in this case much is lost by beginning at the beginning. Readers can remember nothing about their relations with their mothers during the first year of life; no starting point could be better calculated to make the whole subject remote and abstract. The family is a different matter. Relations with parents and siblings are often a still lively problem to which strong feelings are attached, and memories of the history are likely to be green. To begin here is to start where personal experience is most readily mobilized.

This reason for choosing a starting point reflects my belief that the study of personality should indeed be a personal experience rather than a merely intellectual encounter with a realm of knowledge. To keep this subject at a distance from oneself, to treat the people studied as if they were a foreign breed, puts serious obstacles in the way of understanding. We all have personalities. Serious students are likely to encounter themselves on a number of occasions in the pages that follow. They should take this as a good sign. Certain of our own experiences are indispensable for understanding how it is with others, and progress can be assured only if the reader is willing to allow himself to be in the field of observation.

What can be learned from this book will be multiplied if readers try their own hands at studying life histories. In the college course from which the book evolved, part of the students' work consisted of examining the original materials of personality studies—interviews, documents, test records, and experimental protocols—presented without comment or interpretation. Well-known figures from history and literature, especially those who had ventured to write autobiographies, also served the purpose of this educational program. To struggle to organize and find meaning in the known bits and pieces of a person's life is ten times better than just reading a book about it. This book can provide a useful framework for such endeavors. Its contents can be used as an outline for the study of particular personalities. These are the things, awesomely numerous as they are, that one would like to find out if one were attempting to reach a relatively full understanding of another person's life. But no book can take the place of the personal effort at understanding that comes from working with the materials of actual lives.

So much time has gone by since I became a student of personality that it has become impossible to acknowledge my huge accumulated indebtedness to others. A complete list would start with Donald MacKinnon, who converted me from the history of nations to the history of individual lives, and would indicate my long and rich apprenticeships with Henry Murray and Gordon Allport. Too numerous to untangle, however, are my debts from the ensuing years of work in which colleagues and students always had a large part, years during which as a teacher I had the benefit of being educated by those I was teaching. But I should like to thank explicitly, though anonymously, those students and research subjects who have allowed excerpts from their lives to appear in this book, and I am grateful to Lawrence McCready and James Rippe for the use of case material they collected. Of great help during the writing was Margaret M. Riggs, who read the first version of each chapter, criticized the contents freely, and thus improved substantially the quality of the final product.

ROBERT W. WHITE

Contents

1 Sources of Knowledge about Personality

In a period of history marked by an unparalleled rate of change in the conditions of life, we human beings are more than ever before a puzzle to ourselves. In spite of amazing technological progress, presumably aimed at making existence more secure, convenient, and satisfying, we carry a heavy load of discontents. Living in closer contact and communication with other people, we continue to complain about loneliness. Desiring warmth in human relations, we often have trouble evoking it from others and mustering it in ourselves. Seeking freedom to broaden and deepen our experience, we feel hemmed in by conventional expectations and by our own needs for support and approval. Wanting to profit from expanded educational opportunities, we may be tripped up by doubt about their relevance and by the discomfort of sustained application. The search for a meaningful place in the world becomes ever more difficult as organizations grow larger and more impersonal. Yet if we aspire to improve the current social order, we are apt to be discouraged by the slow progress of cooperative endeavors and the fitful enthusiasm of participants. And we are certainly in no position to feel satisfied with our accomplishments in the way of peace and social justice. With justification we continue to be puzzled, frustrated, at times harrowed by our failure to live as we are convinced it might be possible to live.

The understanding of these widespread human problems has to be approached from many directions. One of these is a field of inquiry we shall call *the study of personality*. Like other words that have been battered by centuries of use, "personality" does not mean the same thing to all hearers. It is sometimes used to signify superficial qualities, like affability, liveliness in company, or an air of businesslike efficiency, that can be put on as occasion demands. In careful use, however, it means something more rooted and more inclusive; in the words of one dictionary, "that which distinguishes and characterizes a person." This is the sense in which the term is used in this book.

As a field of study, personality rests today on the growing body of knowledge provided by the behavioral sciences. It presupposes general laws or principles of development that apply to everyone. A person becomes what he is largely through experience, and experience signifies the operation of lawful learning processes. When interest is centered upon personality, however, the object of study is not only the lawful processes that apply to everyone but also their unique outcome under the particular circumstances of the individual case. "It is convenient to define personality," writes Gardner Murphy, "as that which makes a person distinctively himself; it is equivalent, then, to individuality."[1] In a similar vein was Gordon Allport's carefully wrought definition: "Personality is the dynamic organization within the individual of those psychophysical systems that determine his unique adjustments to his environment."[2] As unique adjustments are constantly being evolved and modified, and as their dynamic organization must likewise be a continuing process, the study of personality can hardly avoid being a study of the course of life. Henry Murray proposed that this discipline must be capable of dealing with "the life history of a single man as a unit." It must have the goal of constructing "a scheme of concepts for portraying the entire course of individual development, and thus provide a framework into which any single episode—natural or experimental—may be fitted."[3] The study of personality thus includes the time dimension and is most perfectly represented in the study of whole lives in all their individuality.

In view of the motives that inspire an interest in personality, it is not surprising that individuality should be the central theme. Many people are drawn to the subject by the legitimate hope that it will give them a better understanding of themselves. Many are attracted by the prospect of increasing their insight into the people who make up their immediate personal world, thus improving the possibility of a satisfying life together. Others practice, or think of practicing, vocations in which working with people is of central importance, such as teaching, personnel management, guidance, counseling, nursing, social work, or psychotherapy. For them the study of personality is obviously instrumental to professional competence. It is an asset also in other occupations in which human interactions are of substantial importance.

All of these purposes require an understanding of individuality. They are not sufficiently served by knowledge of general laws of behavior or by information about how the average person is likely to act. Knowledge of oneself, one's parents, one's brothers and sisters, one's friends, one's spouse,

[1] G. Murphy, quoted in E. Norbeck, D. Price-Williams, and W. M. McCord, eds., *The Study of Personality: An Interdisciplinary Appraisal* (New York: Holt, Rinehart and Winston, Inc., 1968), p. 15.

[2] G. W. Allport, *Personality: A Psychological Interpretation* (New York: Holt, Rinehart and Winston, Inc., 1937), p. 48.

[3] H. A. Murray, *Explorations in Personality* (New York and London: Oxford University Press, 1938), pp. 3, 4.

one's children, and one's associates at work is always a question of understanding individual persons who are weaving the pattern of their lives in their own way amidst their own particular circumstances. Deciding what should be done for people who ask for guidance likewise calls for grasping the particularities of each case and each situation. Important as it is that common processes be understood and general laws established, the understanding of the individual case continues to occupy the focus of interest.

Understanding the particulars in a given case means something more than setting them down in a list. The relations among them are not additive but are the result of the "dynamic organization" that Allport included in his definition. To say that a person is the sum of his experiences or the tally of his traits is to overlook the important fact that in order to function in actual life he has got to maintain some degree of order and pattern in himself, some system of priorities amongst his various tendencies, which will allow behavior to go forward instead of being stuck in constant conflict. One of the most exacting tasks in studying personality is to lay hold of individual organization.

It may seem onerous to be charged with the double task of grasping general principles and elucidating individual organization, but this is the price that must be paid for choosing personality as the object of study.

The Study of Lives

Interest in personality is nothing new. It is not a product of modern times or a consequence of recent advances in biological, medical, and social science. It is an ancient human concern that undoubtedly goes much further back than Socrates, who explicitly advised that we should know ourselves and examine our lives. If we imagine a student of personality fifteen hundred years ago, in the 470s, before the Dark Ages and long before the advent of modern science, our first thought might be that he would find very few sources of information. Yet in fact he could learn a good deal from existing literature. To mention only a few monuments, he could consult Plato and Aristotle on such subjects as the education of the young and man's nature as a political animal. He could look to Hippocrates and Galen for a conception of individual differences in temperament that has not entirely lost its significance today. He could read in the *Characters* of Theophrastus thirty illuminating portraits of types of personality organized around dominant traits. For life histories he could turn to Plutarch, whose *Parallel Lives* contains forty-six biographies of great Greeks and Romans. Here he would find an early attempt at comparative case studies, each Greek being paired with a Roman distinguished in the same field, for instance the generals Alexander and Caesar and the orators Demosthenes and Cicero. He would also have available the *Confessions* of St. Augustine, which gives a vivid picture especially of the turmoils of adolescence. A book on personality written from such sources might lack system, but it would be far from thin with respect to insights.

Biography

The complete description of a person would amount to nothing less than a full biography. One of the oldest and best sources of information about personality is the vast storehouse of biographical literature. Authors and readers of this literature are of course not solely interested in the making of individual personalities. Biography is often undertaken for the purposes of describing a person's accomplishments, re-creating his adventures, or shedding light on the historical period and the social circles in which he lived. Thus the information of greatest interest to a student of personality often is not well represented; in the case of historical figures it may already be lost. But many biographers have been interested in the problem of how their subject came to be what he was, and in recent times a good deal more effort has been put into discovering relevant facts of early development and personal life. Some biographies are even proclaimed to be psychological in intent, treating their subjects as problems in the growth and organization of personality. For the student of personality, biography indeed contains much ore to be mined.

The outstanding monument of biography in the English language is James Boswell's *The Life of Samuel Johnson, L.L.D*, published in 1791. Having found in Johnson a "great and good man" who completely commanded his interest and respect, Boswell set himself the goal of showing him "more completely than any man who has ever yet lived." It is instructive to examine what he considered necessary to this end. Because of the conversational form in which he cast large parts of the biography, he has been incorrectly pictured as a faithful stenographer who simply took down the words that fell from the great man's lips. Boswell was in fact a much more active student of his subject. As closely as possible he kept a daily journal of his meetings with Johnson, making good use of an extraordinary memory for details and speech which made it possible to "commit to paper the exuberant variety of [Johnson's] wisdom and wit." Boswell described the conversations in their settings, including who was present and what expressions, gestures, and emotions they showed. "To see Dr. Johnson in any new situation," Boswell wrote, "is always an interesting object to me," and to satisfy this interest he introduced topics of conversation even at the risk of rebuffs and insults; furthermore, he devised and managed a variety of meetings between Johnson and other people which seemed likely to add grist to the mill—an anticipation of the experimental method. In addition he collected letters, manuscripts, and anecdotes, inviting various people of Johnson's acquaintance to contribute their impressions, well aware that to some of them he might have shown quite a different side. It is improbable that Boswell in the eighteenth century would have stopped to consider whether or not he was a scientist, but his painstaking methods of observation splendidly exemplify the scientific spirit.[4]

---

[4] This account of Boswell's methods and the quotations from various of his writings are drawn from P. A. W. Collins, *James Boswell* (London: Longmans, Green & Co., Ltd., 1956.)

At the end of his tremendous and detailed biography, Boswell felt constrained to deal somehow with the problem of organization. "It may be expected," he wrote, "that I should collect into one view the capital and distinguishing features of this extraordinary man." Knowing his subject so well, Boswell found this task difficult. "Man is, in general, made up of contradictory qualities; and these will ever show themselves in strange succession. . . . At different times, he seemed a different man, in some respects." Numerous strange successions are then described—superstition and critical reason, prejudice and fairness, irritability and benevolence, melancholy and wit—so that one wonders whether or not any capital features are going to emerge. Boswell finally arrives at two persistent patterns. One of these had to do with a cluster of central values. Johnson, he said, was "steady and inflexible in maintaining the obligations of religion and morality," wherefore in all his writings "he earnestly inculcated what appeared to him to be the truth; his piety being constant, and the ruling principle of all his conduct." The other was a quality of mind described as follows:

> But his superiority over other learned men consisted chiefly in what may be called the art of thinking, the art of using his mind; a certain continual power of seizing the useful substance of all that he knew, and exhibiting it in a clear and forcible manner; so that knowledge, which we often see to be no better than lumber in men of dull understanding, was, in him, true, evident, and actual wisdom.[5]

Autobiography

In comparison with biography, writing the story of one's own life has a good many disadvantages. However impartially the author may hope to portray himself, he can never be a detached observer. There are many motives for writing an autobiography, but it is virtually impossible to eliminate elements of self-justification, of improving the self-picture, and of enhancing the importance of one's life. But the very fact that author and subject are the same makes autobiography in one respect a unique source of information: it can tell what the life story looked like from the inside, how it felt, how it was related to aspirations, plans, fantasies, daydreams, and the play of moods. Boswell kept journals on Johnson but he also kept journals on himself for the purpose of correcting and stabilizing his own character. These journals, which came to light only many years after their author's death, provide a way of comparing what it means to write about another person's life and to write about one's own.

One of the great monuments of autobiography is *The Confessions of Jean-Jacques Rousseau*, written between 1768 and 1770. Rousseau's place in history is a large one: his writings had a profound effect on social theory, on the thinking of those leaders who carried forward the French and American

---

[5] These quotations are from *Boswell's Life of Johnson*, Vol. 4, ed. G. B. Hill (Oxford: Clarendon Press, 1887), pp. 424–429.

Revolutions, on the history of education, and on the course of romantic literature. One might surmise that a man of such influence, far greater in the end than that of Samuel Johnson, would exhibit remarkably steadfast purpose and organized intellectual power. The autobiography tells a different story. Rousseau describes a mind that was only barely capable of steady application. So wandering was his attention that even when seriously trying to learn something, he could stick to it for only half an hour at a time. Continuity in writing came only when he was surcharged with emotion, and even then his attempts to achieve expression were agonizingly disorganized. Furthermore, the external course of his life was much at the mercy of impulse; he describes several occasions when the fancy of the moment made momentous decisions for him. It is impossible to obtain any understanding of Rousseau's life without insight into the sweep of his feelings, his vast and glowing daydreams, his self-reproaches and convictions of inferiority, and the tortured combination of attraction and suspicion that haunted his relations with the upper levels of Parisian society. This crucial information would be inferred by outside observers with poor success. It is the sort of thing of which only the subject himself, if he is so disposed, can give a valid report.[6]

Much contemporary interest has been aroused by *The Autobiography of Malcolm X*, life story of a man who was leader for a time of the Black Muslims in New York and afterwards a black leader in his own right. The career of this remarkably gifted and influential man, cut short by assassination before his fortieth birthday, could be seen from the outside as a series of inconsistent and disjointed steps that perhaps betokened opportunism and mere love of power. The consecutive meaning of Malcolm X's actions and the distinguishing features of his personality become clear only from the inside story. At the age of 15 he is transformed from a popular athlete and class officer in a mainly white Michigan high school into a rebellious, violent youth in Boston's ghetto who rejects even the black middle class. This sequence becomes intelligible when we learn of the searing wound to self-respect inflicted by a teacher who advised him to reduce his vocational aspirations and choose a humble job at which blacks might be acceptable. Later he is transformed from Malcolm Little, a tough, cynical racketeer on the streets of Harlem, respecting no man, into Malcolm X, a minister of the Nation of Islam, enormously deferential toward its leader Elijah Muhammad and gladly accepting its controlled, austere, dignified pattern of life. This, too, is intelligible when we understand that Elijah Muhammad's doctrines enabled Malcolm X to feel, for the first time since high school, that he was a noble member of the human race with a significant mission to perform. The inner meaning, the unique contribution of autobiography, supplies the key indispensable to this particular life story.[7]

Obviously the understanding of a life will be most comprehensive when sources of information include both biography and autobiography. For

---

[6] J. J. Rousseau, *The Confessions of Jean-Jacques Rousseau* (New York: The Modern Library, Inc., n.d.).

[7] *The Autobiography of Malcolm X* (New York: Grove Press, Inc., 1965).

example, Rousseau's life and writings have become a field of research in themselves. His *Confessions* were written fairly late in life, when suspicion of hostile motives in others had begun to obsess him to an extent that suggests mental unbalance. Under these circumstances it cannot be supposed that he reported all facts objectively, and the biographer's task becomes one of checking from other sources and seeking the reasons for discrepancy.[8]

Naturalistic Observation

Much has been learned about personality simply from shrewd observation of the human scene. The outstanding practitioners of naturalistic description have generally been animated by an interest in some particular aspect of human behavior, which they pick out with a penetrating eye in a large number of situations. Prominent among these objects of curiosity are (1) the strategic aspects of behavior and (2) individual differences in types of mind.

Behavior as Strategy

The idea that human behavior can be a planned strategy designed to achieve certain effects upon one's surroundings was expressed with unadorned clarity in *The Prince* by Niccolo Machiavelli, who lived from 1469 to 1527. In this work, written at a time when his native Italy was divided into a large number of independent princedoms, Machiavelli assembled a compendium of advice to princes on how to keep themselves in power. Because the theme is limited to power this book has come to be considered a monument of crafty, calculating, unscrupulous manipulation. Machiavelli was perhaps not quite as bad as he has been painted; he believed that it is well even for a prince to be "merciful, faithful, humane, religious, and upright." But experience had taught him—"we see from what has happened in our own days"—that cunning dishonesty was often successful, even essential, in the consolidation of power. A prince is therefore advised to maintain the appearance of the virtues while watching the realities of power: "he ought not to quit good courses if he can help it, but should know how to follow evil if he must." Machiavelli certainly believed in maintaining a public image, as we call it today, and his precepts for princes require only minor changes to be suitable for candidates for office in political democracies. Easily overlooked is the impressive scholarship that underlies his treatise. His recommendations rest upon the broad basis of actual political life not only in his own times but earlier in the history of the Mediterranean world. *The Prince* is a considerable feat in the naturalistic description of the striving for political power.[9]

The idea of behavior as strategy was developed in an important way by Friedrich Engels and Karl Marx in the middle of the nineteenth century.

[8] A recent work on the subject is W. H. Blanchard, *Rousseau and the Spirit of Revolt: A Psychological Study* (Ann Arbor: University of Michigan Press, 1967).

[9] Quotations are from N. Machiavelli, *The Prince*, 3d ed., trans. N. H. Hill (Oxford: Clarendon Press, 1913).

Believing that the course of history and the forms of human society are largely determined by the necessities of economic production and by the class divisions that result, these writers proposed that the whole realm of ideas be re-examined as an unwitting expression of class interests. They applied this interpretation to political, religious, philosophical, and even scientific thought, but especially to moral values. "Men consciously or unconsciously derive their moral ideas in the last resort from the practical relations on which their class position is based—from the economic relations in which they carry on production and exchange." Because society "has hitherto moved in class antagonisms, morality was always a class morality: it has either justified the domination and interests of the ruling class, or, as soon as the oppressed class has become powerful enough, it has represented the revolt against this domination and the future interests of the oppressed." Thus, Marx and Engels saw ideas and values as a superstructure built on an economic base, as an *ideology* serving material self-interest. Virtues such as devotion to work, thrift, self-reliance, planning for the future, and fidelity to contracts were clearly appropriate to bourgeois existence but had small meaning for the proletariat. Ideals of tranquillity and the maintaining of law and order prevented disruption of the bourgeois way of life by keeping the proletariat in its place; and religion, as Engels and Marx saw it, emphasizing better things not here but in a future life, could easily be a soporific for the masses.[10]

The theme that ideas are expressions of human—all-too-human—needs was carried forward by the German philosopher Friedrich Nietzsche toward the end of the nineteenth century. Interested in the genealogy of morals—the phrase became the title of one of his works—Nietzsche developed a detailed description of what he called herd morality. "My teaching is this," he wrote, "that the herd seeks to maintain and preserve one type of man, and that it defends itself on two sides—that is to say, against those which are decadents from its ranks (criminals, etc.), and against those who rise superior to its dead level." The origin of morality lies in the instincts of the herd, the need for gregarious security. The man who lives by this code "has no independent value"; he must exhibit the virtues of the herd, and he "*must* not be an individual." Especially galling to Nietzsche was the herd's hatred for superior members of the species, based on "the suspense and the fear to which the great innovating man gives rise." Herd virtues such as "industry, modesty, benevolence, temperance, are just so many *obstacles* in the way of *sovereign sentiments*, of great *ingenuity*, of an heroic purpose, of noble existence for one's self." In addition to the security it provides, herd morality is powered by hatred. Referring to it often as slave morality, Nietzsche saw it as heavily colored by the resentment of those who felt themselves to be disadvantaged. It was therefore necessarily dominated by images of evil, and it generated feelings of guilt that crippled the free flowering of personality.[11]

---

[10] The quotations from Engels and Marx are drawn from V. Venable, *Human Nature: The Marxian View* (New York: Alfred A. Knopf, Inc., 1945).

[11] Quotations are from F. Nietzsche, *The Will to Power: An Attempted Transvaluation of All Values,* trans. A. M. Ludovici (London: T. N. Foulis, 1914), aphorisms 285, 319, 358.

This view of the adaptive or strategic nature of moral values is not, of course, entirely consistent with the Marxian idea. Yet each description provides important insights into human behavior. The difference is understandable if we make allowance for the resentments felt by the authors themselves. Marx's antagonism was toward the capitalist class, the privileged exploiters of other people's miseries. Nietzsche's knife was out for the conventional morality that surrounded him and stifled his inner sense of freedom to develop his unusual powers to the utmost. His dissatisfaction with the constricting effects of middle-class morality corresponds to that often expressed today by well-educated and gifted people.

Types of Mind

Naturalistic description is not inherently motivated by animosity and directed toward unmasking the evil behind the good. Impulses of this sort are less prominent, though perhaps dimly present in the background, in the history of attempts to describe different types of mind. Curiosity about this question arises out of repeated observation of disagreement. Even with respect to abstract topics far removed from immediate self-interest, human beings exhibit large, persistent, seemingly irreconcilable disagreement. This suggests the possibility that minds do not all work alike, that regardless of personal involvements people actually experience things in different ways. Is there not some deep difference between those writers and artists whom we call classic and those we call romantic, a difference in perception, in feeling, in fundamental organization? Are there not basic differences in the experiences of rationalists and those of empiricists? William James wrote as follows about the problem:

> The history of philosophy is, to a great extent, that of a certain clash of human temperaments. Of whatever temperament a professional philosopher is, he tries, when philosophizing, to sink the fact of his temperament. Yet his temperament really gives him a stronger bias than any of his more strictly objective premises. It loads the evidence for him one way or the other, making for a more sentimental or a more hard-hearted view of the universe, just as this fact or that principle would. He *trusts* his temperament. Wanting a universe that suits it, he believes in any representation of the universe that does suit it.[12]

James proposed that there must be at least two different types: the rationalist, who is "tender-minded" and devoted to abstract and eternal principles, and the empiricist, who is "tough-minded" and prefers facts in all their variety.

The outstanding work along this line of thought is Carl Jung's book on psychological types, published in 1920.[13] In this work Jung introduced the distinction between introverted and extraverted types, picturesquely described as "two distinct human natures" and illustrated by such contrasting

[12] W. James, *Pragmatism: A New Name for Some Old Ways of Thinking* (London: Longmans, Green & Co., Ltd., 1907), pp. 6–9.
[13] C. G. Jung, *Psychological Types, or the Psychology of Individuation*, trans. H. G. Baynes (New York: Harcourt Brace Jovanovich, 1924).

thinkers as Plato and Aristotle. The difference between the two types, as Jung saw it, lies in the direction taken by their basic interest-energy. In extraversion the predominant direction of interest is toward what lies external to oneself, including concrete events and the situations and people who make up one's surroundings. In introversion, interest is drawn more toward subjective experience, the thoughts and feelings and dreams and reasonings that accompany and follow external happenings.

There is a rough correspondence between extraversion and James's fact-oriented empiricist and between introversion and the theory-seeking rationalist; indeed, Jung showed that some such distinction as the one he was proposing ran deeply through literary, artistic, scientific, and philosophical thought. But as a naturalistic study of psychological types, Jung's observations went much further than this dichotomy of the direction of interest-energy. He distinguished four varieties of mental function: thinking, feeling, sensation, and intuition. These were apt to be unequally developed; a given individual might lean most heavily, for instance, on thinking as his most congenial asset, leaving feeling and the other functions to a more rudimentary development. As any function could take either an extraverted or introverted form, Jung's description comes to rest with eight basic psychological types. Unwieldy as the scheme may be, difficult as are its finer distinctions, Jung's work still stands as a mighty effort at the refined naturalistic description of types of mind.

The intensive study of individual lives through biography and autobiography and the careful naturalistic description of selected aspects of human behavior continue to be important sources of knowledge about personality. During the last century, however, channels of information have been much enlarged by progress in three areas of research: the experimental study of behavior, the clinical study of psychological disturbances, and the comparative study of societies. These advances have not only increased the available store of information; they have helped to make description more systematic and to engender explanatory principles.

The Experimental Study of Behavior in Animals and Man

Darwin and Evolution

The publication in 1859 of Charles Darwin's *The Origin of Species* proved to be a revolutionary event for the intellectual life of our time. The theory that the different species of living creatures were not separately created but gradually evolved through natural selection is now so widely accepted as to seem commonplace and unexciting. Yet it contains implications that for a long time were bitterly resisted because they changed so radically the previous conception of man's nature and place in the universe. The theory implies that man has evolved from earlier biological versions of himself, which, if traced back far enough, give him a common ancestry with chimpanzees and other higher primates and plant him firmly in the mammalian branch of living creatures. He has come to his present estate by no higher principle than survival. Because living organisms multiply rapidly and compete for resources, only a small number can survive and reproduce their kind, these being the individuals of each generation who are most fit to survive under existing conditions. This story of the origin of the human species is decidedly inglorious when compared to the idea that we were made in the image of God. It is decidedly less attractive than the long-held view that man has a soul and spiritual faculties that differentiate him sharply from animals. The roots of his being and the reasons for his existence now seemed to be made identical with those of all living creatures, and the meaning of life appeared to be crushed into the struggle to survive. It is not surprising that there was sustained intellectual resistance to such belittlement.

After a while it was realized that the implications need not be so devastating. Perhaps Marx was right when he said that Darwin's conception was distorted by images of the British industrial system in which individual owners struggled to make their businesses survive in a fiercely competitive market. But Darwin was aware, even if he did not give it much emphasis, that impulses toward mutual aid existed in animals as well as man, and that in many species the survival of the fittest applied to societies rather than to individuals. Cooperation among the members of a species is dramatically illustrated in the social insects such as ants and bees and in animals that, like beavers, live in colonies and work for certain common goals. These need not, however, be regarded as isolated examples; some degree of interdependence and cooperation is characteristic of a great many varieties of animal life, including all of the mammals, whose immature young survive only through parental care. Such considerations brought back into the evolutionary picture, as relevant to survival, impulses to behave in ways that were of benefit to others rather than to oneself alone. Spiritual faculties were difficult to derive from Darwin's naturalistic scheme of thought, but at least altruism could be rescued in a system that at first seemed to embody pure egoism.[14]

The outstanding effect of the theory of evolution was to eliminate the discontinuity between man and other forms of life. Animals had been seen as creatures of instinct, man as a creature of reason. Early transformations of Darwinism into research quite naturally took the form of looking for reason in animals and for instinct in man. A literature sprang up in praise of the intelligent feats and sensitivities of animals, especially animal pets, while at the same time human nature was being knocked from its pedestal by showing its bondage to irrational urges such as the herd instinct so deplored by Nietzsche. In the course of time these lines of investigation outgrew anecdotal beginnings and combined to form, with the aid of greatly improved methods, a highly important tradition of research.

Laboratory Research on Behavior

Advances in knowledge depend on the availability of suitable methods of investigation. One of the crowning achievements of modern scientific research has been to bring things into the laboratory and study them under con-

---

[14] W. C. Allee, *The Social Life of Animals*, rev. ed. (Boston: The Beacon Press, 1958), esp. Chap. 2.

ditions in which extraneous influences are controlled. Bringing human beings into the laboratory as objects of study raises formidable difficulties, but the theory of evolution suggested a practical way around them. If there is no basic discontinuity between men and other animals, laws of behavior derived from experiments with animals in the laboratory might be supposed to apply also to men. Thus was instituted the long scientific career of the white rat and certain other species whose behavior under controlled conditions has been used to shed light on the general nature of processes of learning.

The picture that first emerged indicated a close connection between learning and motivation. Animal survival depends on the satisfaction of certain needs, such as hunger, thirst, sex, and escape from pain. These needs— the *instincts* of the older vocabulary but now generally called *drives*—create states of tension and restlessness, which the organism can reduce only by securing the object or situation that satisfies the need. Learning appeared to be closely related to such needs. Researchers found that animals learned more quickly when strongly motivated, and what they learned was the series of actions and discriminations that led to need reduction, other available behaviors that produced no such result being discarded. This conception fitted well with the evolutionary emphasis on survival, and when one thought of the importance of rewards and punishments in the lives of children, there seemed to be little risk in assuming that animal and human learning answered to the same laws.

There proved to be some risk, however, in deriving these laws from situations that were too closely controlled. In their natural habitat animals and children alike engage in a good deal of random movement, exploration, and play, and they seem to learn from this behavior even when no strong drive is involved. When these conditions were simulated in the laboratory it turned out that animals are capable of learning about their surroundings without the aid of drive reduction, simply as an end in itself. In human experience the closest parallel is doing things merely out of curiosity. This finding, however, is not at all at odds with evolutionary biology. A tendency toward active exploration, toward what might be called early practice and learning in advance, would clearly confer a survival advantage over creatures that merely sat in the sun until some moment of crisis arrived. Exploratory play increases competence in dealing with the environment, and the attaining of competence, which has little resemblance to drive reduction, must be counted as an intrinsic form of satisfaction. When we consider how much a child has to learn in the way of motor coordination, skills, and language, to say nothing of all that is taught in school, it seems likely that this sort of intrinsically motivated activity plays a significant part in the growth of personality.

It is not difficult to connect the findings of the laboratory with the situations in which children do most of their learning—the social situations of family, school, and playground. Allowing that in the beginning drive satisfaction and confort are largely provided by adult family members, and allowing further that exploratory play often evokes human responses, it is easy to deduce that the child's relations with the people around him will acquire a good deal of force as rewards and punishments. We shall examine in later chapters the complications that exist in what is stated here in skeleton form. It is enough at this point to perceive that principles of learning derived from laboratory experiments with animals can be of use in the more complex human situations in which the growth of personality typically takes place.[15]

The Clinical Study of Psychological Disorders

It seems obvious that mental illness and other forms of psychological disorder can shed light on the normal workings of personality. However, the study of mental illness requires systematic methods of observation, and these in turn depend upon institutional arrangements that permit continuing contact with patients and the keeping of detailed records. Mental hospitals were a rarity in Europe and America until the nineteenth century, and the slow work of systematic description and classification of mental disorders had advanced little by the twentieth century. As part of the province of medicine, mental disorders were pictured as bodily diseases, most likely diseases of the brain. The development of better microscopes led to significant advances in knowledge of the structure and functions of the nervous system. In some instances disordered behavior that was first described in psychological terms, including loss of coordination, mental confusion, delusions and hallucinations, turned out to be correlated with detectable brain injury and deterioration of brain tissue. In other instances such symptoms proved to be associated with drug intoxication and other physiological abnormalities. These findings served to emphasize the connection between experience, behavior, and the functioning of the nervous system, but they left a good deal unexplained. The most common and widespread mental diseases, schizophrenia and manic-depressive disorders, were not associated with detectable physiological abnormalities and did not always seem to fit the traditional concept of disease. Furthermore, another class of disorders, the psychoneuroses, began to appear less like physiological disorders than like difficulties with acquired strategies of living. It became conceivable that neurotic troubles occurred because the patients had learned to live their lives in unfortunate ways.

Freud's Discoveries

An important event in intellectual history began when Sigmund Freud, a Viennese physician who had made a promising start in biological research, turned his attention to the treatment of neurotic patients. If one had to compress into a nutshell the great wealth of Freud's discoveries, his development of the idea of *unconscious motivation*, especially when it had to do with sexual desires, hostility, and the avoidance of anxiety, would seem to be

---

[15] A noteworthy attempt to relate simple learning principles to social learning in the family was made by J. Dollard and N. E. Miller, *Personality and Psychotherapy* (New York: McGraw-Hill, Inc., 1950), esp. Chaps. 3–10.

most central. The idea of unconscious motives is, of course, an old one. The leakage of such motives into overt behavior through slips of the tongue, errors, and humor has often been employed with telling effect in literary characterization. Freud's contribution lay in the discovery of a systematic procedure for investigating at great length motives that were not initially conscious. This method, the technique of psychoanalysis, opened for him a large territory that revolutionized in his time the prevailing ideas about human nature.

Freud discovered his method at a point in his psychiatric practice at which he had come to believe that the cure of neurotic patients depended upon their giving open expression to imprisoned feelings. After trying and discarding several other devices, he hit upon the *method of free association*, which has ever since remained the cornerstone of psychoanalytic practice. Instead of conducting an alert dialogue with the doctor, the patient was asked to lie relaxed upon a couch, to stop giving conscious direction to his thought, and to say whatever came into his head, even if it seemed illogical, embarrassing, or insulting. Freud's idea was to set aside logic and convention so that the flow of thought could fall under the guidance of feeling, permitting imprisoned affects to make their way to expression.

Described in this way, the method of free association sounds much too simple to deserve the status of a scientific technique. Yet its persistent use in psychoanalytic treatment leads to a series of developments that is never observed in any other situation. At first the patient resists the abandonment of his usual methods of talk and interaction; it may take weeks and even months before he can really give himself over to free association. Then further resistances are encountered; anxiety prevents the pursuit of certain lines of thought and chains of memory. Furthermore, patients are upset at the emergence of feelings of love or of hate toward the physician, feelings that seem to have no proper place in a professional relationship. All of these manifestations show that the method does indeed bring feelings to unfamiliar expression. If the anxieties are overcome and the resistances reduced, what comes to light is an array of wishes, fantasies, and attitudes toward other people that have not before been conscious but that can now be seen to have influenced behavior in consistent though subtle ways. Freud was early impressed by the prominence of sexual urges in this material. He was also impressed by the frequent emergence of memories indicative of erotic fantasies in early childhood involving the members of the family circle. Later he gave more attention to aggressive urges and hostile fantasies and to the anxieties that kept such tendencies from open expression. Gradually he formed a picture of development in which certain of our most basic biological urges, notably sex and aggression, emerging early in life, are subjected to repression as the child is taught to meet conventional standards of socialized behavior. Forced out of awareness, they nevertheless cannot be eliminated, and they persist as unconscious motives influencing behavior in ways that may be damaging to personal development.

Freud's discoveries opened up wide new vistas on human nature, and his theories have had a powerful influence on psychological thought.

Others who used his method, however, did not always interpret the findings in the same way. This is illustrated in the work of Alfred Adler, an early associate of Freud's who eventually took an independent path.

Adler and the Striving for Superiority

As Adler listened to the free associations of neurotic patients his attention was caught by a theme other than sex. He seemed to hear everywhere the subtle workings of a striving to surpass, dominate, and triumph over others, a persistent struggle for superiority. The patients did not, however, strive directly for these goals; they employed roundabout means such as controlling the household by being sick and securing the services given to invalids. They seemed to be afraid to assert themselves in direct competition, yet their behavior betrayed an enduring interest in being somehow superior. Adler became convinced that they were troubled by deep feelings of inferiority, that they were driven by a strong urge to compensate for this, but that their confidence was insufficient to risk straightforward tests.

There are many parallels between Freud's thinking and Adler's. Both took their start from the treatment of neurotic patients by methods centered on free association. Both gave prominence to anxiety as a force that interfered with impulse expression and free development. Both assumed unconscious motivation and looked for its origins in early childhood. But Adler diverged in two important respects. In the first place he was less impressed than Freud by infantile sexuality and hostility, and he attached greater importance to a different motive, which might be called an infantile striving for power. Such a striving, as he saw it, is highly vulnerable in childhood. It can be thwarted simply by being the smallest member of the family circle, and the thwarting can be acutely painful if the child has real shortcomings that becomes the subject of belittlement and ridicule. Feelings of inferiority, Adler believed, are intolerable, striking at the heart of all confident action and self-respect; if strong, they inevitably give rise to powerful compensatory urges which get in the way of affectionate impulses and social feeling. Sometimes this results in a successful overcompensation, as in the stutterer Demosthenes, who made himself into a great orator. Sometimes the aim is deflected, as in the traditional girl without beauty who specializes in brains or the traditional boy without brains who specializes in brawn. Compensatory strivings, however, are likely to engender fantasies of wonderful superiorities that in fact are forever out of reach, a situation conducive to enduring disappointment and resentment.

Adler's second important divergence from Freud came from his sharp perception of the strategic aspects of behavior. Freud made notable discoveries about defense mechanisms, thinking of them indeed in a somewhat mechanical way, but Adler paid more attention to continuous purposive strivings aimed at achieving long-range goals. In this connection he introduced the conception of style of life, a pattern of adaptive strategies acquired to meet the problems of the early years and not greatly changed thereafter.

Style of life he considered to be one of the most important aspects of individuality, even though the person himself might be little aware of it. Adler's theories were not as well wrought as Freud's and never became as widely known, but his principal ideas were taken up by clinical workers and entered strongly into what might be called the clinical common sense of the mid-twentieth century.

The Comparative Study of Societies

Light of a different sort has been shed on personality by the work of anthropologists engaged in the comparative study of societies. These far-ranging observers have brought back from all over the globe descriptions of primitive people, often living in small homogeneous societies under widely different conditions. The method of observation calls for living for many months in the society under study, mastering the language, making oneself acceptable even though an eccentric outsider, noticing customs and public festivities, and questioning selected individuals closely about child training, political organization, values, and beliefs. Under such scrutiny no two societies prove to be exactly alike; they exhibit, like people, a large amount of individuality. To bring order into the myriad particulars that make up this individuality, anthropologists introduced the important concept of *culture*.

As used here, culture refers to the total way of life of a society, the heritage of learnings that is shared and transmitted by the members of the society. A culture, to express it a little differently, is a set of shared plans for living, developed by previous generations to meet the necessities of their existence, existing in the minds of the present generation, and taught directly or indirectly to new generations. By providing pretested solutions to many problems, the culture allows us to learn without endless trial and error what to expect of others and of ourselves. The pretested solutions may have to do with small matters of custom: what foods it is proper to eat, what utensils one should use for eating, what clothes one should wear on what occasions, what ways of speaking are acceptable in formal exchanges. Cultural prescriptions deal also with larger matters, such as kinship and marriage customs. In some societies courtship and marriage belong in the sphere of individual enterprise, but in others it is taken for granted that such an important decision must be made by parents in their wisdom and not left to frivolous considerations such as youthful romantic love. Societies differ also in the range of individuals who count as one's kin, with whom marriage is forbidden but mutual help is expected. Culture includes beliefs about the nature of the world and the means of propitiating hostile forces, a task sometimes assigned to ceremonial dances, sometimes to witchcraft, and sometimes to scientific research. Perhaps the most important aspect of a culture is its definition of basic values. The plan for living that is transmitted to children as they grow up includes ideal standards of behavior, and these, too, vary greatly from one society to another. The proper way to live may be seen in one society as gentle, cooperative, and friendly, but another tribe may set the ideal in terms of individual competition, honoring the person who climbs to the top by sharp practice and magic. A third may put a high value on cooperation only as a means of warlike depredations against its neighbors. Taking the whole world into account, as anthropologists have done, there is an astounding range of differences in cultural values.

The comparative study of societies and their cultures has had the effect of challenging many of the things we have taken for granted in our own society. Cross-cultural perspective makes hard sledding for the belief that values are absolute. For the study of personality it was especially illuminating to perceive the force of custom, belief, and moral precept learned half-unconsciously from the older members of the group, who in turn did their teaching half-unconsciously. A lot of our behavior came to be seen as blindly cultural rather than beautifully rational. The culture concept makes it clear how closely we all tend to live according to the habitual life plans prevailing in our society, even when these plans are being made obsolete by changing conditions.

In a large differentiated modern society there are likely to be certain cultural features common to the whole, but the various groups into which the society is divided can be seen as *subcultures* having values and an outlook of their own. The structure of the society, including the subcultures created within it by social and economic stratification and by ethnic groupings, must be taken into account in order to understand each individual's environment of growth.

The three areas of research just discussed—the experimental study of behavior in animals and man, the clinical study of psychological disorders, and the comparative study of societies—have one thing in common. They all attach great importance to learning and especially to the lasting effects of early learning. The first transmitters of the culture are parents, who are also the first participants in the child's emotional development and the stage managers and audience for his acquisition of competence. This convergence upon early life is reflected in the organization of this book, in which there are four chapters on what might be called the social roots of personality—the effects of being brought up in a specific family circle in a specific kind of neighborhood—before we turn to the more detailed chronological account of personal growth.

A Forward Look

The ground to be covered by this book as a whole will be foreshadowed in the next chapter, which consists of studies of two actual lives. It will be apparent from these descriptions that comprehensive understanding requires a great deal of information. The subsequent outline of chapters can be considered also an outline for the making of case studies. These are the things one would want to know if confronted by the problem of understanding another person's life. The scope is admittedly wide, and the possibility of learning so much about a person will not often exist. For practical purposes such as counseling or psychotherapy the inquiry can often be much narrower, concentrating on the problem for which help has been sought. For comprehensive understanding, however, the ideal goal must be to secure information about everything that is likely to have a significant influence on the pattern of a life.

The study of personality differs in one respect from almost any other branch of learning: one's own self is included by definition as part of the subject matter. At first glance this circumstance seems to offer a grave hazard to the objectivity and detachment that we associate with the advance of knowledge. How can we expect to maintain a judicious frame of mind if we keep meeting ourselves on the printed page, if every so often the description touches on one of our sensitive spots? But this risk must be run, because the alternative of total detachment tends to restrict what will be observed. The study of personality becomes less than it should be if it is approached as a survey of a field of knowledge entirely outside oneself. It should be a personal experience, a series of recognitions of oneself and of how one is related to the scheme of human life and society. To avoid these recognitions cuts down on the amount that one can learn, including the amount one can learn about other people, for we can understand certain features of others only through our own experience. Even if it is disconcerting to include oneself in the subject matter of study, the attempt is warranted by the probability of valuable gains.

Misgivings may be felt that the study of personality will lead to a mechanical or otherwise demeaning image of man. Contemporary psychology, psychoanalysis, and social science, using models of thought derived from the physical sciences, have revealed to us a great many ways in which we are pushed around. We have learned to think of ourselves as responding to stimuli, driven by unconscious wishes, and shaped by cultural and social expectations. There is a lot of truth in these images, yet there is room for doubt that they contain the whole truth. The idea that we are simply pushed around is in conflict with our personal experience of effort and initiative, and it seems far from adequate for understanding people like Samuel Johnson, Rousseau, and Malcolm X, who were themselves a source of unmistakable influence on others. To be alive means to be active, a source of energy, and thus to participate in the growth of one's own personality.

2 Two Lives: A Comparative Study

The overture to an opera customarily introduces the main musical themes that will be developed in the body of the work. An overture to the study of personality can best perform a like service by displaying its main themes as they occur in actual life histories. Two lives are here chosen for this purpose, the lives of two men who were studied over a span of time and who have since become well established in their respective spheres. A comparative case study, shifting continually from one subject to the other, may seem less easy to follow than the story of a single life, but it puts a more telling emphasis on individuality. Though different in background, the two men passed through a number of similar situations, with which they dealt in their own individual ways. What does one need to know to understand a person's life? Much more, it will be surmised, than was learned in these two studies, but at least some of the main themes will be apparent in the account that follows.

The subjects of this comparative personality study were first seen when they were college students, each 20 years of age. We shall assign to them the names of John Chatwell and Harold Merritt.[1] Originally engaged to serve as paid subjects in psychological experiments, they were persuaded to expand this role by participating in extensive studies of personality, amounting in the end to more than thirty hours of interviews, tests, and experiments. This voluminous material yields a picture of their development up to that time, but

---

[1] John Chatwell's case has been published by M. Brewster Smith, J. S. Bruner, and R. W. White, *Opinions and Personality* (New York: John Wiley & Sons, 1956), Chap. 5. A version of the comparative study of the two men appears in *The Study of Lives*, ed. R. W. White (New York: Atherton Press, 1963), Chap. 3.

knowledge of their lives does not have to cease at that point, for both men were studied a second time several years later, when they were beginning to be settled in their careers.

The First Studies

Styles of Speech

Independently of the main study, a comparison between the two students was made entirely on the basis of an objective analysis of recorded samples of their speech. Fillmore H. Sanford, author of the study, after giving in detail the precise measurements used, made the comparison in the following summaries of speech style:

> In his verbal behavior Chatwell is colorful, varied, emphatic, direct, active, progressing always in a forward direction. His responses are well co-ordinated, closely interconnected, more evaluative than definitive, and somewhat enumerative. He covers extensive areas verbally and is disinclined to consider details or precision of reference. His speech is confident, definite, independent. In general he appears to use speech not so much to describe the external world and its relations as to express his own individuality and to impress the auditor.
>
> Merritt's speech is complex, perseverative, thorough, uncoordinated, cautious, static, highly definitive, and stimulus-bound. If we go one step further toward synthesis and generalization, we might conceive of his whole style as defensive and deferent. Most of his verbal behavior seems to reflect a desire to avoid blame or disapproval. He is cautious and indirect, rarely making a simple or bald statement. Once he makes a judgment he explains it and presents all aspects of it, leaving little to the auditor's imagination and little for the auditor to question. His concern for the adequacy of every response results in a reexamination of the response and this, in turn, brings about roughnesses in his discourse. His disinclination to venture out "on his own" makes him feel more comfortable in the stimulus-bound situations.[2]

Speech is the main instrument of social interaction, and the two subjects clearly use it with different degrees of confidence. Chatwell sounds as if he expected to be able to impress his hearers and to evoke from them an appreciative and respectful response. Merritt seems less sure of the impression he can make; he speaks as if others were likely to be critical and perhaps belittling, so that it is well to explain, qualify, and soften, thus making his communication less susceptible to challenge. Neither young man is inarticulate, but Chatwell uses the instrument of speech with stronger strokes.

[2] F. H. Sanford, "Speech and Personality: A Comparative Case Study," *Character and Personality*, **10** (1942), 169–198.

Contrasting Family Circles

During Chatwell's boyhood the family circle, which included the parents and a younger brother and sister, was the scene of much lively discussion and some quarreling. Both parents had scientific and other intellectual interests, and the father particularly enjoyed tossing out controversial problems for debate at the dinner table. Chatwell's mother, when interviewed, was a bit apologetic about the high-strung atmosphere of the home, but her eldest son looked back upon it with considerable satisfaction. He made it clear that the quarrels did not run deep: "I never remember an argument on any really important subject such as our education; it was generally on some never-proven point such as the question of who gained or lost the most in the World War." The picture that emerges is one of underlying secure solidarity, which gave the children a feeling of freedom to express and assert themselves. In matters of serious discipline Chatwell was afraid of his father's anger, but in retrospect he registered no complaints against the regime and recollected that his mother worked more through bribes than through punishments. As an undergraduate he considered himself to be highly self-sufficient; yet he felt certain that in any time of trouble he would receive a sympathetic hearing and unquestioning support at home.

Merritt's account of his childhood was a little more somber. His middle-class Jewish parents were much involved in local civic affairs, and he recalled occasions when they would be out for the evening, when his older brother would also go out, leaving him alone and tearful in the house. He complained of "never having the real experience of a close family connection" and reported his envy of friends at whose houses he would find "their parents and brothers and sisters sitting in the front room and talking; this is an experience of which a greater part of my earlier life was deprived." He averred that his parents had never shown much sympathy for his troubles or excitement over his successes. "Everything is taken as a matter of course," he said; "I was never helped or admired." Wistfully he mentioned never having been patted on the back, a deprivation that he rectified in a story, told as part of a test of imagination, wherein a father embraces the son who has done him honor in a football game. In this atmosphere of niggardly affection and respect he had not found it safe to assert himself strongly or to indulge rebellious wishes. He found no injustices in the regime of discipline, and, when punished, he "resolved not to let the situation happen again." He resented it only when his mother continued to scold long past the point at which his inner surrender had been made.

These contrasting pictures justify to some extent Adler's idea that styles of life become set by experience in the family circle. In the intellectually competitive but basically benign atmosphere of the Chatwell home the eldest child, mentally the most mature, found it often possible to impress his parents and put down his sibling rivals. This strategy was not open to Merritt, the younger son whose parents cared less for intellectual brilliance than for a virtuous and respectable way of life; he achieved his best results by restraint and by deference to the implicit moral regime. But if strategies get their start in the family circle it does not necessarily follow that they remain unchanged in other situations. Sometimes the autocrat of the household is timidly cooperative on the playground or the model of domestic virtue proves to be the hellion of the school.

Interactions with Contemporaries

Turning to interactions with other children, we might conclude that Merritt made a quicker start toward social initiative. Chatwell reported himself to have been a cry-baby at the start of school, whereas Merritt remembered at the age of six "inviting all my young friends to play in the yard with me." These sessions in the yard were marred by fits of temper on the part of the host: "I was stubborn and would get angry if they didn't agree to play my games or go where I wanted to go." Apparently arrogance worked no better with his playmates than with his family, for Merritt represented his subsequent social growth as a progress from this selfish assertiveness to an ability to cooperate smoothly with others. By the time he reached junior high school he had many friends and was "well liked by teachers and associates." In senior high school he became president of a political science club, but the organization crumbled through lack of student interest and faculty support. Merritt had clearly not developed into a charismatic leader.

Chatwell's picture of his own social growth was one of overcoming anxiety rather than suppressing anger. Filling out an item about his attitudes, he wrote: "When young, obedient; when older, especially at school, critical, aggressive, belligerent, but often cooperative." With respect to the groups with which he associated, he said: "I was respected, perhaps admired by a few; I certainly wasn't picked on." The earlier tendency to cry was successfully counteracted during the third grade, when a grouchy, rheumatic teacher stimulated rebellious mischief: "A friend and I were kicked out of his class three times a week, but I soon got so that I could go before the principal and be perfectly self-possessed." By the time he entered high school and "had gotten past the shy freshman stage," he was ready to take part in all social activities; he made many friends and was chosen for several offices. It became his "favorite indoor sport" to meet new people, talk with them, and get their point of view. This sounds less spectacular than the kind of verbal assertiveness that could often be made to work at home, but Chatwell's interpersonal strategies were still developing. It was reported by his mother that as a child he was physically timid. Slight of frame, though wiry and boundlessly energetic, he hung on the edges of football scrimmages and knew anxieties and humiliations in the days when physical prowess was all-important. In one of his imaginative stories he told indirectly what happened then. The hero, laboriously playing football with the knowledge that he could never do it well, came to the conclusion that "he didn't like the way the whole sport was organized at college. But instead of merely giving voice to his objections, he suddenly threw himself wholeheartedly into modifying the system. He found that he had just the qualifications for doing this successfully." Chatwell found that he had the qualities—high intelligence, quick wit, and an extraordinarily well-furnished memory—to meet challenges fearlessly and to establish competitive dominance when things could be kept verbal, abstract, and not too deadly serious. By restricting himself to verbal influence he was able to fashion an extraordinarily efficient adaptive strategy.

Self-Descriptions as College Students

Throughout the interviews, especially when alluding to their abilities, the two subjects drew consistently different pictures of their behavior with other people. Questioned about leading and governing ability, Chatwell pronounced himself a good executive who knew how to delegate authority, and said, "Responsibility in emergencies is my meat." Merritt could not recall taking an active part in an emergency. He felt that "as far as leading others is concerned, I can hold my own"; mentioned specific instances in which others had turned to him for advice; and replied to a question about his persuasive skill: "I think I can get my way—well, I mean, if my point is correct I can persuade others." With respect to economic ability, Chatwell described some profitable deals with other students and characterized himself as "the sort of fellow who can get it for you wholesale"; whereas Merritt said, "I don't bargain for a price, but take the salesman's word for it" and revealed that his mother still bought his clothes. Chatwell announced that he tended to monopolize conversations, whereas Merritt put it that he could "hold [his] own in conversation" —but only with men, for he confessed to being shy and awkward with girls.

From various indications it could be inferred that such progress as Merritt had made in "holding his own" with other people represented a counteractive victory over a strong inner tendency to surrender to personal pressure, learned originally through appeasing his parents. His considerable sociability reflected a real dependence on the support of a friendly human environment. Rating himself on a questionnaire, he gave two of his rare top scores to the statements, "I become very attached to my friends," and "I like to hang around with a group of congenial people and talk about anything that comes up"; and he assigned the lowest rating to the thought, "I could cut my moorings—quit my home, my parents, and my friends without suffering great regrets." But if there was much in him that dictated a gently deferent, even submissive attitude toward others, there remains the important fact that he had managed to bring about something firmer in interpersonal relations that was consistent with self-respect. To the extent that he could truly "hold his own" he was by no means at the bottom of the scale of social confidence.

Chatwell's self-picture, in contrast, was so brimming with confidence as to suggest a certain bravado beneath which might lie real residues of anxiety. It should first be noticed that he actually did a great many of the kinds of things he said he did. His zest and versatility made him a treasure to the student employment office, which could use him in response to practically any call. One of his assignments was to arrange a series of radio programs involving information contests between teams of high school students. This entailed persuading school principals, overcoming the prejudices of school boards, and selling to everyone the idea that an educational purpose would be served. "This was duck soup for me," said Chatwell. But his impressive achievements did not leave him without worries. There were aspects of life with which he could not deal by quick and clever mastery. He was aware of a certain lack of content and conviction in himself. Much as he enjoyed argument, it worried him that he could so easily and persuasively take either side; his intellectual virtuosity was not matched by a firm sense of what was important to him. In considerable degree he went through an identity crisis, complaining that he lived wholly in the present and could stabilize no enduring interests or plans for the future. It bothered him that he lost interest in things when there was no more anxiety to overcome, a clear indication that the mastery of fear was getting in the way of intrinsic positive satisfactions. Chatwell's strategy for influencing and dominating his social environment was thus somewhat overdriven, and his concentration on the verbal mode made it sometimes possible to evade serious issues.

Relations with Girls

As a corrective to the idea that a life style is always consistent, it is instructive to notice that both subjects separated their attitudes toward girls from their other human interactions. Chatwell quickly discovered that competitive dominance was of little interest to him in this sphere, and Merritt was regretfully aware that the strategy of "holding his own" with boys did not work the same way with girls.

Chatwell could be considered bashful in his first serious relation, in which he held the girl's hand the first year, kissed her the second, and never did much more. As a college sophomore, however, he fell in love with another girl about whom he wrote rhapsodically, and having already parted with his virginity, he presently "stormed the gates" with her. Despite his martial phrase, their sexual activity was very much a matter of mutual desire and consent in a relation that seems to have been on both sides one of tender appreciation. Before long this girl was swept away from him by a more aggressive suitor, causing him to speculate that he had "not handled her right": he had been an "abject slave," whereas "she should have been." The failure of this strategy caused him to test another one. With his next girl he "mingled more of the cave man" in his behavior, which made her "a bit more respecting," even to the point of becoming a "yes-woman." Having achieved this, however, Chatwell found that it was not what he wanted, and he did not fall in love again until he found the satisfying give-and-take of a more equal relation. In this sphere of being, competitive dominance was not his goal and the strategies for obtaining it were of no relevance.

Chronologically, Merritt might be said to have made a quicker start with girls: long before puberty he had been in a fist fight over a girl whom he wanted to kiss, whereas Chatwell at this age viewed girls with contempt. But

Merritt's head start did not betoken fast progress. He was slow to attain confidence with girls. He wrote as follows, exhibiting in his writing some of the qualities Sanford noticed in his speech:

> I have often been told that I am bashful. While I do not think this is wholly true, I say it is true to a great extent, probably because I am a very poor dancer. It is natural at an informal gathering for some few to start dancing. It is here that I am apt to be shy; for, having little confidence in my dancing ability, I would rather withdraw from the active company and not dance—unless I cannot avoid dancing.

At petting parties Merritt was "not at all too aggressive," leaving the initiative to his partner. When, during the spring of his sophomore year, the petting with one of his girl friends became heavy, he was at first "ashamed" of himself, "but she told me that what we were doing was only very natural." And when he realized that this experience was making him want sexual intercourse, he broke off the relationship: "I felt I would regret it because if I did, I'd be 'hooked'—once we would start, it wouldn't end—I'm sure of that because I know what an attraction that girl had for me." Chatwell had never feared being "hooked"; he felt able to "tell anyone to go to hell" if necessary.

This bit of history suggests, and other material strengthens the suggestion, that in Merritt's childhood sex had been associated with anxiety. He met this anxiety by denial and repression, so that for a time he was truly unaware of the stirrings of sexual inclination. As a sophomore he wrote that he had "never indulged in masturbation." But this successful defensive maneuver created anxieties of its own after puberty. He began to dread that something might be wrong with his manhood, that the strength of his sexual urge might not be normal—and being normal in all respects was a quality often favorably mentioned in his middle-class family. The stilted prose of his sophomore autobiography whenever he touched upon this topic testifies to the strong grip of anxious conflict, to the difficulty of convincing both the reader and himself that he was highly normal but not lustfully inclined. Merritt was actually much reassured when his girl friend's initiative proved to him that his sexual desire was strong. Even without putting himself to the test of intercourse he experienced a gratifying increase of self-respect and confidence in all of his social relations. Entrenched defenses, however, are not easily transcended. Especially with girls he often continued to feel self-conscious, inhibited, and unable, as he expressed it, to "take off this stiff robe and let myself go."

Plans and Prospects

As sophomores, Chatwell and Merritt were both asked to write something about their self-estimates and expectations for the future. In the mantle of prophecy, Chatwell wrote as follows:

> I like people, and I think they like me. I get along well with people and can generally get them to do what I want—within reasonable limits, of

course. I am well enough informed to be able to carry on a decent conversation with people from whom I may learn more, although I might
never admit that to them. Unfortunately, perhaps, I think rather well of
myself, although I realize my limitations. I know that there is some
combination of things that I can do better than anyone else; I also know
that there is no one of them that someone else cannot do better than I.
I have a better than average mind, but I am also more lazy than the
average. I have supreme confidence, if not in my skills, in my ability to
figure out a way to get something done eventually.

Merritt's inspection of the crystal ball yielded a more guarded
picture.

I think that those whom I know have a favorable attitude toward me. I
say this because there are very few people with whom I do not get along.
I am treated well in my society—I can see that those of my associates
who do not go to college respect me because I do. There are members of
my family (whom I have heard speak of me) who say that I ought to be
successful because I have a pleasing personality and can get along with
people. As for my own estimate of myself, I might say that I do think
that if upon graduation the opportunity presents itself, I can make a
success of myself. That is, I feel that I have ambition to graduate from
one position to another, until, after ten years or so, I think I can be in a
fairly "well-off" position. I think that in the right position, that is, one
for which I am cut out, I would be a success, because I hold myself to
be intelligent, willing to learn, willing to work hard for success, and I
think I can hold my own against any equal.

The curiously equivocal ending of the last phrase, possibly a slip, symbolizes
beautifully the underlying uncertainty in Merritt's self-confidence.

The Second Studies

Do our subjects possess the gift of prophecy? Fortunately, the
second studies done approximately a decade later make it possible to find out.

Military Service

Born when they were, these two young men were destined to go very
soon into military service, with the prospect of active duty in World War II.

Merritt's transition to military service was smoothed by the fact
that he had taken an officer-training program in college. After brief further
training he was ordered to an executive office outside the United States. "I ran
into a funny situation," he said; "the commanding officer took an immediate
dislike to me. I excuse myself by saying he felt that way, but I used to ask him
everything I didn't know, and he didn't like being bothered." If the officer's
dislike was immediate, it may have been because Merritt was Jewish, but we

notice also an adaptive miscarriage of our subject's deference, with its hint of underlying uncertainty and dependence. He was next assigned to a unit occupying a remote and barren air transport base in Alaska. Although enemy attack was not particularly likely, the base could not be effectively reinforced and the unit was considered expendable. This created anxiety for all, but it contributed to an excellent *esprit de corps*. Conditions were primitive, but the men were "a swell bunch." Merritt came to feel that "adequate food and shelter and good companionship . . . are mighty important." He was able to take with good grace the ribbing that fell to him as the junior officer, including sarcastic remarks about the use to which he was putting his college education.

Merritt's further career in the service reflected the gains he had made during this assignment. He was exposed to danger but was able to control anxiety and perform responsible duties with scrupulous care. Recalling the political science club in high school that fell apart under his presidency, it is clear that although not a spectacular officer he had made substantial gains in capacity for leadership.

Chatwell was in line to be drafted after graduation, but rather than suffer the inevitable delays, he enlisted at once in the branch of the service he perceived as offering the most likely avenue to officer status. "I found that I adapted to the military life with great ease," he wrote. "In fact, I was enthusiastic about it." Within a week he had applied for officer training; but long before he was eligible, he found a way to improve his position as an enlisted man. Hearing two lectures on mathematics badly given, he applied for the job of mathematics instructor and soon found himself teaching "without difficulty" classes of five hundred men. This job brought him in contact with officers and speeded his progress to officer candidate school, where he found the life "stimulating and healthful," the goals "tangible," and the competition "keen and real, as opposed to the ivory tower that so irked me at college." The training period, with its discipline and his own fired enthusiasm, "produced a systematic, determined, conscientious Chatwell," he wrote, "that would mystify the college authorities."

He was made an instructor in the school, was advanced rapidly, and later went overseas as an intelligence officer. On one occasion the unit was obliged to establish its base in a jungle wilderness. "I must say," he wrote, "that one of the most satisfying things I know of is to go into a jungle and set up a reasonable degree of civilization there with your own hands—water, light, sanitation, etc." Such experiences led to a natural reevaluation of what was important: Chatwell specified "food, independence, warmth, dryness, affection of women, opportunity for productive work, liquor, tobacco—in no particular order." More explicit and detailed than Merritt's list under similar circumstances, it makes no mention of the good companionship which so fortified Merritt at the isolated Alaskan base.

The military careers of our two subjects exhibit strikingly their difference in social initiative. Chatwell started lower in the military hierarchy but ended higher. He was challenged by competition with other men, and he lost no opportunity to advertise his skills and bring himself to the attention of his superiors. His confidence rose and his self-respect became firmer as a consequence of his success; we get less feeling of bravado as we find him constantly "delivering the goods." Merritt was unable to muster such impressive initiative. His first moves were nearly undone by an unwelcome hesitancy and deference. When the atmosphere included good companionship, he was content and functioned well, but he showed no inclination to push his career in any way that would imperil this source of security.

Courtship and Marriage

Like so many of their contemporaries, both young men married during the course of their military service. Chatwell married the girl with whom he had fallen in love in the spring of his senior year, the fourth girl in whom he had had a serious interest. Merritt married the girl who had brought out his sexual interest during the spring of his sophomore year, the only girl to whom he was ever strongly drawn.

As a boy halfway through college, fearing intercourse with its implication of being "hooked," Merritt had rather sternly broken off his relation with this girl and substituted less involving friendships. But the girl continued to be fond of him, and her parents, though possibly not his, had hoped that a match would occur. By a course of events that he could not clearly recall at the time of the second study, he drifted back into her company and became strongly aware of her hopes. She was tearfully present when he was seen off to the war, but he left without committing himself. His own decision took place one night at the Alaskan base, when there was strong rumor of enemy action with its inevitable choice between death and capture. In the midst of his anxiety he said to himself, "If I ever get out of here, I'll go back and marry her"—as indeed he did on his next furlough.

This incident calls to mind the sequence so common in the history of Roman Catholicism, in which a person in grave danger implores the help of a saint and vows eternal devotion and great gifts if the help is granted. No such content is available to a young American Jew, but there is something similar in the underlying feeling. It is as if he said, "If I am saved I shall be greatly indebted," and then, looking around for someone to whom debt could appropriately be paid, he discovered that it was to this girl that he had the strongest feeling of obligation. Yet her only actual claim upon him was her desire to marry him, a desire that up to then he had resisted. The fact that terror should finally shake his resolution on just this point is eloquent testimony to the force with which other people's expectations worked upon him. To be sure, a strong physical attraction took sides with his feeling of obligation, but it was not this that was strengthened by danger. If his life was spared he must give, and the person who wanted him to give was the girl whose tears he could dry by offering himself in marriage.

Merritt's pattern of courtship reflects a continuation of the bashfulness that troubled him in college. He took the first girl who gave him real physical satisfaction; and, overriding his reservations about their ultimate compatibility, he took her more because she wanted him than because he wanted her. He would be lucky if after such a slight search he found an ideal partner. In point of fact, the marriage has worked out, though not as a source of much ecstasy. His wife has had numerous illnesses that have required him to participate rather heavily in the housework, but in an undemonstrative way he likes and is perhaps somewhat dependent on her company, enjoys being a family man, and is quite wrapped up in their young daughter. Apparently the marriage has reached an equilibrium.

Chatwell's final falling in love was the culmination of considerably more experience. As we have seen, he had already gone through the waxing and waning of three love affairs, and he had found his way from a rather abasive to a somewhat more dominant relation. But he by no means sought the competitive dominance that was so dear to him with respect to other men. His girl was lively and intelligent, a proper partner for his conversational talents, but she also provided a welcome sense of peace and security at the end of the day. He described himself as liking busy days but then wanting a place where he could take off his shoes. He was, in his own words, "sunk without firing a shot in about two months," and his only misgiving was that the feeling of security might be influencing him too strongly. His girl seemed to him to be "an ideal combination of intelligence, tenderness, and physical attractiveness." He kept after her, this time with no dying down of interest, for the year that was necessary to persuade her to become his wife; and he was both happy and proud when they were married.

As a married man with two children, Chatwell spoke of his wife as follows:

> I trust her absolutely. There's a feeling of—well, I get intellectual and emotional and all the other kinds of response I want, all at once. We seem to share the same values. . . . We have never gone to bed mad at each other since we were married. She rides me a good bit, but for cause—more than I ride her. I am messy and lazy and it's a cause of dissension. I don't see things to do around the house, and she doesn't like to have to ask me to do them.

He talked freely of disagreements over punishing the children and other common forms of domestic strife, but there was no bitterness or attempt at self-justification. One got the impression of a marriage in which deep devotion could easily absorb the frictions of domesticity.

Finding a Vocation

Occupations, in addition to their economic significance, provide a range of opportunities for the exercise of abilities and the satisfaction of interests; they also offer a variety of patterns of human relation. To the extent that there is room for choice, occupational decisions reflect a strategic attempt to reach the best possible pattern—the best possible compromise—among these numerous kinds of satisfaction. Both Chatwell and Merritt were confronted by a number of options. The choices they made and did not make provide additional insight into several aspects of their personalities.

During the interval between graduation and military service Merritt held a job from which he was fired and a second one in which he was sucessful. The first venture was in a department store, ostensibly in an executive training program. His heart was not in it; after the declaration of war especially, it seemed trivial to be fussing over sales problems. He was actually dismissed for an error in handling some merchandise, but he was told that he was in the wrong line of work. His supervisor informed him that he was far too polite and would never get ahead in such an aggressive business. Next, he found work in a government agency, where he was pleased to find university graduates in charge. Realizing the advantage of a fresh start, he developed the trick of speaking on the telephone "in a deep voice, which I didn't have naturally at that time." He began to develop confidence in himself, but the job was interrupted by his call to arms.

After the war he found a position in the regional office of a large financial corporation. At first he felt, with a diffidence that would have been utterly foreign to Chatwell, that he and other veterans had been put in the false position of supervising people who already knew their jobs. Presently a high official came from the central office to look things over.

> The job of working with Mr. Driver was thrown to me, and I took an interest and got to work closely with him. He had the reputation of being the meanest so-and-so, but I found him upright. I never argued with him. A man who opposed him was fired after two months and I was put in the job, being made chief of one of the floors.

The people on that floor had wanted to promote one of their own men, so Merritt was "in a fairly tough spot, but to this day I don't have an enemy over the place." He continued to enjoy the support of Mr. Driver, who liked both his loyalty and his intelligence and who gave him opportunities for special training in new procedures. He could even have gone to the central office at higher pay, if he had not been disinclined to move away from friends and family connections. On the whole he was well satisfied: "I think I've done pretty well for myself. Someone I think is important thinks I'm important, and that has given me a lot of confidence. That, in turn, lets me do a better job."

In this position Merritt found virtually the perfect way to make use of his preferred social strategies. It came easily to him to be the deferent servant of an overbearing boss, and his inner uncertainties were no longer a handicap when all decisions were made higher up and he could be merely the instrument of company policy. At the same time he managed to melt the antagonism of those below him through conspicuously fair and considerate behavior fashioned by his need for an atmosphere of friendly companionship. One must admire his skill in thus serving two masters. It was not easy, and he often found himself under considerable tension. At the annual Christmas party, for instance, he had to take a clear stand for company policy that no liquor be served and at the same time not spoil the festivities by noticing violations. But he managed well, and thus he fulfilled his own prophecy that "in the right position, that is, one for which I am cut out, I would be a success."

Chatwell emerged from military service with the decision fairly well made that he would become a lawyer. This was certainly a play from strength: he cast his lot with his already well-tried strategy of competitive dominance through verbal channels in the realm of abstract ideas. Presently he was in a position to choose between a large and a small firm, each of which would employ him as a law clerk while he pursued evening study. He made the choice that probably would not have been made by Merritt, who found security in large groups; he chose the small firm, which offered greater chances of advancement through independent achievement. Both then and later the work proved to be another helping of "duck soup." In the law classroom he argued the cases with tremendous zest, holding the floor and sometimes even clashing with the professor. In preparing briefs, he was strongly aided by his excellent memory, wide range of information, and speed of learning, whatever technical matters the case might involve. The pattern of his enthusiasms, intense but short lived, was no handicap in a business where each case had to be prepared rapidly but then put aside for an entirely different one. He was delighted with the combination of legal scholarship, new facts to be mastered, and "constant strife and argument to exact care and method from my disorderly soul." His seniors in the office accepted him as one of them and were, as he put it, "patient with me and kind to my ego, both when I failed and when I succeeded." His own summary varies but little from his sophomore prophecy:

> And so you see that I am very, very happy, busy as hell, with independence, a measure of security in a form in which I can accept it, a future with several broad avenues besides the attractive one I'm on, and plenty of problems—interesting problems, and none beyond my abilities.

In their military service, in their marriages, and in their occupations, Merritt and Chatwell exhibit differences in strategies of living that are consistent with those observed when they were in college. During the period from 20 to 30 years of age we do not see drastic change, but neither do we see a total lack of change. Both men had made gains in confidence and had established self-esteem on a more solid basis. Both had been able to find and then to mold situations that went well with their needs and strategic strengths in human relations. Both had made sacrifices to safety, Merritt rather more than Chatwell; defense against anxiety had in certain respects restricted the process of growth. But both of these men were leading lives designed not just for security but for positive satisfactions: happiness, success, a continuing sense of enlargement.

The Content of Personality

No two case studies can display everything that is involved in personality, but many of the topics taken up in the subsequent chapters of this book are important in understanding these two lives.

The family circles present us at once with a list of differences. The Chatwell family appears to have provided more sense of interest and support, a more lively intellectual climate, and a more liberal tradition. Merritt's parents, who emphasized community service, social acceptance, and a cautiously conservative outlook, failed to convey much feeling of family warmth and cohesiveness. Position within the family was a matter of significance: the eldest of three children is in a different situation from the younger of two boys. To these differences within the family circle must be added the important variables of social status and ethnic membership. The upper-class Gentile surroundings of the Chatwells constituted a different environment from the Merritts' middle-class Jewish neighborhood, and we may well wonder whether Chatwell's assertive tactics during military training would have been as well received if he had been Jewish. The environments in which our two subjects grew up must be rated as different in several significant respects.

The two young men differed, furthermore, in their physical and mental endowments. As nearly as one could tell, the largest difference lay in level of energy. The slender, small-boned, wiry Chatwell was capable of a sustained high output of both speech and activity, a capacity that affected some of the crucial decisions of his life. Merritt, whose physique was softer in outline and tended to thicken as he grew older, was consistently more placid and low-keyed in everything he did. Our two subjects testify to the importance of biological individuality.

The information about earliest development in these studies was not abundant. It is currently assumed, as we have seen, that what the young child learns through the dependent relation on the mother and through his early attempts to attain competence in dealing with the environment is of lasting importance for the growth of personality. For later events our subjects' memories were better furnished, and they provided information about their anxieties and avoidances, feelings of guilt and inferiority, problems in managing aggression, and view of adult expectations. We pick up the thread of their social participation and memberships, and notice in Merritt a dependence on friendly human support that contrasts with Chatwell's self-reliance and enjoyment of competition. Relations with girls and experiences of love played important and somewhat different parts in their personal development. Their use of educational resources was also an individual matter. Chatwell made fast progress in a small private school, impressing everyone with his quick wit, but as a college student he was disappointed at his lack of lasting interest and sustained application. Merritt moved less spectacularly through public high school, studied as a dutiful chore, and found college courses at most mildly interesting; but graduation from college remained an unquestioned part of his life plan. It proved profitable to examine the different strategies employed by the two men in pursuit of their goals, especially their ways of dealing with other people. Here Merritt showed a persistently lower level of confidence and initiative. Finally, the subjects' pictures of themselves and statements of their values provided indispensable clues to the organization of their personalities and the priorities that governed their behavior.

Only two cases are required to demonstrate the diversity of human life patterns. So different were the directions taken by Chatwell and Merritt that at 30 they almost seemed to occupy different worlds. It is hard not to jump to an evaluation—one life pattern must be better than the other—but if such judgments are to be worth anything they must be made with much understanding and tolerance. This problem is taken up in the final chapter of the book.

3 The Influence of Parental Attitudes

During the earliest years of life a child's environment consists almost wholly of home and family. It is in this small world that the important first steps in development take place. A young child's day consists of meals, naps, baths, dressing and undressing, and periods of play, either with objects or with the members of the household. His human contact is likewise restricted; only the immediate family is more or less constantly present, and outsiders are for a considerable time less interesting to the child than household pets. The predominance of this small environment in the young child's experience is shown in the types of situations that evoke fear. The child may take quite lightly events known to adults to be full of peril, like wartime bombing raids, but experience strong anxiety about changes of routine, physical discomforts, absence of the mother, and emotional upsets in the household.

As the child's capacities progressively ripen, of course, he begins to cross the boundaries of home and encounter a wider world of objects and people, including other children of his own age. Presently he goes to school, which brings him into contact with new tasks, new acquaintances, and a new circle of adults. During adolescence the weight of influence continues to shift from family circle to outside world, sometimes smoothly but sometimes as the result of embattled effort. In many societies past and present, and in many sectors of our own society, close contact with the family of origin continues throughout life. The logical end point of complete separation is common only in mobile industrial societies, in which young adults often establish themselves far away from the scenes of their childhood.

The character of a child's experience in the family circle is naturally much influenced by the parents. It is influenced by many other things as well, but the parents are key figures whose behavior is bound to have a powerful effect. This is no modern discovery. A large store of practical wisdom on the subject has accumulated over the years without benefit of psychological research. When child guidance became a matter of serious professional concern during the 1920s, the relation between children's troubles and parents' attitudes assumed immediate prominence, and the topic of parent-child relations was chosen early for research. In this chapter we shall consider what has been learned by studying the effects on children of different parental attitudes. It should not be assumed, of course, that these attitudes alone determine child personality, that the relation is strictly one of cause and effect, or that other influences, including the child's own response to his treatment, are not always in operation. Bearing in mind that personality is formed in a complex field of influences and events, it is still legitimate to select one kind of influence and investigate whether or not it produces detectable average consequences. This is the subject of the chapter—the detectable average consequences of a number of parental attitudes on the growth of personality in childhood.

Acceptance versus Rejection

The first parental attitude to emerge clearly in modern study is one that is usually called *rejection*. This term implies that the parents do not feel affection for the child, or at least not enough affection to moderate their contrary feelings of frustration and anger. Such attitudes on the part of parents were foreshadowed in studies of juvenile delinquency. There was a time late in the nineteenth century when young delinquents were viewed unsympathetically as "bad eggs" with some kind of innate biological defect. This idea was gradually supplanted when serious inquiry was turned to the environments in which delinquent children grew up. Conditions discovered in their homes lent support to the idea that the troublesome behavior was an intelligible response to a difficult environment. Delinquency sprang most frequently, the case records seemed to say, from homes crushed by poverty, where food, clothing, and space were in short supply. It originated very often in broken homes, or in households still intact but tortured by strife and brutality, where efforts at training were conducted with sporadic bursts of angry punishment or streams of belittling criticism. There was nothing remarkable in a boy's preferring companionship on the streets, spiced with the excitement of breaking windows, stealing cars, or otherwise defying authority, if home life meant constantly knuckling under to an abusive, alcoholic father. There was no need to invoke a bad inheritance to explain a boy's running away from home when one learned about a bitter stepmother who required the child to steal food for the household, thrashed him violently whenever he failed, and killed a stray dog which he tried to keep and feed in secret. Details of this sort from clinical histories gave vividness to the idea that parents did not automatically love their children. They could hate their children, and this attitude appeared to be all too common in the family circles of juvenile delinquents.

Overt Rejection

In order to understand more fully the nature and effects of parental rejection, it is necessary to separate the parents' attitudes from other circumstances that are often present in economically depressed areas. A step in this direction can be taken by studying children from such areas who have not taken the pathway of delinquency. In a monumental study of this kind, Sheldon and Eleanor Glueck investigated in detail 500 delinquent boys and another 500, matched as closely as possible with respect to age, intelligence, ethnic background, and residence in disadvantaged areas, who showed no signs of delinquency.[1] Parental attitudes characterized as warm were found in 80 percent of the nondelinquent group, twice as often as in the familes of delinquents, whereas attitudes described as indifferent or hostile were present with greater frequency in the parents of delinquents. Similarly, discipline that was firm but kindly seemed to characterize more than half of the parents of nondelinquents but only 5 percent in the delinquent group. Lax, overstrict, or erratic discipline had higher frequencies in delinquent backgrounds. The Gluecks found that the delinquent boys were more likely than the others to feel rejected at home, claiming that they had never been recognized or appreciated, a finding that has been repeatedly verified in other studies of delinquents' attitudes.[2] More likely to appear also among the delinquents were resentment toward parents, suspicion of other people's motives, and impulsive behavior with poor self-control. In a study based on comparisons between group averages this does not constitute final proof that the parents' behavior caused the delinquent boys' attitudes, but a connection seems probable. Being unappreciated at home, perhaps actively disliked, leads plausibly to resentment, suspicion, and a feeling of alienation from home values. Opposition to these values, which are likely to include self-control and respect for authority, can be well expressed by waywardness and adventures in delinquency.

The effects of parental rejection can be seen at closer range in a study that eliminated the complicating influence of poverty and slum surroundings. Bandura and Walters chose subjects of average or better than average intelligence who came from intact homes in reasonably good neighborhoods and whose fathers were steadily employed.[3] By means of interviews with parents and adolescent sons, they compared 26 boys having histories of aggressive antisocial behavior with a control group of 26 who were free from such behavior. Their study makes the same kind of comparison that was done in the Gluecks' investigation, but the scene has shifted to a middle-class neighborhood.

[1] S. and E. Glueck, *Unraveling Juvenile Delinquency* (New York: The Commonwealth Fund, 1950); *Delinquents and Non-Delinquents in Perspective* (Cambridge, Mass.: Harvard University Press, 1968).

[2] P. C. Goldin, "A Review of Children's Reports of Parent Behaviors," *Psychological Bulletin*, **71** (1968), 222–236.

[3] A. Bandura and R. H. Walters, *Adolescent Aggression* (New York: The Ronald Press Company, 1959).

We can demonstrate the findings best by describing a particular subject and his family. Donald, an only child, had accumulated both a school and a court record for antisocial aggression before he reached his seventeenth birthday. By this time he was strongly committed to an independent pattern of life. In the interviews he declared that he would never ask for help from his parents, from teachers, from counselors, or even from friends, repeatedly stating a preference for working things out for himself. His relations with his parents were distinctly antagonistic, yet he found no compensation with boys of his own age, whom he viewed as untrustworthy and approached with ill-concealed hostility: "I kind of hate them when I first meet them." Even in his early encounters with other children, during his first years at school, he had been irritable and quick to resort to his fists, although a competing anxiety showed itself in a tendency to stand aside from the others. Yet as a baby Donald had often been responsive and affectionate. His mother recalled that he would climb into her lap and kiss her cheek, that he liked to be rocked to sleep, and that when she tried to have him "entertain himself a certain amount" in his room he would quickly rejoin her. What happened that could suppress these urges toward affection and turn Donald into a hostile, suspicious, excessively self-reliant adolescent?

The interviews contain strong hints, even though they may not have touched all aspects of the problem. Donald himself averred that his father did not understand him, was not interested in him, and acted as if he did not like to have him around. For his mother he retained some positive feeling but was sure that she, too, did not understand him and added: "I never rely on her." At 17 he clearly felt rejected by both parents. If his mother's memory was correct, the estrangement had been going on at least since the age of 8, and probably earlier. She remarked of Donald's father that children "got on his nerves" and that he did not make an effort to understand them. Perhaps it was an early feeling of this impatience that caused Donald to reject friendly overtures and wriggle out of his father's lap. Soon the father was advocating independence as if he wanted to have nothing to do with the child, and his attempts at discipline were recounted in punitive language like "thrashing things out," and "knocking things into him." Describing the punishment of taking away Donald's allowance, the father exclaimed: "Boy, that hurts him more than anything." At the same time the father did not hesitate to express belittlement; he seemed easily convinced that Donald's poor school work signified ultimate inferiority in life. Rejective tendencies in the mother were less open and unmitigated, though there is a hint of them in her early desire to have the child play by himself. But she was easily antagonized when at the age of three his initiative and assertiveness rapidly increased: "He and I used to go round and round until I began to think maybe I was too hard on him, and then I would let up." Moreover, she was not able to soften her husband's impact. In a later showdown over sloppy clothes and haircut, she urged him to let Donald do as the rest of the crowd did, but she finally advised her son that her urgings were of no avail and that he had better go along with his father's wishes. It is easy to understand why Donald said that he never relied on her and why he felt that in the last analysis both parents were against him. Thus, as the authors of the study put it, "he remained unloved and unwanted."[4]

It is possible to think of *rejection* as being at one end of a continuum of possible parental attitudes. At the other end would stand attitudes that have been variously described as love, warmth, and affection, but most often by the general term *acceptance*. The acceptance-rejection variable can be pictured as representing the relative proportions of love and hate, or, in milder terms, of affectionate interest and irritated avoidance. It is easy to think of these attitudes in terms of the emotions they sometimes produce, but a fairly central thing, as Baldwin has pointed out, is the extent to which the parent finds it rewarding or burdensome to interact with the child from day to day.

> The obvious reaction to finding the child burdensome is to have as little to do with him as possible. . . . We can see that the desire to reduce social interaction with the child would tend to make the parent dictatorial. The parent must make decisions about the child; he will be asked questions. The response of the parent who does not want to enter into the situation is to make some snap judgment in a final fashion. "No, you cannot go to the movie, now leave me alone," or, "Do whatever you want to, but get out of the kitchen," are answers which reveal the fact that at the moment the child's demands are burdensome. Every parent has felt this on some occasion; the rejecting parents are those who feel this interaction to be an imposition and intrusion whenever it occurs.[5]

Hostility toward a child may be present from the start, as when a step-parent unwillingly assumes responsibility for children not his own. More often it is the result of an accumulation of small frustrations in a parent for whom the burdens of interaction outweigh the satisfactions.

Pleasure in contact with the child is a central theme in the case chosen by Bandura and Walters to contrast with Donald.[6] The father of Raymond sought opportunities to play with his son even when the child was quite small. When the boy became a Cub Scout the father became a Cub Master, and during the subsequent years of scouting he went with the troop on all its trips. The mother took a similar interest in what interested Raymond and expressed great satisfaction in his company. Both parents had to control themselves a bit to let him have the independent life with other children which on principle they considered desirable. For some tastes these parents may seem rather doting, but they illustrate with unusual clarity the affection, interest, and pleasure in interaction that constitute an attitude of acceptance. The interviews indicate that Raymond prospered in this supporting atmosphere without being trapped by it. Outside the family circle his adolescent career was marked by confidence and sociability. His willingness to accept legitimate help contrasts sharply with Donald's surly, isolating independence.

---

[4] Quotations in these two paragraphs are from Bandura and Walters, *Adolescent Aggression*, pp. 313–332.

[5] A. L. Baldwin, *Behavior and Development in Childhood* (New York: Holt, Rinehart and Winston, Inc., 1955), pp. 488–489.

[6] Bandura and Walters, *Adolescent Aggression*, pp. 332–354.

Covert Rejection

The attitudes of acceptance and rejection have been described thus far in their overt forms. One of the possible complications is an attitude that has been characterized as overt acceptance with covert rejection. The most impressive evidence for a pattern of this kind came from the psychoanalyst Karen Horney and was derived from her work in treating neurotic patients.[7] Her sample of patients, mostly wealthy enough to afford private psychiatric treatment, stands far removed from the slum-dwelling delinquent children among whom parental rejection was first clearly discerned. In behavior the neurotic patients were also far removed, displaying a great deal of anxiety and inhibition but a minimum of antisocial aggression. There is no reason to suppose that overt rejection is confined to lower economic levels or covert rejection to higher ones. Covert patterns come to light more easily, however, when it is possible to use the extended probings and rememberings that go on in psychoanalytic therapy. Often it took patients a long time, with recollection of many incidents, to perceive the inconsistent pattern to which they had been exposed.

In Horney's account of her observations the parents were characterized as lacking true warmth and affection for the child. This lack of warmth, however, was concealed behind an overt attitude of solicitude and care, with frequently expressed concern for the child's best interests. The parents seemed to have convinced themselves that they were loving, and might even have cast themselves in the role of ideal parents, all of which made it doubly necessary to remain unaware of their response to the burdensome aspects of having children around. But the elements of hostility that they could not admit to consciousness crept out in indirect ways. The parents might, for example, promise a child a much desired treat on a certain day but change the plan at the last minute because of some seemingly legitimate concern of their own. They might carry out a sensible policy of throwing away broken and dirty toys while never noticing that certain ones had become precious to the child. Similarly they might make unfavorable comments on the child's friends, including those who had become most important to him. In short, their latent hostility, unmodulated by awareness that they had it, might dictate a whole series of moves in which the child's feelings and interests were given not the slightest consideration.

Horney believed that parental attitudes of covert rejection created deep anxiety in the child. "Needless to say," she wrote, "a child feels keenly whether love is genuine, and cannot be fooled by any faked demonstrations." Becoming progressively aware of the small importance ascribed to his wishes in the household, the child experiences "an insidiously increasing, all-pervading feeling of being lonely and helpless in a hostile world." One of Horney's patients drew a spontaneous picture of herself as a "tiny, helpless, naked baby, surrounded by all sorts of menacing monsters, human and ani-

[7] Karen Horney, *The Neurotic Personality of Our Time* (New York: W. W. Norton & Company, 1937).

mal, ready to attack her." Another dreamed that she was a "small mouse that had to hide in a hole in order not to be stepped upon."[8] Confidence is undermined, initiative and enterprise are poisoned with disapproval, and the possibility of trusting the human environment is steadily whittled away. Horney came to believe that this sort of pervasive anxiety was a necessary, though not in itself a sufficient, cause of later neurosis.

Why should overt and covert rejection produce such different results? It would seem to be a good guess that the answer lies in the fate of the child's answering hostility. In either case the child is often frustrated by the parents, but if the rejection is overt he has a chance to perceive the unfair and irrational aspects of his treatment and thus, like Donald, direct his anger back at his parents and the constraints for which they stand. If the rejection is covert, this avenue is closed: the parents believe they are good parents, repeatedly say so, and justify their acts as being in the child's best interests. Anger directed against this solid front of felt virtue is self-defeating. It is met by reproaches and further self-justification, and its only effect can be to weaken such chances of being loved as may still exist. Therefore the child dares to blame only himself, belittles his own feelings, and is trapped in an ever-deepening conviction of helplessness.

Covert Acceptance

There is no logical reason why the pattern of parental attitudes just described should not occur in reverse: overt rejection and covert acceptance. Not much has been made of this possibility in the writings of psychologists, nor have there been systematic investigations of its effects. But there is nothing incongruous in the idea that parents can be deeply fond of their children yet also enough irritated by daily interactions so that a surface air of friction is maintained. Mothers may peck at their children for small faults but proudly relate great virtues when chatting with their neighbors. Fathers may prefer the newspaper to evening interaction with their offspring but put much thought and effort into assuring them opportunities for higher education. Familiar to many families will be the following sequence of emotions:

> The children are going on an all-day hike with a group under capable leadership. They cannot wait to get out of the house away from parental nagging, nor can the parents wait to hear their voices receding into the distance so that a little peace and relaxation can be enjoyed. By lunch time the parents begin to miss the children and complain that the house is too quiet. In the afternoon there are thunderstorms, and when the group fails to return at the stated hour the parents become sick with fear and call up neighbors to organize a search party. Finally the hikers come in, wet and bedraggled, delayed by having missed the trail on their way home. The parents are overjoyed and immensely relieved, though these emotions may be screened by criticism of the leaders for losing

[8] Quotations in this paragraph from Horney, *The Neurotic Personality of Our Time,* pp. 80, 89, 92, 93.

the way. The children, though pride may forbid them to show it, are as glad to be back at home as they were glad to leave in the morning.

The psychological consequences of the pattern of overt rejection and covert acceptance may be presumed to depend upon the proportions between the two and especially upon the extent to which the latent love is made evident to the child. Covert rejection, we have seen, leads to a variety of behaviors showing lack of consideration for the child's feelings, thus causing frustration. Covert acceptance should produce considerate behavior in large matters, but this may be overshadowed by the overt friction. One report is available which bears on this problem. Austin Wood, in a paper on his personal psychoanalysis, described his father as strict and outwardly unloving; the relation consisted chiefly of angry and bitter arguments. One day when the boy was 11 he was injured in a street accident and was carried home by his father, who bade him, "Be a big man and stop crying"—which he did. During the psychoanalysis, he recollected the full emotional significance of this scene: his father holding him tenderly, much concerned, expressing by his tone of voice both his deep love and his respect for his son's manliness.[9] It is clear in this case that overt rejection was sufficiently strong to dominate the relation between father and son; a major crisis was necessary to bring into the open the father's covert acceptance. But it is possible for the balance to tip in the opposite direction. College students looking back on their family experience sometimes report a pervasive confidence that their parents would stand back of them through thick and thin, supporting them in the things that really mattered. Against such a background parental impatience, daily bickering, and high words bandied across the dinner table could easily be tolerated as superficial froth.

Maternal Overprotection

An important historical place is occupied by David Levy's study of maternal overprotection.[10] This maternal attitude is of great interest in its own right, and the findings will also serve to introduce another major dimension of parental attitudes.

Levy's study was a retrospective clinical research based on selected case records from the Institute for Child Guidance in New York. From more than 500 consecutive records, 20 cases were selected that exhibited maternal overprotection in unmistakable and powerful form. The research workers who assisted in the selection were told to include only loved and wanted children, excluding instances in which the mother's protectiveness appeared to be a

[9] A. B. Wood, "Another Psychologist Analyzed," *Journal of Abnormal and Social Psychology*, **36** (1941), 87–90.

[10] D. M. Levy, *Maternal Overprotection* (New York: Columbia University Press, 1943).

compensation for latent hostility. No doubt it was difficult to make this judgment with complete success from clinical records, but at least an attempt was made to choose cases in which the mothers stood high on the variable of acceptance. Levy argued that maternal overprotection provided something close to a natural experiment in which a single parental attitude could be isolated for study. The overprotective mother works hard to exclude other influences, such as that of the father or those of friends, thus making herself the major element in the child's surroundings. When 20 cases meeting the criteria had been selected it turned out that there were 19 boys and 1 girl. Although this is in harmony with a common impression that intense maternal relations are more likely to develop with male children, it should be remembered that the sample was drawn from children referred for guidance. Conceivably the effects of an engulfing maternal relation are more quickly judged serious in boys than in girls.

Levy described maternal overprotection under three headings: (1) *Excessive contact* was shown in the mother's being always there. She offered continuous companionship, prolonged care during illness, and amounts of fondling even up to puberty that were much in excess of common practice. One mother of a 7-year-old boy had given up all social life in order to be at home with her son. Another, whose son was 16, claimed to share his every experience; they went to the movies together and had a common social life. (2) *Infantilization* was displayed in the mother's performing acts of care for the child well beyond the age when such attentions usually cease. The records showed that breast feeding had continued much longer than average. This indulgence was later expressed through, for example, assisting an 8-year-old to dress, accompanying an 8-year-old to and from school, shining shoes for a boy of 14, and fetching a glass of water whenever a son of 15 requested it. (3) *Prevention of independent behavior* was to be seen in regularly helping the child with homework, excusing him from irksome chores, and discouraging if not actually preventing the forming of friendships outside the home. It was characteristic of the mothers to take active steps to preserve their monopoly of influence over the children.

The behavior of the children, however, did not present a uniform picture. They fell into two clear groups, with only one case on the borderline. In 11 cases the behavior that had led to referral was rebellious, defiant, and tyrannizing. The reports mentioned disobedience, impudence, tantrums, spitting and swearing, slapping and kicking, demanding food whenever it was wanted, throwing disliked food on the floor. At school these children did well scholastically but were cocky, selfish, and much inclined to show off in the company of other children. These were the cases in which overprotection had been combined with feeble disciplinary control: the mothers had surrendered to the child's wishes and allowed infantile tendencies, including aggression, a flourishing growth. Most of these children had been referred by their mothers, who wanted help in controlling their rambunctious young. In the contrasting 8 cases the behavior of the children could best be described as submissively dependent. At home the children were docile, neat, obedient, industrious, and helpful around the house; with other children at school they were painfully shy and timid, and showed a strong preference to stay out of playground activities. These were the cases in which overprotection had been combined with dominance and close control. It is noteworthy that the referrals came mostly from teachers, who were worried about the children's social ineptitude. The mothers were not unhappy about the docile pattern.

The behavior of the overprotective mothers seems so excessive, and that of the children so unpromising, that the findings with respect to outcome may come as something of a surprise. Levy did not attribute much change to the clinic's effort, but follow-up information from nine to twelve years later classified all but two of the young people as at least "partially adjusted." For the most part the traits of the earlier time still showed, but in more modulated form, and schoolwork had on the whole gone well. Perhaps it can be inferred that these children had two advantages, in spite of their overwhelming protection. They had never felt unloved or unwanted, and they had been given a head start with their studies, around which self-direction and persistence could eventually become organized.[11]

If the cases in Levy's study were successfully selected according to design, the mothers all stood far toward the accepting end of the acceptance-rejection variable. But they differed widely with respect to the constraints they placed upon their children, ranging from doting indulgence of every whim to intrusive direction of every aspect of the child's life. Clearly another dimension is needed to accommodate this important parental attitude.

High Control versus Low Control

In contrast to the dimension of acceptance-rejection, which expresses the balance between love and hate, is a variable of parental attitudes in which the central theme has more to do with power. There has been little agreement on naming this dimension, which has been variously called dominant-submissive, demanding-indulgent, restrictive-permissive, and autocratic-democratic. The central meaning is best indicated by calling the two ends of the continuum *high control* and *low control*.

The strongly controlling parent undertakes to direct the child's behavior by making and enforcing rules, by curbing impulsive outbursts, by providing information and guidance, and by setting detailed standards of conduct. The implicit idea is that the parent knows best and that the child must be steered toward acceptable adult behavior. The low-control parent shows little of this dominance and leaves the child as much as possible to the dictates of his own impulses and initiative. The implicit value for this parent is that

---

[11] Further evidence of the nature of an intensely possessive maternal relation will be found in G. W. Allport, *Letters from Jenny* (New York: Harcourt Brace Jovanovich, Inc., 1965). These letters describe the stormy course of a mother's possessive relationship with a grown up son.

the child take care of himself and learn through his own experience. Within these extremes there is room for wide variation between high and low control.

When considering the control variable, it is important to be on guard against presuppositions built into the language. If this dimension is perceived as extending from autocratic to democratic behavior, images spring to mind of Mussolini, Hitler, and totalitarian tyranny at one end and the democratic allies fighting for freedom at the other. Not by chance these two designations became prominent in developmental psychology just after World War II. If, as is now fairly common, the high-control end is labeled "restrictive" and the low end "permissive," there is again an aura of evil and good; the images that now leap up are likely to be of arbitrary middle-aged parents trying to *restrict* the freedom of their adolescent sons and daughters who ought to be *permitted* to make their own decisions. When we think of human interactions in general —interactions among adult equal citizens—the advantages all seem to lie with low control; dominating and demanding attitudes are unlikely to produce good human relations. But with parents and children, the interaction is not between adult equal citizens. Especially when the children are small, the relation is inherently unequal in the sense that the mature members have to take care of the immature ones, providing them with protection, economic support, and training for membership in family and society. Parents must bring up children—we all expect this of them. To do so they must on occasion dominate, guide, restrict, and insist upon having their expectations met. Calling the control variable "high guidance versus low guidance" might help to separate it from a value scale going simply from bad to good. High guidance might still be viewed with disfavor, but really low guidance could only mean deprivation of what parents owe their children, reaching its extreme in total neglect. Some degree of control is inherent if parenthood is taken seriously.

At first glance it might be supposed that high control would go more often with parental rejection and low control with acceptance. This turns out to be not at all a reliable rule; the love variable and the power variable can appear in all possible combinations. Bearing in mind that rejection involves interacting with the child as little as possible, it can be seen that such an attitude is not compatible with a real policy of close control and guidance. In his remarkable autobiography John Stuart Mill describes in detail the manner in which his father, James Mill, undertook from the earliest years to control his education and preside over the forming of his mind.[12] Clearly the elder Mill was committed to almost constant contact with his son in order to execute his strenuous plan for the shaping of character. The son describes studying his Greek lessons across the table from his father, who was writing a history of India, and interrupting him to ask the meaning of each new Greek word. He marvels that his father, naturally an impatient man, could have endured this constant breaking of his train of thought. It is indeed a marvel unless we assume that the son whose mind James Mill was shaping was in a true sense

---

[12] J. S. Mill, *Autobiography* (1873) (New York: Columbia University Press, 1924).

the apple of his eye. High control does not necessarily imply rejection, nor does low control inevitably signify love. Indeed, low control is compatible with different attitudes that vary widely along the acceptance-rejection dimension. It may signify doting indulgence, with the child perceived as a treasure from heaven whose wishes should never be crossed. It may signify indifference and even hostile rejection, when the parent finds the child a nuisance and wants him out of the way. Between these extremes it may reflect a considered policy of permissiveness and an attempt at family democracy, but low control is also characteristic of parents who are made anxious by exerting authority or whose values are so confused that they cannot decide what standards to set.

Two Examples of Democratic Child Rearing

To illustrate relatively low control, we take two slightly contrasting cases of upbringing under an explicit democratic philosophy of child care. These cases come from the Fels Research Institute in Yellow Springs, Ohio, and are part of an intensive study of children and their families that has been going on since 1929. Knowledge of the interaction between parents and children was obtained in this study through regular home visits, the findings of which were entered on carefully wrought descriptive scales. Besides being seen at home with their parents, the children were observed at school and tested at the Institute.[13] Both of the two boys to be described, Dale and Leonard, had highly intelligent parents who were strongly committed to a democratic ideal in family life. This meant to the parents a scrupulous respect for the child's unfolding powers of understanding and initiative. They enacted this by minimizing coercion, giving reasons for necessary restrictions, and trying to make the child an active participant in family decisions. As further implementation of these ideals both families had set up the institution of the family council, a domestic legislative assembly in which grievances were discussed and policy decisions arrived at, each member having one vote. The right to vote was attained as soon as the child reached sufficient linguistic maturity to participate in the proceedings of the assembly.

In Dale's case the principles were applied with ingenuity, and with scientific detachment. His mother was unusually inexpressive of emotion, and this made it easier for her to devise consistently democratic policies. When Dale was still very young she tried whenever possible to give him choices of action. By the time he was 5 he was making his own decisions with respect to naps, indoor or outdoor play, and staying at home or visiting neighbors, and he had a voice in the family menu. Reasons were given for every imposed frustration, including his occasional exclusion when the parents' friends were calling or a committee was meeting at the house. Babying and pampering were strictly avoided, but Dale was given maximum intellectual stimulation. Exploratory tendencies were encouraged as soon as he could crawl by hiding toys in unusual places. At 3 he knew how to answer the telephone and put

---

[13] A. L. Baldwin, J. Kalhorn, and F. H. Breese, "Patterns of Parent Behavior," *Psychological Monographs* **58**, no. 268 (1945).

through outgoing calls. Soon afterwards he had absorbed a completely adult pattern of speech and pronunciation. The mother in particular placed a high value on accomplishment and on rational intelligent behavior. Inferior performances were never called bad but were rejected as being what stupid people would do.

It will be noticed that this description entails something more than a democratic attitude. Further qualification is necessary: democratic principles are applied with scientific detachment and a certain coolness, which, though not really rejective, places the parents some distance down from the accepting end of the love dimension. In addition there is great emphasis on intellectual development, resulting in an active program designed to accelerate Dale's academic career. This pressure to accelerate seems hardly consistent with complete respect for the child's preferred and natural ways of growing up, and contemptuous references to stupid people are unlikely to foster a democratic spirit. At all events, Dale at the time of entering school was eager, precocious, and self-reliant, but by no means prepared to be at home in a society of equals. His most prominent social trait was violent, unreasonable aggressiveness, which he directed freely at playmates, teachers, relatives, bystanders, and even other children who were trying to make friendly advances. Such uninhibited belligerence is hardly the intended outcome of democratic child rearing, and it may have had more to do with those aspects of the regime that discouraged gentleness and geared approval to being an intellectual boy wonder. Fortunately Dale was not long in discovering the likely consequences of his aggression and managed to moderate it a little in the interests of being liked by the other children.

In the second example, that of Leonard, democratic principles and low control coexisted with warm, kindly, good-humored enjoyment of children on the part of the parents. Maintaining their policies was not always easy for the parents, who sometimes checked themselves from expressing affectionate feelings that seemed beneath the dignity even of small citizens. They were unusually tolerant of sexual impulses, tried to avoid constraints that might evoke anxiety, and did their best to keep out of squabbles, hoping that the children would learn to settle them by themselves. The Fels observers were favorably impressed by the effects of this warm democracy but did not overlook certain difficulties that resulted from it for Leonard. There were four children in the family, forming with the parents a closely knit circle which was in many respects a satisfying and sufficient human environment. Before going to school Leonard was timid and shy about venturing into the less supportive world outside his home. Furthermore, the parents' policy of letting the children settle their own differences acted to defeat democratic ideals. Inevitable conflicts of interest and competition for parental affection led to power struggles of a crude kind, unmodulated by democratic principles still far beyond the children's grasp. Leonard was put under much belittling pressure, especially from his older brother, who often charged him with being lazy and irresponsible. As a consequence he exhibited rather severe feelings of inferiority, which he carried with him to school and which began to be alleviated only when he began to achieve popularity with his classmates.

Commenting on these and other instances of the effects of parental attitudes of low control, Baldwin draws a conclusion with appropriate reserve.

> Neither a democratic philosophy nor democratic techniques applied in the training of the child can provide an automatically optimum environment. . . . Adequately applied, these techniques *may* facilitate the production of a child who is an independent human being, secure in his relationships, able to appraise himself and his environment, and capable of self-direction and attainment. But these goals of the democratic method can be defeated by the parent who warps the child's personality in some other way, the parent whose own misapplied devotion and confined viewpoint restrict the child's growth and freedom, or the parent who, by his own withdrawal and detachment, makes the child insecure and uncertain in his goals and relationships.[14]

The Authoritarian Personality

Like low control, high control can take a great many forms, some the result of formulated beliefs, others spontaneous and unreflective. One of the possible patterns was brought to light in 1950 in a monumental study by Adorno, Frenkel-Brunswik, Levinson, and Sanford entitled *The Authoritarian Personality*.[15] This work, which has had a lasting influence on contemporary thought, called attention to connections between personality as formed in childhood and later attitudes toward social problems. The study was made at the end of World War II, when the power of fascist ideas over whole nations, and the barbarities to which these ideas could lead, were fresh in memory. It began as an attempt to uncover the emotional roots of hostility toward outgroups. Prejudice against Jews was taken as the leading example, but the focus was more broadly on rigid and bigoted ways of thinking. The authors developed scales for the measurement of ideologies, devising questionnaires that permitted them to test large numbers of people. By this means they selected from a much larger number two groups of young adult subjects, one very high on prejudice and one very low. The selected groups were small enough to make possible an elaborate program of interviews and psychological tests designed to disclose both the present personality and its childhood background in the family circle.

The prejudiced subjects proved to be more likely than the unprejudiced to report parental discipline that was harsh, threatening, and arbitrary. The threat was so great that the only safe course was subservience, with suppression of unacceptable impulses. The disciplinary program was based on power relations: dominance by parents, submission by children. It appeared that the authoritarian parent was likely to be concerned about appearances and social status, holding conventional values for reasons not easily understood by children. These values were likely to be expressed in stereotyped ways as somewhat inflexible clichés, and a strong emphasis was laid on fitting

---

[14] A. L. Baldwin, *Behavior and Development in Childhood*, p. 516.

[15] T. W. Adorno, E. Frenkel-Brunswik, D. J. Levinson, and R. N. Sanford, *The Authoritarian Personality* (New York, Harper & Row, Publishers, 1950).

expected roles and meeting obligations. Such a regime exhibits a high degree of control without much implication of affection: the power dimension obscures the love dimension. It also exhibits an arbitrary and somewhat overconfident way of thinking. Under such forceful pressures the child's relative helplessness and dependent needs dictate submission with acceptance of the proffered values, while his assertiveness begins to find outlets in proclaiming those values with indignant righteousness at the expense of others. Hostility, engendered by a program that frustrates many childish wishes, yet barred from direct expression by fear, now finds its opportunity for an acceptable outlet. Outgroups that are believed not to share the values of family and ingroup, that are imagined to threaten the ingroup in some way, become the object of a hostility that is felt to be entirely legitimate. As the authors put it: "The displacement of a repressed antagonism towards authority may be one of the sources, and perhaps the principal source, of the antagonism toward outgroups."[16]

It was emphasized in this study that the authors were speaking of average differences between two groups of subjects, not of something that always characterized the prejudiced subjects and never the unprejudiced. Because of the urgent social problems created by group hostilities it is all too easy to stereotype the people who chiefly cause these problems and forget that in the realms of personality things are not likely to be so simple. In the present instance the authors' reminder should be heeded that not every subject who displayed a prejudiced outlook also described authoritarian parental attitudes or exhibited authoritarian qualities of his own. There are other ways of arriving at prejudice besides growing up in the particular family constellation called authoritarian.[17] One of these is to live in an environment where prejudice is already widespread, so that accepting it may be simply an unthinking conformity on the part of a person who does not have an unusual need to displace aggression. Furthermore, the displacing of hostility to ethnic outgroups is only one of several ways to deal with the aggression engendered by authoritarian upbringing. Different targets can be chosen, such as "big business interests," criminals, juvenile delinquents, or the "shiftless poor," without reference to ethnic membership. It may even be that the hostility, mainly throttled in a subservient, guilty attitude, will be externalized to outgroups only if the parents ratify such a course through their own prejudiced behavior.

The relation between authoritarian parental attitudes and prejudice toward outgroups is thus not a tight one, being dependent on a good many contingent circumstances. The pattern disclosed in *The Authoritarian Personality* is, however, a valuable contribution toward understanding high control. As described, this high control is also rigid, arbitrary, and unsoftened by affection. These qualifications are necessary in order to appreciate the large amount of hostility engendered in the child. If the control were less stereotyped, more

---

[16] Adorno et al., *The Authoritarian Personality*, p. 482.

[17] D. Byrne, "Parental Antecedents of Authoritarianism," *Journal of Personality and Social Psychology*, **1** (1965), 369–373.

reasonable, and more informed by affectionate understanding, its frustrating effect would be smaller and its acceptance by the child would presumably be less laden with conflict. But high control can be said to exist, whatever the qualifications, when there is a central emphasis on adult dominance—when the parents feel that the twig must be bent if there is to be hope of an acceptable tree.

Longitudinal Investigation

Several other studies, generally involving children's behavior both at home and at school, compare the effects of high and low parental control. A summary by Becker shows that there is substantial agreement among them.[18] "Children of dominating parents were better socialized and more courteous, obedient, neat, generous, and polite," Becker concludes. "They were also more sensitive, self-conscious, shy, and retiring." Children from low-control homes proved to be "more disobedient, irresponsible, disorderly in the classroom, lacking in sustained attention, lacking in regular work habits, and more forward and expressive."[19] The meaning of these two patterns has been illuminated by Baldwin in connection with a study of nursery school behavior.[20] Noticing that children from low-control homes were rather wild and aggressive but also more inventive, original, and confident in using the opportunities provided by the school, Baldwin reflected on the dilemma that is inherent in the socialization of children. "Conformity to cultural demands," he said, "is not easily obtained without robbing the child of that personal integrity which gives him a mind of his own and which supports him in his attempts to satisfy his curiosity and to carry out his ideas and fantasies in dealing with the real world." High control runs just such a risk. "It obtains conformity but at the expense of personal freedom in areas which are not intended to be restricted" —areas such as curiosity and easily expressed affection. Low control, on the other hand, "runs the risk of producing too little conformity to cultural demands." There is an inherent risk that high control will accomplish more than is intended, whereas low control may achieve less socialization than is necessary.

Theoretically, one could resolve the dilemma described by Baldwin by discriminating between the kinds of behavior that should and should not be controlled. In practice this is less easy than it sounds, because in the earliest years the child's cognitive development may not be equal to such discriminations, even when the parents make them. If the young child experiences anxiety when he is reproved for boisterous disturbance or risky exploratory ventures, it is hard for him to realize that social gaiety on a more propitious occasion or adventuresomeness in a less dangerous environment, both of

---

[18] W. C. Becker, "Consequences of Different Kinds of Parental Discipline," in *Review of Child Development Research*, Vol. I, ed. M. L. Hoffman and L. W. Hoffman (New York: Russell Sage Foundation, 1964), esp. pp. 189–199.

[19] *Ibid.*, p. 191.

[20] A. L. Baldwin, "Socialization and the Parent-Child Relationship," *Child Development*, **19** (1948), 127–136.

which *feel* much the same as the previous behavior, now have the status of virtues. Early learning can easily be overgeneralized. This observation suggests that the time dimension is of great importance in understanding the effects of parental attitudes. Consequences are likely to change as the child's cognitive growth advances and he grasps more clearly what is going on. Longitudinal study, difficult as it may be, is clearly in order.

A longitudinal investigation by Kagan and Moss sheds further light on the control dimension.[21] The setting was again the Fels Research Institute, where a substantial number of children studied from birth have now reached adulthood. Kagan and Moss were able to use a series of 89 children, both boys and girls, dividing the study of their behavior and their parents' attitudes into periods (1–3, 3–6, 6–10, 10–14 years), and adding interview material with the child subjects after they had become young adults. Reported results were confined to the mothers' attitudes, on which the information was most complete. The findings showed that restrictiveness had by far its strongest inhibitory power during the earliest period. Restricted boys and girls both showed the docile, submissive, timid pattern described above. The mothers maintained fairly consistent restrictive patterns over the years, more so with the girls than with the boys, but the correlations with child behavior were never again so high. It is to be surmised that other influences competing with the mother, together with the child's growing cognitive capacity, combined to produce this lessening impress of maternal restriction. As adolescents and young adults, both sexes refrained from criticism or hostility toward their parents, though both gave evidence of suppressed aggression. The girls, however, after showing some aggression during the 3–6 period, remained in adulthood rather passive and dependent on their families, whereas the boys, already restive during childhood and preadolescence, turned actively if somewhat anxiously to peer relations as a means, it would seem, of counterbalancing maternal restriction.

This research makes it evident that a parental attitude, even if it is maintained consistently over the years, meets an evolving response as the child's active and cognitive capacities enlarge. There will be progressively less generalization of situations that involve anxiety, more awareness of alternative paths, a sharper sense of injustice, and more shrewd and discriminating ways of protesting. The effects are not necessarily the same for boys and girls; probably the parents' attitudes themselves are not quite the same. In any event it is clear that the effects of parental attitudes cannot be fully understood apart from the dimension of time.

Summary of Effects

One of the steps that has been taken to facilitate thinking about parental attitudes is to arrange them in a *systematic diagram*. Following earlier suggestions, and making a mathematical analysis of the results of four previous

[21] J. Kagan and H. A. Moss, *Birth to Maturity* (New York: John Wiley & Sons, Inc., 1962).

investigations, Schaefer proposed the diagram that is given in Figure 1.[22] The two main axes, hostility versus love and autonomy versus control, correspond closely to what have been described here as the acceptance–rejection and the high control–low control variables. By laying them out as axes, we can locate a number of recognizable attitudes that partake of both variables; these are represented in the diagram by the labeled black dots. The model was developed specifically to describe maternal behavior, but in a rough way it can be

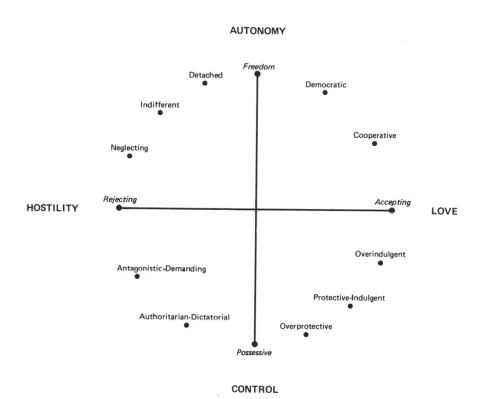

Figure 1. A hypothetical circumplex of maternal behavior concepts. (Adapted from E. W. Schaefer, "A Circumplex Model for Maternal Behavior," *Journal of Abnormal and Social Psychology,* **59** (1959), 232. Copyright 1959 by the American Psychological Association, and reproduced by permission.)

used as well for the attitudes of fathers. An authoritarian parent, for example, male or female, belongs in the lower left quadrant, placed so as to indicate very strong control and a somewhat smaller degree of rejection. Parents of slum-dwelling juvenile delinquents would be more likely to appear in the upper left quadrant, combining rejection with a low control that represents neglect and indifference rather than intended policy. The model does justice to

[22] E. W. Schaefer, "A Circumplex Model for Maternal Behavior," *Journal of Abnormal and Social Psychology,* **59** (1959), 226–235.

those of Levy's overprotective mothers who also dominated their children: they belong in the quadrant that combines love and control. It seems to fail with the truly indulgent overprotective mothers, who in that particular sample exhibited in some respects a minimum of control; however, remembering Levy's three criteria of overprotection, control in certain spheres is implicit in protectiveness. This slight problem in placing certain mothers serves as a reminder that there is nothing magical about a diagram of this kind. The diagram is an aid to thought to the extent that it permits an easier grasp of possible relations among attitudes. Carried beyond this point, it might impede thought by diverting attention from the variety and individuality of actual parental behavior.

Even the most basic feature of the diagram, the two main axes, is not without its critics. Baldwin, for example, believes that a diagram has to be three-dimensional in order to encompass observed parental attitudes.[23] Becker, examining several studies made after the publication of Schaefer's model, introduces in agreement with Baldwin a third axis, labeled *anxious emotional involvement* vs. *calm detachment*.[24] Overprotective mothers, whatever their position on the control axis, would certainly be found clustered at the anxiously-involved end of this new variable, whereas highly educated parents consciously practicing a democratic child-rearing philosophy would run to the calm-detached end. These suggestions serve to underline the provisional nature of all attempts to capture parental attitudes in a systematic scheme.

Even dealing with two main axes makes it necessary to consider the *interaction* between the two chief variables. In his survey of research Becker puts the chief clear findings into the four squares of a table that represent all four possible combinations.[25] The effects of parental attitudes on child personality can be provisionally summarized in the following brief statements.

Acceptance and High Control

When dominance is combined with acceptance and communicated in a kindly and reasonable way, the child is likely to incorporate parental expectations in his own behavior and adapt himself to the requirements of authority in school and community. Hostility will be little evoked and easily controlled. The child will behave well, perhaps being thoughtful of others and applying himself steadily to schoolwork, but he may also lack the confidence to express warm feeling, assert himself, or risk flights of inventiveness and imagination. He will perform better in structured than in unstructured situations.

Acceptance and Low Control

Loved but left relatively free, the child under reasonably favorable circumstances is likely to develop qualities of confidence, assertiveness, and independence. Learning many things through trial and the exertion of his own

[23] A. L. Baldwin, *Behavior and Development in Childhood*, p. 519.
[24] W. C. Becker, "Consequences of Different Kinds of Parental Discipline," pp. 172–176.
[25] *Ibid.*, p. 198.

energy and inventiveness, he will have a good power of initiative and will perform well in unstructured situations. Parental attitudes will not impede social outgoingness, and leadership may come to be within his powers. There will be little at home to evoke hostility, but in the normal frustrations of competitive peer life he will be unpracticed in control, so that cooperative activity may come hard. He likewise tends to be ill-schooled in doing things without the agreeable push of spontaneous interest; persistence through the monotonous parts of long-range tasks may greatly bother him, and versatile superficiality may seem more rewarding than consistent accomplishment.

Rejection and High Control

When combined with rejection, high control still exerts a pressure for docile compliance, but there is now a problem connected with hostility. Rejecting parents offer the child a meager ration of love in return for his sacrifices of freedom. He submits mainly out of fear, and with resentment. A variety of consequences follow, which are most easily understood as different dispositions of the hostility. This may be directed at the self, creating a sense of guilt that eats away at self-confidence and that sometimes plays a part in the development of neurosis. It may injure the relation to other children, promoting either a quarrelsome tendency or, to avoid this, a withdrawal from contact. It may produce half-hearted compliance with authority in which socialized behavior is performed with sour resignation. It may be displaced to more remote objects such as outgroups seen as enemies of sound values. It may finally come into focus on the parents or on authority in general, producing a belated and often difficult rebellion.

Rejection and Low Control

The path of rebellion is most easily taken when the parents frustrate by rejection but do not intimidate by control. Motives for compliance are weak, aggression is not subjected to restraint, and the way is open for early migration to peer groups and a career of delinquency. Inducements to persistent effort are minimal, and even mere attendance at school may be felt as an intolerable restraint. But self-reliance and initiative in other spheres of action may be strongly developed. Performance will be better in unstructured than in structured situations.

In reading this summary it is important to keep in mind the limitation of its focus. The propositions are intended to express the influence that different parental attitudes have on the child's growth, but they do not imply that this influence stands alone. The variables represented by the two axes are often called *interaction variables;* they refer to the daily stream of direct interactions between parent and child, characterizing the nature of the parent's initiatives and of the child's probable responses. But a child's life contains much more than daily interactions with parents. As we saw in the second chapter, personality develops in a field of influences by which it is affected in complex ways. Particular cause-effect sequences have to be considered in the light of everything else that is happening. For this reason it would be premature to draw sweeping conclusions about child-rearing practices. Much as we would like to know how to create the most favorable conditions for growth, the prescription cannot be deduced simply from what has been learned about parental attitudes; there is always more to it. To illustrate this point we shall consider the problems involved in a system of child rearing that has had a great deal of popularity and influence in recent years.

Permissive Child Rearing

In the diagram of parental attitudes permissive child rearing belongs in the upper right quadrant: it is high on acceptance and low on control. The appeal of this position is evident if high acceptance is equated with love and low control with democracy. Parental attitudes characterized as loving can be expected to show themselves in direct expressions of affection, in providing support and encouragement, and in making children feel wanted and valued. Parental attitudes of democracy are consistent with respect for individuality, permissiveness toward impulse expression, and confidence in children's capacity to learn from their own experience. Should not this happy combination produce the liberated, confident, creative generation needed to cope with the problems of today's world and to find happiness in it?

This view receives strong support from what has been learned about the acceptance-rejection axis. Students of childhood find little to say in favor of rejection. They are widely agreed that an affectionate atmosphere is important and that its presence will compensate for superficial blunders in child management and for temporary states of parental annoyance. One should not, of course, be satisfied to talk about anything so evanescent as an "atmosphere." Acceptance, if it is real, must be something that is communicated in behavior and expression meaningful to the child. Affectionate feeling tends to do this. It dictates interacting with the child and being interested in him, and this to some degree translates itself into grasping his outlook and being in tune with his needs, thus creating a truly responsive relation. The trend of research clearly indicates that acceptance works as a favorable influence. The one flaw that shows here and there in the research results has to do with transition to life outside the home. If the child's income of appreciative interest is set too high in the family circle, the amount obtainable even from a benign outside environment may be experienced as a deprivation and rejection. Harm can come of this, though we do not know to what extent it is likely to be lasting.

With respect to the control dimension, the deductions concerning child rearing are not so simple. A good deal of control is implicit in bringing up children while they are still young. The baby cannot be allowed to crawl into the fireplace or the toddler to march into the street. The child who is never thwarted when in a tantrum, when snatching toys, or when hitting out at other children is on his way to more serious later frustrations. In some aspects of early training there are permissive options, but they are apt to be small. Feeding a baby when he is hungry rather than by the clock is one such option, available if the mother is in a position to respond at once to the cry of hunger.

Unhurried, gentle toilet training is another, but no one is going to be well satisfied, least of all the child, if the parents do not insist upon ultimate success. Dogmatic permissiveness is clearly unrealistic in the early years when those who are immature need frequent guidance and training from those who are mature. To apply the permissive philosophy in an enlightened way means accepting parental responsibilities, leaning toward permissive options when possible, and moving steadily toward the low end of the control axis as the child grows up.

Varieties of Permissive Patterns

Permissive statements are more uniform than permissive practices. Leaving a lot to the child's initiative might seem easy, but often it proves difficult. Sometimes the parents' patience fails. Much patience is required to endure a child's first experiments in feeding himself with a spoon, and democratic family councils can be as wearing as adult committee meetings. Sometimes it is parental courage that fails. When a 14-year-old decides to hitchhike to the far ends of the continent, or when a 16-year-old announces a decision to get married, parents are easily flooded by anxiety and convinced that the actual dangers and difficulties have not been anticipated.

A common pattern that results from an amalgam of parental desires, impatience, and anxiety might be described as *overt permissiveness* with *covert control*. Because the parent does not fully accept his controlling tendency, it comes out in indirect ways. It may take the form of nudging the child toward a certain course of action by saying that it is what a sensible person would do or by praising the neighbor's child for having decided to do it. It may appear in the form of pressing upon the child information that shows how the parent thinks something should be done. Parents may attempt psychological manipulation through management of praise and blame, reward and punishment, while freedom of choice continues to be the announced policy. Control may surface suddenly in a major crisis like choosing a mate or an occupation, and the parents may find themselves claiming a veto power that is not in the constitution as the whole family has previously understood it. Sometimes a young adult, looking back after an acute family crisis, realizes that he has been brought up in an atmosphere that might be expressed in these words: "You are absolutely free to choose whatever occupation you like provided you take over your father's business and settle down here in town."

There is another variant of the permissive pattern, quite common at the present time, which consists of *principled low control* in many areas of life with what might be called *pockets of high control*. Permissiveness is faithfully maintained with respect to emotional expression, sex life, conventional manners, and many forms of independent behavior. When the children are in high school, for instance, the parents will defend their right to choose their own styles of dress and haircut, will support them if they do battle with school regulations, will allow them to take full charge of their sexual behavior, and will permit them much freedom to roam and travel. But in two spheres there is high control and continuous undisguised pressure: the children must be great academic successes and they must be socially adjusted. These, of course, are areas of strong anxiety for ambitious parents. High academic and social skills look like the critical things for advancement, success, and ultimate affluence in the world as it is organized today. These opportunities could easily be thrown away, the parents think, if they do not take steps to combat their offspring's laziness, wayward impulses, esoteric interests, or taste for solitude. From the very start of school life the child may be hounded to bring home a report card with top grades and be put under pressure to mingle with other children, take part in group activities, and become both well liked and prominent. For parents so disposed, dropping out of school is the ultimate disaster. In such a crisis they may express their combination of low and high control in words like these: "You can sleep with anyone you please but you *must* get your degree."

Still another version of the permissive pattern occurs when parents are seriously unsure of themselves. Lack of certainty is common in a historical period of rapid change, when old values are being reexamined. The resulting child-rearing pattern might be called *low control by default*. Confused about their own values, the parents do not convey a clear or consistent pattern of expectations; they let the child's inclinations prevail because they have no guidelines of their own. If the interaction variables were all that mattered—if high acceptance and low control told the whole story of permissive child rearing—low control by default should have the same consequences as low control embedded in a democratic philosophy. But this proves to be at variance with the facts. A considerable body of research dealing with subjects in nursery school, in late childhood, in high school, and in college supports the proposition that confused parents produce confused children.[26] Competence, initiative, self-esteem, and true independence are more likely to appear in children and adolescents brought up amidst clear parental expectations and clearly expressed values. This tends to be true regardless of the child's ultimate acceptance of the values; even the rebel is a stronger character if he has a clear idea of what he is rejecting. Confused parents and parents who stand for something create different environments even if in practice they are both permissive.

The Summerhill Experiment

Permissiveness in a context of definite values can be illuminated by briefly considering the Summerhill experiment, an educational program that has a strong appeal to advocates of permissiveness.[27] Summerhill is a coedu-

[26] See, for instance, D. Baumrind, "Child Care Practices Anteceding Three Patterns of Preschool Behavior," *Genetic Psychology Monographs*, **75** (1967), 43–88; S. Coopersmith, *The Antecedents of Self-esteem* (San Francisco: W. H. Freeman & Co., 1967); E. B. Murphy, E. Silber, G. V. Coelho, and D. A. Hamburg, "Development of Autonomy and Parent-Child Interaction in Late Adolescence," *American Journal of Orthopsychiatry*, **33** (1952), 643–652.

[27] A. S. Neill, *Summerhill: A Radical Approach to Child Rearing* (New York: Hart Publishing Company, 1960); A. S. Neill, *Freedom—Not License!* (New York: Hart Publishing Company, 1966).

cational boarding school in England founded by A. S. Neill in 1921. "My view is that a child is innately wise and realistic," says Neill. "If left to himself without adult suggestion of any kind, he will develop as far as he is capable of developing." To fashion a school in accord with this belief and to encourage the growth of "healthy, free children whose lives are unspoiled by fear and hate," he endeavored to create a democratic society, symbolized in the General School Meeting "at which all school rules are voted by the entire school, each pupil and each staff member having one vote." All lessons were made voluntary, children being permitted to skip them for months and even years if they so desired. In many other respects the children were left unusually free, though Neill felt obliged to compromise on one point, realizing that if adolescent students were allowed to live out their sexual inclinations in the totally uninhibited way of which he approved Summerhill might run into serious financial and legal difficulties. The result of the regime of freedom, equality, and mutual respect was, in Neill's words, "possibly the happiest school in the world," one from which students graduated without academic handicap and possessed of unusual confidence and maturity.

Summerhill surely qualifies as an accepting, permissive educational environment, but it is also a society, just as the family circle is a society. The effect on the children cannot be deduced wholly from the affectionate, low-control attitudes of Neill and his staff. It is not irrelevant that Neill is a strong, consistent advocate of his ideals. "I get out of small children's rooms if they tell me to get out," he writes, and when he has grievances such as damage to his garden, he brings them before the General School Meeting just as the children bring theirs. This firm enactment of equality and respect for the rights of others differs sharply from permissiveness by default, which contains no inherent principle of justice. Furthermore, Summerhill is a school. Attendance at lessons may be voluntary for the students but it is not for the staff, and every child must be aware that going to classes and learning academic skills are considered desirable by the school society as a whole. Indeed, irregular attendance brings down the wrath of other children because the wayward member falls behind and holds up the class's progress. A crucial test of how a school would run "without adult suggestion of any kind" would require that *some* of the staff live a bohemian life, careless of the rights of others, attending classes only when so inclined, and letting it be known that they considered academic pursuits a waste of time. Summerhill is a striking contribution to educational enlightenment, but not solely because it is permissive. It is an instance of a permissive philosophy operating within the framework of a school society in which the adults express their values clearly, enact democratic attitudes faithfully, give frequent evidence of respect for the rights of others, and make no bones about the fact that they consider education a good thing.

Conclusion

The example of Summerhill makes it clear that what has been described in this chapter is only a beginning of what is needed to understand the social roots of personality. The child does not grow up in a pure culture of interactions with parents, in a world fully characterized by the acceptance-rejection and the high- and low-control variables. To be sure, these variables are important; they have, as we have seen, detectable effects on the growth of personality. But they do not stand alone. They cannot be used as the sole basis for working out a philosophy of child rearing, just as they cannot serve as a complete description of the influence of parents on children's development. The family circle is a social system in which the nature and lines of influence can be highly complex. Even when not interacting directly with children, parents convey information through their behavior about the nature of that social system and its values. The family may be stable or unstable, the household cooperative or quarrelsome, the values sober and goal-directed or impulsive and hedonistic. As individuals the parents will differ from each other and from other parents with respect to such characteristics as consistency, personal competence, and emotional security. The presence of brothers and sisters adds an additional complication to acceptance and control, introducing questions of alliance, rivalry, favoritism, and the capacity of the parents to administer justice. Finally, the family circle is part of the larger society of neighborhood and community. It may be an integral, harmonious part or it may stand in some conflict with its environment.

These inescapable features of his surroundings are not lost on the child. As we shall see in the next three chapters, the two parents and other adult relatives, the brothers and sisters, and the surrounding community all form a vital part of the social system within which the growth of personality takes place.

4 The Family as a Social System: Fathers and Mothers

At the outset of two chapters on the family as a social system it is appropriate to consider what is implied by describing any group of people as a system. A group waiting for a bus would hardly merit such a description, nor would an audience gathered to hear a speaker or the thronging guests at a large reception. A system implies a more lasting set of relations. It implies that these relations cannot be treated as separate transactions and described one at a time. The events in a system are interconnected, part of a constant process of reciprocal influence. The group waiting for the bus does not have this interconnectedness. What one person says to another may not be influenced at all by what a third says to a fourth. The family is clearly not of this nature. Each member has important and enduring relations with every other member, and any one relation is importantly influenced by its position in the pattern as a whole.

Suppose, for instance, that a father's attitude toward his son is discerned to be one of high control, with a stern insistence on certain standards of conduct. If the family is studied as a system it is necessary to go beyond this single relation and discover the surrounding network. Father and son both interact with mother, and all three interact with sister. It may be that father and mother have a happy and harmonious relation, that they agree perfectly on high control, and that they apply this control alike to the son and daughter, at the same time providing acceptance and stability, which dispose the children to conform to expectations. But one might start from the same father-son relation only to discover a different set of surrounding interactions, which put the initial one in quite another light. Father and mother are dissatisfied and disharmonious, with mother believing in greater lenience. Father is irked because mother undercuts his authority with the boy and yields to her son's wishes more readily than she yields to his. Mother on her part is a little jealous because father's liking for his daughter seems to detract from his interest in her. Under these circumstances, father's dominance over the son is sharp and uncompromising, with an edge of anger, whereas the daughter is controlled with a looser rein. The boy harbors rebellious feelings because of the injustice and is resentful toward his sister, while the girl has grounds for resentment at her mother's apparent preference for the son, yet both children may find satisfaction in being one parent's favorite. Treating the family as a system brings all these connected attitudes to light. It is easy to see what large misunderstandings might arise if one relation in the family were studied out of context. High control that is sensed to be principled and fair is vastly different from high control that is unfair or that carries a latent message of resentment.

A further characteristic of systems is that they have a life of their own, so to speak, that is more than the sum of the parts. The family has functions, like living together and making up a household, that it performs only through joint activity. It has goals, such as maintaining a certain reputation, that can never be the handiwork of a single member. If the Joneses are seen by the neighborhood as socially successful, the Smiths as trying to keep up with them, the Browns as industrious and reliable, and the Jukeses as ne'er-do-well, these characterizations are probably based upon real qualities exhibited by the families as a whole, though perhaps in different degrees by individual members. Indeed, if a young Brown and a young Jukes join in a mischievous escapade, the former will be described as a black sheep and the latter as behaving just like a Jukes; family characterizations are not changed by occasional negative instances. The group waiting for the bus has no such character as a whole. It performs no joint functions and has no reputation to maintain with other groups waiting on other corners. The family, in contrast, is anything but evanescent and impersonal. It is an enduring, vital social system within which each child arrives at his own first pattern for living in social systems.

Studying the Family as a Whole

Family life has always been an object of human interest and curiosity. That the subject is today a good deal less than a finished science must be laid not to lack of zeal but to lack of method. There are not many circumstances in which a family is willing to disclose to outsiders the candid story of its inner life, especially if this life includes secret shortcomings and painful strains. It is often said that nothing can be gained by washing dirty linen in public, and as the scientific observer is bound to want to see the dirty linen along with the clean this attitude is enough to bar his way forward. Quite recently there has been a softening of reticence about family life. Belief in the trustworthiness and respectability of social scientists has somewhat increased, and in some circles quite a virtue is made of being willing to tell all to a professional investigator on the ground that the information may be of value in promoting human welfare. But it is not without significance that simultaneously with this change there has been rising public controversy over the invasion of privacy by social scientists. The right of a person not to be studied if he does not want to be is certainly a right that ought to be protected.

There are circumstances, however, in which otherwise reticent people become strongly motivated to lay their secret bewilderments before a trained expert. In this respect the advent of *psychoanalysis* was an important historical milestone. According to the theory advanced by Freud, neurotic disorder has its roots in emotional conflicts in the family circle, and these conflicts can be resolved, and health restored, only by prolonged total disclosure of every memory, thought, and feeling that comes to a patient's mind. Motivated by the desire to be cured, and assisted by Freud's technical devices of free association and dream interpretation, neurotic patients produced large quantities of evidence about the secret inner life of their families. These lives appeared to be filled with jealousies and hatreds, crude sexual fantasies, unmitigated self-love, anxieties, and damaging defensive processes; no one could complain of a lack of dirty linen. The scientific harvest from psychoanalytic treatment was abundant; it has produced in our time a substantial change in the whole conception of human nature. But as a means of studying the family as a social system, the method had a serious defect. The information came from a single observer, the patient, who could hardly be expected to describe things with balanced objectivity.

Family Psychotherapy

What was learned through individual treatment led to a growing conviction that the person who came in as a patient was not necessarily the only disturbed member of the family, and might not even be the one who was most disturbed. The location of the difficulty was not one person; rather, a relationship was causing trouble, and this involved at least two, if not more, members of the family circle. When psychiatric treatment was extended to children it quickly became standard practice to treat both child and mother. Change in the child often seemed to depend on the mother's changing at the same time. From here it was in theory a short step to treating the family as a whole, but in practice there were great difficulties in taking this step. The whole family is not likely to think of itself as sick. Even if it can be convinced that everyone is involved in the trouble, there are many practical obstacles to plans of treatment that involve all the members. Thus family psychotherapy, regarded today as a sound and desirable idea, has not yet realized anything like its full potential for illuminating the family as a social system.

One of the foremost advocates of family therapy, Nathan Ackerman, makes a practice whenever possible of interviewing the whole family at the outset. The members enter the office where there are chairs enough for all but no guidance as to who shall sit where. The order in which the members enter the room, the way they distribute themselves among the chairs, the conversations that may take place over where to sit, and the matter of who starts speaking to the doctor about the problem at hand can all be taken as preliminary indications of the structure of the family. It may be the father or it may be the mother who leads the way, designates seats, and opens the interview; or there may be competition between the parents for the leading role or, in contrast, each may defer and try to make the other take the lead. As the conversation proceeds, the observer may become aware of alliances, rivalries, and exclusions that divide the family into distinct subgroups. Father and eldest son, nodding agreement and confirming each other's statements, may prove to be allied against mother and younger son, whose remarks they criticize and disparage. Perhaps the child who is considered to be the patient stands alone, excluded from the alliances, or perhaps he is embedded in a minority party that is damagingly dominated by the majority.[1] It has often been observed in the course of psychotherapy that as the patient gets better other members of the family get worse. The equilibrium that has been achieved to the patient's disadvantage is being upset, and the strains begin to show in other parts of the system.[2]

Methods of Investigation

Family therapy has thus opened a large door to the study of the family as a whole. It has led to methods of observation more precise and controlled than those that are possible when therapeutic considerations are necessarily uppermost. Researchers can learn something by giving psychological tests, including tests of imaginative productions, to each member of a family. A good deal can be discovered by systematic interviewing that includes each member, provided the family is willing to participate in such an endeavor. Some workers have undertaken a kind of participant observation in which the researcher lives with the family for a period of time, noticing the casual and habitual interactions among members as well as those of which they are more conscious. Other workers have created experimental situations that, though artificial, are intended to reveal characteristic features of family interaction under controllable conditions. A father, mother, and adolescent child, for example, may be brought to a research room and asked to discuss certain controversial topics, their conversation being recorded and later transcribed for detailed systematic analysis. When experiments of this kind are described they sound rather wooden, but it often happens that the participants become really involved in their discussion so that their ways of talking to one another—their rivalries, supportive relations, condescensions, uncertainties—may approximate those of spontaneous home life.[3]

[1] N. W. Ackerman, *The Psychodynamics of Family Life* (New York: Basic Books, Inc., 1958); *Treating the Troubled Family* (New York: Basic Books, Inc., 1966); "Family Psychotherapy Today: Some Areas of Controversy," *Comprehensive Psychiatry*, **7** (1966), 375–388.

[2] The idea of disequilibrium, and of treatment as reequilibration, is developed by J. P. Spiegel, "The Resolution of Role Conflict Within the Family," *Psychiatry*, **20** (1957), 1–16.

[3] Descriptions of different methods, by different authors, for studying whole families have been assembled by Gerald Handel, ed., *The Psychosocial Interior of the Family* (Chicago: Aldine Publishing Co., 1967), Chaps. 2–7.

In an attempt to learn more about family processes in general, without reference to pathology, Hess and Handel undertook an intensive study of "nonclinical" families living in the vicinity of Chicago.[4] Families were found in which all the members agreed to take part in extensive interviews and psychological tests as a contribution to scientific knowledge. The authors were interested especially in processes clearly characteristic of the family as a whole, processes that transcend individual behavior and represent the action of a social system. The family has to evolve some kind of compromise between the inevitable separateness of individuals and their equally inevitable connectedness in a social system. It has to mediate, as the authors put it, between the individual member's effort "to become his own kind of person" and his effort "to find gratifying connection to the other members." It has to achieve, furthermore, a workable congruence of the images that each member has of every other member, so that there can be "some sort of stability or predictability of preferred behavior." It must similarly establish the boundaries of the family's experience—how much of the outside world will be considered safe and welcome, what ranges of experience will be held appropriate for open discussion or individual evaluation. All of these processes came to light in the studies and provided a basis for individual differences among families. It is easy to imagine a family that makes a real fetish of togetherness at the expense of individuation, that tries to stereotype the images the members have of one another, that discourages individual judgments, and that pictures itself as a small sanctuary of light in a hostile world. At the opposite extreme is the family in which members come and go as they please, interaction is minimized, and no regular mealtimes are observed, so that home is experienced as a convenient facility rather than as a center of emotional warmth. Family processes can be worked out in a large variety of patterns.

Influential Aspects of the Family as a Social System

The family as a social system affects in several different ways the growth of the child's personality. In the last chapter, concentrating on direct interactions between parent and child, we followed what is probably the inadvertent tradition of the research literature and spoke as if only one parent and one child were involved, or as if the two parents were united in a single attitude with respect to acceptance and control. In a typical family consisting of two parents and more than one child, the interactions themselves are bound to be more complicated; furthermore, the child is influenced by the properties of the domestic social system as a whole. The following features of family life appear to have significant consequences for personal development:

1. The functions of the family, including bringing up children, can be fully performed only through cooperation by the two parents. This involves

[4] R. D. Hess and G. Handel, *Family Worlds: A Psychosocial Approach to Family Life* (Chicago: University of Chicago Press, 1959). Quotations from pp. 5, 6.

division of labor and the differentiation of masculine and feminine roles. The child is affected by the parents not only as two individuals but as persons performing related tasks in an organization. *Role differentiation based on sex differences* is the most conspicuous aspect of the parents' part in the system. Children soon infer something about the implicit power relations between the parents and come to expect that they will be treated differently by father and mother.

2. Parents' behavior is influenced by the *conceptions of family life* they have initially brought to their marriage and subsequently evolved in the course of their shared life. These conceptions are in part derived from the parents' own experience as children in a family. Their response to their children is colored by this background of personal experience and by expectations as to the part children should play not just as individuals but as family members.

3. Parents respond to one another in a variety of ways, ranging from predominant harmony and affection to degrees of strife and bitterness that may end by breaking up the family. Even mild differences between them can become the basis for alliances and rival groups involving the children—a differentiation of the family social system into subunits—and when the level of controversy is high, there is little chance that the children will not be drawn in. The *personal relation between the two parents* has influential repercussions on children's development.

4. Many family circles include *grandparents and other adult relatives* living either in the house, in the neighborhood, or at a distance that permits occasional visits. The importance of these relatives differs greatly from one family to another, but they are always a potential source of further models, different conceptions of family life, and additional positions in the pattern of domestic alliances and subgroups. Departed grandparents whose memory is kept green may continue as models to be emulated, or occasionally as bad examples to be avoided.

These four aspects of the family as a social system and the influence they are likely to have on the growth of the child's personality will be examined successively in this chapter. Another influence, that of *brothers and sisters*, is of such great importance as to require a chapter of its own.

Roles in the Family

In the study of social systems the concepts of *position* and *role* have proved to be of outstanding importance. Behavior within a social system means behavior that is monitored and guided by the expectations of those who make up the system. The guidance may take the form of physical restriction, as when a baby is prevented from climbing out of a playpen. It may take the form of direct verbal statement, as when a child is told that it is bad to grab toys from other children and good to put his own toys away at night. Typically, however, the constraints of the system work through demands and expectations that are communicated by less sharply focused signals of approval and disapproval. When a person tells a joke in a group that offends certain members, the weak perfunctory chuckles followed by freezing silence may well constrain him more powerfully than if someone had hit him. The demands and expectations of a social system emanate more or less continuously and form a vital part of each individual's environment.

The related concepts of position and role are of great value in understanding such processes. Role has been defined by Newcomb as "the ways of behaving that are expected of any individual who occupies a certain position."[5] The positions that exist in the family circle are defined primarily by age and sex. In the language of positions, father and mother are adult male and adult female; the children are immature males and females, with further specification according to age, there being different expectations for adolescent, older child, younger child, and baby. From the surrounding social system there is very real cultural pressure on the occupants of these positions to exhibit the appropriate role behavior. The parents are expected to fulfill roles of caretaker, educator, and socializing agent. In time of sickness or distress their behavior may be virtually confined to the caretaker role. The children are expected to act their age and to behave toward the other members of the circle, and to those outside, in the manner dictated by age and sex roles.

It is a virtue of the concept of role that it allows for the force of social expectations without obscuring the part played by individual wants and peculiarities. The role concept, as Levinson has pointed out, makes room for both these aspects of behavior while showing more or less precisely how they are related, thus forming a bridge between the concerns of sociology and of psychology.[6] Role expectations are rarely specified down to the last detail. They consist of ranges of behavior considered appropriate for a given position. Within these ranges, the individual can perceive and perform role behavior in a manner quite his own. For instance, it may be that a 10-year-old daughter's age and sex roles include the specification that she is to wash the dinner dishes. Though there is no escape, role behavior requires only that she get the dishes washed. The rest of her role enactment is largely her own. She may do the work cheerfully, singing a happy tune, strengthening her image of willing, beloved mother's helper. She may work with brisk efficiency to demonstrate how much better she can do the job than mother or older sister used to do it. She may enact her role in a spirit of martyrdom, emitting sighs and groans, pointing out how exhausting it is to clean sticky pots and pans. She may express resentment by inexplicable breakages, by comments audible to father and brothers on the unfair lot of women, or by accusing her mother of hiding

[5] T. M. Newcomb, *Social Psychology* (New York: Holt, Rinehart and Winston, Inc., 1950), p. 280.

[6] D. J. Levinson, "Role, Personality, and Social Structure in the Organizational Setting," *Journal of Abnormal and Social Psychology*, **58** (1959), 170–180.

the soap powder or using more dishes than were necessary. The role of family dishwasher can be enacted with many variations, which serve to achieve a variety of personal goals.

Parental Roles

The roles of parents are in the first place defined and sanctioned by the culture. The two parents are expected to live together and to produce children whom it is their duty to protect, nurture, and induct into the ways of the society. This cultural requirement is virtually universal, so much so that exceptional instances, such as bringing up children in institutions, and variant patterns, such as the child-rearing programs in the Kibbutzim in Israel, become objects of strong scientific curiosity. As between the two parents the cultural expectation calls for differentiated masculine and feminine roles based on a division of labor. The assignment of functions starts from the biological imperative that child bearing and suckling shall be the province of the woman. Other biological factors, such as the man's better muscular equipment for heavy work and sustained exertion, play their part in the assignment of duties. The differences between masculine and feminine roles may be further enlarged by a cultural expectation that interests and mental outlook will be far apart. Whatever may be their precise content, these role expectations are early communicated by deed and word to the young members of the family, upon whom they are likely to make a strong impression.

Close to the heart of parental roles is the division of functions between breadwinning and homemaking. Analyzing this distinction, Parsons and Bales describe the father's role as mainly *instrumental*, the mother's as predominantly *expressive*.[7] These terms signify that the mother takes the larger part in child care and in matters having to do with the expression and regulation of feeling among the members of the family, whereas the father has a larger share in the instrumental acts of breadwinning and managing the family's effectiveness in the outside world. This distinction is based simply on division of functions. Its wide diffusion is revealed in newspaper accounts of fires in which it is stated that the father led his wife and children to safety. If the father is absent the mother may be reported to have led her children to safety, but one never hears of the wife leading husband and children to safety; the adult male is the one who is supposed to know about such instrumental things as the route to safety. The instrumental-expressive distinction is undergoing a number of changes in contemporary society. Yet in spite of all the variations that now exist, the breadwinning-homemaking distinction still exerts tremendous power.

The impact of parental sex roles on children has been investigated in a number of studies in which children were asked to describe parents, either through direct questions or through interpreting pictures. In two studies Emmerich showed that children with some consistency differentiate the male

---

[7] T. Parsons and R. F. Bales, *Family, Socialization and Interaction Process* (New York: The Free Press, 1955).

and female parent roles in terms of the variables used in the last chapter: the mothers are more love-oriented, the fathers more power-oriented.[8] Two studies by Kagan and associates indicate that children of both sexes perceive father as more powerful, more punitive and fear-inspiring, and also more competent in dealing with the outside world. This leaves mother with the prize only for nurturance, but it allows her the consolation of being considered the "nicer" of the two.[9] It is evident that the differences between masculine and feminine parental roles are not lost on the children.

A Literary Illustration

Sometimes literary description is more successful than formal statement in conveying a sense of the forces at work in human affairs. The power of community expectations with respect to masculine and feminine roles was the central theme of a novel by Dorothy Canfield published in 1924.[10] The story centers upon a family beset by ill health and emotional turmoil. There is a gentle husband, burdened by chronic indigestion, who drags himself daily to a small business job that he hates and performs so poorly that advancement never comes. There is an energetic wife who exhausts herself in bringing up the three children and keeping a perfect home; she is occasionally tempted by community activities but cannot spare them the time. Her high standards of neatness and propriety cause her to be constantly frustrated by the children, who cannot escape her nagging voice and are given either to ill health or to compulsive naughtiness. The situation is abruptly changed when the husband has an accident that leaves both legs paralyzed. Moving about in his wheelchair, he is able with the children's help to become the homemaker, a feat much applauded by the community. The wife assumes the instrumental role and is in her turn applauded when she proves successful in an executive position. The atmosphere at home changes sharply for the better. The wife, spared the daily irritation of children, feels fulfilled as a successful businesswoman. The husband discovers in himself a deep interest in the children, whose developmental needs he now has time to observe and patience to support. The children begin to flourish; illness and naughtiness both disappear, as does the father's indigestion. One evening the youngest child is endangered when a curtain blown over a lighted candle bursts into flames beside his bed. In the nick of time the father rips down the curtain and extinguishes the blaze; then, turning, he sees the wheelchair standing at the other side of the room. Ener-

8 Walter Emmerich, "Young Children's Discrimination of Parent and Child Roles," *ibid.*, **31** (1960), 315–328; "Family Role Concepts of Children Ages Six to Ten," *Child Development*, **32** (1961), 609–624.

9 J. Kagan and J. Lemkin, "The Child's Differential Perception of Parental Attributes," *Journal of Abnormal and Social Psychology*, **61** (1960), 440–447; J. Kagan, B. Hosken, and S. Watson, "Child's Symbolic Conception of Parents," *Child Development*, **32** (1961), 625–636.

10 Dorothy Canfield, *The Home-maker* (New York: Harcourt Brace Jovanovich, Inc., 1924). Quotation from p. 309.

gized by the emergency, he has crossed the room on his own legs and he knows that he is on the way to becoming once more a well man.

How can this story end? Reversal of the roles of breadwinner and homemaker has proved to be an advantage to everyone. Both parents have found their true vocations. Viewing the matter with detached rationality it would seem simple to let the reversed roles stand even though the husband regains his health. But the novelist knows better.

> He knew that this was impossible. The instant he tried to consider it, he knew that it was as impossible as to roll away a mountain from his path with his bare hands. . . . Every unit in the whole of society would join in making it impossible, from the Ladies' Guild to the children in the public schools. . . .
> "What is your husband's business, Mrs. Knapp?"
> "He hasn't any. He stays at home and keeps house."
> "Oh. . . . ."
> "My Papa is an insurance agent. What does your Papa do for a living?"
> "He doesn't do anything. Mother makes the living. Father stays home with us children."
> "Oh, is he sick?"
> "No, he's not sick."
> "Oh. . . . . . ."
> He heard that "Oh!" reverberating infernally down every road he tried.

Under the pressure of role expectations, quite ordinary but so powerful, would he be able to maintain self-respect as a homemaker? Would his children become ashamed of him, so that he would lose his influence and be of no use to them? Would his wife be able to resist the assumption that she would go back to her children? So great is the novelist's respect for the power of widely accepted role expectations that she ends the story with the husband and his doctor conniving in the fiction that the paralysis cannot be cured.

Current Trends with Regard to Masculine and Feminine Roles

Still fairly common in our society is a conception of sex roles that maximizes the differences. More is involved, according to this view, than a division of labor; men and women are fundamentally so different that it is natural for them to play virtually separate parts in the family. The father is not only the breadwinner; he is also the natural boss. He gives orders to his wife and disciplines the children, and in family grievances he is the supreme court. He lives in a world of masculine interests: business, sports, social life with other men at bars and clubs. The wife is the housekeeper and looks after the children. She must do her husband's bidding and leave family decisions to him. She lives in a world of domestic interests, gossips with her women friends, and pursues feminine interests such as art and music. A college dean once received a letter from a wholesale grocer describing the qualities of his freshman son, who was about to arrive on the campus. After describing a few virtues, and detailing lamentable shortcomings that had come to light when the boy worked half-heartedly in the family business, the father wrote, "His mother says that he has some talent in art and music." For this father art and music lay so far outside a grown man's sphere of interest that no one would expect him even to have noticed them.

This extreme view of masculinity and femininity has crumbled a good deal in recent years. The most pronounced change has come about in the distribution of authority. The husband as boss and lawgiver is not everywhere dead, but his privileges are decidedly on the wane. The weakening of paternal authority is part of an historical change that has been in progress for more than a century, starting with the woman's suffrage movement and the campaign for equal rights, a campaign that is still in progress. On the whole, the distribution of authority between parents that is expected today is more nearly equal. Furthermore, the actual distribution of power in daily family life may depart widely from cultural role expectations. The father may be the theoretical head of the family while at the same time qualifying as a henpecked husband. Not uncommonly a young person will report that in his family the mother was the real power. Perhaps she exerted this power inconspicuously, through tactful indirection and in gentle tones, but children are often aware of the extent to which she thus dominated the household. The research worker has to untangle in each case the actual power relations in the family. It cannot be prejudged by cultural stereotype.

In the matter of authority masculine and feminine roles have become much less differentiated, but with respect to breadwinning and homemaking the trend has not been simple. Some features of contemporary society tend to separate fathers more widely from their homes, while other features draw them closer to the heart of the family circle. Industrial and technical progress has long ago reduced the economic functions of the household. When the fortunes of the family depended upon working the surrounding land or upon household industry, the children saw both parents laboring in a common cause and soon became themselves a part of it. If the father goes out to work, however, and if the nature of his work is obscure to the children, he himself becomes preoccupied with a world outside the home and the children perceive him somewhat as a visitor rather than an integral part of home life. The father's occupation may be so technical that there is no way of explaining what he does even if he tries. Yet he may feel strong pressure, from his home as well as his own needs, to be successful, and the price of success is likely to be the devotion of more time, energy, and interest to his work. The briefcase brought home at night symbolizes the dilemma. On occasion it may be opened to reveal toys for the children and a present for the wife, but more often it contains papers that must be mastered in order to make a good showing next day at the office.

This aspect of the evolution of parental roles has been widely recognized. As Nash points out in a review of relevant writings, it is often said that in Western society child care has become more and more matricentric, the exclusive province of the mother, a realm from which the father tends to exclude himself.[11] This can mean that boys and girls alike are brought up in an atmosphere disproportionately dominated by feminine models. Particularly in the United States, where most public school teachers in the younger grades are women, this predominance of the feminine may continue even into adolescence. A number of studies included by Nash in his review suggest that this situation may be disadvantageous for boys, who are expected to behave like young males but not sufficiently assisted by appropriate models of masculinity. To some extent boys are left to define the role through the crude models of comic books and television screen or the spontaneous assertiveness of their bolder contemporaries, patterns that do not hasten their growth toward modulated adult masculinity. Furthermore, it is reasonable to suppose that there is a reciprocal relation between paternal preoccupation outside and maternal preoccupation inside the home. The more strongly the mother needs the children for companionship and intimacy, the more easily is she drawn into overprotection and pampering, as well as into friction.

The picture has been largely drawn from a social level at which men carry briefcases. Pressure to immerse oneself totally in the job falls most heavily on professional men and rising business executives. Yet a similar conception has been applied at the opposite end of the economic ladder. Studies of lower-class neighborhoods show a high frequency of households that are literally mother-centered because the father for one reason or another has disappeared. Recent surveys of urban slums indicate that a substantial proportion of the families have a female head. Under these circumstances the mother very likely tries to make a home, but she is overburdened and cannot give the children much time. The situation differs in important respects from what has been observed at higher social levels, but at least one of the same consequences for boys has been deduced: both the urge and the expectation to be masculine operate in a vacuum of adult models and assume a crude form. It has been suggested that a need to deny femininity and prove one's masculine toughness might be an important ingredient of delinquent behavior.[12]

Treating the family as a social system is of value in analyzing the differences between father-absence at the briefcase level and father-absence in the slums. The preoccupied professional father, little as he may see of his children, is still a member of the family circle. He comes home at night, he is likely to provide ample material support, and he probably also gives his wife a sense of moral support in her homemaking role, a thing that may be of great value to her morale.[13] If he is shadowy as a role model for his sons, he is nevertheless there as an object of respect and as proof that a valued instrumental role is possible. The absent father of the urban slum presents the children with a wholly different relation. The mother is unsupported in her role,

---

[11] John Nash, "The Father in Contemporary Culture and Current Psychological Literature," *Child Development*, **36** (1965), 261–297.

[12] W. B. Miller, "Lower Class Culture as a Generating Milieu of Gang Delinquency," *Journal of Social Issues*, **14** (1958), 5–19.

[13] L. Bartemeier, "The Contribution of the Father to the Mental Health of the Family," *American Journal of Psychiatry*, **110** (1953), 277–280.

probably conveys her contempt for male irresponsibility, combines in herself the instrumental and expressive functions, and provides the only model of adult adequacy. The two forms of father-absence are not at all the same in their effects on the social system of the family and hence on the children's development.[14]

There are other forces at work in contemporary society that tend to increase the participation of fathers in family life. Nash's paper contains considerable evidence for such a trend. The five-day working week, for example, provides fathers with more time to be at home with their children if they choose to use their leisure in this way. The fact that many married women have jobs reduces the distinction between breadwinner and homemaker, and often increases the father's participation in the household. Most important is the gradual decline of legal and customary inequalities between the sexes. What results is an increased freedom for men and women to define their roles more in accord with their feelings and interests. If it is no longer disgraceful for a woman to work beside a man in factory, business office, or research laboratory, it is also no longer disgraceful for a man to cook a meal, play with his children, or change the diapers, though on this last point he may occasionally sigh for the good old days.

A study by Tasch in 1952 gives strong support to Nash's argument and seems to be in accord with more recent observations of young parents, especially those who are thoughtful about their roles.[15] In interviews with 85 fathers in the New York area, representing great diversity of social background and educational level, Tasch found little to support the idea of an exclusively breadwinning male role. On the contrary, the fathers perceived themselves as active participants in child rearing: most of them reported taking a regular part in daily routine care, discipline, and play with their children. The majority counted companionship with the children as one of their important satisfactions, and there were many complaints when this was obstructed by the demands of jobs. Findings of this kind suggest that fatherly feelings may be as natural as motherly ones if cultural expectations do not block them. In a discussion of this subject Josselyn points out that American society has tended to assume deep biological and psychological roots beneath motherliness but has pictured fatherly behavior as simply a response to a social obligation without intrinsic rewards.[16] Evidently the question of male nurturance and tenderness needs to be reconsidered.

On the whole the current trend is in the direction of minimizing, as much as circumstances permit, the differences between masculine and feminine roles. It is beginning to be more widely felt that too sharp a definition of

[14] L. Rainwater, "Crucible of Identity: The Negro Lower Class Family," *Daedelus, Journal of the American Academy of Arts and Sciences*, **95** (1966), 172–216. Reprinted in G. Handel, ed., *The Psychosocial Interior of the Family*, Chap. 18.

[15] R. J. Tasch, "The Role of the Father in the Family," *Journal of Experimental Education*, **20** (1952), 319–361.

[16] Irene M. Josselyn, "Cultural Forces, Motherliness and Fatherliness," *American Journal of Orthopsychiatry*, **26** (1956), 264–271.

the social roles prevents both men and women from developing their potentialities to the full. There is something false about trying to exclude men from the realms of aesthetic sensibility and tender feeling, or women from assertiveness, self-confidence, and knowledge of the world. Socially defined roles are not, as we have seen, so binding that they altogether prevent divergent and highly individual role enactments, but they tend to discourage such departures from the norm and to surround them with conflict. Sex differences are real, division of labor in the family is necessary, but there is a strong contemporary trend to limit the definition of masculine and feminine roles to these necessities, leaving as much as possible to individual preference.

Parents' Conceptions of Family Life

Next to be considered is a second influential aspect of the family as a social system. More is involved than the manner in which husband and wife enact their parental roles. The system is also colored by the expectations and hopes brought to it by each parent as an individual. The two people who enter upon marriage are themselves veterans of life in families. Each has been a child in a family circle, and each brings from this experience a set of preconceptions about the virtues and faults of family life. The two parents, having had different experiences, may operate with different expectations and hopes. Often some degree of accommodation is reached, but sometimes these differences lead to conflict. In any event, parental expectations reach expression in direct interactions with the children and thus become an influence on the growth of personality.

Four aspects of parental expectations will be examined: (1) the *personal meanings* attached by parents to family life on the basis of their own experience as children; (2) the *family traditions* they carry over from the past and evolve in the present; (3) the *family fictions* that may develop to keep the system in workable balance; and (4) the tendency of parents to *perceive selectively* those aspects of their children's behavior that were problematical in their own development.

Personal Meanings of the Family

In their study of sample families in the Chicago area, Hess and Handel made a special attempt to discover each parent's conception of the meaning of family life.[17] In several instances it came out that the family atmosphere was intended to be an improvement upon what the parents had experienced in their own childhood days. Thus for one father, who had suffered in an impoverished, broken home and been passed around among relatives, the dominant concern was that the family should be financially secure and personally stable. Striving to create this security, he was less aware of other

[17] Hess and Handel, *Family Worlds: A Psychosocial Approach to Family Life.*

possibilities such as initiative in the neighborhood, and the children seemed more anxious than circumstances warranted about asserting themselves away from the house. For one mother, whose own mother had been forbiddingly stern and whose sister had been the successful competitor for meager rations of favor, the family was excellent to the extent that it minimized competitive friction and created an atmosphere of warm appreciation. In pursuit of this goal the mother made a strong virtue of cooperation and a strong vice of self-ishness, the latter signifying interference with family harmony for the sake of personal desires. Neither child was allowed to win a dispute or to profit from selfish behavior. This high standard of internal harmony made it difficult for the children to come to terms with their aggressive impulses in any but a strongly suppressive way. In another family, in which the father was capable in the professional sphere and the mother energetic in community activities, values centered around independent but useful participation in the surround-ing world. The mother in particular was aware of a lack of these virtues in her own upbringing, saying of the grandmother that she permitted too little free-dom of choice and "tried to do our thinking for us." The expectation that each member would achieve creditable things in his own right proved highly congenial to the competent, sociable elder son, who won several top offices in school. It was not as easy for the quieter, more imaginatively inclined younger boy, who accepted the goal but felt inadequate to reach it.

All three of these families, different as they are, illustrate expecta-tions designed as improvements upon what the parents had experienced in childhood. This is one of the ways in which betterment in the conditions of life can take place from one generation to the next. It involves the risk that in compensating for the shortcomings of their own childhood, parents will swing too far and neglect aspects of family life that may be real sources of strength. Expectations, of course, often express a desire to reproduce what the parents experienced in their day as satisfying and constructive features of the family circle. In this way what is good may be preserved. It can easily happen, how-ever, that changed conditions make some of these features obsolete, so that the attempt to maintain them tends to cloud the perception of what is new in the world.

Family Traditions

Interviews and home visits often bring to light the existence of fam-ily traditions that form an important part of the system of domestic values. These usually have some reference to the family's past, and there may be two wholly separate traditions for the two sides of the family. Traditions may turn on physical prowess, perhaps with recollections of feats of strength performed by grandfather working his farm. They may be based on characteristics such as possessing common sense, being good in a crisis, having an artistic flair, or being devoted to good works in the community. Possibly the tradition is dram-atized by recollection of an individual in the past who disgraced the family.

Traditions can exert an effective influence even if they are simple and unpretentious. It is one thing to grow up in a janitor's family that has a record of reliability, perhaps in the form that father and his father before him never missed a day of work; it is quite another thing to be the child of a janitor who has lost a succession of jobs because he worked only when he felt like it. Whatever its content, tradition exerts a certain normative pressure on the children. Because they are members of the family they expect to be strong, reliable, artistic, or whatever the traditional excellence may be. Matching their forebears, if not surpassing them, may be important in what they come to expect of themselves.

The power of family tradition is well illustrated in the account given by a Jewish shopkeeper whose parents were immigrants from Russia.[18] Grandfather had been a scholar, the sage of the Hebrew community in which he lived. Father was trained to a highly skilled trade, but upon coming to the United States and finding that this trade required working on the Jewish Sabbath he turned to a much humbler occupation. This forced him to take up residence in a noisy, crowded, run-down neighborhood. The son remembered his home as "an oasis in the desert." Family boundaries were strictly drawn, contact with neighboring children being strongly discouraged, but within the circle life was "extremely pleasant, stimulating, and close knit." Books were read and discussed, family excursions were made to parks, zoos, and museums, and the phonograph provided an early introduction to classical music, as a result of which the children learned to play instruments and became amateur musicians. Father was the arbiter and censor of taste. When a new record could be afforded he presided over the long, careful listening at the record shop that preceded final selection. Unlike the neighbors who gladly bundled their children off to the movies, he selected films for family attendance, first going himself to make sure that the entertainment met his standard of being "worthwhile." With this background of traditional scholarship and foreground of sober self-improvement along intellectual and aesthetic lines, it is not surprising that the children aspired to levels of education unknown to the population surrounding the oasis.

The effectiveness of family traditions and values is much affected by the way the parents enact them. If the father of the family just described had spent his evenings watching television, pipe in one hand and beer can in the other, and had merely told his children that it was a fine thing to read books, go to museums, and practice music, it is doubtful that his ideals would have become so important in their lives. Actions begin to speak louder than words perhaps earlier in childhood than is generally supposed. A household that offers lip service and small donations to the improvement of social conditions while denying itself little in the way of sports, pleasures, and showy new cars affects its younger members differently from one in which substantial time and energy are devoted to social causes. The effect of serious value enactment is shown in some recent research. Keniston, for instance, in a study of young

18 M. B. Smith, J. S. Bruner, and R. W. White, *Opinions and Personality* (New York: John Wiley & Sons, Inc., 1956), pp. 210–218.

radical leaders in a program of community organization, found that several came from homes in which working for radical causes was the accepted pattern of life, and that virtually all had been brought up in an atmosphere of "consistent orientation to principle."

> Somehow these parents communicated, often without saying outright, that human behavior was to be judged primarily in terms of general ethical principles; that right conduct was to be deduced from general maxims concerning human kindness, honesty, decency, and responsibility; that what mattered most was the ability to act in conformity with such principles.[19]

In studies of northern civil rights volunteers working in the South, comparisons have been made between those who stuck with the work over an extended period of time and those who came for a single summer and did not return. The former proved to be more likely than the latter to come from families in which dedication to some good cause, not necessarily civil rights, had established a visible example of faithful devotion to what the cause required, regardless of momentary inclination and comfort.[20]

Family Fictions

Sometimes, unusual circumstances or exceptionally strong needs on the part of parents lead to expectations that depart widely from the actual situation. Possibly family traditions are always a little tinged with fiction, but the term *family fiction* should be reserved for beliefs that diverge radically and stubbornly from things as they are. The best studies of this form of irrationality have been made with the families of schizophrenic patients. It should not be concluded from this that fictions are unique to families in which mental disorder occurs. Examples are easily found in families no member of which has suffered a mental breakdown. The tendency of family fictions, however, must be to interfere with reality testing. If one or both parents habitually distort the surrounding actualities, it will be harder for the children to find out what is really there.

A group of workers headed by Theodore Lidz at Yale University has made intensive studies of the families of schizophrenic patients.[21] Fifteen such families were studied over several years by means of repeated interviews, and opportunities were seized to observe family members interacting with one another. In some cases it seemed that fictions arose out of a powerful need to feel blameless, to keep self-esteem at a peak by attributing shortcomings to the outside world. One of the mothers in the study believed that her twin sons

---

[19] Kenneth Keniston, *Young Radicals: Notes on Committed Youth* (New York: Harcourt Brace Jovanovich, Inc., 1968), p. 66.

[20] N. J. Demerath III, G. Marwell, and M. T. Aiken, *Dynamics of Idealism* (San Francisco: Jossey-Bass, Inc., 1971).

[21] T. Lidz et al., *Schizophrenia and the Family* (New York: International Universities Press, 1965).

were geniuses. Her own self-esteem required this belief so vehemently that she could not accept evidence to the contrary. When the twins, supporting each other in mischief, broke into and robbed a house and set fire to a dock, the mother ignored the delinquencies and put the whole blame on other children. When the twins were ostracized in the neighborhood, the mother insisted on moving to another community, but only, she maintained, to find a school system worthy of her sons' superior abilities. The father, completely dominated by his wife, did nothing to counteract the evolution of these fictions. Only when the twins argued with their mother did she find any fault with them, but it was an impersonal fault. For years the boys thought that constipation meant disagreeing with mother because she met their arguments by saying that they were constipated and needed enemas, which she forthwith administered. In such an atmosphere there would seem to be little chance for the twins to develop a good sense of responsibility for their own behavior.

In other cases irrationality was centered on feelings and motives within the family. The precarious self-esteem of one or both parents required the maintaining of drastic fictions about their contributions to family life. In one of the families in the study, the father had appeared to make a brilliant start on his career, but upon the early death of his gifted partner he proved quite unable to maintain the pace. His income dwindled and he spent most of his time on petty scholarly work, drowning the perception of his sagging career in a liberal use of alcohol. His wife required the fiction that he was still the great man she had married, and although she had to take a job and become the serious breadwinner, the household operated on the principle that father's work was all-important, his pronouncements the peak of wisdom, and his comfort the responsibility of all the other members. The presence of a gross fiction of this kind makes it difficult for the children to discover what is real in human behavior and to make any sense out of their own feelings. Lyman Wynne and his associates have described *pseudo-mutuality* in families, a fiction that everyone is happy and secure in togetherness. As the fiction allows no place for anxieties, hostilities, real intimacy, and a sense of one's own individuality, the tendency of this family pattern is to make it difficult for children to be aware of their feelings and to grasp the linkages between feelings and events. The splitting off and suppression of so many affects may even encourage a way of living that is experienced as mechanical and meaningless.[22]

Selective Perception of Children's Behavior

In studying the family as a social system, it is important to understand how children become targets of specific parental attitudes. A parent's experience as a child in his family of origin results in a special sensitivity to the situations that were most fraught with emotion; this leads to a strong response when like situations arise in his own family. The two parents bring with them different sensitivities, and their own relation may eventually be much

---

[22] L. Wynne, I. Ryckoff, Juliana Day, and S. Hirsch, "Pseudo-mutuality in the Family Relations of Schizophrenics," *Psychiatry*, **21** (1958), 205–220.

affected by their selective perceptions of what goes on among the younger members of the household.

The mere fact of the child's sex may start the process of selective perception. The personal meaning attached to having been a boy or a girl in one's own family affects what parents perceive in the interactions among their sons and daughters. A mother who once suffered because her brother was a privileged favorite will be keenly attuned to evidence of like injustice to her daughter. A father, veteran of nagging encounters with a belligerent sister, will be irked by his daughter's attempts to assert herself against his son. It is not, of course, a binding rule that parents will favor like-sexed children; the opposite is certainly common, perhaps more common, there being many influences at work in a matter of this kind. Perceptions guided by the parents' own sex role problems should be listed, however, as one of the influences that bear on the attitudes they take toward children.

A similar influence may be exerted by position in the family. Each parent has occupied a position: eldest, youngest, somewhere in the middle, or only child. Such occupancy is likely to have left a legacy of expectations and feelings that are easily revived by events in the nursery. There is no one pattern for eldest children, as will be seen in the next chapter, but whatever it meant—privilege, respect, deference from the younger ones, being the target of envy, shouldering unwelcome responsibility, bearing a miserable burden of housework or of caring for the younger children—the parent who was an eldest child understands his own eldest child in terms of his own experience of that position. Strong emotional response is evoked when a parent witnesses two of his own children in a struggle for dominance or favor that repeats the battles of his past. Position and sex easily combine in guiding these selective perceptions. If a family consists of two children, older boy and younger girl, and if each parent came from just such a family, it is easy to see how the two males and the two females might come to form rival coalitions.

The children's appearance, particularly their resemblance to one or the other parent, can easily stimulate selective perceptions. The clinical literature is full of instances of this sort. When there is serious parental conflict, the unthinking tendency to assign a child to one side or the other because of appearance may have damaging consequences. If a mother is angrily anxious because her red-headed freckled husband has taken to drink and other women, she may react violently to small signs of waywardness in her 7-year-old red-headed freckled son, whom she pictures as joining his father in the downward slide to ruin. In a family of several children, it is often easy for parents or for outsiders to judge that certain children are like the father's family while others favor the mother's side. These mysterious outcomes of the genetic process may have a decided influence on the attitudes taken by the parents.

Of somewhat similar nature are perceptions derived from a parent's own developmental problems. A parent may attach high value to certain traits because he has attained them in his own life with great effort; he will view other traits with alarm because he has experienced them as painful handicaps and has tried to suppress them in himself. To take a common example, a parent who in childhood learned with great difficulty to control outbursts of anger and who still sometimes feels like exploding may be badly upset by the normal tantrums of his children and may act harshly to bring them under quick control. Another currently common example is the parent whose childhood self-esteem was damaged by a timid lack of social initiative; such a parent hopes for social virtuosity the moment the child enters nursery school and is dismayed if the teacher reports slowness in mingling with the group. Examples could be multiplied endlessly; the principle to bear in mind is that parents, influenced by their own developmental histories, respond to their children in ways that show the imprint of those histories.

It should not be supposed that these influences have the sole effect of falsifying the parents' perception of their children. We tend to assume an ideal of perfect objectivity in which every aspect of the child's behavior is faithfully perceived in its true proportions; selective perception then seems to imply an overemphasis or underemphasis that departs from the objective ideal. If the nature of our actual understanding of other people is kept in mind, however, selective perception appears in a better light. If at times it falsifies, at other times it deepens the parent's comprehension of what is going on in the child. Satisfactions and frustrations, joys and sorrows, triumphs of pride and wounds to self-esteem can be fully inferred in others only through comparable experiences of one's own. The parent who perceives his children in the light of his own experience will be wrong when their experience is in fact different from his own, but when he is right he will be more right, so to speak, than it is possible to be in any other way. Only through such use of his experience will he be able to give a child the reassurance of being fully understood and sympathetically supported. Selective perceptions sometimes breed error, sometimes wisdom.

Relation between Parents

A third significant aspect of the family as a social system is to be found in the relation between the parents. This relation varies along a dimension from an ideal affectionate harmony to a maximum of conflict. Although this obviously oversimplifies a complex matter, the dimension of harmony versus conflict has been shown in several research studies to be correlated with important outcomes in the children's lives. Westley and Epstein, for example, in a study of "emotional health" in college students, found parental harmony to be a highly significant variable. "The root of emotional health in children," they concluded, "was a good relationship between their parents." This conclusion may be too sweeping, but there is a reassuring logic behind it. Because happy couples meet each other's needs and support each other's self-esteem, they do not have to use their children so much for these purposes and are better able to treat them as individuals in their own right.[23] There is less to obscure the children's real interests.

If the parents are harmonious and in substantial agreement, the

---

[23] W. A. Westley and N. B. Epstein, *The Silent Majority* (San Francisco: Jossey-Bass, Inc., 1970).

impact of their shared values and expectations is likely to be strong. If they do not agree but are reasonably tolerant about it, the child still may not find it impossible to please them both. Thus a girl may please her father by taking an intelligent interest in politics and her mother by developing good taste in clothes. Differences in parental values also make it possible for the child to play off one parent against the other, turning to the one who is most apt to be lenient with respect to the problem at hand. But if the parents' differences are accompanied by personal disharmony and anger, the child's position is more difficult: if he pleases one parent he displeases the other. The situation is polarized—there is no middle ground—and the easiest solution, which is to side with one parent and reject the values of the other, is still fraught with a good deal of danger.

When a child has to make a choice of this sort, he is influenced in an important way by what he senses to be the power relation between his parents. Where, as is fairly common, the father attempts high control in a noisily assertive if not abusive fashion, it may appear dangerous to side with the mother even if she is affectionate and indulgent; the child dares not risk evoking paternal wrath. Much depends on the mother's ability to protect the child from the father. Clinical cases could be cited in which the child sensed that in a showdown mother would give in and father would prevail. Some years ago August Aichhorn, a discerning and remarkably successful worker with juvenile delinquents, advanced the hypothesis that the combination of dominant, unsympathetic, strong father and loving, indulgent, weak mother was peculiarly conducive to male delinquency. The boy's relation to the father produced simmering resentment against authority, the relation to the mother fostered the attitude that what one wanted could be easily obtained, and neither parent lent encouragement to persistent, constructive effort.[24] But the situation is decidedly different if the mother is strong enough to assure protection. A familiar literary example, which gives every evidence of being drawn straight from life, is the Morel family in D. H. Lawrence's *Sons and Lovers*.[25] Taking the father, a coal miner given to drink and abusive rages, and the mother, disappointed in marriage and concentrating affection on her children, one might suppose that Paul Morel's situation would resemble the one described by Aichhorn. But psychologically they are miles apart. Mrs. Morel is the stronger parent, and it is her influence that becomes crucial for the son's development. Paul shares his mother's contempt for the father. He adopts her aspirations for a different and better kind of life, and he enjoys the support of her appreciative interest in everything he accomplishes. This is by no means without its problems, but they are not problems of alienation from adult values or of juvenile delinquency. The push created by his family takes an entirely different direction.

[24] A. Aichhorn, *Wayward Youth* (New York: The Viking Press, 1935). The pattern was illustrated in the case of Donald described in the last chapter. Another instance is given in R. W. White, *The Abnormal Personality*, 3d ed. (New York: The Ronald Press Co., 1964), pp. 68–76.

[25] D. H. Lawrence, *Sons and Lovers* (1913) (New York: The Modern Library, No. 109).

When parents are in open and irreconcilable conflict, they may use the child crudely to score points and inflict wounds in the battle. But if the parents are motivated to maintain the family circle in spite of conflict, they may use a child unwittingly as a means of keeping the system intact. In a paper on this subject by Vogel and Bell, based on the study of families having an emotionally disturbed child, the idea is advanced that the sick child has been made a scapegoat in conflicts that the parents do not dare to express directly to one another.[26] When the mother, to use one of their illustrations, is driven by fierce ambition and is bitterly disappointed at her husband's lazy work habits, while the father in turn bitterly resents his wife's lack of respect and failure to make the home a haven of peace, the family can remain intact only by avoiding open quarrels. But hostile tension is still there, and it may be deflected upon a child who in some way becomes a suitable target, symbolizing the issues between the parents. The conflict just described, for example, is most easily visited on a child who makes a poor start in school. The mother is quick to perceive laziness and to start a campaign of nagging demands; the father springs to the victim's defense, excusing poor achievement and implicitly encouraging low effort. Caught in this crossfire, confused by the forceful but irreconcilable pressures, the child finds no way out and becomes emotionally disturbed. The family stays together but at the cost of one member's health.

Grandparents and Other Adult Relatives

In a society that is predominantly urban, industrial, and mobile, it has become customary to think of the family as a small unit consisting only of parents and children. This could also be called the minimal family, the smallest unit that can be moved from place to place as industrial opportunity dictates. For most families, however, the cast of characters is somewhat larger. The minimal nuclear family turns out to be a convenient concept rather than a widespread actuality. The typical family in our society today is not isolated but has its existence within a network of kin relationships.[27] Constant uprooting is not universal, ease of travel reduces the effects of distance, and so in a very real sense the family circle may include grandparents, uncles, aunts, and cousins. When these relatives are frequently seen, and especially when one or more of them live under the same roof, their influence will certainly be felt by the children. They must be included if the workings of a given family are to be properly understood.

The kind of error that can result from thinking of the family always

[26] E. F. Vogel and N. W. Bell, "The Emotionally Disturbed Child as a Family Scapegoat," in *A Modern Introduction to the Family*, ed. Vogel and Bell (New York: The Free Press, 1960).

[27] Margaret Blenkner, "Social Work and Family Relationships in Later Life," in *Social Structure and the Family: Generational Relations*, ed. E. Shanas and G. F. Streib (Englewood Cliffs, N.J.: Prentice-Hall, Inc., 1965), Chap. 3.

in its isolated two-generational form can be illustrated by the problem of the scapegoat just described. If the parents with their irreconcilable attitudes constitute the whole environment of adult relatives, it is difficult to escape the trap created by their conflict. But the grip of irrationality will be less powerful if there are other adults in the family circle whose outlook is more objective and reassuring. Parent-child relations as described in the previous chapter further illustrate the limitations of the isolated family concept. The effects of parents' attitudes on the child's development will be diluted when other family members are important in his life. Cross-cultural studies that include societies having a widely extended family system give evidence of this dilution. When the household includes grandparents, uncles, and aunts, the children tend to be better controlled yet less harshly disciplined; their aggression, for instance, is heavily prohibited, but spanking and yelling at them are less frequent.[28] The diffusion of authority among several adults in the household gives a somewhat less personal meaning to high control, though increasing its effectiveness. Furthermore, it has been found that "in extended families where the mother's mother or sister is available to minister to the young child's needs, emotional ties between the child and his biological parents are likely to be less intense."[29] The parents do not have monopolistic control over the child's security and satisfactions, and this may give greater freedom to his development.

Roles of Adult Relatives

Understanding the influence of adult family members other than the parents is facilitated by considering the nature of their roles. In our society the parents are held responsible for bringing up the children; other adults, even if they assist, seldom assume central responsibility. A possible role for a maiden aunt has been described by Katharine Butler Hathaway, who made clear the deep difference between this and the maternal role. The best maiden aunts, she wrote, indeed "the only true and valuable maiden aunts," are those who have been disappointed in their own desire to marry.

> Their unspent love and the compensating talent, which they so often possess whether they develop it or not, can do certain things for children which no good mother ought to be able to do, since it happens that a good aunt makes a very bad mother, and a good mother could not possibly be a good mother if she had the wild erratic qualities which belong to the good maiden aunt.
>
> Everybody knows that a good mother gives her children a feeling of trust and stability. She is their earth. She is the one they can count

---

[28] J. W. M. Whiting and B. B. Whiting, "Contributions of Anthropology to the Methods of Studying Child Rearing," in *Handbook of Research Methods in Child Development*, ed. P. H. Mussen (New York: John Wiley & Sons, Inc., 1960), pp. 918–944.

[29] J. A. Clausen, "Family Structure, Socialization, and Personality," in *Review of Child Development Research*, Vol. 2, ed. L. W. Hoffman and M. L. Hoffman (New York: Russell Sage Foundation, 1966), pp. 1–54.

on for the things that matter most of all. She is their food and their bed and the extra blanket when it grows cold in the night; she is their warmth and their health and their shelter, she is the one they want to be near when they cry. She is the only person in the whole world or in a whole lifetime who can be these things to her children. There is no substitute for her. Somehow even her clothes feel different to her children's hands from anybody else's clothes. Only to touch her skirt or her collar or her sleeves makes a troubled child feel better. And often when a child wants her this is all that a mother has time to give. She is always moving. She has so many things to do. She can't sit down in a chair and talk nonsense right in the middle of a busy day. Sometimes a child has a great urge to talk what its mother calls nonsense. Sometimes even a child's worry about death and about the beginning and the end of the universe seems like nonsense to the busy mother when she knows by taking one quick animal sniff of him that there is nothing wrong with him.

This is where the good maiden aunt comes in. . . . The good maiden aunt is the one who is as free and nonsensical (and sad, at times) as the children are themselves, and who will never tire of paying attention to anything they do or say. She is the one grown-up person in their acquaintance who will never look at a clock and tell them to hurry up because it is time for them to get ready. She would rather let them be two hours late to a dressmaker and three hours late to school than ever say this to them. Yet their mother could not possibly be like that and the children could not bear it if she were. The good aunt has the same uncorrupted cosmic sense of leisure that the children have, and together they carry on conversations and enterprises which haven't any end. They lie on the floor and write and draw pictures. They make up songs, they make up games, they look at things through a microscope, they make things with scissors out of colored paper. There is no limit to what they may think of or invent. They discover wonders and talk about subjects that the mothers and fathers haven't any idea of.[30]

This account represents one of many ways in which adult family members who are not centrally responsible for upbringing can find congenial roles that complement, and even at times oppose, parental roles. Uncles who have time to take their nephews fishing or to induct them into the secrets of repairing a car can similarly complete what a busy father may not have time to do. Sometimes adult relatives who take indulgent roles create for the child a conflict of loyalties and may arouse the parents' jealousy, but under favorable circumstances they constitute an enrichment of the child's human environment. It is by no means certain that the isolated minimal family provides the best conditions for the growth of personality.

These considerations help in understanding the parts played by grandparents. It might be supposed that in a period of history when child-rearing practices have tended to move toward permissiveness, grandparents would

[30] Katharine Butler Hathaway, *The Little Locksmith* (New York: Coward-McCann, Inc., 1943), pp. 160–162.

stand for strictness and would try to impose higher control on the grandchildren. No doubt this sometimes happens, but the opposite relation appears to be more common. A study by Apple shows that grandparents and grandchildren rather frequently have close, warm relations.[31] Another study by Young and Willmott, made among working-class families in London, reveals that grandparents sometimes become the children's allies in opposing parental sternness.[32] The visits of grandparents are often seen by parents as a decidedly mixed blessing. Useful as the older people may be as sitters, there is a risk that they will be indulgent to the point of spoiling, that they will weaken the parents' authority, and, most unreasonably of all, that they will let the children get away with things they never allowed the parents to do when they were young. This last unfairness is an understandable cause of resentment, and it may be true. Not having central responsibility for grandchild rearing, the grandparents are free to take pleasanter, more indulgent roles, and to enjoy these children more than they dared enjoy the ones for whose upbringing they alone were answerable.

Partly because of this freedom, adult relatives can produce a variety of influences, many of which serve to mitigate the impact of the parents. As Clausen, speaking specifically of grandparents, expresses it, they provide the child "with an opportunity to see his parents as subject to the commentary of an older generation, perhaps rendering the parents less remote, more humanly fallible in their judgments. At the same time, the grandparents provide another model of what adults are like, a model to which the child can relate with comfortable familiarity."[33] The presence of adult relatives also enlarges the possibility that the child will find allies within the family circle.

Adult Relatives and Family Subgroups

If a family circle is carefully analyzed, it is usually possible to detect subsystems within the whole. Even when there is strong unity and little conflict, the observer can often perceive evidences of pairings and groupings based on a sense of congeniality. In discussing this idea of subsystems within the family, Henry and Warson use the illustration of a little girl who could be said to live in five families, one that included her grandmother and her sister, one that included her parents and her sister, and so forth.[34] These overlapping subsystems were activated under different circumstances, but when activated they provided the child with the support of an ingroup against other members of the family, who for the time being constituted an outgroup. Alliances within a family may be firm and lasting, but sometimes, like alliances among nations, they are subject to rearrangement when a particular crisis is past. These sub-

[31] Dorian Apple, "The Social Structure of Grandparenthood," *American Anthropologist*, **58** (1956), 56–63.

[32] M. Young and P. Willmott, *Family and Kinship in East London* (London: Routledge and Kegan Paul, Ltd., 1957).

[33] J. A. Clausen, "Family Structure, Socialization, and Personality," p. 7.

[34] J. Henry and S. Warson, "Family Structure and Psychic Development," *American Journal of Orthopsychiatry*, **21** (1951), 59–73.

systems, unlike the family as a whole, which is a publicly recognized institution, are private alignments that can be revised to meet new circumstances.

Children are placed in a difficult position when a sharp cleavage is formed between the mother's and the father's sides of the family. This hazard, possible in any marriage, is especially likely to be real if the two families are of widely different backgrounds or different ethnic groups, thus starting with little common experience and easily slipping into rivalry. In neighborhoods with a relatively stable population, grandparents may be part of the daily environment. The London study by Young and Willmott showed surprisingly frequent contacts between mothers and maternal grandmothers, contacts in which the children often took part. As many as half the mothers visited their mothers every day; many more made at least weekly visits. Such contacts can perfectly well be reassuring and pleasant for the children, especially if the grandmother is affectionate and indulgent. Studies of disturbed children, however, have sometimes disclosed disturbance in the parents that involved the grandparents as well.[35] In the daily visits to grandmother the mother may be seeking comfort for her disappointment in father, an ally in proclaiming him unworthy, or a stronger hand in disciplining the children. If the children are then taken to visit the paternal grandparents they may hear their father giving details about his wife's shortcomings and receiving confirmation of his own conduct. Conflict between parents is difficult for a child; when it is extended to include larger family coalitions the difficulty may well be compounded.

More favorable consequences follow for the child when adult relatives hold themselves aloof from parental conflicts and make themselves havens of security. Disillusionment with quarreling parents may be much mitigated if there is a grandparent, an uncle, or an aunt who remains sufficiently detached yet takes enough interest to serve as an anchor. This relative may help to interpret the conflict and lower the anxiety it generates, but even without this aid to understanding the child may feel fortified simply by having an ally within the family circle. Pressure to take sides in parental disputes, and thus to place oneself definitely in one or the other subsystem, is lightened when membership in a third subsystem is an open possibility.

The potential value of grandparents in child development is illustrated by Coles in a study of a black family involved in the school desegregation crisis in New Orleans in 1961.[36] The family consisted of the grandmother, her only son and daughter-in-law living next door, and their 6-year-old daughter Tessie, who might be said to live in both houses. Tessie's parents' house was new and neat, with polished floors, whereas her grandmother's house was battered and messy. Tessie spent a good deal of time in the less constraining atmosphere of the old house, and her pet dog lived there all the time. The child's environment was much enriched by this second home,

[35] N. W. Bell, "Extended Family Relations of Disturbed and Well Families," *Family Process*, 1 (1962), 175–193.

[36] Robert Coles, *Children of Crisis: A Study of Courage and Fear* (Boston: Little, Brown & Company, 1967), pp. 86–97.

less exacting in its requirements. When desegregation was ordered, Tessie was one of three little black girls who entered the previously all-white school. The school was at once boycotted and picketed, so that attendance necessitated walking between lines of whites who screamed, cursed, spat, hurled insults, and threatened serious reprisals. Tessie was first escorted by her father, but the dangerous duty was presently taken over almost wholly by the grandmother. Tessie's mother confessed afterwards that she could not have held out against the insistent threats and harassments if her husband had not done so, and he could not have done so without the defiant determination of the grandmother.

Grandparents and Family Traditions

Grandparents, whether present in fact or only in memory, may occupy an important place in family traditions. Sometimes, to be sure, family aspirations require turning one's back on the grandparents, rejecting and trying to forget what they stood for. This is likely to be the case when upward mobility is an important goal or when the grandparents were immigrants who adapted with difficulty to the customs and language of their new land. Personality studies of college students bring to light many instances in which grandparents are remembered hardly at all, are felt to be irrelevant to current concerns, or have been a source of social embarrassment; sometimes the parents, too, are experienced as incongruous with the social environment in which the student is becoming immersed. Sometimes, however, family pride has been sustained through periods of misfortune and impoverishment through recollection of the status achieved by grandparents. Forebears who have had distinguished careers set a high standard of achievement for the coming generation. Models of this kind can stimulate exertion and emulation. There can be little doubt that the exploits of grandfathers have often lodged firmly in their grandsons' minds, constituting a push toward a similar level of achievement even when the direction of interest is quite different. If the father has been less successful there is added satisfaction in surpassing him and restoring the family's reputation. But sometimes distinguished examples have the opposite effect: they become oppressive and generate feelings of inferiority. For instance, a male undergraduate during World War II, rejected for military service because of a minor physical defect, deserted by his male friends who had gone to war, attending predominantly female classes, experienced grave difficulty in maintaining a bearable level of self-esteem. Nobody criticized him for being there, and he might have counted himself lucky to be legitimately excused from danger, but in fact he was miserably depressed. For three generations the men who bore his family name had occupied conspicuous positions of public service, which made them nationally known. It was against such standards, a living part of his own personality, that he measured his unfitness to serve his country in time of grave need. The example is an extreme one, but it serves to illustrate the difficulty sometimes created by a family tradition of high achievement. Some people may regret that their forebears amounted to so little; others may regret that they amounted to so much.

Conclusion

At the end of Chapter 3, parental attitudes were gathered on two main dimensions called acceptance and control, a circular diagram was presented on which combinations could be located, and research was cited showing the average expectable effect of these attitudes on the growth of personality in children. Had we been able to leave it at that, the study of personality might have seemed encouragingly simple.

But obviously there is more to it. The present chapter has added the notion of the family as a social system in which the child has membership. This change of focus brings in all the members of the circle, and it calls attention to properties of the family as a whole that exert a significant influence on individual members. If one undertakes to study personality by means of life histories and begins each case by trying to establish the influence of the family, one must of course discover the attitudes of the parents in terms of acceptance and control, but only as the first step of the inquiry. The average expectable effects of these attitudes may fade to the point of disappearance owing to other characteristics of the family social system. Information must be obtained about the parents' enactment of their respective masculine and feminine roles, the harmony or conflict in their relation to one another, their conceptions of family life, their selective perceptions of the children's part in it, the goals and traditions they espouse, and the extent to which they set concrete examples of family values by practicing what they preach. Information must also be gathered about subsystems within the family and thus about grandparents and other adult relatives who often form a part of these internal alliances and provide alternative sources of comfort, interest, and example. It is amidst such complexities of influence that personality grows, and one cannot understand personality if he overlooks or oversimplifies them.

Students of personality must observe facts not singly but embedded in a network of other facts. The fact of a broken home, for instance, often means an unstable household and a paucity of adult control, but if the departed father was a contentious and disturbing influence, and if the mother is now consistently backed by a strong grandmother, the breaking of the home may produce an environment both more stable and more controlling. The fact of harmonious alliance between parents often implies an atmosphere conducive to security and confidence. In a given instance, however, especially if there are no adult relatives to mitigate the parental united front and no sibling allies to help oppose it, it may mean that the child is overwhelmed by parental influence and feels constantly inferior and anxious. Only a study in great detail can disclose the way things hang together in the individual case.

Mention of sibling allies calls attention to an aspect of the family social system that has not yet been included in this account. Brothers and sisters are obviously a vital aspect of any family, as potential competitors for privilege, rivals for the parents' love, allies and sharers of fun, and members of subgroups within the whole. The picture of the family as a social system must now be completed by a sketch of the rest of its junior membership.

5 The Family as a Social System: Brothers and Sisters

The importance of brothers and sisters in the family can be attested by anyone who has them. It can be further affirmed by the prominent places they occupy in the lives of children referred to clinics because of emotional problems. Curiously enough, when one turns from everyday knowledge and clinical experience to the research and theory inspired by brothers and sisters, it seems at first glance that siblings do not count for very much. But the thinness of the experimental and theoretical literature is not in this case a judgment of importance. It is a confession of the difficulty of carrying out scientific propositions. There is reassuring regularity in the biological circumstances that every child has a father and a mother, never more or less. On this foundation was built, for better or worse, the abstract model of the isolated three-person family; on it rested the hope that parent-child relations could be captured in systematic theory. But when it comes to siblings, the variety of patterns seems designed to defeat orderly thinking. There may be no brothers and sisters, there may be a lot of each, the numbers and sex distribution can fall in an almost infinite variety of patterns, and as a crowning insult to systematic thought, Nature every so often throws in a multiple birth.

How can such a topic be investigated with profit? How can one formulate questions that are sufficiently limited so that definite answers can be extracted from the findings? If a problem were selected concerning the mutual effects of a sister and brother on each other's development when the sister was the elder and there were only two children in the family, and if the procedure called for studying a fair number of such pairs and arriving at a group average, the results would have meaning only when compared with all the other sister-brother patterns, including families of more than two children. The subject is certainly not inviting for research designed in this way. Indeed, questions framed in terms of group averages, implying that the effects of certain family positions can be separated from all surrounding circumstances, do not necessarily represent the best scientific strategy. In actual life, pairs of siblings cannot be isolated from their surroundings. They are embedded in the social system of the family, and the way in which they affect one another's development is always subordinate to the total pattern of influences prevailing in the family. The first step toward greater knowledge is to deepen one's understanding of these total patterns, taking note of the traps they set for traditional research design.

What is known about the developmental effects of brothers and sisters thus depends fairly heavily upon the disclosures of patients during psychotherapy, the observations of professional workers studying the family, and the material provided by life history studies of normal people. There are, however, three lines of research along which systematic investigation has been pressed, and these will be considered first in this chapter. (1) *Family size*, the measurement of which offers no problem, may be an important influence on the child's development. Comparative studies have been made between children brought up in small families and children brought up in large families. (2) *Sibling rivalry*, sometimes an acute clinical problem, lends itself to observation in at least one of its many manifestations, the behavior of the first-born child following the birth of a sibling. (3) *The effects of birth order* have attracted the most attention. For a time, great effort was directed at establishing the average consequences of being an eldest child, an only child, a youngest child, or a child placed somewhere in the middle of the family. Interest in the subject then seemed to dwindle, but in the last few years fresh findings and new controversies have renewed its lease on life.

Effects of Family Size

In 1948 appeared an entertaining book called *Cheaper by the Dozen*, describing what it was like to be brought up in a family of twelve children.[1] Though not intended as a contribution to science and clearly weighted toward the brighter side of things, the book brings before its readers a number of happy consequences of being part of so large a brood. The huge household could not go on without active participation by the children, who felt themselves to be a vital part of the enterprise. Recreations, whatever their nature, could easily assume the form of huge hilarious picnics. Sibling rivalry was blunted by the large number of competitors and the diffusion of parental interest. Uncomfortable episodes like measles and whooping cough did not have to be borne alone. Above all, by outnumbering their parents six to one, the children could mobilize effective opposition through mutual support, and there were always enough companions to carry out imaginative adventures in mischief. It is illuminating to contrast this picture of family life with the sober

---

[1] F. B. Gilbreth, Jr. and Ernestine Gilbreth Carey, *Cheaper by the Dozen* (New York: Thomas Y. Crowell Company, 1948).

household in which Jean-Paul Sartre grew up as an only child with his mother and grandparents, or with the tense, guilt-producing three-person family described by Arthur Koestler in his autobiography.[2] Childhood environments more utterly different can hardly be imagined. The large family and the very small family are different worlds.

In an exploratory study of families with six or more children, J. H. S. Bossard, a long-time student of family life, found a number of characteristic features that are illustrated in *Cheaper by the Dozen*.[3] As contrasted with small families, he concluded, the large family puts a high value on organization and cooperation. The necessary division of labor, the assignment of special tasks among the children, tends to make the members closely interdependent and to create a sense of family unity. The parents, dispersing their time and energy, are not likely to be possessive, nor do they demand a strong emotional interaction with any one child. As regards discipline, they tend to act autocratically and to rely on fixed rules; this inflexibility is increased if the rules are administered by older children required to help in bringing up the younger ones. Opposition to rules, however, is more easily expressed in the large family: children "back-talk" more frequently.

The picture drawn by Bossard appears to be confirmed in several particulars by other research on large families.[4] However, a great many variables get in the way when the attempt is made to compare large families with small. It is important to know, for instance, whether many children were planned and wanted, were accepted as a duty, or just happened through lack of planning. Obviously there is a world of difference between an intended large family and an accidental one. Consideration must also be given to the family's economic level: it is one thing to have many children who can be well enough supported, quite another to have too many mouths to feed. Large families in urban slums do not exhibit the organization and corporate feeling that is characteristic under more favorable circumstances. Far from being rule-bound, discipline in such neighborhoods is likely to be haphazard and inconsistent.

The effects of family size on the development of the child's personality have been studied particularly with respect to intelligence and achievement. Studies in Great Britain and the United States indicate that intelligence test scores, educational attainment, and motivation for achievement are all a little higher in children from small families.[5] The differences are small, the complications are many, and it is impossible to say much about underlying

[2] Jean-Paul Sartre, *The Words*, trans. B. Frechtman (New York: George Braziller, Inc., 1964); Arthur Koestler, *Arrow in the Blue* (New York: The Macmillan Company, 1952).

[3] J. H. S. Bossard and E. S. Boll, *The Large Family System* (Philadelphia: University of Pennsylvania Press, 1956).

[4] See the summary by J. A. Clausen in L. W. Hoffman and M. L. Hoffman, eds., *Review of Child Development Research*, Vol. 2 (New York: Russell Sage Foundation, 1966), pp. 9–15.

[5] See, for example, G. H. Elder, Jr., "Family Structure and Educational Attainment," *American Sociological Review*, **30** (1965), 81–96.

causal connections. If parents take a long view of the future, which they are more likely to do when gifted with good intelligence, and if they hold achievement in high esteem, which they are more likely to do when their economic level makes the prospects good, they may elect to have a small family in order to give maximal advantages to each child. These are no doubt the circumstances under which children achieve more, but whether this higher achievement is due to innate endowment, economic advantage, parental rewards and encouragements, or a combination of all three remains an elusive question. People may choose to have a small family for very different reasons: difficulties of childbirth, dislike of children, protecting one's own career from interruption, or simple fear of being unable to provide support. It seems unlikely that such parental motives would create an atmosphere conducive to exceptional achievement. Only a much closer knowledge of what is going on in each family system can reveal the full meaning of obtained average differences.

If small families slightly favor achievement, it might be supposed that large families would at least slightly favor certain other qualities like cooperation and sociability. Such evidence as there is does not support this idea. A study made in small towns and rural areas of the Midwest showed slightly more evidence of feelings of inferiority and problems of social adjustment in children from large families.[6] It has been noted elsewhere that children from large families are a little overrepresented in child guidance clinics. These findings are confounded, however, by the variable of social and economic level. A study of families in relatively favorable situations might show that the large family had its own peculiar virtues.

These slender results, based on the comparison of groups of large and small families, should not be taken to mean that family size is a matter of tiny significance. Rather, standard effects of family size do not come through strongly in research that lumps together large numbers of families. It is probably correct to conclude that family size has no marked standard effects that will appear through thick and thin, regardless of other circumstances, but this does not mean that it has no effects. Being an only child is obviously different from being one of twelve, and the difference is continuously present throughout the whole time in which the family is the chief influence on the growth of personality.

Sibling Rivalry

The ethical injunction that children in a family should love one another owes its existence to strong proclivities in the opposite direction. If love were the only possibility there would be no need to uphold it as a virtue. In the Old Testament, which is not given to glossing over the less attractive features of human nature, sibling rivalry is introduced with the very first pair of

---

[6] G. R. Hawkes, L. Burchinal, and B. Gardner, "Size of Family and Adjustment of Children," *Marriage and Family Living*, **20** (1958), 65–68.

brothers. When Cain the farmer and Abel the herdsman brought their ceremonial offerings, the Lord showed a preference for the animals, at which Cain was "very wroth, and his countenance fell"; soon afterwards "it came to pass, when they were in the field, that Cain rose up against Abel his brother, and slew him." This is only the beginning. Going no further than the Book of Genesis, there are accounts of severe trouble between the twin brothers Esau and Jacob, a bitter childbearing race between the sisters Leah and Rachel, who were Jacob's wives, and a long resentful contest between Joseph the dreamer, his father's favorite, and the brothers who hated him.[7]

At a much later point in history the familiar phenomenon was given new depth by psychoanalysis. In the recollections, fantasies, and dreams of patients undergoing analytic therapy brothers and sisters often appeared in major roles, sometimes in connection with incestuous wishes, often as objects of the feelings experienced by Cain toward Abel. Surface friendliness with a sibling, even a warm alliance, did not necessarily preclude latent half-conscious or unconscious rivalry and hostility. These latent impulses, moreover, had a way of persisting into adult life even though the childhood situations that brought them into being had long since faded into the past. Patients sometimes became aware that they were still competing with grownup siblings for the favor of parents who might be aged, senile, or even long dead. Sometimes patients came to realize that new rivalries, for instance with business associates or professional competitors, aroused feelings more bitter and anxieties more disturbing than the circumstances warranted; the legacies of competition in the family circle prevented them from responding with intelligent discernment to contemporary realities. If sibling rivalry could leave such lasting marks it must certainly have been important in the early growth of personality.

The Birth of a Younger Child

Freud's single venture into child analysis, his study of a phobia in a 5-year-old boy, disclosed among other things the child's heavy preoccupation with his mother's pregnancy and the birth of his younger sister.[8] With the growth of psychiatric treatment for children it became possible to observe sibling rivalry not as a recollection from the past but as a current happening. Studies by David Levy were particularly influential in bringing the problem to professional attention.[9] When a hitherto only child has to start sharing the parental attention to which he has become accustomed, it is understandable that he will not like it, but hostility toward the newcomer or toward the par-

[7] Genesis, Chaps. 4, 25, 29, 30, 37.

[8] S. Freud, "Analysis of a Phobia in a Five-Year-Old Boy" (1909), reprinted in *Collected Papers*, Vol. 3 (New York: Basic Books, Inc., 1959), pp. 149–289.

[9] D. M. Levy, "Hostility Patterns in Sibling Rivalry Experiments," *American Journal of Orthopsychiatry*, **6** (1936), 183–257; "Release Therapy," *ibid.*, **9** (1939), 713–736.

ents proves to be quite the wrong strategy for regaining his place in the sun. Levy showed that this trap could have serious consequences: it could produce symptoms such as night terrors, loss of acquired bowel and bladder control, head-banging and other self-injurious actions, and even disorders of speech. He saw these symptoms as outlets, indirect and symbolic, of impulses locked in conflict: jealous hatred that would not go away, and dread of what would happen if destructiveness went out of control. In treating the young patients he tried to lighten the burden of their anxiety by encouraging them to express hate symbolically. This was accomplished through play with dolls, during which the smashing of the baby dolls and mother dolls was blandly accepted, sometimes even initiated, by the therapist. It is noteworthy that the children sometimes felt better after these sessions, as if their right to feel hatred had been ratified, but that they never undertook to practice their new freedom on the characters at home.

The birth of a sibling does not, of course, ordinarily lead to emotional disaster, and sibling murder is exceedingly rare. More common is a kind of indirect psychological warfare that is tempered by parental restrictions and gradually further moderated by the gains that can come from friendship and alliance with siblings. Even though the newborn sibling is too small to be of much use, the child can often find a few redeeming features. Occasional services to the smaller one can serve as gratifying evidence of superior grownup competence, and playing with the baby may eventually become a pleasure in its own right.

Some years ago an anonymous pair of parents made a detailed record of the behavior of their 4-year-old daughter Evelyn in response to the birth of a baby brother, Bert.[10] For some time, even before the pregnancy, Evelyn had been advocating a baby sister, and had even proposed that if her mother were too busy to have the baby she would have it herself. Thus she was looking forward to the newcomer, but was somewhat miffed when it proved to be a boy. The most significant thing about the diary of the little girl's behavior is its evidence of conflicting feelings, some positive and some negative. The child was observed to use a varied repertory of actions and attitudes as if she were dealing with the puzzle by trying out an array of possible solutions. For a short while she called the baby "she," but soon gave this up when nobody concurred. With intense interest she watched the baby nurse and once expressed the fantasy that she had pulled the blanket out from under him. She expressed her discontent with Bert as a playmate by saying, "All the baby does is drink and wet and mess his pants." She aimed a toy pistol at him with shouts of "Bang, bang!" but rather quickly threw it aside. At other times she took a different tack, saying, "You're more my mother than his, because I was born first and I'm going to grow up first." Perhaps one of her earliest comments, made the day mother and baby came home from the hospital, went closest to the heart of the difficult problem: "You like me, don't you? And you

---

[10] Anonymous, "Ambivalence in First Reactions to a Sibling," *Journal of Abnormal and Social Psychology*, **44** (1949), 541–548.

like the baby, and you like Daddy." Can such catholicity of liking be grasped and accepted by a 4-year-old? Several times Evelyn pretended that she was a baby, drinking from her doll's nursing bottle and requiring her parents to enact appropriate caretaking roles. At other times she played out the fantasy of giving birth to a baby and taking care of it; one day the mother's ministrations to Bert were matched step by step by Evelyn's attentions to her doll. Slowly, sometimes with grumbling but sometimes with pride, she began to participate with her mother in taking care of Bert. By Bert's sixth month she often wanted to hold him, was pleased that by talking to him she could sometimes stop him from crying, and shared her possessions generously with him, even reserving part of her candy for the day when he would be able to eat it. Yet there were still residues of negative feeling expressed in conversations about death and in hostile fantasies directed now at her parents.

In all probability this pattern of experimenting, marked by changes of feeling and trying out many different actions, is what most children do when coping with the birth of a sibling. The age of the older child is an important consideration, influencing both his understanding of what is taking place and the repertory of behavior at his disposal. In an early study Sewall showed that jealousy occurred most frequently when the age difference between the two children was between 18 and 42 months.[11] It can be presumed that before 18 months the child's cognitive development does not permit a true grasp of the situation, whatever discomfort he may feel, whereas after 42 months his repertory has enlarged to a point where many alternatives are available. Sewall's study also suggested that parental attitudes might be involved. Rating the families in her series as poorly adjusted or well-adjusted, she found that 63 percent of the children in the former group, but only 10 percent in the latter group, manifested strong signs of jealousy. Other workers have found evidence that jealousy of a newborn sibling is most common in first-born children, who have had no previous experience of sharing their parents with another child. It has further been shown that jealousy occurs with slightly greater frequency when the newborn is a boy. Parental attitudes must certainly be implicated in this last result.[12]

Because the early literature dealt with clinical cases in which sibling rivalry was considered to have contributed to emotional breakdown, much thought was given to ways of preventing jealousy among brothers and sisters. It cannot be prevented altogether. The arrival of a new baby necessarily means a change in the distribution of the mother's attention and to some extent of the father's. The older child is bound to feel this difference and to be pained by it. If the child has wanted the baby as a playmate, disappointment is in store; all that the newcomer will do, as Evelyn so well expressed it, is "drink and wet and mess his pants." As the baby grows and becomes more demanding, conflicts may very well increase at a faster rate than occasions for agree-

[11] M. Sewall, "Two Studies of Sibling Rivalry, I. Some Causes of Jealousy in Young Children," *Smith College Studies in Social Work*, 1 (1930), 6–32.

[12] Catherine Landreth, *The Psychology of Early Childhood* (New York: Alfred A. Knopf, Inc., 1958), pp. 199–200.

able exchange. For a young child, having a newborn sibling does not present enough intrinsic advantages to counteract the inevitable loss. "Children have justification," writes Landreth, "in looking with disfavor on a new arrival." Landreth summarizes as follows the inherent frustrations and the things she believes parents can do to soften them.

> A child could be helped by being informed of a new family member's arrival shortly before the event. He might also be prepared by seeing new babies and the kind of care they need so that he is not disappointed in his expectations. Further the new baby can be made something of an asset by letting the child have some part in preparing for him and later, if he wishes, some share in caring for him. At this time too a child can learn that being older has its advantages in freedom of activity, play with friends, eating at table with parents, and enjoying an association that is unique to himself and his age. Finally, parents can accept their child's *feelings* of jealousy while modifying its *expression* into socially acceptable forms.[13]

Rivalry in Later Childhood and Adolescence

The birth of a younger sibling is a definite event that lends itself to observation. It has therefore absorbed most of the research and much of the theorizing on the subject of sibling rivalry. Displacement by a newborn baby, however, is only one of a variety of situations that can give rise to jealousy. An older child will have many later occasions to feel envious of what seem to be the privileges and exemptions of the younger ones. Being the family sitter, or having to escort younger children and keep them from harm, may create the feeling that an elder child's lot is not a happy one. But the other side of the coin is equally important. Not at first, but often in the course of time, younger siblings have occasion to be jealous of older ones. Parental attitudes contribute, but once again inherent features of the situation make it difficult to avoid competitive feelings. If it is not always agreeable to an older child to watch over a younger one, it is likewise not always agreeable to a younger child to be watched over by an older one. Older children have built-in privileges appropriate to their age, and there are bound to be times when these awaken envy and look unfair. "You let *him* do it, why can't *I*?" is one of the protests most persistently heard in the family circle. Sometimes a youngest child clamors to be allowed to go to school because this is seen as a privileged badge of maturity that is being withheld. One victim of this injustice greatly annoyed her older sister by pretending that she, too, had been to school and recounting fictional happenings far more glamorous than the real ones experienced by the sister. Each step in development, each granting of a privilege, revives and perhaps strengthens such feelings. The older sibling's being allowed to go to bed later and use lipstick and have dates and drive the car all keep alive for some children a painful jealousy of those who through no virtue of their own have qualified for special privileges.

[13] Landreth, *The Psychology of Early Childhood*, pp. 200–201.

Once infancy is past, rivalry with older siblings is likely to be carried on at some disadvantage. The heart of the issue, of course, is the love and respect of the parents, and the older child has had more experience in dealing with parents. The older child's cognitive grasp is more mature and his capacities more varied. This gives him an advantage in competitive maneuvering and in the art of making himself appear to be in the right. If the younger child senses that a situation is being manipulated to his disadvantage but cannot see how to oppose it, he may simply become violent in word or deed, but this is usually a tactical defeat in gaining parental approbation. The older competitor is likely to be more skilled both in pleasing the parents and in managing them. The younger one may score points with the pathetic appeal, but this eventually is incompatible with self-respect. The advantages of being older may, of course, be lost entirely if one or both parents favor the younger child. Developmental maturity is nevertheless an inherent asset in the competitions engendered by sibling rivalry, and the victories to which it leads may seem extraordinarily unfair to the younger contestants.

In autobiographical papers submitted by college students, sibling rivalry emerges as a fairly common theme, and it is by no means a dead issue at college age. The sharp sensitivity that may surround this problem during childhood is shown in the large variety of situations described. One student, much alienated from his family, remembered with bitterness that his older brother was warmly praised for grades of *C* on his report card whereas he himself was expected to bring home *B*s and was congratulated only for *A*s. Perhaps the brother was scholastically handicapped, but this did not alter, especially from a child's point of view, the gross unfairness of parental expectations. In another case the situation was almost reversed: the less gifted of two brothers bitterly resented parental rejoicing over his brother's high grades and the unequal allocation of family resources to his higher education. In still another instance a girl described an earlier orthopedic handicap that had necessitated some months in a hospital; she experienced this period as an unfair desertion by her parents who were mostly at home with the other children, but the siblings were miffed that their parents rushed to the hospital every day and lavished so much attention on the privileged invalid. Keenly sensitive as they are to their status in parental affection, children find evidence of injustice and favoritism in a great variety of situations.

Observational studies thus show that sibling rivalry can sometimes leave deep marks on personality. These marks will appear chiefly in situations that involve competition for the esteem of people in a position analogous to parents, such as teachers or superiors in one's occupation. Something akin to sibling rivalry is often experienced by graduate students, whose careers are much influenced by the impression they make on their senior professors. It is also experienced in business organizations where many are employed but few are promoted. The issues are contemporary, but the feelings and fantasies that arise may betray the enduring residues of earlier competitions. But the residues of rivalry may extend beyond the personal sphere so that they influence attitudes toward more abstract issues. The sense of justice is involved. A person who has known the sting of injustice in the family circle may be quick to detect infringements of justice in public affairs and may become a staunch champion of civil rights. A person who was often defeated at home by a self-righteous sibling may develop an unusual capacity to see and expose whatever is pompous, arrogant, and condescending in public life and communication. Frustrations in the family circle are sometimes destructive in their consequences, but when they are transcended in this fashion they may contribute to important social accomplishments.

Effects of Sibling Death: An Illustrative Case

The depth of feeling involved in sibling rivalry sometimes comes out in striking form when a sibling dies. What happens when a hated rival disappears from the family scene? Obviously something more complex than plain rejoicing. A young man who will be called Graham provides illustration. Graham was 14 years old when his brother died. This brother was barely a year older, was the eldest child, bore the father's name, and was clearly the mother's favorite if not also the father's. Rivalry between the two boys was of long standing. One of Graham's earliest memories was of "Junior and myself arguing over which one of us would marry mother when we grew up." Recollections included a good many fights and a certain smugness on Junior's part that often reduced Graham to tears. There were two summers of intense happiness at camp when Graham was conspicuously successful in sports and surpassed his brother, but presently Junior pulled ahead again and made teams that the younger boy failed to make. Then came the usual series of adolescent privileges for which Junior qualified first. But at 15 Junior was sent away to boarding school and Graham came into his own: he drove the car, smoked, drank, and seized "every possible opportunity for dissipation." He wrote, "This was my first opportunity to live my life the way I wanted to, and in spite of my parents' disapproval I don't think I have ever been quite so happy."

It is significant that Graham reached peaks of happiness first when he bested his brother in competition and later when, with equal privileges at last, he found happiness and excitement in a round of life with other teenagers and could afford to shrug off his parents' approval. He started to take the path that often attracts those who feel themselves less loved: turning one's back resentfully on the unbreakable alliance of parents and favorite child and seeking one's happiness among contemporaries, often with some flouting of adult values. At this point Junior became fatally ill. The final scene at the hospital was acutely agonizing, with the mother beseeching the dying boy not to leave them. In the ensuing days of family grief Graham was surprised to discover that he felt little sadness or inclination to cry. While Junior had been at boarding school he had not missed him and he did not miss him now. Yet something momentous had happened, something that dominated his life up to the time he was studied nine years later. "Undoubtedly," he wrote, "the most important single experience of my life has been the death of my brother."

At the time of the death Graham's best friend, his companion in dissipation, told him that now he would have to be particularly kind to his parents and be two sons to them. The parents seemed ready to fit into this prescription and concentrate affection on the son who was now their eldest. Yet almost at once Graham stayed out with the car far beyond the prescribed hour, terrifying his parents and drawing violent blame for breaking a promise. He could not step into Junior's place, even if it were really there. The displays of grief had only confirmed that Junior was the parents' real favorite and strengthened Graham's resentment against them. He could not find it in himself to comfort them by being a good second-best son, especially if this entailed sacrificing his career as a somewhat rebellious, independent adolescent. Far from following his friend's well-meant counsel, he began having as little as possible to do with his parents, and he continued to seek excitement and dissipation in the company of his contemporaries. Perhaps it was a concession to the family that he became more serious about his schoolwork, but his life with his friends was the real center of his being.

But now this life no longer worked. Escapades and minor delinquencies gave pleasure that was ever more fleeting and that progressively failed to alleviate a bleak mood. His health began to decline; at length a bothersome digestive disorder that resisted treatment became the chronic uncomfortable background of his existence. Stories he wrote at 23 as part of a psychological testing program were filled with themes of discouragement, unhappiness, and the contemplation of suicide, though with occasional outbursts of anger and violence. From his actual life such outbursts were absent, but his feelings closely resembled those of his weary characters: no joy could be found in the present, and even a lifetime of hard work would yield only "an infinitesimal amount of happiness." Clinical studies have often linked depression with feelings of guilt and tendencies toward self-punishment. Graham was certainly depressed, and guilt was not far below the surface.

In Graham's case guilt was more complexly organized than it would be for a young child. Undoubtedly he felt deeply troubled over his inability to comfort his parents and restore their happiness by becoming a devoted and loving son. Even his friend, who otherwise shared his values, saw this as the appropriate way to behave. But when there has been such a long history of sibling rivalry it is difficult to stop hating the parents for their unfairness; the inclination to comfort them is blocked by resentment. Furthermore, there is likely to be residual anger at the sibling, however unreasonable this may appear. By dying, Junior put his brother into a nasty box just when Graham was solving the problem of being the less-favored son. Junior deserted his post as the one who kept the parents happy, moved into a realm in which his memory was quickly idealized, and placed himself where he could never be bested in future competition. If he had done this on purpose it would have been a dirty trick, and Graham's feelings were like those in earlier incidents he experienced as dirty tricks—feelings that included guilt at hating the parents' favorite son. The total load of guilt that came up after his brother's death was too much for Graham to manage without paying heavy tribute in the form of depression and ill health.

The Favorite Child

The tendency in psychological studies to concentrate on jealousy and its disturbing consequences should not obscure the fact that being a favorite child also has consequences for the growth of personality. The favorite child has one great advantage: he is secure in the feeling of being loved and es-teemed. By itself this is conducive to self-confidence and a sense of well-being, indeed to the whole pattern of traits associated with parental acceptance as summarized at the end of the third chapter. Being the fav-orite, however, is not wholly free from difficulties. One of its effects may be a reluctance to leave the family circle. Neighboring homes, the school, and the playground may afford an unpleasant contrast with home, offering nothing better than treatment as an equal, which is less than the favorite child has learned to expect. A second possible consequence is the growth of a self-righteous attitude that others, especially other children, are likely to find disagreeable. At his worst the favorite child may be serenely convinced that he is always right; when others oppose him they are simply being unreasonable. This seems to be what Graham had in mind when he attributed smugness to his older brother. It is a quality that can interfere badly with learning to see things from another person's point of view. Still another consequence may follow from occupying a favored position: the child may learn constant vigilance both to keep pleasing the parents and to defeat the machinations of disgruntled sibling rivals.

Of particular interest are reports by college students who have been the family favorite and have come to realize it. Arrival at this insight may be far from pleasant. Feelings of guilt may follow the realization that one has occupied a position of unjust privilege, and the favored child may resent the parents for their departures from fair practice. Thus the favorite child may offer restitution to the siblings by acts of assistance and intercede with the parents to give the other children a better break.

Studies of Birth Order

Research on the child members of the family circle is hampered by variations in number, sex, age, and age interval; the resulting combinations approach infinity. Searching for something to hang on to, research workers have seized upon order of birth, which has the virtue of being measurable without error. The chief positions studied are those of eldest child, youngest child, intermediate child, and only child, usually without reference to sex or to age intervals. Does it make a difference to the development of personality to grow up in one of these positions rather than another?

Eminence

In 1874 Sir Francis Galton published a book called *English Men of Science* based on biographical information collected from the outstanding scientists of his time and country. He reported in this book a finding that in various guises has been cropping up ever since: there were more only sons and first-born sons among the eminent scientists that there should have been by chance. In Victorian England the finding occasioned no surprise. The eldest son under the law of primogeniture inherited his father's whole estate and thus more often had the means to follow what was then an unprofitable career. Galton further speculated that only and eldest sons were given more adult companionship and responsibility; the latter trait particularly made them pursue their scientific labors with devotion and persistence. The explanation in terms of inherited wealth was shattered when J. M. Cattell published a survey of eminent American scientists, raised in a land in which laws of primogeniture had long been abolished, and found a similar predominance of the first-born.[14] Cattell's survey produced another finding that had also been made by Havelock Ellis in England.[15] Youngest sons appeared among eminent persons significantly more often than intermediate sons, though proportionally not as often as eldest sons. If eminence were one's goal it was best to be first-born, next best to be last-born, and poor to be in the middle. These findings, especially with respect to the eldest, have been corroborated by considerable subsequent research.[16]

Intellectual Ability

Terman, in his well-known research on gifted children, studied the effects of birth order from a different point of view. He defined intellectual giftedness as having an I.Q. of 140 or higher on a standard test of intelligence, the Stanford Binet. His findings were surprisingly parallel to those of Cattell: first-born and last-born children were overrepresented.[17] Research based on college aptitude tests and on performance in the National Merit Scholarship Competition confirms the predominance of eldest children in highly gifted groups but does not support Terman's findings with respect to

[14] J. M. Cattell, "Statistical Study of American Men of Science," *Science*, n.s., **24** (1906), 658–665, 699–707, 732–742.

[15] H. Ellis, *A Study of British Genius* (London: Hurst and Blackett, 1904).

[16] W. D. Altus, "Birth Order and Its Sequelae," *International Journal of Psychiatry*, **3** (1967), 23–32.

[17] L. M. Terman, "Genetic Studies of Genius," *The Mental and Physical Traits of a Thousand Gifted Children*, Vol. 1 (Stanford, Calif.: Stanford University Press, 1925).

the youngest, who may even be less represented than intermediate children. Furthermore, there is reason to suppose that the demonstrated birth order effects are confined to the most gifted level of the population, fading out if the investigator takes a sample that is a little below the top 2 or 3 percent.[18] The time is past when the I.Q. was regarded as a measure simply of innate intelligence. Measures of intellectual ability and scholastic aptitude are virtually certain to reflect the consequences of education and stimulation as well as innate potential. It is therefore legitimate to interpret the superiority of first-born children not as a weird genetic phenomenon but as in some way a consequence of an advantageous position in the family circle.

College Attendance

Understanding of this advantage is assisted by still another angle of investigation, the frequency of the different positions among those who go to college and to graduate school. In 1963 Stanley Schachter published a paper summarizing a large amount of research on this question by himself and others.[19] Once more the first-born are found in greater than chance numbers, significantly so in college and still more markedly in graduate school. A check on students in high school showed that at that level there was no disproportion; the emergence of first-born and only children apparently occurs at the point of transition to college. Youngest children are not overrepresented in either the college or the graduate school populations. The findings of Cattell on scientific eminence and of Terman on high intellectual ability do not have a parallel here with regard to youngest children, but the theme of the advantages of the first-born comes through again with striking consistency.

It is of course reasonable to suppose that intellectual ability, higher education, and eminence stand in a fairly close relation. "The repeated finding of a surplus of first-borns among eminent scholars," writes Schachter, "appears to have nothing to do with any direct relationship of birth order to eminence but is simply a reflection of the fact that scholars, eminent or not, derive from a college population in which first-borns are in marked surplus." This brings the problem to a focus on those points in life at which a person does or does not enter the pathways to higher education. The advantage of being the eldest has its impact particularly at the time of entrance to college and again at entrance to graduate school. Conceivably the advantage could be simply an economic one: family resources tend to be concentrated on the first child and are sometimes not equal to educating the others. This explanation, however, appears to be wrong. In a study of successful graduate students Bayer found no evidence at all that the greater proportion of eldest children had anything to do with economic circumstances.[20]

[18] Altus, "Birth Order and Its Sequelae," pp. 25–27.
[19] S. Schachter, "Birth Order, Eminence and Higher Education," *American Sociological Review*, **28** (1963), 757–768.
[20] A. E. Bayer, "Birth Order and the Attainment of the Doctorate: A Test of Economic Hypotheses," *American Journal of Sociology*, **72** (1967), 540–550.

The hypothesis is advanced by Altus that the critical thing is a difference in parental treatment. There is evidence that parents are stricter with the first-born, being new to their job, and that they treat later-born children in a more relaxed, permissive fashion.[21] The difference in handling, taken together with the fact that the first-born enjoys exclusive parental attention in the beginning, results in a stronger dependence on adults, acceptance of their norms and expectations, and motivation to secure their approval. When these qualities are later displayed at school they win the approbation of teachers, and this still further encourages the child to do what is expected of a student. "If the first-born, by virtue of his different treatment in the home, takes to school more readily, works harder, persists longer, then it might be expected that he may well increase his intellectual stature in the process."[22] Eldest children, in short, are more strongly influenced in the family to develop qualities that make later on for academic success. In the most gifted segment of the population these traits make a difference in the pursuit of higher education and in the possible attainment of eminence.

It will be noticed that this hypothesis turns the spotlight on qualities that are not primarily intellectual. The suggested traits have more to do with motivation toward academic goals and with the organizing of behavior to achieve them. Conceivably birth order has effects upon a much wider range of personality traits.

Traits of Personality

Among workers with a background in psychoanalysis Alfred Adler held the most explicit views about sibling relations. He emphasized particularly the struggle for power between the oldest and next oldest child. In this struggle the advantages lay with the elder, whose strategy was likely to be superior and who could thus often goad the younger into ineffective rage. "The oldest child," Adler wrote, "is usually the one whom one accredits with enough power and common sense to be a helper or foreman of his parents." Adler attributed to the first-born a trait of conservatism, and he likened the attitude of the second-born to "the envy of the poor classes; there is a dominant note of being slighted, neglected in it."[23] Adler's idea of the parents' foreman is beautifully illustrated in the autobiography of John Stuart Mill. After being minutely guided and supervised by his father in a phenomenal educational program that began at the age of 3, Mill was required at 8 to become the teacher of his younger siblings, being held responsible for the success with which they recited their lessons to their father. Mill, however,

---

[21] R. R. Sears, E. Maccoby, and H. Levin, *Patterns of Child Rearing* (New York: Harper and Row, Publishers, 1957); J. K. Lasko, "Parent Behavior toward First and Second Children," *Genetic Psychology Monographs*, **49** (1954), 97–137.

[22] Altus, "Birth Order and Its Sequelae," p. 31. See also R. W. Bradley, "Birth Order and School-related Behavior: A Heuristic Review," *Psychological Bulletin*, **70** (1968), pp. 45–51.

[23] A. Adler, *Understanding Human Nature* (New York: Greenberg, 1927).

quickly became an unwilling foreman; "I well knew," he wrote, "that the relation between teacher and taught is not a good moral discipline to either."[24] Apparently the younger Mills resented their brother's favored position and made things hard for him in the schoolroom. The picture drawn by Adler suggests greater satisfaction in the foreman's role because of its advantages in the power struggle.

In the course of time, workers for whom the power struggle occupied a less central place than it did in Adler's thinking began to put more emphasis on the conservatism of the eldest child. Sears reported that mothers in one study and teachers in another rated first children more dependent than second children.[25] More dependent implied less rebellious, more conscientious, and more fully identified with parental values. The conservatism of the first child meant having a greater stake in conserving these values, whatever their content, which might, of course, be liberal or radical in the political sense.

The theme of greater dependence and conformity among first-born children has been the topic of quite a few investigations since 1960. Reviewing this evidence, Warren concludes that it is substantial, but the methods used restrict what has been demonstrated to the proposition that "first-born are more susceptible than later-born to social pressure."[26] The social pressure used in most of the recent studies comes from experimentally induced opposition between the subject's judgment on some matter and the judgment of his contemporaries. Conforming in such situations implies low confidence in one's own judgment compared to that of peers, and it may not be a faithful reflection of dependence on adults and espousal of their values.

Clearer light on first-born personality traits comes from an earlier investigation by McArthur, using data of a more natural kind.[27] The subjects are more than 200 college men who as sophomores had taken part in a study of adult development, and with whom contact was maintained for twelve or more years to secure continuing information. These participants had been given fairly thorough study on the first occasion, interviews with their parents being included. Four sources of material were examined with a view to detecting differences in the way first and second children were described: the participants' descriptions of themselves on a self-rating questionnaire when they were sophomores, descriptions of the participants by their parents at approximately the same time, descriptions of the participants by psychiatric interviewers, and, jumping on a dozen years, the participants' descriptions of their own children. All descriptions were elicited in the course of gathering general information and were not pointed toward birth order comparisons.

[24] J. S. Mill, *Autobiography* (1873) (New York: Columbia University Press, 1924).

[25] R. R. Sears, "Ordinal Position in the Family as a Psychological Variable," *American Sociological Review*, **15** (1950), 397–401.

[26] J. R. Warren, "Birth Order and Social Behavior," *Psychological Bulletin*, **65** (1966), 38–49.

[27] C. C. McArthur, "Personalities of First and Second Children," *Psychiatry*, **19** (1956), 47–54.

Findings were based on a count of the adjectives used in these spontaneous descriptions. The first-born were more often described as serious, adult-oriented, conscientious, studious, and shy; the second children were more often considered not studious, cheerful, easygoing, friendly, and placid. As McArthur summarized the findings, "The first child in a family is more commonly adult-oriented, while the second child is more likely to be peer-oriented. Of the various traits that arise from first-born and second-born orientation, sensitive seriousness in the first and easygoing friendliness in the second seem best documented." It will be noticed that Graham and his older brother, described earlier, almost perfectly exemplified this pattern.

The findings reviewed in this section show a certain consistency. Whether the research starts from eminence, intellectual ability, college attendance, or traits of personality, first-born children are more likely than later-born to be oriented toward adult values, to be sensitive to parental expectations, and to be dependent, serious, and studious. The differences between first-born and later-born children are often statistically significant, but they are usually not of great size. In every study there are some people, often quite a few, who come out the opposite way. There are intermediate children who are adult-oriented, attend college and graduate school, are intellectually highly gifted, and attain eminence, and there are first-born children who take paths deplored by their families. A personnel director would hardly be thought astute if in looking for someone to fill a responsible post he decided to consider only first-born sons. Undoubtedly there is lawfulness behind what has been found about the first-born, but it is not the kind of lawfulness that permits a simple statement of cause and effect. There is nothing inevitable and irresistible about being born first that regularly produces a certain pattern of personality. The findings say only that a certain pattern occurs a little more often in first-born children than in children who occupy other positions.

Is it possible to come closer to lawful processes? One can do so only by adhering strictly to the idea that the family is a social system within which individual members come to occupy differentiated roles.

Differentiation of Sibling Roles

The study of sibling roles can best be introduced through comparative case studies. We first select cases that are similar in a good many respects but sharply different as regards the points to be investigated; we then search the case material exhaustively for explanations of the difference. For the present purpose, we choose two cases, each of which involves a first and second child. The family backgrounds and circumstances are similar, and in both cases the first child is a girl, the second a boy. But the roles are entirely different. In the first family the girl is the "good" child and the boy the "bad" one; in the second family it is the boy who is adult-oriented and serious, the girl whose outrageous behavior becomes a family problem.

Comparative Study of Two Families

In both of the families to be described, the father was a Protestant minister in a liberal denomination. The atmosphere at home was conspicuously serious-minded, with emphasis on high ideals and the transforming power of love. Neither family was given to overt strictness of discipline, and high control of the authoritarian type was absent, but the standards of expected behavior, especially the control of aggressiveness and selfishness, were on the high side. Economic circumstances were moderate but not desperate, the parishes were in upper-middle-class neighborhoods, strong cultural interests prevailed in the homes, and college attendance was part of the expected pattern, whatever its cost. In such families, in which ideals of conduct are prominent and the encouragement of worthy behavior is part of the father's job, it is easy for roles of "good" child and "bad" child to become sharply polarized. But how did it happen that the first child in one case, the second in the other, came into possession of the good child role, and how did this choice move the two other siblings to adopt the character of renegades?

In the first family, the Kingsleys, the parents had every reason to be delighted with the daughter, Joyce, who was their first-born.[28] As Joyce herself put it in an autobiography written when she was in college, she was "docile and willing," "never did anything to offend mother or father," and "always followed the baby books." She was a lively and pretty child, considered charming by her father's parishioners, who showered her with gifts. For her father and mother this was indeed a happy introduction to parenthood, but it did not prepare them for what was to come. Joyce's earliest memory had to do with a birthday party in her honor: brother Albert in his high chair had to be forcibly removed when his loud screaming disrupted the festivities. Albert is described as always having had a bad temper and as being given to drastic action. Too young to be dressed up like Joyce and taken to church, he found his way, clad in a dirty play suit, by a side door into the chancel where his father was conducting the service. The Kingsley parents were shocked and bewildered by their son's rambunctious behavior. Albert's outbursts of fury reduced them to helplessness, for they were determined not to respond in kind. They sought the advice of friends on how to control their small savage, and at one point Mrs. Kingsley retired to a rest home to recuperate from the strain. It is of interest that Joyce, who had a stake in Albert's being properly punished, invented an imaginary companion, an older woman whose special skill lay in appreciating good children and firmly controlling bad ones.

What started the role differentiation of these two children? In a later chapter on temperamental differences it will be seen that even newborn babies do not behave alike. Joyce's happy docility and Albert's vigorous impatience may have been present from the very start of their lives. The par-

---

[28] This case is described at length in R. W. White, *Lives in Progress*, 2d ed. (New York: Holt, Rinehart and Winston, Inc., 1966), Chap. 7.

ents' attitudes contributed importantly. Committed to values of love and cooperation, they were paralyzed by the punitive impulses evoked by their son's assertiveness. Out of such beginnings the pattern became established that Joyce was the good child and Albert the naughty one. As the role assignments began to crystallize, each child became increasingly motivated to enact his role in such a way as to maximize its possible benefits. Joyce strengthened her position as the ally of her parents, endeavoring to meet their expectations and suppressing any tendencies in herself toward resentment or waywardness. Even as a senior in college she described how "we" felt about various issues public and private; this meant how she and her parents felt but did not include Albert, who was often one of the issues about which "we" had feelings. Joyce became adult-oriented, conscientious, serious, and hard-working, depended a good deal on the sustaining power of parental values, and as a college senior did not feel entirely comfortable with her contemporaries. Albert got away from home as soon as possible, dropped out of college, lived in an unconventional way, and became an absorbed and skillful technician in scientific work. The predictions that could be derived from McArthur's research on first and second children were largely fulfilled.

How then does one account for the first and second children of the Liveright family, who came out just the opposite? The focus of study in their case was the second child, Sam, a sophomore in college, but his sister Bella became a part of it when two years later, on her brother's urging, she came to the research center to seek counsel about her problems. Sam at this point in his career was in many respects like Joyce Kingsley. He, too, was adult-oriented, conscientious, and highly serious, and he complained of not feeling at ease with his peers. The adjectives he chose to describe himself were "likable, patient, kind, trustworthy, responsible." He pointed out that he liked to "make a favorable impression on everyone, and consider highly the opinions of others concerning myself." He was inclined to admire his teachers and "sought their friendship through good marks," while living "rather an unsocial life" and feeling inferior to his friends in athletic and assertive prowess. "In morals," he wrote, "I go by conventions, not by what I believe to be true. Conventions produce order and peace." Sam's personal development was far from finished; his later career showed that he outgrew the timid conservatism of his sophomore sentiments. But at the time of study this second-born child almost perfectly exemplified the characteristics more common in the first-born.

His sister Bella, in contrast, like a second child leaned toward peer-orientation. In her brother's words, she was "the type that cannot be happy by herself; she needs people around her." She admired Sam and respected his opinions. But she felt herself to be painfully inferior, was jealous of his close alliance with their mother, and in moments of stress would denounce him as a "goody-goody" and even express the wish to kill him. Her turning toward peers was accentuated when she went to college, where with the tutelage of a sophisticated roommate she improved her social skill and went out with many boys. Unfortunately, her social life proved incompatible with studying, so that she flunked out at the end of her first year. Next year she enrolled in an art school and lived at home, but this made unbearably acute the conflict between home values and the satisfaction she had discovered in late hours, alcohol, and boyfriends. Nagged by her mother, lectured by her brother, she became increasingly unhappy and disorganized, on which account she finally consented to ask for professional advice.

There is evidence in the Liveright family history that role differentiation made an early start. Its beginnings are obscure, but a crucial event was the death of the father when the children were respectively 4 and 2. There was a large discrepancy in age between the father and the mother; the clergyman, widowed in middle age, had married a zealous young worker in his parish and embarked upon a second family. The children's mother thus became a widow early in life, still very much in love with the older man she had married, and now much inclined to idealize his memory. The most direct remaining link with him was the son who bore his name, so that Sam, even when he was only 2 years old, was destined in his mother's imagination to become the man of the house and the reincarnation of his father's good life. Maternal images do not necessarily have the power to produce the desired result. If Mrs. Liveright pictured Bella as a zealous parish worker, she did not succeed in making this dream come true. But Sam was made happy by her preferential treatment and accepted the role of good child, developing it strongly. With the "good" role thus preempted, and with no hope of securing equal rewards by emulating it, Bella became increasingly disposed to make what she could out of the "bad" role.

Role Assignment and Role Development

The two families just examined illustrate with unusual clarity the roles of good child and bad child. From the parents' point of view a "good" child can almost be defined as one who is adult-oriented; that is, one who accepts the values that are cherished by the parents and substantially guides his behavior according to their expectations. A "bad" child is one who resists what the parents desire, shows temper, creates friction, and perhaps turns eagerly to peer values if these are incompatible with those of the home so that they provide an avenue to rebellious independence. "Good" and "bad" are intended here not in an absolute sense but simply as each set of parents defines them. "Good" must therefore not be stereotyped as adherence to what are sometimes called conventional moral values. In Communist countries children greatly disappoint their parents if they show interest in such bourgeois values as religion or property, and in American families with strong liberal views a child may evoke sharp disapproval by mowing down toy soldiers, wearing a reactionary campaign button, or showing reluctance to play with a child from another ethnic group. Roles of good child and bad child can be defined only in relation to the specific values prevailing in the family circle.

It is important at this point to take account of the distinction between formal and informal roles. A *formal* role is one that is recognized by the whole society, good examples being masculine and feminine roles or the breadwinner and homemaker roles described in the last chapter. Behavior in a formal role is importantly shaped by widely shared social expectations, and the pressure of public disapproval will be felt if the expectations are violated. Thus the breadwinner who fails to provide bread and walks out on the family generally tries to get lost and move as far as possible from the contempt of his neighbors. *Informal* roles do not have this sort of public sanction. They exist in the minds of a more restricted group and are not determined by biological facts such as sex differences or by inescapable necessities such as breadwinning and homemaking. The roles of good and bad child are strictly informal roles, which, if they exist at all, develop within the family circle and are maintained almost wholly by family expectations. This does not imply that the weight of expectation is necessarily light: a child can feel tremendously constrained by his role assignment in the family. Informal roles come into existence in the first place because they serve some purpose in the family social system, helping at least to describe the members, define their relations, and make things somewhat more predictable. They continue as long as they serve this purpose and perhaps, out of inertia, for some time beyond; but if the pattern becomes too frustrating for one member, or if it ceases to perform its function for the group, informal role assignments may change or fade out.

The beginnings of assignment to the roles of good and bad child are undoubtedly complex. Anything that makes parents like or dislike a child can contribute to the process. Temperamental traits that make caring for the child easy or hard may start maternal preferences early in life, as may personal appearance and resemblance to other members of the family. Being a boy and bearing the father's name may have something to do with it, though this influence may be opposed by a preconception that girls will be good and boys naughty. If these and other factors lead to preferential treatment, the favored child will then have his liking for the role progressively strengthened by parental approval. The other child, becoming aware that his sibling is the favorite and seeing no way to outstrip him in goodness, finds less and less to be gained by sacrificing his desires to parental expectations. The roles of good child and bad child can easily have a reciprocal relation: as one child becomes increasingly allied with the parents, the other becomes increasingly disgusted with goodness and inclined to get all he can out of the bad role. This seems to have happened fairly steadily in both the Kingsley and Liveright families. As the roles developed they continually pushed each other farther apart, reaching just about maximum contrast when the subjects were of college age.

It is possible, of course, for two or more children to occupy roles of relative goodness. Parents may succeed in managing so that persistent favoritism is avoided and more than one child can feel happy when fulfilling parental expectations. But this more or less implies that no one child has enacted the good role as a total pattern of behavior, thus preempting it at the expense of others. When everyone behaves badly some of the time, including the one who is closest to being the parents' foreman, then everyone is living in a glass house and hesitates to throw the first stone. But although it is possible to avoid role assignments along lines of goodness and badness, and observant parents may try their best to keep this cleavage from developing, the division is a natural one in the rivalrous life of childhood. How one stands in parental affection and approval is tremendously vital to a child, so vital that the perception of siblings as rivals is all but inevitable. In an autobiographical essay a college student who was a second son described his brother as everything the parents desired and himself as trying to be a second good child by following in his brother's footsteps. At the age of 10, when his brother, 15, was laid up for months with an injury, he took pride in assuming his brother's family duties and earned much parental praise. But the brother, when he recovered, felt a need to reassert his position by critical attacks on the substitute who had replaced him a little too well. The parents, believing that the younger boy should fight his own battles, did little to protect him from the campaign of belittlement. This left embers of resentment, but emulation still seemed the most profitable course, especially when the older boy was brilliantly successful in high school. The second son was if anything more successful, but now the parents expected success and hardly bothered to express any special praise. The role of second good child, starved of rewards, at last proved itself worthless in the coinage of parental esteem. Now willing to face vehement parental disapproval, the student turned to a field and vocational path representing interests of his own, where he could moreover feel supported by his peers. The second good child had proved, after all, to stand distinctly second in parental esteem, and this made the sacrifices of the role intolerable.

Being the parents' adult-oriented, conscientious child involves a considerable sacrifice of easily imagined pleasures. There is often a detectable undertone of envy in the remarks of good children about their naughty siblings. The sacrifices required to stand first with the parents are made worthwhile by a high income of affection, and the bargain is spoiled if this coin is paid out indiscriminately to siblings who have not earned it. The reverse of the picture is seen when a bad child learns that a good child has gotten away with some secret sin. The consolations of the bad role lie in satisfying one's impulses, treating responsibilities lightly, having fun with contemporaries, perhaps even seeking the excitement of delinquency. That a supposedly virtuous sibling should bootleg some of these rewards while continuing to hold his monopoly on parental approval is an infuriating piece of injustice. Sometimes it seems as if rivalrous siblings use a precise arithmetic on the balance of rewards and sacrifices in their respective roles.

Good child and bad child are far from being the only types of role open to children. They have been singled out to illustrate role assignment and role development because they bear directly on the effects of birth order. The characteristics found through research to occur with greater than chance frequency in first-born children—adult-orientation, dependency, seriousness, studiousness—turn out to be the characteristics of those who occupy the role of good child in the family circle. The birth order research indicates that this role is somewhat more likely to be available to first-born children than to those born later. Reasons have been suggested for supposing that parents might assign it more often to the first-born and that eldest siblings would be more successful in developing it at the expense of younger children. But birth order is hardly more than an incidental influence in the lawful sequence of events. It is only one of a large number of factors that incline parents to prefer a particular child and that incline a particular child to accept and flourish in the role of good child. When other factors steer parental interest to a later-born child, as happened in the Liveright family, the first-born position proves powerless to produce the characteristics of the adult-oriented child. The influences at work upon Bella and Sam Liveright are not at all mysterious or unlawful. The two children are not exceptions to a general rule; they are illustrations of a general rule. It is understandable that research should have concentrated on something objective like birth order, but one can discover the meaning of the findings only by looking much more closely at the patterns of influence at work in the family system. If one could pick out a group of children favored by parents and compare them with a not-favored group—regardless of birth order—the average differences in personality might well turn out to be large.

Varieties of Childhood Role

Many roles in the family are available to children. One child, for instance, may be the family handyman who mends things and builds things to facilitate household routines. Another may be cast as the hard-headed one who calms emotional storms and deals coolly with neighbors and tradesmen. Another may be seen as hopelessly impractical, a dreamer who goes around with his head in the clouds, but perhaps acceptable if he gives some evidence of scholarly capacity or genius. There may be a family pet, usually a young, small, pretty child who is not expected to assume responsibilities. There may also be an actual invalid whose role becomes defined very differently from those of the healthy children. The family entertainer or clown is a well-known figure whose role is like that of a court jester: providing amusement, he is privileged to weave in a certain amount of criticism, but his humor tends to blunt the sharp edges in serious disputes. One child may be considered an adornment because of unusual attractiveness or social skill, his social virtuosity serving to create a good impression for the family as a whole on the larger community. Some role assignments, such as the sullen one, the black sheep, and the scapegoat, explicitly emphasize alienation from the family. There are a great many possibilities, too numerous to be readily cast in a systematic scheme, but the elucidation of these roles in studies of families is always a matter of importance.

Writers have thus far been more successful than scientists in capturing the full significance of family roles. A vivid example is to be found in Thomas Wolfe's highly autobiographical novel, *Look Homeward, Angel*, in which the parents, Gant and Eliza, and the six Gant children are drawn with striking clarity and differentiation. The eldest child is Steve, a vain and pretentious ne'er-do-well who early drifts out of the family circle and returns on occasion only to make trouble. Next is Daisy, a sensitive girl who plays the piano and comes to have contempt for her tumultuous, disorderly home. She is not really a part of it, and marries and leaves at the earliest opportunity. In contrast, Helen is very much a part of it, motivated by powerful maternal feelings to take care of everyone, but torn by conflict over the resulting intrusions on her own life. The next child, Ben, is known as "the quiet one"; intensely secretive, self-sufficient, and overtly critical of his family, he nevertheless lives at home, stealing in and out, and is deeply devoted to the family welfare. Luke, the fifth child, tagged as "the generous one," occupies the role of good child. His tremendous hunger for approval leads him to develop the visible and audible traits most valued in the community, while his high energy and low sensitivity make him at an early age a phenomenal success as a magazine salesman. He is, however, "determined to occupy alone the throne of goodness," and this makes him a thorn in the flesh of the youngest boy, Eugene, whose preoccupation with reading and whose "deep inward turning of the spirit" Luke interprets as unforgivable selfishness. These large differences are not the result of whimsical role assignments by the parents. Wolfe assumes that each child started with strongly marked innate characteristics. He makes Helen divide the children into Gants and Pentlands, those who take after their word-spouting, histrionic, violent, unstable yet fascinating father, and those who take after their mouth-pursing, frugal, constricted, yet dimly devoted mother. But Wolfe makes it plain that Helen has oversimplified the contribution of heredity; as he describes them, each child represents a novel combination of the Gant and Pentland traits. Thus individuality is there at the beginning, but what the author portrays with such rare skill is the manner in which role assignments and role enactments operate with given differences to produce a further steering of the growth of personality.[29]

Being cast in a family role tends to promote growth in certain directions and restrict it in others. Roles exist in the minds of those concerned and are felt as a series of expectations as to how one will behave. If on certain occasions a child is shy and the parents begin to think of him as the shy one, every meeting with a stranger will be affected by the cues emanating from these expectations, so that the trait of shyness is progressively strengthened. In like fashion, family role expectations can strengthen qualities of a more desirable kind: confidence, poise, friendliness, and consideration for others are all more easily developed in an atmosphere that presupposes their existence. The restrictive aspect of roles derives from what they implicitly exclude. It may be difficult for the court jester to get his family to take him seriously, for the hard-headed practical one to stray into whim and idle fancy, or for the family dishwasher to let it be known that she would like to dress up and go out on a date. When roles in the family are narrowly defined, stereotyped,

[29] Thomas Wolfe, *Look Homeward, Angel* (New York: Charles Scribner's Sons, 1929), esp. Chaps. 10 and 18.

and crudely used for control—"you are a person who does these things but does not do those things"—they can have a decidedly restrictive effect on growth. When they have greater breadth and softness of outline, so that not all behavior is forced into them, their effect can be highly supportive.

Sibling Alliance

Rivalry is not the only possible relation among children. Brothers and sisters can serve one another as objects of love, admiration, nurture, companionship, and support. If parental behavior is grossly inadequate, the presence of siblings may mean salvation. No study of personality could be considered complete if it dealt with sibling relations wholly in terms of rivalry and did not allow for the developmental consequences of alliance.

The point is well illustrated in *Look Homeward, Angel*. In a family circle that put highest value on the garrulous, heavy-handed Luke, there would seem to be little chance of congenial support for Eugene, who, emerging from babyhood and the baby's role, stretched into a lanky, awkward, extremely sensitive boy with a powerful secret life of imagination. But there was also Ben, the "quiet one," eight years older, who found Luke and his parents unbearable and who understood what it was to have an inner life, though he never disclosed a hint of his own. When he was at home Ben spent many hours playing with Eugene, sometimes giving him presents, sometimes cuffing him, but managing to establish with him "a secret communication to which the life of the family had neither access nor understanding." He was also the younger boy's defender, criticizing his parents unsparingly when they demanded too much or were neglectful of Eugene's interests. He thus somewhat stemmed the tendency for Eugene to become a misunderstood outcast, at the same time reducing his own sense of isolation by nurturing and leading another human being who responded with affectionate admiration.

Alliance and rivalry stand in a reciprocal relation. Love among siblings is natural if rivalrous feelings do not get in the way. Some positions are undoubtedly less likely than others to evoke rivalry. Thus a large age difference such as separated Ben and Eugene reduces the probability of competition, and it might be expected that a brother and sister would more easily become allies than two siblings of the same sex. More important, however, is the strength of siblings' need for one another and the likelihood of their having a sense of common interest. Alliance is certainly favored by sharing a common plight and by needing strength in a common cause. Sometimes two less-favored children discover that by acting in concert they can score points against the favorite and put up a stronger case when the parents are umpires of a dispute. Alliance against parents can similarly strengthen the bonds among siblings. Acting thus in a common cause may well cleanse their own relation of its rivalrous elements and make them devoted comrades in arms.

Sibling Positions and Later Development

The most thorough attempt to put sibling positions into a systematic scheme and to assess their immediate and remote effects on personal development is to be found in the work of Walter Toman.[30] His thesis is straightforward and provides a needed correction to the idea, derived from some of Freud's theorizing, that interpersonal attitudes are mainly determined by the child's relations with parents. Toman argues that experience with the grownup members of the family circle is indeed important for later attitudes toward people who are older or people who occupy positions of authority through which they influence one's destiny. Relations with contemporaries, on the other hand—especially close friends and marriage partners—are more importantly colored by one's history of interactions with the near-contemporary members of the family circle, the brothers and sisters. Experience in dealing with peers is first acquired at home in dealing with siblings. As a lesson in the history of science it is instructive to notice how easily this simple proposition has been overlooked. Many developmental psychologists date the beginning of peer relations at the time when the child first ventures outside the family circle and meets children of exactly his own age on the playground, in the streets, or at school. But when this moment arrives many children are already veterans of life with siblings, and in the ensuing years, even with daily school attendance, it is siblings who are continuously present, sharing the house and the round of domestic life. A time-count would probably show that in the average family with school-age children, sibling contacts outweigh those with schoolmates and friends. An interaction study would probably show that they are more prominent in those sharings of everyday life that later on will characterize close and intimate relations. The relative importance of siblings in a child's life declines, of course, with the years, but not so early or so quickly that we can disregard their effects on the course of development.

To bring out more systematically the nature of sibling relations, Toman distinguishes eight major types of position, using for this purpose only the two objective variables of age and sex. At first glance the list looks formidable and abstract; it is as follows:

1. The oldest brother of brother(s)
2. The youngest brother of brother(s)
3. The oldest brother of sister(s)
4. The youngest brother of sister(s)
5. The oldest sister of sister(s)
6. The youngest sister of sister(s)
7. The oldest sister of brother(s)
8. The youngest sister of brother(s)

[30] W. Toman, *Family Constellation: Its Effects on Personality and Social Behavior* (New York: Springer Publishing Co., 1969).

This is not, obviously, an exhaustive list of all possible positions; that would be endless. It is a list of those positions that best lend themselves to characterization with respect to type of social experience. Other positions, such as the oldest brother of both brothers and sisters, or any of the middle positions having siblings both older and younger, can then be described as combining in various ways the social experience and the effects of these "pure" positions.

Inspection of the list suggests at once that it brings out something of importance. It is certainly not the same kind of experience to be the oldest brother of brothers as it is to be the first-born son followed by sisters. Equally different are the positions of youngest sister of sisters and youngest sister of brothers. The oldest brother of brothers, for example, becomes deeply experienced with the problem of maintaining his position of power and authority. If other circumstances are propitious he uses the available role of parents' foreman to this end, and with his superior size, strength, and cognitive maturity accumulates experience in managing the younger boys while keeping them in their place. It is easy to see how this experience will serve him in good stead if he moves toward leadership in school or perhaps into a managerial position in later life. On the other hand, in certain respects his experience in the family circle might be called impoverished. He remains a novice at dealing with peers just a little older, and he does not have the kind of familiarity with girls that comes from growing up with them in a family. Toman hypothesizes that he will tend to be something of a "tough guy with women," expecting admiration but treating them like younger brothers who must "live up to his assignments." Quite different in this respect is the oldest brother of sisters, who is "a friend of the ladies"; however, a woman he cares for "must always keep in mind that she is a woman and that, in this very capacity, she has to be the subordinate, the submissive, patient, and wise friend." The boy who has only younger sisters has a more secure position in the family than the boy with younger brothers and does not have to spend so much energy defending it. He is unschooled, however, in dealing with other boys and may have his difficulties with girls who do not take a role similar to that of a younger sister.

Given these first descriptions, representing the consequences simply of age position and sex, it is not difficult to work out the strengths and weaknesses of experience that result from the other six types of position. The youngest brother of brothers is trained, so to speak, to let other males take the lead and assume the responsibilities; he has little experience of women's interests and tends to be, in Toman's words, "shy, awkward, almost innocent." The youngest brother of sisters, on the other hand, will tend to be a "girls' boy" who gets and expects a great deal of care from his sisters and invites a continuation of this care in the relations of later life; he is not well trained either to work with or to compete with other men.

The oldest sister of sisters is in a position to become expert in managing and instructing younger women, and may make them a good boss in business, but she will have no early-acquired skills in dealing with men. The youngest sister of sisters learns to get along by being "charming, quick, capricious," qualities that may attract men but do not make for a lasting relation.

The oldest sister of brothers has the opportunity to become an expert in taking care of men and understanding them, though she may dominate them more than they like. Toman suggests that in a business office she will keep everything congenial for the male employees but hardly notice the females and be inclined simply to use them. Finally, the youngest sister of brothers receives training that can make her a huge success with men, learning to be everything a man wants a woman to be, but she, too, will tend not to notice other women and will easily seem unfriendly toward them.

The logic of these derivations seems to imply that it is an advantage to have both brothers and sisters. This makes possible a varied domestic social experience and forestalls those shortcomings of understanding that come from having siblings of only one sex. A middle child with both an older brother and sister and a younger brother and sister might be expected to be most versatile. Least favorable would be the position of an only child. Toman does not shrink from this deduction: the only child "is not really prepared for any peer relationship at all; he will rather be looking for mother and father figures." Nothing in the scheme serves to rescue the only child from the long-ascribed fate of being a spoiled brat in relation to his peers.

The logic of Toman's descriptions is plain, but one immediately wants to know whether or not things generally work out this way in real life. What is the evidence for these propositions? What is the evidence, in other words, that the patterns of social training that result from interaction with one's siblings are sufficiently durable to show later on in friendships and marriage? It is easy to see that in actual lives there would be many complications. The parents are clearly an additional influence. Natural differences among the children and the development of informal roles may alter substantially the situation created by age and sex alone. Division into alliances and other subgroups means that the siblings will not have an equal influence on any one member. If there is much friction and resentment, learning to get along may mean learning how to conduct cold wars. Furthermore, in spite of the admitted importance of siblings throughout childhood, there are other opportunities for acquiring social experience—with playmates, companions, and friends—where new attitudes can be learned and old ones modified, where even the luckless only child can start learning to get along with equals. Can we believe that the consequences of sibling experience will come through in adult life, surviving the impact of so much intervening social learning?

The obvious way of testing these hypotheses is to study directly the social traits of people whose sibling positions are known. Several investigations of this kind are described in Toman's book.[31] It was found, for instance, that oldest brothers predominated at more than a chance level among leaders of male youth groups and among high school students elected presidents of their class. Among housemothers of children's villages and orphan homes there was a similar preponderance of older sibling positions, and the housemothers came from families with an unusually large number of children

[31] *Ibid.*, pp. 246–249.

(an average of nine). In another type of study, high school students were asked to write character descriptions of their siblings; their composite portraits for each position were very much in line with theoretical expectations. The composite portraits were then given to other students who were asked to pick those that best fitted their brothers and sisters; the theoretically "right" portraits were selected with much more than chance frequency. More research of this kind is desirable to clinch the point, but results so far indicate that social experience with siblings is indeed important and may well last into later life.

More impressive at the moment, however, are results obtained from a study of the effects of sibling position on marriage compatibility and stability.[32] Prediction was based on the "duplication theorem": marriages would be most congenial and stable when each partner's relation to the other duplicated an earlier sibling relation. The most complete complementarity occurs when both age and sex positions are duplicated, as when an oldest brother of sisters marries a youngest sister of brothers, or when a youngest brother of sisters marries an oldest sister of brothers. Complementarity is lowest when both age and sex positions are conflicting: an oldest brother of brothers and an oldest sister of sisters, for example, would compete for seniority and also have little understanding of the other sex, and there would be similar trouble for a youngest brother of brothers and a youngest sister of sisters except that their competition would be for "juniority." Obviously there are a great many intermediate positions characterized by partial rank or sex "conflict." The duplication theorem can be tested by comparing married couples with those who are divorced. In a first comparison of 16 married couples and 16 divorced couples, matched with respect to age, time since marriage, and other relevant considerations, Toman found that in the first group 12 couples "were fully or partially complementary according to their sibling positions, whereas this was true of only one of the 16 marriages that had ended in divorce." This investigation was followed by a field study in two Central European cities involving more than 2,000 families. Among the 108 divorced pairs found in this sample there was a significant predominance of poor or non-complementary matches and a significant shortage of completely complementary ones. Furthermore, when the divorced group was subdivided into later divorces (after 13 or more years) and earlier divorces, complementary sibling relationships were found significantly less often among the early divorced partners.

These findings bear testimony to the lasting importance of siblings in the formation of personality. The social experience gained in growing up with brothers and sisters becomes an embedded part of one's repertory of attitudes and understanding. The consequences show themselves no doubt in a variety of later relations but especially in those that are close and continuous with people of approximately one's own age, marriage partners being the perfect example. As with so many processes of personality, however, the

[32] *Ibid.*, pp. 239–241.

finding of a significant connection between earlier and later events does not mean the discovery of a rigid cause-effect sequence that works out the same way every time. Many other things besides age and sex position enter into sibling relations, as we have seen; many other things influence later happenings such as friendship and marriage. The discovered relation reflects something lawful, but the law does not work in such a simple way as to be taken as a guide to conduct. A couple contemplating marriage would not be wise to let the decision hang on whether or not they are complementary with respect to their sibling experience. Knowledge of this kind cannot render obsolete the slow process of discovering mutual congeniality, but when conflicts arise, it may increase the partners' awareness of how their earlier experience may be slanting their present behavior. Insight of this sort can improve one's ability to deal with the current problem in its own right.

In later life, direct interactions among siblings are likely to be of diminishing importance. Unless unmarried siblings remain in one household, the contacts are less frequent and the spheres of interest more separated. But when rivalrous feelings have been strong, they may be quickly fanned afresh by later events. There can be competition over who has the best spouse, the nicest children, and the best-paid job, and sometimes the divison of property upon the death of the parents sends middle-aged children up the old ramparts. Even so, the solidarity among brothers and sisters can be surprisingly strong. This is more than a feeling of obligation toward one's closest relatives. It is a residue from the experience of having lived together as children, having been in the same boat during the early years, and having developed a deep familiarity with one another that is different from any other relation.

Further Reflections on Child Rearing

At the end of Chapter 3 it was pointed out that practical wisdom about child rearing could not be distilled without studying the family as a social system. We have now studied the family in detail. What bearing does this have on the bringing up of children?

The question arose in connection with the permissive philosophy of child rearing. Research on the effects of parental attitudes indicated that permissiveness, embodying relatively high acceptance and low control, would be most likely to encourage a happy combination of security, personal warmth, confidence, and creative initiative—a "liberated" personality well suited to present conditions. But there was a disquieting suggestion that these traits, standing alone, might not be compatible with the patient, sustained endeavor that lies behind valuable human accomplishments, and that permissiveness by default, in a vacuum of parental values, might leave a child badly confused about what was important both in himself and in the world. The example of Summerhill, a school designed to embody the permissive philosophy, suggested that a high degree of freedom might require for constructive results the support of a social system in which there were strong values, strong expectations, and strong personal examples. The growth of personality is inevitably affected by *all* the characteristics of the system.

Chapter 4 examined the family circle with special reference to parents and other adult members. As a social system it has a number of characteristics that are likely to be important for the children. From the manner in which their parents divide the labor of the household and enact masculine and feminine roles the children obtain their earliest and strongest impressions of sex roles and cooperative living. If there is sharp conflict and disharmony between parents, the children's sense of security may be seriously undermined; they may be swept into the battle and damaged by it. Then there are subsystems within the family, composed of grandparents and other adult relatives as well as siblings, the result being a series of internal alliances that may strongly affect a child's sense of security and appreciation. It is one thing to be a disfavored child who has the support of a grandparent, uncle, or aunt; another thing to stand alone. Families to some extent develop traditions and values of their own, adding to or varying from those that are common to their culture. These values and their enactment are an effective part of the environment of growth. In one family permissive parents may be remembered chiefly for their fidelity to some highly valued cause or their steadiness when confronted by obloquy and threats; another pair of permissive parents may be recalled mainly for the lively cocktail parties they gave. All such characteristics of the family social system must be included to understand the growth of personality and to grasp the multiple problems of fostering that growth.

In this chapter brothers and sisters were added to the picture, and this is no small complication. Even the most thoughtful child-rearing philosophies often come to grief over sibling relations. There is no escaping the circumstance that although siblings can be friends, allies, and sources of mutual aid, they stand in a position of rivalry for parental affection and for privileges in the household. The permissive philosophy meets its most grueling test in dealing with more than one child. The presence of at least two children raises in sharp form the question of fairness—of maintaining justice—and justice is not permissive; it entails the application of principles in an even-handed way that may well frustrate the desires and hopes of both parties to the controversy. If parents do not adhere to the principle that privileges increase with age, but yield to the screams of younger children for equal treatment right now, they teach that age and maturity have no intrinsic value and that you get what you scream for, lessons that offer little prompting toward growing up. If parents, bent on encouraging self-reliance, leave the children to settle their own quarrels, the oldest or strongest may always triumph, and all may deduce that nothing really pays except crude power. Parents can be a veritable showcase of high principles, good example, and intended love, but if one of the children feels that another is always subtly favored he will come to view the parental virtues as just so much hypocrisy. It is on this account that a single family can produce such contrasting offspring as a cautious, conserv-

ative parents' foreman and a reckless, cynical revolutionary. Their environment is in many respects the same, but as regards justice it is utterly different.
And justice is a highly important aspect of the family social system.

It is because of these many complicating features that child-rearing
philosophies cannot be compressed into simple statements of value and a
conveniently short set of precepts. In recent years careful clinical observation,
studies of families, and longitudinal investigations have made substantial
contributions to knowledge relevant to the bringing up of children. This has
helped to free parents from relying on folklore and custom or from bringing
up their children exactly as they themselves were brought up. It lays the
foundation for a more carefully considered, more rational outlook on purposes and methods. But it has not turned child rearing into a clear-cut
applied science. There are always a great many things to consider. Personal
systems and social systems interact in ways that are inherently complex. Add
to this the fact that the events of family life usually take place so fast that
no one has time to reason out all possible consequences, and it is clear that in
practice child rearing still calls for a strong dash of intuitive art even though
our theoretical understanding of it has improved.

6 Varieties of Environment: Social Status and Ethnic Group

Babies and small children spend their time in the family circle, and this daily interaction gives the family environment great weight in the early growth of personality. But the family is obviously part of a much larger environment extending outward through neighborhood, community, region, nation, and even in a sense to the whole world. In the course of time the growing child will enter some part of this larger environment and experience its direct impact, but even before he stirs outside the family he is influenced indirectly by wider surroundings. The family is affected by the neighborhood of which it is a part, and the neighborhood in turn is influenced by the surrounding community; thus the wider world constantly makes itself felt in each household. Children are a favorite topic of conversation among mothers. The atmosphere of a child's supper hour and bedtime routine may be perceptibly affected by tales of nursery management absorbed by his mother from her neighbors during the afternoon. Further influence may be subtly present the next morning if the mother read in her evening newspaper a column of advice to parents, watched a relevant television program, or dipped into a popular paperback on how to bring up children. The family circle is never impermeable.

For any given family, however, interaction with the larger community is limited. No one can have contact with the whole world. In the United States, for instance, with its great size, diverse ethnic origins, tremendous specialization, and advanced division of labor, there are a large number of social subdivisions in the population, and each of these has an outlook and values sufficiently different to make it a sort of subculture. The most important of these subdivisions are those connected with *socioeconomic status*. The population is stratified into levels, often described as *social classes*, which owe their existence to a variety of economic, social, and educational circumstances. The differences in way of life that distinguish different social levels are so great that they tend to overshadow anything that could be called a national character. It is true that Americans as a whole differ in certain respects from the English as a whole, the Germans, the Japanese, or the people of a Latin American nation. Widespread impressions to this effect have been supported by extensive research.[1] But even within a single nation there are differences of no small magnitude, such as those that separate, say, an itinerant farm worker from a corporate executive or the inhabitant of an urban slum from a wealthy suburban professional man. In a closely packed city, high-rise luxury apartments, rows of neat but drab walk-up flats, and the crumbling buildings of a black ghetto may stand on adjacent blocks. The physical distances that separate them are small, but the social distances have the depth of canyons.

The social distances that separate *ethnic groups* are sometimes no less significant. Even a superficial acquaintance with American communities brings to light a marked ethnic clustering in residential areas. This is most conspicuous in urban centers, where ethnic homogeneity may create a Chinatown, a French Quarter, a Little Italy, or a black ghetto. The same phenomenon, though usually in less dramatic form, can often be observed in small towns and rural areas. Tiny villages in which nobody is rich may prove to have detectable ethnic areas, possibly each with its own church and social hall. The much-publicized recent exodus from central city to suburbs might be expected to reshuffle the population and break up established ethnic groupings, but often this is not what happens. A new real estate development consisting of rows of standard houses on straight streets may become differentiated from the start into ethnic neighborhoods. Even when there are no differences in socioeconomic level and no deprivation of access to public schools and other facilities, children living in these ethnic neighborhoods are brought up in different subcultures. At home they will be made more or less aware of their cultural heritage, perhaps also of a special religious tradition. In the immediate neighborhood they will play with children of like background, but a few streets away and at school they will meet other groups with other backgrounds, and they will become aware of intergroup attitudes and ethnic stereotypes. The difference of experience becomes huge when, as with blacks in the United States, an ethnic group has been surrounded by powerful prejudice, excluded from major opportunities, and even assigned the status of a permanent inferior caste. The subculture formed in this way creates special problems for the growth of personality.

[1] See, for instance, Alex Inkeles and D. J. Levinson, "National Character: A Study of Modal Personality and Sociocultural Systems," in *Handbook of Social Psychology*, 2d ed., Vol. 2, ed. G. Lindzey and E. Aronson (Reading, Mass.: Addison-Wesley Publishing Co. 1968); also Daniel Bell, "National Character Revisited: A Proposal for Renegotiating the Concept," in *The Study of Personality: An Interdisciplinary Appraisal*, ed. E. Norbeck, D. Price-Williams, and W. M. McCord (New York: Holt, Rinehart and Winston, Inc., 1968), Chap. 7.

Whether we like it or not, social stratification and ethnic grouping are stubborn facts that the student of personality must take into account. The conditions under which personality develops are not the same in different parts of the society. Even the physical environments are not the same, and there are bound to be differences in outlook, goals, and values. "The social class of the child's family," as Davis and Havighurst put it, "determines not only the neighborhood in which he lives and the play-group he will have, but also the basic cultural acts and goals toward which he will be trained. . . . Thus the pivotal meaning of social class for students of human development is that it defines and systematizes different learning environments for children of different classes."[2]

The Study of Social Stratification

The tradition of democracy in the United States has tended to discourage open recognition of social stratification. It has not prevented stratification from existing, but except in the South it has kept it from being institutionalized and marked by standard outward signs. The idea of a fixed social hierarchy with titles and other symbols of rank is incongruous even to those who stand high on the ladder. The tradition is maintained symbolically in the fact that the President, even when he is receiving a twenty-one-gun salute or inspecting a military formation in rituals derived from much earlier times and circumstances, always appears in ordinary civilian clothes, perhaps even rumpled ones. If an American citizen were bluntly asked about his social class membership, he would probably experience real difficulty in giving an answer. Aware though he might be of people with whom he would not be asked to associate, and of others with whom he does not want to associate, it would not occur to him that these private exclusions put him in a distinctive social class or attach him to a definable rung on the social ladder. When social scientists in the 1920s and 1930s began a serious study of stratification in the United States they could not ask their questions with blunt directness. They had to work their way gradually into a community and discover by indirect questioning where the lines of discrimination and exclusion actually lay.

Significant in the study of social stratification is the work of W. Lloyd Warner and a group of associates, who developed the first really satisfactory method of getting at the facts of the matter. These investigators adopted the plan of entering a chosen community in the spirit of an anthropologist who comes to stay for a while and gets to be familiar to many of the inhabitants. When a basis of confidence has been established, the visitor can begin to ask questions that will lead him to discover the latent social structure. He may start by asking who are the most important people in town, the ones who are

[2] A. Davis and R. J. Havighurst, "Social Class and Color Differences in Child-Rearing," in *Personality in Nature, Society, and Culture,* 2d ed., ed. C. Kluckhohn and H. A. Murray (New York: Alfred A. Knopf, Inc., 1953), p. 309.

listened to and who control things. If the community is not too large, this line of inquiry yields surprisingly consistent results from people at various social levels. The members of the community can easily point to those who are most influential, who most strongly affect the course of business and politics, and who are thus the holders of power. With relatively high agreement they will report that this one's word is practically law whereas that one is rarely taken seriously. By pursuing this line of questioning through the various aspects of community life—the educational system, the health system, religious institutions, social service, cultural activities, recreation, as well as politics and business—the visitor can construct a fairly detailed chart of social positions mainly in terms of relative prominence and influence.

This, however, is only the beginning. The inquiry must proceed to more personal and delicate questions having to do with each individual's sense of his own position in the social structure. The investigator must find out with whom the respondent associates most freely, whom he believes to be a cut above him, and whom he considers to be below him. It is in the realm of intimate associations that social distinctions have their real being. Warner concluded that the three most important criteria for establishing class lines were visiting, inviting to meals, and intermarriage. The man in the apartment halfway up the building does not think of calling on the family in the penthouse, does not expect to be invited there to dinner, and knows that his teen-age son would not be welcomed in the role of suitor. At the same time he sees the janitor only on business; it does not occur to him to invite the janitor's family up for a meal, and he will be dismayed if his son appears to be finding a love interest in the basement apartment. Quite unreflectingly he sticks to his own floor, where the inhabitants have the very important quality of being "people like us."[3]

This feeling that there are "people like us" and other people who are "not our kind" forms the subjective aspect of social status. With the people to whom he has intimate access the individual feels a certain group solidarity, a sense of "we-ness," with common interests and a shared outlook. This comes out most clearly when a person is questioned about groups immediately above and below him. In a study of social structure in the white population of a southern city, people fairly low on the socioeconomic scale described themselves in such terms as "we poor folks" and "poor but honest folk." Those directly above them they pictured in less tolerant language as "people who think they are somebody" or "people who are up because they have a little money," while those below were dismissed as "shiftless people" or a "no 'count lot." These same "poor but honest folk," however, appeared to those above them at best as "good people, but 'nobody,' " whereas in the eyes of the "no 'count lot" they were "snobs trying to push up."[4] Awareness

---

[3] W. Lloyd Warner and associates, *Democracy in Jonesville: A Study in Quality and Inequality* (New York: Harper and Row, Publishers, 1949).

[4] Allison Davis, B. B. Gardner, and M. R. Gardner, *Deep South: A Social and Anthropological Study of Caste and Class* (Chicago: University of Chicago Press, 1941).

of social levels and of one's own position in the hierarchy is undoubtedly sharper in communities like this southern city, in which the composition of the population and the basis of its economy have remained relatively stable over a period of time. Rapid turnover and vast, impersonal size tend to interfere with group solidarity, leaving not so much a classless democracy as a state of disorganization and isolation.[5] It does not take long, however, even in newly formed and rapidly changing communities, for intimate social interactions to form themselves on a hierarchical basis, thus bringing a social ladder into existence.

The semiprivate nature of the processes whereby people who are "not our kind" are excluded from intimate social interaction makes it difficult to set up a scheme that will faithfully represent in general terms the actualities of social stratification. The existing lines of inclusion and exclusion do not fall automatically into a ladder of fixed social classes. Social *stratification* is a fact—groupings based on socioeconomic status are real—but social *classes* are more in the nature of constructs developed by social scientists to bring order into their thinking. To give a name to a social class, to designate it as "middle class" or "working class," makes it possible to talk about stratification and bring out important differences in the associated learning environments, but it also suggests a fixity of class structure that can be seriously misleading. Significantly, investigators have not agreed on the number of social classes in the United States. Schemes of four, five, and six classes have all had their advocates.[6]

Fortunately the student of personality can learn much to his purpose without waiting for this conceptual problem to be settled. It is simply necessary to remember that social classes are not sharply differentiated, homogeneous entities. Within any one class there will be wide individual differences of outlook and values; some people who are classified in a given status on the basis of economic and educational criteria may prove to have the perspective and ideals that are more common at another level. Furthermore, *social mobility*—movement of individuals or families from one status to another—is a well-documented fact of American life even though it may not be easily accomplished. American society is far from being fully open and fluid, but it is not so fixed as terms like "class structure" and "social ladder" might imply. One must approach it without losing sight of variation, mobility, and human individuality.

With these precautions against rigidity and stereotypes in thinking,

[5] For an important early perception of this problem of the changing community, see James S. Plant, *Personality and the Cultural Pattern* (New York: The Commonwealth Fund, 1937).

[6] The problem of classification is discussed by M. M. Tumin, *Social Stratification: The Forms and Functions of Inequality* (Englewood Cliffs, N.J.: Prentice-Hall, Inc., 1967). In a detailed study of a city of a million inhabitants, R. P. Coleman and B. L. Neugarten, *Social Status in the City* (San Francisco: Jossey-Bass, Inc., 1971), find a five-class scheme roughly suitable but distinguish thirteen strata for more adequate understanding.

we can proceed to a description of social classes as environments for the growth of personality. For this purpose we shall employ the five-class scheme that is currently much used by social scientists, consisting of (1) an upper class or elite, (2) an upper middle class, (3) a lower middle class, (4) a working class, and (5) a lower class. Ethnic groupings will be taken up later in the chapter and considered here only incidentally.

Upper-Class Status

The designation *upper class* or *elite* refers in all schemes to a numerically small segment of the population, usually estimated as between 1 percent and 3.5 percent. Membership in this class is importantly based on the possession of wealth, but further elements are always involved. Recalling Lloyd Warner's method of investigating a community, it will be seen that prominence and influence form part of the picture; some criterion of power or importance is usually added to that of wealth. Furthermore, influence is possessed most often by people whose families have enjoyed wealth and prominence for more than one generation. These other criteria may be so important as to override present economic status. A once-prominent family in reduced financial circumstances may continue to experience the upper class as "people like us," with a common tradition and interests, while viewing as "not our kind" those much richer families whose money is just being made. Respect for the time dimension is more than a snobbish device for keeping the group small and excluding ambitious newcomers. As Kahl points out, an attitude toward life is involved in being a member of a social elite; "only by being born into such a family can one fully learn its manners and mores."[7] Among these manners and mores is an attitude toward wealth that can come only from growing up secure in its possession. Under these circumstances money is no longer needed for display or as testimony to one's individual success. It can be more readily taken for granted and used to support comfortable living, personal enjoyment, and cultivation of the arts.

Seen at their worst, the members of the upper class have been described as economic parasites with a lust for power, an arrogant assumption of superiority, and a disdainful refusal to admit the newly rich as social equals. Hollingshead, basing his account on "Elmtown," a relatively small midwestern community with an industrial emphasis, calls attention to the extensive ownership by upper-class families of business, urban, and rural properties, a situation that leads to tight control over local politics in the interest, among other things, of keeping down the tax rate. While there is no such thing in the United States as a true leisure class, Hollingshead pictures these community leaders as performing a minimum amount of work and setting aside large amounts of time for amusements such as sports and travel. Fussy in main-

---

[7] J. A. Kahl, *The American Class Structure* (New York: Holt, Rinehart and Winston, Inc., 1957), p. 189.

taining a formal social code, they exert financial and moral pressure on their children to visit, to play, and ultimately to marry within their class.[8] When a community is ethnically less homogeneous than Elmtown, upper-class ramparts may be all the more vigorously manned against newcomers from a different ethnic group. Thus in a later study of New Haven, Connecticut, Hollingshead and Redlich distinguished a core group within the upper class consisting of long-established New England Protestant families who actively rejected all other ethnic groups.[9] This exclusiveness forced the other groups into parallel channels toward upper-class status. The situation was symbolized by the existence, as in a good many other American communities, of what might be called a Protestant country club, a Jewish country club, and a Catholic country club.

Seen at their best, the members of the upper class have been described as a highly civilized group having a stable family life, a strong sense of community responsibility, and an appreciation of the finer aspects of living. In the New Haven study Hollingshead and Redlich take notice of family stability, calling attention to a strikingly low divorce rate. This stability appears to be an aspect of the long-standing solidarity of the core group; it is not characteristic of the newly rich families. These observers also find that a sense of obligation to the community is a commonly held upper-class value. Both men and women spend a great deal of time working in voluntary organizations devoted to welfare, education, and cultural improvement, and they consider it their obligation to provide the necessary financial support.[10]

That the security afforded by upper-class membership is an advantage in discovering certain intrinsic values is suggested by a research study by McArthur.[11] The measuring instrument used in this study was the Thematic Apperception Test, a procedure that consists in putting before the subject a picture and inviting him to make up a story for which the picture might serve as an illustration. The pictures used in the test are dim, ambiguous, and lacking in definitive detail, permitting a wide variety of interpretations and thus making it necessary for the subject to draw heavily upon his imagination. In thus carrying out the task in his own way the subject is likely to give evidence of his preferred themes, suppressed desires, and preconceptions about the social world and the nature of human interactions.[12] Five pictures from

[8] A. B. Hollingshead, *Elmtown's Youth: The Impact of Social Classes on Adolescents* (New York: John Wiley & Sons, Inc., 1949), esp. pp. 84–90.

[9] A. B. Hollingshead and F. C. Redlich, *Social Class and Mental Illness: A Community Study* (New York: John Wiley & Sons, Inc., 1958), esp. pp. 69–85. The historical origin of such a group, once more open to recruitment from below, is described by E. Digby Baltzell, *An American Business Aristocracy* (New York: The Free Press, 1958).

[10] Hollingshead and Redlich, *Social Class and Mental Illness*, p. 83.

[11] C. C. McArthur, "Personality Differences between Middle and Upper Classes," *Journal of Abnormal and Social Psychology*, **50** (1955), 247–254.

[12] C. D. Morgan and H. A. Murray, "A Method for Investigating Fantasies," *Archives of Neurology and Psychiatry*, **34** (1935), 289–306; H. A. Murray, *Explorations in Personality* (New York: Oxford University Press, 1938), esp. pp. 530–545.

the series were given as part of a larger test to freshmen in Harvard College, and the stories were then sorted into two groups, those told by students who had entered from private preparatory schools and those who had come from public high schools. This division was only an approximate way of separating upper-class and middle-class students, but it rested on the assumption that the private school group would be more heavily weighted with boys from upper-class homes. There proved to be significant average differences in story content between the two groups, the following being most pertinent with respect to class status. The private school students were less likely to refer to college as an avenue to success, less likely also to represent parents as pushing and ordering their sons. In stories told about a picture showing a young boy with a violin, for instance, the private school subjects were less likely to create a situation in which parents demanded hard work and persistent practice on the part of their child with a view to his becoming an outstanding musician. They were more likely to see playing the violin as a means of self-expression and as a way of finding personal satisfaction through the creation of beauty. When parents appeared at all in these stories, they were more likely to be represented as models and examples rather than as sources of ambitious pressure. The results suggest that it is easier to appreciate the intrinsic value of artistic expression and the enjoyment of experience when one's position is secure and there is freedom from pressure to attain higher status. Obviously these values exist at other socioeconomic levels, but their development is less hampered under conditions of status security.

As an environment for the growth of personality, upper-class status offers many advantages. Children are likely to have the best of health care, good diet, and a relatively safe environment with space for play and exploration. They are likely to be well supplied with toys and other objects that are conducive both to enjoyment and to the growth of competence. They benefit from family stability, from growing up in an intact family circle. The personal attention and stimulation that are favorable for development are likely to be available to them. Furthermore, they are likely to have the security that comes from living in one place and being part of a stable neighborhood. Allison Davis has pointed out that "by defining the group with which an individual may have intimate clique relationships, our social class system narrows his training environment."[13] This principle is well exhibited in those upper-class families who narrow their children's educational path by sending them early to private schools, where both the traditions and the faculty represent the socioeconomic elite. The consequences of this continuing isolation in a small world, which may be perpetuated even beyond the school level, are not good with respect to the individual's ultimate understanding of the rest of humanity. But in the early stages it may be easier to grow up in an environment narrow enough to maximize a feeling of membership,

[13] A. Davis, "American Status Systems and the Socialization of the Child," *American Sociological Review*, 6 (1941), 345–354.

participation, and solidarity. And even when children attend public schools, the group patterns and cliques into which they fall seem to be guided more strongly by neighborhood, status, and other familiar ties than by an abstract conception of democracy.[14]

At some point in his progress along the narrowed path, the child will become aware of his privileged position. To feel oneself privileged and superior is inherently gratifying and may be helpful in developing early social confidence and self-esteem. It can contribute, however, to a number of trends that are less desirable for society and may even come to stand in the way of personal happiness. Feelings of privilege may dispose a child to shun what is irksome and unpleasant, to balk at consistent application to any task, and to exploit others with an expectation that they will do the dirty work. Privileged young people may drift through college without intellectual awakening, leading mainly a lively social life, knowing that a secure place awaits them after graduation. Upper-class surroundings are capable of providing a child with systematic training in irresponsibility, especially when the family values are smugly social or crassly materialistic. Such values, however, are not an inevitable consequence of upper-class status. When there is emphasis on community service and support of cultural institutions, and when parents visibly enact these values, the atmosphere may be conducive to a strong sense of responsibility.

As is true of other levels of social stratification, upper-class status in the United States is undergoing marked historical change. Great fortunes are trimmed down by high rates of taxation, servants are no longer plentiful, large houses are too expensive to build or to maintain. The mansions of the 1890s and the 1920s have either been torn down or turned into institutions, and the era has clearly passed in which a legendary estate owner complained that the price of swans was exorbitant. But more important than the shrinking of the once-extreme economic gap is a considerable change of attitude, especially on the part of young people brought up in privileged status. Typically, in an earlier time, they spent the summer with their parents at resorts or country places, engaging mainly in sports. Today, they often travel in simple style without their parents or take full-time jobs, sometimes working for the disadvantaged, sometimes even as laborers. This choice of activities reflects a clear downgrading of the values of wealth and status. More general awareness of social problems and the consequences of economic inequality has produced a sharpening of social conscience, a discontent with unfairness in the distribution of opportunity. In some instances it has produced an explicit determination to use one's economic and educational advantages in the service of those who have not had them. Upper-class young people seem less willing than before to accept status ascribed by wealth and family rather than earned by personal attainment. Only by meeting the demands of life at a common level is it possible to affirm one's worth as a human being.

---

[14] Hollingshead, *Elmtown's Youth*, esp. Chap. 9.

Upper-Middle-Class Status

It may seem an affront to clarity that the designation *middle class* is not used exclusively for people in the middle of the status system. In the language of social science, the middle class starts where the upper class ends, which means that not more than 2 or 3 percent of the population is placed above it. At the other end are the working class and the lower class, which between them are likely to take in from half to two-thirds of the population. Middle-class membership thus always implies being above the middle and possibly close to the top. This stretch of social territory, however, is far too large to be treated as a unity. There is a vast difference in outlook between the self-made bank president in his luxurious corner office and the tellers, bookkeepers, and secretaries who work at impersonal rows of desks. For this reason it is important to distinguish between upper- and lower-middle-class status.

In upper-middle-class status belong the business leaders and prosperous professional people whose income may equal that of upper-class persons but who lack the tradition of wealth and security that further defines that status. The men are successful and influential in their line of work, and both men and women are of considerable prominence in the community. Salaried administrative personnel in large government and business offices, and the owner-operators of small businesses, should be included in upper-middle status. What is characteristic of this status is a certain amount of influence over decisions and policy, together with the power to exercise some choice over the course of one's occupational career. The upper-middle-class family typically lives in a single house of ample size, often located in a suburb; the house and its surroundings are objects of pride and are kept in excellent condition. Being in a good neighborhood is important in selecting the home, and there will be distress if the neighborhood changes so that it no longer qualifies as good. The inhabitants are neighborly and participate actively in community life through membership in associations that support education, religion, the arts, health, and civic improvement, resembling the upper class in this respect. Through such participation they both extend the range of their acquaintance and assure themselves of a voice in what is going on around them.

If one looked for a single word to describe the central value of those in upper-middle-class status, that word would be "career." As Kahl expresses it, "Their whole way of life—their consumption behavior, their sense of accomplishment and respectability, the source of much of their prestige with others—depends upon success in a career. The husband's career becomes the central social fact for all the family." Kahl continues with a description of what this involves.

There are prerequisites for admission into career competition: a certain minimum of intelligence, a personality that is sufficiently outgoing and flexible, a motivation for success strong enough to lead one to work and plan and often to sacrifice for it, an appropriate education in intellectual and social skills. Birth into a middle class family vastly increases the chances of meeting these prerequisites, and most middle class sons remain in their class of birth. However, our system of formal education permits many working class sons to climb into the career competition if they start early enough.[15]

As the central social fact for the family, the husband's career requires support from the rest of the family circle. The wife can, if she wants to, contribute importantly to it by encouragement, by maintaining a home that reflects prestige, by making appropriate social contacts in the community, and by accepting such frustrations as her husband's working at night and going on business trips. Her supportive role is more endurable if she fully shares her husband's values and is pleased to be carried upward on the status ladder. The children's contributions are forced upon them: they must get used to a preoccupied, exhausted father who gives them little time. Business and professional career advancement often entails moving from one community to another. Their father transferred from the Chicago to the Los Angeles office, then put in charge of the Atlanta branch, and finally recalled to headquarters in Dayton, the children must somehow survive continual uprooting from their schools and neighborhood companions and develop skill in entering new social situations. A college student who had had fourteen homes in twenty years reported that at a certain point, to reduce the repeated pain of parting from friends of whom he had grown fond, he resolved to keep a cool distance and not become involved with his contemporaries in the next community. The rising business executive may be able to set his family down in advantageous communities, but if his career line calls for moving he cannot give them continuity, tradition, or an assured sense of belonging. For the children the easiest outcomes are skill in superficial social adjustment and a deep inner loneliness; these can, unfortunately, exist together.

Three values assume prominence in a great many upper-middle-class families. The first is related to the enduring competitive aspect of business and professional advancement. For these families, it is desirable that boys, at least, should develop assertiveness and initiative, giving evidence of ability to compete successfully and stand out as potential leaders. The second is related to another aspect of contemporary business and administrative life, the increasing importance of the large organization in which advancement depends not so much on what one produces as on how well one fits into the system of social and bureaucratic interactions.[16] What is valued here is often referred to as a "well-balanced" personality, which commonly signifies

[15] Kahl, *The American Class Structure*, p. 194.

[16] The classic account of this situation was given by W. H. Whyte, Jr. in *The Organization Man* (New York: Simon & Schuster, 1956). Aspects of it figure in novels by John Marquand (*Point of No Return*) and Sloan Wilson (*The Man in the Gray Flannel Suit*).

an ability to interact harmoniously with those above, those in equal status, and those below in the organizational hierarchy, thus contributing to the frictionless operation of the whole. As a parental value this is felt by children in the form of pressure to interact with other children, to get started early and progress steadily in the curriculum of becoming a "well-balanced" social being, all things to all men. The third value is the importance of doing well in school. Educational advancement can become such an obsession that parents pick their place of residence because the local high school has an outstanding record for vaulting its graduates into colleges of high prestige.

Illustrative of upper-middle-class expectations is a study by Aberle and Naegele of successful business and professional families in an affluent suburb.[17] Fathers were interviewed with a view to finding out what problems worried them in their high school sons. The fathers proved to be most worried if their sons did not seem to be exhibiting the following traits and achievements: responsibility, initiative, good school record, assertiveness, athletic success, and emotional stability. Fastening on athletic success, the interviewers inquired gravely whether the father wanted his son to become a professional athlete. This was, of course, not the case: the fathers pictured their sons as attaining an occupational status equal to their own, and athletic success at school was merely a sign of having the assertiveness necessary to climb a competitive ladder. Worries about daughters fell into an entirely different pattern: they must not fail in personal attractiveness, popularity, and social charm. It could be inferred that their fathers saw them in the future role of wives supporting their husbands' careers.

Lower-Middle-Class Status

As a rule of thumb, though certainly far from precise, it is often said that the line between the lower middle class and the working class is drawn by the color of one's shirt: white-collar jobs mark one as middle class, blue-collar jobs as working class. There is no like symbol to separate lower-middle from upper-middle status unless one believes that the growing popularity of gaily colored sports shirts at the upper level is destined to create another collar-color line. There are many occupations in the white-collar category that are not associated with burgeoning careers, social prominence, or prospects of wealth. The positions of secretary and accountant have already been mentioned, to which should be added such semiprofessional activities as photographer or draftsman. Most public school teachers, having only modest opportunities for either income or advancement, are classified as lower middle class. Relative to the classes below it, this status signifies a good level of education. Both men and women are typically high school graduates who

[17] D. F. Aberle and K. D. Naegele, "Middle Class Fathers' Occupational Role and Attitudes toward Children," *American Journal of Orthopsychiatry*, **22** (1952), 366–378.

have received additional training such as four years at a teachers' college, a short course at business school, or a curriculum in accounting. Full college education for the children has recently become a more or less standard expectation. Residence, if not in an urban apartment, is likely to be in a small single house neatly kept, and the emphasis on a good neighborhood is hardly less than at the upper-middle level.

Lower-Middle Environment and Values

As one moves down to the more modest middle-class occupations the goal of a career progressively loses its force. In lower-middle-class status, where the job may be relatively secure and pleasant but not likely to lead to conspicuous achievement, aspirations for the children may be kept high, but personal goals are scaled down to maintaining one's position and preserving one's good repute. The experience of men and women working at the middle level of an organization is strongly colored by the fact that their security, and whatever modest advancement they can expect, depends upon giving satisfaction to those above them who control the organization. A secretary can rise to the position of being the president's secretary, but only if she is both highly efficient and highly skilled in understanding how to expedite her boss's work. A bookkeeper can become head of his department, but only through accuracy and prompt responsiveness to the demands of the company. A teacher in a public school system can perhaps become a principal, but she can keep her job at all only if her conduct meets with the approval of her superiors and of the community in which she works. Such a position in the status system lowers the importance of initiative, assertiveness, and zest for competition. Stability, efficiency, responsibility, and getting along well with others are important values, but another virtue, which might be called "respectability," can perhaps be considered the keystone of the value system. White-collar status is cherished, and with it the qualities of being neat, clean, and presentable, polite and correct of speech, and willingly deferent toward those who stand in control of one's fortunes. It is important to be well thought of in the community; the family's reputation must not be blemished by behavior likely to elicit disapproval. At no level is conventional behavior more strongly emphasized.

Parents in lower-middle status may be intensely ambitious for their children, but they may also be fairly well satisfied with their mode of life and consider it sufficient for the next generation. This point is brought out in a report by Kahl, who chose from a much larger studied population two groups of high school boys, one planning to go to college, the other not.[18] The two groups were matched with respect to family income and social status. They all came from two-family houses in good repair, a type of residential neighborhood that even the casual observer knows is very different from one with two-family houses in poor repair. The boys were likewise matched for I.Q.,

[18] J. A. Kahl, "Educational and Occupational Aspirations of 'Common Man' Boys," *Harvard Educational Review,* **23** (1953), 188–201.

and these several matchings made it unlikely that either scholastic ability or social status accounted for the difference in aspirations. The roots of this difference were found to lie in the particular values that prevailed in the families. Parents of the college-bound boys were dissatisfied with their status, were keenly aware that lack of education had limited their advancement, and had resolved to spare their sons this handicap to success. The other group of parents was well enough pleased with their position and did not suppose that their sons' continuing in it would be helped by a college education. Parents of these two types were found to look upon each other with a certain contempt. The college-oriented parents could not understand their counterparts' lack of ambition, their lazy disinclination to get ahead and better themselves. Parents indifferent to college saw the others as anxiously driven and as not knowing how to relax and enjoy life. Wide differences of value can exist within the not-very-different walls of two-family houses in good repair.

Psychological Problems in Upward Mobility

Certain psychological problems are likely to arise when parents are strongly motivated to project their children into a status decidedly higher than their own. Common enough in any event, this situation occurred with especial frequency in parents who grew up during the Great Depression of the 1930s and were forced to leave school and sacrifice their own aspirations. A child of such parents wrote that her mother, first a stenographer and then a housewife, had stood second in a high school class of 427 students—an odd bit of information to be preserved in the family tradition except that it reminded everyone what mother might have been under more fortunate circumstances. The root of the difficulty lies in the fact that the parents, still lingeringly disappointed at the limits imposed upon their own lives, want too strongly to see their children live out for them their own frustrated ambitions. "At last everything can be set right, my son can be the doctor I wanted to be" —but the dream may grow to the point that it suppresses recognition of what the son wants to be. This creates for the child what often prove to be bewildering conflicts of feeling and attitude.

Resorting again to the method of comparative case study, we can illustrate these problems from the life histories of two college students taking a premedical program.[19] In both cases the projected career in medicine was an unquestioned part of the family value system. Both families had worked their way from the working-class status of their youth into the lower edge of the middle class. One of the fathers, Irish and of Roman Catholic faith, had built himself a small but secure business; the other, an accountant of Jewish faith, had lifted himself by special training from the immigrant status of the previous generation. The pattern of parental pressures was a

---

[19] The Irish Catholic student, given the name Joseph Kidd, is described at length by R. W. White in *Lives in Progress: A Study of the Natural Growth of Personality*, 2d ed. (New York: Holt, Rinehart and Winston, Inc., 1966). The other case is unpublished.

little different in the two households. In the Catholic family the mother was the true apostle of upward mobility. Before her marriage she had been a servant in wealthy homes, and her heart was set on seeing her children climb the educational ladder to situations of affluent prestige. In the Jewish family the father was the more vocal advocate, constantly reminding his son and daughter of the prizes to be won by respectively being a doctor and marrying a doctor. Both sons had been exposed to a great deal of training designed to fit them for the elegant future. Angry scenes took place at table upon any exhibition of sloppy manners or careless slurring of speech. Both sons had been heavily briefed on the sacrifices being made for them: the careful saving, the long extra hours of work, the imperiling of parental health so that there would be money enough for the sons to attend the chosen college, perhaps even to live there and get the benefit of college life, though commuting was possible.

What does it mean psychologically to be the object of this particular kind of pressure? The parents certainly place themselves high on the control dimension, and their attentive interest in their children's ultimate welfare might suggest a like high position with respect to acceptance. But their love is of a peculiar nature, mingled as it is with self-love to be gratified vicariously through the children's success. It is a pattern that children find difficult to fathom, so that even at college age they may still be struggling to sort it all out. As children the two sons accepted the briefing about parental sacrifices and the good life ahead. But this exposed them to very strong feelings of guilt whenever they strayed from the sober required path, whenever a wayward impulse, a moment of laziness, a disinclination to study, or a desire to fool around with other kids made them feel that they were wasting the opportunities so painfully given them. The Catholic son became virtually immobilized between the pain of studying uncongenial scientific subjects and the guilt of throwing away the chances for which his parents had worked so hard. The Jewish son, whose father had instructed him that making contacts was the true avenue to success, experienced misery when, yielding to rather strong shyness, he sat alone behind a newspaper in the dining hall and missed an opportunity to make a useful acquaintance. It is strenuous to be a worthy son of so much sacrifice.

Under these circumstances ultimate resentment can hardly be avoided. By the time they were well into college both sons were beginning to realize that their parents were in many ways powerless to help them. The parents had no experience of life at the new educational and social level; they could not train their sons how to behave there. Thus the Catholic parents made a scene over their son's espousal of the theory of evolution, which because of their uninstructed conception of the matter they believed to be contrary to their religion. The Jewish son suffered numerous embarrassments with girls in the college community because he did not know the more sophisticated social conventions, and nobody at home could tell him. Further cause for resentment arose as the sons became fully aware that they were being expected to do difficult things their parents were comfortably avoiding.

The Catholic son came to be angry at the thought of his father spending evenings of sociability and song while he himself was painfully boning up for a quiz in organic chemistry. The Jewish son, trying to control his anxiety as much as possible in order to make the prescribed social contacts, realized that his father fairly regularly avoided contacts. In the end both students experienced doubt and confusion over the nature of their parents' love. The Irish mother was finally perceived by her son as motivated by a curious blend of real devotion and fierce determination to make her children enact her will and fulfill her life. The Jewish student, recalling especially an occasion when his parents moved to a more pretentious neighborhood and in so doing ruthlessly uprooted him, despite a tearful protest, from a highly congenial group of friends, realized that his parents had often been governed by their own fantasies of mobility rather than a real appreciation of what was good for their son. Yet these insights do not quickly bring peace of mind over the resentments that have been felt. However thoughtless and selfish the parents may have been, the wound of failing to live out their aspirations may seem too cruel to inflict. Both subjects managed eventually to veer somewhat from parental expectations, but the growth of the necessary insights on the part of the young men and their parents was neither rapid nor easy.

Changes in Middle-Class Values

Middle-class values have been the object of sharp criticism in the writings of social scientists. It was held that they were likely to deform the growth of personality, producing anxiety and neurotic tendencies, whereas the less strict training of the lower classes encouraged a more natural and wholesome development. These interpretations were undoubtedly influenced by Freudian psychology, in which the repression of instinctual tendencies was closely linked to neurotic disorder. Middle-class ideals seemed hostile to the impulsive side of human nature. They require an extensive sacrifice of present enjoyments and spontaneous inclinations in favor of future goals attainable only through disciplined behavior. Being neat, clean, and presentable is not one of childhood's natural delights. Like sitting in school and studying one's lessons, it requires a continuous curbing of childish inclinations. What this training leads to in adult life is too far ahead to become a real childhood motive, so the force behind it has to come straight from parental demands. Middle-class children were being sacrificed and made neurotic, the argument ran, in order to attain the future status desired for them by their parents. In contrast to this grim picture, it was easy to romanticize lower-class status as a place where impulses flowered unchecked and neurotic anxieties never took root. In retrospect it seems evident that more than a dash of fantasy crept into this interpretation of working-class and lower-class child rearing. Actual studies gave little support to the picture of blissful spontaneity.

Recently the middle class has been emerging in a better light. In a searching review of relevant studies from 1930 to 1958, Bronfenbrenner has shown that over the entire period middle-class parents are reported to be more acceptant and more equalitarian than working-class parents. Even where in the early studies they were stricter, as in feeding, weaning, and toilet training, they came out after World War II as more lenient, and their attitudes toward children's expressed needs and wishes moved steadily in the direction of permissiveness.[20] Research by Kohn leads to the conclusion that middle-class parents are now typically interested in their children's motives and feelings, sympathetic toward impulse, and in many matters truly concerned with happiness and self-direction.[21] To be sure, in spheres about which they are anxious, especially educational success and getting along with others, parents are still likely to push their children with fierce puritanical zeal, but in other matters like the expression of sex, aggression, and initiative, they are a good deal more permissive than their counterparts in lower status. Both upper- and lower-middle-class parents have been responsive to trends of opinion among experts in child development. College courses in psychology, books of advice on child rearing, government bulletins, magazine articles, and newspaper columns have found a receptive audience at this social level, leading to substantial progress toward a better understanding of children.

Working-Class Status

To designate one section of the population a *working class* sometimes evokes protest from hard-working members of other status levels. The accountant and the small businessman may put in longer hours than the assembly-line worker in a union shop, and the man who is building his career may be the longest and hardest worker of them all. Perhaps the line might be better drawn by calling this part of the population the *wage-earning* class, bearing in mind that even lowly white-collar workers are apt to refer to their pay as a salary. In the literature on social stratification, however, the attaching of names to levels has always been a problem, and *working class* is perhaps as good a designation as any for that part of the population engaged occupationally in skilled or semiskilled manual work, the kind of employment for which a blue collar symbolizes the appropriate costume. Speaking of the skilled trades in the New Haven study, Hollingshead and Redlich mention auto body repairers, electric welders, linemen, linotype operators, masons, typographers, and railroad yard superintendents; semiskilled workers are most often found on the assembly lines of large manufacturing concerns, but others are employed as checkers, receivers, repairers, truckers, and wrappers.[22] In a community less exclusively urban this general status would be occupied also by gardeners, woodsmen, fishermen, quarry and mine

---

[20] U. Bronfenbrenner, "Socialization and Social Class through Time and Space," in *Readings in Social Psychology,* 3d ed., ed. E. Maccoby, T. Newcomb, and E. Hartley (New York: Holt, Rinehart and Winston, Inc., 1958), pp. 400–425.

[21] M. L. Kohn, "Social Class and Parent-Child Relationships: An Interpretation," *American Journal of Sociology,* **68** (1963), 471–480.

[22] Hollingshead and Redlich, *Social Class and Mental Illness,* p. 105.

workers, and agricultural laborers regularly employed. Throughout the United States the working class is large, almost always the largest segment of any sizable community, accounting on the whole for something like half the population. In the sense that its members are the people who do the actual work with material objects—rather than with persons and papers—it can appropriately be called the working class and recognized as the foundation of the whole economic system.

The Working-Class Situation

There have been a good many studies of industrial workers on assembly lines, whose attitudes toward life and job afford important insight into working-class values. The work itself is easily learned and highly monotonous. Repeating a small operation several hundred times a day is not conducive to developing an interest in one's job. Furthermore, the rate of pay does not go up much over the course of time; seniority may increase security but does not bring with it a sharp rise in income. Reputation is not a matter of intense concern: hiring practices are so impersonal that if jobs are available a reasonably good work record is all that counts. These circumstances militate against investing personal feeling in the job. The industrial worker is often described as alienated from his work, his interest being only in the paycheck, comfortable working conditions, shorter hours, and such security as can be had from fringe benefits. Improvement in these matters depends not on individual performance but on organized union activity in which the average worker has but a tiny part. Small wonder that for the working man daily life really begins when he leaves the shop behind him and goes home. The center of value in his existence is the part of the day when his time is his own. His home, of course, is the scene of his wife's working hours, which may be considerably longer than his, and a common cause of domestic friction is the ratio between his assisting with children and chores and his being the tired worker who must have his rest and recreation. Home and family, nevertheless, are likely to lie at the heart of working-class values and happiness.

In an earlier period, existence at the working-class level was perilously hand-to-mouth. Even in good times wages were too small to permit savings, and in an economy little protected from fluctuations of business activity there were many rainy days of unemployment. With the decline of immigration, with the strong growth of labor unions producing much-improved wage levels and job security, and with national policies designed to dampen business cycles, there has emerged in the United States a stable working class with the prospect of maintaining a decent standard of living. Kohn describes this group as typically wanting to feel secure, to live in modest comfort, and to enjoy their homes and amusements. Ownership of a car is no longer a rarity, and the house is more than likely to contain an electric refrigerator and a television set. With individual exceptions, working-class persons have no great interest in upward social mobility and no great enchantment with education. Their outlook tends to be conservative. Between union strength and business prosperity the worker is likely to feel that he is doing all right in the present economic system and that he can expect further gains. Alienation from work continues, but improved domestic prospects lead to an increasing concern with respectability. As working-class life improves, there is progressive absorption of the value pattern that was once most characteristic of the lower middle class. Increasingly the working-class child comes under pressure to make his behavior respectable.[23]

The Working-Class Outlook

In order to obtain fuller understanding of this status as an environment for the growth of personality, it is necessary to consider in more detail the outlook that develops in the working-class round of life. The members are not well educated. They may complete high school, but often they drop out before graduation to start looking for a job. In either case, they do not involve themselves deeply in high school studies, most of which are not impressively relevant to the way lives are led in their neighborhood. The shift from student status to wage earning is a move into adulthood, and if school is not interesting there can be little motive to postpone growing up. But leaving school means a tapering off of involvement just in that period of adolescence when more eager students rapidly expand their horizons from home and community to the nation and the world, transcending the narrow, parochial outlook of childhood in favor of a worldwide perspective and the framing of experience in generalized, abstract terms. People in working-class status are typically not readers. Their fare is restricted to a daily paper and a magazine or two, and these are likely to stress sensation and excitement more than important happenings. Their largest channel of information is the television set, in front of which they spend much time. It is possible to learn a lot about the world through this medium, but a judicious selection of programs can easily keep one's mind from being stretched. The range of interests and concerns of most working-class families stays small.

Characteristic also is a lack of participation in the community. On this point the overall contrast with the middle class is sharp, although the new working-class emphasis on respectability may presage a change. Though his fortunes depend directly on the effectiveness of his union, the average worker is hardly at all involved in union meetings or strategy. He and his wife take little part in voluntary organizations except those that are purely social.[24] Even visiting and inviting friends to meals tend to be less frequent than they are in the middle class. These patterns of social behavior further restrict exchange of information and enlargement of the sphere of personal involvement. Working-class people have practically no influence on the powers that control their fate. Decisions in the community, in the unions, and

---

[23] Kohn, "Social Class and Parent-Child Relationships," p. 476.
[24] R. W. Hodge and D. J. Treiman, "Social Participation and Social Status," *American Sociological Review*, **33** (1968), 722–740.

in business management are made by remote figures with whom contact is impossible, and the consequences of these decisions usually have to be accepted as if they were immutable decrees of nature. Such a situation disposes a person to an attitude of resigned acceptance, and he is all the more encouraged to make what he can of life within his small sphere of relative freedom.

Like any other parents, working-class fathers and mothers bring up their children with a view to the kind of lives they expect the children to lead. Independence, initiative, and decision making are not part of the expected life pattern; what is important is to follow explicit rules set by authorities and to learn how to please those who control one's destiny. There is thus pressure to conform to external requirements: to be neat and clean, to respect adults, to behave according to the rules. How the child feels does not bulk large in the training process. There are too many situations in life that have to be accepted whether one likes it or not. The emphasis in punishment is therefore on the external consequences of behavior rather than on the intentions behind it. Comparative studies at different class levels show that working-class children, in contrast to middle-class children, perceive their parents on the average as less accepting, less supportive, less interested in them, and somewhat more punitive and controlling. At the same time they see their parents as less effective people: less smart and ambitious, more inclined to be shy, nervous, and worried, thus providing a poorer pattern of independent assertiveness.[25] The earlier stereotype of the children of the poor as paragons of happy spontaneity is far from the truth. On the average, working-class children grow up with less overtly expressed love and interest, more frequent and arbitrary punishments, and fairly strong pressure to constrain the expression of impulses.

Status Misunderstanding

Professional services like medicine and education are supposed to be available alike to all segments of the population. Members of the professions would count it a grave ethical blemish if a doctor refused to treat an injured person who could not pay, or if a public school teacher knowingly discriminated against the children of the poor. The individual conscience in such matters has been strict, but in a system of free enterprise, under which professional people are held free to better themselves and live and work where they please, it has come about that the poor do not receive equal services. With the growth of the idea of a welfare state this attitude is changing, but evidence has now come in that there is an important further difficulty in extending professional services to lower socioeconomic levels. Professional people, by virtue of their educational attainments if not by previous status,

[25] B. C. Rosen, "Social Class and the Child's Perception of the Parent," *Child Development*, **35** (1964), 1147–1153; P. C. Goldin, "A Review of Children's Reports of Parent Behaviors," *Psychological Bulletin*, **71** (1969), 222–236.

belong firmly in the middle class. This may lead them to misunderstand seriously the way their less-favored clients think and feel.

The difficulty was brought to light in striking fashion for psychiatry by Hollingshead and Redlich's study of mental health services in the New Haven community.[26] In publicly supported clinics, where therapists are on salary and the patients' financial arrangements are made with someone else, it was found that senior psychiatrists preferred to work with patients of middle-class status, turning over patients of lower status to interns and medical students. The basis of selection was the impression made by the patient on the doctor in their earliest meetings. The doctors could not be accused of snobbishness, which was certainly far from their intentions; they were responding to more relevant cues, many of which, however, were related to class status. Conversation of an intimate kind is an important tool of psychiatric treatment. If a patient talks freely and intelligently, seems inclined to reflect on his experience, is somewhat aware of his feelings, and is felt to "speak the same language" as his listener, the doctor is likely to conclude that an effective helping relation can be established and decide to work with the patient himself. A person making such an impression, of course, is just about certain to be at least of middle-class background. The working-class patient, less educated, verbally less facile, less accustomed to think about his feelings or to suppose that talking about them has anything to do with health, is far less likely to impress his sophisticated listener as a good therapeutic risk. The study showed that patients of limited education and working-class or lower-class outlook tended to think of emotional maladjustments as if they were physical diseases caused by infections or bumps on the head. They expected treatment to take the form of an injection, a pill, or some other manifestation of medical authority, and could see no sense in protracted talk. Insight into their own feelings was as foreign to them as insight into the feelings of a child who needed to be brought into line by punishment. The goals of self-understanding and self-realization through a method such as psychoanalysis were understood only by those on the higher rungs of the educational and social ladder.

Status misunderstanding can be so great that it interferes with what the psychiatrist thinks of as a purely medical judgment. Suppose that he is consulted by a working-class patient who has become depressed by chronic quarreling in his household. Sooner or later the doctor will have to decide whether or not the patient is restored to health. The psychiatrist has reached his own position through much sacrifice and a long course of training, sustained by great faith in higher education, and his only personal worry at the moment is that his son in high school may not be showing the proper signs of competitive assertiveness and social virtuosity. One day the patient reports complete restoration to health. Cheerfully he relates that he can again spend

[26] Hollingshead and Redlich, *Social Class and Mental Illness*, esp. Chaps. 11 and 12.

the evening in comfortable relaxation drinking beer and watching television, and that a pleasant family atmosphere has been restored since his son stopped griping about high school and decided to drop out and look for a job. Can the psychiatrist perceive this as a restoration to health? Can he avoid taking it for granted that a man must still be depressed who shows no interest in his son's going to college, in bettering his own position, or in mingling with friends? People in upper-middle-class status engaged in fashioning professional careers often unthinkingly identify mental health with driving ambition. Such limitation of insight can seriously interfere with extending professional services to the whole population.

In the realm of public education, it is now well documented that status misunderstanding contributes to the relatively poor performance of working-class and lower-class children. Public education is a huge enterprise calling for the recruitment of large numbers of teachers. The recruitment is not a random affair drawing equally on all segments of the population. The situation is vividly described by Friedenberg, who points out that "the role of schoolteacher is the least costly and most readily available role commonly accepted as of professional status." The educational requirements for entering the profession are not difficult to fulfill, the nature of a teacher's activity is well known through having been a pupil, and if the financial rewards are small, so also are the risks.

> A teaching career provides security against the kinds of economic vicissitudes to which small businessmen and clerical employees are subject. The kind of security that people who think of themselves as working class derive from a strong union, teachers obtain in some measure from a licentiate and tenure regulations. Public school teaching therefore attracts a disproportionate number of persons to whom security is more important than real freedom in the conduct of their life or their professional activity. Teachers do not usually desire to rebel against the social attitudes of their community, though they may resent or fear their application to particular events in their lives; on the whole they share these attitudes and were themselves brought up to have little respect for privacy and to expect little deference to the demands of the inner life.[27]

From this description, it is easy to infer that public school teachers are heavily drawn from the upper level of the working class and lower level of the middle class, precisely the status levels at which respectability is likely to be a central value. Facing their classes every day, they find most congenial those students who are intelligent, in the sense of being alert, interested, and quick to learn, and cooperative, in the sense of sitting still, following instructions, and keeping out of mischief. They are also attracted by the children who are neat, clean, orderly, nicely dressed, and well mannered. In other words, they like the children who resemble what they themselves try to be.

[27] E. Z. Friedenberg, *The Vanishing Adolescent* (Boston: The Beacon Press, 1959), pp. 78–80.

For obvious reasons they dislike behavior that disrupts the class, but they are also put off by lack of manners, crudeness of speech, carelessness of dress, and boredom or indifference to the lessons. These preferences on the part of teachers work to the disadvantage of many working-class children and of virtually all children from the lower class. Very likely without intending to do so, the teachers respond more warmly to the congenial students, giving them encouragement and words of praise. In slight ways they communicate their disapproval to the children of lower status, their remarks being studded with criticism and exhortation. Using the dimensions already described for parent-child relations, the teachers stand lower on acceptance and higher on control in dealing with the less favored students. The latter become aware that they are treated differently. Studies show that they feel uncomfortable and inferior at school, that their self-esteem suffers, and that in consequence their scholastic performance falls below what it might otherwise have been.[28] Differences of aptitude are not ruled out by an explanation of this kind, but it seems clear that status values and status misunderstandings can discourage the full use of capacity.

Lower-Class Status

Throughout history, poverty has been the lot of the great majority of people. Many societies of the past, and some of the present, are prominently stratified into two main groups, a privileged aristocracy and the masses. Karl Marx, writing in the earlier stages of the industrial revolution, drew a sharp line between the bourgeoisie and the proletariat, the former a small though controlling group. In the United States, which has reached an advanced stage of the industrial revolution, the time-honored scheme does not square well with the facts. The working class, numerically the largest part of the population, is far from corresponding to the masses of the past, and its relative security, stability, and not wholly discontented outlook distinguish it sharply from the historical pattern of a proletariat. The American stratification system bulges in the middle, the lowest status being occupied by a minority that rarely numbers as much as 20 percent of the population and is often estimated at 10 percent. This group at the bottom, the lower class, is described by Kahl in the following paragraph:

> Every town and city contains a sizable group of people who live in decrepit houses in slum areas, work irregularly at unskilled or semiskilled jobs, and are usually suffering from poverty. This group contains an undue proportion of Negroes and foreign-born, yet there are also many families with as long a line of Yankee forebears as the local old-family

[28] See, for example, Hollingshead, *Elmtown's Youth*; A. K. Cohen, *Delinquent Boys: The Culture of the Gang* (New York: The Free Press, 1955); and especially W. Lloyd Warner, *Democracy in Jonesville* (New York: Harper & Row, Publishers, 1959), Chap. 5.

elite. Many studies confirm the same conclusions: although the actual rates will vary according to the business cycle, these people contribute far more than their proportionate share to the relief rolls, to crime and delinquency rates, to the list of unmarried mothers, to divorces and desertions. They are the least educated group in the population and the least interested in education.[29]

Why are they there? The high representation of Negroes and recent immigrants suggests that ethnic prejudice is a force that consigns people to poverty and keeps them there. The presence of Yankee families and the fact that there is a lower class even in ethnically homogeneous communities suggest that limitations of ability can have something to do with it. There are doubtless other contributing influences, but it appears to be also true that conditions of life in this status produce attitudes and an outlook that impede moving out of the status. To adapt to poverty may lead to a kind of entrapment in poverty.

Lower-Class Conditions of Life

Lower-class dwellings are disagreeable and crowded. In cities the aging apartment block, battered and patched, drearily bare, and more than likely structurally unsound, in rural areas the tarpaper shack, cobbled together out of crates and other discarded materials, never provide enough space for their occupants. Not uncommonly a family of five or more members lives in two rooms, a kitchen–living room and a crowded bedroom, and the sanitation facilities may be far below middle-class standards, as the visiting social worker's nose will quickly inform her. The family itself may not conform to traditional patterns. The husband and wife may be married or they may be living together by private agreement alone, but in either case the relation tends to be unstable. Half or more of the families have been broken by death, desertion, separation, or divorce. Many are the households in which the father is no longer present and the mother is struggling to take care of the children while also bringing in money by working outside as a cook, waitress, or cleaning woman. Even when the family is intact the husband's employment is intermittent and the wife is not wholly exempt from breadwinning. If the lower-class community is reasonably settled and stable, there will probably be relatives who can be drawn in to assist with the children. When the neighborhood is one of rapid change, even this advantage is lacking. The men, particularly, may change jobs frequently. They are not always forced to; they are quick to drop a job if they consider the work too hard or the boss disagreeable. When there is never enough money, no cushion of savings, no certainty that the week's rent can be paid or the week's meals provided, it might be supposed that this adversity would increase family solidarity and steadiness on the job. It has the opposite effects, and this proves to be no paradox when all the conditions are understood.

[29] Kahl, *The American Class Structure*, p. 211.

The members of the lower class live in an even narrower world than the working class. Their education having stopped during or soon after grammar school, they read almost not at all, and their main source of information is what they choose to see and hear on television. They almost never take part in community activities, and their social contacts are largely restricted to relatives and close neighbors. The narrowing of life is further increased by a feeling that much of the world is hostile. These people deeply distrust authority figures. They see the police as obvious enemies, but also suspect clergymen, teachers, doctors, social workers, and the people who exert political power. Those who represent society at large are pictured as running a racket for their own personal benefit, exploiting the poor at every opportunity. We cannot dismiss this as a total misperception. No doubt blame of others serves to bolster self-esteem, but to a degree it is a legitimate interpretation of the experience of being in the lower class. Lower-class people are indeed victimized by self-seekers and racketeers, are virtually powerless to get things set right, and, as we have seen, meet condescension and disapproval even from those who, like public health doctors and public school teachers, are there for wholly benign purposes. Suspicion and guardedness are justified, but they tend to increase the feeling of isolation and hopelessness. Even enlightened programs of assistance may be rejected as the work of meddlesome do-gooders.

Central to the lower-class outlook is an estimate that the situation is hopeless. It will always be desperately hard to make both ends meet, even if one goes on relief. The struggle to keep everybody fed, clothed, and sheltered ceases only with incapacitating illness or death. If the future is not going to be any better, there is no point in sacrificing for it. What makes life worthwhile is the pleasure that one can obtain in the present, and this pleasure is all the more valuable if it is strong enough to drown one's awareness of daily misery and frustration. This attitude puts a high premium on sexual gratification and sexual adventures, lends special charm to alcohol and drugs, favors a search for strong stimulation and excitement, and enhances the value of the television set. There is little in this pattern to encourage control of one's desires or delay in acting upon them. Enduring a boring job or checking the aggression generated in domestic friction do not come easily; hence the frequency of job changes and of broken homes. Orientation is strictly to the present, and thus acts to the disadvantage of those aspects of life that need continuity, like bringing up children.

The Environment of Growth

Some of the circumstances in which lower-class children grow up can be derived directly from the foregoing description. The children are constantly in close contact with other people, often to an extent that promotes conflict. They have few things to investigate, few toys. The atmosphere around them is likely to be dominated by weary preoccupation with getting the work done, irritable outbreaks, and noisy quarrels among the adults. The mothers love their babies, but as the children become more numerous and are too much underfoot, maternal patience will snap many times a day. At night the children are supposed to sleep, but they are likely to be aware of adult sexual life, especially when it goes on in the same room. Going to school is required, but parents give its purposes—other than getting the children out of the house—little explicit support. In urban areas, going outdoors means entering yet another crowded human environment. The life of the streets may be more conducive to adventure, but it is also highly competitive and often violent, awakening anxieties and calling for constant alertness. Street life continues the child's education in matters of sex and strengthens his sense of opposition to law, order, and the police. The child has plenty of opportunity to learn lower-class values and very little way to avoid learning them.

On the face of it, this kind of environment is not likely to foster an ability to rise in the world by climbing the educational ladder. Everything seems weighted against steady application and progress in school. Close observational studies of the interactions between mothers and their young children suggest a further source of developmental handicap. Comparative studies of verbal interaction at different social levels show that it is less frequent at the lower-class level—only half as frequent as in professional families. These studies show further that the content is significantly different from class to class: restraining commands such as "Don't do that," "Shut up," and "Go away and leave me be" form a much larger proportion of lower-class communications than of higher-class communications, and they are accompanied less often by explanations—such as "Can't you see I'm busy getting dinner?"—which might direct the child's attention to reasons behind the words of command. Interactions of this kind invite passive compliance rather than an active attempt to understand. In this additional sense the lower-class home environment must be classified as unstimulating to mental growth. When the child is old enough to migrate to the street, he will probably find the company of his peers more stimulating, but not in directions that lead to an appreciation of school learning.[30]

The nature of lower-class surroundings as an environment for growth is illuminated in a book published by an anthropologist, Oscar Lewis, which consists of the spoken autobiographies of four members of a family living in a slum in Mexico City.[31] That the family is Mexican does not make it different, Lewis believes, from families similarly situated in the United States; there is a "culture of poverty" that in its main features is much the same in all lands. For the student of personality Lewis's study has the advantage of preserving individual differences in full relief. In spite of their membership in a single family in a "culture of poverty," the children of Sanchez come out as four distinct individuals.

[30] J. McV. Hunt, *The Challenge of Incompetence and Poverty* (Urbana, Ill.: University of Illinois Press, 1969).

[31] Oscar Lewis, *The Children of Sanchez: Autobiography of a Mexican Family* (New York: Random House, Inc., 1961).

The Children of Sanchez

At the time they were interviewed and asked to tell their life stories the children of Sanchez had grown up. The two boys, Manuel and Roberto, were 32 and 29, the two girls, Consuelo and Marta, 27 and 25. Their mother had died when Marta was 2; they were then brought up by their father and a succession of women engaged to take care of them. The father, Jesus Sanchez, 50 years old, was unusual in the slum environment in that he held a steady job and earned enough to keep the family out of acute want. In other respects his values were not unusual. As a parent he believed the children should be beaten but not heard; his adult sons were still intimidated in his presence. He imposed little restraint on his sexual inclinations: the services of women hired to help with the children included nocturnal obligations to the father which were certainly no secret in the one-room home. He founded families without legal or religious formality, not even limiting himself to one at a time; two other households were being supported while these children were growing up. The father was thus fairly typical of the "culture of poverty" except in his working habits and faithful economic support of his families. His children suspected that as a food buyer for a restaurant he ran a few little rackets that kept his income equal to its formidable task.

Manuel, the eldest son, came closest to the pattern of traits held to be typical in a disorganized slum environment. He recalled little about his home life, though his brother and sisters remembered all too well his crude assertions of authority when father was not at home. Having an "aversion to routine," as he put it, he remembered only "the exciting things," and these occurred mainly with his gang of friends who soon became the most important part of his life. Stocky and strong, he was from the first a good fighter and earned the other boys' respect. One of his fiercest fights, started to defend his brother, led oddly to a firm friendship; he and his new companion became inseparable, exchanged many confidences, and for years supported each other during emotional hard times. Manuel did poorly in school, which after the sixth grade he gladly gave up in favor of jobs, pocket money, and girls. At 13 he was inducted into sexual intercourse, after which "the fever, this sex business," got hold of him "in such a way that all I did was to go around thinking about it. At night my dreams were full of girls and sex. I wanted every woman I saw." Presently he fell into the grip of another fever, gambling at cards. "If a day passed without a game," he said, "I was desperate." This fever soon mounted to a point where he would bet a whole week's pay, but when he won he would go out with his friends and "throw it all away." Regretfully he recalled that he "never did anything practical" with his winnings. There is a certain charm about Manuel. His narrative is full of vitality and drama, and he sometimes reveals generous impulses, especially toward male friends. On one occasion he took over a sick friend's job to hold it for him, thereby sacrificing a much better job of his own. On another occasion, set up in a small business making shoes, he paid his three helpers so well that he went bankrupt. This mishap extinguished an already feeble spark: "I lost the little confidence I had in myself and lived just from day to day, like an animal. I didn't have the will power to carry out plans." At 15 he started a family and presently had four children. He never provided a home for his family, which finally became part of his father's household, and he increasingly neglected his wife, staying away and having a torrid affair with another woman. When his wife died he was grief-stricken. With his boyhood companion he departed for some months to work and gamble elsewhere, leaving the children to his father's support. No doubt this behavior contained some element of revenge for the humiliations and belittlements received from his father, but there was a strong undertone of shame and sadness in Manuel at having led a life "so sterile, so useless, so unhappy."

In Roberto, the second son, the feeling of worthlessness was more painful and chronic. "I don't know why," he said, "but I have always felt less than a nobody. Never in my whole life did I feel that there was anyone who paid attention to me." He further described himself as a bad egg from the beginning; at 5 he was already stealing things from the house. At 29, with a dishonorable discharge from the army and three penitentiary terms behind him, it was still hard to shake the image of a bad egg. Roberto's troubles were increased by his conspicuously dark skin, which earned him the nickname of "Negro." But he was deeply scarred by his mother's death, which occurred when he was 6 years old. "I cried for years," he said; "I still miss her. I believe if my mother were still alive I'd be very different." Family legend about the cause of death ascribed part of it to his own bad behavior, so that both loneliness and guilt became his chronic burden. Roberto himself was aware of deep restlessness, which took the form of playing hookey from school and, after the age of 11, running away from home. "I feel calm," he remarked, "only when I run away, when I go off as a vagabond." Intermittently he held jobs—"by the time I was 13, I had been a stevedore, a locker boy, a glass worker, a baker and a mason"—but he always got tired of them, a feeling with which he could cope only by moving on. Although he availed himself of the plentiful opportunities to display virility and secure sexual pleasure, he fell in love only with his half-sister, whom he met when both were 14. Romance was thus blocked, and the fact that he was "a first-class avoider of obligations" kept him single much longer than was customary in the neighborhood. His own story of his life is to an astonishing extent a history of fights. His other burdens no doubt increased his irritability, but his fighting assumed the intensity of an addiction or fever such as Manuel described for sex and gambling. His freely flying fists and drawing of the knife always carried at his belt momentarily drowned his misery and afterwards produced chaos in his life.

What is there for the girls in this kind of environment? Consuelo tried to reject it and better herself, but at 27 she was beginning to despair. Marta, who accepted and enjoyed it as a child, was faced at 25 with bringing up four children already deserted by their father.

Consuelo remembered her childhood as "nothing but bitterness and a feeling of being alone." She suffered from the loss of her mother, from rough treatment by her brothers, and from injustice on the part of her father, whose favorite was Marta. She was thin and often in poor health—nicknamed "Skinny"—and she did not consider herself attractive. Afraid of children her own age, she kept apart from others at school, hung about the teachers, and preferred the company of older women like a neighbor who taught her to sew. She liked the controlled environment of the classroom, where she did well and earned good conduct badges. At home, however, the personal frictions bordered on the unbearable, and her moments of escape into pleasant daydreams were always shattered by derisive commands to wake up. She learned that the single-room home is too small for introversion. Particularly painful were her feelings about her father's successive sexual partners, who robbed her of his attention. Bent on getting out and finding a better life, she went to a commercial school where she enjoyed a brief period of happiness, feeling solidarity with a group of girl friends. Her attitude toward sex was curiously Victorian. When she at last consented to live with a man her chronic resistance to the repugnant sex act brought the relation to an early end. Before long she discovered that even as a secretary, still more in seeking any further advancement, she could get nowhere without offering the bribe of her body. Her determination was strong to make for herself a cleaner, quieter, more secure and rewarding kind of life, and she hoped to provide this life also for Manuel's children, of whom she had become fond. But eventually she gave up the hopeless struggle. Her savings wiped out and her health undermined by an abortion that became necessary as a consequence of an attempt to get a better job, she gave up her apartment and returned to her father's crowded house. Here she tried to resign herself; in her own words, "I want to quiet the pain and anxiety I feel in my breast and look with indifference on the four children I have loved so much. It wasn't right for me to expend all my moral and physical strength to offer them a better life, only to fall in a faint. I will live half blind, like the rest of the people, and so will adapt to reality."

Marta was very different from her sister. Nicknamed "Chubby," she was bursting with health and vigor. She recalled her childhood as "the happiest any girl could have," mentioning her father's favor, her power over the household helpers, her sense of freedom, companionship in adventures with her brother Roberto, and her dominant position in her circle of friends. School she disliked—"I couldn't stand being shut up in a room"—and the lessons seemed irrelevant—"I never planned to be anything in life, like a nurse or a dressmaker: Tarzan was my favorite and I wanted only to be his companion." Until the age of 12 she was a tomboy, fighting alike with girls and boys, but she changed easily to a young lady interested in her clothes and careful of her appearance. With the other girls she tried smoking, drinking, and sexually sophisticated conversation without letting any of these become a fever. The tenor of her recollections suggests a comfortable adaptation to her surroundings; under the right circumstances, including those that prevail in the family circle, the lower-class environment is compatible with a happy childhood. For Marta, however, childhood was all too soon past. At

15 she found her mate, at 16 bore her first child, and in her early twenties was responsible for bringing up a family of four. Relations with her husband deteriorated steadily as the children arrived. The husband, himself anything but faithful, constantly accused her of infidelities, and their life turned into a series of violent quarrels, walkings out, and reconciliations. Her patience exhausted, Marta retired with her family to her father's house, where Manuel's children were also living. There was an interlude with a man ten years older, father of several families, but as her fifth pregnancy got under way his financial support dwindled. "What am I waiting for?" asked Marta; "I'm waiting for nothing, exactly nothing! . . . I'm not worried about myself, but about my children. If it hadn't been for them I would have wiped myself off the map long ago. But I know very well that they need me. Without me, they would be through, because no one would love all of them the way I do." Maternal love was the sole surviving positive feeling when everything else seemed to have failed.

Socialization for Violence

According to a common stereotype, life in the lower class has been held to represent human nature in the raw, unfettered by socializing constraints. This is what we would all be like—lazy, improvident, irresponsible, sexually insatiable, jealous and competitive, touchy and aggressive even to the point of murder—were it not for a forcibly applied process of socialization that teaches us to control ourselves and guide our energies into civilized living. Occasionally lower-class life is romanticized, becoming a modernized version of the South Sea Islands in nineteenth-century fiction, where play, song, dance, kindness, and sexual enjoyment flourished unhampered by civilized inhibitions and ambitious tensions. Familiarity with life at this level quickly splinters the stereotypes. The inhabitants of slums are not at all free from socializing pressures, and they are anything but happy. The young people of Lewis's report, vital and strong as they often appear, are far from representing the happy flowering of unspoiled human nature. Now that they have grown up they all live with a strong undertone of misery and desperation; they have all thought of suicide. Like everyone else, moreover, they are surrounded by cultural pressure, and in their different ways each testifies to the power of that pressure. Especially eloquent is the testimony of Consuelo, who tried most strenuously to be deviant. She aimed for a quiet and orderly existence, a pretty home, steady employment, improved security and status; she wanted to avoid sexual promiscuity, to get rid of quarreling and fighting, and to create an atmosphere in which it was possible to listen to daydreams. On every count the culture of the slum put her down hard, as if she were propounding wicked heresies.

Human nature shaped by what Lewis calls the "culture of poverty" is not human nature in the raw. It is human nature made raw by cultural prescription. Every group of people arrives at certain solutions to the problems of living and then passes these on to the next generation. If the problems are difficult, if anxiety and despair can only just be held in check, the solutions are passed on all the more urgently. When the economic position is hopeless, the paths to betterment blocked, and the powers that control one's fate remote and hostile, one can make life endurable only by maximizing the satisfactions of the moment, especially those that can crowd everything else out of mind. This is the cultural wisdom that is passed on in disorganized lower-class neighborhoods. The individual must become tough, mistrustful, self-sufficient, and aggressive if he is to endure the life that lies before him. Generosity, kindness, sensitivity, and feeling for others have no place in the picture and must not be allowed to get in the way. The widespread preoccupation with sex, which on closer inspection turns out to be overdriven and shrill with jealousy, is not the simple expression of an uninhibited biological urge; it is a cultural imperative designed to maximize this accessible form of pleasure in a world of great deprivations. Learning to fight is similarly pushed as the only possible way to relieve frustrations, preserve rights, and attain self-respect. The two boys in Lewis's report recalled a time when they felt no hostility toward other boys and were timid about getting into fights. The culture of the streets took care of this dangerous weakness. In several respects, to be socialized in slum societies means to be brutalized.

Cultural pressure to heighten the expression of aggression is vividly described in Claude Brown's account of his childhood in Harlem's black ghetto. "Throughout my childhood in Harlem," Brown writes, "nothing was more strongly impressed upon me than the fact that you had to fight and that you should fight."[32] It was permissible to be scared but disgraceful if the fear were not overcome. In the end, boys were "more afraid of not fighting than they were of fighting." If two little boys started fighting, the older boys and men gathered around and urged them on; never was the fight stopped. Brown recalls that at 7 or 8 he was offered a dollar by an adult—a huge financial inducement—to tangle with another boy of the same age. He describes a scene in which his father, meeting him at the door in flight from two bigger boys, threatens to beat him up if he does not go back to face them. It was necessary first to establish one's reputation as a fighter and then to keep living up to the reputation. "Most girls in Harlem," Brown adds, "could fight pretty well themselves, and if other girls bothered them, they could take care of themselves." Odd as it sounds, natural aggressiveness is clearly distrusted in the society Brown describes. It must be strengthened by vigorous cultural pressure if self-respecting citizenship on the streets is to be attained.

Upward Mobility as a Motive

The literature on social stratification, dealing as it does with the characteristics of groups rather than of individuals, sometimes begets the view that class status and upward social mobility are universal preoccupations.

---

[32] Claude Brown, *Manchild in the Promised Land* (New York: The Macmillan Company, 1965), Chap. 10.

Facts such as those discussed thus far in this chapter dispose some observers to believe that the desire to scramble upward and climb higher in relation to other people must be a motive of extraordinary generality and power. By concentrating on this aspect, one can give a status interpretation to a great deal of behavior. A family's move into a larger house can be seen as an example of "conspicuous consumption" designed to show the world that the family's financial fortunes have improved. One can see attendance at a concert as an attempt to make a good impression on the best people in the community, who have sponsored the event. Joy at being admitted to a good graduate school can be interpreted as delight at the prospect of prestige by association and of employment advantages at the end of training. One can thus make upward social mobility a touchstone for interpreting behavior. This interpretation has the added attraction (because people often deny any desire to increase their status) of convincing the researcher that he is penetrating false fronts and disclosing the latent snobbishness that actuates us all.

Touchstones, however, are highly unlikely to fit the facts of personality. As we have seen, simple and sovereign explanations violate the complexity that is inherent in human behavior. The kinds of behavior generally taken as examples of status striving almost always have other goals as well, which would be sought even if social prestige were not involved. A larger house means less crowding and clashing, more privacy, more scope to create beautiful surroundings indoors and out. Attending a concert means enjoying music; many people go with no interest at all in the status of other listeners. Going to graduate school develops one's skill and knowledge in a sphere of proven interest, and the choice of field may have nothing to do with its claims to prestige. The concept of striving for upward social mobility becomes badly blurred if it is allowed to include all movement toward further education, self-improvement, bettering the conditions of life, and enjoying and enriching one's experience. Most actions serve more than one purpose. Understanding requires that the purposes be carefully sorted out and their intrinsic goals distinguished.

As a motive, upward social mobility has to be defined in relation to an existing system of stratification. It depends upon having at least in the back of one's mind a conception of higher and lower status, an imagery of a social ladder, and it takes the form of wanting to move up so as to be with people of higher status. Inherent in the goal is *one's placement on a prestige scale in relation to other people*. The operations used by social scientists to learn about status make this clear: upward mobility implies being accepted by a superior group as an intimate member with whom there will be visiting, inviting to meals, and the possibility of intermarriage. It is always a question of being with others who are ahead of others, so to speak—of affirming superiority over other people through group membership with those who are already superior.

The roots of such a motive in earlier experience are not hard to trace. Long before social status as such becomes comprehensible, the child's experience familiarizes him with some of the relevant feelings. In the family circle, as we have seen, questions of status in the affection and esteem of parents are of immense importance. Being closer to the household's "ruling class," being accepted and enjoying its confidence, is for younger children one of the surest ways to attain superiority over sibling rivals. In school, where the number of potential rivals is much larger and competition for the teachers' esteem inevitable, regardless of the school's educational philosophy, there is further development of feelings having to do with comparative status. When children become more clearly aware of social stratification in the adult sense they are already experienced with placement on a prestige scale in relation to other children. The manner in which they transfer this experience to the larger social scene is of course greatly influenced by their actual position and by the attitudes expressed and enacted by parents and neighbors. None of us, however, encounters social stratification as a wholly new experience.

These considerations at once suggest that there will be marked individual differences in children's responses to social stratification based on their experience in the family circle and during the early years of school. The student of personality cannot ignore these differences, which require careful assessment in each individual case. But the assessment should not be confined to the pattern of personal feelings brought to the problem from childhood; it must include an equally discriminating grasp of the parents and their values, where again there is a wide field of individual variation. To assign a family to upper-middle-class status on the basis of general criteria, like income and education, does not tell us that it will necessarily have the outlook and values that *on the average* are characteristic of that group. Each family has its own version, which sometimes departs widely from the average. This is true even in the perception of what constitutes superiority. Professional people, for instance, commonly put much more emphasis on education than on money. They seek membership among people with serious interests who are well read, talk intelligently about world affairs, and are at home with the arts. Such people are felt to be substantially superior to those whose interests are symbolized by stepping out of a large new car at the door of the leading golf club.[33]

Upward social mobility, then, cannot properly be cast as a universal motive with simple and sovereign power over human social behavior. This is not to deny that it is strong and widespread; the studies of social stratification show plainly that it is at work in many people and in many contexts. But these same studies have shown that satisfaction with modest status is often possible, and closer psychological analysis reveals variations in personal goals that cannot be forced into the conception of upward social mobility. Very important as evidence of their relation to external circumstances is the fact that attitudes toward status in the United States have undergone marked historical change. Prior to the Depression of the 1930s, throughout the whole preceding half century, attitudes on this subject took forms that today

---

[33] The need to assess each family's values as variants of the average status pattern is shown in R. W. White, *Lives in Progress*, esp. pp. 121–122 and 264–266.

seem incredibly harsh. Economic free enterprise, profiting from a rapid expansion of industrial technology, kept producing ever-wider differences of wealth. These differences were justified as an expression of natural endowments: the shiftless poor, the restricted middle class, and the enterprising rich were made that way and enjoyed the financial status they deserved. This tradition is not dead, but it has been greatly softened by increasing knowledge of economic and social processes and of human development. Ideas that are widely accepted today—control of the economy, the welfare state, taking steps to provide equal opportunity, attempting to create environments conducive to personal growth—all work to reduce the sharpness of social stratification and tend to weaken upward mobility as a personal goal. Many people, especially younger people, in the upper half of the status system take less pride in being there than in knowing how the other half lives through mingling with them, finding grounds upon which to like and respect them, and doing something to improve their opportunities. As a value social status is slipping, but as a fact it has not yet slipped so far that the student of personality can neglect it as part of the environment of growth.

Ethnic Groups

Conceptually, it is possible to make a sharp distinction between ethnic grouping and status grouping. In the United States, however, the two variables have become deeply intertwined. Ethnic groups are far from being equally distributed along the status ladder, and prejudice against some of them has often been compounded by rejection of people in lower status. This situation resulted from the historical course of immigration into the once thinly settled land. The first large wave of immigration, starting early in the seventeenth century, consisted almost entirely of English and Scotch Protestants; smaller groups, like the Dutch around New York, were also Protestant and from the northern part of Europe. This relative homogeneity of national origin, culture, and religion continued well into the nineteenth century, and the descendants of this population, generally described as white Anglo-Saxon Protestants, are still a majority in many parts of the country, though often a minority in particular regions. During the nineteenth century, industrial development improved prosperity in northern Europe, decreasing the inducements to leave, but overpopulation and poverty became more acute in the still agricultural nations of central and southern Europe. Large numbers of Irish immigrants, spurred by an acute famine in their homeland, came first, to be followed by a wave of Italians and later by substantial numbers from the several peoples of central Europe. The great majority of these immigrants were Roman Catholic, and a small minority were Jewish. On the West Coast there was eventually a similar influx of Chinese with smaller numbers of Japanese. These newer immigrants, mostly desperately poor, entered an already existing system of social stratification at the lowest level. They were unfavorably regarded for both their social status and their ethnic and religious difference, and therefore continued to cluster in distinct ethnic groups even when their economic position began to improve. In the meantime, starting early and continuing into the nineteenth century, forced immigration of blacks from Africa created in the South first a lower class in the status of slaves, and later, following legal emancipation in 1863, a class marked off by skin color and kept in inferior status by systematic withholding of rights and opportunities. In this instance, too, ethnic membership and low economic and educational status reinforced one another in the pattern of rejection.

That the two are separable is best shown by the fact that status systems emerge even in groups that are ethnically homogeneous. Old New England villages were just as stratified when inhabited only by Protestants of English origin as they were later following the newer immigration. Furthermore, any ethnic group that is prevented from moving freely into the larger status system is likely to develop an internal stratification of its own. In New York City at the turn of the century, there was a partially independent Jewish status system extending all the way from riches to rags. Stephen Birmingham, in a book about the prominent Jewish families of New York, a self-made elite of wealth and manners, describes their dismay when large numbers of their coreligionists poured into the lower East Side, their contempt for this "uncouth and unwashed" population, and their grudging admission that some of the newcomers might be "witty and interesting personalities."[34] In both northern and southern cities, careful studies have disclosed a black status system that repeats many of the features of the white one, lending itself to similar designations like upper- and lower-middle class, working class, and lower class.[35] Readers of Malcolm X's autobiography will remember his contemptuous description of the "snooty-black neighborhood" in the Roxbury section of Boston, where the blacks living on "the Hill," a stone's throw from the ghetto, kept their houses and yards in middle-class fashion and prided themselves on their superior culture.[36]

There are clearly many problems connected with ethnic membership that are of interest to students of personality. Strong ethnic tradition that is honored by observances, patriotic or religious, that connect the present with a long past, may be experienced as a source of pride and as an aid to self-definition. When the group is already in advantageous status, tradition may be used to harden a conservative if not reactionary outlook, but it may also generate a desire to emulate the constructive achievements of ancestors by like achievements appropriate to the present. When an ethnic group is handicapped in the main status system, tradition of this kind provides an alternative basis for the feeling of personal worth. The Jewish student previously

[34] Stephen Birmingham, *Our Crowd: The Great Jewish Families of New York* (New York: Harper & Row, Publishers, 1967), Chap. 37.

[35] Allison Davis and John Dollard, *Children of Bondage* (New York: American Council on Education, 1940); St. Clair Drake and Horace R. Cayton, *Black Metropolis* (New York: Harcourt Brace Jovanovich, 1945).

[36] *The Autobiography of Malcolm X* (New York: Grove Press, 1966), Chap. 3.

described,[37] whose parents' values were wholly secular, materialistic, and upwardly mobile, so that their son experienced being Jewish simply as a handicap, spent a summer shortly after graduation at an institute designed to develop a deeper understanding of the Jewish cultural and religious heritage. This expanding of background gave him, he said, "something to be proud of, a positive reason for retaining one's Jewishness, because it made for a bigger person."

Membership in an ethnic group that rejects other ethnic groups undoubtedly leaves its marks on the formation of personality. Studies of anti-Semitism, including those of authoritarian personality structure mentioned in Chapter 3, show the relation of ethnic prejudice to the management of blame and aggression in personal life. The presence of a scapegoat group upon which both blame and hostility can be turned makes it easier to maintain a conviction of rightness and strength when these are shaky. Serviceable in this sense, the strategy has an obvious social cost in intergroup hostility and a developmental cost in the impairment of the desire and capacity to understand other people. The question of insight into others has a special significance for students of personality. Is it possible to have an appreciative understanding of people if they are objects of one's contempt or hate and if these feelings are serving to support one's own sense of superiority and self-esteem? James Baldwin has proposed that whites can never understand blacks because such understanding would require them to recognize in themselves profound depths of anxiety, hate, and savagery.[38] There is certainly a point to this warning, though fortunately it has not led whites to give up the attempt.

The Experience of Ethnic Rejection

Numerous as are the problems connected with ethnic groups as environments for growth, we shall concentrate here on the one that in recent years has received the most public attention and technical research. This is the effect on personality of ethnic rejection, of being a member of a group that experiences prejudice by the dominant group in the population. The crucial feature of this situation is the constant presence of an irrational hostility in the human environment. To a child growing up, this hostility is as unaccountable as a tornado or a flood, an ugly characteristic of the world before which one is helpless. It is met repeatedly, coming up on all kinds of unexpected occasions, and it never makes sense as a relevant or fair response to one's own behavior. As one is born into ethnic membership and is in no way responsible for it, the child experiences attitudes of rejection on this count alone as singularly unjust. Yet it becomes plain that such attitudes are virtually beyond influence and are only increased if met with righteous indignation or anger. This is the situation to which members of a rejected minority must somehow manage to adapt.

As an illustrative example we take first the early history of a Jewish

[37] See page 132.
[38] James Baldwin, *Notes of a Native Son* (Boston: The Beacon Press, 1955).

professional man who grew up twenty-five years ago in a comfortable upper-middle-class neighborhood, son of a successful and respected lawyer. His educational path led from public grade school to private preparatory school and thence to college and graduate study. An upper-middle-class Gentile boy of like intellectual gifts could expect to follow this path with a relatively unbroken sense of welcome and membership in the successive social environments. The Jewish boy was not as fortunate. In a family that was generally mild in its discipline, "One thing," he wrote, "was made explicit: if one was a Jew, he had to be better than good in order to succeed." When he was 5, three children who lived across the street refused to speak to him; puzzled at the time, he realized in retrospect that this was his first collision with ethnic prejudice. At 8 he was called a "dirty Jew" by a boy with whom he was having a heated argument. In junior high school his teacher asked him to give a monologue as part of a school entertainment, the sketch being entitled "Finkelstein Sells a Suit"; years later he recalled this with anger but did not remember any special feeling about it at the time. Having chosen scholastic achievement as the sphere in which to be better than good, he secured admission to a mainly Gentile preparatory school where the room he shared with three Jewish classmates was immediately nicknamed "The Ghetto." At college an essay he wrote at white heat on Nazi Germany was called "puerile and vituperative" by the instructor who, however, refused to discuss it with him and point out the faults. This incident finally taught him "that there are certain individuals with whom one cannot reason." The expressions of prejudice in this history are relatively mild, but they still stick out as evidences of irrational hostility in a human environment that in other respects was far from being crude and cruel.

The most searching studies of growth in an environment of prejudice have taken as their object blacks in the United States. All the problems inherent in ethnic rejection can be seen here in sharp and magnified form. Skin color, an obvious criterion except in a small number of borderline cases, serves to define ethnic membership, and the long history and tradition of slavery has still further hardened the boundary between whites and blacks.

The Black Role and Its Effects on Personality

An established status system calls for all parties to enact appropriate roles. In the present instance, as Pettigrew expresses it:

> The white must act out the role of the "superior"; by direct action or subtle cue, he must convey the expectation that he will be treated with deference. For his part, the Negro must, if racist norms are to be obeyed, act out the role of the "inferior"; he must play the social role of "Negro." And if he should refuse to play the game, he would be judged by the white supremacist as "not knowing his place," and harsh sanctions could follow.[39]

[39] T. F. Pettigrew, *A Profile of the Negro American* (Princeton, N.J.: D. Van Nostrand & Co., 1964), pp. 3–4.

The point is made even more sharply by Grier and Cobbs, black psychiatrists who have observed the subtle persistence of the role in contemporary black patients:

> Slavery required the creation of a particular kind of person, one *compatible* with a life of involuntary servitude. The ideal slave had to be absolutely dependent and have a deep consciousness of personal inferiority. His color was made the badge of that degradation. As a final precaution, he was instilled with a sense of the unlimited power of his master. . . . The black man was brought to this country forcibly and was completely cut off from his past. He was robbed of language and culture. He was forbidden to be an African and never allowed to be an American. After the first generation and with each new group of slaves, the black man had only his American experience to draw on.
>
> The culture of slavery was never undone for either master or slave. The civilization that tolerated slavery dropped its slaveholding cloak but the inner feelings remained. . . . The minds of our citizens have never been freed.[40]

The enactment of a role originally based on involuntary servitude entails damage to many aspects of personality. Particularly obvious is the difficulty of developing self-esteem and a sense of identity as a person of worth. In direct contact with whites, expectations of inferiority are likely to be communicated in one way or another. Looking around in the world, a black can easily see that important positions in American society are rarely held by people of his skin color, and his difficulties in securing employment will soon teach him how effectively the usual avenues to advancement are blocked. These obstacles exert a destructive action that has caused a great many blacks to believe in their own inferiority and to feel self-hate, tendencies that today are being purposefully combatted by the motto, "Black is beautiful," and by programs of study emphasizing black accomplishment in America and Africa. The usual situation offers powerful inducements toward deference, passive compliance, good-natured acquiescence in an inferior role, along with no small amount of vigilance as to what the white majority expects. It is not a role that can provide foundations for self-esteem.

Being in the black role has further far-reaching consequences. Grier and Cobbs call attention to its interference with a sense of womanhood, a sense of manhood, stable family life, a sense of responsibility, and a commitment to education. For women the feeling of being desirable is undercut by a conviction that black cannot really be beautiful and that sexual exploitation by white men is without love or respect. For men, assertiveness and aggression in particular cannot be accommodated in the role. A black man is under pressure to remain anonymous, "held back by some inner command not to excel, not to achieve, not to become outstanding, not to draw attention to

[40] W. H. Grier and P. M. Cobbs, *Black Rage* (New York: Basic Books, Inc., 1968), Chap. 2.

himself." In this connection Grier and Cobbs give instances of black male patients who, after achieving with great effort some measure of success, fall victim to psychiatric or psychosomatic disorders, as if the inner command not to be conspicuous created a conflict incompatible with health.[41] In family life the basic disintegrative circumstance is that a black father, if the climate of racial prejudice is strong, cannot protect his wife or children from mistreatment by whites, and he cannot resist such harassments as verbal abuse, unlawful search of his home, or seizure of his property. Where the wife is the principal breadwinner, it is hard for him to be a significant member of the family circle. Developing a sense of responsibility with respect to property and finances requires a dependable environment, and the black man's environment is often made undependable by arbitrary and illegal white activity. Property owned or a business successfully run too often become targets of cupidity and are confiscated, leaving the black owner with no effective legal recourse. Having a stake in education and encouraging children to take it seriously do not make sense if black schools are notably inferior and if opportunities after graduation do not exist. Faith in education, furthermore, will burn dimly if one has a deeply indoctrinated conviction of being slow and stupid in comparison with whites.

Black children often grow up in a human environment that has been powerfully shaped in these several ways by the requirements of the black role. Such is the culture that is transmitted to them.

The Environment of Growth for Black Children

The children who grow up in this environment become aware quite early in life of the problems connected with skin color. The fact of different colored skins arouses their curiosity during the third year of life and enters into the stream of questions that is so characteristic of this age. By the time they enter school at 5 or 6 they have picked up a certain understanding of their inferior status. Robert Coles, in a book that includes detailed study of children involved in the school desegregation crises in the South in 1960, points out that differences of status and privilege are already being represented in spontaneous crayon drawings.[42] A black girl of 6, for instance, drew white children in considerable detail and, considering her age, in relatively good proportion, but she had difficulty with black subjects. Characteristically she drew them smaller, lacking in detail, even a little distorted, and for some time she would not use brown or black crayons, outlining black and white children alike in orange or red. A boy of 7, asked to make a picture including his black chum and some white boy from the school, drew the white boy in colorful detail at the top of a hill and the chum, disproportionately small and all brown, at the bottom. He explained that the black boy might like to be at the top too, but he is used to being where he is, so he

[41] *Ibid.*, Chaps. 1 and 4.
[42] Robert Coles, *Children of Crisis: A Study of Courage and Fear* (Boston: Little, Brown & Company, 1967), Chap. 3.

would be afraid up there and might get dizzy. If he carried some food up to the white boy he would come right down again because the white boy would not like to have him stay and because "he might slip and get killed if the two of them were there when there's only room for one."[43] The symbolism of this boy's drawing and explanation could hardly be more telling. What is remarkable is that he has gathered so much about his social environment at such an early age.

Black parents take it as one of their obligations to teach their children to keep out of trouble with whites. The consequences of failure are serious and the instruction must not be allowed to go unheeded. One mother in the South expressed the problem as follows:

> We have to live with one another, black and white, I mean. I keep on telling that to the children, and if they don't seem to learn it, like everything else, I have to punish them to make sure they do. . . . Just the other day my Laura started getting sassy about white children on the television. My husband told her to hold her tongue and do it fast. It's like with cars and knives, you have to teach your children to know what's dangerous and how to stay away from it, or else they sure won't live long. White people are a real danger to us until we learn how to live with them. So if you want your kids to live long, they have to grow up scared of whites; and the way they get scared is through us; and that's why I don't let my kids get fresh about the white man even in their own house. If I do there's liable to be trouble to pay. They'll forget, and they'll say something outside, and that'll be it for them and us too.[44]

Training thus begins early and continues forcefully to induct the child into the black role with its required inhibition of assertiveness and aggression directed at whites.

The environment of growth provided by the schools is often unable to rectify the effects of home training. However the educational system is organized, black children are unlikely to enter it on what seems to them an equal basis with whites. If the school is segregated it is usually inferior in fairly obvious ways. If it is integrated, the black pupils may feel at the start the burden of the legend that they are stupid, and they will be lucky indeed if this is not reinforced, intentionally or not, by the attitudes of the teachers. As the content of what they are taught begins to be more heavily weighted toward current events, social studies, and history, all seen largely from the white point of view, black students are likely to become still further convinced that education really belongs to someone else and is not for them. Doing well in studies increasingly acquires the meaning of being like the white students and becoming separated from black companions. Most important of all is a corrosive doubt that education will have any use in the future. It is certainly not relevant to the type of work being done by the majority of

---

[43] *Ibid.*, pp. 67–68.
[44] *Ibid.*, p. 66.

black parents, and the prospect that schooling will lead to better jobs in competition with whites is not good enough to arouse enthusiasm.

This last problem is illustrated in a dramatic episode already mentioned in the life of Malcolm X, an episode that proved to be a turning point in his career. In junior high school in a community in Michigan where there were but a handful of blacks, Malcolm was an outstanding student and athlete and was elected president of his class. One day a teacher asked him about his plans for a career; he replied rather casually, having given the matter little thought, that he might like to be a lawyer. The teacher explained to him that this was not a realistic goal for one of his race, recommending instead that he use his skill with his hands to become a carpenter. The effect of this dose of "realism" was devastating. The same teacher, he soon learned, had encouraged white children's plans, but the campus leader, because he was black, was supposed to content himself with a humble trade. Malcolm became depressed, pulled away from whites, gave up plans for senior high school, and moved away to join his half-sister in Boston, where in a black section of the city an entirely new phase of his career began.[45]

For black children the environment of growth contains severe and lasting restrictions. It is conducive to an attitude of suspicion toward white people and their laws and institutions. It discourages continuous effort and optimistic plans for the future. It begets chronic resentment difficult to control, dangerous to express. Clearly it calls for remarkable human resilence.

Conclusion

In retrospect on this chapter, it is necessary to recall once more the importance of historical change. Social stratification and ethnic grouping are not fixed and final. In recent years there has been a steady growth in understanding how these social processes work; they can no longer be denied and swept under the rug. With this has come an increasing sense of outrage at the spectacle of unfairness and at the consequent deformations of human potentiality and human dignity. The social environments surrounding the growth of personality, seen more clearly through carefully controlled observation, are being judged to stand in great need of improvement.

The excesses of ethnic prejudice practiced by Hitler's regime in Germany produced a revulsion of feeling that has strengthened the hands of those who work to make prejudice a thing of the past. As a result the grip of anti-Semitism in the United States has been perceptibly weakened. The Supreme Court decision on school desegregation and the civil rights movement initially led by Martin Luther King have increased the crumbling of white prejudice toward blacks. Recent repeated opinion surveys testify to measurable progress in this direction. But as everyone knows, the rate of progress is painfully slow. The habits and attitudes produced by growing up

[45] *The Autobiography of Malcolm X*, pp. 35–36.

in a particular social environment are too deeply embedded for rapid change; learned expectations of how things should be block the perception of how things might be improved. If two groups of people are brought up, as we have seen, in something like a master-and-slave relation, they learn the roles of master and slave to a degree that makes change a difficult process.

Not, however, an impossible process. We shall consider later in this book the ways in which environmental shaping can be transcended. We are not enslaved by our training and surroundings to the point of being unable to imagine a better world or to initiate events leading to social change. If the influences described in this chapter were totally binding there would be no possibility of social change, but also no explanation of how society came into its present form. The improvement of conditions depends upon the fact that there is more to human beings than a capacity to be shaped by circumstances. What more there is will occupy us in the ensuing sections of this book.

7 Biological Individuality: Constitution and Temperament

The central fact to which the preceding four chapters pointed is that personality develops from the very beginning in a social environment. So numerous and impressive are the social influences surrounding individual growth that theorists have sometimes been tempted to make them the whole explanation of personality. The person, in such a view, is what the people around him have made him. Based on the assumption that a child is wholly plastic and can be molded to any shape, the theory crumbles in the presence of actual children, lively creatures who display initiative, produce drastic effects on their surroundings, and often seem able to resist attempts at social control. Looking at children reminds us that personality has individual, organic roots as well as social ones. It is an attribute of a living system, one that is often described as having a will of its own. Its locus is a self-regulative, partly autonomous organic system in a more or less constant state of activity.

When attention is turned to this aspect of personality, we run at once into the clear fact that infants are not standardized. Biological methods of production have little in common with industrial ones. The plan of nature seems to be to use a fresh combination of ingredients in each single item produced, a scheme that wildly violates industrial standards of efficiency in which all articles coming off the assembly line are exactly alike. Much can be said for it, however, in that genetic variability is a distinct asset in the survival of a species when external conditions change. The mechanisms of heredity are geared for variation and produce uniquely endowed individuals. The genes are freshly shuffled, so to speak, on each occasion, creating a degree of biological novelty in each new life. If a person says that there has never before been anyone like him, we should reflect, before accusing him of unbounded conceit, that he might have meant merely to utter a simple biological truth. There has never been anyone just like him, nor will there ever be.

The Nature of Genetic Endowments

Three types of genetic endowment relevant to the growth of personality will be considered in this chapter. The best starting point, because it is visible, is *physical constitution.* This includes stature, shape, sexual differentiation, coloring, facial features, and tendencies with respect to weight. These characteristics are ever-present accompaniments of our lives. Many of them are apparent at birth, most of them are relatively stable over the years, and together they provide the chief cues for the remarkable human ability to tell people apart even when met by the thousands. Another set of qualities, less easy to measure but still often apparent to the casual observer, is displayed more directly in behavior. We might describe these qualities as preferred ways of experiencing and acting, but here we shall call them preferred *styles of functioning.* Prominent among these is the activity-passivity variable, but there are other dimensions of style of functioning, including extraversion and introversion, impulsiveness, and sensitivity. Our interest here is in those that can be recognized early and that seem to persist as individual characteristics throughout the course of life. Finally there is *temperament,* which refers more specifically to the realm of feeling. Allport defined it as referring to "the characteristic phenomena of an individual's emotional nature, including his susceptibility to emotional stimulation, his customary strength and speed of response, the quality of his prevailing mood, and all peculiarities of fluctuation and intensity in mood, these phenomena being regarded as dependent on constitutional makeup, and therefore largely hereditary in origin."[1] This sphere of experience will be taken up in this chapter in connection with prevailing moods and stability of moods.

How much importance for subsequent personality should be attached to innate endowments of this kind? Especially with respect to styles of functioning, it is well to remember that learning begins at once, that experience starts to leave its impression perhaps in the prenatal period and certainly from the moment of birth. Does this not mean that experience will fairly soon blot out all traces of genetic endowment?

This result would probably follow if innate traits and learned traits were separate entities engaging in free competition. This, however, would be a serious misconception of the relation between them. "The influence of heredity on behavior is always indirect," says Anastasi. "No psychological trait is ever inherited as such."[2] Genetic endowments are not finished traits. They can be better described as predispositions that favor the development through experience of certain qualities rather than others. They exert a consistent influence over the learning process, giving it a certain slant without controlling exactly what will be learned or producing a preordained result. A

[1] G. W. Allport, *Pattern and Growth in Personality* (New York: Holt, Rinehart and Winston, Inc., 1961), p. 34.

[2] A. Anastasi, "Heredity, Environment, and the Question 'How?'," *Psychological Review,* **65** (1958), 197–208.

strong physical frame predisposes a schoolboy to become an athlete but does not automatically produce this result; environmental influences may lead him to disdain sports and make use of his strength only in useful labor, or even not make use of it at all. A high degree of sensitivity makes it easier to experience the beauties of nature and of art, but if the environment discourages the developing of such interests, the potentiality may be left to lie fallow. It is possible to conceive of genetic endowments in terms of the ease and speed with which one learns different kinds of things, the naturalness with which one performs different kinds of acts, and the sense of congeniality one feels in pursuing different kinds of interests. Endowments thus have a gentle tendency to steer experience but not, except in extreme cases, to produce a fixed result or to impose a precise destiny on personal growth.

In examining this subject it is important to consider the manner in which genetic proclivities enter the learning process. Presumably they do so from the very start: the mother interacting with her newborn child is immediately affected by the baby's characteristics, such as level of activity and prevailing pleasantness of mood. The child's endowments make themselves felt in the family circle. Parental attitudes do not act on a schematic average child but on particular children, and are themselves influenced in specific ways. Parents may be predisposed toward high control, but given three children, one who actively resists, one who passively complies, and one who typically disarms them with a winning smile, they will come to display three quite different versions of their original attitude. Children, from the very beginning of their membership in the household, show distinct individuality. It is crucial to know how the parents respond to their children's characteristics. Do they like the child's pattern of traits? Do they understand such qualities? Do they adapt their requirements to the child's preferred way of doing things, or do they struggle to change him around? Similar interactive questions arise in relation to brothers and sisters, and the whole drama continues as the child enters social environments outside the family circle. The consequences for growth that arise from these interactions will be considered with respect to each of the constitutional and temperamental variables now to be described.

Physical Constitution

The most successful attempt to systematize the measurement of physique was made in the 1930s by William Sheldon.[3] Trying to give precision to earlier impressionistic studies, Sheldon developed a technique of photographing the human body at a standard distance and in three standard positions—front, side, and back. The basic observations were made with a sample of 4,000 young men of college age. The photographs were used for a

---

[3] W. H. Sheldon, S. S. Stevens, and W. B. Tucker, *The Varieties of Human Physique* (New York: Harper & Row, Publishers, 1940).

variety of exact measurements on the basis of which Sheldon concluded that there are three main components of physique and that individual differences can be largely accounted for by the relative strengths of these three components.

The easiest way to describe the components is to imagine individuals, actually rather rare, in whom a single one is heavily predominant. The first component, to which Sheldon gave the name *endomorphy*, seems designed to favor the digestive viscera, which are large relative to other structures; the body form is otherwise characterized by soft roundness and has this shape even when there is little deposit of fat. This body form had been previously described in the literature as the "round" or "digestive" type. The second component, *mesomorphy*, shows itself in somatic structures such as bone, muscle, and connective tissue and tends to give to the body a shape that is hard, firm, strong, and somewhat rectangular. As these somatic structures have to do with motility and exertion it is not surprising that older writers had used expressions such as "motor" or "athletic" type. When the third component, *ectomorphy*, predominates, the body is slender, poorly muscled, and rather flat-chested, creating an impression of delicacy and even fragility, especially in contrast to an extreme mesomorph. In earlier work the predominantly ectomorphic physique had been described as an "asthenic" (weak) type or more flatteringly as a "cerebral" type. In most young men, of course, one component does not totally dominate the other two. Yet variability is still high: only a small number of Sheldon's cases had an equal score on all three components. With respect to physique the average person has something of everything, but with a definite accent on one or another of the components.

The conception that physique has measurable components and that individual differences result from their relative strength is an advance over the older idea of types. The concept of type implies something discontinuous: you belong in one type and are not supposed to have any of the qualities of another type. As this division into compartments never squares with the facts, typologies are always eventually vitiated by talk about "mixed types." A scheme of varying components avoids this difficulty, recognizes that we are all mixed types, and at the same time produces a workable method for dealing with individual differences, in this case of physique. When Sheldon uses the term *somatotype* (type of body), he is referring not to type in the usual sense but to a person's score on the relative strengths of the three components.

The terms used by Sheldon may be abstract and unfamiliar, but it is easy to recognize in his descriptions the qualities of physical constitution that have long been a part of common observation and popular wisdom. In a rough sort of way we all recognize connections between visible physique and other personal qualities. We would accuse a Shakespearian director of bad miscasting if he gave us a wiry, quick-moving Falstaff, a craggy, broad-shouldered Hamlet, or a comfortable, plump Othello, or if he let Cassius have other than the "lean and hungry look" appropriate to a plotting thinker. No doubt there is some tendency here to think in stereotypes, but they are far too persistent to be considered idle. We easily accept the description of a face as thin and sensitive but would feel surprised if told about a round sensitive face or a square-jawed sensitive face. We would find it incongruous if a writer described a character as tall, very thin, earthy, and given to resounding belly-laughs and noisy belches. Something certainly would seem wrong in images of a thin, tense, motherly woman; a buxom, rosy-cheeked, high-strung girl; or a young woman with the heroic proportions of Brunhilde who did exquisitely refined art work with the delicacy of Japanese paintings.[4] It should be noted that none of these combinations is impossible. They simply strike us as unlikely; we have not often seen or heard of qualities going together in such patterns.

In a later work Sheldon and Stevens reported a study in which components of physique were related to a large number of personal qualities ascertained through interviews.[5] The correlations with clusters of traits were very high, but the research design was not sufficiently protected from contamination of judgments, and other workers attempting to investigate the problem have found at most rather small correlations.[6] This is in accord with the idea that physique is simply one of a great many influences that enter into the sequential growth of personality. Being genetically determined, physique might conceivably be correlated with internal genetic factors having a direct effect on behavior: for example, qualities of nervous organization responsible for preferred styles of functioning. But until we have more telling evidence for such relations it is advisable to ascribe to physique only such effects on development as can be directly observed.

Physique and Personality

Physical constitution affects the growth of personality in two chief ways. It influences what a person can do, and thus affects the responses of others to his actions. It also is responsible for how he looks, and thus affects the reactions of others to his appearance.

On the side of doing, the mesomorphic component tends to produce strength, relatively high energy, and a liking for physical exertion and exercise. A predominantly mesomorphic male is likely to have a strong voice and a solid tread, and his handclasp will rate anywhere from firm to crushing. Physical labor, sports, and adventurous expeditions appeal to him, but sitting

[4] The scheme of the three components of physique applies also to the female body, except that the second or mesomorphic component is relatively less important and the first or endomorphic component more so. Sheldon's measurements have to do with the solid frame of the body and are not affected by fat deposits, which can vary a good deal at different periods of life.

[5] W. H. Sheldon and S. S. Stevens, *The Varieties of Temperament* (New York: Harper & Row, Publishers, 1942).

[6] Sheldon's work is summarized and evaluated by S. Diamond, *Personality and Temperament* (New York: Harper & Row, Publishers, 1957), pp. 138–150; and by H. G. McCurdy, *The Personal World* (New York: Harcourt Brace Jovanovich, 1961), pp. 318–331.

still creates an unpleasant restlessness, and he is apt to be both clumsy and impatient with things that require finely coordinated dexterity. Patience and relaxation are qualities more often associated with a predominantly endomorphic constitution. Physical comfort is more agreeable than exertion; sitting and talking is therefore a congenial way to spend time. This constitutional quality thus favors social interaction and may contribute to an eventual reputation for comfortable companionship. The ectomorphic component favors a pattern of action characterized by quick motion, alert vigilance, and dexterity, along with tendencies to become tense and to shrink from rough contacts. In these ways different physical constitutions go with different capabilities, with different patterns of things that one can do most adequately, comfortably, and naturally.

Three boys, each representing the predominance of one of the components, might be imagined to apply for jobs in a supermarket. They will be happiest if the mesomorph is assigned to wheeling out truckloads of goods to replenish the shelves, the endomorph to serve as even-tempered checker at one of the exits, and the ectomorph to dart from exit to exit putting the purchased articles deftly in paper bags. If the three go to the airport to meet a girl they all know, things will work out best if the girl asks the mesomorph to carry her bags, the endomorph to straighten out a misunderstanding about her ticket, and the ectomorph to repair the watch strap which broke while she was disembarking. Each of the boys could do any of these things, but each is likely to find one of them more congenial than the others. The respect that a person elicits from other people is closely bound up with what he can do, especially what he can do with natural ease and skill, and to this his physical endowment may make a significant contribution.

The other channel of influence, personal appearance and the social response to it, may well have its moments of greatest importance during adolescence.[7] A girl who has long been overweight, or a boy who has long understood that he looks like a plucked chicken, will experience these defects with a maximum of pain when the question arises of attractiveness to the other sex. Although tastes vary from culture to culture and even from time to time, it is likely to be clear at any given moment what bodily forms and facial features are esteemed most attractive and exciting, especially in a society that makes extensive use of physical beauty in advertising and entertainment. Beauty of face can occur with any bodily structure, but beauty of form is heavily weighted in favor of certain somatotypes. One has only to think of the physical types that appear in the movies only in comic roles or character parts. It is certainly possible in the American high school culture for a girl to believe that she is so fat or that she is so skinny, especially if her figure is not well developed, that no boy can possibly take a serious interest in her. Softly rounded boys and skinny boys can likewise easily assume that if a girl ever looks at them it must be out of pity. Physical defects or blemishes only

[7] C. B. Zachry, *Emotion and Conduct in Adolescence* (New York: Appleton-Century-Crofts, Inc., 1940).

increase the probability that one's body will be experienced as a thing of ugliness and inferiority, a cause of shame and a reason to be pessimistic about future happiness. Fortunately, human tastes are not all alike; fortunately, also, physical constitution is not everything.

Early and Late Maturity

The two kinds of influence on the development of personality—action and its consequences, appearance and its consequences—are illustrated in the problem of deviations from the average in the time of sexual maturation. A report by Bayley and Tuddenham in 1944, based on the California Adolescent Growth Study done at Berkeley, showed that early-maturing girls, big for their age, and late-maturing boys, small for their age, were especially likely to exhibit temporary problems of maladjustment.[8] The findings for boys were sustained by further research with the California subjects. Jones and Bayley showed that at the age of 16, late-maturing boys tended toward immaturity in social behavior, being less relaxed and matter-of-fact, more active and talkative in an attention-seeking sense, than a comparison group of early-maturing boys. Furthermore, on the basis of a reputation test it appeared that other adolescents viewed them in the same light, as attention-getting, restless, talkative, and bossy, as well as less attractive in appearance.[9] Carrying the research further, Mussen and Jones used tests of fantasy and deduced from these that late-maturing boys were more inclined to feel rejected and to think of themselves as inadequate.[10] This form of test disclosed one asset: "Fortunately for the late maturers' subsequent adjustments, they seem more willing to face their feelings and emotions." Finally Jones, in a follow-up study using early subjects who were now men of 33, showed by means of two standard personality tests that the qualities associated with adolescent late maturing had to some extent carried over into adulthood.[11] Although they had long since caught up in their physical development, the men who had once been late-maturers could still be described on the basis of their test responses as more inclined than the comparison group to be rebellious, touchy, impulsive, self-indulgent, and insightful, and as a group they had had more difficulty adapting to their vocations.

The original finding for girls has not been sustained by subsequent research with the California subjects. A later study by Weatherley, using different methods and different subjects at another time and place, confirms

---

[8] N. Bayley and R. Tuddenham, "Adolescent Changes in Body Build," *43rd Yearbook, National Society for the Study of Education* (1944), pp. 33–55.

[9] M. C. Jones and N. Bayley, "Physical Maturity among Boys as Related to Behavior," *Journal of Educational Psychology*, **41** (1950), 129–148.

[10] P. H. Mussen and M. C. Jones, "Self-Conceptions, Motivations, and Interpersonal Attitudes of Late- and Early-Maturing Boys," *Child Development*, **28** (1957), 243–256. The test of fantasy was the Murray-Morgan Thematic Apperception Test.

[11] M. C. Jones, "The Later Careers of Boys Who Were Early- or Late-Maturing," *Child Development,* **28** (1957), 113–128. The tests used were the California Psychological Inventory and the Edwards Personal Preference Schedule.

the main findings with respect to late-maturing boys but indicates that early maturing is not a problem for girls.[12] It is an interesting speculation, though nothing more, that during the 20 years from 1944 to 1964, attitudes toward sex became so much more favorable that an early blossoming by girls, once felt to be embarrassing if not alarming, turned into something more like an asset. The same trend, however, could offer no comfort to late-maturing boys.

In evaluating this research it is important to remember that the differences between groups were never large. Late sexual maturing in boys creates a push toward a cluster of traits centered around feelings of inadequacy and rejection, but it is not such a strong push that all late-maturers exhibit the traits, nor is this the only situation in life that is capable of encouraging them. It would be a bad mistake to infer that a person who had feelings of inferiority and rejection must have been once a late-maturing adolescent. Bearing in mind the limits of these findings, however, it is still possible to allow that in boys late sexual maturation can become an obstacle to the development of self-respect. On the side of action, there is the frequent circumstance of delayed growth spurt, so that one's friends leave one behind in size and strength. Along with this the friends show a sudden increase of interest in girls, an inclination that the late-maturer does not as yet discover in himself. As to appearance the rejection by others may be real enough: the mature boys and the girls easily think that their own earlier condition is a little inferior. Some of the late-maturers' traits are compensatory in character, as if the boy said, "I may be young and small but notice me anyway." And it is not to be overlooked that the patterns of behavior and feeling evolved in this crisis of physical constitution may outlast the original occasion and to some extent persist in later life.

Styles of Functioning

The second group of individual differences to be examined in this chapter, styles of functioning, does not lend itself easily to measurement or to division into clear-cut components. Physique is visible and measurable, but styles of functioning as exhibited in behavior offer obstacles both to measurement and to systematic thinking. This is not to imply that they are always subtle or difficult to observe. There can hardly be a plainer fact, as we shall soon see, than the difference between an active and a passive child. The trouble lies in deciding what dimensions are of truly fundamental importance. Individual differences that could be classed under styles of functioning are so numerous that they cannot be handled intelligibly without being reduced to a smaller number of basic dimensions or components. A number of proposals along this line have been made, but there is not as yet a system of nonoverlapping basic variables that commands widespread acceptance. One

---

[12] D. Weatherley, "Self-perceived Rate of Physical Maturation and Personality in Late Adolescence," *Child Development*, **35** (1964), 1197–1210.

can imagine a day when styles have been reduced to simple components such as speed, intensity, and lastingness of response, when differences can be detected and measured soon after birth, and when the stability of these measures over the course of life can be tested. That day has not come, and it is to be feared that organic systems are not put together along such simple lines. In the meantime we must struggle with variables that are overlapping and hard to measure.

The history of the subject has actually followed a different course, without much reference to origins in early life. A great deal of serious reflection and keen observation has been directed toward global qualities such as preferred ways of using one's mind or preferred styles of dealing with one's problems, and the findings have often been expressed in terms of discrete types rather than continuous dimensions. Speculative studies of this kind have generally been based on observation of sophisticated adults, less attention being paid to the early emergence of the traits in infants and young children. But the problems raised are so recurrently important in human affairs that they deserve notice in their own right.

Extraversion–Introversion

A landmark in this line of thought is Jung's book on psychological types.[13] It was in this work, as we saw in the first chapter, that Jung introduced the distinction between introverted and extraverted types. The two terms have passed into popular speech and have become the basis for self-rating questionnaires, but at least in the United States they have been thinned out to designate superficial attitudes rather than the deep differences of psychological functioning that Jung had in mind. Extraversion and introversion should not be used as if they meant sociable and unsociable. If this were all that was meant, there would be no need for the more technical terms.

In Jung's thinking, extraversion signified a predominant direction of interest toward objects external to the self: concrete things like a job to be done, a meeting to attend, or a trip to be taken. Introversion signified a predominant direction of interest toward subjective experience: the thoughts generated by the job, the feelings aroused by the meeting, the dreams awakened by the projected trip. This difference in direction of interests affects all aspects of life and betrays itself clearly in preferred ways of observing and thinking. Commenting on the differences between Plato, "an intellectual mystic, poetic, other-worldly," and Aristotle, "a physician and scientist, prosaic, this-worldly," McCurdy draws the following contrast:

> Even when they dealt with exactly the same topic, the result was different. For example, from Aristotle we learn that dreams are produced by stimulation of the sense organs and by memory of prior sensory experience, helped along by disturbed digestion, and are on the whole

[13] C. G. Jung, *Psychological Types, or the Psychology of Individuation* (1920), trans. H. G. Baynes (New York: Harcourt Brace Jovanovich, 1924).

> quite commonplace and insignificant; whereas, if we look at the matter as Plato did, we regard dreams as revelations of the depths of personality, visions of the evil and darkness below the surface of things, convulsions of the soul.[14]

Either way of experiencing has its assets and liabilities. An extreme extravert, according to Jung, can become "caught up in objects, wholly losing himself in their toils," and he may thoughtlessly accept conventional values just because they are there.[15] The introverted liability is in the opposite direction: a one-sided interest in the subjective aspects of experience may lead to distortion of how things really are in the outside world.

Jung's concepts of extraversion and introversion were defined in terms of direction of interest, but include cognitive styles. Murray, in an analysis that separates cognitive attitudes from evaluative ones and from social traits, describes the cognitive dimension as *extraception-intraception*.[16] This difference is of great contemporary interest as the spheres of the scientist and the humanist draw ever farther apart. The strongly extraceptive person, as Murray describes him, "perceives and understands the world as it affects his senses, particularly the sense of touch, hard substance being for him the ultimate fact." The strongly intraceptive person, "being chiefly influenced by psychic processes, perceives motility and behind motility the working of energies and directive forces." From this it follows that the extraceptive person "is at his best when dealing with inorganic matter"; the intraceptive, "when dealing with human emotions."[17] It is to be hoped that the twain will continue to meet and keep up an attempt at communication, but if they differ in their perception of the world, to say nothing of what they value, an easy harmony is not to be expected.

Extraversion and introversion might be described as big variables in the sense that they gather up in a single interpretation a considerable number of specific qualities or traits. But they are not merely impressionistic descriptions; there is impressive evidence that this dimension is a real and fundamental one in the organization of personality. This evidence is found in the work of H. J. Eysenck, which is based on a large number of tests given to a large number of people, the results being handled by the mathematical method of *factor analysis*. This method, when properly used, can be made to disclose significant patterns of correlation among test scores, the resulting clusters pointing to higher-order factors that are common to several tests. Under proper conditions it might enable one to perceive, for instance, that individual differences on thirty specific tests amounted in the main to differences with respect to two or three fundamental variables. Proceeding in this

[14] H. G. McCurdy, *The Personal World* (New York: Harcourt Brace Jovanovich, 1961), pp. 339, 340.

[15] Jung, *Psychological Types*, pp. 418, 420.

[16] H. A. Murray, *Explorations in Personality* (London and New York: Oxford University Press, 1938).

[17] Murray, *Explorations in Personality*, pp. 237–238.

fashion with a large variety of tests—ratings, questionnaires, objective tests of behavior, measures of physiological functions, measures of interests and attitudes—Eysenck has shown that a higher-order variable persistently emerges from the factorial analysis of each type of material, and he calls this variable extraversion-introversion.[18] Defined in terms of the tests used rather than by Jung's unsystematic though shrewd observations, extraversion-introversion undergoes some change of meaning, but it is still plausibly related to the original concept. Apparently this dimension is entitled to be considered a basic feature of the organization of personality. That it expresses differences in genetic endowment is not, of course, a safe deduction from research with adult subjects, but it is certainly not easy to understand extraversion-introversion as a pure consequence of experience without help from any initial proclivity.

It is something of a jump to think of measuring such a variable in the earliest months of life. Investigators of infancy have not used this formulation but have tried instead to discover what differences in styles of functioning can actually be observed in young children. Two detailed studies of this problem, one by Escalona based on direct observation of infants in Topeka, Kansas, and one by Thomas, Chess, and Birch using young children in New York City, make use of variables of a simpler kind.[19] In pursuing styles of functioning further we shall make a selection of relatively well-studied qualities, starting with activity level, which plays an important part in both the Topeka and the New York studies.

Activity Level

More than two centuries ago Rousseau set down the following observation: "One nature needs wings, another shackles; one has to be flattered, another suppressed."[20] He was referring partly to one of the most important and readily observable ways in which children differ, even before they are born: the level of activity. Mothers report great differences in the amount of "life" they feel during the last months of pregnancy, and these signs of fetal movement in the womb predict fairly well the level of the infant's activity after birth.

In 1935 a systematic study of activity level was begun by Margaret Fries, who started her observations with newborn infants.[21] Estimates were

[18] H. J. Eysenck, *The Structure of Human Personality* (London: Methuen & Co., Ltd., 3rd ed., 1970).

[19] S. K. Escalona, *The Roots of Individuality: Normal Patterns of Development in Infancy* (Chicago: Aldine Publishing Co., 1968); A. Thomas, S. Chess, H. G. Birch, M. E. Hertzig, and S. Korn, *Behavioral Individuality in Early Childhood* (New York: New York University Press, 1963).

[20] J. J. Rousseau, *La Nouvelle Héloise* (1760), Book V, p. 3.

[21] M. E. Fries, Psychosomatic Relationships Between Mother and Infant," *Psychosomatic Medicine*, **6** (1944), 159–162; M. E. Fries and P. J. Woolf, "Some Hypotheses on the Role of the Congenital Activity Types in Personality Development," *Psychoanalytic Study of the Child*, **8** (1953), 48–62.

based on the amount of motor activity shown in certain situations during the first ten days of life. It was possible to group the infants under five headings, which actually represent a continuum from the lowest to the highest activity. Most of them were classified under one of three headings considered to lie in the normal range—quiet, moderately active, and active. A few extreme instances at either end were given labels suggestive of pathology—hypoactive and hyperactive. Interestingly, Pavlov some years before had classified laboratory dogs on a similar dimension (inhibitory, quiet, lively, excitatory) and had shown that the different types performed differently under standard experimental conditions.[22] Human infants showed differences in feeding behavior, spontaneous motor activity, behavior during routine caretaking, and response to stimuli experimentally introduced. Quiet infants sucked with less vigor, occasionally dozed off during the feeding, lay peacefully wherever they were put, and made relatively small motor responses when startled. Active infants were more vigorous in their feeding, constantly moved their arms and legs, twisted and squirmed during diaper changes, kicked off the covers when in their cribs, and moved a good deal even when asleep. Differences in activity were found to be fairly stable when measured again in later months and were still in evidence at the end of five years.

Longitudinal studies by other workers confirm the impression that measures of activity in early life are at least somewhat predictive of later activity level. The Topeka infants studied by Escalona later became subjects in a longitudinal study directed by Lois Murphy. It was thus possible to arrange an experiment in prediction in which the early investigators had no knowledge of how the children, now between 3 and 5 years old, had been appraised by the later team of workers.[23] With respect to activity level the "blind" predictive statements, based on how the infants had behaved in their first thirty-two weeks, proved to be 67 percent correct. Two right guesses out of every three is not remarkable, but it is a good deal better than chance guessing. Another study, made by Kagan and Moss, covered a longer period of development, extending from birth to early maturity.[24] The subjects were children studied over this span of time at the Fels Institute at Yellow Springs, Ohio, as described above in Chapter 3. The authors were impressed by the stability of passive behavior during the childhood years:

> Intensive study of the observations on the school-age children who fell at the behavioral extremes of this dimension suggested that the tendency toward passivity during preadolescence was already apparent during the first two years of life. Passivity during the first three years was significantly associated with a consistent cluster of school-age behaviors (ages 6 to

---

[22] I. P. Pavlov, *Conditioned Reflexes and Psychiatry*, trans. W. H. Gantt (New York: International Publishers Co., Inc., 1941).

[23] S. K. Escalona and G. Heider, *Prediction and Outcome* (New York: Basic Books, Inc., 1959).

[24] J. Kagan and H. A. Moss, *Birth to Maturity* (New York: John Wiley & Sons, Inc., 1962), esp. Chaps. 3 and 9.

10): avoidance of dangerous activity, absence of physical and verbal aggression, conformity to parents, and timidity in social situations. Moreover, the boys who were passive during Period I avoided sports and other traditional masculine activities during the preadolescent and adolescent years. The four boys who were rated most passive during the first six years chose intellectual careers as adults (music, physics, biology, psychology). The four least passive boys chose more traditional masculine vocations (football coach, salesman, and two engineers).[25]

It was noticed, however, that in spite of striking continuity in extreme cases, the prediction of adult activity-passivity from the early years worked well only for girls, not for boys. Kagan and Moss interpret this difference to mean that with respect to passivity girls are allowed to go along much as they please, whereas boys are subjected to social pressure in the direction of activity as part of the masculine role. As a result many boys at school age struggle to counteract passive tendencies in themselves and do so with some success. These findings demonstrate both that initial proclivities tend to remain stable over the years and that they can be to some extent modified by strong motives and social expectations.

Activity level is measured in infancy by the amount and force of motor activity. It does not by itself reflect other qualities such as sensitivity or even intelligence. Quiet children may be quite as intelligent as active ones. Activity level signifies nothing more than the frequency and force of motor expression. Even in this restricted meaning, however, level of activity has far-reaching effects upon development. It immediately colors interactions with the mother, who cannot fail to be influenced by the character of the baby's response to her ministrations. Mothers are likely to enjoy feeding a baby who sucks with vigorous enthusiasm. It is hard not to feel a little downcast if the baby goes to sleep while being offered the gift of maternal nourishment. The active baby will seem at first more interesting and responsive and more fun to play with, and the mother may feel that his liveliness gives promise of successful development. But the advantages are not all on the side of activity. The quiet baby will be much easier to wash and dress and will put much less strain on maternal vigilance. When walking, manipulating, and exploring begin to ripen, a high activity level may suddenly seem to the parents to be the worst possible trait. They will heartily agree with Rousseau that some natures need shackles, and their attempts at control may lead to stormy relations. It is now the quiet or moderately active children who make pleasant companions and are fun to have around. Yet when the time comes for venturing out among other children, the parents may turn to the view that some natures need wings and try to force their children to become socially airborne. Activity level is bound, in the nature of the case, to have an important influence on parental attitudes, and this influence is likely to change during different periods of development.

Although not necessarily correlated with intelligence or adaptability,

[25] Kagan and Moss, *Birth to Maturity*, p. 79.

activity level has an influence on cognitive development. Active children explore their surroundings more thoroughly and try out more frequently their power to make things happen. In this way they seem to take more rapid steps toward self-sufficiency and mastery of the environment. Quiet children, on the other hand, tend to be observant: eyes and ears are frequently at work even when the large muscles are quiescent, and a knowledge of the surroundings may be stored up that escapes those who rush around. Fries drew a contrast between two little girls, one of whom "early began to overcome all possible obstacles by herself," gaining mastery through activity, whereas the other, rather quiet and slow, absorbed experience through visual and auditory channels and learned how much she could get done by influencing adults to help her.[26] Adaptation requires different things at different times. Some situations are best dealt with by prompt and abundant action; others require reflection and may be spoiled by haste. The child's characteristic level of activity may predispose him to specialize in one direction at the expense of the other.

Several points concerning activity level are illustrated by a brother and sister described in a study by Lois Murphy, the more strikingly because the two children reverse common expectations about sex differences.[27] Steve, the elder by two years, is described as soft, quiet, and easygoing; Sheila as robust, forthright, and forceful. These children, drawn from a group of average families in the Topeka study and well within the normal range of child behavior, had first been carefully studied at the age of four weeks, at which time their later styles were clearly foreshadowed:

> Sheila protested what she did not want; she terminated feeding decisively when she was finished; she demanded, and, as her mother later reported, "always" succeeded in getting what she wanted. Steve was by contrast a quiet, passive infant who, though he sucked efficiently, did not even withdraw his lips from the nipple when he had had enough, but let the milk dribble down his chin and chest. In both the positive and negative sense he was a child who tended to "take what comes" and this mode of response was expressed in the oral zone par excellence. He was never a go-getter. Sheila was sturdy, Steve was easily fatigued. . . . Throughout the ten to twelve years we have watched the two children, the decisiveness of Sheila, her firm stance, and her capacity to protest have continued to be characteristic, while Steve has continued to avoid conflict or direct encounter with opposition.

The study of these children included a careful investigation of their parents. In Steve and Sheila's family there was no convincing evidence that attitudes toward the two children had been radically different. The mother was fond of children, was generally permissive, had abundant milk, and

[26] Fries and Woolf, "Some Hypotheses on the Role of the Congenital Activity Types in Personality Development," p. 52.

[27] L. B. Murphy, *The Widening World of Childhood* (New York: Basic Books, Inc., 1962), pp. 322–326.

nursed both infants a long time. Apparently she made little attempt to tamper with their endowments; Steve and Sheila were allowed to take their natural course. Of the two, Steve was apparently the more contented. Sheila's assertiveness did not lead regularly to enjoyment; her face often wore a frown and her voice rose in protest over issues like being laid down after being held, situations that Steve could easily take in stride. Both children, as they developed, seemed to be capitalizing on their natural strengths. Steve continued to be peace-loving but showed perceptual gifts and an artistic sensitivity that at 12 years were already suggesting choice of career. Sheila's destiny at 10 was less clear, but few would hesitate to predict that she would be a force in her social orbit.

What happens when parental attitudes generate serious conflict with preferred temperamental style? An instructive contrast in this respect is given by Chess, Thomas, and Birch from their longitudinal study of middle-class parents and children in New York City.[28] The authors describe two highly active boys called Larry and David, alike in their propensity for energetic and rapid movement. As babies their arms and legs were never still, as toddlers they left no corner of the house unexplored, on the street they were constantly darting into danger, on the playground they quickly reached the top rung of the jungle gym, and when friends came to the house they entertained them by noisy running, leaping on furniture, and daring programs of acrobatics. Larry's parents were equal to this exhausting behavior. Good-humoredly referring to him as "the monster," often terrified for his safety, they nevertheless bore with his motor exuberance and patiently introduced rules only as he became able fully to grasp them. Relations between parents and child continued to be friendly, and Larry tried his best, often with small success, to contain his behavior within limits. David's parents were more bothered by "the streak of lightning they were harboring in their house." Frequently annoyed, they issued a stream of admonitions to sit still, stop running, and put things down that the boy was literally unable to obey. He could not distinguish clearly what was acceptable and what was forbidden, so he gave up trying to curb his actions. When he reached school his uncurbed behavior brought additional criticism from teachers and other children: "The more he was criticized, the bigger grew the chip on his shoulder." His parents desperately tried to discipline him by removing privileges such as TV, but he met these tactics by renouncing interest in whatever was taken away, a contraction that boded ill for his future growth. Thus David had progressively worse relations with his parents, became defiant, and gave up any attempt to modulate his extremely active constitutional endowment.[29]

In adult life the influence of early activity level is overlaid by the

[28] S. Chess, A. Thomas, and H. G. Birch, *Your Child Is a Person* (New York: The Viking Press, 1965), pp. 41–43.

[29] T. B. Brazelton, *Infants and Mothers: Differences in Development* (New York: Delacorte Press, 1970), gives profiles in depth of three very different babies—active, average, quiet—during the first year; all developed normally with characteristic pace and style.

effects of learning. Common experience indicates that circumstance and motivation strongly influence one's actual level of activity. Emergencies bring out unsuspected resources in everyone, and friends may scarcely recognize a person whose energy output has been elevated by a challenging and significant new job. Case studies sometimes disclose the opposite change: activity may fall off sharply if guilt or anxiety undergo an increase or if future prospects become discouraging. Yet in spite of this undeniable plasticity, there is evidence that constitutional activity level is still a live issue in adulthood. Often a young man who finds himself in a desk job experiences a primitive physical restlessness that can be set right only if he makes time for frequent "workouts." Often a young wife wonders at her exhaustion, not stopping to think that housework and child care, keeping her constantly on her feet, put a heavy toll on energy. It seems plain, moreover, that a variety of illnesses, including those called psychosomatic, arise from attempts to follow a pattern of life that one's constitutional endowment cannot support. Some jobs in contemporary society sound as if they had been designed for Larry and David and no one else—jobs typified by the man with the briefcase who is always boarding a plane, or by the appointment schedule so crowded that committee meetings have to be tucked in on Sunday mornings. When those who were quiet or moderately active babies try to fill such jobs their physicians will soon be telling them to slow down, take a vacation, stop burning the candle at both ends if they expect to keep their health. Other jobs may be too quiet for those who hold them; sometimes a change yields a striking improvement in health because the new work satisfies a craving to move about, expend energy, and assert oneself in a variety of situations. The art of living in accord with one's constitutional means is a subtle one. One can easily use the idea that one is "made that way" as an excuse for not trying or for failure. The only sure way to know is to try, but if this results in difficulties, one might at least consider the possibility that his constitutional limits are being exceeded.

Impulsion-Deliberation

A person who sought guidance from aphorisms would find it awkward to reconcile "Haste makes waste!" and "Look before you leap!" with "He who hesitates is lost!" He might well conclude that these pieces of advice should be reserved for different occasions, for it is certainly true that precipitous speech or action can be ruinous in some circumstances whereas in others delay may be fatal and quick action imperative. Yet it is easy to observe that a great many people have a fixed preference for one style or the other, regardless of circumstances. Haste makes waste except where he who hesitates is lost, but rare is the person who can always perfectly suit his speed to the occasion.

This dimension of style of functioning is called *impulsion-deliberation* by Murray, who describes as follows its manifestations in adult behavior.

> *Impulsion* is the tendency to respond quickly and without reflection. It is a rather coarse variable which includes: (1) short reaction time to

social press, (2) quick intuitive behavior, (3) emotional drivenness, (4) lack of forethought, (5) readiness to begin work without a carefully constructed plan. The subject is usually somewhat restless, quick to move, quick to make up his mind, quick to voice his opinion. He often says the first thing that comes into his head, and does not always consider the future consequences of his conduct.

Deliberation is easier to observe than Impulsion. It is marked by: (1) long reaction time to social press, (2) inhibition of initial impulses, (3) hesitation, caution, and reflection before action, (4) a long period of planning and organizing before beginning a piece of work. The subject may have obsessional doubts: a "load" of considerations which he must "lift" before beginning. He usually experiences difficulty in an emergency.[30]

This variable naturally appears in a simpler form in early childhood. We do not expect young children to take thought of the morrow or to be guided by long-range plans. Yet something resembling impulsion-deliberation constantly crops up in research on individual differences. Kagan, for instance, in studying problem solving in children in the early grades at school, noticed a dimension of preferred tempo that he characterized as *impulsivity-reflection*.[31] Kagan observed this difference in children to whom he presented problems with several response possibilities, asking them to select the best answer. The children who have what Kagan calls a "fast conceptual tempo" come out impulsively with the first solution that seems halfway appropriate, making numerous errors; the reflective children delay their replies until they have considered the alternatives, and make few errors. Habits acquired in school may play some part in this, but the difference still shows when research is pressed back into earlier years with tests of a simpler kind. A relation has been shown between reflectiveness at 6 years and long sustained play with toys at 2½ years.[32] A study by Reppucci using children 27 months old showed positive associations among several test situations: the children who qualified as reflective played longer with toys during free play periods, gazed longer at visual stimuli, and took longer in tasks characterized by uncertainty and conflict.[33] Conceptual tempo has early roots and seems to be plausibly an outcropping of the more general variable of impulsion-deliberation.

Further information on this variable comes from the research already mentioned by Thomas and others, who studied attention span in young chil-

[30] H. A. Murray, *Explorations in Personality* (New York: Oxford University Press, 1938), pp. 205–206.

[31] J. Kagan, "Information Processing in the Child," in *Readings in Child Development and Personality*, ed. P. H. Mussen, J. J. Conger, and J. Kagan (New York: Harper & Row, Publishers, 1965), pp. 313–323.

[32] F. A. Pedersen and P. H. Wender, "Early Social Correlates of Cognitive Functioning in Six-Year-Old Boys," *Child Development*, **39** (1968), 185–194.

[33] N. D. Reppucci, "Individual Differences in the Consideration of Information among Two-Year-Old Children," *Developmental Psychology*, **2** (1970), 240–246.

dren and noticed a wide range of differences with respect to distractibility and persistence.[34] The researchers estimated distractibility by noticing the ease with which the children's attention turned from the main activity of the moment. Some children sucked steadily at the bottle through thick and thin; others were likely to stop if the telephone rang or if someone came into the room. Similarly, handing a diverting toy to a crying child stopped some from crying more quickly than it did others. Persistence as a general trait was best estimated from situations like gazing at a cradle gym or working to get hold of a toy just out of reach. The infant who stared intently at the cradle gym for half an hour at a time was likely to be found a year later playing a long time with a single toy, whereas short attention span in the crib went with later flitting from one toy to another. As with all these variables, some children were rated in the middle; it is a question not of two distinct types but of a dimension along which individuals are spread.

The effect of these differences on interaction with parents depends importantly on the parents' understanding of the traits in question. Chess, Thomas, and Birch illustrate the point with two girls, both of whom were strongly persistent and nondistractible. One girl's parents were well accustomed to the trait, having themselves a marked capacity to become absorbed and even buried in what they were doing. They were pleased by their little girl's tenacity, appreciated her ability to amuse herself, and took calmly the occasional inconvenience of prying her away from a deep preoccupation that interfered with routines. The other parents seemed remarkably different from their daughter. Lively, expressive, and enthusiastic, they were puzzled by the child's solemn determination, her protracted work on jigsaw puzzles, her unsmiling struggle when only 3 to sew a button on a piece of cloth. They felt that she ought to be more relaxed and joyful, and they were frustrated by her lack of overt emotion, which they interpreted to mean that she was unsatisfied with the things they did for her. The little girl lost out in parental favor to her two more distractible but more responsive brothers and became in effect a rejected child.[35]

The individual differences in impulsion-deliberation that are so readily observable in adult life are of course no longer pure expressions of biological individuality. Endowment in this respect—the degree of deliberateness that is most natural and feels most comfortable—has by this time been open to a great deal of influence by experience and may have yielded somewhat to individual adaptive requirements. An impulsive style of functioning, as we shall see in a later chapter, can be developed into a strategic style of living. One can cultivate deliberateness in order to deal with situations in which care and reflection are clear assets. But in some persons impulsivity or deliberation holds its place so stubbornly, whether appropriate or not, as to suggest an endowment too strong to be altered. Teachers of graduate seminars are aware of the difference between students who leap into discussion with the first idea

[34] A. Thomas et al., *Behavioral Individuality in Early Childhood*, pp. 41–42.
[35] Chess, Thomas, and Birch, *Your Child Is a Person*, pp. 44–46.

that comes to mind and those who slowly disentangle their thoughts before taking an active part. Discontent can result from being in an occupation that calls for speeds of response and decision making that are at odds with one's natural style.

Sensitivity

The next dimension to be considered is less clear-cut than activity level and more ambiguous in definition than the impulsive-deliberative style of functioning. There is a widespread impression that children differ greatly in their natural sensitivity. Parents with several children can often easily designate the most sensitive member of their brood, sometimes also the least sensitive—the child whom nothing seems to bother. But when it comes to pinning down the meaning of sensitivity, and especially when it comes to devising measurements, there is serious lack of unanimity.

The simplest measure is sensory threshold: the level of stimulation required to elicit response. Babies clearly differ in this respect. Those with a high sensory threshold are not awakened easily or startled by loud sounds, are not bothered by strong light, seem little troubled by discomforts of temperature or clothing, and do not react with distress to being soiled or wet. Other babies seem to experience pleasure, discomfort, and pain from their surroundings on much slighter provocation. Individual differences of this kind have been measured as early as the first five days of life. In a study by Birns, four controlled stimuli were applied during these days—a soft tone, a loud tone, a cold disk, and a pacifier—and measurements were made of the intensity of response. Already the 30 babies could be differentiated. Some responded strongly, some moderately, some mildly, these differences being relatively consistent for all four types of stimulation and relatively stable from the second to the fifth day.[36] Differences in responsiveness to stimulation clearly make an early start.

This kind of responsiveness does not, of course, include all that is usually implied by sensitivity. An older child or adult may be called sensitive because he responds strongly to natural beauty or to works of art. In the social sphere a person may be considered sensitive because he readily understands the feelings of others or, in a different meaning, because his own feelings are easily hurt. These more complex meanings suggest general qualities of responsiveness that go beyond the thresholds of sense organs. At the same time they spread out so broadly as to weaken the assumption that a single dimension is involved. Thus far the tendency in research has been to work with a meaning that sticks fairly closely to response to sensory stimulation. Restricted in this way, individual differences in sensitivity appear to be somewhat stable over time. In the study by Escalona and Heider already described, in which predictions were made from observations during the first 32 weeks

---

[36] B. Birns, "Individual Differences in Human Neonates' Responses to Stimulation," *Child Development,* **36** (1965), 249–256.

to behavior at 3 years, predictive statements with respect to the variable called "perceptual sensitivity" were correct 70 percent of the time.[37]

The sensitive end of this dimension is illustrated in a study by Bergman and Escalona.[38] The observations were based roughly on level of sensory threshold, and in the cases described a low threshold seemed to exist for all sensory modalities. Thus the extremely sensitive infant was fearful of loud sound, oversensitive to light, and easily hurt. One of the young children, when being taken in the car at night, ducked and turned away whenever the headlights of an approaching car appeared. Another was much disturbed by loud music. The good side of the picture showed itself with respect to enjoyment: moderate stimulation often produced signs of great pleasure and delight. The child who disliked loud music was enchanted by quiet music and always touched the piano keys gently, in striking contrast to the average toddler's preference for muscular fortissimo. A girl of 10 months "almost leaped out of her mother's arms when she saw some red flowers," and the touch of velvet put her into paroxysms of joyful laughter. Enviable as the capacity for intense enjoyment may be, in these children it was carried to a fault. Their sensitivity was so extreme and their distractibility so great as to constitute a handicap to development in an average environment.

Temperament

Variations in mood have always occupied a large place in discussions of individual differences. To some extent, moods can be seen as appropriate accompaniments of one's actual situation. If we are happy when blessed with good fortune and success, or if we are depressed after losses and failures, the connection seems so natural that we do not easily regard it as a psychological problem. But down through the ages it has been observed that mood is not always so responsive to circumstances. It seems to enjoy a certain autonomy, as if governed by internal processes with laws of their own, and its influence can sometimes be so strong as to color every aspect of experience, including one's perception of the world.

Among the earliest recognized forms of mental disorder were mania and melancholia, the former characterized by a highly elated mood, the latter by a severely depressed one. In patients so afflicted it was difficult to discern a connection between mood and events. The affective state seemed to be altogether excessive and in some instances wholly inappropriate, as when a manic state followed directly upon a great personal loss. There were also instances in which depression occurred at regular intervals regardless of events, as if controlled by an internal biochemical cycle. So frequent were cases in which one extreme mood abruptly succeeded the other that the whole group

[37] Escalona and Heider, *Prediction and Outcome*, pp. 255–256.
[38] P. Bergman and S. K. Escalona, "Unusual Sensitivities in Very Young Children," *Psychoanalytic Study of the Child*, 3/4 (1949), 333–352.

of mood disorders came to be designated as manic-depressive psychosis. A genetic predisposition was suggested by statistical evidence of a tendency for this disorder to run in families.

It is possible to measure something like mood in very young children. A study by Washburn records the development of smiling and laughing during the first year of life.[39] Observing 15 babies closely, Washburn found it not at all difficult to make a fourfold classification: those in whom crying predominated over smiling, those in whom smiling took the lead over crying, those in whom both responses occurred with high frequency, and those in whom both responses were of infrequent occurrence. The infants remained true to type through the first year of life, which strongly suggests differences in temperamental proclivity. The ratio of happy expressions—cooing, gurgling, smiling, laughing—to unhappy ones—fussing, crying, sobbing—has proved to be useful in subsequent research as a means of rating infants on a variable of *positive versus negative mood*. Washburn's "expressive" group, showing many feelings both positive and negative, suggests a second dimension, which can be called *stable versus variable mood*.

Positive versus Negative Mood

It is not difficult to imagine the effects of a prevailingly happy or unhappy mood on the interaction between infants and their parents. Most parents, even those who are most convinced that life later on is sober, hard, and disappointing, prefer that children should be happy and are favorably influenced by contented gurgles and bursts of hilarity. A happy infant is thus likely to move his parents toward acceptance on the acceptance-rejection axis, and he may considerably mitigate high control in parents so disposed. The effect on the household is quite different when the prevailing sounds from the nursery are those of fussing and complaint. In the long run such sounds can build up a substantial amount of worry, irritation, and feeling of incompetence on the part of the parents. As a result of these effects it may well be that conspicuously happy babies grow more happy, their temperamental proclivity being strengthened by the delight they evoke, whereas the early grumblers produce results that give them more to grumble about. This vision of the rich growing richer and the poor growing poorer is softened by the recollection that with respect to positive and negative mood the majority of infants are located in the middle.

In a study of positive and negative moods in college students, Wessman and Ricks called upon their subjects to make a record of affective experience every day for a six-week period.[40] Each evening, subjects marked a set of "personal feeling scales." These scales "covered such important affective dimensions as elation-depression, energy-fatigue, tranquillity-anxiety, har-

---

[39] R. W. Washburn, "A Study of the Smiling and Laughing of Infants in the First Year of Life," *Genetic Psychology Monographs*, 6 (1929), 397–537.

[40] A. E. Wessman and D. F. Ricks, *Mood and Personality* (New York: Holt, Rinehart and Winston, Inc., 1966).

mony-anger, and sociability-withdrawal, and feelings regarding such matters as love and sex, and work." Subjects were asked to indicate the highest and lowest points they had reached on each scale during the course of the day. From the averages of these self-ratings it was possible to derive scores that placed the subjects on a dimension of happiness-unhappiness, a complex version, perhaps, of what infants portray in the ratio of smiling and crying. In the college men and women, mood was sewn into a rich fabric of life, some of which was disclosed by intensive concurrent studies of personality. Mood at this age was no longer sufficiently described just in terms of feeling; it carried additional connotations, such as the fullness or emptiness of the world or the size of the felt gap between actual self and ideal self.

With a group of 18 men for whom life history information was abundant, Wessman and Ricks summarized the difference between the happier and the less happy subjects and looked for possible origins of these differences. With respect to both college work and interpersonal relations the happy men were more optimistic, self-confident, and genuinely successful. In their studies they found continuity and meaning, in their relations with other people a constant source of interest and satisfaction. The unhappy men, in contrast, found more that was irksome than rewarding in their studies and more tension than pleasure in social life, from which they were often tempted to withdraw. Looking back over the histories, the investigators saw, as one would anticipate, much individuality of pattern, but certain generalizations could be made. The currently happy men appeared to have had "warm and supportive home environments that were conducive to growth and the gradual development and assumption of responsibilities." They had been able to identify with respected models, and they had moved with little friction into the wider environment of school and peer groups. The currently unhappy men were more likely to give histories of parental conflict, to be cynical about the models of behavior to which they had been exposed, and to describe hampering timidities in human relations during their school years.[41]

If these young men had begun their lives as subjects in a longitudinal study it would be possible to say whether or not the happy men of today were the gurgling, smiling babies of yesteryear. In view of all that can happen in twenty years one would hardly expect to find a perfect relation. The moods described in this study tend to be appropriate reflections of successful involvement in both academic and social spheres, which makes it impossible to estimate the extent, if any, to which mood level influenced the success in the first place. Furthermore, when information about childhood has to be derived from the subjects' own reports there is danger that present mood will color the recollection of the past. It is a matter of common experience that when feeling successful we take a more generous view of past family life than we do when burdened by frustration and failure. Yet it is fair to say that at any age a cheerful disposition tends to evoke amiability in one's environment, and that if one starts out as a naturally cheerful baby the environment

---

[41] *Ibid.*, esp. Chaps. 2 and 6. The contrasts are illustrated by two case studies.

will be gently pressed toward favorable response. Such pressure may not be sufficient to produce perceptible results when the environment is heavy with troubles and hostility, but under more favorable conditions it may well leave its mark.

Stable versus Variable Mood

People of relatively stable mood, who feel pretty much the same from day to day unless something very unusual happens, are apt to suppose that theirs is the normal condition and that strong experiences of mood are a little pathological. Others, more labile in their affective life but by no means emotionally disordered, testify to the importance of mood in all aspects of their experience. Following is an excerpt from a diary kept by a young man while he was in college. Mood fluctuations such as he describes occurred from day to day, sometimes even in the course of a day, in this student's life.

> Sometimes I feel that life is zestful, I am young with much before me, and the world is good. Sometimes I feel that the world is empty, a mockery, a tale told by an idiot, with no purpose, or reason, or end. When I feel bad I cannot imagine the arguments that could be advanced for feeling good, and when I feel good I cannot imagine feeling any other way. . . .
>   I think the thing that characterizes these wonderful seizures most is the tremendous abounding *interest*, fascination with the world, my mind running from one thing to another provoking thing, suddenly magic. . . . I want to read by the volume. I can stare at a wall or a sunset and think and think, my mind on fire. . . . My mind seems to bore through any problem, to run out in all directions at once.
>   [On bad days] I am tight, nervous, with heart beating hard, worried, ill-at-ease, prone to mistakes, afraid of fear, undirected, trying to fool myself . . . lousy, small, failing and incompetent . . . slow and inefficient . . . no matter what I try it will sooner or later go bad. . . . I want to shut out the world. When I feel glum I want to be alone. I feel sad, listless, morose, sort of what's the use.[42]

A dimension of mood running from stable to variable can be observed, as we have seen, during the first year of life. It becomes more apparent in the course of time, when the child of stable mood, be it cheerful or glum, clearly differs from one in whom there are mercurial changes of weather. The effect of these mood patterns on the household will be much affected by the parents' own experience of mood. The stable child has the advantage of predictability; the parents know what to expect from day to day and will be less often bewildered by unexpected emotional responses. The child of variable mood tends to keep the parents off balance, but if enough of the expressions are happy the child may be esteemed as colorful and interest-

[42] *Ibid.,* pp. 74–76.

ing. This dimension of mood may also have an effect on the patterning of the child's experience. When mood is highly variable, when today's experience is colored very differently from yesterday's, a sense of the continuity of existence may be more difficult to establish. The student's diary just quoted shows how hard it may be to think of things in any other way than that dictated by a strong present mood. Thus instability of mood may be conducive to instability of cognition and of self-perception.

In a study for which college women served as subjects, Wessman, Ricks, and Tyl investigated the relation between mood fluctuation and self-concept.[43] The "personal feeling scales" filled out every day provided measures of both average level and fluctuations of mood. The subjects were also handed self-rating tests to be filled out twice, once when mood was at its best and once when it was at its worst. These tests consisted of statements, printed on cards, describing a large variety of personal qualities. Using what is called the Q-sort method, the subject's task was to sort the cards into seven piles ranging from "—3, least characteristic," through "0," to "+3, most characteristic." On each occasion the Q-sorts were made twice, once "to give the most accurate picture of yourself as you really believe you are now" (self-concept), and once "to give a picture of yourself as the kind of person you have hoped to become or have fancied yourself to be; the picture you describe should be the personal ideal for you" (ideal concept). Comparing the "elated" with the "depressed" Q-sort descriptions for each subject, the ideal concept of self underwent relatively little change, but the concept of actual self became much less favorable when mood was low. This had the effect of increasing the discrepancy between what one was and what one would like to be. Moreover, those young women whose daily "personal feeling scales" showed a relatively high frequency and intensity of mood swings were also those with the most marked instability of the self-concept. Fluctuation of mood went with fluctuation of self-concept; the attainment of a stable sense of self is inherently more difficult for those who are given to large mood variability.

Even in a relatively homogeneous population such as a group of college men or college women there are large individual differences in mood variability. The behavior and experience of a highly stable person differ greatly from those of a highly variable one. It is not plausible that such widely different mood patterns are simply appropriate responses to different surroundings. Mood variability has internal determinants that color the way the environment is interpreted. Most people, even the essentially stable, have enough daily rhythm to know the difference in outlook between their mentally fresh and mentally fatigued states. Most women have experienced fluctuations of mood in connection with the menstrual cycle. Mood comes partly from within, and it enjoys a certain autonomous influence upon the course of life.

[43] A. E. Wessman, D. F. Ricks, and M. McI. Tyl, "Characteristics and Concomitants of Mood Fluctuation in College Women," *Journal of Abnormal and Social Psychology*, **60** (1960), 117–126.

It does not necessarily follow that mood variability is a direct consequence of a temperamental trait observable in the early months and consistent
thereafter. Studies begun at college age have not thrown clear light on the
developmental side of the problem.[44] As with positive and negative mood,
one would expect the intervening history to have some shaping effect on
whatever exists at the beginning in the way of innate proclivity. There is,
nevertheless, persistent evidence for the relative permanence of characteristics
that correspond to the dimension of mood described here. Something very
like it repeatedly appears in studies based on the factor analysis of large
numbers of test scores.[45] Individual differences cannot be fully understood
without it.

Conclusion

For those who want facts to be nicely ordered with clear-cut definitions in consistent theoretical systems, the study of individual differences in
constitution and temperament is something less than a paradise. To be sure,
the formal definition of these qualities as unlearned proclivities is logically
sharp, but this sharpness is hard to carry over into observation. Even when
young children are chosen as subjects, the effects of experience cannot be
wholly excluded; observable consistent differences may already have been
affected by subtle differences in parental care. Physical constitution alone
lends itself to uncontaminated measurement. Styles of functioning and variables of temperament never present themselves in pure form; their existence
has to be inferred from such signs as early manifestation, stability over time,
and a consistent slanting of experience. Further frustration for tidy thinking
lies in the difficulty of reaching certainty with respect to basic dimensions
or variables. Not all the dimensions described in this chapter have an air of
finality. Especially the different styles of functioning, even those that have
been most extensively studied, are not clearly independent of one another and
must be suspected of overlapping. The careful devising of tests and the application of mathematical methods like factor analysis, as in the work of
Eysenck and of Cattell, are paths toward progress in this respect; long-range
longitudinal studies would be even more informative. But anything like finality appears to be a long way ahead. With regard to natural endowment we
cannot suppose that we have yet gotten to the bottom of it.

In spite of this lack of sharpness, however, differences of constitution
and temperament cannot be dismissed as of no account. Observation of infants and young children shows individuality well beyond what can plausibly

[44] Two studies of college women, the one by Wessman, Ricks, and Tyl, the
other by J. Becker and C. H. Nichols, "Communality of Manic-Depressive and 'Mild'
Cyclothymic Characteristics," *Journal of Abnormal and Social Psychology*, **69** (1964),
531–538, appear to have contradictory implications in this respect.

[45] R. B. Cattell and J. R. Beloff, "Research Origins and Construction of the
IPAT Junior Personality Quiz," *Journal of Consulting Psychology*, **17** (1953), 436–442;
R. B. Cattell, *Personality and Motivation: Structure and Measurement* (New York:
Harcourt Brace Jovanovich, 1957).

be laid to differences of experience. Physical constitution is in large part a genetic endowment, which can have an important influence at various stages of the growth of personality. Styles of functioning such as activity level, impulsion-deliberation, and sensitivity, and variables of temperament such as the quality and stability of mood, can be reliably estimated in the early months of life and then predicted with better than chance success up to 3, 5, and occasionally more years. Careful observation of adult behavior discloses differences like Jung's extraversion-introversion that ramify so widely through behavior and experience as to suggest deeply placed variations in biological organization. Results to date are only a beginning of what might be accomplished in longitudinal studies planned to shed light on the genetic aspect of personality.

Individual differences in constitution and temperament have been discussed at this point in the book, directly after the social roots of personality, in order to clarify the part they play in development. Basically, their influence consists of a gentle persistent slanting of experience that gives what might be called a coloration to the traits that are acquired through learning. Stating it another way, they weight the learning process in certain directions, increasing the probability that certain kinds of behavior will be well learned and other kinds less well learned but by no means insuring this result. It is therefore important to place them at once in the earliest setting in which learning goes on, the family, and to consider their probable effects on interactions with parents, brothers, sisters, and other relatives. If parents apply standard methods of child rearing, the child soon proves to them that he is not a standard article but an individual who responds to their ministrations in his own way. This tends to change the character of the ministrations; thus the child affects the attitudes by which he, in turn, is affected. A newborn infant starts at once to give his behavior a personal stamp. Helpless as he may seem, he is already capable of "doing his own thing," and it is his own because it is a property of his unique biological endowment.

Surprising as it may seem in view of the badly tainted political history of notions about heredity, recognition of biological individuality can be regarded as a step in developing respect for other people. The personal stamp that every infant gives to his behavior has its effect on the parents and challenges the illusion, if they harbor it, that they are omnipotent stimuli in complete control of the baby's responses. Parents who have been seasoned by bringing up several children can sometimes describe precisely what they could and could not do in dealing with each child. Respect for individuality and a willingness to cultivate it is of substantial advantage to society. Only a narrow-minded autocracy wants its citizens to be all alike. As Aldous Huxley expressed it, "Physically and mentally, each one of us is unique. Any culture which, in the interests of efficiency or in the name of some political or religious dogma, seeks to standardize the human individual, commits an outrage against man's biological nature."

Knowledge about individual differences in constitution and temperament has important practical applications. These can be indicated in a single question that arises in many connections: What proportion of effort should be allotted to building up one's strengths and what proportion to overcoming one's deficiencies? The question recurs again and again in the course of life. It is asked by parents in bringing up their children, by teachers in dealing with their pupils, and by guidance counselors whose clients are trying to direct their lives wisely. It is asked by people about themselves when they must make important decisions or when strains develop in the conduct of life. The question cannot always be answered in the same way; the proportions cannot always be the same. Social living and practical management both make certain basic demands that every normal child should meet, the price of failure being an isolation from others and an impracticality in dealing with the environment that severely handicap further development. Some qualities and inclinations are worth overcoming even when doing so is painfully diffi-cult and uncongenial. But in other spheres the path of wisdom may be to develop one's strengths, to cultivate one's best talents, and to listen closely to promptings from within. When one's own inclinations and interests declare themselves strongly, it may be better to follow their lead even if it means failing to become a well-rounded personality.

Finally there is the question already raised about living within one's constitutional and temperamental means. Much personal unhappiness and even ill health results from trying to do a job or fill a role that is badly out of harmony with one's mood characteristics and preferred styles of functioning. Unfortunate chains of circumstances may place a person of slightly depressed mood in a job of sales promotion, cast a ruminative introvert as a cruise direc-tor, tie a former athlete to a desk job, plant an impulsive girl behind a calcu-lating machine, and put someone who is never relaxed with strangers in the task of interviewing strangers eight hours a day. Positions and roles are de-fined by external requirements—by the job that has to be done. If there is a bad mismatch between these external requirements and the individual's in-ternal requirements, the job can be done well only at painful personal cost. This cost may show itself in boredom and discontent, in tension and anxiety, in a consuming need for the relief provided by weekends and vacations, and in grievous low spirits when it is necessary to return to the grind. Such states of mind are not conducive either to continuing good performance or to con-tinuing good health.

In the absence of adequate ways of assessing the strengths and limi-tations that have their beginnings in constitutional endowment, judgments have to be arrived at through personal experience. It is easy to make natural endowment a scapegoat for failure and for laziness, or to lean upon it as an excuse for not attempting things that awaken anxiety. When a person says with a shrug that he is "just made that way," we are entitled to wonder whether or not he has put his nature to sufficiently rigorous tests. On the other hand, it is easy for a person to believe that he can do anything that anyone else can do and that he is a failure if he cannot keep up. This may lead to driving oneself in uncongenial directions to the point of breakdown, physical or emotional. How to live in tune with one's natural proclivities is part of the art of living that stands to benefit substantially from further well-designed research.

8 Dependence and Attachment in Infancy

In this chapter we begin to describe in a relatively systematic way the course and crises of the growth of personality. To do so is valuable in its own right for those who want to improve their understanding of children during each period of life. Whether it is equally valuable for understanding the adult personality is a matter of persisting controversy. As was pointed out in the first chapter, the leading lines of investigation that have influenced the current study of personality—the experimental study of behavior, the clinical study of psychological disorders, and the comparative study of societies— have all converged on the idea that what is learned in early childhood is highly significant for all later development. It has been argued that the main lines of personality are firmly set by the age of 5 and that later changes are bound to be slight and superficial. But it has also been argued that real change occurs in later life, as situations change and fresh learning takes place. This question cannot be settled easily. We should keep it in mind, though, as we ponder the beginnings of personality in childhood.

The Mammalian System of Care

Dependent tendencies are not the product of a single drive. They are a necessary accompaniment of the mammalian system of reproduction whereby the young are born relatively helpless and in need of prolonged care. The fact of dependence is obvious in a creature born with so little power of manipulation and locomotion as the human infant, a creature that needs some fourteen years to attain adult size and capability. Dependent tendencies arise from helplessness, but the human animal also develops strong feelings and important attitudes toward the objects on whom it depends.

In view of the child's actual helplessness it can be considered a biological advantage that he has a large capacity to become lovingly attached to his caretakers. The infant's repertory of behavior, inadequate as it is at first to influence physical realities, contains a number of items that tend to galvanize the caretakers into helpful action. There is of course the cry of distress, a sound that seems to be primitively disturbing to any adult hearer. There is also the smile, which is likely to melt the hardest adult heart. Clinging, nestling, reaching, playful vocalizing and laughing, all products of strong positive affect, elicit from the caretakers the nurturant feelings and the services that promote the child's well-being. Loving dependence on one side and loving care on the other seem to create the perfect reciprocal arrangement for the early stages of growth, laying a foundation for all that is to come.

There is an important liability in the otherwise desirable meshing of dependent and nurturant needs. The situation is going to change. The child will become progressively less dependent; his ties with others will have to move toward equality of giving and taking, and beyond that to his becoming himself a caretaker. For these developments the dependent tendencies are no longer appropriate, and to the extent that they are not replaced by other strivings they may act as a hindrance to further growth. Although it is usual to say that a child loves a nurturant parent, this love is not the same as what will be needed in an adult love relation. The dependent infant expects an enormous return for his few small signals of distress or affection. Food, comfort, entertainment, stimulation all come from the caretaker, the child's executive agent whose services he can command by pathetic appeals or seductive charm. An adult with an infant's dependency would be a self-centered autocrat who expects everyone to jump to his bidding. Few are the friends or spouses who are willing to play the parent's part for any other adult.

The problem of adult dependency has sometimes bred the conception that dependence is a necessary evil that should be discouraged as early as possible in the young. Seen in more tolerant fashion, however, dependence is the natural and appropriate condition of infancy, and the strengthening of attachment during the first year of life may well be considered a constructive aspect of growth. Common to several schools of thought is the idea that deprivation of maternal care has extensive consequences that are often disastrous for later development, and that a strong relation between mother and infant is vital for healthy growth. But this view of the matter is not universal. In societies with a less individualistic tradition, notably Russia and the communal farming communities of Israel, group care is considered more desirable than maternal care. The issues thus raised are important both practically and theoretically.

The Tie with the Mother

The outstanding feature of an infant's environment in a family is the primary caretaker, in most cases the actual mother. Her prominence comes from her being the chief agent in reducing need-tensions, removing discomforts, and providing gratifications. It is not to be supposed that the young infant understands the situation in just this light. Absence of the mother is not a signal for anxiety until the child has had six months or so to make some order out of the perceptual world; until then, anyone will do who provides the usual services in the usual ways. In the course of time, a relation between infant and mother evolves, the nature of which deserves careful consideration.

Nature of the Tie

The most striking service the mother provides is nourishment. Well-fed adults who always know where the next meal is coming from may have to stretch their imaginations—or, better, observe babies in action—to appreciate the primitive force of hunger, the distress that accompanies its frustration, and the delight that goes with feeding. For at least the first eight months the eagerness for feeding and the evident pleasure that accompanies it give the impression that it is the infant's outstanding affective experience. The mother as the provider is thus the source of great rewards upon which a strong tie can be established. Her position as reducer of the hunger drive is a commanding one.

Evident as this seems, it was not the central idea in Freud's conception of orality. According to psychoanalytic theory the oral zone during infancy is the chief locus of libidinal excitability. The lips are highly sensitive, and their contact with the nipple is supposed to yield libidinal pleasure independent of the satisfaction of hunger. Evidence for this contention is found in thumb-sucking, which may occur in replete infants, as if the hunger of the lips for pleasurable stimulation outlasted the hunger of the stomach for food. Experiments with bottle-raised puppies were done to show that those who were fed through large, freely flowing nipples showed more of the canine equivalents of thumb-sucking—sucking the experimenter's finger, each other's ears, and so on—than those who exhausted their oral libido as well as their hunger by long labored work on nipples with niggardly apertures.[1] There seems to be little doubt that the lips provide independent pleasure even if one does not assume, as Freud did, that this particular pleasure is the paramount influence on the course of development.

The nature of the tie between infant and mother has been given a somewhat more complex interpretation by Bowlby.[2] In addition to feeding and the seeking of oral pleasure, the infant has certain other tendencies that play their part in the making of a strong dependent relation. One of these is clinging, a pattern that was undoubtedly of great survival value in man's arboreal ancestors but which serves the present human species more as a warm pleasure that invites an answering embrace. Another is crying; we have

[1] D. M. Levy, "Experiments on the Sucking Reflex and Social Behavior in Dogs," *American Journal of Orthopsychiatry*, **4** (1934), 203–224.
[2] J. Bowlby, "The Nature of the Child's Tie to His Mother," *International Journal of Psycho-Analysis*, **39** (1958), 350–369.

already commented on the power of a child's cry to disturb listeners and stimulate action to relieve his distress. A third tendency is smiling, and we can again test the primitive effectiveness of this stimulus by trying to remain deadpan when smiled at by a baby. Bowlby summarizes as follows:

> It is my thesis that, as in the young of other species, there matures in the early months of life of the human infant a complex and nicely balanced equipment of instinctual responses, the function of which is to ensure that he obtains parental care sufficient for his survival. To this end the equipment includes responses which promote his close proximity to a parent and responses which evoke parental activity.

All these tendencies, then, contribute to a relation that soon becomes central in the early growth of personality.

Significance of the Mother-Child Relation for Development

The infant's relation with the mother can be supposed to establish several patterns of lasting significance. Her *provision* of the necessities of life gives the child his first experiences with the gratification of basic needs. She is the chief regulator of his *security*, enabling him to form his first crude estimates of the balance he must expect between serenity and anxiety. The relation is *social*, and it therefore provides the child's first experiences bearing on attitudes toward other people. It is an *intimate* relation involving both love and hate, which makes it the first chapter in a person's history of relations with love objects. It is a relation of *mutuality*, in which the child takes some of the initiative; thus it gives him early experience of competence or lack of it.

Freud's emphasis on the oral zone led to the conception of oral character types. One of these patterns, called "oral dependent" or "passive receptive," was presumed to result from highly satisfactory feeding experience leading the adult to expect abundant provision without much effort. Another pattern, which might be described as "demanding dependence," had its origin in feeding frustrations, including those connected with weaning, in which the infant forced provision out of a reluctant mother by violent sucking, biting, or vigorous vocal protest. It became a part of psychoanalytic theory that the attitudes thus formed would continue to influence not only social behavior but also general expectations of life. Satisfactory oral experience laid the ground for an optimistic outlook. The world's pessimists, on the other hand, were recruited from those whose nursing histories were full of frustration, disappointment, and anxiety.[3]

---

[3] The oral stage was first described by S. Freud, "Three Contributions to the Theory of Sex" (1905), in *The Basic Writings of Sigmund Freud* (New York: The Modern Library, 1938); the concept was developed by K. Abraham in "The First Pregenital Stage of the Libido" (1916), published in K. Abraham, *Selected Papers on Psychoanalysis* (London: Hogarth Press, Ltd., 1927).

The place occupied by the mother-child relation in the infant's sense of security has been described with especial care by Sullivan.[4] According to this observer, the chief source of anxiety in the infant is anxiety in the mother. The infant is fairly well protected from the external dangers that may affright him when he is a little older, but he is not protected from anxiety and its consequences in his chief caretaker. It was Sullivan's opinion that maternal anxiety is transmitted to the infant by an empathic process and that it interferes gravely with normal pleasurable functioning in both mother and child. Anxiety might first interfere with the mother's own tenderness and mothering skills, and thus would spoil things for the infant; feeding from an anxious mother is simply not the usual good experience. When the mother senses the child's disturbance, her own upset is increased, setting up a circular process of mounting tension. The infant, having few other resources, may finally deal with his own rising tension by becoming apathetic and somnolent, a reaction that dampens both his frustrated needs and his anxiety. Sullivan saw in the apathetic reaction an ominous prototype of schizophrenic withdrawal in later life. The mother's anxieties may be wholly extraneous, having to do with troubles in her adult world, but they may also be connected with aspects of her maternal duties, taking the form, for instance, of obsessively strong concern about feeding or cleanliness. Children are likely to show disturbance in the development of the function about which the mother worries, and such disturbance may be seen as a possible root of psychosomatic disorders in later life.

Dollard and Miller made an analysis of the feeding situation of a somewhat different sort, based on reinforcement learning theory.[5] Their emphasis falls particularly on the social learning that occurs in this situation. The basis of sociability, of liking to be with others, can be experiences of happy feeding, loving care, and play, the pleasantness of which easily becomes attached to the person providing the gratifications. "Since the mother or caretaker stands at the very head of the parade of persons who become 'society' for the child, it is very important that she evoke such benign and positive responses." The opposite result, a generalized dislike of human company, would be expected if feeding were the occasion of frustration and apprehensiveness, or if the mother forced food on the child when he was already replete. Dollard and Miller point out an additional social pattern that can become established if parents allow their baby's hunger to mount without responding to him, until it produces acute anxiety. The highly negative affects of hunger and anxiety may become so strongly attached to the absence of human company that the child develops a fear of being alone. If this fear persists in adult life, the person cannot tolerate solitude and is compulsively driven into social contacts.

[4] H. S. Sullivan, *The Interpersonal Theory of Psychiatry* (New York: W. W. Norton & Company, Inc., 1953).

[5] J. Dollard and N. E. Miller, *Personality and Psychotherapy* (New York: McGraw-Hill Book Company, 1950), Chap. 10.

The mutuality of the relation of infant and mother is most fully recognized in Erikson's account of the first year. He chooses "trust" and "mistrust" as the words best suited to express what the infant is learning.

> For the first component of a healthy personality I nominate a sense of *basic trust*, which I think is an attitude toward oneself and the world derived from the experience of the first year of life. By "trust" I mean what is commonly implied in reasonable trustfulness as far as others are concerned and a simple sense of trustworthiness as far as oneself is concerned. . . . The firm establishment of enduring patterns for the balance of basic trust over basic mistrust is the first task of the budding personality and therefore first of all a task for maternal care.[6]

There is some resemblance here to the earlier psychoanalytic view about optimism and pessimism, but Erikson makes it clear that confidence is a result not only of what the environment can be expected to provide, but also of what influence the individual's action and initiative can exert upon it.

Separation Anxiety

One way to study the character and importance of the tie between infant and mother is to see what happens when it is broken. Circumstances such as illness or death may take the mother abruptly from the scene, or the child may have to be hospitalized or may be sent to a safer area in time of war. There has been active research on this topic, spurred on by the recognition that separation sometimes has grave effects on a child and by the hope that ways can be found to minimize such effects. As is so often true with problems of personality, the occurrence of separation anxiety depends upon a large number of relevant circumstances. This complexity is not displeasing to those who work with children. Usually they cannot prevent separations from happening, but they can at least lessen the severity of the experience.

Some years ago in a series of studies at a children's hospital, Margaret Ribble gathered evidence that infants prosper better when they are held, cuddled, patted, rocked, and "mothered" rather more than is strictly necessary for daily care. Such treatment had a favorable effect even on physical development, promoting stronger respiration, firmer sucking and swallowing, and better digestion. Ribble's observations included cases of severe disorder, both physical and emotional, when "mothering" was interrupted and no adequate substitution of attentive care was possible. Her findings suggested that a long-known but unexplained cause of infant mortality, a "disease" called marasmus, might consist simply of lack of a stimulation essential for survival and early growth.[7] One is reminded of Sullivan's views about apathy in response to frustration and anxiety.

[6] E. H. Erikson, "Identity and the Life Cycle," *Psychological Issues,* **1**, no. 1 (1959), 55–56.

[7] M. A. Ribble, *The Rights of Infants* (New York: Columbia University Press, 1943).

These observations soon received support from two studies by Spitz, which shortly became landmarks in the literature on child care. In one of these studies Spitz showed that when children of six months or so are abruptly separated from their mothers, they sometimes develop a markedly depressed and lethargic condition. If continued, this *anaclitic depression* appears to arrest their whole development.[8] The other study led to the now familiar concept of *hospitalism*. Spitz made a comparative study of young children reared in a foundling home and children reared in the nursery of a penal institution for women. In the foundling home each worker was responsible for the care of seven or more children and thus had little time for mothering. At the penal institution, in contrast, the children's own mothers, having little else to do, could spend a great deal of time playing with their babies in the nursery. Spitz reported striking differences between the less-mothered and the more-mothered children. The former had a higher rate of mortality and were more susceptible to disease, even though the health precautions in the foundling home were excellent. The less-mothered children were also relatively retarded in motor and language development, and they were more given to expressions of distress, fits of screaming, and odd repetitive behavior. Spitz called this combination of inactivity, distress, and retardation "hospitalism" to signify its connection with impersonal institutional care, in contrast to individual mothering.[9]

The findings of Ribble and Spitz had an immediate strong effect on the climate of American child training. Earlier in the century, under the joint influence of Watson's uncompromising behaviorism, a worship of science, progress in dealing with health and sanitation, and the final crest of an economic philosophy of rampant individualism before the Great Depression of the 1930s, impersonality in child care had been made a virtue. Mothers were advised to attend to their children's health and cleanliness but otherwise not to fuss over them or be sentimental about them. It was good for them to cry, wait for their food, and be left to their own devices—good training for the self-sufficiency and hard struggle that lay ahead. Suddenly, with the studies of Ribble and Spitz, the nurturant impulses were vindicated. Science switched to the other side and showed that "mothering" was essential for healthy, normal development. The hugs, caresses, and delighted play with infants released by this change of outlook must be far beyond counting. A generation later, the change is still generally reckoned a good thing. Active mothering, harmonious with the mammalian system of reproduction, is exhibited in the way animal mothers fuss over their young, and it fitly expresses the nurturing impulses that are strong in many women and some men. But as students of the growth of personality we must beware of oversimplifying the situation. Spitz did not show that children in unstimulating foundling homes were necessarily sick and retarded, or that separation from the mother led inevitably

---

[8] R. A. Spitz, "Anaclitic Depression," *Psychoanalytic Study of the Child*, **2** (1946), 313–342.

[9] R. A. Spitz, "Hospitalism: An Inquiry into the Genesis of Psychiatric Conditions in Early Childhood," *Psychoanalytic Study of the Child*, **1** (1945), 53–74.

to anaclitic depression. He showed that such results happened in some cases but not in all.

To understand what else may be involved in separation anxiety, we must consider the now abundant research. A full review has been made by Yarrow of literature up to 1964.[10] According to Yarrow, "analysis of the literature emphasizes the diversity of experiences associated with separation and their varied meanings for the child." He calls attention first to the importance of age. As already mentioned, cognitive development must proceed a certain distance before the child can perceive his mother's absence in its true light. Up to six months of age, on the average, the infant tolerates separation easily, provided his wants are being met by substitutes. The most vulnerable period, during which separation has its most drastic effect, appears to be between six months and two years. This is also the time during which the tie between infant and mother is predominant in the infant's emotional life.

Of course the length of the separation is important; if the mother returns in a reasonably short time, the effects of her absence may be substantially wiped out. Yarrow points out that separation from the mother must be qualified by the amount of real change that is involved. If the relation with the mother was not satisfactory, its loss may not be much of a letdown, especially if substitute caretakers are able to perform just about as well. The effect of further reinforcing experiences should not be overlooked. The mother's death or permanent departure may consign the child to institutional care or perhaps to a succession of foster homes that cannot compensate for the attentive relation that has been lost. Finally, there is reason to suppose that constitutional differences have a good deal to do with the reactions to separation. Anaclitic depression, with its lethargic retardation of functions, for instance, would seem far more likely in a constitutionally passive infant than in an active one.

The intensity of separation anxiety, in short, depends not just on the shock of separation but on a pattern of contributing circumstances that regulate, so to speak, the size of the shock. This discriminating knowledge of how it works has been of great practical importance in the management of necessary separations between mother and child, as when one or the other requires treatment at a hospital. Much can be done to reduce the anxiety that was once supposed to be inevitable in such situations.[11]

Lasting Consequences of the Mother-Child Relation

There is no doubting the importance of the relation between infant and mother during the beginnings of personality growth. But now the question returns: How powerful is this relation in shaping the future course of growth?

[10] L. J. Yarrow, "Separation from Parents during Early Childhood," in *Review of Child Development Research*, Vol. 1, ed. M. L. Hoffman and L. W. Hoffman (New York: Russell Sage Foundation, 1964), pp. 89–136.

[11] J. Robertson, ed., *Hospitals and Children* (New York: International Universities Press, Inc., 1968).

Can we expect to find in adult personality enduring residues of what the infant experienced in relation to his mother? If we can measure in later life such attributes as passive dependence, demanding dependence, a tendency toward apathetic withdrawal, sociability, fear of solitude, level of optimism, and feelings of trust or mistrust, will it turn out that the strength of these attributes is correlated with the weight of the corresponding experiences in the infant-mother relation? On purely abstract grounds the question could be answered in either way. It could be supposed that learnings that came first, involved powerful needs, and elicited strong affects would necessarily leave an indelible impression. On the other hand it might seem that in view of the long continuous history of learnings after infancy, the early traces would be gradually extinguished and would endure only if circumstances conspired to keep them reinforced.

Most of the evidence in favor of lasting consequences came originally from psychoanalytic sources. The painstaking recovery of memories that often occurred in lengthy psychoanalytic treatment, though it did not lead to recollections from the first year of life, was quite likely to disclose chains of consistent attitudes, reappearing at different ages, that plausibly went back to the mother-child relation. Evidence of this kind can be impressive with its wealth of detail, but it is imperfect on two counts. In the first place it is derived from a limited sample, the people who have undergone psychoanalytic treatment—conceivably people whose early experiences have had an unusually strong grip on their later development. In the second place, there is a chance that in the production of these memories the analyst and the patient unwittingly conspire to select those items that best fit their preconceptions about infantile origins. In spite of these risks, however, psychoanalytic case studies often provide valuable information, especially ones like the following, in which dependent attitudes lead to constant frustration but are not thereby extinguished or outgrown.

A Clinical Example of Compulsive Dependence

Childlike dependent attitudes that persist into adult life and spoil adult relations can best be illustrated by an unusually marked example. Karen Horney described such a case in Clare, a woman in her late twenties undergoing psychoanalytic treatment interspersed with periods of systematic self-analysis.[12] At one point Clare recalled a daydream with which she had frequently played, especially during her college years.

> It circled around the figure of a great man, endowed with superior intelligence, wisdom, prominence, and wealth. And this great man made advances to her because beneath her inconspicuous exterior he had sensed her great potentialities. He knew that if given a good break she could be beautiful and achieve great things. He devoted all his time and energy to

[12] K. Horney, *Self-Analysis* (New York: W. W. Norton & Company, Inc., 1942), esp. pp. 47–52, 75–88, 190–246.

her development. He did not merely spoil her by giving her beautiful garments and an attractive home. She had to work hard under his guidance, not only at becoming a great writer but also at cultivating mind and body. Thus he made a beautiful swan out of an ugly duckling.[13]

Except for the element of working hard, this daydream shows a completely childlike dependence on a partner to whom is assigned all initiative in loving her, in recognizing her worth, and indeed in developing her personality.

No doubt many people have daydreams of this character, but in Clare's case the wishes behind it were compulsively strong. Unwittingly she tried to force precisely this relation on the actual partners in her life. These included, just after college, an older writer who encouraged her and for a while seemed willing to make himself her mentor; a husband to whom she was married for three years; and finally a confident young man named Peter with whom she had a close friendship at the time of her analysis. In each case she fell deeply in love, perceived her partner as a demigod, felt that the relation would be eternal, and reveled in security and happiness. The relation was complete in itself; she needed no other friends and indeed looked upon others with a certain contempt. All went well while the partner was in his first enthusiasm for her, while he gave her presents, and while she could command instant attention by giving expression to distress. But soon there were difficulties. Peter, for example, had to be away on business trips; she was desperately lonely without him, anxiously depressed if he returned late or seemed tired or preoccupied, and greatly irritated by any evidence of inattention. Gradually she would come to feel that her partner did not give her what she wanted, yet life without him seemed meaningless and impossible. It was the strain of these later stages of a relation that made her seek the aid of psychoanalysis.

By slow degrees Clare came to realize what she was demanding of her partners, how little she cared about them for themselves, how consumingly she expected them to provide the initiative and meaning in her own life. She also uncovered the childhood roots of her dependency, which lay in the family. The first of her admired, overvalued partners was her mother, but this bond was injured when she grew old enough to realize that her mother much preferred her older brother, the two having a close relation from which she was excluded. No compensatory attention came from her father, who was busy and not fond of children. For a time Clare whined and was discontented, but mother and brother alike blamed her for her sourness and she came to think of herself as indeed an ugly duckling. The only salvation lay in admiring her mother, who liked to be admired and could then treat her as the wonderful daughter of a wonderful mother. This solution, however, was fatal to Clare's contact with her own feelings and sense of self. She did not really admire her mother, and when trapped into doing so she became alienated from her true feelings, especially her assertiveness and aggression. In the light

[13] *Ibid.*, pp. 202–203.

of this history the power behind her persistent daydream and the compulsive force of her dependent tendencies become clear. She needed an all-loving partner to rescue her, to discover her self, to affirm her value, and to supply her lost power of initiative.

Research Findings

Are there ways of bringing the problem of lasting consequences to more critical tests? Considerable research has been undertaken with this end in view, but there are grave difficulties in subjecting the relevant variables to measurement. The problem has been approached in a number of ways.

1. Several investigators have measured personality traits in adult subjects and correlated these with certain ascertainable facts about infancy, such as breast feeding versus bottle feeding or the time and abruptness of weaning. After a thorough review of nineteen such investigations, Caldwell reaches the following judgment: "One would have to conclude from this group of research reports that no clear adjustment patterns had been demonstrated to appear as a consequence of any aspect of feeding experience."[14] This gives no support to the idea of lasting consequences, but it is important to realize that the scientific foundations of the research plan are somewhat shaky. Easily scored self-rating questionnaires may not be subtle enough to measure the qualities under consideration. Measurement of the circumstances of infancy that are based on external criteria like time of weaning and do not get at what the infant actually experienced may be even less satisfactory. One research report avoided these difficulties through extended individual observation of babies in the nursing period and again of the same children when approximately 3 years of age.[15] The method made it possible to rate the children on something of indubitable importance, oral gratification as shown by eagerness, zest, and signs of subsequent satisfaction in feeding. Oral gratification in this sense was found to be correlated with a number of 3-year-old traits signifying confidence, freedom from anxiety, and effective strategies of adaptation. This study was made, however, with a fairly small number of subjects, and prediction to 3 years is not the same as prediction to adulthood. The strictly oral origins of the so-called oral character traits has not yet been given convincing demonstration.

2. Another way of creeping up on the problem is to compare the childhood histories of patients having disorders plausibly associated with maternal deprivation and other patients with disorders of quite a different kind. This line of research has been pursued by Bowlby, among others. His comprehensive survey for the World Health Organization in 1951 did much both to stimulate research and to bring about more humane handling of separations

---

[14] B. M. Caldwell, "The Effects of Infant Care," in *Review of Child Development Research*, Vol. 1, ed. Hoffman and Hoffman, pp. 9–88.

[15] L. B. Murphy, *The Widening World of Childhood* (New York: Basic Books, Inc., 1962).

by medical and social agencies.[16] In an early study of juvenile thieves, Bowlby selected a group of 14 "affectionless characters" showing serious difficulties in interpersonal relations. The life histories showed that 12 had been separated from their mothers in infancy or early childhood, a much higher proportion than in the rest of the thieves.[17] Further research has shown that the connection is not quite as strong and simple as this might suggest. Several variables are involved, such as age of separation, and there is always difficulty in disentangling the effects of the initial separation from those of subsequent deprivations. The weight of evidence thus far, however, seems to be that maternal deprivation occurs with suspicious frequency in the histories of people whose troubles include marked impairments in affectionate relations.[18]

3. The most satisfactory situation for investigating the lasting consequences of infant-mother relations is one in which subjects have been carefully observed in infancy, followed during subsequent years, and examined again when they reach adulthood. Continuous longitudinal studies best achieve this situation. It was partly realized in an influential series of investigations by Goldfarb on the later status of children who had spent the first three years of their lives in institutions.[19] In one of these studies, 15 such children were matched with another 15 whose first three years were spent in the more favorable climate of foster homes, where the initial maternal deprivation was compensated by foster mothering. Tested at around 12 years of age, the institutional children differed most conspicuously with respect to interpersonal relations; they were rated much lower in friendly contact with the examining adults and in close ties with other children. They differed also in being more impulsive, less planful, and less controlled; and in an experimental game they more often broke the rules without signs of guilt. Finally, they gave evidence of intellectual retardation, especially with respect to concept formation and abstract reasoning. This cluster of impairments in human relations, personal control, conscience, and intellectual development poses interesting problems. It is worth noting, however, that other followup studies have not regularly verified the relation between maternal deprivation and intellectual impairment.

Conditions for research were highly favorable in an investigation conducted by Heinstein using subjects continuously studied from birth to 18 in the Berkeley Guidance Study.[20] This research produced evidence that maternal

---

[16] J. Bowlby, *Maternal Care and Mental Health*, Monograph Series, No. 2 (Geneva: World Health Organization, 1951); M. D. Ainsworth et al., *Deprivation of Maternal Care: A Reassessment of Its Effects*, Public Health Papers (Geneva: World Health Organization, 1966); both published in one volume (New York: Schocken Books, 1966).

[17] J. Bowlby, "Forty-four Juvenile Thieves," *International Journal of Psychoanalysis*, **25** (1944), 1–57.

[18] Yarrow, "Separation from Parents during Early Childhood," pp. 103–105.

[19] W. Goldfarb, "Emotional and Intellectual Consequences of Psychologic Deprivation in Infancy: A Revaluation," in *Psychopathology of Childhood*, ed. P. H. Hoch and J. Zubin (New York: Grune & Stratton, Inc., 1955), pp. 105–119.

[20] M. I. Heinstein, "Behavioral Correlates of Breast-Bottle Regimes under Varying Parent-Infant Relationships," *Monographs of the Society for Research in Child Development*, **28**, no. 4 (1963).

warmth in the early years was associated with fewer behavior problems in the course of later development. Most of the findings, however, were of a more complex nature. Separate analyses for boys and girls disclosed, for instance, that late-weaned boys had more behavior problems in middle childhood than early-weaned boys, but that this relation did not hold for girls. Estimates of maternal stability, on the other hand, were associated with fewer behavior problems in girls but not in boys. Furthermore, there were numerous complicated relations among single variables, known technically as interaction effects. Duration of nursing, for example, interacts with a variable called favorableness of interpersonal environment, with the following result: boys in poor environments had fewer adjustment problems if nursed for a shorter time, whereas boys in good environments fared better with adjustment if nursed for a longer time. And for girls? Exactly the opposite. Readers may find their heads spinning at this point, and it is probably premature to attempt an interpretation of such findings. Yet it is clearly inevitable that quantitative studies of development should assume this unwelcome complexity of form. We must expect large amounts of interaction among variables if we elect to study such a phenomenon as personality.

Much as we would like to believe that developmental problems can be brought squarely to the bar of research and given decisive answers, it seems fair to say that investigations of the lasting consequences of the infant-mother relation have thus far given only hints. Considering the nature of the problem and the technical difficulty of investigating it, perhaps this is all that they can ever give. For the present, at all events, we must be content with considerable uncertainty. With respect to oral character traits, where the evidence is decidedly weak, it seems likely in retrospect that the original hypothesis was weak. That the adult traits of passive dependence, demanding dependence, and surly rejection of dependence should be derived straight from infantile feeding experience is much too simple a postulate. Constitutional differences in level of activity probably play a large part in the development of these traits. Subsequent history should have a considerable voice in deciding how strongly they will endure. This is a situation in which simple cause-effect reasoning is inappropriate. Multiple determination of the so-called oral traits should be considered the more plausible hypothesis, though it is teasingly difficult to test.

One hint, however, comes through so strongly and repeatedly that we can hardly question its significance: things do not go as well, either in early childhood or in later life, when mothering is lacking, is cut off, or is coolly impersonal. Experiences of warmth, security, satisfaction, and pleasure in the infant's relation with the mother make for more rewarding human relations in later life and have something to do with establishing basic trust as Erikson uses that expression. This consequence has the strongest claim to being lasting.

It is well to keep in mind the possibility that the effects of the mother-child relation may be more lasting for some people than for others. This idea is especially relevant when the relation has been such as to produce chronic frustration and severe anxiety. When the situation is so bad that the infant must withdraw into apathy or use primitive defense mechanisms, his potential for development may be subject to enduring limitations. The fact that clinical literature on the subject seems more ready than the experimental literature to favor lasting consequences may simply reflect the fact that people who seek help are more likely to have had difficult histories from which they have been unable to extricate themselves. Conceivably those who have had a happier early experience are left more free to meet the present on its own terms, and thus to change.

Early Development under Group Care

In describing thus far the growth of personality during the first five years of life, we have stayed within the outlook of individualistic societies. There is a sense in which the family is universal, reflecting as it does certain requirements of the mammalian system of reproduction and care of the young. In an organized society, however, these necessities do not require bringing up children in single family units in which the relation of infant to mother is the paramount experience. If communal living rather than individual development is taken as the goal of upbringing, it sounds reasonable to try to start it as early as possible. Would it not be better to bring up children from the very beginning in groups under trained caretakers? To do so would diminish the importance of the family circle and lead the child instead to anchor his security and loyalty to the other children in the communal nursery. Trained experts, who could perform their task with more objectivity, would displace the mother, an amateur at child rearing. Schemes of this kind have been put in operation in the Kibbutzim in Israel, agricultural communities founded originally to promote an ideal communal way of life. In the Soviet Union since 1956 there has been a somewhat analogous program of children's collectives, established as a means of creating a "new Soviet man" whose central loyalty is to the purposes of the state. Even in the individualistic United States there has recently been an increase of interest in group care. Where mothers are important to family support, there is an obvious need to supply day care for their small children.

From what we have studied thus far, what would we expect to be the consequences and hazards of group upbringing? It is a question difficult to approach with an open mind. At an early conference at which a psychiatrist reported his conclusions after observing the experiments in Israel for four years, the participants themselves became aware of their tendency to find fault with group upbringing and to pounce upon evidences of emotional disturbance in the children. One would suppose that a gathering of experts on psychiatry and child care would be peculiarly aware of the defects of parental upbringing, but their basic conviction still was that sound development is uniquely a product of good mothering.[21] Thinking in this tradition we would expect that children separated early from their mothers and brought up under conditions unavoidably like those of an institution would exhibit some of the signs of hospitalism and of anaclitic depression. We would look for apathy, low affect, retardation of development, and signs of emotional upset. We would expect habit training to be difficult without the rewards that parents can give. We would imagine latent anxiety, doubting that young children could find security in one another and could socialize themselves, so to speak, without having first been socialized by their parents. We might even predict evidences of deep-seated disorder in later life.

It would be satisfying to turn now to the facts and test the accuracy of these several expectations. Unfortunately the conditions for decisive experiments are not met. The children's collectives in the Soviet Union, which take children as early as three months of age, are largely day care centers; individual family life continues outside working hours and during holidays. In the typical regime of a Kibbutz, the mother visits the very young child in the infants' house, and a little later the child makes regular daily visits to the family. The system is thus mixed, with parents still playing a significant part in the child's emotional life even though all matters of training are considered the province of the caretakers. The perfect experiment is further vitiated by practical difficulties in manning the nurseries with real experts. The Soviet plan aims at three years of training for nurses in charge, but there are not enough such people to go around, and much of the work is done by less-trained apprentices. In the Kibbutzim the caretakers often have less than a year of training. The Soviet ideal of two adults to every eight children is likewise often not realized in practice. Finally, there is great difficulty in determining the results of group upbringing; precise measurement is not easy.[22]

Trying to extract some valid conclusions from a considerable number of reports, we can say first that group upbringing, which under the circumstances might also be called multiple mothering, appears to be harder for young children than straight maternal care. This is evidenced by a high incidence of signs of emotional upset and by slower early development than is found in comparison groups.[23] At least for the first three years the infant's adaptive task can be regarded as inherently more difficult in group upbringing. He must shift back and forth between mothers, he must endure the greater

---

[21] G. Caplan, "Clinical Observations on the Emotional Life of Children in the Communal Settlements in Israel," in *Problems of Infancy and Childhood*, ed. M. J. E. Senn (New York: Josiah Macy Jr. Foundation, 1950); reprinted in *Psychopathology: A Source Book*, ed. C. F. Reed, I. E. Alexander, and S. S. Tomkins (Cambridge, Mass.: Harvard University Press, 1958), pp. 724–754.

[22] D. R. Meers and A. E. Marans, "Group Care of Infants in Other Countries," in *Early Child Care: The New Perspectives*, ed. L. L. Dittman (New York: Atherton Press, 1968), Chap. 10.

[23] Caplan, "Emotional Life of Children in the Communal Settlements in Israel"; A. I. Rabin, *Growing Up in the Kibbutz* (New York: Springer Publishing Co., Inc., 1965); B. Bettleheim, *The Children of the Dream* (New York: The Macmillan Company, 1969).

need-frustrations of a scheduled existence, and he must cope very early with other children of equal age. The difficulties are even greater when staff inadequacies and monotonous surroundings create conditions unfavorable for the natural growth of competence. These problems have led to a certain amount of debate in Communist countries about the value of children's collectives. In some places this debate has resulted in renewed efforts to improve the day care centers, in others to a decision to delay entrance until the age of 3 in order to avoid the "inevitable hurt and sorrow" experienced by younger children.[24] It is of interest that mothers in the Kibbutzim, even when devoted to the communal ideal, sometimes chafe at turning over to the caretaker so much of their child's upbringing and seek to increase their own contacts.

If these findings score a point for individual mothering, the advantage is blunted by another persistent trend in the reports, especially those from Israel. There is no evidence that the handicaps of early group care lead to lasting impairments. Rabin's study is typical in this respect. He compared Kibbutz children with the children of independent farmers in Israel. Although he noted the "slower early developmental tempo" of the Kibbutz child, he was unable to detect any "long-range deleterious effects upon personality development." Studying samples of subjects at different ages all the way to adulthood, he concluded that "the Kibbutz child surges forth subsequently under conditions that are conducive to accelerated further growth and development".[25] We cannot disregard the evidence cited earlier in this chapter that linked early maternal deprivation with certain lasting consequences. But it may be that for most children early handicaps are more reversible than we had been led to suppose. At all events, the average slow-starting Kibbutz child has shown no evidence of later shortcomings either as a member of child society or as a soldier defending his embattled nation.

When communal living is taken as the highest value, the success of the experiments with group upbringing is judged chiefly in terms of consequent group membership and solidarity. Whether or not the child is developing toward becoming a good parent, for instance, is irrelevant in a society that minimizes parental functions. The child in a Kibbutz grows up in the constant company of the small group of age-equals with which he started. The reports suggest that solidarity with this group is difficult at first before the child can control aggression and anxiety, but that a real bond presently develops. Even at the age of 3 the children show some degree of identification with their own group and some hostility toward other groups. "We" and "ours" figure much more largely than "me" and "mine" in their conversations. Sharing and taking turns are better developed than in American nursery schools, and there are more frequent manifestatons of sympathetic feeling and helpfulness.[26] Of course these are not spontaneous groups; they are under

[24] Meers and Marans, "Group Care of Infants in Other Countries," p. 257.

[25] Rabin, *Growing Up in the Kibbutz*, esp. Chaps. 9 and 10.

[26] H. Faigin, "Social Behavior of Young Children in the Kibbutz," *Journal of Abnormal and Social Psychology*, **56** (1958), 117–129.

the caretaker's direction, and when the children correct one another it is often in the caretaker's precise tone of voice. Under this regime the children perform outwardly well as group members, but there is debate about the inner quality of this early socialization. Even in the Kibbutzim voices are occasionally raised claiming that a subtle rule of the strong over the weak is really going on and that an anxious conformity underlies the outward cooperation. In effect these critics are questioning the proportions of love and fear that enter into the visible solidarity. Western observers wonder about the amount of room left for individuality, but this, of course, is not a major value in the ideal of communal living. The whole problem is clearly suffused with observers' values, making it difficult to allow the data to speak for themselves.

Something approaching an experiment was reported in 1951 by Anna Freud and Sophie Dann.[27] A group of six children, all between the ages of 3 and 4, separated from the start from their parents through the exigencies of war and internment camps, had remained together while being brought up in the most haphazard fashion in one situation after another. These children were products not even of multiple mothering but of something resembling no mothering at all. For each child the only stable element in the human environment was the other five children. The group was finally brought to an English house with the curious name of Bulldog's Bank, where they were studied for a year by Anna Freud and cared for under her direction. At the outset it was noticed that positive reactions were predominant in the children's relations with one another. They treated each other with natural affection and warmth, and there was little to suggest even latent jealousy, rivalry, and competition. Occasional outbursts of anger occurred, but aggression was mainly apparent in an attitude of suspicion and hostility toward the outside world. A certain frustration of needs for closeness could be inferred from the large amount of thumb-sucking and masturbation, and toilet training was sufficiently precarious to break down in the new environment. Developmental retardation was marked with respect to manipulative skill, motor coordination, speech, and mental operations. Until their arrival at Bulldog's Bank the children had existed under barren institutional conditions with restricted space.

The psychoanalytically trained workers who now entered the scene were convinced that what these children needed was good mothering. Progress is described almost wholly in terms of the growth of individual ties to the adults. The marked retardation with respect to competence disappeared within the year; the children quickly reached the manipulative, motor, and linguistic levels of average 4-year-olds. Freud and Dann mention the coincidence of this progress with "the growth of the child's emotional interest in the adult world," but one should not overlook the fact that the children had suddenly been provided with an environment rich in objects and opportunities for the

---

[27] A. Freud and S. Dann, "An Experiment in Group Upbringing," *Psychoanalytic Study of the Child*, **6** (1951), 127–168. An abridged version is printed in *Readings in Child Development*, ed. W. E. Martin and C. B. Stendler (New York: Harcourt Brace Jovanovich, Inc., 1954), pp. 404–421.

natural growth of competence through exploratory play. With respect to the formation of individual ties the experiment was not in its own terms so dramatically successful. Such ties appeared: children became attached to their particular caretaker, formed a "dependent and erotic" relation, acted as if they wanted to belong to an adult, and were resentful when the mother-substitute had to be absent. But these new ties never overtook in strength the older ones within the group. The children's loyalty to one another remained largely unshaken.

In her previous wartime work with separated children at the Hampstead Nurseries in London, Anna Freud had shown that strong affectionate and dependent ties to mother-substitutes interfered with ties to other children. Given the chance to focus on a mother-relation, the Hampstead children began to treat each other more like rival siblings with a sharpening of jealousy and hostility.[28] She considered this loss acceptable because it was accompanied by a general blossoming of personality once the mother-relation was established. In her view, interactions among children between 2 and 4 lead only to "a primitive form of social order, a rough-and-tumble kind of justice and morality, where might goes before right, but where the individual without really changing his nature or transforming his impulses learns to adapt himself in his behavior to a limited number of restrictions."[29] Such a superficial achievement is worth sacrificing for the more profound benefits of maternal care: warmer interactions, a sense of trust, and a willingness to accept the restrictions of training in exchange for affectionate care.

We may suspect that an ardent advocate of communal living would give a more favorable interpretation to the early ties among children, seeing these ties as much more than a superficial achievement. One could also argue that the warm mothering described by Anna Freud is far from being universally achieved, and that maternally deprived children are worse off for having no alternative attachments to other children. A counter argument would be that inept group caretakers would not succeed in creating a favorable child society for their charges. It does not look as if this question, about which it is so difficult for culture-bound observers to be objective, would find a prompt, decisive answer.

In the meantime we have to be satisfied with tentative conclusions: that good maternal care is correlated with more satisfactory living in later childhood and adult life; that deprivation of maternal care has deleterious effects both immediate and long-lasting; that residues of the early experiences sometimes exert a strong influence on adult behavior; that maternal upbringing is less stressful and more satisfying to young children than multiple mothering or group care, but that the products of group care in communal societies do not on the average exhibit lasting handicaps in later life.

[28] A. Freud and D. Burlingham, *Infants without Families* (New York: International Universities Press, Inc., 1944).

[29] A. Freud, "The Bearing of the Psychoanalytic Theory of Instinctual Drives on Certain Aspects of Human Behavior," in *Drives, Affects, Behavior*, ed. R. M. Loewenstein (New York: International Universities Press, Inc., 1953), p. 273.

9 The Early Growth of Competence

The human organism is conspicuous in the animal kingdom for its capacious brain and for its success in mastering important features of the environment. The two things are obviously related. Human beings can be considered a far-out evolutionary experiment involving maximal helplessness and ignorance at birth together with maximal development of a capacity for learning about the nature and utility of the surrounding world. The experiment has been successful in meeting the standard of survival: we are here. But very likely we would not be here if the endowment had consisted of a brain without any corresponding inclination to use it. Properly considered, the brain is not simply a mechanism but a living organ that is inherently inclined toward activity. From this springs the restless urge to find out about the environment and to test the effects of actions upon it. Though such a striving is seen in a multitude of forms, its central biological significance seems well described as an urge to attain competence in dealing with the environment.[1]

Exploratory Play

The strongest evidence for an independent motive of this kind is the ceaseless activity of young animals and children during their waking hours. This activity is variously described, depending on circumstances, as exploration, manipulation, or simply play. Activity occurs, of course, when the young creature is hungry, uncomfortable, or fearful, but it occurs also when hunger is satisfied, discomforts removed, and security established.

[1] R. W. White, "Motivation Reconsidered: The Concept of Competence," *Psychological Review*, **66** (1959), 297–333.

The play of kittens and puppies has the air of a spare-time activity rather than one that is immediately concerned with survival and safety. This quality is still more evident in the play of young children, who by the end of the first year spend something like six hours a day at it, and even mingle it with the serious business of being fed, washed, and dressed, to the detriment of the mother's efficiency. Close study of the child's exploratory play shows that even though it may change focus fairly rapidly it exhibits a directedness and persistence that bespeaks motivation rather than a random overflow of energy. Though it may be only in short spurts, all play seems to involve finding out what can be done with the environment.

Jean Piaget, one of the most careful observers of early play, who used his own three children as subjects, reports that as early as the fourth month the activity begins to be "centered on a result produced in the external environment."[2] For a while the behavior can be described as "rediscovering the movement which by chance exercised an advantageous action upon things." The child Laurent, for example, discovers accidentally that pulling a string causes the rattles suspended over his bassinet to emit sounds. In the course of several days he rediscovers the correct movement to produce this result and proceeds to use it with various degrees of force, laughing gleefully at the succession of sounds. By 9 months the children have become quite systematic in their investigation of new objects, the sequence including visual exploration, tactile exploration, a slow moving about of the object in space, and a trying out of their repertory of actions such as shaking the object, striking it, swinging it, rubbing it on the side of the bassinet, sucking it, and so forth, "each in turn with a sort of prudence as though studying the effect produced."[3] Still before the first birthday Piaget observed unmistakable patterns of active exploration. At 10 months and 11 days of age Laurent, surely not yet cognizant of Galileo's experiments with falling bodies, engages in the following piece of research:

> He grasps in succession a celluloid swan, a box, and several other small objects, in each case stretching out his arm and letting them fall. Sometimes he stretches out his arm vertically, sometimes he holds it obliquely in front of or behind his eyes. When the object falls in a new position (for example on his pillow) he lets it fall two or three times more in the same place, as though to study the spatial relation; then he modifies the situation. At a certain moment the swan falls near his mouth; now he does not suck it (even though this object habitually serves this purpose), but drops it three times more while merely making the gesture of opening his mouth.[4]

These early instances of exploratory play provide a formula for the many processes of cumulative learning whereby the originally helpless

[2] J. Piaget, *The Origins of Intelligence in Children,* trans. M. Cook (New York: International Universities Press, Inc., 1952), p. 51.

[3] *Ibid.,* p. 255.

[4] *Ibid.,* p. 269.

infant attains competence in dealing with the world around him. The infant who can only cry and squirm when he is too hot may grow up to design an air-conditioning system, but only after years of directed, persistent explorations on the pattern of Laurent's work with the celluloid swan. It is by such means that children learn to coordinate hand and eye, to develop the power of locomotion, to attain the motor skills seen in sports or in craftsmanship, to master the complexities of language, and to become adept at thinking, planning, and carrying out large undertakings. The young may learn some of this under the influence of needs such as hunger and avoidance of danger, but in the course of evolution a great advantage for survival must have lain with those members of a species who stored up knowledge in advance of a crisis. Animals that explore their surroundings with a curiosity that may seem idle are actually strengthening their position in the world: in time of crisis they will more quickly find escape routes or paths to probable nourishment. It is thus understandable that we come equipped with a strong persistent motive to explore, to manipulate, and to play. In man, this motive lies at the root of the far-reaching physical and mental accomplishments whereby the environment has been brought under control and made serviceable for civilized living.

Nature of the Motive

What, exactly, is the urge toward attainment of competence? Mc-Dougall was one of many in the early years of this century to attribute to animals and man an *instinct of curiosity*.[5] It is not uncommon today to find researchers with animals speaking of an *exploratory drive*. Much research has been aimed at discovering the conditions in the environment that set off approach and exploration.[6] This work shows the importance of novelty in patterns of stimulation and suggests that perceived departures from the familiar, when not great enough to precipitate anxiety, increase the level of activity and elicit exploratory behavior.[7] It has further been postulated that human beings have a positive *need for varied sensory stimulation*, which might even be called "stimulus hunger" or "perception hunger," and that they actively seek the higher interest and excitement provoked by variety.[8] This line of thought has been related to contemporary information theory in the phrase, a *need to engage in information processing*.[9]

[5] W. McDougall, *An Introduction to Social Psychology*, 16th ed. (Boston: John W. Luce & Co., 1923), p. 59.

[6] D. E. Berlyne, *Conflict, Arousal, and Curiosity* (New York: McGraw-Hill Book Company, 1960).

[7] D. O. Hebb, *The Organization of Behavior* (New York: John Wiley & Sons, Inc., 1949).

[8] D. W. Fiske and S. R. Maddi, *Functions of Varied Experience* (Homewood, Ill.: The Dorsey Press, 1961).

[9] J. McV. Hunt, "Intrinsic Motivation and Its Role in Psychological Development," in *Nebraska Symposium on Motivation*, ed. D. Levine (Lincoln: University of Nebraska Press, 1965), pp. 189–282.

Such conceptions are somewhat weighted on the cognitive side, emphasizing the attainment of knowledge rather than the attainment of competence, to which in broad biological perspective knowledge serves as a means. The active side had an early advocate in Karl Groos, who, in his classical analysis of play, called attention to the child's *joy in being a cause* as shown in making a lot of noise, throwing things around, and playing in puddles, where he can produce particularly dramatic effects. He wrote, "We demand a knowledge of effects and to be ourselves the producers of effects."[10] These picturesque expressions are entirely in accord with the psychological outlook of John Dewey, who insisted upon the adaptive nature of behavior and who therefore emphasized the results of acts and the feeding back of information about these results.[11] Piaget, as we have seen, noticed the preference of his children for objects they were able in some way to influence. A like preference has been demonstrated by Welker in an experiment with young chimpanzees. When he gave the animals two objects at a time, they spent longer times with objects that they could light up, make to emit sounds, or move about in varied ways.[12] A round ball, with its versatile powers of motion, has always enjoyed special popularity as a plaything with kittens, puppies, otters, raccoons, and human infants. Adult sports such as baseball, basketball, football, tennis, golf, and bowling testify to its enduring challenge to human competence. A ball has a unique appeal to joy in being a cause.

Can these different conceptions be given the single heading of a motive to attain competence? Scientific inquiry often advances by making finer discriminations, and should doubtless do so in this case. But for the student of personality it is important not to lose sight of what all the processes have in common: their bearing on the development of effectiveness in dealing with the environment. If in our thinking about motives we do not include this overall tendency toward active dealing, we draw the picture of a creature that is helpless in the grip of its fears, drives, and passions; too helpless perhaps even to survive, certainly too helpless to have been the creator of civilization. It is in connection with strivings to attain competence that the activity inherent in living organisms is given its clearest representation—the power of initiative and exertion that we experience as a sense of being an agent in the living of our lives. This experience may be called a *feeling of efficacy*.[13] This expression certainly sounds better than "feeling of dealing with the environment," yet it should imply dealing in a broad sense: being actively engaged in some way, perhaps inter-

[10] K. Groos, *The Play of Man*, trans. E. L. Baldwin (New York: D. Appleton, 1901).

[11] J. Dewey, *Interest and Effort in Education* (Boston: Houghton Mifflin Company, 1913).

[12] W. I. Welker, "Some Determinants of Play and Exploration in Young Chimpanzees," *Journal of Comparative and Physiological Psychology*, **49** (1956), 84–89.

[13] R. W. White, *Motivation Reconsidered*, pp. 297–333.

preting perceptual input, perhaps exerting oneself in motor output, perhaps straightening out ideas that have been recalled or conjured up inside one's head. The feeling of efficacy thus goes with all forms, direct and indirect, of learning how to deal with the environment.

Sense of Competence

Over the course of development, seeking of feelings of efficacy leads to the building of actual competence in dealing with the environment, and it leads also to a subjective *sense of competence*. For various reasons these two may not be in perfect correspondence: we all know of people whose sense of competence seems either too high or too low for what we judge to be their actual ability. But in a rough sort of way a person develops a strong sense of competence in those spheres in which he has had predominant success, and a sense of incompetence in realms that have baffled and defeated him. The difference shows most clearly in the confidence with which new experiences are approached. A child entering a new school, for instance, may run swiftly to the playground, grip firmly the bars of the jungle gym, and quickly become absorbed in a series of creative acrobatics, confident and expertly coordinated in a sphere of previous triumphs. But when the bell summons him indoors and he is set in front of the arithmetic lessons he has always found bewildering, he will groan and squirm in his chair, pick up the pencil with a weak hesitant grasp, find that it needs sharpening, and have great difficulty keeping his mind on the dreary chore of figuring out the problems. Sense of competence, as we shall see later in this book, is a very important aspect of the organization of personality and of ego identity.

For purposes of exposition, we have thus far described competence mainly with respect to the inanimate world. It applies equally well to dealing with the human environment. The child has a stake in finding out what effects he can have on the people around him and what effects they will have on him. He takes an active interest in human beings and may, for example, conduct an intensive investigation of his mother's face. But the crucial issues have to do with discovering how responsive the human environment can be made to be to the child's major needs and wishes. The outcome of this striving, the degree to which a *sense of interpersonal competence* is attained, is of high significance for the ultimate pattern of personality. In adult life the feeling of being able to have some effect on people, to get them to listen, provide some of the things we need, do some of the things we want, receive some of the love and help we want to give, provides a substantial foundation for security and self-respect.

Growth of Competence in Early Childhood

At first the most concentrated form of activity is visual exploration, though babbling and gross motor movements are also present. Halfway through the first year comes what Gesell called the *heyday of manipulation*, when grasping is an "eager and intent business." Hand and eye become increasingly coordinated and the infant increasingly understands the properties of objects as he picks things up, puts them in his mouth, turns and looks at them, passes them from hand to hand, uses them for banging, drops them, recovers them, and a little later purposefully throws them away. Gesell described the use of the hands for manipulation as a "compelling urge." We can be certain that the infant is not moved by the solemn purpose of preparing for future exigencies. He handles things just for fun. But his fun does in fact help him toward the biologically important goal of competence.

Stimulation, as we have seen, plays an important part in the growth of competence. The child needs something to work on, so to speak, and his level of activity is increased by varied stimulation. Animals reared in restricted environments show decrements in certain aspects of their development. Infants in institutional surroundings develop measurably better if provided with varied stimulation even in the impersonal form of colorful patterned crib sheets and moving objects suspended overhead.[14] This line of research illuminates one of Spitz's findings concerning hospitalism. Spitz believed that loss of mothering produced motor and cognitive retardation; we can now supply an intervening term and recognize that when such retardation occurs it is probably due to the low level of stimulation that followed separation from the mother. People are a source not only of nourishment, security, and love but also of fun and entertainment. The child happily passing objects back and forth with another person, playing peek-a-boo, hiding behind chairs, or engaging in the hilarious pastime of being chased while creeping, testifies to the arousing properties of animate companions and suggests their contribution to motor and cognitive growth. In a grim, preoccupied, disadvantaged, anxious family there may be not only a shortage of love but a shortage of the benign, agreeable, varied stimulation that is conducive to the growth of competence.

During the second and third years the child makes astonishing gains in competence. As regards locomotion he starts as an awkward toddler but soon becomes a restless runabout who gets into everything and who experiments with his prowess by stunts such as walking backwards or pushing his own carriage. By the third birthday he may be coordinated enough to start riding a tricycle. Parallel growth in manipulation is seen in carrying objects about, filling and emptying containers, tearing things apart and fitting them together, lining up blocks and eventually building with them, and digging and constructing in the sandbox. This picture of persistent motor activity led Mittelmann to postulate a *motility urge*.[15] He even called this the dominant urge of the second and third years, and he saw motility as "one of the most important avenues for exercising such functions as mastery, integration, reality-testing, and control of impulses." The attainment of competence and the related feeling of self-esteem is an important issue during this period of growth.

As these developments go forward it becomes evident that the child,

[14] B. L. White, "An Experimental Approach to the Effects of Experience on Early Human Behavior," in *Minnesota Symposium on Child Psychology*, Vol. 1, ed. J. P. Hill (Minneapolis: University of Minnesota Press, 1967), pp. 201–226.

[15] B. Mittelmann, "Motility in Infants, Children, and Adults," *Psychoanalytic Study of the Child*, **9** (1954), 142–177.

as Stern expressed it, "realizes himself as a living entity, a one complete center of power; he wishes to affirm himself, his existence, his importance, and to increase it."[16] This growth of a sense of autonomy is clearly illustrated in the child's desire to *carry actions to completion*. The helpful adult who hands down the out-of-reach toy suddenly finds himself greeted by signs of frustration and anger; he has missed the point of the child's attempts to reach it, which was to get the toy by his own efforts. Levy sees a clear early manifestation in the "battle of the spoon," the time when the child seizes the spoon and undertakes to feed himself. When this is done actively and with persistence it is perfectly clear that the motive is not either to increase nourishment or to please the mother. The spoon, on what Gesell described as its "hazardous journey" from dish to mouth, is quite likely to arrive upside down and empty, and the mother, even if in theory she admires independence, cannot rejoice heartily at the prospect of cleaning up afterward. The true meaning of this behavior and of similar manifestations that multiply during the second year of life lies, as Levy puts it, in "a general movement towards the autonomy of the whole person . . . the first flowering of self-determination."[17] The core of satisfaction in such behavior is the feeling of efficacy that results from producing an intended result through one's own effort.

The urge to be thus efficacious is at the root of the social behavior often described as *negativism*, which comes to a peak on the average around the age of 2½. Adult observers use such expressions as "willfulness," "obstinacy," and "defiance"; if the children could put their side of it into words they might speak of "a heroic struggle for independence." Linguistic development has something to do with it: the battle takes place most conspicuously over the use of commands and the consequences of the word "no" when uttered by oneself. To illustrate the child's defiance Stern described a mealtime episode in which his little daughter Eva, impatient at slow serving, issued the rash command, "Father, pick up the spoon." A clash of wills followed because she had not said, and would not say, "please"; her obstinate refusal to pronounce this conciliatory syllable resulted in her having no dinner.[18] To contemporary readers, less concerned than was Stern's generation about politeness, the punishment does not seem to fit the crime, but the episode clearly shows that Eva was engaged in testing her interpersonal competence both by giving a command and by refusing to obey one. To interpret this kind of transaction wholly in terms of aggression is to miss the point. Tests of interpersonal competence can easily stir up aggression on both sides, but their more fundamental meaning is to discover what range of effects one can have on the human environment.

The child's sense of interpersonal competence undergoes repeated tests in connection with parental training and discipline. As his powers of

---

[16] W. Stern, *Psychology of Early Childhood* (1914), 2d English ed., trans. A. Barwell (New York: Holt, Rinehart and Winston, Inc., 1930), p. 492.

[17] D. M. Levy, "Oppositional Syndromes and Oppositional Behavior," in *Psychopathology of Childhood,* ed. P. H. Hoch and J. Zubin (New York: Grune & Stratton, Inc., 1955), pp. 204–226.

[18] Stern, *Psychology of Early Childhood*, p. 499.

manipulation, locomotion, and language increase, he learns that there are many restrictions on his freedom. There are a lot of things he feels inclined to do but is not supposed to do, like ordering parents and older siblings around or going off on solitary trips. There are other things he does not feel inclined to do but is expected to do, like sharing toys with other children or keeping himself neat and clean. Many of the requirements of social living must necessarily seem mysterious and arbitrary to a young child, yet he must make some sort of accommodation to them. Toilet training is for most children an arbitrary requirement. In Freud's thinking it was the central battle-field, the prototype of all discipline, because libido had supposedly become concentrated in the anal zone, investing evacuative processes with a precious instinctual pleasure that the child was loath to give up. In certain cases toilet training may deserve this centrality, but most of the deductions Freud made about its consequences fit more coherently into the concept of interpersonal competence.[19] Bowel training is but one of many situations in which the dictates of inclination collide with social requirements and create a conflict of power.

During the fourth and fifth years the child's capacities continue to expand and his initiatives and those of the people around him continue to interact. Erikson calls attention to developments at this time in three spheres of competence: locomotion, language, and imagination.[20] Locomotion advances from a difficult stunt to a serviceable tool, reaching a nearly adult degree of competence. The child becomes skilled enough in other motor accomplishments, like throwing a ball and using simple tools, to suggest comparison with adults and older children. Language develops enough to support wider understanding and social exchange. The child can now expand his learning about the world vastly by asking questions. Taxing as the endless stream of 4-year-old interrogation may seem to those who are expected to provide answers, the child is making an important initiative in the direction of competence. Besides extending his knowledge about the world, he is securing practice in expressing himself and in listening with comprehension to what others have to say. Imagination also assumes during these years a more well-rounded form. This is the time when the child can first maintain the fantasy of an imaginary companion. It is the time when he can begin to understand roles and to experiment with them by dressing up in adult clothes, imitating adult behavior, and pretending to be a powerful figure like a schoolteacher or a truck driver. All of these developments invite a comparison with adults. They signify an increasing capacity to think of oneself as a person among other persons. There is obvious risk in such comparisons. The 5-year-old is still small, his skills are still immature, and if he lets his pretensions go too far he can easily become an object of derision.

The development of competence and the evolution of a sense of per-

---

[19] R. W. White, "Competence and the Psychosexual Stages of Development," in *Nebraska Symposium on Motivation*, ed. M. R. Jones (Lincoln: University of Nebraska Press, 1960), pp. 97–141.

[20] E. H. Erikson, *Childhood and Society*, 2d ed. (New York: W. W. Norton & Co., Inc., 1963).

sonal competence continue throughout life. We break off the chronological story at this point—the age of 5—only temporarily, with a view to giving the subsequent history more extended coverage in later chapters. The sense of competence ramifies widely into a great many aspects of personality. It has a significant place in social development, in intellectual growth, in strategies of living, and in self and ego identity. Having inspected the early childhood origins of the sense of competence, we shall now consider the effects of the childhood history on personal development both at the time and for later life.

Significance of the Sense of Competence for Development

The problems that surround the growth of competence lie in what we generally refer to as confidence and self-respect. Typically the child acts in an exploratory way; his initiative and effort elicit a response from the environment, a response that may vary all the way from tractable compliance to forceful counterattack. The success of his attempts to influence the environment affects his sense of competence and hence the level of confidence at which he confronts new situations. It affects the degree to which he experiences himself as an autonomous being and center of initiative, an agent in his transactions with the environment. The child, of course, attempts to influence his world in many different ways, and success is not likely to be uniform. Motor coordination may become a source of pride, whereas social charm seems unattainable, or it may be the other way about. Gradually a cognitive map is formed on which are entered, we might suppose, the probabilities of being competent in a large variety of situations. But the child is not an inventory; he is a living system. However differentiated the sense of competence may become in actual practice, the child very early experiences it also as an overall attribute. Injury at one point in the system may spread to become injury to the whole. Adler, as we saw, maintained that a person could emerge from early childhood with a lasting inferiority complex. This did not imply that the child had done everything badly and had achieved no success. It meant that in certain critical situations, those that mattered most, he had experienced belittlements so painful as to cripple confidence in all directions and turn the self-picture into that of an inferior person.

Consequences of Success and Failure

We can grasp the effects produced by the vicissitudes of competence most easily by thinking of relatively simple actions. Successes in this sphere, including the coordinated management of one's body and mind to produce appropriate skills, result in feelings of confidence, security, and self-respect. There is an obvious inverse relation between sense of competence and anxiety: to the extent that things can be dealt with they need not be feared. Failures lead to hesitant approaches, avoidance, feelings of awkward helplessness, lack of self-respect. The child perceives the outcome of these initiatives from direct feedback, without social ratification, though this may be added if onlookers are present. As soon as acts involve intention, the realizing of the intention becomes the basis for success or failure. A girl who tries to make herself a dress or a boy who tries to mend a broken tricycle can have clear knowledge of success or failure before any other person offers an opinion on the subject. They may even reject that opinion. Erikson observes that "children cannot be fooled by empty praise and condescending encouragement."[21]

Interpersonal competence works basically in the same way, but the situation is complicated by the powerful feelings of dependence, love, and hate that surround the most important human objects. In his attempts to influence the human environment, a child is handicapped by being young and unable to do without the continuing favor of those he would like to influence. There is the further complication that other people have a stake in their own sense of competence and may respond touchily to any challenge to their power or authority. Commonly, parents have believed that when a young child begins to assert himself it is vitally important to keep him in his place, cut him down to size, let him know who is the boss; otherwise there can be no hope of bringing him up as a socialized being. A final complication with respect to interpersonal competence is that the child's initiatives sometimes bring down upon his head a series of expressed judgments—"naughty child," "fresh kid," "smarty pants"—that seem to apply to him as a person, not just to the transaction that elicited them. Attaining a sense of interpersonal competence in the early years is no mean achievement. The human environment often seems little disposed to welcome it.

Example of Unusual Initiative: Benjamin Franklin

To illustrate the full flowering of initiative and self-confidence during the course of life we take the example of Benjamin Franklin, who toward the end of his career wrote an autobiography that is illuminating on this point.[22] Franklin qualifies as one of his country's great men by virtue of contributions to science and to public affairs, most notable of the latter being the diplomatic and financial achievements that supported Washington's military skill in winning the Revolutionary War in 1783. The autobiography was written to instruct young people in the ways of success, and allowance must be made for the selectivity that would result from this goal, but there is no reason to doubt the essential truth of what the author chose to set down.

From his childhood he cites instances of leadership in enterprises with other boys, but the most outstanding example of his initiative takes the form of a zeal for learning. This is the more remarkable in that it came largely from within and was only in small part a product of family expectations or of pressure from such schools as existed in his boyhood. While apprenticed

---

[21] E. H. Erikson, *Childhood and Society*, p. 235.
[22] B. Franklin, *Autobiography* (1791) (London: J. M. Dent & Sons, Ltd., Everyman's Library Edition, 1908).

to a trade, young Franklin spent his lunch hour and spare time studying. Among other things he taught himself the French language, and he carried out a systematic scheme for improving his writing of English prose, giving the project an amount of time and patient labor that would amaze any schoolmaster. At the age of 22 he established himself as a printer in Philadelphia, made a success of the business, and soon emerged as a man of prominence in his community.

Franklin's high sense of competence, backed by unusual intellectual gifts, shows during his adult life in a pattern of alert perception, sustained reflection, and prompt, confident initiative. His experiment with a kite in a thunderstorm is only an especially dramatic instance of the curiosity and ingenuity that made him in his day an international scientific authority on electricity. The same qualities kept reappearing in practical ways. Reflecting on the large loss of heat up the chimney in the ordinary fireplace, he designed what came to be known as the Franklin stove, which used less firewood and circulated more heat into the room. Noticing that street lamps with round globes grew dim with soot in the course of the night and were easily broken, he designed new lamps with air inlets at the bottom and flat panes of glass that could be readily replaced. Mud and dust prompted him to draw up plans for regular street cleaning; destructive fires led him to organize the first fire-fighting company; and lack of available books inspired him to start the first subscription library, forerunner of the public libraries of a later day. Many of his city's prominent institutions, including the University of Pennsylvania and the Pennsylvania Hospital, came into being because of Franklin's alert eye for public need and his ceaseless initiative in getting something done. To an extraordinary extent his mind let nothing rest without at least a try at bringing about improvements.

Franklin's confidence with the inanimate world was matched by a strong sense of interpersonal competence. He learned from frustrations and modified his behavior appropriately. Describing his efforts to start the library, he reflected as follows on the art of persuading people to give money:

> The objections and reluctances I met with in soliciting the subscriptions, made me soon feel the impropriety of presenting one's self as the proposer of any useful project, that might be supposed to raise one's reputation in the smallest degree above that of one's neighbours, when one has need of their assistance to accomplish that project. I therefore put myself as much as I could out of sight, and stated it as a scheme of a *number of friends*, who had requested me to go about and propose it to such as they thought lovers of reading. In this way my affair went on more smoothly, and I ever after practis'd it on such occasions.

In similar fashion, having been highly disputatious as a youth, he learned to sacrifice vanity in order to improve his power to influence others.

> I made it a rule to forbear all direct contradiction to the sentiments of others, and all positive assertion of my own. I even forbid myself the

use of every word or expression in the language that imported a fix'd opinion, such as *certainly, undoubtedly*, etc., and I adopted, instead of them, *I conceive, I apprehend*, or *I imagine* a thing to be so or so; or it *so appears to me at present*. When another asserted something that I thought an error, I deny'd myself the pleasure of contradicting him abruptly, and of showing immediately some absurdity in his proposition; and in answering I began by observing that in certain cases or circumstances his opinion would be right, but in the present case there *appear'd* or *seem'd* to me some difference, etc. I soon found the advantage in this change in my manner; the conversations I engag'd in went on more pleasantly. The modest way in which I propos'd my opinions procur'd them a readier reception and less contradiction; I had less mortification when I was found to be in the wrong, and I more easily prevail'd with others to give up their mistakes and join with me when I happened to be in the right.[23]

Franklin's method of improving his interpersonal competence involves curbing personal vanity in order to consider the feelings of others. He was, moreover, a man of high moral principle in public affairs, so that the influence he sought to exert upon people was in the service of improving human welfare. But he gives his account with a certain cool detachment, with perhaps a hint of pleasure in being able to make people do what he wanted, that serves to remind us that interpersonal competence yields satisfactions capable of growing into a sheer love of power. Furthermore, there is no intrinsic connection between competence and good causes. The great villains of history have often been highly competent and supremely self-confident people; that is why they have been able to do so much harm. In our time, with its multitude of information media, the cold manipulation of people's wishes in the interests of commercial gain and the crude shaping of their attitudes for the sake of political power show that interpersonal competence can coexist with a cynical contempt for other human beings. The motive we have been examining must be studied for just what it is: an urge to explore one's environment, to try one's efficacy in having an influence upon it, and thus to attain competence in dealing with the world in which one lives. Whether the forms of competence attained are admirable or not is quite another matter.

Influence of Parental Attitudes on the Growth of Competence

From the child's point of view, it would seem ideal if his initiatives were always allowed to prevail and if his achievements were regularly greeted with respect. Sometimes parents aspire to take this benign position, but unfortunately nothing guarantees that the child's initiatives will stay within the bounds of safety or of what the parents can tolerate. We should recall the plight of the indulgent overprotective mothers in Levy's study, who desperately sought help to recapture some sense of maternal competence in dealing with their demanding, tyrannical, insufferable children. The low control that

---

[23] The two excerpts are from pp. 139–140 and 162–163 of the *Autobiography*.

was characteristic of these mothers, and the doting nature of their love, encouraged initiatives in a great many directions, but offered no training in living with other people and respecting their rights. Children brought up in this way are in for a bad time when they arrive at school and discover that they cannot deal with teachers and other children just as they please.

At the other extreme is a touchy sense of parental competence that requires constant display of superior wisdom, knowledge, and power. Overtly or implicitly, parents with this attitude belittle the child's initiatives at every turn and show him no respect. The child's resources for dealing with this atmosphere are not extensive. Anxious compliance with distrust of his own initiatives offers the readiest accommodation. The result is the opposite of Franklin's serene self-confidence. The child would learn French and improve his English only if some adult authority insists upon it. He would endure inefficient chimneys, smoky street lamps, and destructive fires with resignation rather than change the way things had always been done. If prospective donors refused to contribute money to a good cause, he would draw the conclusion that it was wrong to ask. He would feel no need to temper self-assurance in arguments; he would assume from the start that the other person was right.

These two extreme types of consequence suggest that a parental middle ground is more likely to be conducive to a realistic and socialized sense of competence. This hypothesis is congruent with the conclusions drawn in Chapter 3 with respect to the variable of high and low control. The exact pattern of encouragements and restraints will always depend upon a specific situation. It will also be affected by the child's activity level—whether he needs shackles or wings—and by other relevant constitutional qualities. But the problem can be made less abstract, and perhaps thereby less difficult, if we bear in mind the nature both of the restraints called for in child training and of the parental behavior that is most conducive to self-respect.

It is a mistake to picture childhood as wholly a battle of wills. Even Freud's prototype of toilet training does not justify representing the child as an all-out champion of free instinctual gratification struggling against impositions of an evil society. The hypothetical anal pleasures are not being snatched away; they are being restricted merely with respect to time and place. This is generally true, as Murray has pointed out, with respect to training and discipline. Cultural and parental prescriptions do not call for total suppression of the child's needs but for their expression at the right times, in the right places, in the right modes, and with the right objects.[24] Being able to meet parental expectations is thus something of an accomplishment, not a surrender, and it may be a real source of satisfaction to the child. Psychological theories that put all the emphasis on instinct, drive, and impulse, and picture socialization as a long dreary process of giving up what the child really wants, have obscured the obvious fact that children like to grow up. Children have a stake in their own sense of competence, want to

[24] H. A. Murray, *Explorations in Personality* (Fairlawn, N.J.: Oxford University Press, 1938), p. 136.

be respected as adults as much and as soon as possible, and may be positively eager to accomplish what is necessary to this end. There is plenty of room for respect and for self-respect in the child's learning to fit his initiatives into the channels of socialized behavior.

The most important way in which parents can support a child's initiative is to feel and communicate *respect*. This does not necessarily mean to feel love; it means to notice and appreciate the child's ability, as shown in his manifestations of competence. Parental respect for a child appears in its purest form in the experience of astonished admiration for something the child has said or done, the kind of experience that causes the parent to muse: How did he get to have such fortitude, such wisdom, such skill, such perceptiveness so early in life? Respect dwindles, of course, if the parent starts congratulating himself on having brought the child up well, displacing the credit to himself. It may be that he deserves some credit, but respect implies giving credit to the other person. Evidences of respect go far to make a child feel that he is fundamentally valued, and they soften the pain of such restraints as may be necessary.

Lasting Consequences of Early Striving for Competence

What are the lasting effects of experiences in the sphere of competence during the first five years of life? Is the child's history in dealing with the inanimate world fateful for his adult confidence in managing the physical environment? Is his experience with interpersonal competence, mainly with parents and siblings, decisive for his adult relations with other people?

Clinical evidence again favors the idea that the consequences are lasting. There are plenty of case histories in which the effects might be described as cruelly lasting. The work with patients that led Alfred Adler to his conception of the inferiority complex and the striving for superiority convinced him that the first five years were decisive for a basic sense of competence. Memories brought forward in psychotherapy are sometimes heavily loaded with episodes of belittlement and shame created by parents or older siblings. Most people can remember incidents from the ages of 4 and 5, and those that bred shame are not infrequently represented. This evidence is, of course, imperfect, but there is probably no reason to doubt that adverse experience with the sense of competence in early childhood has strongly lasting effects in some cases. What we do not know is the generality of the proposition. Do good experiences produce lastingly good consequences, and can we suppose that in an unselected adult population individual differences in self-respect would be correlated with early childhood experience?

One line of research, inspired by Freud's ideas about toilet training and the anal stage, has led to a dead end. After examining 17 studies in which a relation was sought between elimination training and later personality, Caldwell draws the conclusion that significant relations have not been demonstrated.[25] Elimination training, however, is but a small part of the larger issue of the growth of a sense of competence.

The larger problem has thus far received little attention from research workers. The report that comes closest to bearing on the issue is one by Macfarlane based on a longitudinal study in which a group of normal subjects was examined at frequent intervals from birth to the age of 30.[26] Many of the subjects judged to be competent as adults had also been competent during childhood, as shown in both schoolwork and social interaction, but this was not always true. Some of the outstanding adults had earlier been conspicuous for academic difficulty, disciplinary trouble, and social ineptitude. The reverse side of the picture was similar: some children who were competent during the early years turned into adults full of burdensome problems. Commenting on these results, Wenar remarks that "while it may be generally true that 'nothing succeeds like success,' it is not inevitably true. Something must be missing from the simple formula."[27] As we have seen, a lot is usually missing when a formula about personality is made too simple.

It seems a reasonable conclusion, not inconsistent with Macfarlane's report, that in a general way those children who develop a good level of effectiveness and sense of competence will continue to exhibit these qualities as adults, while those who are less successful in these respects will carry the burden of inferiority feelings into their adult lives. It is not impossible, however, for such continuities to be markedly interrupted by events and circumstances along the way, with the result that some children do not live up to their early promise while others arrive at a belated flowering. This conclusion can hardly be said to qualify as a tightly specified scientific proposition, and it will not become so until research based on an intensive knowledge of subjects' lives makes it possible to state the conditions under which the early level of competence does or does not continue into adulthood.

[25] B. M. Caldwell, "The Effects of Infant Care," in *Review of Child Development Research*, **1** (1964), esp. 41–55.

[26] J. W. Macfarlane, "Perspectives on Personal Consistency and Change: The Guidance Study," *Vita Humana*, **7** (1964), 115–126.

[27] C. Wenar, *Personality Development from Infancy to Adolescence* (Boston: Houghton Mifflin Company, 1971), p. 72.

10 Anxiety, Defense, and Aggression

Two characteristic human tendencies—anxiety and aggression—create serious problems for civilized living. If we were not so easily moved to fear and so quickly aroused to anger we would be spared many of our most difficult problems, both in personal development and in peaceable existence with our fellow men. The survival value of swiftly triggered powerful responses to danger and to frustration is easy to imagine, especially under precivilized conditions, but we could do with less of these evolutionary assets when it comes to growing up in relatively civilized communities and trying to be citizens of the crowded world. Even a fortunately situated person can discover in himself, if he cares to look, how often feelings of anxiety and anger are at least mildly aroused. He is unlikely to get through his daily newspaper without several arousals of these feelings. When development takes place under conditions of real danger, deprivation, and hostility, it is not strange that anxiety and anger become dominant affects, usually to the detriment of other aspects of growth.

Under certain conditions flight is a competent way of dealing with the environment. In the face of a real danger that cannot be met with available resources, flight is the only sensible course of action. Under other conditions, such as the presence of an obstacle, aggression in the form of heightened effort to remove the obstacle also qualifies as sensibly adapted behavior. Ideally the course of growth is marked by a general increase in competence, which allows us to deal more adequately with dangers and obstacles, thus reducing the occasions for terror and rage. But this desirable outcome can never be complete. We continue to have occasions for dread and for wrath, and these emotions can be so strong that they block further appraisal of the situations that set them off. As this chapter will show, it is a difficult matter to bring these two powerful and primitive tendencies under the kind of control that would be most advantageous for civilized living, and attempts at control can sometimes distort the process of growth. In their different ways fear and anger are difficult members of the household of personality.

Anxiety and the Avoidance of Danger

In a work of no small influence in its time, William McDougall undertook to catalogue the principal instincts of man, emphasizing those that we share with other animals.[1] It was part of his plan to show that the arousal of each instinct carried with it a characteristic emotional experience. First on the list he placed "the instinct of flight and the emotion of fear." He gave them this position of priority because of their great force: their power to interrupt and take precedence over other activities. Fear, once aroused, McDougall wrote, "haunts the mind; it comes back alike in dreams and waking life, bringing with it vivid memories of the terrifying impression. It is thus the great inhibitor of action, both present action and future action, and becomes in primitive human societies the great agent of social discipline through which men are led to the habit of control of the egoistic impulses."[2] McDougall's vocabulary may be rather out of date, but he set the themes for what today we would be more likely to express as the place of anxiety in human affairs and in the growth of personality.

Fear and anxiety have occasioned confusion in systematic thinking because in ordinary usage the terms are not sharply distinguished. One of the rough distinctions most often proposed is that *fear* should be used when the object of danger is clearly perceived, *anxiety* when the object is dimly discerned or unknown. The difference is not easy to establish in practice, and in any event there seems to be no doubt that we are dealing with a single biological tendency, the goal of which is the avoidance of danger. *Anxiety*, which refers to the affect rather than to any pattern of avoidant actions, is the word most often encountered in the literature of personality. In most cases the context shows that this word is standing as a shorthand expression for a strong biological urge that could be spelled out as a tendency to avoid dangers and the unpleasant emotions to which they give rise.

Origin and Nature

Anxiety is displayed early in infancy. There has been speculation that it may first occur during the events of birth, which impose severe and difficult stimulations on the infant. Watson, in the early experiments whereby he tried to establish the innate stimuli to various emotions, concluded that fear was elicited by loud sounds and by loss of physical support, as when the

---

[1] W. McDougall, *An Introduction to Social Psychology* (1908), 16th ed. (Boston: John W. Luce & Co., 1923).

[2] *Ibid.*, pp. 57–58.

infant was quickly lowered or loosely held.[3] The list may well not be exhaustive, but it is not hard to perceive the survival value of a very strong response to these particular threats. The range of stimuli to fear is rapidly enlarged in the course of childhood through direct experiences of pain and through instruction by other people; children learn to fear more things than they are born to fear. The earliest form of response was described by Watson as catching the breath, clutching with the hands, closing the eyes, puckering the lips, and then crying. Subsequent research has refined this description especially with respect to a more or less uniform immediate pattern known as the *startle response*.[4] One of the problems of the young infant in coping with danger is that the motor processes necessary for effective flight have not yet developed. The loud cry is well adapted to getting something done, but for some time the human animal has to put up with a high degree of helplessness in escaping danger and dispelling anxiety.

The relation between action and feeling can be seen more clearly in fully developed adult experiences with danger. Basing his work on the unusual and lasting dangers of modern warfare, Emilio Mira, a psychiatrist for the Spanish Republican Army in 1938, described an evolution of fear from mild anxiety to acute panic.[5] In the early stage, when fear is still mild, the emotion appears to serve the useful purpose of "arousing, sustaining, and directing activity,"[6] with increased vigilance toward outside events and a preparation of bodily resources for strenuous activity.[7] A person may sense mild risks in civilian life, such as facing an audience or starting down a ski slope, as agreeably arousing and challenging, causing him to put forth his best efforts. If the danger is somewhat greater the unpleasantness of anxiety becomes more evident, and behavior is increasingly cautious and restricted. This trend is shown in dramatic form when troops advancing through supposedly safe territory suddenly encounter enemy sniper fire. They take cover as best they can, and their movement is now strictly limited by considerations of safety, their attention fiercely concentrated on sources of danger, and their emotional state sharply unpleasant. Still greater dangers lead to higher levels of anxiety, incessant preoccupation with danger, disorganization of thought and action, and what Mira describes as "an extremely unpleasant sensation of losing one's mental balance." If the trend continues further, the end result is complete disorganization and a nightmare state of panic. The anxiety reaction is pushed beyond its point of biological utility and now simply adds to its victim's helplessness.

[3] J. B. Watson, *Psychology from the Standpoint of a Behaviorist* (Philadelphia and London: J. B. Lippincott Co., 1919), Chap. 6.

[4] W. A. Hunt and C. Landis, "The Overt Behavior Pattern in Startle," *Journal of Experimental Psychology,* **19** (1936), 312–320.

[5] E. Mira, *Psychiatry in War* (New York: W. W. Norton & Company, Inc., 1943), pp. 31–35.

[6] R. W. Leeper, "A Motivational Theory of Emotion to Replace 'Emotion as Disorganized Response,'" *Psychological Review,* **55** (1948), 5–21.

[7] W. B. Cannon, *Bodily Changes in Pain, Hunger, Fear and Rage,* 2d ed. (New York: Appleton-Century-Crofts, 1929), esp. Chaps. 2 and 12.

It is clear that a basic biological endowment of this kind, consisting of a sensitivity to danger, a strongly arousable impulse to avoid the danger, and an emotion the mounting unpleasantness of which adds strength to whatever actions are undertaken, has enormous value for animals in the struggle for survival. This endowment is of no less value for human beings in circumstances that approximate those in which animal survival is challenged. Civilization, however, has in several respects changed the human situation, and anxiety proves to be a mixed asset for the growth of personality. Anxiety is so unpleasant that relief from its tension serves as a tremendous reward. Behavior that leads to anxiety reduction is easily learned, indeed easily overlearned so that its modification becomes difficult, a point that has been demonstrated even in animal experiments.[8] Because the human infant is so helpless, the reduction of his anxieties is accomplished very largely by the people who are taking care of him. Within a fairly short time the infant learns to respond to absence or inattention on the part of these people as signs of danger, and their presence or attention take on the power to reduce anxiety. Safety and security become strongly attached to the behavior of other people, so that children sense danger in parental ill humor, punishment, or rejection, in unfairness or defeat by siblings, or in disapproval by other members of the community. McDougall's perception of fear as an agent of social discipline should not be restricted to primitive societies. Socialization in civilized societies, too, depends in part on the child's need for the security provided by an attentively supporting human environment. For the sake of this security —this anxiety reduction—he will shape his behavior at least in some degree to meet parental and cultural expectations.

The effects of anxiety on the development and later economy of personality can best be shown in examples in which this influence is fairly great. Cases of neurosis would serve the purpose, but even more instructive at this point are life patterns that bear the marks of large sacrifices to anxiety yet within their limits are relatively organized and stable. It will be evident that social class status makes a contribution to this outcome.

Example of a Constricted Personality

An example of such constriction with stability is a man who will be called Clarence Clark, a 41-year-old accountant whose life story was examined during a study of political attitudes.[9] Clark was the son of a school janitor, a reliable but very cautious man whose aspirations in later life became centered on the prospect of a pension. His mother was of middle-class origin with a high school education; it was largely because of her wishes in the matter that their home was in a "better than average" neighborhood that strained the

---

[8] R. L. Solomon and L. C. Wynne, "Traumatic Avoidance Learning: The Principles of Anxiety Conservation and Partial Irreversibility," *Psychological Review*, **61** (1954), 353–385.

[9] M. B. Smith, J. S. Bruner, and R. W. White, *Opinions and Personality* (New York: John Wiley & Sons, Inc., 1956), pp. 203–210.

family finances. Clarence was early made to understand the difficulties of making both ends meet. He was obliged to help out with part-time jobs from the age of 13 until he finished his education through high school and a two-year business college. Both parents were strong advocates of education as the route to success in life. Both frequently spoke of the sacrifices they were making so that their son and daughter might enjoy this great benefit. When Clarence misbehaved his father talked to him seriously, reminding him of these sacrifices and of the worry he was causing his parents. This appeal to sympathy caused the boy to decide to improve his ways. Play with other children was also shadowed by uneasiness, partly because Clarence was small and thin, partly because his mother discouraged rough games, fortifying her timid overprotection with a theory that his bones were brittle.

It appears from these details that Clark's personality developed in an atmosphere of dangers. He feared parental displeasure and rejection, the roughness and competitiveness of other children, the possibility of not doing well in school, the threat of what the neighbors might think, and the more general possibility of economic failure with its attendant social contempt. The only safe course he could discover through these dangers was more or less complete submission to the demands and expectations of those around him. Hard work and self-discipline appeared to be the only possible routes to cconomic capability and self-respect. There was no room in the program for wayward impulses, idle curiosity, or risky adventures. His rejection of such tendencies was so complete that it colored his performance even on standard psychological tests. With tasks that were clear and objcctive, in which there was always a right answer, he worked well; his I.Q. of 125 put him in the top 4 or 5 percent of the population. With less structured tasks, however, and with tests requiring a free use of imagination, he was often hopelessly at a loss and eager for guidance from the examiner. Even telling what he saw in the Rorschach inkblots, where by definition there are no objectively right answers, seemed to him adventurous to the point of real discomfort. He played it safe by restricting himself to a few obvious and conventional percepts.

The pattern of constriction shown in the psychological tests was equally apparent in the way he led his life. At 41 he had become head of a four-man accounting unit in a large manufacturing corporation. There was no chance for further advancement, but his position was secure and he was not looking for opportunities elsewhere. Giving orders to his three subordinates bothered him and led him occasionally to do their work for them; largcr responsibilities would have been distinctly alarming. At home he spent most of his time puttering around the house and dealing with finances: "My one ambition in life," he remarked, "is to get my bills paid up." When he played with his children it was with strong emphasis on their improvement in the serious business of life. Except for certain company-organized activities, always with groups of familiar people, he had no interests outside his home and job, no participation in the surrounding community, and no concern about politics. His information on controversial issues was likely to be sparse, and his opinions had a soft quality that suggested a desire to avoid controversy and commitment—to avoid dealing with the issue at all. He lived in a small world, which was precisely the way he wanted it.

Clarence Clark illustrates the manner in which anxiety can be kept down by a general constriction of interests. For the sake of safety he leads a planful, orderly life confined to a small environment with which he has learned to cope. The price for this reduction for anxiety is that his days are routine and colorless, his ambition is restricted, and his assertiveness is smothered to the point of making it hard for him to maintain a pleasing self-picture. These sacrifices, perhaps with some jealousy of the freedom of less constricted people, generate a certain resentfulness that comes out in fault-finding and petty criticism of others. Yet on the whole the scheme may be said to work, in the sense that Clark is not given to disorganizing anxieties, that he lives stably, and that he gets a certain quiet enjoyment out of his life. It is possible that temperamental qualities like those discussed in an earlier chapter play a part in his docile adaptation. There is no independent measure of this, though everything about him—slight physique, gentle manner, flat tone of voice, blandness of affective expression—suggests that under no circumstances could he have been a firebrand or a man of overflowing zest. But in any event his personality must have been largely made, not born, and in this process the workings of the basic motive of avoiding anxiety are conspicuously clear.

Defense Mechanisms

Freud is still known as the man who laid bare the secrets of sexuality. But it may be that as time passes his fame will depend even more on his unmasking of the devious workings of defenses against anxiety. His genius for perceiving an erotic undertone in the free associations, dreams, and behavior of his neurotic patients was matched by an equally penetrating insight into the mental maneuvers whereby human beings protect themselves from the painful experience of fear. Freud's most striking disclosures along this line are embodied in his concept of mechanisms of defense. These are relatively primitive devices, almost wholly unconscious, which involve distorting one's cognition of oneself or of the environment in order to feel secure. As his theory of neurosis developed, Freud came to see that anxiety and its avoidance formed the central problem in neurosis. Neurotic patterns of life could be understood as the ultimate consequence of defensive inhibitions learned early in childhood as a means of avoiding the dangers, real or fancied, that attend meeting parental expectations and discipline. Neurosis, in other words, sprang from an undue thwarting of instinctual drives by the anxiety incident to becoming socialized.

Freud's eye-opening discoveries about defense mechanisms stimulated an impressive series of observations of the part played by anxiety in the growth of personality. Defense mechanisms were soon seen as only a starting point in describing the role of anxiety. As personality develops, defensive maneuvers also develop, with the result that if the earlier anxieties persist the defenses against them may become widespread and highly elaborated. One of Freud's early followers, Wilhelm Reich, introduced the picturesque idea of *character armor*.[10] This expression refers to traits or habits, seemingly superficial and far removed from present danger, which nevertheless serve as a protective front line against the arousal of deeper anxieties. For example, formality of manners, formality of dress, and formality of speech may all combine to keep relations with other people distantly impersonal, allowing one to avoid dangers associated with intimacy. The more genial trait of cheerful chattering about everyday matters may perform the same service, by keeping the conversational initiative in the speaker's hands and thus blocking more serious, more threatening talk. Protective traits of this sort, however, are not likely to stand in isolation. Other workers in the psychoanalytic tradition, notably Karen Horney, developed the idea of a *protective organization* that manifests itself more or less consistently in many aspects of life.[11] Using again as an example a person who has carried over from childhood a strong anxiety about close human relations, his whole pattern of life might be laid out so as to minimize this danger. Thus he might choose an occupation that entailed minimal social interaction and much concentration on objective work; he might live not in a sociable neighborhood but in an impersonal apartment building; he might avoid marriage, or marry someone who demanded no more than a cool companionship. Protective organization of this sort can restrict growth in many areas.

As adaptive devices the mechanisms of defense disclosed by Freud have a serious shortcoming: they impede the obtaining of further information. They are called into action under circumstances of acute stress, when anxiety threatens to mount to a real state of panic. One relieves the anxiety either by blocking out part of the cognitive field or by subjecting it to a major interpretative distortion; in either case, one sacrifices further relevant information. As far as our knowledge of defense mechanisms goes, derived largely from psychoanalytic treatment, they are adaptive in the short run. They cause trouble in the long run because they contain no provision for learning anything new about sources of danger. Closing the cognitive field is a static solution, guaranteeing that dangers will not be reexamined and may, therefore, retain their original power to precipitate anxiety. Thus defense mechanisms can be considered poor devices, the work of which must sometimes be undone for the sake of psychological health.

Repression

These points are illustrated in the case of repression, the best known of the defense mechanisms. As revealed through psychoanalysis, this mechanism is called into play chiefly when one's own impulses or feelings are on

---

[10] W. Reich, *Character-Analysis*, trans. T. P. Wolfe, 3d ed. (New York: Orgone Institute Press, 1949), esp. Chaps. 4 and 9.

[11] K. Horney, *Our Inner Conflicts: A Constructive Theory of Neurosis* (New York: W. W. Norton & Company, Inc., 1945).

the point of creating a dangerous situation; when, for instance, a child is intensely angered at his parents but also intensely frightened of the consequences of giving vent to this anger, or when a person becomes aware of a sexual impulse the enacting of which would produce horrified rejection by the community. One restores safety not by denying the consequences but by banishing one's own impulse from consciousness. One of Freud's patients recalled after prolonged treatment that on the occasion of her sister's death, standing at the coffin beside her brother-in-law, she had been visited by the thought, "Now he is free to marry me." Such an impulse, especially at such a time, shocked her so deeply that she instantly repressed it and for several years remained totally unaware of anything but a kindly interest in her brother-in-law. Is is unusual, of course, to be able to recapture in this way the memory of an impulse just before its swift and silent erasure from consciousness. The bulk of the evidence for repression comes from the phenomenon of *resistance* in psychoanalytic treatment. This consists of the blockages, evasions, and other difficulties of recall that occur even in a situation designed to make the recovery of past experiences easy. Often, inclinations denied at the outset and believed by the patient to be furthest from his thoughts work their way slowly into consciousness in the form of increasingly clear memories of their previous existence.

Although repression is often listed as one of several mechanisms of defense, there is reason to believe that it is more fundamental, more drastic, perhaps more primitive than the rest. Anna Freud, in her book on defense mechanisms, puts the problem as follows:

> Theoretically, repression may be subsumed under the general concept of defense and placed side by side with the other specific methods. Nevertheless, from the point of view of efficacy, it occupies a unique position in comparison with the rest. In terms of quantity it accomplishes more than they, that is to say, it is capable of mastering powerful instinctual impulses in face of which the other defensive measures are quite ineffective. . . . It is also the most dangerous mechanism. The dissociation from the ego entailed by the withdrawal of consciousness from whole tracts of instinctual and affective life may destroy the integrity of the personality for good and all. . . . The consequences of the other defensive methods are not less serious, but even when they assume an acute form they remain more within the limits of the normal.[12]

To speak of *repression* technically, as Freud did, it is necessary to constrast it with some word such as *suppression*. This term covers all ordinary instances in which desires are subjected to control, postponement, or even abnegation without being lost to consciousness. Repression can then be assigned its place as a more drastic mechanism, a truly primitive inhibitory process, the consequence of which is that the inhibited urges lose their right of representation in consciousness.

[12] A. Freud, *The Ego and the Mechanisms of Defence* (London: Hogarth Press, Ltd., 1937), pp. 52–55.

Although repression is often described as if it took place on single drastic occasions, Freud clearly thought of it as a continuing process. Central to his conception was the idea that impulses, especially those of sex and aggression, could not be successfully imprisoned by mere mental maneuvers; even when excluded from awareness they remained active and pushed for expression in disguised, roundabout, and sometimes disturbing ways. It was in order to understand these derivatives of repressed tendencies that Freud became so much interested in dreams, errors, and slips of the tongue, and he was convinced that the symptoms of neurosis were also byproducts of repressed urges. He saw repression as a continuous process, one that put a drain on energies and thus lowered the person's capacities to deal with problems. Repression and the other defense mechanisms might be initiated at moments of acute stress, but in order to perform their security function they had to be kept at work, and in this way they exerted a continuing influence upon the growth of personality.

Freud's conceptualization of these happenings in terms of energies was an appropriate guess in his own time, but we may understand them better by thinking of them more in the language of cognition and action. Suppose that a child, in the familiar trap of being angry at parental discipline but fearful of parental wrath, becomes one day so furious that he all but loses control and is sure his parents will throw him out forever if not actually kill him. Repression comes to the rescue, fury is knocked out of consciousness, the parents are appeased, safety is regained. If this were simply a case of conscious *suppression* we can imagine it being verbalized, something like this: "That was a near thing, I'd better be careful not to get so mad again and not to make them so mad." If the child handled his anger this way, he would not lose awareness of the possibility of anger, and it would be useful on subsequent occasions to attempt cognition of his own and his parents' incipient feelings in order to forestall a clash. The way would thus be kept open for exploratory behavior through which the child could gradually discover that neither his own nor his parents' anger was as terrifying as it had seemed on that critical occasion. If panic came so near, however, that *repression* ensued, these avenues to fresh learning would be effectively closed. The consequence of repression, if it were turned into words, would be, "I wasn't angry, so they weren't angry and everything is fine." This solution entails *not* looking at one's own angry impulses, not risking the discovery that they are still there. This narrows the realm in which cognition and action can function freely. The child will be free to interact with the parents only in ways that are placating, conforming, and ingratiating; he can make no move that evokes a parental frown or a faint hint that one is beginning to boil. The necessity to avoid friction with parents takes such precedence that it crowds out whole sectors of cognition and exploration—those sectors having to do with expressing anger, asserting oneself, arguing for one's rights, even seeking a fair compromise. Only the docile sector remains safe.

It is apparent from these considerations that repression does more than provide relief from anxiety in specific crises. Its use tends to impose restrictions on the subsequent course of development. This way of looking at the matter is more discriminating than Freud's metaphor of drained energies, which suggests merely a kind of generalized feebleness in all aspects of behavior. The repressed sector is likely to be somewhat specific, and there need be no impairment of development in other directions.

Projection

Anna Freud's idea seems applicable to the defense mechanism called *projection*, which compared to repression appears to "remain more within the limits of the normal." Projection is usually defined as the unconscious attribution of one's own thoughts, feelings, and impulses to other people. If the girl standing beside her sister's coffin had made use of projection she would have believed that her brother-in-law was thinking that he was now free to marry her, and she could have felt indignant that he should have such a thought at such a time. To be able to attribute one's own wish to another person, and to be indignant about it, implies being unaware that it is one's own; thus the projective device of relocating the forbidden impulse achieves the same result as repression with respect to consciousness. The lengths to which projection can go are shown in the delusional beliefs that occur fairly often in serious mental disorders. Thus it may be that a patient, outwardly docile in his humdrum hospital life, believes that the doctors are in league with a group of power-drunk political figures who want to keep him confined so that he cannot expose their evil machinations and assume his own rightful powers. Other patients suppose themselves to be objects of unwanted sexual attentions or to be victims of constant conspiracies having an exploitative content. In such cases the defensive processes have indeed destroyed the integrity of personality. The insistence that all initiative and all impulse comes from others makes it impossible to gain adequate information either about one's own true nature or about the true nature of other people. For security's sake the world has been fatally falsified.

But if this is projection are we not all projectors, and does this mean that we are all slightly mad? For it is certainly a widespread trait to dislike being at fault and to try to pin the blame on others. The tennis player who indignantly inspects his racquet after missing a shot and the housewife who asserts that the temperature control is out of order when the food is over-cooked both illustrate the power of the urge to prove that when things go wrong it is not our fault. It is easy to detect the origin of this device in the attempt to soften parental punishments and to preserve self-respect in the eyes of other children, but it is disconcerting to realize how extensively we still do it when supposedly grown up. But this everyday maneuver is not full-blown projection unless it is followed by a true and stubborn loss of aware-ness of one's own possible part in the transaction. Most of us are not really fooled by the fictions we improvise in moments of injured pride; we do not go on to have the offending racquet restrung or the temperature control re-placed. A confirmed projector would carry things much further, even to the point of charging that enemies had damaged the racquet in the locker room or that a hostile neighbor, knowing that guests were coming, had tampered with the temperature control.

In these examples the extremes are clear enough, but there is real difficulty in limiting the zone within which projection can be described as a defense mechanism. This difficulty becomes clear when we take into account the way we come to understand other people and their motives. We could never understand them without assuming that some of their thoughts and feelings and desires are like our own. We can attribute an inner life to other people only because we know about our own. Thus a kind of projecting is involved, a kind of attribution of our own urges to others, even in the most accurate and successful attempts to understand people. This sort of thing was what Anna Freud seems to have had in mind when she wrote that defense methods other than repression "remain more within the limits of the normal."

An attempt to deal systematically with this paradox has been made in a paper by Theodore Kroeber.[13] The central argument is that defense mechanisms are special cases of the adaptive processes that operate to produce normal development. What makes them special is the presence of so much anxiety that anxiety reduction takes precedence over all other considerations. We accomplish this, as was remarked earlier, by blocking out or distorting information. Although this strategy may be adaptive at the moment, it destroys the long-run effectiveness of the process that is involved. Thus the normal process of observing other people, empathizing with them, and thus learning to understand them is employed in the defense mechanism of projection, but it is used in a constricted fashion because of the overriding need to visit upon others the impulses one cannot tolerate in oneself. Kroeber argues that each defense mechanism can be paired with a flexible strategy of adaptation; each is the anxiety-ridden, primitivized, blindly inflexible form of a wholly legitimate way of dealing with experience. Thus *projection*, with its mistaken attribution to others of one's own objectionable tendencies, is paired with *empathy*, through which a person "sensitively puts himself in the other fellow's boots" and is able to "imagine how the other fellow feels."

Reaction Formation

Like projection, reaction formation eliminates from consciousness impulses that would lead to anxiety or humiliation. This defense mechanism can be defined as the development of tendencies or traits that are the very opposite of what we fear in ourselves. If a child fears the force and consequences of his own aggression, situations may arise in which mounting rage produces mounting panic; the child restores security by becoming the very picture of reasonableness, gentle deference, or kindly consideration. If a child comes to feel ashamed of dependence and is on occasion painfully ridiculed by his friends for signs of it, he may banish dependent longings altogether from

---

[13] T. C. Kroeber, "The Coping Functions of the Ego Mechanisms," in *The Study of Lives*, ed. R. W. White (New York: Atherton Press, 1964), Chap. 8.

consciousness and act thenceforth in the image of a frontiersman who can do everything without help. In either case the use of this defense mechanism immobilizes the offending impulse—the aggression or the dependence—but imparts rigidity to the opposite behavior, which is helping to counteract the impulse. A reaction formation against anger means that anger will never be shown or felt, even in situations where it might be appropriate. Similarly, a reaction formation against dependence will make a person compulsively independent, so that he will hate to borrow a nickel or ask for a direction when lost, and if he is sick in bed he will be a thoroughly difficult patient who cannot let others take care of him.

In Kroeber's scheme, *reaction formation* is paired with *substitution,* which signifies the free and unconstricted use of the same process. In everyday life most children become at least mildly ashamed of dependent and babyish ways, and nothing can be more sensible than to try out such forms of independent, grownup behavior as are within their reach. The value of these tactics was clearly shown in the Bethesda studies of transition from high school to college. Attempts of this sort to counteract shortcomings do not imply that the original problematic impulses have been banished from consciousness or that the new behavior is rigidly uncompromising. This is the way we all go about improving ourselves in our own eyes and the eyes of others.

The three defense mechanisms described here—repression, projection, and reaction formation—are probably the most common ones, but they are merely a sample of the longer lists represented in psychoanalytic writings.[14] Once again, however, our concern is not to construct a complete inventory of these primitive defensive maneuvers but to take account of their general effects on personal growth.

It is important to emphasize the primitive nature of the mechanisms of defense described by Freud. Literally they can be classed as strategies of adaptation, but they represent only a fraction of the resources available to human beings in dealing with the problems of their lives. This will become apparent in Chapter 15, in which we take up the full range of strategies of living.

Anger and Aggression

Of all our biological endowments, anger and aggression are the most problematical. We are forever destined to be social creatures, yet we have within ourselves impulses that all too easily lead to the destruction of socialized living. Today we are often in despair at our repeated failures to fashion a society that can maintain peaceful conditions and cope with the causes of

[14] A. Freud, *The Ego and the Mechanisms of Defence,* esp. Chap. 4; O. Fenichel, *The Psychoanalytic Theory of Neurosis* (New York: W. W. Norton & Company, Inc., 1945), esp. Chap. 9.

frustration and anger. Not all the blame, of course, should be put on aggression; other motives, and especially the fact of competition for limited resources, contribute to the enduring difficulty of living together in concord. But certainly the problem would be much less severe if we did not get angry so easily and build up resentments instead of dealing competently with causes of frustration.

Nature of Aggression

Watson, in his well-known search for innate emotional responses in infants, detected a pattern which he called *rage*. "Observation seems to show," he wrote, "that the *hampering of the infant's movements* is the factor which apart from all training brings out the movements characterized as rage."[15] Interference with activity and restriction of movement produce a characteristic pattern of response consisting of general struggle, vigorous flailing of the arms and legs, and screaming. As motor coordination advances, the flailing movements can be described as kicking, slapping, pushing, and even hitting, and they may be of considerable service in getting rid of the restraint.[16] In a more recent work Buss points out that noxious stimuli of various kinds, including attack, should be included among the antecedents of rage, but he still assigns a major position to blocking of free movement and interference with goal-directed activity.[17]

The biological significance of anger cannot be in much doubt. We have it in order to get out of tight places, both literally (restraint of movement) and figuratively (being cornered in an argument). The service it does for us is that of raising the level of activity in order to push aside and get rid of an obstacle or a restraint. The increase of intensity can be observed dramatically in the furious fight of a cornered wild animal. It is neatly disclosed in man when tempers are lost in the course of a competitive game. If a boys' boxing match degenerates into a fight the contestants will hit harder and faster, fouls will increase, and it may prove impossible to stop the match at the end of the round. Like other strong emotions, anger tends to subvert judgment and rationality. In a laboratory experiment in which subjects were purposely made angry, those who had a chance to dissipate their anger did better on a test of mental alertness than did those who were left simmering.[18]

Not until the child's second year can we observe an aggressive intent in his anger. At this time, according to Mittelmann, striking and kicking may be "carried out with a mischievous facial expression and with clear signs of enjoyment." Only by the third year is it clear that the child "realizes that what he does *hurts*. The child has experienced pain and discomfort from aggression

---

[15] J. B. Watson, *Psychology from the Standpoint of a Behaviorist*, p. 220.

[16] B. Mittelmann, "Motility in Infants, Children, and Adults," *Psychoanalytic Study of the Child*, **9** (1954), 161–162.

[17] A. H. Buss, *The Psychology of Aggression* (New York: John Wiley & Sons, Inc., 1961).

[18] P. Worchel, "Catharsis and the Relief of Hostility," *Journal of Abnormal and Social Psychology*, **55** (1957), 238–243.

directed toward him, and he now connects his inner experience with his own overt activity."[19] Rage has ripened into a capacity for purposefully aggressive action, in which destructive consequences are to some extent foreseen and intended.

According to a widely held idea, supposedly deduced from Darwin's theory of evolution, aggression exists in great force in animals and helps them to survive by tooth and claw, whereas in human beings, dwellers in groups and makers of civilization, aggressive urges are much attenuated. This view may be flattering, but it is certainly wrong. Careful observers of animals in natural settings have shown that there is little unnecessary, unadaptive aggression among them. Except when one species is the food supply for another, animals of different species typically occupy the same territory in peace. Furthermore, as Lorenz has shown in detail, fighting among members of the same species occurs only under quite special conditions, and has often become ritualized into threats, gestures, and restricted attack from which the loser retreats without really serious injury.[20] With this picture the human record compares most unfavorably. During the course thus far of the twentieth century, in many ways the apex of civilized living, the number of human beings killed by other human beings as objects of homicide, as victims of massacres, and as casualties of war runs into a great many millions. The history of punishment and torture and the records of what takes place when victorious armies overrun a civilian population give force to a statement once made by Durbin and Bowlby that no species of animal is "more aggressive or ruthless in their aggression than the adult members of the human race."[21] Seen in perspective, we look like such a quarrelsome, cruel lot that our concurrent capacity to be civilized becomes something of a miracle.

What this means in terms of motivation has been thought of in two rather different ways. According to one view, aggression is an instinct or drive like hunger or sex, building up energy that sooner or later will overflow into destructive behavior even without external instigation. The mischievous 3-year-old who seems to enjoy giving pain might be taken as a symbol of this view. According to the other view, aggression is a pattern of responses that occurs only when elicited by stimuli of a frustrating nature. In the second view destructive behavior will appear only to the extent that it is called forth, whereas the first assumes a deep innate malignity in human nature.

The first view was taken by Freud in his concept of the *death instinct,* a drive that, when directed outward, overflowed in general hostility toward others. "Men are not gentle, friendly creatures wishing for love, who simply

---

[19] Mittelmann, "Motility in Infants," pp. 161–162.

[20] K. Lorenz, *On Aggression*, trans. M. K. Wilson (New York: Harcourt Brace Jovanovich, Inc., 1963), esp. Chaps. 7 and 11.

[21] E. F. M. Durbin and J. Bowlby, "Personal Aggressiveness and War," in *War and Democracy: Essays on the Causes and Prevention of War*, ed. E. F. M. Durbin and J. Catlin (London: Routledge & Kegan Paul Ltd., 1938). See also D. Freeman, "Human Aggression in Anthropological Perspective," in *The Natural History of Aggression*, ed. J. D. Carthy and F. J. Elbing (New York: Academic Press, Inc., 1964).

defend themselves if they are attacked; a powerful measure of desire for aggression has to be reckoned as part of their instinctual endowment."[22] Freud's conception of an instinct entailed a fund of energy generated internally, producing unpleasant tension unless relieved by action of some kind, in this case hostile action. He therefore considered aggressive acts to be intrinsically satisfying, which justified him in speaking of a *desire* for aggression.

The other view was stated in its most downright form by Dollard and co-workers: Aggression is a response, and it is always to frustration.[23] The infant does not thrash and scream and get red in the face for the fun of it, so to speak, but only when subjected to restraint or some other noxious stimulation. According to the *frustration-aggression hypothesis,* this is the true model for human aggressive behavior. With a sufficiently refined analysis it would be possible to show that all instances of aggression, even the most hideous historical examples, were in some complex and cumulative way responses to frustration.

The issue between these two conceptualizations appeals to lovers of debate, perhaps all the more so because it cannot be settled by turning to the facts. To be sure, the results of physiological research seem to lie on the side of the frustration hypothesis. Summarizing these, Scott writes as follows:

> Thus the study of the physiology of aggression leads to the conclusion that there is a complex network of causal stimuli, no one of which entirely accounts for aggressive behavior. . . . The important fact is that the chain of causation in every case eventually traces back to the outside. There is no physiological evidence of any spontaneous stimulation for fighting arising within the body. . . . We can also conclude that there is no such thing as a simple "instinct for fighting," in the sense of an internal driving force which has to be satisfied. There is, however, an internal physiological mechanism which has only to be stimulated to produce fighting.[24]

These findings may give some readers a sense of relief, but the last sentence effectively spoils it. If we do not have an overflowing destructive instinct, it looks as if we had something just about as bad.

Unequivocal proof of a destructive instinct from direct observation of behavior would require instances of aggressive behavior in which antecedent frustration could be ruled out. With human beings it is virtually impossible to meet this condition. Delays in satisfaction, discipline, sibling rivalry, and many other circumstances serve to elicit aggression in some degree almost from the start, so that there can be no such thing as a certified frustration-free child.

[22] S. Freud, *Civilization and Its Discontents* (London: Hogarth Press, Ltd., 1930), p. 85.

[23] J. Dollard, L. W. Doob, N. E. Miller, O. H. Mowrer, and R. R. Sears, *Frustration and Aggression* (New Haven: Yale University Press, 1939).

[24] J. P. Scott, *Aggression* (Chicago: University of Chicago Press, 1958), pp. 63–64.

Furthermore, it is characteristic of human aggression that it can be delayed, concealed, and displaced to other objects. If a child is suddenly rough with the family dog or starts to smash his toys, it may turn out that an earlier event, such as a scolding or the forbidding of something much desired, has been perseverating in his mind. Indeed, the human capacity to think and to daydream makes it possible to keep the wounds of frustration open for long periods of time. Rebukes suffered from traffic officers may be remembered for decades, each time with feelings of anger, elevation of blood pressure, and invention of a still more crushing reply. Thus what appears to be a bottomless reservoir of aggressiveness may actually be fed from a bottomless reservoir of frustrations preserved and accumulated in memory.

These considerations do not rule out the possibility of an instinctive desire to be aggressive. The extent of human malignity continues to strike some observers as requiring this concept even though specific proof is impossible. But the understanding of personality can still go forward without settling this particular issue. It is clear that in the study of individual lives an important place must always be assigned to the vicissitudes of anger and aggression.

Control and Channeling of Aggression

Childhood aggression expresses itself in relatively crude forms such as the tantrum. Even the most permissive parents cannot long submit to this tyranny, and steps are taken to make the results of the tantrum unsatisfactory. This sets in motion a long series of exchanges that tend toward the control of aggression and its direction into acceptable channels. To the extent that parents respond to anger with anger of their own the child's aggression may be inhibited by sheer terror. If the parents are more restrained in evincing their displeasure, the child may still feel strong anxiety over loss of love. The control of aggression, however, is not wholly imposed from without. Violent anger is very often an ineffective way of dealing with a frustration, as anyone knows who has taken a hammer to an alarm clock he is unable to repair. Children presently realize that they have a stake in controlling the more impulsive manifestations of aggression; they are more likely to master obstacles, win arguments, and persuade parents if they stay cool enough to keep their wits about them. Strivings for competence thus become allied with parental training in the management of aggression.

It is possible to divide the reactions to frustration into three general types. Rosenzweig names these *extrapunitive*, *intropunitive*, and *impunitive* types of reaction.[25] The reaction is extrapunitive when we perceive objects or other people as being to blame for the frustration and direct anger at them. It is intropunitive when we see ourselves as to blame and are angry at ourselves for being clumsy or stupid or tactless. It is impunitive when our main response is to minimize the aggressive elements in an event, seeing the

[25] S. Rosenzweig, "Types of Reaction to Frustration," *Journal of Abnormal and Social Psychology*, **29** (1934), 298–300.

whole thing as of no consequence and not to be taken seriously. In the right circumstances each of these reactions is appropriate, but most people show a preference for one type or another and tend to give their preferred reaction in situations where it is not appropriate.

The stability of these preferential tendencies and their probable origins in childhood were investigated by Funkenstein, King, and Drolette in a study for which male college students served as subjects.[26] After some search, a frustrating task was found that seemed to divide the subjects not too unequally according to reaction type. The subjects were asked to read a passage, then give the substance of it aloud in their own words. They had to do this while attached to an apparatus called the sonic-confuser, which fed back to them through earphones the sound of their voices with a slight delay. Normal speaking is regulated by the feedback of hearing one's own voice, and this slight interference with the pattern produces stammering and other upsets that make it irritatingly difficult to concentrate on the given task. Subjects were interviewed immediately afterwards and categorized as Anger-Out (blaming the task and the experimenter), Anger-In (blaming themselves for doing poorly), Anxiety, and No-Emotion, the latter perhaps corresponding to the impunitive reaction type. Through a variety of procedures it was ascertained that the behavior in the experiment was consistent with the subjects' reactions to frustration in everyday life. Using life history materials the investigators found certain significant average differences among groups in the pattern of parental relations. Most pertinent here are those that differentiated the Anger-Out and Anger-In groups. In the former, the fathers were important as role models and sources of authority, but relations with them were full of friction. In the latter, fathers were again important but relations with them were close and affectionate. Apparently the preference for outwardly or inwardly directed aggression becomes established fairly early, and in boys depends importantly on the relation with the father. It is of interest that the subjects who were most heavily involved with their mothers because father was either weak or absent fell mostly into the Anxiety group. Findings for the No-Emotion group were not particularly clear.

The results of this experiment bring us back to the importance of parental attitudes, a topic already examined in Chapter 3. We saw there that the effect of the parents on the child's aggressive tendencies is always a matter of consequence. Parental rejection, for instance, evokes aggression but also anxiety. If the rejection is overt and unreasonable it may be possible for the child to respond with anger and rebellion (Anger-Out). If the rejection is covert, hidden beneath a façade of consideration, the child is constantly obliged to swallow his aggression (Anger-In). The parental pattern of control likewise exerts an influence on the child's expression of hostility. Loveless authoritarian control, as we saw, is capable of producing extrapunitive tendencies deflected from family to outgroups and other scapegoats.

[26] D. H. Funkenstein, S. H. King, and M. E. Drolette, *Mastery of Stress* (Cambridge, Mass.: Harvard University Press, 1957, esp. Chaps. 4, 15.

Inhibited Aggression

There is a reciprocal relation between competence and aggression, just as there is between competence and anxiety. In spheres in which a person has become competent he will be exposed to less frustration, hence less arousal of anger. There are situations, however, in which anger is constantly stimulated but effective action is impossible, either because of internal inhibition or because the outward situation defies change.

An an example of the blocking of aggression from within we take the following excerpt from an autobiographical study by a male college senior.

> In examining my own recent experiences I found a disturbing absence of aggression. In general, I find myself somehow unable to take part in "heated discussions," quite a handicap at an institution where there is a constructive clash of ideas going on all the time. Specifically, I am incapable of getting into arguments with my roommates, even though I sometimes feel ample reason to do so; and vice versa, I feel very anxious about their getting angry with me, making a constant effort to keep them on friendly terms with me. They are both basically easy-going, but when they do get into one of their infrequent arguments, I feel extreme anxiety and have to try to stop the argument or at least shunt it off into a more friendly level.
>
> Perhaps the best example of a situation in which control of emotions has become a frustrating nightmare is the trip I took across Europe last summer, during which I travelled for a while with a girl I previously had known only slightly. She was very flighty, impractical, and never willing to admit she was wrong. As a result, she was continually getting lost, making us miss trains, or locking us out of our hotel room when I was off taking a shower and clad only in a towel. All this bothered me no end, even though outside of these traits I liked the girl very much. These episodes I could have put up with, but over time they built up increasingly. A brief outburst of self-righteous anger would have set the situation straight and shown her my feelings. Unfortunately, I was quite incapable of verbalizing my anger and further frustrated by not understanding why I was incapable. The best I could do was make cold, biting remarks or simply ignore her, which did not help our relationship at all. She interpreted this as "aloofness" and a "prep-schoolish lack of emotion," but when she did sense my suppressed anger towards her, she told me I would feel much better if I could bring myself to have a good yell at her once in a while. Even then, though I agreed with her, I still could not get openly angered, only inwardly frustrated.

The girl's prescription is a common one, based on the theory that a catharsis of anger is better than bottling it up. But it seems clear that she was also trying to maintain her extrapunitive stance: her friend was wrong to be cold and sarcastic, he must mend his ways by blowing up and then being friendly again—there is no mention of her becoming a bit more careful about schedules and keys. The metaphor of catharsis with respect to anger takes attention away from the real nature of the young man's problem and the development he needs to undergo. Learning to have tantrums is not an adult goal. What is needed is to develop competence in expostulating when another person's behavior appears to be inconsiderate and unjust; expostulating with anger, but not to the extent of getting off the point, storming, and blocking the possibility of understanding and compromise. This is what is needed to get at the real causes of interpersonal frustration. When aggression is associated with so much anxiety that even the least hint of it produces inhibition, this competence fails to develop. But the feeling that others can never be opposed makes for great helplessness and weakens the growth of self-respect. In these circumstances working up one's power of expostulation by slow degrees is probably the best way to set development in motion.

The Effects of Chronic Indignation

When the source of frustration lies in the outside world, chronic indignation can be experienced with painful force. The most vivid examples are found in those who are obliged to live under conditions of continuing injustice. This may be true for a child whose parents markedly prefer a sibling. Unfairness will then manifest itself repeatedly, in large things and small, and the less-favored child will feel that there is absolutely nothing he can do about it; every attempt at expostulation is turned into a defeat. In adult life the same emotional impasse is created by chronic social injustices. In his autobiography, *Black Boy*, the novelist Richard Wright portrayed this situation vividly. Brought up in Mississippi, as a young child he had no contact with whites, though his family training gave him advance practice in being the object of harsh injustice. When he began to understand the caste system— "that there existed men against whom I was powerless, men who could violate my life at will"—there commenced an endless struggle with seething anger that never could be safely expressed.[27] A striking account is also given by James Baldwin, 16 years younger than Wright, for whom *Black Boy* was "an immense liberation and revelation" because it openly expressed "the sorrow, the rage, and the murderous bitterness which was eating up my life and the lives of those around me."[28] Baldwin writes as follows about his first drastic encounter with white prejudice, which took place when he went to work in a war industry in New Jersey during World War II.

> I learned in New Jersey that to be a Negro meant, precisely, that one was never looked at but was simply at the mercy of the reflexes the color of one's skin caused in other people. . . . That year in New Jersey lives in my mind as though it were the year during which, having an unsuspected predilection for it, I first contracted some dread, chronic disease, the

[27] R. Wright, *Black Boy: A Record of Childhood and Youth* (New York: Harper & Row, Publishers, 1945), pp. 64–65. Wright's life is described in some detail in Chapter 16, below.

[28] J. Baldwin, *Nobody Knows My Name* (New York: Dell Publishing Co., 1962), p. 191.

unfailing symptom of which is a kind of blind fever, a pounding in the skull and fire in the bowels. Once this disease is contracted, one can never be really carefree again, for the fever, without an instant's warning, can recur at any moment. It can wreck more important things than race relations. There is not a Negro alive who does not have this rage in his blood—one has the choice, merely, of living with it consciously or surrendering to it. As for me, this fever has recurred in me, and does, and will until the day I die.[29]

Richard Wright and James Baldwin, gifted and influential writers, do not in their own lives illustrate the full possible consequences of intense chronic indignation with no outlet whatsoever. But Wright in one of his novels, *Native Son*, attempted to describe them in the character of Bigger Thomas. The paradoxical nature of this novel has been much discussed. The whole last part is an account of the black boy's trial, which is a monument of racial prejudice, but the enlisting of sympathy for Bigger is made difficult by the fact that he has murdered a white girl, stuffed her in a furnace, tried to extort ransom for her, and murdered his black girlfriend lest she give him away. Why should a black author put his principal black character at such a huge disadvantage in his trial by whites? But in this particular novel Wright attempted to convey a different message.

> During the last two days and nights he had lived so fast and hard that it was an effort to keep it all real in his mind. So close had danger and death come that he could not feel that it was he who had undergone it all. And, yet, out of it all, over and above all that had happened, impalpable but real, there remained to him a queer sense of power. *He* had done this. *He* had brought all this about. In all of his life these two murders were the most meaningful things that had ever happened to him. He was living, truly and deeply, no matter what others might think, looking at him with their blind eyes. Never had he had the chance to live out the consequences of his actions; never had his will been so free as in this night and day of fear and murder and flight.
>
> He was more alive than he could ever remember having been; his mind and attention were pointed, focused toward a goal. . . . His being black and at the bottom of the world was something he could take with a new-born strength. . . . No matter how they laughed at him for being black and clownlike, he could look them in the eyes and not feel angry. The feeling of being always enclosed in the stifling embrace of an invisible force had gone from him.[30]

Wright describes in these passages the feeling of power, the experience of self-direction, and the sense of being alive that comes from carrying out in actuality the savage impulses so long stifled by white society. By implication he describes the previous consequences of chronic indignation without outlet:

---

[29] J. Baldwin, *Notes of a Native Son* (Boston: The Beacon Press, 1955), pp. 93–94.

[30] R. Wright, *Native Son* (New York: Harper & Row, Publishers, 1940), pp. 224–225, 141–142.

helplessness, lack of initiative, apathy, a sense of deadness. He is dealing here, of course, not just with the dynamics of aggression but with frustrations that affect many aspects of personality. If one's entire path of life and possibility of enjoyment are blocked by unfair social restraints, the effects are greater than the effects of more circumscribed frustration. The case of Bigger Thomas represents the devastation of all that is constructive in personality when chronic far-reaching frustration arouses chronic intense indignation and there are no effective ways to alter things for the better. Under these circumstances, Wright tells us, the only way to feel alive and capable may be to break out in acts of crude violence. This piece of insight on the novelist's part is of value in understanding the seemingly senseless violence that sometimes breaks out among people who are seriously disadvantaged.

Conclusion

Anxiety and aggression, both of which are deeply rooted parts of human nature, emerge in this chapter as sources of difficulty in the growth of personality. This is not because there is no room for them in adult life. The world is full of present dangers about which it is appropriate to be fearful. It is also full of possible future dangers that can be averted only by the persistent effort and planning to which anxiety is a proper spur. The world is also full of other people whose purposes differ from our own, whose interests collide with ours, and whose actions may constitute a chronic frustration. There is plenty of useful work for our capacities for fear and anger, provided we can keep them in appropriate channels and shape them toward carefully chosen purposes.

This proviso, however, points to the heart of the difficulty we have with these tendencies. All too easily they overflow appropriate channels and interfere with intelligent reality-testing. Especially in early life they quickly mount to desperate panics or to blind rages and tantrums. Furthermore, they are often aroused together in the course of socialization: parental restraint evokes anger, but anger against one's caretakers evokes fear of their anger and the loss of their love. Primitive defense mechanisms thrown into action to avoid anxiety must often serve also the purpose of avoiding anger. It is especially these early defensive operations that tend to block new learning and reality-testing, thus obstructing certain directions of development and narrowing the scope of future growth. Anxiety, as we have seen, tends to constrict personality in part or as a whole, requiring large sacrifices for the sake of safety. When aggression is severely inhibited, the paralysis may extend to all forms of self-assertion. Chronic indignation may become so preoccupying as to stunt the flourishing of other interests. On the other hand, aggression too little governed leads to constant friction with others, and anger channeled into hostility toward outgroups is likely to have disastrous social consequences. Clearly there are many ways in which development associated with anxiety, defense, and aggression can go astray. To such problems the solutions can never be simple.

11 Identification and Conscience

As one moves ahead chronologically in studying personal growth it becomes increasingly necessary to take account of cognitive development. The older the child, the more pertinent it is to ask how he understands his environment, how he construes the behavior and expectations of those around him, what personal meanings he gives to the events of which he is a part. This does not imply that motivation can be neglected. What a person is striving for is always an essential aspect of what he does. But in the course of time motivation is increasingly steered by cognition, so that one can discover the nature of the striving only by knowing how the situation was perceived. Sometimes a remark that sounds innocuous evokes a violent response from the person to whom it is addressed. The discrepancy makes sense only when we learn that the remark was perceived as a slur, an insult, a threat to pride. Much misunderstanding results from failure to detect personal meanings.

The cognitions most important for personality have to do with other people and with the nature of the social environment. They have to do with expressions of parental love or rejection, with rules and constraints and what is considered acceptable, and with the possibly unstable climate of parental feelings. They come to include the role structure of the family, the relations among family members, and the framework of expectations within which one's own behavior takes place. As the horizon enlarges it becomes necessary to grasp the nature of the surrounding society, including social status and ethnic groupings. These are the learning problems that are most fateful for personal development. The understanding of such phenomena, which are often elusive and indirectly communicated, is a considerable achievement in cognitive organization. Children arrive at it only as rapidly as their state of development permits.

In this chapter we shall take up a series of topics having as their central theme the manner in which children learn to live with the surrounding social world. First to be considered is the guidance provided us by theories of *learning* and of *cognitive organization*. Then we shall take up the topic of *identification*, an active process whereby the growing individual makes use of existing models of behavior in shaping his own. A somewhat different problem has to do with grasping and responding to the *expectations* that emanate from other people. Special attention will finally be given to the origins and evolution of *conscience*, a topic that has broad implications for later membership in adult society and for the values that will come to prevail in the adult world. All of these developments are likely to leave their marks on personality and contribute to the characteristics of each individual life.

The Concept of Reinforcement

It is impossible to go far in the psychological literature bearing on personality without discovering the prominent position occupied by the concept of reinforcement. This concept was derived originally from experiments in which animals gradually learned to solve problems set for them by the investigator. Reinforcement refers to the strengthening of some form of behavior, such as taking the correct turn in a maze, so that it occurs more promptly or more frequently on later occasions. What strengthens the response is its connection with a reward, which in animal research usually means reduction of a drive like hunger, thirst, sex, or escape from pain. Reinforcement through drive reduction is a formula of wide applicability in research. on animal learning. It is also useful, especially when amplified by the idea that rewards of a more social character, like expressions of love and esteem, can serve as reinforcers, in understanding how children pick up sequences of behavior that are instrumental in securing what they want and avoiding what they fear.[1]

Reinforcement in Childhood Development

In the earlier chapters of this book the principle of reinforcement has frequently been implied. It is clear, for instance, that overprotective mothers reward their children with love and approval for staying at their side (positive reinforcement) and punish them with criticisms and displays of hurt feelings (negative reinforcement) for independent steps away from home. These mothers also reinforce their children's habits of studying by bestowing attention, help, and praise on this activity. By one pattern of giving out rewards the mother can raise the frequency of docile, obedient behavior; by

---

[1] The relation between this concept of learning and the growth of personality is summarized by C. S. Hall and G. Lindzey, *Theories of Personality*, 2d ed. (New York: John Wiley & Sons, Inc., 1968), Chap. 11.

another, she can increase the probability that her children will make arrogant demands for services. Children are dependent on their parents in a great many vital respects, and they learn early to respond to the signs of parental pleasure and displeasure. The rewards are not as crude as in animal experiments, but there is some degree of analogy between children, so much of whose security and satisfaction is tied up with parental favor, and laboratory animals, who can assuage their drives only by behaving according to the design the experimenter has in mind for them.

The use of simple forms of reinforcement in experiments with children is illustrated in the following study. Azrin and Lindsley designed a situation in which it was possible without explicit verbal instruction to reward a certain act of cooperation.[2] Pairs of subjects between the ages of 7 and 12 years, facing each other across a table, played a game that involved inserting a stylus into holes on the board that each one had in front of him. Whenever the two children chose corresponding holes at the same time, reward appeared in the form of a jelly bean. Subjects learned perfect cooperation under these circumstances without specific instruction in about ten minutes; among other things, they agreed on division of the jelly beans, which came out of the apparatus one at a time. This part of the experiment was immediately followed by an extinction procedure during which no rewards were given for the correct combination of holes or for any others. Under these circumstances cooperative behavior fairly rapidly disappeared, and the only sign of its previous existence was its almost immediate reinstatement once the flow of jelly beans was renewed.

Readers who allowed themselves to hope that the subjects were being imbued with a lasting spirit of cooperation will be disappointed at the children's opportunism: they cooperated only as long as cooperation paid off in jelly beans. The experiment was not designed to exhibit the acquisition of lasting traits and enduring principles of conduct. As we shall see, these require learnings more complex than those evoked by playing a game for jelly beans. But it does call attention to an important matter consistent with a conception of personality as a partially open system in constant transaction with the environment. The concept of reinforcement has value for understanding not only the *acquiring* of behavior but also the *maintaining* of behavior. Skinner writes on this question as follows:

> Behavior continues to have consequences and these continue to be important. If consequences are not forthcoming, extinction occurs. When we come to consider the behavior of the organism in all the complexity of its everyday life, we need to be constantly alert to the prevailing reinforcements which maintain its behavior. We may, indeed, have little interest in how that behavior was first acquired. Our concern is only with its present probability of occurrence, which can be understood only through an examination of current contingencies of reinforcement.

    [2] N. H. Azrin and O. R. Lindsley, "The Reinforcement of Cooperation between Children," *Journal of Abnormal and Social Psychology*, **52** (1956), 100–102.

This is an aspect of reinforcement which is scarcely ever dealt with in classical treatments of learning.[3]

It is not inconceivable that even a trait that seems deeply ingrained and highly generalized, so that it continues to govern behavior despite many immediate disappointing consequences, will eventually fade out if it never leads to rewarding effects. Even a committed idealist may turn cynical and self-seeking if he finds himself bucking a system that never lets him prevail.

Much of the behavior of children in the family maintains its stability because the contingencies of reinforcement do not greatly change. Parental favoritism, for instance, is likely to show itself fairly constantly in a variety of situations, thus maintaining the reinforcement of such roles as "good child" and "bad child." An important principle in dealing with children's behavior problems is to diagnose the reinforcement contingencies that may be maintaining the problematic behavior in spite of everyone's expressed desire that it stop. If these maintaining conditions can be discovered, treatment can be effectively aimed at changing them. Peterson states as follows the questions that one must ask when seeking to devise a program for beneficent change:

> What, in specific detail, is the nature of the problem behavior? What is the person doing, overtly or covertly, which he or someone else defines as problematic and hence changeworthy behavior? What are the antecedents, both internal and external, of the problem behavior and what conditions are in effect at the time the behavior occurs? What are the consequences of the problem behavior? In particular, what reinforcing events, immediate as well as distant, appear to perpetuate the behavior under study? What changes might be made in the antecedents, concomitants, or consequences of behavior to effect desired changes?[4]

Peterson illustrates these principles in the case of a timid boy whose anxiety attacks, fear of heart failure, and spells of weeping were found to be subtly reinforced by concerned school officials and worried parents alike. The problem behavior produced consequences such as excuse from disagreeable tasks and expressions of sympathy, interest, and underlying affection. These reinforcements were by no means the whole explanation of the boy's trouble, but they suggested points at which it was possible to make a beginning of favorable change. It was proposed to the teachers that they try to avoid making the boy's anxiety attacks the occasion for granting him favors. The parents were likewise urged to express their interest and affection at other times and in connection with other types of behavior. The therapist lowered the value of the old reinforcements by gradually showing the patient that he considered the boy's attacks and the resulting excuses unworthy of a

---

[3] B. F. Skinner, *Science and Human Behavior* (New York: The Macmillan Company, 1953), p. 98.

[4] D. R. Peterson, *The Clinical Study of Social Behavior* (New York: Appleton-Century-Crofts, 1968), p. 57.

boy of his age. These changes in the contingencies of reinforcement had a favorable effect on the boy's behavior, reducing the frequency and intensity of his attacks.[5]

Limits of Reinforcement as an Explanation of Behavior

If we confine ourselves to children silently rewarded by jelly beans, the analogy with animals reinforced by pellets of food does not seem strained. But when we shift to a less artificial situation, as in the clinical case just described, the postulated reinforcements prove to be of quite a different order. It is a question now of social reinforcements, of satisfaction gained by eliciting from other people expressions of interest, love, and esteem. Although such expressions might be received with pleasure from anybody, they are much more reinforcing if they come from certain people important in one's life, such as teachers and especially parents. The reinforcing properties of affection depend, furthermore, on the character of the situation. One may construe sudden expressions of this kind from a stranger as instrumental to an unwanted seduction or a swindle, in which case their reinforcing value will probably be negative.

In the case just described, the whole program for changing reinforcement contingencies necessarily involved altering the cognitive fields of the participants. Teachers, parents, and the patient himself had to perceive the situation in a new light if the pattern of reinforcements was to be cast in a new shape. Care must be taken, then, to keep reinforcement from degenerating into a tag word that obscures part of what is really going on.

Reinforcement cannot be regarded as simple, virtually mechanical, once we go beyond the simplest kinds of behavior, in which animals and people may be a good deal alike, and begin to include the more highly developed cognitive fields of which only people are capable. The strengthening of behavior through need-satisfying or security-giving expressions is certainly a legitimate concept, but if it is necessary to specify in detail the circumstances under which such reinforcements will take place, we have already made the subject's cognitive field an essential part of the explanation. How does a person construe the events of which he is a part? Only if we know this can we understand what he will find rewarding about them.

This point is illustrated in a line of research begun in the 1950s called *verbal conditioning*. The suspicion had sometimes been voiced that in long-term psychotherapy the preconceptions of the therapist as to what was likely to be important would influence what the patient talked about. Thus the patient of a Freudian analyst would soon be concentrating on childhood sexual fantasies whereas the Adlerian patient would speak only of inferiority feelings and compensations. Such results could be attributed to selective reinforcement by the therapist through gestures and remarks expressive of interest when the patient touched upon the favored topics. In the experimental work initiated by Greenspoon and carried on by Krasner, Ullman, and many others,

[5] *Ibid.*, pp. 144–183.

it was shown that a therapist could influence markedly the content of a subject's conversation, even the frequency with which he used certain words, simply by saying "mm-hmm" or "good" or nodding his head or smiling whenever the chosen topics were mentioned or the chosen words uttered.[6] This seemed to exemplify social reinforcement in a form not too different from jelly beans dropping from an apparatus. The finding outraged the sensibilities of those who dislike the idea of being unwittingly manipulated, and it shook confidence in theories of personality derived from extended psychotherapy. But very soon it became apparent that the results were highly unpredictable; only under certain circumstances did the experimental reinforcers have their intended effect. Careful inquiry following the conditioning procedure revealed that the subjects introduced a number of variables over which the experimenter had no control. Presumably unlike animals, they wondered about the purpose of the experiment, were frustrated if they could not understand it, liked or disliked the experimenter, varied in their willingness to cooperate, and thought about a variety of things extraneous to the experiment. What started as an attempt to demonstrate the modifiability of verbal behavior by simple methods turned into a program of research that had to take account of the thoughts and feelings, the cognitive fields, and what Kanfer has called "the self-evaluating, self-motivating, and self-instructing aspects" of human subjects.[7]

Free use of the concept of reinforcement has had at least one highly unfortunate consequence for understanding the growth of personality. It has encouraged a belief that the power to deliver reinforcers lies wholly in the hands of parents, teachers, or other adults who are responsible for the guidance of development. Thus the shaping of behavior is seen as a one-way process by which adults through a careful manipulation of rewards and punishments mold the child's behavior into an acceptable form. This is, of course, an instance of the use of cause-effect reasoning and mechanical analogies where organismic and transactional thinking is required. The concept of reinforcement has played into this recurrent shortcoming of our powers of thought and has thus obscured the fact that social rewards cannot be paid out like coins having always the same value. Mothers briefed on reinforcement come to believe that they can encourage a trait like creativity by payments of praise, overlooking the circumstances that this praise will be valueless if the child himself judges his work to be badly done, and that it will be nearly valueless to a child who believes that a sibling rival received just a little more of it. Flattering as it may be to suppose that one has an endless bank account of reinforcers with which to buy other people's behavior, it is a plain misrepresentation of the facts.

[6] J. Greenspoon, "The Reinforcing Effect of Two Spoken Sounds on the Frequency of Two Responses," *American Journal of Psychology*, **68** (1955), 409–416; L. Krasner and L. P. Ullmann, *Research in Behavior Modification: New Developments and Implications* (New York: Holt, Rinehart and Winston, Inc., 1965), esp. Chaps. 9–11.

[7] F. H. Kanfer, "Vicarious Human Reinforcements," in Krasner and Ullmann, *Research in Behavior Modification*, p. 252.

The most serious distortion that results is a failure to appreciate any satisfactions other than social rewards. A picture of motivation is created in which all we live for is the good opinion of other people. The fallacy in this has already been discussed in connection with the growth of a sense of competence; it will be met again in later chapters because it runs deeply through current thought about personality. Some workers, bent upon keeping reinforcement as their central concept, meet the difficulty by speaking of *intrinsic reinforcement*, for instance, the inherent satisfaction of doing something competently or of making something beautiful, and of *self-reinforcement*, by which is meant the evaluations one puts upon one's own conduct without waiting to hear what other people think. These extensions correct the fallacy but give the originally simple concept a highly complex meaning.[8]

It helps keep things in perspective to remember that reinforcement is a game at which two can play. No one can observe the sequence of expressions on a child's face when persuading his parents to give him a treat without wondering who is the real expert in delivering reinforcers. A subject in verbal conditioning has at times caught on to what the experimenter is trying to do to his pattern of speech and has tried his hand at affecting the experimenter's pattern.[9] An amusing skit could be composed on what might be called the battle of reinforcements between two people determined to influence each other's behavior.

Cognitive Organization

"Whatever else personality may be," wrote Gordon Allport, "it has the properties of a system wherein all parts are mutually related. Quasimechanical views of learning"—such as conditioning and reinforcement—"stress fragmentary acquisition. Hence we must accept additional principles to account more fully for pattern and organization within the total personality system."[10]

The most general of these additional principles is that of cognitive organization. The need for such a concept becomes apparent the moment we observe a child silently contemplating a baffling puzzle and at last solving it in a way not clearly derived from his previous attempts. Even chimpanzees are capable of such insights—sudden solutions not arrived at through overt manipulation.[11] What happens in such instances may best be thought of as

---

[8] H. M. Lefcourt, "Internal vs. External Control of Reinforcement: A Review," *Psychological Bulletin*, **65** (1966), 206–220.

[9] This is embodied in an experiment by H. M. Rosenfeld and D. M. Baer, "Unnoticed Verbal Conditioning of an Aware Experimenter by a More Aware Subject: The Double-Agent Effect," *Psychological Review*, **76** (1969), 425–432.

[10] G. W. Allport, *Pattern and Growth in Personality* (New York: Holt, Rinehart and Winston, Inc., 1961), p. 109.

[11] W. Kohler, *The Mentality of Apes*, trans. E. Winter (Harcourt Brace Jovanovich, Inc., 1922).

cognitive organization. This term refers to an internal working over and patterning of experience that does not depend on the reinforcement of overt responses. This notion is crucial in understanding the growth of personality.

Cognition as Active Construction

The character of cognition at early stages of development has been brilliantly revealed in one of Jean Piaget's most characteristic pieces of research. With infinite patience he observed the evolution of intelligent behavior during the first two years of life of each of his own three children.[12] Besides observing, he arranged objects and played games with the children in order to disclose the widest possible range of their cognitive prowess. It became evident that the children no less than their father were given to active intervention. They did not let a novel object just sit there, but within the limits of their repertory of behavior they explored it, tested it out, and discovered what it could be made to do. Before their first birthdays they were behaving in ways that remarkably foreshadow the activities of adult scientists, conducting what can only be described as experiments through which they gradually learned about the properties of the environment.

From such observations Piaget came to the conclusion that the child *constructs* his knowledge of the world around him. In a similar vein, Kelly said that man typically forms constructs of his environment and tries them on for size. These constructs are intended to "aid him in his predictive efforts," and Kelly saw anticipating and predicting the events in which a person took part as the most characteristic feature of human behavior.[13] The starting point for learning about the nature of the world and one's place in it is the fact that information is all the time pressing itself upon us. We receive it, however, in the controlled and edited form determined by selective attention; we may increase its impact and detail by exploratory action; we construe or interpret it in the light of past experience; we may engage in active testing to provide additional feedback; and we may just plain think, trying to make a more coherent pattern of the information already received. The effectiveness of such processes increases in the course of development, but children exhibit them early and use them constantly in their traffic with surroundings. Being involved in overt action and exploration is conducive to learning. Children can gather much information, however, simply by observing the interactions of other people and by listening to what they have to say about the world. Ordinary conversation around the dinner table provides a child with a fund of impressions about human nature, all the more so if the adults are given to gossip.

[12] J. Piaget, *The Origins of Intelligence in Children*, trans. M. Cook (New York: International Universities Press, Inc., 1952); *The Construction of Reality by the Child*, trans. M. Cook (New York: Basic Books, Inc., 1954); see also J. H. Flavell, *The Developmental Psychology of Jean Piaget* (Princeton: D. Van Nostrand Co., 1963); and for a brief summary, A. L. Baldwin, *Behavior and Development in Childhood* (New York: Holt, Rinehart and Winston, Inc., 1955), pp. 299–313.

[13] G. A. Kelly, *The Psychology of Personal Constructs*, Vol. 1, *A Theory of Personality* (New York: W. W. Norton & Company, Inc., 1955), pp. 6–12.

There are also television and books, possibly a more reliable guide if one can find the time to read them. But the listener, the watcher, and the reader can be considered passive only in the sense that they are sitting still. Information input contributes to cognitive organization only when it is met by mental activity—when it is received with interested attention, construed in the light of previous experience, and thus effectively worked into the body of knowledge that guides future behavior.

The learning of language provides an especially clear illustration. To understand what others are saying and to make known one's wants through speech is of high personal relevance even for a child who is just starting the attempt. It is also a cognitive puzzle of no small magnitude, for language, with its different sounds, parts of speech, and grammatical arrangements, the latter often anything but regular and consistent, is a thing of formidable complexity. Learning that a certain word stands for a certain object is simple enough, but simplicity ends at about that point. Language is obviously not something that can be imprinted upon the child's mind. It can be learned only by experimenting, first with speech sounds, then with words, finally with grammatical forms. If we come out in the end with speech that is very much like what is used around us, this is merely because we have abandoned those variations that failed to communicate or that were called incorrect. In an early study of children's speech Wilhelm Stern showed that children try out all kinds of grammatical combinations and learn only through experience to limit themselves to those that are customary. This is most evident when a child produces a seemingly legitimate but actually "incorrect" extension of grammar or vocabulary. By analogy with other past participles he may say "drinked" even when familiar with the word "drunk."[14] One morning a small boy remarked that his dog seemed to be very "barkative" today, and when no cause could be detected for her excitement he concluded that she was "barking through her hat." Though such "wrong" linguistic ventures are eventually weeded out of habitual speech, their inventiveness shows that even correct speech results not from flat copying but from active experimentation. Each child to a certain extent constructs for himself the traditional language that is used around him.

The concept of cognition as an active organizing process is indispensable for understanding the social learnings that are most significant for the growth of personality. In coming to comprehend other people, their relationships, and the nature of the social environment, the child embarks early on a lifelong course of study. The materials of the social curriculum are plentiful, varied, often confusingly inconsistent and ambiguous, and likely to be conveyed by subtle cues and implications rather than in the form of clear information. Only an attentive learner can put together out of this unsorted abundance even the minimum organized understanding necessary to live with others.

[14] W. Stern, *The Psychology of Early Childhood*, 2d ed. (New York: Holt, Rinehart and Winston, Inc., 1930).

Identification

In recent years the concept of *identification* has occupied a conspicuous place in theories of development. The idea, however, is far from new. It is a precept of long standing that parents should provide their children with examples of good conduct and protect them from early exposure to bad examples. Implicit in this precept is the idea that children copy the behavior of those around them, using especially adults and older children as models in making their own behavior older and more adult. Growing up in a world of other human beings, the child is not obliged to construct all his patterns of conduct by piecemeal trial and error. He is surrounded by models at home, at school, at play, and on the television screen, and as development goes forward he becomes increasingly able to copy the behavior of these models in large chunks. Identification refers to this aspect of personal growth.

Unfortunately the concept of identification, like that of reinforcement, has not always been kept within reasonable bounds. Its value has been impaired by indiscriminate use, and it can be said to have run riot especially through the clinical literature, degenerating from a legitimate explanatory principle to a verbal tag for a variety of processes having little in common. This mishap to clear thinking is one of the unintended legacies of psychoanalytic theory. Freud gave identification a central place in normal development, attributing to it "a great share in determining the form taken by the ego."[15] But the growth of the ego, the development of personality in its realistic and capable aspects, was not one of Freud's deep preoccupations. In retrospect his thoughts about it appear somewhat casual, and in different writings he used the concept of identification in ways that even his best friends, to say nothing of his critics, have been unable to make consistent.[16] Small wonder that an idea blessed by Freud, given an abundance of meanings, and assigned the leading part in understanding normal development should rather quickly get out of hand. Yet the concept is a valuable one, worthy of both serious attention and careful restriction.

Meaning of Identification

Identification, which involves producing in oneself the observed behavior of a model, belongs under the general heading of *imitation*. It is characteristic of imitation that the behavior that is copied must already exist in some approximate form in the subject's repertory. This principle is illustrated during the first year of life in the imitation of speech sounds. The

[15] S. Freud, *The Ego and the Id* (London: Hogarth Press, Ltd., 1927).

[16] These problems are discussed at length by N. Sanford, "The Dynamics of Identification," *Psychological Review*, **62** (1955), 106–118; J. Kagan, "The Concept of Identification," *Psychological Review*, **65** (1958), 296–305; and R. W. White, "Ego and Reality in Psychoanalytic Theory," *Psychological Issues*, **3**, no. 3, Monograph 11 (1963), Chap. 6.

infant can copy only those sounds produced by others that he has already produced himself in the course of playful babbling. In this sense, copying another person's behavior is not an abrupt new action; the child can imitate only what he can already almost do. But this way of putting it should not lower our respect for the process of imitation. When as a result of observing another person a child is able to combine the elements of his repertory in a new pattern, he may start to behave in decidedly new ways. As Bandura and Walters point out, citing relevant research, "When a model is provided, patterns of behavior are typically acquired in large segments or in their entirety rather than through a slow, gradual process based on differential reinforcement."[17] This testifies to an active process of internal reorganization even when no overt responses are being made.

Identification is a particular form of imitation. Its distinguishing mark can be found by contrasting the two phrases, "wanting to do something that someone else has done" and "wanting to be like someone else." When a salesman shows you how to work a gadget you are buying, you want to be able to do what he has done, but you do not care about being like the salesman in any other respect, any more than you want to be like the instruction book that comes with the gadget. Wanting to be like another person implies something more, something that is not confined to single acts but is both more global and more personal. A boy who identifies with his father wants to be like the person who can drive the car, run the power lawn mower, give orders to repairmen, assert his wishes in the family, and generally display assured competence in dealing with the environment. Bronfenbrenner defines identification as "a motivated attempt to resemble a specific other person."[18] It is, then, a particular form of imitation in which copying a model, generalized beyond specific acts, springs from wanting to be and trying to be like the model with respect to some broader quality such as competence or attractiveness to other people.

Wanting to be like someone implies feelings such as admiration and envy. It is not necessarily a manifestation of love. This is one of the points upon which Freud was conspicuously inconsistent. In different works he described as identifications the little boy's loving relation with his father and the ties of tenderness and loyalty that bind the members of a cohesive group. Yet in another place he declared it "easy to state in a formula the distinction between an identification with the father and the choice of the father as an object. In the first case one's father is what one would like to *be*, and in the second he is what one would like to *have*."[19] If one sticks to this distinction there is no difficulty in understanding those instances in which a model is copied who is feared and even hated. Anna Freud describes a process which

[17] A. Bandura and R. H. Walters, *Social Learning and Personality Development* (New York: Holt, Rinehart and Winston, Inc., 1965), p. 106.

[18] U. Bronfenbrenner, "Freudian Theories of Identification and Their Derivatives," *Child Development*, 31 (1960), 15–40.

[19] S. Freud, *Group Psychology and the Analysis of the Ego* (London: Hogarth Press, Ltd., 1922), p. 106.

she calls "identification with the aggressor," a copying of aggressive or threatening models motivated mainly by attempts to avoid anxiety.[20] Bettelheim, making a study of concentration camps in which he was confined in Nazi Germany, describes prisoners who came to admire and emulate their guards, whose power they could not help but envy in spite of hatred and fear. Older prisoners behaved aggressively toward newer ones, inflicted suffering upon them, and were noisy in enforcing even the most arbitrary rules. They even risked punishment by sewing their own uniforms in such a way as to resemble those of the guards.[21] It is true that in studies of American school boys ranging from kindergarten to high school a positive correlation has been found between strength of masculine interests and a perception of fathers as nurturing and affectionate.[22] This certainly suggests that a loving relation provides more fertile soil for copying parental models, but love is not indispensable for identification. The key element in wanting to be like another person is wanting to create in oneself the model's social competence, effectiveness, and attractiveness to other people.

Imitative behavior occurs very early in life, but true identification becomes prominent during the fourth and fifth years as the child's growing mastery of locomotion and language enables him to behave more like an adult. When a child can dress himself without assistance, handle objects competently, explore the neighborhood, and talk with something like adult sentence structure and grammar, the stage is set for those programs of make-believe that adults find often entertaining and sometimes painfully disconconcerting. Possibly donning adult clothes, the child may imitate dramatic instances of parental competence by pretending to drive the car, run the vacuum cleaner, telephone orders to the repairman—whence comes that tone of complacent arrogance?—or act as host or hostess at an imaginary party —why do the expressions of cordiality sound so spurious? When a child's repertory of behavior and comprehension permits him to act a little like an adult, he begins to use identification as a means of becoming still more like one, making use of the available models. For better or for worse, identification thus serves as a shortcut to the mastery of complex adult patterns of behavior.

The following incident illustrates identification and at the same time suggests the force of a child's desire to be respected as a serious member of the adult world. A farmer's son received his first pair of overalls shortly before his third birthday. Proudly clad in this garment, which in every way resembled his father's, and limping slightly as his father did, the boy appeared at the barn door announcing that he was going to help. Unfortunately the father

[20] A. Freud, *The Ego and the Mechanisms of Defence* (London: Hogarth Press, Ltd., 1937).

[21] B. Bettelheim, "Individual and Mass Behavior in Extreme Situations," *Journal of Abnormal and Social Psychology*, **38** (1943), 417–452.

[22] P. Mussen and L. Distler, "Masculinity, Identification, and Father-Son Relationships," *Journal of Abnormal and Social Psychology*, **59** (1959), pp. 352–356; P. Mussen, "Some Antecedents and Consequents of Masculine Sex-Typing in Adolescent Boys," *Psychological Monographs*, **75**, no. 2 (Whole no. 506) (1961).

found the sight of his tiny helper so comical that he burst out laughing, thereby inflicting a wound to pride that reduced the boy to tears. But when the father realized the deeply serious intent with which help had been offered, he took on the new agricultural laborer, who was soon hard at work wielding a short-handled broom. This was the beginning of a cooperation in the work of the farm that proved highly advantageous to both parties.[23]

Analysis of Examples

The complex way in which the process of identification may operate can be seen in more detail in the following example described by Erikson.

> During the last war a neighbor of mine, a boy of five, underwent a change of personality from a "mother's boy" to a violent, stubborn, and disobedient child. The most disquieting symptom was an urge to set fires.
>
> The boy's parents had separated just before the outbreak of war. The mother had moved in with some women cousins, and when war began the father had joined the air forces. These women frequently expressed their disrespect for the father. They cultivated babyish traits in the boy. The father, however, did well in war; in fact, he became a hero. On the occasion of his first furlough the little boy had the experience of seeing the man he had learned not to be like become the much-admired center of the neighborhood's attention. The mother announced that she would drop her divorce plans. The father went back to war and was eventually lost over Germany.
>
> After the father's departure the affectionate and dependent boy developed more and more disquieting symptoms of destructiveness and defiance, culminating in fire setting. He gave the key to the change himself when, protesting against his mother's whipping, he pointed to a pile of wood he had set afire and exclaimed (in more childish words), "If this were a German city, you would have liked me for it." He thus indicated that in setting fires he fantasied being a bombardier like the father, who had told of his exploits. . . .
>
> When the worst of this boy's dangerous initiative had subsided, he was observed swooping down a hill on a bicycle, endangering, scaring, and yet deftly avoiding other children. They shrieked, laughed, and in a way admired him for it. In watching him, and hearing the strange noises he made, I could not help thinking that he probably imagined himself to be an airplane on a bombing mission. But at the same time he gained in playful mastery over his locomotion; he exercised circumspection in his attack, and he became a virtuoso on a bicycle.[24]

The situation described in this narrative is one that called forth an abrupt and therefore highly visible identification with the father. The changes

---

[23] E. Yates, *Is There a Doctor in the Barn?* (New York: E. P. Dutton & Co., Inc., 1966), pp. 35–37. The boy grew up to become a veterinarian.

[24] E. H. Erikson, *Childhood and Society* (New York: W. W. Norton & Company, Inc., 1950), pp. 210–212.

in the boy's cognitive grasp of his world occasioned by the father's visit were too sudden and too great for his 5-year-old adaptive powers; therefore, the first manifestations of new behavior were full of conflict, anger, and pointless destruction. Well trained to be a good little boy, yet also in a sense the man of the house, the son was suddenly displaced and downgraded by the father's return. This precipitated an attempt to construe what it must be that enabled a man to enjoy general admiration and to recapture his wife's love. The conclusion was inescapable that the path to such enviable goals was to enact the masculine role with a maximum of competent mastery, daring, self-assertion, and destruction. Within the limits of his comprehension the boy at once began to do likewise. Only gradually was the behavior set off by the identification moderated to fit the actual circumstances of his life.

Commenting on this example, Erikson points out that identification with a model often accomplishes a synthesis of previously unchanneled wants and capacities. This boy in his tame domestic role had not found full employment for the activity and motor coordination dictated by his constitutional endowment, for the energy and initiative that reach something of a peak at the age of 5, or for urges to dominate, impress, and assertively win the respect of others, including other children. "Where such synthesis succeeds," Erikson writes, "a most surprising coagulation of constitutional, temperamental, and learned reactions may produce exuberance of growth and unexpected accomplishment. Where it fails, it must lead to severe conflict, often expressed in unexpected naughtiness and delinquency."[25] The son of the bombardier illustrates something of each outcome.

The synthesizing function of identifications is not confined to early childhood nor to the family circle. It can be illustrated in the case of the college sophomore described in an earlier chapter, whose ambitious Jewish parents were pushing him from lower-middle-class status into a career in medicine.[26] Having reached his second year in college, removed from direct parental pressure and very much on his own in an intellectual and social environment for which neither his parents nor his schooling had been able to prepare him, this student was decidedly at loose ends as to his own capacities and inclinations. He had absorbed the family goals of making contacts, becoming a doctor, and getting ahead, but he moved toward them with anxiety and reluctance, unkindled by any vision of his own. At this point he took a course taught by a renowned professor who had impressive power to communicate his enthusiasm and love of his subject. The experience was memorable: the student at last saw and felt what it might be to achieve intellectual and social success. Aiding the identification were the circumstances that the professor had a medical degree and that he proved himself a nurturant mentor by making extensive and sympathetic comments on the student's term paper. In this man the student perceived what he construed to be the fruits of making contacts and struggling to get ahead: economic security, firm social status,

[25] *Ibid.*, p. 212.
[26] See above, Chap. 6, p. 133.

confident assurance, and wide personal acquaintance with prominent people. He also perceived an additional bonus, absorption in the pursuit of knowledge and joy in communicating it, which he was only just beginning to experience in his own life. The identification with this teacher produced a significant change in the student's behavior, as if he had shifted to a higher gear. Exuberance of growth and unexpected accomplishment truly followed the synthesis achieved through the model.

Some Lasting Consequences of Identification

It must often be true that the consequences of identification become mingled with other factors in the course of development and thus to all intents and purposes lost to view. Only on certain occasions is it possible, as in the two examples just discussed, to observe fairly drastic changes of behavior and to secure evidence of the underlying identification from the subject's own report. A good deal of the evidence for lasting consequences comes from the self-disclosures of patients in psychoanalytic treatment; supplementary evidence, usually inferential, can be derived from case studies of normal growth. Identifications with family members, chiefly with parents but sometimes with others, probably leave the most lasting impressions. Often it happens that the subject himself has not realized until his attention is called to it that images from so long ago are still alive in his mind. Thus he may discover with surprise that his own unreflective enactment of the male role in adult life does not simply reflect a general cultural pattern but contains elements peculiar to his father, to his older brother, perhaps even to one of his grandfathers. Maybe he has always assumed that men would be gentle and considerate toward the members of their families, and has failed to notice that this pattern practiced by his father is far from universal in society. Subtle assumptions of this kind can result from a person's own constitutional and temperamental preferences and from experiences outside the family, but they can also be the direct consequences of early domestic identifications.

In clinical work, problems connected with sex roles and sex behavior have sometimes been traced to early identifications. Most children probably identify in certain respects with both parents. Circumstances may occur which disproportionately strengthen opposite-sex at the expense of same-sex identification, circumstances strong enough to overrule the sex role expectations of the culture. The daughter of an admirable father but erratic, irresponsible mother may want to be like her father to the point of rejecting the feminine role altogether. When the mother is the admirable one and the father a hopeless alcoholic, the son may similarly reject the compromised masculine role. These reversed identifications, although they are likely to make social development harder, by no means necessarily interfere with later sexual behavior, which is subject to numerous other influences. They crop up, however, with what looks like more than chance frequency in clinical cases of disturbed sexual functioning.

Early identifications sometimes have a similarly lasting effect on the expression of aggression. If a man is conspicuously docile and ingratiating, letting others push him around, older relatives may correctly recall that his father at the same age was a similar doormat. If a woman intimidates her family and neighbors with formidable displays of angry belittlement, old friends may remind each other that her mother was a wildcat in her day.

Some of the conditions that increase, maintain, and reduce the expression of aggression have been studied in a series of experiments on imitation by Bandura and associates.[27] In a typical experimental situation the subjects, preschool children, were shown films of an adult in a playroom that contained, among other things, a large inflated plastic doll. One group saw a film in which the adult—the model—paid no attention to the doll; another group witnessed a violent display of aggression in which the doll was knocked down, kicked, and hit with a hammer. Afterwards each child was slightly frustrated and left in the playroom, where his behavior clearly showed the influence of the recent model, especially in those cases from the second group in which the model's ways of attacking the plastic doll were copied in detail. The experimenters also established the fact that the amount of punishment visited on the doll was influenced by the previously observed aftermath of the model's behavior. In one film the model was shown being punished for maltreating the doll, in another being praised and rewarded for it. The children who saw the second film were significantly more rough in their treatment of the doll.

The experiments, of course, took place in an artificial situation and may be presumed to have evoked largely transient hostile impulses and imitations. But it may not be stretching things too far to say that if one's chief identification figure in the family circle, the same-sex parent, is constantly observed expressing aggression and getting away with it, the probability of copying this behavior becomes high. In contrast, if such behavior usually gets the identification figure into trouble or if it never occurs at all, the likelihood of its appearing in the child is much smaller.

Limits of the Concept of Identification

Valuable as the concept of identification may be, its indiscriminate use obscures other aspects of development that are of no less importance. As we have seen, identification is a form of imitation; it involves copying the behavior and characteristics of a model who is in some respect admired. The value of the term is washed out the moment we separate it from the idea of motivated copying and apply it to situations that entail merely learning from others or doing what others desire. If someone asks me to do an errand for him, my doing so may suggest that I want him to like me, but it does not imply that I want to be like him, nor is any copying involved in my doing what he is too lazy to do for himself. We come to understand many important

[27] Bandura and Walters, *Social Learning and Personality Development*, Chap. 2.

aspects of the personal world through experiences in which there is no element of wanting and trying to be like another person.[28]

Two points are especially noteworthy. In the first place, patterns of behavior are constantly being provided by the expectations of the human environment. Starting from what parents expect of an infant, every child grows up in a widening circle of social expectations, including those that lie behind social roles and cultural values. Responding to these expectations, as we shall see, cannot be reduced to imitation. While still young, children are not expected to copy adult behavior in all respects and may even be forbidden to do so. The child has to construct the world of social expectations that surrounds him just as he has to construct the world of inanimate objects. This implies an active process of internal organization, making use of cues that are often diffuse and sometimes inconsistent.

In the second place, almost any carefully made case study will show a striking selectivity in the use of identification. Family members supply obvious models, but even here the child does not copy everyone indiscriminately, nor does he necessarily fashion himself in all respects like the same-sex parent. It is not impossible for a boy to imitate his father's playfulness and tenderness but not his drunken rages; or he may make the opposite choice. Which of the figures exposed to him on the television screen will a given child use for identification? Which children on the school playground will he select as models for his own behavior? Which aspect of his best friend will he single out to incorporate in himself? These questions are all legitimate, because the individual is from the start choosy. He is drawn into an identification only when something about a model represents a step in development that he would like to take, that it feels congenial to take, perhaps that he is ready to take without realizing it or knowing how to go about it. For very young children just awakening to the possibility of copying adults, global imitation of a parent may be the first step, and these initial steps may leave traces that can be detected in later behavior. Very soon, however, identifications become selective, and we can understand the choices only in terms of a fit between inner needs and outer models.

Responding to the Expectations of Other People

Among girls who have a younger sibling, a not uncommon early memory is of the occasion when mother went to the hospital to have the baby. The memory is often centered upon father and has to do with the little girl's attempt to take mother's place during her absence, perhaps by helping with the housework, perhaps by making adult conversation at the dining table. There is a good measure of identification here, copying mother's

---

[28] For a critical and experimental analysis of this problem see A. P. Bell, "Role Modelship and Interaction in Adolescence and Young Adulthood," *Developmental Psychology*, **2** (1970), 123–128.

characteristic ways of behaving and speaking, but the copying is instrumental to another goal, that of attracting father's affection. Seizing the moment when mother has turned her attention away from both of them, the little girl tries to prove that she can be as good a wife to her father, perhaps even a better one. This can be the starting point of what is in any event an important aspect of the growth of personality. A girl may want to be like her mother, but she also wants to be the kind of woman her father likes, and unless mother is a flawless wife this suggests a variety of improvements upon the available model. Similarly a boy is likely to want to be the kind of man mother likes, bettering wherever possible the husband with whom she is actually stuck. Improvement upon the model implies understanding just what the other parent finds unsatisfactory about it. The little girl at the breakfast table will try to make herself a fountain of sparkling conversation only if she comprehends that mother's grumpy silence is displeasing to father. The boy must correctly read mother's annoyance at her husband's delays in fixing things around the house if he is to become a contrasting picture of alacrity in carrying out her requests. Success depends upon picking up cues to the parents' feelings and of constructing out of these cues a conception of parental expectations that goes well beyond what is directly communicated. Even in this relatively simple situation it is a cognitive accomplishment of no small magnitude to construct a map of what other people expect.

It will be evident at this point, as it must have been throughout the chapter, that cognition is not here used in a sense that implies full conscious recognition. To speak of unconscious cognition is likely to outrage some readers—what can knowing mean if not a conscious process?—but there is certainly no strangeness in the thought that we can act on information, call it a hunch or an intuition, without being able to say exactly what it was or where it came from. A map of other people's expectations, especially a child's map of them, may not be looked at and reflected upon, yet it contains real information, derived from cues and silently organized, that serves as a guide to behavior. We know much more than we know that we know, to put it paradoxically; that is, we act upon a much larger store of information, not necessarily accurate, than we are ordinarily aware of. The little girl chattering brightly at the breakfast table is probably not aware that her father is pained by grumpy silence and that she is making a play for his favorable attention, but it is hard to describe her behavior without assuming internal guides of just this kind. Cognitive organization is for some purposes at its best when fully conscious and cast in communicable form. But we do not always live at such cognitive peaks, and our capacity to receive and process information without giving it conscious attention must be rated for many purposes a valuable asset.

Parental Expectations

It is not surprising that children should be strongly motivated to understand and accommodate themselves to expectations of their parents and the other family members. From these expectations, the child learns what is desirable and what is undesirable. He can do what is desirable partly by being like his parents, copying them with respect to cleanliness, good manners, and control of angry impulses. But parents may also expect quite different behavior: going to school while parents go to work or stay at home, going outdoors to play while parents stay inside, going to bed early while parents stay up. There is a realm of adult privileges that is forbidden to children. Moreover, there are expectations with respect to sex roles, where copying must be restricted to members of the same sex. Furthermore, as we have seen especially in families where upward social mobility is greatly desired, parental expectations may be heavily freighted with implicit advice to behave not as *we* do but as *they* (the envied occupants of a loftier status) do. If in certain respects parents invite identification, in other respects they discourage and even prohibit it. Any child who fully understands what is expected of him has accomplished a remarkable feat of cognitive organization.

Informal roles within the family, however they start, are maintained by expectations. This can be observed with striking clarity when the roles of good child and bad child are sharply differentiated. If sounds of mischief or of a quarrel between the two children break out, the parents start shouting at the bad child before they have time to find out what actually happened. It testifies to the force of parental expectations that they can strengthen the seemingly painful role of bad child. Because everyone expects that the child will be bad, he comes to anticipate bad behavior himself and to behave worse and worse. In work with emotionally disturbed problem children who are given residential treatment away from their homes, an early and sometimes protracted task is to demonstrate that the staff does not expect behavior to be outrageous and destructive.

One of the difficult cognitive problems many children face is to make sense of conflicting expectations. Sometimes crudely, but sometimes subtly, two parents may convey expectations that cannot be reconciled. The conflict may come to a focus on almost any issue, even a seemingly small one like how one should look when setting off for school. Out of a welter of directions, comments, and sneers the child may construe father's message as a warning not to be like his neat, fussy, prim, inhibited mother, and mother's message as advice to avoid resembling his sloppy, lazy, impulsive, good-for-nothing father. We have seen that those situations are difficult for children. Part of the difficulty is the purely cognitive one of sorting out and grasping a complex and inherently not very sensible pattern of parental desires and expectations.

Double-Bind Communication

The problem becomes even more formidable when conflicting expectations emanate from a single person. Communication can be carried on through multiple channels, or at different levels; what is transmitted by the spoken word may not be congruent with what is conveyed by tone of voice or gesture. Furthermore, a spoken message may carry conflicting implications, and two messages occurring in sequence may have exactly opposite meanings.

Examining these possibilities, Gregory Bateson and a group of workers at Palo Alto described a form of communication which they named a *double bind*.[29] This term signifies a communication that contains an injunction of some kind, a second injunction contrary to the first, and at least implicitly a third injunction against recognizing the inconsistency. By way of example the authors give the following illustration:

> A young man who had fairly well recovered from an acute schizophrenic episode was visited in the hospital by his mother. He was glad to see her and impulsively put his arm around her shoulders, whereupon she stiffened. He withdrew his arm, and she asked, "Don't you love me any more?" He then blushed, and she said, "Dear, you must not be so easily embarrassed and afraid of your feelings."

In this example the mother's first communication, her stiffening gesture, is an injunction against showing love; her first words, however, are a request for love, while her second statement, a command to show love, completes the contradiction with her original gesture; yet throughout there is an implicit prohibition against charging her with being senseless. Mishler and Waxler's comment is appropriate: "This is a 'damned if you do and damned if you don't' situation for the child, who is trapped by the incongruent demands and forbidden to call attention to his predicament."[30]

Undoubtedly the transmission of conflicting messages is a common failing in human communication. A husband during a disagreement can address his wife as "dear" in a voice that vibrates with irritation. A father can say that a punishment is for his child's good in tones that betray the annoyance he is about to relieve. Anxiety and reassurance are likewise easily condensed into what appears to be a single message. Students of school phobias have concluded that anxiety over separation may be as much the mother's as the child's and may be communicated in such statements as, "I know you are not going to be afraid of anything at school," or in such gestures as firmly grasping the child's trembling hand (it is not always clear whose hand is trembling).[31] In Bateson's illustration the mother seems to be motivated by a desire to be always right, and it is the son's acceptance of her rightness that completes the double bind. True double binds seem most likely to occur when parents are full of conflict about their children and when the children, because of youth, dependence, or overtraining, accept the fiction of parental infallibility. Attempting under these circumstances to respond adequately to incongruent expectations, the child is hardly likely to develop the kind of cognitive field that favors clear and confident action.

[29] G. Bateson, D. D. Jackson, J. Haley, and J. H. Weakland, "Toward a Theory of Schizophrenia," *Behaviorial Science*, 1 (1956), 251–264.

[30] E. J. Mishler and N. E. Waxler, "Family Interaction Processes and Schizophrenia: A Review of Current Theories," *The Merrill-Palmer Quarterly*, 11 (1965), 269–315. Reprinted in *The Psychosocial Interior of the Family,* ed. Handel, Chap. 22.

[31] L. Eisenberg, "School Phobia: A Study in the Communication of Anxiety," *American Journal of Psychiatry*, 114 (1958), 712–718.

It is possible to escape from the bind of conflicting messages if the incongruity can be recognized and a response chosen—if, for instance, the school child had the aplomb to laugh at his mother and point out that she was the scared one, as an older child might do. It is possible also to mitigate the effects of double-bind communication from one parent if the other parent, or some other member of the family, communicates more clearly and sets a more rational pattern of interaction. Conflicting communications do not create true binds simply in their own right. They do so when a child is trapped by his own needs in a vital relation and either cannot or dares not bring his critical capacities to bear on the confused messages he is being given. An alert child who was not tied in this way to her temporary sitter, a nervous aunt who favored play in the fresh air but feared colds, simply put the cool question, "Well, which do you want me to do, go out or stay in?"

Group Expectations

The expectations of friends and acquaintances become increasingly important in the course of development, and here again imitation accounts for only a part of the resulting behavior. In a relatively organized group an accepted leader does not want or expect anyone else to act as a leader, a right-hand man does not encourage anyone to usurp his place of privilege, and the group's established entertainer and clown does not look with favor on someone who caps all his sallies. Role expectations play a prominent part in the social life of children and adolescents. Their forceful sustaining effect is perhaps most vividly experienced when a person wants to graduate from an informal role that has stood him in good stead but is no longer compatible with what he is hoping to become. It is a commonly reported fate of childhood clowns and early adolescent humorists that they cannot get their friends to take them seriously. When they try to speak in a sober conversation the face of every listener sets itself in an anticipatory smile, awaiting the gem of wit that is about to fall. Similar difficulties beset the person who has stood in a deferential relation to a friend and now seeks equality, or the person with a brilliant athletic record who starts wanting to be respected for intellectual accomplishment. Going against established expectations reveals their force not alone in other people's minds but in the expectations built up within oneself. Can the humorist really be serious, the athlete intellectual? It takes hardihood to find out.

When a newcomer enters a group he may pick up in a remarkably short time its pattern of expectations. The signals are constantly being given out; all that is necessary is for him to receive and grasp them. This cognitive work does not have to be clearly conscious. If it were so, it might well prove to be based not on stated values but on a synthesis of magic words and sneers. There are circles in which the tenor of conversation shows that being hardheaded and having common sense are unquestioned virtues; characterizations such as sensitive, imaginative, and impractical are made to sound like epithets. In other circles people are called sensitive and imaginative in tones of voice that convey admiration, but when they are described as hardheaded it is with a note of contemptuous amusement. Withering comments—remarks that everyone accepts as withering—serve to define quickly what the group does not like. Expressions like the following speedily convey to the newcomer what attributes are held in low and high esteem: "Well, with his background what would you expect?" "Oh, you know, it's so middle class," "The trouble is he hasn't any protest," "But what has he ever actually done?" "Yes, but is it really creative?" If one has any interest in being an accepted member of a group, communications of this kind are far from neutral. They define a set of expectations the sharing of which is the price of acceptance. The process is the same as the one by which the culture as a whole makes its impact on individual behavior and values.

The Evolution of Conscience

In the recent history of thought the idea of conscience has become strangely confused. In the past, conscience has been described as man's noblest possession, the source of his consideration for others, the power that transforms self-seeking into altruism, the seat of the loftiest ideals, and the origin of the most admirable deeds. It still retains much of this connotation. Notable instances of self-guidance according to ethical convictions, like Thoreau's going to jail rather than pay taxes for a war he judged to be unjust, are described as manifestations of conscience and are generally admired. In such cases the person is seen as acting according to internalized ethical principles and thereby placing his conduct in opposition to conventional expectations, easy conformities, and perhaps opportunities for graft and personal gain. But the historic conception of conscience was not of an agency that acts only on spectacular occasions. As a general attribute of personality it was seen as guiding countless daily decisions, leading many of Thoreau's fellow townsmen, for instance—less heedful of distant implications—to pay their taxes as a matter of duty and in other ways to behave in accordance with their ideas of decent and respectable living. In a given individual conscience might not be properly awakened, and it might be overwhelmed by impulse and desire, but it was considered to exist as a potential and highly desirable attribute of every person.

In modern thought, however, conscience has not always kept its good repute. Nietzsche thought of it as mean and pinched, the representative of the herd instinct, agreeing with Hamlet that it "makes cowards of us all." Freud added to its bad name by pointing out the disastrous inhibitory part that it played in neurosis. Spurred on by these insights, observers began to see that children sometimes used moral precepts to justify domineering and hostile attitudes toward other children, and the history of warfare, especially of religious wars, was reexamined to show the bellicose consequences of a conviction of moral superiority. So great was the revulsion against conscience in certain quarters that the lack of it came to be cast as a virtue. It began to be perceived as an irrational inner agency that stood in the way of intelligent ethical judgments.

The upshot seems to be that conscience can sometimes play the enlightened part attributed to it by earlier thinkers but that it can also go badly astray. Freud opened the path toward understanding the latter possibility by unearthing the early start of internalized control in childhood. Much of the trouble stems from the fact that moral training begins at a time when the child cannot possibly understand what it is about.

Freud's Concept of the Superego

In the course of psychoanalytic treatment a curious phenomenon came to light that seemed to make no sense in the patient's current life. Freud described this as the "negative therapeutic reaction," a paradoxical sequence of getting better and immediately getting worse. The patient might leave one day illuminated by a piece of insight, feeling buoyantly free from certain inhibitions, only to return for his next session down in the dumps, depressed, in the grip of severe feelings of guilt. These feelings of guilt were clearly irrational, in the sense that they obstructed the patient in his avowed intent of recovering from neurosis. It seemed as if he had to punish himself for trying to get well. What Freud had observed was a persisting, uncompromising sort of conscience. The patient's behavior was ruled at critical junctures by a feeling of what was right and wrong, a feeling that was not formulated in adult terms but that was strong enough to overrule conscious intentions. Karen Horney described these moral compulsions and scruples as "ego-alien": "The individual seems to have no say in the matter of the self-imposed rules; whether he likes them, whether he believes in their value, enters as little into the picture as his capacity to apply them with discrimination."[32] The reason for this irrational power lay in the circumstances under which the rules came into being. Freud described the situation in terms that applied to any transaction of discipline and punishment.

> Small children are notoriously amoral. They have no internal inhibitions against their pleasure-seeking impulses. The role which the superego undertakes later in life is first played by an external power, by parental authority. The influence of the parents dominates the child by granting proofs of affection and by threats of punishment which to the child mean loss of love and which must also be feared on their own account. . . . It is only later that the secondary situation arises, which we are far too ready to regard as the normal state of affairs; the external restrictions are introjected, so that the superego takes the place of the parental function, and thenceforward observes, guides, and threatens the ego in just the same way as the parents acted to the child before.[33]

[32] K. Horney, *New Ways in Psychoanalysis* (New York: W. W. Norton & Company, Inc., 1939), p. 208.

[33] S. Freud, *New Introductory Lectures in Psychoanalysis*, trans. W. J. H. Sprott (New York: W. W. Norton & Company, Inc., 1933), p. 89.

Superego was the term Freud chose for this internal representation of parental authority. The introjection of parental standards and values takes place in the beginning through relatively simple learning processes. Freud's theory that the superego was introjected, as if a whole value system were swallowed at a gulp, is simply a picturesque way of describing what can easily be analyzed into specific learning processes. This analysis is made in some detail by Bandura and Walters, who make reference to numerous experimental studies bearing on the development of self-control.[34] One way in which parents try to make children responsive to their prohibitions is simply by punishment. In the language of learning theory this is described as "the presentation of a negative reinforcer," which results in "response inhibition." The authors note, however, that "the use of aversive stimulation as a disciplinary measure is more likely to be associated with avoidance of the disciplinary agents" than with real control from within. They cite substantial evidence that a regime of punishment, especially if there is a shortage of warm affection, leads a child to be smart about avoiding punishments but otherwise to get away with everything he can. The superego is best introjected—controls are most strongly internalized—under conditions that have sometimes been called "psychological punishment," conditions that presuppose parental acceptance and affection. Undesired behavior is met by "withdrawal or withholding of positive reinforcement," by taking away a privilege and by making the child feel unloved and unworthy. Reinstatement of these rewards becomes contingent on the child's compliance or on attempted restitution, which has the effect of reinforcing this behavior and increasing the probability that on future occasions it will be strong enough to prevent the undesired behavior. Bandura and Walters make it plain, however, that more is involved than positive and negative reinforcement. Changes in the strength of self-controlled behavior can occur through the imitation of models, in other words through vicarious learning without any direct reinforcement. The authors also recognize that parents try to encourage internal control by reasoning with children, by pointing out consequences and suggesting more socialized ways of doing things. Changes in future behavior can thus occur simply from a changed understanding of what is involved. Children can redraw their cognitive maps both by observing others and by listening to them describe their cognitive maps.

Cognitive development proves to be of central importance in understanding not only the superego as Freud described it but also the course of events that leads to a mature and enlightened conscience. The internal controls that constitute the superego are necessarily subject to all the limitations of childish understanding. At 4 and 5 years a child's comprehension of the meaning of rules and prohibitions is bound to be primitive. In a historically important investigation of expressed moral judgments, Piaget showed that young children think of a rule as if it existed like a physical object. He called this *moral realism*, in contrast to the *moral relativism* that would ensue later

[34] Bandura and Walters, *Social Learning and Personality Development*, Chap. 4.

when the child discovered that rules were made by people for certain human purposes and might be changed if these purposes changed. While still a moral realist, the child perceives rules in such an absolute way that they cannot be adapted to meet circumstances. Accidentally breaking all the cups on a tray while trying to be helpful seems much worse to the child than angrily throwing down one cup with the intention of breaking it, as if the size of the crime could be measured wholly by the volume of broken china.[35] If moral values are heavily overlearned in childhood, so strongly that they resist the cognitive enlargement that can happen only in the course of time, they will continue to have a primitive, absolute, inflexible character that under certain circumstances will be experienced as alien to the current personality. It was primitive moral compulsions of this kind that Freud observed in the psychoanalysis of neurotic patients.

Stages of Moral Understanding

The problem of the gradual enlargement of children's moral understanding has been pursued further by Kohlberg using a technique similar to Piaget's, that of presenting problems and talking them over with children of different ages.[36] On the basis of findings with boys between the ages of 7 and 17, Kohlberg proposes that the child's moral understanding develops through a series of detectable stages. These stages "seem primarily to reflect cognitive development, as is suggested by the fact that they are related to I.Q. as well as age." In the first stage, prevailing often enough as late as 10 years, the children think of obedience and conformity simply as a matter of avoiding punishment. In this spirit a boy of 10, given the problem of whether or not to report an older brother's misdeed to their father, weighs only the alternatives that his brother might beat him up for telling and that his father might spank him for not telling. The second stage amends this grim conception by allowing that conformity has practical value in obtaining rewards and having favors returned. Thus a 13-year-old subject contemplates that he might someday want to commit a misdeed and decides not to squeal on his brother now lest his brother squeal on him then. Kohlberg characterizes these outlooks, with their self-centered and almost calculated self-interest, as *pre-moral*. In the next two stages morality rises to the level of *conventional role-conformity*, which is seen as desirable in order to maintain good relations in the family and a position of rightness with respect to society's immutable requirements. Stage 3 is described by Kohlberg as that of *good-boy morality* in which the motivation is to enjoy the approval of others. A 16-year-old respondent noted that if his failure to report his brother's misdeed were discovered, his father would no longer be able to trust him; the boy's silence

---

[35] J. Piaget, *The Moral Judgment of the Child* (New York: Harcourt Brace Jovanovich, Inc., 1932).

[36] L. Kohlberg, "Development of Moral Character and Moral Ideology," in *Review of Child Development Research*, Vol. 1, ed. M. L. Hoffman and L. W. Hoffman (New York: Russell Sage Foundation, 1964), pp. 383–431.

thus would injure a mutually satisfactory relation that included parental interest and support. Stage 4 is reached with the emergence of a conception of
morality as a categorical order of rights and duties legitimately maintained by
authorities such as society or religion; feelings of guilt are now seen as the
appropriate consequence of violations. Given the ethical problem of a mercy
killing to relieve pain, a subject in this stage judged such conduct immoral on
the ground that neither a doctor nor anyone else has the right to take a human life. Only in the last two stages, reached typically at about 16 or 17, are
right and wrong understood to be based on *self-accepted moral principles*.
Kohlberg describes Stage 5 as representing a "morality of contract, of individual rights, and of democratically accepted law" in which the motive for
conformity is "to maintain the respect of the impartial spectator judging in
terms of community welfare," somewhat akin to the greatest good of the
greatest number. In Stage 6, morality is still more completely internalized,
being derived from principles of individual conscience the violation of which
would lead to self-condemnation. In this perspective feelings of guilt might
visit a person who timidly failed to violate a law when convinced that doing
so was required by a higher value.

Because of the heavy reliance on verbalization in experiments of this
kind it might be supposed that the stages reflected merely a growth of verbal
habits or verbal sophistication. Kohlberg rejects this interpretation and takes
the view that the stages "form an invariant developmental sequence." Careful
examination of the children's responses indicates that there is no skipping of
stages; each stage is attained only after the previous one has been mastered.
"The successive moralities of the child," says Brown in commenting on this
study, "are not a set of graded lessons taught by adults but result from the
child's spontaneous restructuring of his experience." If the same child is tested
at different age levels he seems to deal with the problems in quite a different
way, as if he took off from a new set of assumptions. Brown points out a
similarity between what is involved in acquiring moral concepts and what is
involved in learning to use grammar. "To speak a language one must have
a system of general rules by which infinitely many sentences can be constructed. To distinguish right from wrong one must have another such
system."[37] Only by slow degrees and by successive approximations built out
of his own cognitive resources does a child come to understand the complexities of relationship that are implicit in human value systems.

There is an embarrassing side to these studies of development. Much
as we would like to suppose that only Kohlberg's last two stages will be found
among adults, it is all too easy to think of examples that refute this flattering
view. Many staunchly upheld adult value systems are based on the simple
perspectives and absolute assumptions that are characteristic of earlier stages.
We often judge things to be right and wrong in an arbitrary, rule-bound fashion
that excludes consideration of their actual human consequences. Furthermore,
plenty of adults seem to have real difficulty in seeing things as another person

[37] R. Brown, *Social Psychology* (New York: The Free Press, 1965), p. 407.

sees them. But of course there is no novelty in the idea that we do not always think and behave with perfect rationality. This generalization proves to be true even in that person whom we would most like to exempt from it.

To advance to a fully adult conscience is a considerable feat of cognitive organization. The adult must transcend the idea that moral restraints represent simply what you have to do to please your parents or to avoid criticism by the neighbors. Progress is assisted to the extent that the child can make his own judgments of the consequences of actions and take account of relevant circumstances. Unfortunately, this growth is not always pressed with zeal. "Many people," as Kierkegaard put it, "reach their conclusions about life like lazy schoolboys; they copy the answers from the back of the book without troubling to work the sums out for themselves." All too often this laziness is encouraged by the surrounding culture. A great deal of our customary training with respect to values is done with more emphasis on conformity than on inquiry. It is not surprising, therefore, that conscience and morality, which at their best can be such important attributes of maturity, are often compromised by their early origins, continuing to exhibit some of the shortcomings of a child's understanding of rules.

The path toward a more enlightened conscience, capable of discriminating the actual consequences of acts in particular situations while still valuing certain consequences more than others, is a cognitive accomplishment that is assisted by social experience. As we shall see in the following chapters, social experience occurs in a variety of forms, each of which has its effects on the growth of personality.

12 Social Competence and Membership

Under ordinary circumstances children are no novices at social interaction when they first enter the company of other children of their age. The social curriculum begins in the family circle, and a child has usually passed a course or two before he becomes mobile enough to get around outside. He cannot deal with children his own age, however, simply by drawing upon a practiced repertory. They present a new version of an old problem. Learning to deal with this version soon becomes a theme that is of large consequence in the growth of personality.

Considered as a whole, social development can be pictured as consisting of several themes, each of which continues into an aspect of adult life. Group experience, the subject of this chapter, is the ground on which attitudes are formed and strategies developed for getting along with others in competitive situations, cooperative work, and everyday social mingling. Two-person interactions, on the other hand, constitute steps toward intimate relations such as those with a close friend, a spouse, and one's children. In the course of time, relations with younger people give rise to attitudes ranging from crude dominance to considerate nurturance. All the while, interaction continues to broaden and to affect later attitudes toward becoming adult and assuming adult authority.

The World of Peers

For the sake of brevity the word *peer* has come into widespread use to designate another child of the same age, a strict contemporary. In all probability children do not immediately prefer the company of their peers, but social institutions give them little choice in the matter. In societies that have attained a certain density of population the child will sooner or later, but never very late, find himself propelled into an age-graded group in which all the other members are right around his chronological age, size, and level of development. If he lives in a kibbutz in Israel the age-grading may begin at once in the infants' house; in the Soviet Union he may find himself in a day-time children's collective as early as 3 months; in an American suburb he may be taken to nursery school at 3 years; and in any advanced nation he will be enfolded in a graded school system as long as his formal education continues. It should not be assumed that because this age-grading is inevitable it is necessarily the best way of promoting social development. The village school, providing constant interaction with children both older and younger, offers a more natural and flexible situation for social growth, whatever its intellectual shortcomings. But as population grows more dense, age-grading becomes more rigid, and learning to get along with peers becomes an increasingly important adaptive task.

Bearing in mind that the social experience of a child of 3 has been almost wholly with people older than himself, 3-year-old peers will not at first seem especially desirable companions. Compared to adults they show a singular lack of interest. They appear preoccupied in what they are doing, and they display no gifts whatever of anticipating one's wants or understanding one's imperfectly expressed verbal communications. They compare favorably only with babies, who are even less disposed to interact. But with further time and exposure it becomes evident that peers offer a special challenge as well as a special opportunity. The child eventually has to show what he is good for in a society of equals. This may signify what he is good for in motor development, in combat, in adventure, in initiative, in the things the others do; it may also mean personal attractiveness, helpfulness, pleasant companionship, conversational ability, and capacity to provide entertainment. The dimensions of excellence are many, but their testing with peers eventually comes to have a certain centrality. Where nobody has handicaps or advantages due to age, one's sense of worth receives its sharpest exposure.

A Scheme of Social Needs

Lest we fall into the error of an earlier time, when the Darwinian image of a competitive struggle for survival got in the way of observing what actually goes on among children, it is important to keep in mind the full spectrum of satisfactions that can be derived from peer group experiences. Murray distinguishes eight forms of positive social satisfaction that can be desired, singly or in patterns, in the company of other people.[1] These are as follows:

> *Dominance*—a desire to influence other people to act in accordance with one's wishes, expressing itself through suggestion, persua-

[1] H. A. Murray, *Explorations in Personality* (Fairlawn, N.J.: Oxford University Press, 1938), Chap. 3.

sion, command, and attempts to organize their activities. This need is in part derived from the general motive of attaining competence.

Exposition—a desire to inform others, to share one's knowledge with them, expressing itself in verbal exposition of what one knows and in showing people how to do things. Satisfaction lies in expounding and explaining, not necessarily in dominating the behavior of others.

Recognition—a desire to elicit from others appreciation of one's worth and praise for one's accomplishments, expressing itself by calling these things to the attention of others, either subtly or by blowing one's horn a bit. The end sought is to be of worth in the eyes of others.

Exhibition—a desire to make a dramatic impression on others; as Murray expresses it, "to excite, amaze, fascinate, entertain, shock, intrigue, amuse or entice." This desire expresses itself in behavior that is colorful, conspicuous, and self-dramatizing; other people are preferred in the role of audience.

Play—a desire to do things for fun without further purpose, expressing itself in joining others for sports, parties, card games, amusing conversation, and general relaxed good times. Any companions will do provided that they also are bent on play.

Affiliation—a desire for the company of one or more congenial, friendly people, for mutually enjoyed, enduring, harmonious relations. In contrast to the play motive, the characteristics of the other person are of great importance and a true congeniality and reciprocity is sought.

Deference—a desire to be guided and inspired by a respected person considered to be superior in wisdom or effectiveness. This desire expresses itself in admiration, eager alliance, willing assistance, and adoption of the goals and values of the respected person. Deference is a positive motive, the deferent relation being a source of real satisfaction; it is to be distinguished from the unwilling subordination that might result from anxiety or the sheer vigor of another person's dominance.

Abasement—a desire "to submit passively to external force," to accept criticism, admit error, belittle oneself, "take a back seat," "allow oneself to be 'talked down.' " While it may be hard to think of abasement as an intrinsic positive need unrelated to anxiety, it may become an end that is sought and enjoyed as the only way to feel comfortable in the company of others. It is a way of showing others that you intend to offer them no competitive threat.

It is clear from Murray's list that there are many dimensions to what people desire from the company of others. In studying the individual case it is always necessary to look for the exact pattern of these desires and to describe them in discriminating terms.

Social Behavior as Exchange

One of the things a child has to learn through experience is which kinds of satisfaction he really wants, which ones are worth the effort. In a useful formulation of this problem Homans describes social behavior in terms of exchange, analogous to an exchange of material goods but obviously including important nonmaterial ones such as approval and prestige. Social interaction in these terms can be said to contain values and to incur costs. Values and costs can also be called positive and negative reinforcements, but the exchange analogy draws more vividly the picture of a person trying to get the most for his money out of social interactions—the best balance between satisfactions and costs.[2] It can perhaps be assumed that any child is capable of feeling satisfaction in any of the eight ways described by Murray, but these are not likely either to be equally attractive or to incur equal costs. The terms of exchange are already an individual matter by the time a child seriously encounters his peers.

Adaptation to peers is an aspect of development to which constitutional differences can be expected to make a distinct contribution. One is more sharply aware of differences of *physique*—size, shape, muscularity, agility, attractiveness—when comparing oneself with age-mates. A fat boy or a skinny boy can win recognition in athletics, or a tiny, round-faced, soft-voiced girl become the dominant member of a group, only at great cost in effort. Differences in *level of energy* are clearly related to costs and satisfactions. For a passive child, maximum value may prove to lie in a quiet combination of affiliation, deference, and abasement. The variable of *sensitivity* fits well into the exchange metaphor. Children with high sensitivity may find that peer society, with its inevitable buffetings, does not often yield satisfactions that equal its costs in pain. Early learning in the family circle, itself influenced by constitution, likewise produces tendencies such as dependence, confidence, inferiority feelings, or guilty inhibitions that markedly affect the value-cost ratio in peer relations. Each child has to find out what he wants in this sphere relative to what it costs him to obtain it. It is misleading to express this in the language of fixed social traits. The process is better described as an evolution of strategies for striking the best bargain, under prevailing and changing circumstances, between what is found valuable in peer-group memberships and what must be paid in costs.

As we shall see, the positive values of membership may be considerable. Simply being a member of a group, even though an inconspicuous member, adds appreciably to an individual's sense of power. There is strength in numbers, and a group can do things that would far surpass individual daring and capacity. Group membership counteracts loneliness and may become an alternate or preferable source of security for children who get little of this boon at home. Good and bad morale, which have so much to do with the outcome of cooperative undertakings, are understandable only as phenomena of the group. A feeling of belonging is of great importance in human experience. This may mean simply acceptance in one's immediate circle, but it seems often to have a cognitive content in which the central element is being part of something larger and humanly more important than oneself.

[2] G. C. Homans, "Social Behavior as Exchange," *American Journal of Sociology*, **63** (1958), 597–606.

Cognitive Difficulties in Understanding Human Relations

Mistakes can occur in understanding the growth of personality through failure to take into consideration the level of cognitive development. We all know that children do not necessarily understand things as adults do, but it is not easy to see things again through a child's eyes. The child's understanding of human relations is likely to be complicated by wishes and anxieties, but part of the problem is simply cognitive. Human relations are no easy matter; a long accumulation of experience is required to grasp all that may be involved. Developmental processes like identification and responding to the expectations of others have to take place within the child's cognitive capacity, determined in part by his age. Cognitive capacity has its own laws of unfolding.

Early in his work, Piaget contributed an important insight into this problem in his concept of egocentrism. This concept has at times been carelessly misused to imply selfishness or preoccupation with self, but this was far from Piaget's intention. What he meant was that a young child cannot put himself in the position of another person or see things through another person's eyes; he is locked in his own perspective. Experiments by Piaget and his co-workers indicated that this rigidity applied even to physical perspectives. Children were shown a large picture of mountains and asked how the mountains would look to a person far to the left in the picture and to another person far to the right. The younger children were unable to entertain the idea that the mountains would look different when seen from different positions. The same cognitive shortcoming appeared in thinking about the members of the family circle. Asked if he had a brother, a small boy said that he had one, Paul; asked if Paul had a brother, he replied in the negative. Piaget interpreted this sort of mixup as a sign that the child was unable to transcend his own perspective, imagine himself in Paul's position, and therefore realize that he himself was a brother to Paul.[3]

Egocentrism clearly puts limits on understanding human interactions. This was well brought out in an experiment devised by Eugene Lerner on the growth of perspectives during childhood.[4] Children were told a story involving a piece of behavior that from an adult point of view would be judged differently by the different characters involved. In the story a teacher tells his class that Frank, who is doing badly, is lazy and must learn to work harder; he therefore forbids the other children to help him with his lessons. In spite of this command one of the boys, Paul, feels sorry for Frank and helps him anyway. Having told this much, the experimenter asks the child how Paul

---

[3] J. Piaget, *The Judgment and Reasoning of the Child* (New York: Harcourt Brace Jovanovich, Inc., 1928). For a survey of Piaget's thought, see H. Ginsburg and S. Opper, *Piaget's Theory of Intellectual Development: An Introduction* (Englewood Cliffs, N.J.: Prentice-Hall, Inc., 1969).

[4] E. Lerner, "The Problem of Perspective in Moral Reasoning," *American Journal of Sociology*, **43** (1937), 249–269.

regards his own act, whether he thinks it was good or bad, right or wrong; then follow questions about what the teacher thought of it, what Frank thought of it, what Frank's mother and Paul's mother thought of it, and so on through all the characters. The younger children, up to 8 or so, frame the problem in simple terms: everyone, including Paul, regards the act as bad. A year or two later, however, comes the first break in this ironclad conception of a rule; Paul is allowed to believe that he did the right thing, although Frank and Frank's mother still view the deed as utterly wrong. Not until 10 or 11 could the majority of the children interpret the incident with due regard for each character's probable outlook: the teacher's wrath at the flouting of his command, Frank's pleasure in receiving friendly help, Frank's mother's delight that someone loved her boy, Paul's mother's acceptance of her son's generous impulse but worry about his disobedience and about the effect on Frank. Even the simple incident chosen by Lerner for the story turns out to contain a complex pattern of human relations, which children only gradually come to understand.

In a research using pictorial rather than verbally described situations, Dorothy Flapan showed excerpts from a commercial film to her subjects, girls of 6, 9, and 12 years, and asked simply for a description of what happened before putting questions designed to amplify the spontaneous report.[5] The excerpts consisted of scenes involving children and parents living on a farm. In one sequence, for example, the father, finding his little girl sad because she has accidentally killed a squirrel, makes her a present of a newborn calf. The girl happily relates this at dinner, but the mother, not knowing what has gone before, says that the farm animals belong to the family, not to anyone in particular. The girl is now sad again, but when the father explains what he did, the family decides that it would be desirable for the girl to have full responsibility for bringing up the calf. In describing this sequence the 6-year-old subjects confined themselves largely to a factual reporting of what was done and said. Features that an adult would consider incidental were reported with as much fidelity as those that carried the plot; one subject, for instance, detailed the moment at which each person around the dinner table began to eat, and included an incidental dialogue on taking big mouthfuls. At 9 years, and more fully at 12 years, reporting was amplified by explanations of the action and dialogue, at first largely in terms of the objective situation, but increasingly passing over into inferences and interpretations that included what the characters felt, what they intended, and how they understood the feelings and thoughts of other characters. It was interesting to observe how often the youngest children, while apparently enjoying the film, failed to get the point of it in terms of human relations. They seemed to view the film as a series of events that happened successively without any internal connection; the girl's sadness over the squirrel and the father's gift of the calf might be two quite

---

[5] D. Flapan, *Children's Understanding of Social Interaction* (New York: Columbia University, Teachers College Press, 1968).

separate happenings. Understanding human relations is difficult. It involves putting things together that do not occur simultaneously, and it also calls for a considerable amount of reading between the lines. No wonder it has not gone far at the age of 6, for it is something we keep on learning all our lives.

The Early Course of Interactions with Peers

In considering the course of social growth it is necessary to keep in mind not only the child's social inclinations but also the level of cognitive sophistication. We cannot properly understand how a child feels about his peers unless we know how they look to him. The age of 3 is often mentioned as the right time for starting nursery school, and it is with respect to the first three years that the greatest amount of doubt has been expressed in Communist countries about the value of children's collectives. What is there about age 3 that makes it more suitable for peer interactions? In part it is a question of perceptual differentiation. A 2-year-old, seeing something he wants, may toddle straight through another child's mud pie or sand castle on the way to his goal. A 3-year-old is more likely to see and avoid these treasures of another child's industry. Nursery workers are aware that group play at 2½ is hazardous, deteriorating almost at once into unrestrained impulse and conflict. Not that everything is smooth sailing after the third birthday, but children are then at least somewhat more capable of being onlookers of each other's behavior and of interacting for brief periods.[6]

Observations at Nursery Schools

The relation of cognitive repertory to behavior is well illustrated in children's first weeks at nursery school. The new world opening before them consists of adult women, play materials, and children all of the same age. With adult women and play materials the child is already somewhat familiar, but the novelty of such a profusion of equal-age "siblings" may simply be frightening. It is noticed that at first the child's attention goes more to the teachers than to the other children. Security is sought in the mother-substitutes: it is far more important to be sure that these women will provide for one's needs and protection than it is to begin testing out the other children. The child perceives the situation according to his previous experience as another version of a family, and he must first discover how well the teachers are going to perform the parental role. Parents of a nursery school child, looking hopefully for social virtuosity, are often frustrated and even alarmed by their candidate's indifference to those among whom he is supposed to shine. But the child's strategy is sound. He is using his previous experience as best he can, and his security would indeed be small in a group of 3-year-olds unsupervised by adults.

[6] A. Gesell and F. L. Ilg, *Infant and Child in the Culture of Today* (New York and London: Harper & Row, Publishers, 1943), esp. Chaps. 17 and 18.

Once a certain security is established it becomes possible to take the other children into account. This may start simply by watching. Landreth describes a girl who sat for most of several days in a swing contentedly watching what was going on. Although she took no social initiative at all during this period, she asked the teacher about a child who was absent, and at home she talked about the children and sang nursery school songs. She was developing a cognitive map of the human environment prior to taking active steps.[7] A slightly more advanced step consists of parallel play, playing a game of one's own with one's own materials but simultaneously observing the games of other children nearby. Verbal overtures and perhaps some exchanging of materials pave the way for play that is more interactive and that presently becomes truly cooperative. In an observational study at a nursery school where there was a younger group between 2 and 3, the tally showed that solitary and parallel play accounted at this age for three-quarters of the playtime; this dropped to less than half for the group between 3 and 4 years.[8] Real exchanges with one's peers represent a considerable advance in daring and in social perception.

It is probably premature to speak of group membership at nursery school age. Spontaneous grouping among the children is fleeting. Even when they exhibit bursts of affection for one another, these feelings are not usually sufficient to cement lasting pairs, much less groups of three or more. In an early study of this question Parten observed spontaneous nursery school groups in the fall, in the winter, and again in the spring. The groupings proved to be highly transient, and even the phenomenon of leadership changed markedly from one period to the next. Six of the nine children given a high leadership rating in the winter, for example, received low ratings in the fall and spring.[9] Nursery school experience can help children a great deal in getting used to the company of other children and in discovering the rudiments of rewarding interaction. For children of 3 and 4, however, the social curriculum still has a long way to run.

Observations During the Early School Grades

Progress in relations with peers is illustrated in a study by Biber and associates of 7-year-olds at school.[10] One of the things studied by the investigators was spontaneous conversation at lunchtime. The children talked freely, using language with ease and considerable maturity, so that the lunch room had much the same background noise, only pitched a little higher, as if it held a gathering of adults. Conversations had to do with happenings in the

[7] C. Landreth, *Education of the Young Child* (New York and London: John Wiley & Sons, Inc., 1942), Chap. 9.

[8] C. Landreth, *The Psychology of Early Childhood* (New York: Alfred A. Knopf, Inc., 1958), p. 220.

[9] M. B. Parten, "Leadership among Preschool Children," *Journal of Abnormal and Social Psychology,* **27** (1933), 430–440.

[10] B. Biber, L. B. Murphy, L. Woodcock, and I. Black, *Life and Ways of the Seven-to-Eight Year Old* (New York: Basic Books, Inc., 1952).

children's lives, but they were occasionally spiced with references to world events as the children understood them. The investigators also turned their attention to free play on the playground during recess. Here they were able to observe cooperative play in a form suggestive of a Western thriller. The children became members of a task force, so to speak, some rushing around and pretending to fire guns while others took supporting roles in the drama. These two situations indicate a marked advance over what nursery school children could do. School-age children show budding awareness of role differentiation, a start on taking reciprocal roles, and an increased awareness of both being and having an audience. It should be noted that in these situations strict age-grading is probably not most propitious for development. Slightly older children provide models for the younger ones to emulate.

These gains are impressive, but one should not exaggerate the interactive sophistication that underlies them. It is well known, for instance, that a first grade functions as a real group only for the briefest periods. There is still no lasting group structure or continuous leadership, and there is still a marked instability even of pairs and groups of three children.[11] Furthermore, the plot of the Western thriller is improvised from moment to moment, and the members of the cast wander in and out of the production as individual inclination dictates. Close examination shows that the children play mainly for themselves and stop the moment the presence of the other players ceases to yield immediate enjoyment. This is also somewhat true of children's conversations. In one of his earliest studies Piaget, introducing the concept of egocentrism, pointed out that children's dialogues at around the age of 7 were often in reality *collective monologues* in which one speaker uttered a thought, another uttered an unrelated thought of his own, the first speaker pursued his own thought a little further, the second pursued his a little further, and so on indefinitely, socialization being indicated only in the convention of not both talking at once.[12] This defect in communication, not unknown in adult conversations, indicates that the power of listening and of entering the other person's point of view is not as well developed as the buzz of lunchtime conversation might suggest.

The limitations of sustained group organization are shown in an episode described by Biber in which the 7-year-olds put on a strike for shorter rest periods. The plan called for a sit-in with refusal to rest or to go anywhere else until the demand was granted. This action caught the Establishment in a weak posture, because the school favored independence and group activity and the teachers admired the children's spunk in thinking of such a plan. The teacher of the striking group thus occupied the awkward position of trying to bolster group morale in an action directed against herself. But in

[11] C. Buehler, "The Social Behavior of Children," in *A Handbook of Child Psychology*, 2d ed., ed. C. Murchison (Worcester, Mass.: Clark University Press, 1933), pp. 374–416; A. Gesell and F. L. Ilg, *The Child from Five to Ten* (New York: Harper & Row, Publishers, 1946).

[12] J. Piaget, *The Language and Thought of the Child*, trans. M. Warden (New York: Harcourt Brace Jovanovich, Inc., 1926), esp. Chaps. 1 and 2.

spite of her best efforts the strike was a failure. The attention of individual members quickly strayed, the momentary feeling of group strength rapidly melted away, and the strikers wandered off separately into the routines of school life. Group cohesion was not yet real enough to achieve a serious collective purpose.

The Juvenile Era

The period from about 6 to 12 was described by Harry Stack Sullivan as the juvenile era.[13] It is evident from his account that he had in mind chiefly children's spontaneous, unsupervised interactions—what they did on the playground, on the streets, and in the fields and woods rather than how they behaved in situations dominated by adult presence. Sullivan attributed to this type of experience a highly significant part in the growth of personality.

> The importance of the juvenile era can scarcely be exaggerated, since it is the actual time for becoming social. People who bog down in the juvenile era have very conspicuous disqualifications for a comfortable life among their fellows. A vast number of important things happen in the juvenile era. This is the first developmental stage in which the limitations and peculiarities of the home as a socializing influence begin to be open to remedy. The juvenile era has to remedy a good many of the cultural idiosyncrasies, eccentricities of value, and so on, that have been picked up in the childhood socialization; if it does not, they are apt to survive and color, or warp, the course of development through subsequent periods.[14]

The course of growth during the juvenile era was in Sullivan's view neither smooth nor comfortable. He described it as a time of "shocking insensitivity to feelings of personal worth in others," and further characterized it as a period "when a degree of crudeness in interpersonal relations, very rarely paralleled in later life, is the rule." The following comment from the autobiography of C. S. Lewis, made in connection with his experience at an English boarding school, is relevant:

> For boyhood is very like the "dark ages" not as they were but as they are represented in bad, short histories. The dreams of childhood and those of adolescence may have much in common; between them, often, boyhood stretches like an alien territory in which everything (ourselves included) has been greedy, cruel, noisy, and prosaic, in which the imagination has slept and the most unideal senses and ambitions have been restlessly, even maniacally, awake.[15]

It will be noticed that Lewis limits his strictures to boyhood and that Sullivan, who as a psychiatrist specialized in work with male schizophrenics, usually

[13] H. S. Sullivan, *The Interpersonal Theory of Psychiatry* (New York: W. W. Norton & Company, Inc., 1953), Chap. 15.

[14] *Ibid.*, p. 227.

[15] C. S. Lewis, *Surprised by Joy* (New York: Harcourt Brace Jovanovich, Inc., 1955), p. 71.

sounded as if he were talking about boys. It does not follow that girls, already sex-typed in their own and others' minds in a less assertive and competitive image, exhibit the alleged juvenile characteristics to anything like the same degree.

If the juvenile era is a hard school it is nevertheless capable of teaching valuable lessons. Sullivan stated the two chief topics as *competition* and *compromise*. Both of these tendencies can be called natural in the sense that competition inevitably results from the assertiveness and expansiveness of growing children and that compromise inevitably emerges as the only possible check on endless struggle. In a society that values competition there is likely to be strong cultural encouragement of its manifestation during the juvenile era, but compromise is also encouraged both by the staff of the school and by the juvenile society itself. Sullivan made these two tendencies equivalent to the ends of a single variable of dominance-submission. This connection is shown in his description of the possible lasting consequences of an extreme development of either pattern.

> Both competition and compromise, while very necessary additions to one's equipment for living with one's fellows, are capable of being developed into outstandingly troublesome traits of the personality. In what I call chronically juvenile people one sees a competitive way of life in which nearly everything that has real importance is part of a process of getting ahead of the other fellow. . . . Under some circumstances compromise also becomes a vice, so that we find people going on from the juvenile era who are perfectly willing to yield almost anything, as long as they have peace and quiet, as they are apt to put it.[16]

Describing the extremes in this way, Sullivan clearly implies a process akin to the fixation hypothesized by Freud for earlier developmental levels. It was central to Sullivan's thinking, however, that strategies overlearned at one stage were often remedied through natural growth during a subsequent stage. If juvenile behavior, whether competitive or abasive, lasted into chronological adulthood, it might be because the situations in late childhood and adolescence had not been favorable to learning anything better.

The experience of being out among one's peers and at the same time subordinate to new kinds of adult authority is conducive to rapidly widening cognition of the human environment. Whereas the newcomer at nursery school sees before him a slightly changed replica of the family, the school-age child becomes acquainted with new ranges of peer behavior and with new and more specialized types of authority. He and his companions talk about their parents and visit each other's homes. This encourages the insight that parents have different characteristics and values: things are allowed in another house that one could never get away with at home. Teachers are found to have characteristics different from parents, and the sphere of their authority, as of other agents such as the police, proves to be not identical with that

---

[16] Sullivan, *The Interpersonal Theory of Psychiatry*, p. 232.

of the authorities at home. All these discoveries, discussed with one's companions and perhaps also at home, lead towards a more discriminating understanding of roles, perspectives, and the structure of the surrounding society. This new understanding tends to diminish the absolute position of the home, which continues, however, to be highly important during the juvenile era.

Valuable as is Sullivan's perspicacious description of this period of growth, it should not be taken as an account of an unvarying stage of development. The description sounds a little too rough-and-tumble for a contemporary well-ordered suburb where such a large part of children's time is taken up in organized activity under adult supervision. It sounds somewhat wrong for children growing up in a kibbutz, who at 6 are already veterans of peer interaction but who are never far from an adult's eye. But it does not sound rough-and-tumble enough for the life of the streets in an urban slum, where, as we saw in an earlier chapter, fighting is virtually forced on boys and girls alike and where aggression is encouraged rather than controlled.[17] The character of a child's experience during the juvenile era is very much a function of the social setting. This is a point that requires careful investigation in understanding individual cases and in drawing conclusions about consequences for the growth of personality.

Emergence of Group Self-Management

At about the age of 9, according to Gesell's observations, the first evidences appear of intentional, planned group formation, usually for some specific purpose. Children can form themselves into a club to build a hut in the woods, to play scrub baseball, to work on stamp collections, bake cookies for a sale, and make scrapbooks for the children's wards of hospitals.[18] These groups may not be destined for a long life or for stable organization, but the fact that they can exist at all is indicative of important psychological development. There must be some understanding of the interests of other children and of the possible satisfactions to be gained from a mutual pursuit of interests. There must be a capacity to plan ahead and pursue goals over periods of time. To play an organized game such as baseball, children must grasp something of the interlocking roles of the different players and adjust their behavior to what the others are doing. Capacity to function as a group is shown also in classroom behavior. In contrast to the fluid impermanence of first grade social organization, a fifth grade class can take on considerable enduring structure. There may be class officers and committees, and the children who are considered to be the important ones in the autumn are likely to occupy the same status in the spring.[19]

Observations show that at 9 and 10 years children begin to have a

---

[17] See above, Chap. 6, pp. 148–149.
[18] Gesell and Ilg, *The Child from Five to Ten*, pp. 205–206.
[19] Buehler, "The Social Behavior of Children."

fairly good sense of what may be called power relations. It does not take them long to discover which members of a group have high social competence in the sense of exerting an influence on others. This was brought out clearly in a study by Lippitt, Polansky, and Rosen made at a boys' summer camp.[20] Each boy was asked the question, with respect to his seven cabin mates, "Who is able to get the others to do as he wants them to do?" Within each cabin there was substantial agreement among the eight boys as to the degree of influence exerted by each member; a clear hierarchy had formed itself. This would not be surprising toward the end of the summer after extended interaction. Presumably this sort of influence-grading is most readily established by an actual testing of one another. But the investigators noticed that the hierarchy existed almost from the start, suggesting that there was already a certain skill at picking up clues relevant to this important matter.[21] It is evident that functioning as a group will be more successful if the influence hierarchy is quickly perceived and at least tentatively accepted, obviating a bitter power struggle whenever a new group comes together.

The manner in which groups at their best manage themselves is brought out in a study by Rausch and Sweet.[22] The setting for these observations was a hospital subunit usually devoted to residential treatment of highly aggressive boys between the ages of 9 and 12. During a fortnight's holiday when the young patients went home, the investigators brought in for purposes of comparison a group of normal boys of the same ages. The adult caretakers were surprised to discover how little they were needed. Accustomed to an unending series of acute crises calling for instant intervention and management, they were astonished at the ability of the normal children to regulate themselves. One child might call another's attention to a danger, warning him not to throw a ball so near a window. One might help another, lending a hand or finding a needed tool. Sportsmanship was apparent in a loser's congratulating a winner on his good game. Disintegrative tension rising through stages of giggling, laughter, horseplay, and excitement was sometimes neutralized by a more controlled child who changed the subject of conversation, reminded the others of a goal toward which they were working, or simply told them to shut up and sit down. Particularly impressive were evidences that the boys were capable of respect for each other's self-esteem and might try to repair it when injured, for instance, by encouraging a depressed baseball player who had made several errors. There were manifestations also of interest in others' creative work and accomplishment. One boy, for example, was much impressed by another's drawing, and called the attention of the whole group to the excellent piece of work. On the whole we are likely to take this kind of thing for granted and perhaps dismiss it as incul-

[20] R. Lippitt, N. Polansky, and S. Rosen, "The Dynamics of Power," *Human Relations,* **5** (1952), 37–64.

[21] D. Cartwright, ed., *Studies in Social Power* (Ann Arbor: University of Michigan Press, 1959), esp. Chaps. 6 and 8.

[22] H. L. Rausch and B. Sweet, "The Preadolescent Ego: Some Observations of Normal Children," *Psychiatry,* **24** (1961), 122–132.

cated good manners. But one cannot become aware of another person's self-esteem by fiat. What is seen in these observations, and often in real life, should be considered a momentous achievement in group behavior, one that subordinates egotistical needs to the continuing cohesion of the group.

To what extent is a group of children capable of complete self-management? The question is speculative because it is so difficult to rule out the influence of adults. William Golding in *Lord of the Flies* tells a story that contains his own implicit speculations on the theme.[23] He places a large group of boys, the oldest 12 years of age, on a remote island where as the result of an airplane crash they are left without adult supervision and must fend for themselves. As food is abundant, the building of huts is the only immediate necessity, and they are otherwise free for adventurous play. There is, however, the question of their ultimate rescue. They can attain this, if at all, only by keeping up a large fire, the smoke from which might attract a passing ship. This entails hard work and continuous day-and-night watching, postponing immediate gratifications for an uncertain future event. As Golding tells the story, social organization begins to emerge in the interest of keeping to this distant goal. Leadership is assumed by Ralph, one of the oldest boys, who is attractive, responsible, but not especially perceptive; but his defect is remedied by his right-hand man Piggy, dumpy, awkward, and extremely near-sighted, who functions as the brain behind the throne. Almost at once a rival faction forms itself out of a group of boys who before the trip had been members of a choir. The story turns on a power struggle between Jack, the leader of the choir, who encourages hunting, excitement, and impulse gratification, and Ralph, who stands for ordered political procedure and future goals as typified by the signal fire. If we take the outcome of Golding's story not just as a single happening but as a symbol of what might be expected to happen in a society governed by 12-year-old boys—and Golding seems to have had an even broader symbolism in mind—then his speculation is that social organization will collapse. Ralph steadily loses followers to Jack's side, where primitive fears and dark destructive impulses are increasingly taking command. As the story ends, several boys, including Piggy, have been killed and Ralph is a hunted fugitive, rescued from certain death only by the intervention of adults landing from a naval vessel. Golding is writing fiction, but he provides unforgettable images of the fragility of social organization and rational control when circumstances bring to the surface man's propensities for destructiveness.

Returning to the realm of planned observation, there is a piece of research that bears upon interactions within groups and that also sheds valuable light on relations between groups. Sherif and associates chose groups of boy campers, 11 and 12 years of age, to study in a controlled sequence the formation of groups, the effects of competition between groups, and the

[23] W. Golding, *Lord of the Flies* (New York: Coward-McCann, Inc., 1954; Capricorn Books, 1959).

modification of rivalry in the direction of cooperation.[24] Two groups of boys were taken simultaneously on a three-week camping trip in Robbers Cave State Park in Oklahoma. Conditions were arranged so that the two groups, each of 11 boys, had no contact for the first week. This provided each group with an opportunity to develop social solidarity and an influence hierarchy while taking part in the work and amusements of camp life. At the end of this time the existence nearby of the other group was made known, together with a challenge to a baseball game. The counselors, following the experimental design, built this up into a four-day tournament of baseball games, tugs-of-war, and contests of putting up tents, with prizes for the side that scored the most points. This procedure, which does not depart widely from common camp practice, was intended to maximize rivalry by specifically making one group's gain the other's loss. The maneuver was almost alarmingly successful. The groups now christened themselves the Rattlers and the Eagles, made flags, played fiercely in the contests, shouted at each other a mounting series of derogatory names, took to burning each other's flags, raided each other's quarters, and refused to have anything to do with one another apart from the tournament. Meanwhile internal dissensions dwindled and ingroup solidarity grew stronger.

The final stage of the experiment called for bringing about cooperation between Rattlers and Eagles. Simple contact in a pleasurable activity, such as seeing a movie or sending up fireworks, proved ineffective. The experimenters finally achieved success by setting up superordinate goals that were of serious concern to both groups and could be attained only by joint action. A contrived stoppage in the water pipe from the central supply caused inconvenience and thirst for everyone and yielded only to an investigation by both parties. The truck that was used daily to procure food broke down, and the boys could start it only by pulling it with the tug-of-war rope, this time with intermingled Rattlers and Eagles pulling in the same direction. Involved in such situations during the final week, the erstwhile fighting rivals were able to spend the last evening in joint entertainment and to ride home together amicably in the same bus.

It is beneficial to students of personality to include in their thinking such results as those obtained in the Robbers Cave experiment. If we were to follow a single boy through the three weeks at camp it is entirely possible that we would characterize him during the first week as a markedly cooperative camper, during the second week as a markedly competitive and verbally hostile athlete, and during the third week as a boy with marked initiative in intergroup cooperation. We would see consistency in his activity level, sense of competence, and initiative, but is he an aggressive boy or a cooperative one? These latter "traits" are not fixed characteristics; their strength is influenced

[24] M. Sherif, O. J. Harvey, B. J. White, W. R. Hood, and C. W. Sherif, *Intergroup Conflict and Cooperation: The Robbers Cave Experiment* (Norman, Okla.: Institute of Group Relations, University of Oklahoma, 1961).

by the channels and encouragements provided by the social environment. The observation that changes in these encouragements, so quickly affect behavior teaches us to have a more discriminating view of what is relatively fixed in personality and what is more largely a function of interaction with the surrounding social system. The belief that the juvenile era can remedy some of the harmful consequences of family upbringing appears more reasonable in this light. The juvenile world is a new experience, and if part of a child's behavior in it is simply a rough repetition of previous strategies, another part takes account of the properties of the new situation. Unfortunately, as the Robbers Cave experiment shows and as Golding's story implies, juvenile groups may not always be on the side of remedy. They can also contribute to the loss of patterns that favor cooperative living. But in either event the concept of personality as a partially open system interacting with social influences is necessary to account for what can be observed.

Adolescent Groups

Certain of the trends that have been described in children's social interactions continue through adolescence and beyond. There is an increase in the stability of groups, in their enduring structure and pursuit of long-range goals. There is also a diminishing need for adult supervision and help; adolescent groups soon become competent to manage their own affairs. At college age, students run efficiently such enterprises as a campus daily, a monthly literary magazine, large-scale social events, entertainments, and various forms of social service. It seems possible that high school students are more capable of doing this kind of thing than has usually been supposed. Implicit in such activities is a high level of social organization and cooperation that is beyond the reach of children at the age of 12.

Two things about adolescent groups are somewhat new. In the first place, they rather quickly assume a central place in the individual's security and sense of worth at a time when there is an urge to outgrow the family circle. In the second place, they have to accommodate the interest that boys and girls take in each other after puberty. The social life of American high schools and the system of values that constitutes what is often called the *youth culture* have been the objects of considerable investigation in recent years. It is evident that an individual's experience as a member of high school society is of tremendous importance to him at the time, and it seems reasonable to suppose that the consequences of that experience are of lasting importance for the directions of subsequent growth.

Social Life in High School

The social system in which high school students are immersed consists, as Gordon pointed out, of three subsystems.[25] There is first the formal sys-

[25] C. W. Gordon, *The Social System of the High School* (New York: The Free Press, 1957).

tem of the school itself, with the expectations, values, rules, and regulations that emanate from the administration and teaching staff. Second, there are the semiformal systems represented by sponsored organizations such as athletics, dramatics, and school clubs. Third, there are informal systems such as cliques, leading crowds, and factions, which arise spontaneously regardless of adult blessing or disapproval. The latter groupings are called informal because they have no institutional forms such as curricular requirements or club offices. They simply exist, but their informality should not be taken to signify lack of importance. Membership in a clique or crowd can be the most weighty social fact of all.

The nature of high school cliques was illuminated in Hollingshead's well-known study of youth in Elmtown.[26] Hollingshead introduces his discussion with a quotation from a high school teacher who said:

> This school is full of cliques. You go into the hall and you will find the same kids together day after day. Walk up Freedom Street at noon, or in the evening, and you'll see them again. These kids run in bunches just like their parents. This town is full of cliques, and you can't expect the kids to be any different from their parents.

The high school cliques in Elmtown were small, having from 2 to 12 members with an average of 5. Membership expressed itself in going places and doing things together. Hollingshead reached the conclusion that these associations "consume most of the interest, time, and activities of the adolescents." Interviewing his subjects with great care, he secured a bundle of comments on "who cliques with whom," on how the members get together in the first place and how it is decided whether or not a new candidate will be allowed to run with the group. Being neighbors had a lot to do with it, but Hollingshead's study disclosed with striking clarity that membership in a clique was strongly influenced by social class status. The students did not express it this way, but they were already adept at characterizing other people as "not their type," the concrete specifications for this judgment making it plain that status considerations were important. A study of dating patterns as reported by the students revealed the same influence; roughly two-thirds of all dates were between members of the same social class, and only a tiny number were more than one class level away. These findings should not be interpreted to mean that high school adolescents are natural snobs. Adolescents need small groups for security and support, and they gravitate most readily to neighbors whose similar experience and outlook makes for easy solidarity. But neighborhood residence patterns reflect social and economic status, and adult briefing on who is and is not "their type" is likely to run along the same lines. The effect of high school clique formation is thus to perpetuate the existing status system.

The existence of a *leading crowd* in high school society is well docu-

---

[26] A. B. Hollingshead, *Elmtown's Youth: The Impact of Social Classes on Adolescents* (New York: John Wiley & Sons, Inc., 1949), esp. Chap. 9.

mented in Coleman's study of 10 high schools.[27] The leading crowd is much larger than a clique, consisting of a considerable group of students who are prominent and who dominate the semiformal systems by holding most of the offices. Students do not find it odd to be asked about the leading crowd, nor is it difficult for them to identify its members. In some schools there proved to be a second or rival leading crowd, but this complication was not universal. Systematic inquiry into what it takes to be a member of the leading crowd revealed that the most important attribute was "having a good personality." Coleman comments that "the importance of having a good personality, or, what is a little different, 'being friendly' or 'being nice to the other kids,' in these adolescent cultures is something that adults often fail to realize. Adults often forget how 'person-oriented' children are."[28] For girls good looks, good clothes, and a good reputation followed a good personality as qualifications for membership in the leading crowd; for boys, being an athlete was more important than looks and clothes, and having a car emerged as a distinct asset. Good scholastic standing was a much less significant matter, only slightly outranking having money. Coming from the right neighborhood was rated even less important, something of a contrast to Hollingshead's study more than a decade earlier, and all the more surprising because Elmtown was one of Coleman's 10 high schools. The students were questioned also on the requirements for popularity. Boys gave the first place to being an athlete, boys and girls alike stressed being in the leading crowd and a leader in activities, and girls made a point of having nice clothes. It was noteworthy that scholastic excellence was thought to contribute to the popularity of boys with boys and of girls with girls, but its importance in cross-sex popularity was rated quite small.

One of Coleman's questions gave the students a chance to imagine being someone different from themselves.

"If I could trade, I would be someone different from myself." The pathos inherent in this statement has peculiar relevance for a teenager. He cannot choose, as yet, the social situation or the activity that will make him feel at one with himself. He must see himself through the eyes of a world he did not make, the adolescent world of his community, into which the accident of residence has thrust him. If, in its eyes, he has done well, then he can be at peace with himself; if he is not accepted, recognized, looked up to, nor given status of any sort, he finds it hard to escape into another place in society where he can find recognition and respect. Instead, he turns inward; he must question his very self, asking whether it would not be better if he were someone quite different.[29]

27 J. S. Coleman, *The Adolescent Society: The Social Life of the Teenager and Its Impact on Education* (New York: The Free Press, 1961).
28 *Ibid.*, p. 37.
29 *Ibid.*, p. 221.

The answers to this question underlined the importance of group membership and acceptance by peers. Students in the leading group were less interested in being someone else, as were students who had friends. Those who had neither friends nor membership in the leading group were most liable to wish themselves different. There are, of course, other kinds of success and other channels of interest that can produce self-esteem without social prominence. An adolescent who is low in the requirements for popularity may be considered fortunate if he has alternatives of this kind. But it is still difficult not to be affected by status with one's peers. Unfortunately for the high school's educational purpose, scholastic excellence does not contribute greatly to this status. As Coleman concludes, "For the boys, it is the best athletes who have the most positive feeling about themselves; for the girls, it is those most popular with boys."[30]

Developmental Outcome of Group Experiences

Unlike family influences, the consequences of which have been zealously investigated, the place of peer interactions and group memberships in the growth of personality has received surprisingly moderate attention. We owe this curious imbalance to a situation common in the history of knowledge: a breakthrough at one point tends to absorb interest and produces a neglect of other problems that at the moment seem less amenable to study. When the psychoanalytic method and its various offshoots began to implicate early family influences in the causation of later maladjustment, peer relations were further exempted from serious study by being cast as the automatic road to health. Thus for a time the normal growth of personality was pictured as a process of disengaging oneself from the evils of the family in order to partake fully of the blessings of peer relations; the story ended when the last apron string had been cut. That this achievement could have any resemblance to jumping from the frying pan into the fire came along as a somewhat later insight. We can now, however, be less gullible about social adjustment. The peer group is no more an infallible socializing agent than the family group. There are developmental hazards in being *isolated* from the society of one's peers, but there are also developmental hazards in being *enslaved* by the society of one's peers. Both types of hazard will now be considered, but against the background of the positive consequences that can follow from a fortunate childhood and adolescent social experience.

Social Participation

Membership in a group entails the grasping of group norms, the cognition of group expectations, and the taking of reciprocal roles. Starting from an inevitable egocentric outlook and an absolute conception of rules, the

[30] *Ibid.*, p. 232.

child must discover the relativity of human viewpoints and the purposes served by restraints. He must come to understand what others are doing and thinking and feeling in the course of their daily interactions and group enterprises. These forms of cognitive development can occur in the family circle or in the adult-dominated formal school system, but the peer group is the least ambiguous setting for this learning. Especially in informal games, which are played for fun without any shadow of adult-defined duty, the nature of norms and reciprocal roles becomes abundantly clear. Experience with this kind of group membership makes it possible to grasp the implications and acquire the strategies of participation. A person who does well in this part of the social curriculum should find it relatively easy to take part in the occupational organizations, community activities, and cooperative enterprises of adult life.

Another contribution of peers is to be a source of varied information about the human environment. The youth culture, not always noticeably tolerant, provides an opportunity to compare notes on families, to learn about fathers and mothers and siblings different from one's own, and to discover differences of family values. The same broadening service can be performed with respect to teachers, whose personal qualities may be the subject of zestful psychological analysis on the way to and from school. In high school and later, peers may turn the searchlight on their own society and contribute to each other's education by exchanging views about rival cliques and leading crowds. Successful handling of this portion of the social curriculum should be conducive to relativity of perspectives and to a widening awareness of the varieties and vagaries of human behavior.

Participation in groups can also be conducive to a sense of interpersonal competence, which is derived from the experience of exerting an influence on other people. While this way of expressing it may suggest a power drive and a joy in throwing one's weight around, interpersonal efficacy does not depend for most people on such crude manifestations. Making others laugh, telling them something that awakens interest, contributing a useful idea to a discussion, providing reassurance, expressing love and respect and eliciting like expressions from others—all these benign ways of affecting people contribute to a feeling of comfortable confidence that the human environment is responsive rather than formidable. Interpersonal competence also implies being able to manage an unfriendly situation. It includes dealing with arguments, competition, insults, and attempts to put one in a disadvantageous position. We usually have this aspect of competence in mind when we speak of learning to stand on one's own two feet or of being able both to take it and to dish it out. Social life is thus the arena for discovering the range of one's power to affect other people, and one of its possible rewards is an increasing sense of interpersonal competence.

To these accomplishments in social understanding and strategy should be added the motives and feelings that form part of the process of growth. Participation in peer groups yields a variety of satisfactions, including security, agreeable stimulation, a feeling of worth in the eyes of others, and the various forms and degrees of corporate feeling. The degree and manner of participation that will be most satisfying, in terms of benefits obtained and costs incurred, is discovered gradually in the course of experience with peers. Although adolescent society tends to put a high premium on popularity and prominence, adolescents can obtain many of the satisfactions of participation without being prominent at all and without standing high in popularity. There are people in every group who are simply there, who take unobtrusive roles, but who are missed if they are absent. Successful experience in this aspect of the social curriculum should be conducive to a positive, comfortable feeling about being with others.

All these consequences are predicated on successful and satisfying experiences in peer relations. Peer society, however, is a natural phenomenon, not a device set up to promote successful and satisfying experiences for all. What else can happen to one's personality in his attempts to get along with groups?

Social Enslavement

Often, what looks like a good adaptation to a group turns out to be a true enslavement. This may betray itself in painful loneliness and anxiety when not in the company of one's friends, but its most characteristic manifestation is a compulsive conformity to group expectations. The person's preferences, tastes, and opinions are those that are sanctioned by the group, and he takes no chances of giving offense or incurring disapproval. Some adolescents show awareness of differing impulses in themselves but have no courage to assert them; others truly lose contact with what is inside and define themselves entirely in terms of what others want and expect. Compulsive conformity takes a heavy toll on individuality. It makes for difficulty in experiencing initiative and in thinking of oneself as an autonomous agent. Conflict can be intense if one is a member of two groups that turn out not to have just the same values. Under these circumstances the proper court of appeal is what one really thinks and feels, but social enslavement effectively puts this court out of business.

This description of social enslavement may sound like a relatively extreme pattern of behavior, but some of its components are far from rare. Observers who contemptuously liken human groups to flocks of timid sheep seem to have embarrassingly little difficulty in finding illustrations. They can point, for instance, to our susceptibility to fashions. Who dares wear a skirt that is three inches the wrong length, even though this length was just right two years ago and may be just right again in two years' time? Who can diverge with perfect equanimity from the hair styles, whether male or female, that are in vogue in one's chief circle of acquaintance? These symptoms, to be sure, are superficial, but they point to a widespread difficulty in feeling and declaring oneself to be different from other members of the flock. Everyone has probably experienced a sudden weakening of resolution upon realizing that a suggestion he has made is not liked by the rest of the group. Everyone has allowed his behavior to be guided, perhaps more than he likes to admit, by thoughts of what his friends would say. Even an ardent revolutionist who feeds on opposition to the surrounding society may experience great difficulty when it comes to risking the good opinion of the other members of the revolutionary group. We do not have to look for extreme cases in order to understand the nature of social enslavement. There is a touch of it in all of us.

Social enslavement is a product of anxiety. It occurs when membership is desired but acceptance is experienced as precarious. This difficulty can happen first, of course, with respect to the family circle, so that the child may enter peer relations with a strong hunger for secure acceptance but a low expectation of finding it. As Sullivan pointed out, the peer group is capable of remedying this situation if it is generous with acceptance, but we can by no means suppose that this will always be the case. Spontaneous groups of children or adolescents are not dedicated to developmental goals, and for some members they may have precisely the opposite effect. They can be cruel toward a member who is slow, awkward, and no good at favored group activities. Peculiarities of appearance, handicaps, skin color, and ethnic and class status differences can be crudely seized upon as grounds for ostracism. Opposition can be intimidated and conformity bought by threats of ridicule or physical violence. If the group is controlled by one or two highly assertive members who bully the others, its internal structure may be similar to that of an authoritarian family. Acceptance is far from being an automatic consequence of interaction with peers. For many it can be bought only at the price of enslavement.

An influential study that bears on this problem was published in 1950 by David Riesman.[31] Based on extensive interviews with young people during the just preceding years, the study reflects a shift from a character type that Riesman called *inner-directed* toward one called *other-directed*. Inner direction signified being governed by a set of values and ideals inculcated by parents early in life. These ideals were likely to have a content of achievement and success, along with qualities such as self-reliance and moral restraint that were conducive to such goals. Values of this kind were appropriate in a period of American economic development when individual enterprise and free competition, exploiting vast untapped resources, had seemed to justify themselves by producing a rapid growth of national wealth. But changing economic conditions, with greater material abundance and a trend toward large organizations in business, were leading to a different social character type, especially among urban young people in relatively comfortable economic status. Riesman described the other-directed type as follows:

> The hard enduringness and enterprise of the inner-directed types are somewhat less necessary under these new conditions. Increasingly, other people are the problem, not the material environment. . . . What is

[31] D. Riesman, *The Lonely Crowd: A Study of the Changing American Character* (New Haven: Yale University Press, 1950).

common to all other-directeds is that their contemporaries are the source of direction for the individual—either those known to him or those with whom he is indirectly acquainted, through friends and through the mass media. This source is of course "internalized" in the sense that dependence on it for guidance in life is implanted early. The goals toward which the other-directed person strives shift with that guidance: it is only the process of striving itself and the process of paying close attention to the signals from others that remain unaltered throughout life.[32]

Being other-directed carries with it the risk of loss of individuality. Guidance by others means dependence and a strong need for approval; nonconformity produces diffuse anxiety; thus conditions are created that are likely to increase social enslavement. Riesman noted the tendency of many young people to want to be like one another, even to the point of shunning a prominence that would make them stick out in a crowd, trends that have also been documented by Friedenberg in two studies of high school adolescents.[33] This attitude creates a problem both for differentiated development and for a sense of autonomy. Riesman concluded his book with these words:

> If other-directed people should discover that their own thoughts and their own lives are quite as interesting as other people's, that, indeed, they no more assuage their loneliness in a crowd of peers than one can assuage one's thirst by drinking sea water, then we might expect them to become more attentive to their own feelings and aspirations. . . .
>   Men are created different; they lose their social freedom and their individual autonomy in seeking to become like each other.[34]

A somewhat similar conception had been advanced shortly before by Erich Fromm in a description of what he called the *marketing orientation*.[35] Fromm's account of economic change emphasized the fact that success had come to depend less on skilled accomplishments connected with production, more on personal acceptance and being able to work well with others. He spoke of a "personality market."

> Success depends largely on how well a person sells himself on the market, how well he gets his personality across, how nice a "package" he is. . . . If it were enough for the purpose of making a living to rely on what one knows and what one can do, one's self-esteem would be in proportion to one's capacities, that is, to one's use value; but since success depends largely on how one sells one's personality, one experiences oneself as a

---

[32] *Ibid.*, pp. 18–22.

[33] E. Z. Friedenberg, *The Vanishing Adolescent* (Boston: The Beacon Press, 1959); *Coming of Age in America: Growth and Acquiescence* (New York: Random House, Inc., 1965).

[34] Riesman, *The Lonely Crowd*, p. 373.

[35] E. Fromm, *Man for Himself: An Inquiry into the Psychology of Ethics* (New York: Holt, Rinehart and Winston, Inc., 1947).

commodity or rather simultaneously as the seller *and* the commodity to be sold. A person is not concerned with his life and happiness, but with becoming saleable. . . .

Self-esteem depends upon conditions beyond his control. . . . The degree of insecurity that results from this orientation can hardly be overestimated. If one feels that one's own value is not constituted primarily by the human qualities one possesses, but by one's success on a competitive market with everchanging conditions, one's self-esteem is bound to be shaky and in constant need of confirmation by others. Hence one is driven to strive relentlessly for success, and any setback is a severe threat to self-esteem; helplessness, insecurity, and inferiority feelings are the result. If the vicissitudes of the market are the judges of one's value, the sense of dignity and pride is destroyed.[36]

The marketing orientation as described by Fromm tends to produce a character type that is decidedly other-directed. The effects on autonomy and individuality are of the same destructive sort. What Fromm's account adds to Riesman's picture is that the conditions of existence in the business world, indeed in any occupation that has moved in the direction of large organizations, tend to perpetuate and increase in adult life the pattern of social enslavement.[37]

Social Isolation

Circumstances may conspire to make it difficult for a child to enter readily into the society of his peers. The trouble may lie with the available groups, which may be inconsiderate and crudely unwelcoming. It may lie in the individual, who may be naturally shy and tense or who may have become incapacitated for child society by a domestic regime of excessive favor or overprotection. Under these circumstances the first social ventures outside the family can go badly enough to discourage further effort and to initiate a feeling that membership with peers is not worth the price. We can assume that this feeling is not easily made permanent. The mere existence of peers, even if one feels distinctly an outsider, keeps up a certain curiosity about them and a desire to share in what they seem to enjoy. Thus it often happens that after a lonely childhood a person belatedly discovers a congenial group, perhaps somewhat isolated from the main society but held together by strong common interests, wherein he quickly starts to make up for lost time in learning the arts of membership. It is possible that the beneficial consequences of peer group membership can be fully reaped by a person who is never in the mainstream of child or adolescent society but who participates with satisfaction in small peripheral groups. There are doubtless a number of different paths along which social development takes place.

Negative experiences with other people, however, yield consequences

---

[36] *Ibid.*, pp. 69–72.

[37] A penetrating analysis of this problem is to be found in W. H. Whyte, Jr., *The Organization Man* (New York: Simon and Schuster, Inc., 1956).

that may accumulate to the point of becoming a real obstacle to further social growth. If a child's attempts to fraternize are met with indifference or rejection, the most elementary frustration is to the urge toward competence. The attempt has failed; other people have proved to be resistant to influence. Anxiety and shame may also add their negative tone to the feelings of inefficacy. If repeated experience strengthens the lesson the child may come to regard peers as no more responsive to his initiatives than locked doors or unscalable cliffs. Being with others comes to mean being pushed around by the tides of their desires and the shifting winds of their interests with no guarantee of important satisfactions for oneself. Once these conditions have been established, social life becomes a bad bargain, and the child prefers to stay at home or go off by himself, maximizing the satisfactions that can be found in solitary activities wherein things are at least somewhat responsive to his initiatives.

This sequence is usually described as *withdrawal*, and it is looked upon by others with a curious combination of hurt feelings and moral indignation. How can anyone prefer staying alone to being in our delightful company? What right has anyone to bury himself in his own little preoccupations, worse still to indulge in selfish daydreaming, while the rest of us deal so bravely with cold hard reality? The child who shows tendencies to avoid companionship thus evokes in his peers a certain suspicion and resentment that do not improve his chances of feeling comfortable in future social interaction.

But *withdrawal* is a verbal tag that obscures part of what is going on. Short of becoming a true hermit, it is virtually impossible to withdraw from human interactions. Other people are constantly with us, whether we like it or not. Furthermore, in the present climate of opinion, which makes adjustment to peers an important virtue, the adult world is likely to take an active stand against solitude. Anxious parents may hustle a shy child to parties and oblige him to have friends in to play. Teachers may undertake to lure him into group experiences and school counselors may urge him toward more active participation. The child for whom interpersonal action is so uncomfortable, perhaps so anxiously tense, that he usually cannot act effectively even in friendly situations, experiences relief when it is actually possible to withdraw. The heart of his problem lies in the fact that he must frequently interact with others and that when doing so he will be under the influence of a strong urge to escape.

Under these conditions it is unlikely that interactions will yield experiences of competence in dealing with others. If the child's goal is to end the meeting, he will best accomplish it by agreeing, yielding, appeasing, or making excuses to depart. To respond with interest and enthusiasm will tend to prolong the meeting, so it is better to remain uninvolved. Disagreement and assertiveness will raise the tension and will likewise prolong things while the others argue and assert themselves in return. Thus the child will try few roles except a submissive one, will feel little mutuality, and will perceive others mainly as unwelcome intrusions. Strategies of avoidance and extrication may be developed to a point of considerable skill, but none of the learning will contribute to a feeling that participation can be rewarding and consistent with self-esteem. If relations with peers thus constantly force one into evasive and humiliating roles, anger is likely to compound the difficulty of getting along. When the presence of others means tension, discomfort, and feelings of incompetence, it is no pleasure to see people coming. The human environment may come to be experienced as an endless irritating intrusion.

When social experience is unfortunate enough so that events take this course, the person tends to be shy, retiring, homebound, and limited in his interests to things that he can do by himself. He does not develop skill in competition and compromise, does not experience the give-and-take of group membership, and remains a stranger to convivial good fellowship. He may create great roles and audiences in fantasy, but these cannot dispel grave uncertainties about his actual position in the social organism. Developments that involve separation from home and family will come hard. Without the support of age-mates at adolescence, it will be difficult for the person to disengage himself from home life and move toward a wider range of relationships. Unless he has developed talents along other lines that bring about favorable contact with people, his feelings of isolation and insignificance may well increase in the course of time.

Some people combat these feelings by taking a derogatory attitude toward society. They see cliques as snobbish and stupid, the leading crowd as superficial and socially ambitious, adolescent group life as cheap and callow, popular folkways as primitive superstitions, middle-class values as irrational oppressions. None of these things, of course, is above criticism, but criticism is not likely to stay within reasonable bounds if it must provide a social isolate with self-esteem. Arrogant disdain for the commonplace that one has never truly encountered does not open a path either to well-rooted self-enlargement or to valuable social action. This particular form of aloofness cannot easily ward off the underlying feelings of isolation, ineffectiveness, and resentment.

Retrospect: Peer Groups and Socialization

The parent of today is so firmly convinced of the developmental value of interaction with peers that it is hard to realize how differently the problem has been viewed in other times. The parent of yesterday had no such faith in the power of children to socialize each other. In the literature of advice to parents a century ago can be found explicit recommendations to keep children out of each other's company. No good was expected to come from gatherings of peers. Unless strictly supervised by adults or responsible older children, the effect of age-equals on one another was merely to stimulate excitement, mischief, and riotous lack of control. This attitude was by no means a peculiarity of nineteenth-century America. Taking a long historical view, it was probably nearer some kind of norm than is our present emphasis on early social adjustment. In the past, what was most feared was that children would not develop the control of impulse, the habits of application, and the inner organization that would fit them for adult life—virtues most easily assimilated through adult supervision and example. Contemporary parents often give the impression that what they most fear is failure of their children to get along happily and comfortably with other people. They are permissive about control and application, but insist upon social adjustment at all costs and begin social training at the earliest possible moment.

The contemporary attitude is the result of a number of developments in our society. As schools grow larger, as age-grading becomes sharper, as population becomes more dense, and as institutions move increasingly toward the pattern of the large organization, there is perhaps a greater premium than ever before on interacting successfully with large numbers of people. Increased awareness of the destructive consequences of intergroup hostilities has further emphasized the desirability of wider and more enlightened group experience. Simultaneously the crumbling of a number of traditional values has undermined parental confidence in what to stand for as adults and led parents to hope that the missing standards would somehow be found through wider social contact. Finally, a spurious contribution came from popularized knowledge about mental disorders, especially the alleged relation between social withdrawal and schizophrenia. Recent research has overthrown the claim that withdrawal causes schizophrenia; nevertheless, quite a few parents were exposed to the intimidating thought that solitude and fantasy were breeders of mental breakdown.

In this chapter we have seen that interactions with peers can be a source of highly desirable developments. It has also become plain that group experience is far from a cureall for personal or even for social ills. Individuals can become socially competent, flexible, and happily affiliative, but they can also be inhibited into enslaved conformity or constricted isolation. Groups can be constructive and magnanimous but also authoritarian, cruel, rivalrous, and hostile. There is no magic about group experience, just as there is no magic about families. Both can be good and both can be bad for the development of personality.

The current trend to push children quickly and continuously into the company of their peers has certain serious hazards. Social enslavement and social isolation alike are increased by anxiety. Ideally a child should work his way gradually into peer interactions, moving at his own speed, following his own inclination, giving his anxieties a chance to subside. He should have scope, in other words, to develop his own social strategy. If parental anxiety and impatience result in pushing a child into company for which he feels unready, and if further this company is represented as being, like vegetables, good for him, the chances of his performing well and having a happy experience are exceedingly small. The more common outcome will be either an anxious deference that is the first step toward enslavement or an equally anxious inhibition and abasement that makes interaction feel like a bad bargain. Social participation is one of the many aspects of growth that can easily be spoiled by pressure. This is a sphere in which a relaxed parental attitude has much to recommend it.

13 Intimacy, Love, and Sex

At first thought it might seem arbitrary when considering social development to make a special case out of the group of two. Is there anything different in principle between a pair and a trio, a dyadic relation and a triadic one? Often there is not; the dyad is merely the smallest possible human group. Yet we are all aware that under certain circumstances two is company but three is a crowd. This saying is a reminder that interactions can take place between two people, even when they do not involve sexuality or being in love, that cannot take place even in the friendliest trio or larger group. It is often far from a happy event when a mutual friend walks up to the table of a pair dining together at a restaurant and suggests joining them. Each may be an intimate friend of both of the others, but the ensuing conversation will necessarily lack something of intimacy. The dyad may have significance for the growth of personality quite different from that of group memberships.

This point becomes clearer if one notices that among adults there is no necessary connection between skill as a group member and capacity for intimacy. There is nothing incongruous about a housewife who shuns the women's club and parent-teacher association, who feels uncomfortable and tongue-tied at a morning coffee, but whose individual relations with husband, children, and perhaps a close friend or two are experiences of great depth and meaning. The opposite pattern is candidly described by Arthur Koestler, who admitted that in earlier years he was the type of person who "feels sure of himself when addressing a meeting or holding forth at a crowded party, but becomes the more insecure the smaller the audience, and reveals his basic

296

timidity when alone with one other person."[1] It is, of course, not out of the question to be both a lively group member and an intimate friend, but these must be viewed as two very different kinds of developmental achievement.

The Nature of Intimacy

To keep the distinction in mind it is necessary to reserve the word *intimacy* for its original and proper meaning. It is used carelessly in everyday speech. "I know him intimately" may mean only that one sees him often at meetings, is abreast of the external details of his life, or knows a lot of gossip about him. The word is also used euphemistically for an illicit sexual union, without any guarantee that the parties enjoyed intimacy in the proper sense. Thus it could be said colloquially that Benjamin in Charles Webb's *The Graduate* was intimate with Mrs. Robinson, his father's partner's wife, but nothing could be less intimate than the conversations that take place between them in the bedroom.[2] Intimacy means close and confidential friendship. Recurrent in its dictionary definitions are expressions such as "proceeding from within" and "pertaining to the inmost being." The thing that is characteristic of an intimate relation, that is exceedingly unlikely in a trio and impossible in a crowd, is an exchange of thoughts and feelings coming from one's inmost being. The special warmth that often accompanies intimate friendship comes from sharing what is otherwise private.

The Chum Relation

No one has championed the developmental importance of intimacy more strongly than Harry Stack Sullivan, who attributed to it the possiblity of remedying a number of unfortunate legacies from both family and group experience.[3] Not earlier than 8½, and more likely not before 10, a new type of interest emerges, "interest in a *particular* member of the same sex who becomes a chum or a close friend." Novel in this situation is the appearance of "a real sensitivity to what matters to another person." "And this is not," Sullivan continued, "in the sense of 'what should I do to get what I want,' but instead 'what should I do to contribute to the happiness or to support the prestige and feeling of worthwhileness of my chum.' "[4] On the cognitive side this represents, of course, a complete transcendence of the egocentric perspective. The child can now see things, including himself, through the eyes of his friend. But having a chum is clearly more than a cognitive achievement;

[1] A. Koestler, *Arrow in the Blue: An Autobiography* (New York: The Macmillan Company, 1952), p. 81.

[2] C. Webb, *The Graduate* (Philadelphia: J. B. Lippincott Company, 1963).

[3] H. S. Sullivan, *The Interpersonal Theory of Psychiatry* (New York: W. W. Norton & Company, Inc., 1953), Chap. 16.

[4] *Ibid.*, p. 245.

the importance assumed by the other person and the wish to enhance his self-esteem show that love is involved, a love that is free from the unequal and dependent implications of love in the family circle. It is not too much to say that in this type of relation children have their first experiences of something like love in its adult form.

Sullivan perceived these experiences of late childhood or, as he called it, *preadolescence*, as fateful for later intimate relations, not only for close friendships but also for future family relations. But he saw something of even more general importance, which he expressed by saying that intimacy "permits validation of all components of personal worth." He contrasted this sharply with experience in the preceding juvenile era, when habits of competition, cooperation, and compromise can be acquired without a deep understanding either of others or of oneself. Group membership encourages being reserved about a whole range of experiences that are not consistent with keeping up a social front and that might bring down ridicule. In a close relation with a chum these reserved matters can gradually be brought forward and shared, so that not merely one's social front but all of oneself can be compared with another's experience. It can be a great relief to discover that someone else has a similar interior life. One's friend, too, has worried about physical maturation, has felt unattractive, has experienced odd fears and bad dreams, has entertained daydreams of an extravagant sort, and is not in his heart quite the same person that is known to the public. To have another person know everything about you is an enlarging experience, provided the confidences are mutual and are given as expressions of love and trust.

It was Sullivan's view that preadolescent intimacy could be so beneficial that "warped juveniles," as he called them, sometimes "can at this stage literally be put on the right road to a fairly adequate personality development."[5] Among the warps that might be remedied he mentioned protracted egocentrism, attitudes of suspicion, envy, and conceit, and what might be called a derogatory strategy. If group memberships had failed to modify these qualities or if isolation had increased them, there was a chance that close friendships might create a more congenial climate and do a better job. Social isolates might find with chums a way into society that did not overwhelm them with anxiety. Even highly successful group members could learn valuable lessons about using their gifts in ways that would be considerate of the self-esteem of others. There is, of course, no magic about such results. They depend upon favorable experiences with friendship, just as earlier developments depend upon favorable experiences in the family and with groups. But Sullivan, more alert than other workers to the self-corrective possibilities of different periods of development, performed an important service in spelling out the position of intimacy in the growth of personality.

Close friendships do not necessarily come into being all at once at a given point in development. Helene Deutsch has pointed out that a partner may be useful in helping a young person move away from dependence on

---

[5] *Ibid.*, p. 251.

parents even before the relation assumes much emotional intensity. Establishing one's autonomy requires having secrets, and Deutsch describes the manner in which a girl between 10 and 12 makes secrecy less lonely by finding a partner similar in age and interests "with whom she giggles and titters, with whom she locks herself up in her room, to whom she confides her secrets."[6] The sexual facts of life may be part of the secrets, but Deutsch's studies indicate that overt sexual expression and true tender feeling between the partners is exceptional at these ages. The relationship reduces guilt by allowing the pair to share supposedly guilty secrets and obtain support in emancipation from adult control. So important is this service, however, that Deutsch, like Sullivan, considers the lack of special friendships at this point in life to be a serious developmental handicap.

Preadolescent close friendships are likely to be with a member of one's own sex. When interest in the opposite sex begins to increase, exploration of the nonsexual components of personal worth may continue to be of predominant importance. As Erikson describes it, "To a considerable extent adolescent love is an attempt to arrive at a definition of one's identity by projecting one's diffused ego images on one another and by seeing them thus reflected and gradually clarified. That is why many a youth would rather converse, and settle matters of mutual identification, than embrace."[7] It is sometimes reported by the participants that when a relation that has started in this way becomes openly sexual, the original kind of interaction is crowded out. If the tables are turned so far that the couple would rather embrace than converse, they can soon feel, paradoxical as it sounds, a loss of true intimacy.

Empathy and Altruism

The achievement of intimacy represents a psychological development that is far from simple. Writing about sympathy, which is an important aspect of this development, Lenrow points out that "complex relations between affective responses of two persons" must necessarily be considered. "How does it happen," he asks, "that an individual can be aware of the personal interests of a stranger and want to further those interests, even when this alliance offers no apparent rewards to the first individual?"[8] It has been shown by L. B. Murphy that even at nursery school age there can be flashes of sympathy between children, and that this happens most easily when one child suffers a distress that the other has already experienced.[9] A good many years must go by—years of impressive cognitive growth—before such feelings

[6] H. Deutsch, *The Psychology of Women: A Psychoanalytic Interpretation*, Vol. I (New York: Grune & Stratton, Inc., 1944), p. 13.

[7] E. H. Erikson, *Childhood and Society* (New York: W. W. Norton & Company, Inc., 1950), p. 228.

[8] P. B. Lenrow, "Studies of Sympathy," in *Affect, Cognition, and Personality: Empirical Studies*, ed. S. S. Tomkins and C. E. Izard (New York: Springer Publishing Co., Inc., 1965), Chap. 9, p. 264.

[9] L. B. Murphy, *Social Behavior and Child Personality* (New York: Columbia University Press, 1937).

can be supported by a sensitive awareness of another person's innermost interests and the real roots of his self-esteem. Yet it seems likely that the affective transaction is basically similar. One can understand another person's inner life because one has had analogous experiences. Only by having known shame can one understand the effects of a humiliating experience on another person; only through previous joy can one resonate to another's joy. This process of *empathy* is basic to relations between chums and intimate friends. Wanting one's friend to be happy is derived from wanting to be happy oneself. If this implies that altruism is simply transformed egotism, the emphasis should rest on the fact that it is transformed. The happiness of the other person becomes a true goal.

A considerable amount of experimental work has lately been attempted on altruistic behavior in children. These studies, being oriented to external behavior in somewhat artificial situations, cannot shed much direct light on the affective aspects of intimacy. What they show most clearly is that children "learn some norm which dictates their aiding others, and that allegiance to this norm increases with age, at least until 9 or 10 years."[10] This lends itself to the interpretation that laboratory self-sacrifice, for instance, sharing one's winnings with another child or donating them to a good cause, is merely a question of pleasing the adults who run the experiment. But this explanation, doubtless true up to a point, does not cover all the facts. When the experimenter's expectations are built into the design so that the child is in some instances made clearly aware of them, the tendency to share or to donate proves to be imperfectly related to these expectations, as if something more were involved. Furthermore, the studies contain strong hints that altruistic behavior is more likely to occur in children from families that favor the expression of affect, including sympathy, and that provide models of helping behavior; less likely in children whose families stress competition and status. Such findings suggest that readiness to experience one's own feelings, openness to one's own inner states, has something to do with responding to another person's feelings and taking supportive action. Lenrow's experiments with young adult subjects provide further evidence in favor of such a view.[11]

Most children in late childhood and early adolescence have a considerable number of acquaintances. The emergence of a close friendship is therefore a selective process, and in order to prosper it must be selective on both sides. Discovery of similarities of experience has a good deal to do with eliciting empathy and turning the friendship into an intimate one. This of itself may dictate the choice of a friend of the same sex, and many of the favorable developmental consequences of intimacy require this much similarity in life experience.

It is obviously possible for the urge toward intimacy to lead to frustra-

[10] J. H. Bryan and P. London, "Altruistic Behavior by Children," *Psychological Bulletin*, **73** (1970), 200–211. See also H. Kaufman, *Aggression and Altruism* (New York: Holt, Rinehart and Winston, Inc., 1970); and J. R. Macaulay and J. Berkowitz, eds., *Altruism and Helping Behavior* (New York: Academic Press, Inc., 1970).

[11] P. B. Lenrow, "Studies of Sympathy."

tion, rejection, and even exploitation by the other party. Overtures from one side may not be answered by real interest or understanding. A need for intimacy in one partner may arouse only a need for erotic experience in the other. The tendrils of friendship are easily frostbitten, and rebuffs are likely to increase wariness, reserve, and protective privacy. Just as there is no developmental magic about the family circle or about peer group memberships, so there is no magic about intimate relations. To do good they have to be good.

Patterns of Intimacy: Some Examples

Because the developmental possibilities and vicissitudes of intimate friendships have thus far cut a small figure in the systematic study of personality, it is desirable to become familiar with a number of examples.

The Diary of Anne Frank

A remarkable self-portrait of psychological growth is contained in the diary that Anne Frank kept from her thirteenth birthday until shortly after her fifteenth.[12] The diary was begun in June, 1942, just before Anne's father and his partner, Jewish businessmen in Amsterdam, decided to try to ride out the Nazi occupation by taking their families into hiding. At the back of the tall, narrow city house where the business was conducted were some tiny upstairs rooms so placed that their occupancy might escape detection. Into this hideout the families disappeared; the Dutch employees continued to operate the business in the front of the house and also smuggled in the necessary supplies. The quarters occupied by the eight refugees were cramped to a degree that has to be seen to be believed—the house is now preserved as a museum —and the tenants could never set foot outside. They lived there undetected for more than two years, but in August, 1944, they were discovered by the Nazi police and taken to concentration camps where most of them, including Anne, were killed. It is difficult for any reader to detach his mind sufficiently from the hideous political circumstances to view the diary as an account of a young girl's growth. Yet Anne started to write before she knew about the plan for hiding. Obviously she could not foresee that her very personal pages would one day be picked up from the floor of a ransacked hiding place to be published in many languages, made into plays and films, and taken as an astonishing testament of human worth and wisdom.

Anne started the diary because she was lonely. This, in spite of the fact that she had a great many friends, both girls and boys, and was the very opposite of a social isolate. But something was lacking in all the sociability, with its fun and joking: she could not get close to anyone in order to confide

---

[12] A. Frank, *The Diary of a Young Girl,* trans. B. M. Mooyaart-Doubleday (Garden City, N.Y.: Doubleday & Company, Inc., 1952). See also E. Schnabel, *Anne Frank: A Portrait in Courage,* trans. R. and C. Winston (New York: Harcourt Brace Jovanovich, Inc., 1958).

"all kinds of things that lie buried deep in my heart." The diary was to be the needed close friend until a real one could be found. She named it Kitty and made the entries in the form of letters addressed to "Dear Kitty." "I hope," she wrote, "I shall be able to confide in you completely, as I have never been able to do in anyone before, and I hope that you will be a great support and comfort to me."[13] It is possible that Kitty, even though imaginary, did provide some sense of support and comfort during the twenty-five months of hiding. At all events she received an extraordinary series of confidences.

The need for a companion must have increased sharply once the door closed upon the occupants of the secret quarters. Anne had already made an active life for herself outside the family. Suddenly she found herself the youngest member of a closed circle consisting of the four parents, a dentist friend, her own sister (16), Peter (15), son of the other couple, and herself, just turned 13. She was a lively child, clever and sometimes pert, and she soon discovered that it was now her lot to be jumped on and criticized practically without respite. It is easy to imagine the tension prevailing amongst the eight people, crowded together, depending for their lives on not being discovered; the youngest member, least restrained and least careful about the security measures, was an easy scapegoat. What kept things from becoming completely intolerable for Anne was the program of study and reading arranged by her father, who himself set an example of scholarly effort. Trapped physically in the company and importunities of the others, Anne found in her books a wider world and a series of absorbing interests stretching forward into the postwar future. The focus of her self-respect shifted from the vivacious, assertive Anne, now constantly battered, to a thoughtful, serious, idealistic Anne about whom she wrote at length to Kitty. But this deeper Anne remained insecure with nothing more personal to validate her than the pages of her notebook.

After more than a year in hiding Anne had her first menstrual period, which she welcomed as a sign that she was an adult like the others. One night she dreamed that a boy she had once known was laying his cheek against hers; for days afterward she kept recapturing as a beautiful memory the unique feeling of warmth. After a year and a half Peter, now 17, suddenly became an object of interest to her, and she sought his company in the tiny garret where he studied. It is clear that emerging sexual feeling played an essential part in drawing her to Peter, but the erotic element was virtually lost in the greater hunger for intimacy. Thus the first kiss was important to Anne as a sign that Peter could give something of himself. Anne had to take the lead in getting Peter to talk, but she was greatly elated when they could exchange comments about their parents, their problems, and each other. After a season of being in love, however, she decided that Peter was really not satisfactory as a confidant. Passive, intellectually sluggish, easily discouraged about future prospects, he proved resistant to Anne's eagerness to help, limited in his ability to exchange deep confidences. Important aspects

[13] *Ibid.*, p. 9.

of Anne's worth remained unvalidated in this friendship, yet something favorable had happened. Her feelings of loneliness were not again as acute, and a new note of self-reliance occasionally sounded in the later pages of the diary. Through Peter she came more quickly to perceive her gaiety as superficial "defensive armor" and to discover her "inward happiness," her "boundless desire for all that is beautiful and good." Under the circumstances this must be counted as remarkable progress. Anne's day-by-day comments on the course of the relation provide extraordinary insight into the nature of the need for intimacy.

The Complementary Element: Ben and Jamie

Intimacy requires a large amount of mutual appreciation, but this does not imply that the partners must be just alike. Friendships at all ages can have part of their strength in a complementary relation. Each member can supply the other with something he lacks, at the same time serving as a model from whom the desirable quality can be copied. Thus there may be a relation of leader and follower between a pair of chums, the leader gaining an ally and the follower being bestirred by his friend's initiative; in the meantime the follower learns something about leadership and the leader about followership. The complementary relation is more obvious in boy-girl friendships, but it can play a prominent part in same-sex pairs, as the following example shows.

A subject who will be called Ben took part in a personality study during his adult years and recalled in great detail his relation with his chum Jamie, which started when both boys were 15 and continued through college. Ben was brought up in an urban, achievement-oriented segment of society, and he had every reason at 15 to consider himself a success. As models he had used his two older brothers, almost consciously drawing upon their very different qualities to make a combination of his own. Among his peers he had become a recognized leader, exhibiting high competence and being respected as one who "could always make things happen." His sexual attainments—he had had intercourse with a number of girls by the time he was 15—added greatly to the image of competence. But these exploits left him with a feeling of incompleteness. He never fell in love with any of the girls, "not even for a moment"; the physical pleasure was agreeable, but he did not sense in these companions any possibility of deeper exchange. An urge for intimacy was at work, however, and when he met Jamie he was able to recognize the dawning of a new kind of relation.

Ben attributed the start of this intimacy to its complementary quality. "He had something I didn't have, so there was something new. . . . And I had something he didn't have, so that together we became something larger than we were prior to the chum relationship." Ben, whose school experience had been so unstimulating that he never read a book beyond those assigned, discovered in Jamie a lively spirit of intellectual inquiry and an exciting knowledge of politics and history. Here was a whole world to which his friend opened the door and provided guidance. Jamie discovered in Ben a world previously closed to him, that of confident interaction with other people. Each admired the other, each copied the other, each used the other for practice. In Ben's words: "You see how I was almost consciously expanding my image of myself to include attributes which he already had, so that I felt extended, both of us felt extended by the intimacy."

To this extent, we can understand the friendship between the two boys as a way by which each sought additional areas of competence. There quickly developed, however, something nearer to the heart of intimacy, a feeling of openness and of total security in each other's company. "There is complete ease in the exchanges between the people in the chum relationship. There are no real hassles; there is no static," Ben said. He further described the situation as one of "a wonderful physical security, that when confronted by this other human being the exchange will be efficient, you will know what it's all about. You won't get caught thinking, 'we're on different channels, he doesn't get it, I don't get it, we just don't get it,' with all the unrest and sweat that that produces between people." If Ben and Jamie had merely used each other for acquiring new realms of competence their relation might have been full of envy, competition, and static; such pairs certainly exist. But the satisfaction of being understood and of cherishing each other's purposes subdued these elements, giving the relation a warmth that became for Ben an enduring ideal. It was through this close and mutual relation, Ben believed, that he had learned to understand women. Though the first person he admitted to the secrets of his heart was his male chum, what he learned through this sharing helped him to become increasingly open, observant, and appreciative with his female partners.[14]

Failure of Attempted Intimacy: The Case of Laura

Something that might be called an intimacy famine was described by Laura, who took part in a personality study during her middle twenties. Up to the fourth grade she had had a sort of chum, but from then until shortly before the time of the study she had been without a close friend. This lack of intimacy did not result from an absence of desire. Laura saw herself as having constantly searched for close relations and as being constantly rebuffed. She said:

> I was hurt in grammar school, high school and college and no matter how many times I was hurt I'd still feel some faith in people. I love doing things for people. I love to let them know that I care. I still do, but now I wait: I'm not as quick to jump into it. It's taken me a long time to learn that people really just don't care and that people are basically selfish, that they themselves are the first thing in their lives.

[14] The combination of love and completion of the self in the chum relation is remarkably portrayed by Thomas Mann in the story "Tonio Kröger" (1903), *Stories of Three Decades*, trans. H. T. Lowe-Porter (New York: Alfred A. Knopf, Inc., 1936).

I was always the one person who would listen. If anyone ever wanted anything they knew that they could just come to me. If boys in high school wanted to meet girls, wanted to have a house to come to, wanted a good time, a party, they would always come to me. This was true in college as well. A friend of mine, Helen, got pregnant and borrowed money from me. I gladly gave it to her. But yet, nights when I'd be depressed, it's not easy for me to bother someone and say, "Would you listen to me?" But on the same night Helen would come and expect me, not even ask if I was busy, to want to listen to her. I don't know why people single me out to listen, but every once in a while you get so frustrated and so hurt because you know that they don't really care about you. People just don't give a damn. It's not hard to say, "Laura, would you like to talk to me?" And yet it doesn't get said.

Laura, like Ben, soon learned to take pleasure in sexual relations, but this did not open any channels to intimacy. Her male partners were as backward as her female acquaintances when it came to inviting her to talk. Reading her description, one suspects that Laura contributed somewhat to the lack of interaction by her hesitancy in asking to be heard and her abasive eagerness to please. She was a "soft touch" who in a way invited exploitation. But it is easy to understand the hurt feelings of a sympathetic listener to whom nobody will listen. Few will have escaped the experience of having friendly impulses and incipient affection met by chilling responses, from indifference and self-preoccupation through thoughtless exploitation to cruel contempt. Intimacy can exist only under certain conditions, only when there is a certain readiness on both sides. There is no guarantee that its benefits will be available to everyone. Ben and Jamie might never have met, and we cannot take it as certain that each would have found someone else who would have served equally well. Laura was fortunate enough to find intimacy at 25 with a young woman of her age. As can easily be imagined, it took her a long time to feel real trust in this friend, but eventually the relation flourished. The two traveled together, shared an apartment, and became able to exchange their inmost thoughts. At last Laura found someone who listened; her friend, she said, "knows everything that I know about myself." Able now to express the whole range of her feelings, she realized how much they had been choked off during the intimacy famine. She had trained herself to a cynical expectation that none of her feelings would be of interest to anyone else, and she had consequently ceased to explore them.

Friendship

One of the difficulties that besets understanding of the realms of personal growth considered in this chapter is the lack of an accepted precise vocabulary. Just what is designated by the words *intimacy, friendship, love*? Since Freud we also have to ask just what is designated by *sex*, which assumed in his writings a meaning extraordinarily broad. In daily usage these terms are likely to be tossed around with a blithe disregard for exact meaning. Some people say that they have lots of acquaintances but no friends. Others seem to be trying to say the same thing when they put it that they have lots of friends but no one to whom they can really talk. The varying uses of *intimacy* have already been mentioned, and the varying uses of *love* are perhaps too obvious for comment. The trouble, however, is not just one of careless, un-standardized usage of words. The phenomena themselves flow so freely to-gether that strict definition is impossible. Anne and Peter had a friendship which involved sexual interest, intimacy, love; all the words are appropriate and all the phenomena were to some extent present. Even if one thought up a vocabulary of ugly technical terms it would be difficult to apply it with precision.

Thus far in this chapter we have used *intimacy* to signify a phenom-enon that is of special importance for growth during late childhood and adolescence. The pure case, so to speak, is two young persons of the same age, same sex, and similar background of experience who find in one another the possibility of exchanging deeply personal communications and who cher-ish each other's self-esteem. It is the sharing and the cherishing that are cen-tral. In other respects there can be various degrees of departure from the pure case. Intimate exchange between boy and girl and between man and woman is obviously possible. Differences of age may not create insuperable obstacles, especially during adult years. Varied backgrounds may contribute to a mutual expansion of outlook. In general, however, and especially during the first explorations in late childhood and early adolescence, intimacy is made easier by similarity and is made harder by differences of experience.

The use of *intimacy* in this restricted sense makes it necessary to have another word for those numerous dyadic relations in which the sharing of deeply personal experiences is not of central importance. These will here be put under the broad heading of *friendship*. Calling intimacy a deep relation makes it seem logical to consider these other dyads superficial, but they can be of major significance to the people involved. It is not uncommon for a pair of boys or a pair of girls to do everything and go everywhere together, to be inseparable, but never to exchange a single syllable about their inmost secrets. One might say figuratively that they stand side by side looking out at the world but never look at or into each other. Friendship in such instances does not involve intimacy, but it may be characterized by firm loyalty, strong mutual support, and a certain shared validation of external experience. By providing dependable companionship it deals partially with the problem of loneliness. The two boys who went fishing together in their school days may be found still together on their annual fishing vacation half a century later. They never talk about their troubles, their wives, or any topics about which they disagree, yet they find plenty to talk about and have a splendid time. The two girls who were companions at school may spend their later years sharing a house, never discussing the troubles they had with their late hus-bands or with the rearing of their children, simply being company for one another in their current lives. Superficial in one sense, these friendships may have a strong hold on the two people involved and may even be a cornerstone of their existence. The death of one partner may leave a grievous hole in the other's life.

Friendships often involve complementary patterns, in which case it is not necessary that the friends be of equal age. One such pattern might be called that of stimulator and responder. One of the pair may supply the initiative, the excitement, or the intellectual stimulation, while the other, glad to be aroused, may serve as a steadying influence who brings things back to earth. Nurturance and dependence can form the basis of a friendship that can be deeply satisfying both to the partner who wants to provide care and to the partner who wants to receive it. There are even competitive pairs who seem to be constantly squabbling but who are actually trying out their ideas on each other and providing the boon of blunt criticism; they never come to blows, and each would defend to the death the right of the other to be so stupid. Friendships, it might be said, come in all sizes and shapes, and not much would be gained by trying for an exhaustive list or classification of the possible patterns.

As stated at the beginning of this chapter, dyadic relations serve purposes that cannot be served by triads or larger groups. Intimacy is the most striking possibility, but the other forms of friendship play important parts in the pattern of life. In a study of individual lives, there is a risk that this pattern will be incomplete and perhaps not fully intelligible if information has not been obtained on the dyads of which the subject was a member.

Friendship and Latent Sexuality

Intimacies and friendships in which there is no overt sexual expression are sometimes interpreted as manifestations of latent, possibly repressed, sexual attraction. This way of looking at it owes much to Freud, who sometimes succeeded in unearthing buried sexual fantasies where they were least suspected in a patient's relation to a close friend, or even to the doctor himself. Could it be that all human attachments are sexual in character, that an erotic element is always present even in relations that are not particularly deep? Freud's ear for erotic undertones was keen, and having observed their unexpectedly wide presence in the free associations and newly remembered fantasies of his patients, he went on to answer this question in the affirmative. He advanced the hypothesis that human behavior is mainly motivated by two instinctual drives, the erotic and the destructive, called by him the life instincts and the death instincts, Eros and Thanatos. It is important to notice that once these massive generalizations had been made, all human relations that were not destructive were automatically classed as erotic. In his zeal for a comprehensive theory Freud gave to "erotic" a meaning so broad as to include virtually every kind of positive response that one person can make to another. Friendship without overt sexuality was therefore *by definition* a manifestation of latent sexuality.

Most people cannot comfortably follow Freud in this generalization.

Scholars of Freud's work have shown that he himself slid back and forth between the poetic conception of Eros and the everyday meaning of sexuality. In the everyday meaning, a sexual element in friendship would imply some degree of physical attraction to the friend, some feeling that the friend was beautiful and nice to touch, and it might be imagined that this attraction was merely the civilized outcropping of an unconscious wish to climb into bed with the friend. It is certainly true that intimacy and friendship can co-exist with overt sexual interest, and that sexual attraction, as we saw in the case of Anne Frank and Peter, can help open the way for personal closeness. It is also true that sexual interest can be kept controlled, even kept out of awareness, when overt expression would lead to trouble, as when the two friends are of the same sex or when one partner believes that the other does not share the feeling. These are all possibilities; they all occur. The question therefore reduces itself to whether or not sexuality is an *indispensable* aspect of *all* dyadic relations, justifying us in assuming its latent presence when there are no overt manifestations.

Two of the illustrations given in the preceding section are important in this connection. For both Ben and Laura, sexual interest flowed fairly freely to a succession of partners, but these relations opened no doors to enduring friendship or to the benefits of intimacy. Correspondingly in Ben's description of his chum and in Laura's description of her late-discovered intimate friend, no physical attraction is indicated. If it were present it must have been of trifling importance compared to the satisfactions of mutual understanding, exchange of innermost experiences, and respect for one another's self-esteem. Ben and Laura, in other words, seem to say that sexual interest and friendship can be run as wholly separate enterprises, and that the values received from intimacy are sufficient to explain it without postulating a secret sexual fantasy. It would seem arbitrary, furthermore, to insist upon an erotic tie between the two men taking their fiftieth annual fishing vacation together, when enjoying a shared hobby explains the relation so adequately. Friendship and intimacy both contain intrinsic values that do not require a boost from the sex drive.

It may seem that this question is not worth laboring, but the way it is answered has a marked influence on the climate of development. The popularization of Freud's views in the 1920s and 1930s created an atmosphere of disapproval for close and intimate friendships. Group relations were seen as all right, being public and relatively impersonal, but pairing, especially in early adolescence, was interpreted either as a dangerous homosexual attachment or as a dangerously premature heterosexual adventure. We should allow that this was not exactly what Freud meant, but it was what people thought he meant. The effect of pressure by anxious parents and others, we can now see, was to superficialize human relations, discourage awareness of inner personal experience, block the mutual exploration of such experience, and bring young people to the threshold of marriage with a minimum of previous practice in intimacy. This pressure has somewhat abated as attitudes toward sex became more relaxed, and in any event the rewards of friendship were often clear enough to the participants to enable them to resist adult clamor for group-mindedness. But the lives of young people especially in their early teens were not made easier by the thought that every friendship is sexual and that every chumship may mean that you are "queer."

Sexual Behavior after Puberty

The appearance of menstruation in girls and the capacity for ejaculation in boys opens a new chapter in development. According to the biological schedule it is now time to start giving attention to the reproduction of the species. Girls and boys, to be sure, are unlikely to think about what is happening in such long-range terms, but they are in some sense aware that an important event has occurred that has vital implications for them in the years ahead. Young people may accept the ripening of these biological capacities with joy, as a sign of admission to adulthood. But they may also have misgivings. Any forward step awakens a certain anxiety and regret at the loss of established securities. Furthermore, sexual knowledge may be so inadequate and the surrounding atmosphere so disapproving that the adolescent may look upon the new bodily manifestations as injurious, unhealthful, shameful, and even rather disgusting. Comfortable acceptance is not helped by the close anatomical connection of sexual with excretory functions. But even when the climate is wholly favorable, when parents and peers have encouraged a welcoming attitude toward the signs of sexual maturation, it does not follow that the next months and years will be free from problems. Puberty brings important affective changes, including a much more forceful desire for sexual pleasure and a frequently puzzling change of feeling toward other people. It takes time to find out what to do with it all.

The first effort in this direction is likely to take the form of masturbation. The cultural attitude toward this solution varies greatly at different social class levels and in different historical periods. Historical change at an enlightened level can be traced in successive editions of a bulletin of the United States Children's Bureau called *Infant Care*.[15] In 1914 the bulletin informed parents that childhood masturbation was a highly injurious practice that "easily grows beyond control" and is capable of wrecking a child for life. By 1951 parents were being reassured that the practice was ordinarily harmless and told to pay no attention to it. A similar change of attitude has occurred with respect to adolescent masturbation. Earlier, it was widely believed to produce nervousness, genital injury, sterility, a weakening of physical stamina, mental retardation, and especially insanity. Keeping a sound mind in a sound body was felt to imply total abstinence from genital self-stimulation. The great majority of young people who absorbed this severe standard soon discovered themselves to be deficient in will power. They had to

[15] M. Wolfenstein, "Trends in Infant Care," *American Journal of Orthopsychiatry*, **23** (1953), 120–130.

struggle both with feelings of shameful inferiority and with anxiety about the supposedly direful consequences. When more open inquiry began to reveal that adolescent masturbation was well-nigh universal, whereas insanity remained relatively rare, the idea of direful consequences lost its force. Parents enlightened on this point began to pay no attention to masturbation, and some even thought it their duty to express explicit approval so that the child would attach no shame or anxiety to sexuality. The culture, however, is far from uniform, and negative feelings about masturbation are still undoubtedly widespread and deep. In any event, one may feel some sense of shortcoming about this method of satisfying the sexual need. Anatomy and the culture alike speak for sexuality as a shared activity. Self-stimulation and even mutual masturbation clearly do not qualify as the ultimate solution.

A Study of High School Boys

The course of events for boys immediately after puberty is disclosed in a study of normal adolescents by Daniel Offer.[16] The subjects were found in two suburban high schools drawing students from middle-class and working-class backgrounds, with weaker representation of the lower class. The sample was selected in such a manner as to emphasize normality in general adjustment, excluding boys with marked difficulties along with those who got along uncommonly well. The picture drawn thus has moderately wide but by no means universal applicability. The tests and interviews show how average boys in reasonably favorable circumstances negotiate the passage through the high school years. Practically all of the boys (94 percent) had reached puberty by the end of the freshman year, but only a little more than half (55 percent) had gone out with girls. By the end of the junior year 77 percent of the boys were dating, yet somewhat irregularly and as if their meetings with girls were not of major importance; the 23 percent who did not date expressed no particular concern about their indifference. Up to this point, according to the subjects, "if anyone felt that teen-agers should date, it was the parents and especially the mothers." The boys typically talked over their dating experiences with other boys. Proving oneself to be socially competent and learning to become more competent seemed more important than any deep interest in the girls. By the senior year, however, there was a marked change.

> We noticed a striking difference in our subjects when we interviewed them toward the end of their senior year. By then 95 per cent were dating, and girls had begun to occupy a much more prominent place in their lives. The change was dramatic. It was not limited to the fact that most of the teen-agers were dating. More significantly, almost all our subjects looked forward to their dates and enjoyed their relationships with the girls. At this point the few teen-agers who did not date stated openly that they wanted to date but lacked the courage. . . .

[16] D. Offer, *The Psychological World of the Teenager* (New York: Basic Books, Inc., 1969), Chap. 6.

As their anxiety diminishes in their relationships with girls, they begin to enjoy the encounter more, and eventually can look forward to a date simply because they like the girl and want to share their experiences with her and her alone.[17]

This description shows how far one can go astray by thinking of dating simply as a manifestation of the sex drive. By some standards, especially those of the urban slum, these boys were being pretty slow; they acted as if they did not know what it was all about. Why should not the sex drive go straight to its fulfillment the moment puberty is reached? Evidently this was not the way the problem presented itself to this sample of high school boys. The shared enjoyment of sex, being a social experience, requires first that they develop a certain level of competence in social interaction: a knowledge of how to ask a girl out, how to treat her, where to take her, how to take part in conversation, how to establish some degree of friendship while perhaps experimenting with only the milder forms of sexual arousal. It is not correct to infer that the boys had cruder sexual satisfactions with other girls about whom they did not care. In the survey at the end of the junior year only 10 percent of the boys reported that they had had sexual intercourse, and only half this number reported visiting prostitutes. Whatever inaccuracies may have entered the reporting process, it seems safe to conclude that the typical expectation was to find sex with girls of one's daily acquaintance, which would require the development of a certain social sophistication.

In addition to this aspect of the problem the boys gave evidence of another reason for not proceeding too swiftly. Questioned about their views on premarital intercourse, 80 percent gave it their approval with the proviso that it be after high school. Repeatedly the interviewers heard expressions such as these: "In high school we're not mature enough to handle it; we just are not ready for it; adults know what they are doing, teen-agers don't." It was as if, as the author put it, "too much sexual closeness was frightening." The boys were uneasy not only about their social competence but also about the consequences of surrender to feelings so compelling, so possibly disturbing, as those they believed might possess them during the sex act. In construing sexuality in this way they differed from disadvantaged slum boys, whose construction tends to take the simpler form that sexual intercourse is simply a demonstration of physical prowess, a pleasurable proof of manhood. Presumably the subjects in Offer's study were influenced also by doubts about their skill and potency in carrying out the sexual act, but the deliberate pace that most of them set for themselves gives testimony to their awareness of the social and emotional complications by which human sex is surrounded. They were at least partially aware that sex can "have to do with all that we are," and "the growth of all that we are is not something that can be rushed."[18]

---

[17] *Ibid.*, pp. 80–82.

[18] D. W. Baruch and H. Miller, *Sex in Marriage* (New York: Hart Publishing Co., Inc., 1962).

Object Choice

Another possible reason for the deliberate pace set by the boys in Offer's study is that they were still working on object choice. They were still finding out, not as a matter of knowledge but as a matter of feeling, that girls were the appropriate objects of their sexual inclinations. This statement would have been thought mad in 1900, when the general assumption was that the sex instinct included built-in object choice, as appeared to be the case with animals. Naturally boys got interested in girls and girls in boys; how could it be otherwise? Sometimes, of course, it was otherwise, but lack of interest could easily pass for prudence and self-control, and homosexuality, being rather rare, could be attributed to a mysterious biological abnormality. Heterosexual object choice happens for most people so smoothly as to appear automatic, so that even today a certain skepticism is aroused by the idea that it is not instinctively determined. And it is indeed possible that this choice is favored by something innate; we do not know that such is *not* the case. What we do know, however, is that in human beings learning plays a tremendous part in development, and there can be little doubt that it has a voice in sexual object choice. At first it was their parents, said the high school boys, who thought they ought to have dates. Possibly this coaching should not be regarded as superfluous. All adolescents, when one stops to think of it, are exposed to a heavy program of cultural propaganda in favor of the heterosexual choice. Even when this takes the overt form of warnings against sexual involvement it conveys the covert message that involvement is what one really wants. The convention of the chaperone defined for generations of young people how helplessly they would be gripped by passion if no chaperone were present. Perhaps an innate biological choice is taking its inevitable course, but the culture seems more than eager to help it along.

The problem of object choice appears in its true complexity if we do not limit consideration to the gross fact of heterosexual preference. In spite of the standard models of female beauty and male handsomeness with which viewers of the moving picture and television screens and scanners of the advertising pages are deluged, everyone develops his own version of what is most attractive. Girls may prefer boys who look rugged and strong, but they may favor those who appear relaxed and good-humored, those who are quick and competent, or those who are intriguingly mysterious, and some may secretly prefer boys who are small and sensitive and look as if they needed feminine care. Boys may have similar sets of personal specifications for the truly attractive girl, and they may harbor a virtually exclusive preference with respect to physical characteristics, being strongly drawn, for instance, only to blondes or only to brunettes or only to redheads. But beyond all this is the phenomenon of instant object choice commonly known as love at first sight. The object is seen as beautiful and attractive beyond all others. Such choices are highly individualized. A girl may be smitten by a certain boy when none of her girl friends think he is worth a second look. It is hard to attribute such highly personal preferences to an instinctive mechanism of object choice.

A beautiful description of a boy's first falling in love is given in the story "Tonio Kröger" by Thomas Mann.[19] At 16, Tonio discovers himself to be in love with Inge. She is a neighbor whom he has seen a thousand times, but on a certain evening he suddenly sees her differently. It is not that they are together; he sees her talking to a friend at a little distance, observes her gestures, and hears the warm sound of her voice. This is sufficient to set his heart throbbing with ecstasy, and the images stay with him for hours, sending shivers through him and preventing him from going to sleep. Tonio realizes that this is love and that it can bring pain and destroy peace, but he welcomes it and gives himself up to it, wanting above all things to be "vital and rich" and somehow sensing that love will make him so. Mann made this all happen in a single evening, as the result of a new look at a familiar girl, and this is not necessarily literary license. Many people can testify, even if they are strangers to dramatic forms of love at first sight, that finding another person attractive can be almost instantaneous and can depend on cues and images as fleeting as those that so profoundly smote Tonio.

Sexual object choice after puberty is neither wholly new nor wholly old. Each person already has a history of object choices entailing considerable feeling. Mother and father and brothers and sisters are usually the primary objects, and friends become increasingly important in later childhood. Although the attachments and the feelings of love that go with them are not of precisely the same quality as those that follow puberty, they are nevertheless real and often strong, and they may lay down a sharply defined set of object preferences. The high school adolescent looking around for partners of the opposite sex already has a past that affects his conceptions of personal attractiveness. But this past learning is not entirely a blessing. As the adolescent's feelings become more unmistakably sexual, they are increasingly complicated by the taboos against incest and homosexuality. The object choices that have been made most obvious by past experience turn out to be culturally forbidden as well as, in the long run, not very practical. The appropriate partner, who must be of opposite sex, of equal age, and outside the family, must be novel in some respect.

This aspect of sexual development came to light through Freud's delvings in the childhood histories and fantasies of his patients. He made the assumption that libidinal energy is first invested mainly in family members and that after puberty it must be withdrawn from these now prohibited objects and reinvested in appropriate ones. To use the theory in a sophisticated way, one must recognize the distinctions Freud made between pregenital and genital sexuality. The imagery of just the same libido being withdrawn from some objects and applied to new objects oversimplifies the process; genital sexuality is different enough so that pregenital choices are not mechanically repeated.[20] But it is clear that appropriate object choice after

[19] In Mann, *Stories of Three Decades*.

[20] G. S. Klein, "Freud's Two Theories of Sexuality," in *Clinical-Cognitive Psychology: Models and Integrations*, ed. L. Breger (Englewood Cliffs, N.J.: Prentice-Hall, Inc., 1971).

puberty represents a reworking of already existing preferences. The hampering effect of the earlier object choices was often evident in Freud's neurotic subjects. Men who had married replicas of their mothers, or women who had sought happiness with mates just like their fathers, often became entangled in the incest taboo and had sexual difficulties, besides finding the new dependent relation inimical to their own maturing. On the other hand, those who fled to an object utterly unlike the parent to whom they were still attached sometimes found that this kind of forced choice resulted in personal incompatibility in every way except sex. That the pregenital choices were likely enough to include objects of the same sex could also be a cause of difficulty. Here, too, a reworking of earlier preferences might be necessary to fit the norm of adult sexual interest and behavior.[21]

From this account it is plain that sexual object choice regularly involves a certain amount of relearning. It is somewhat unlikely that the appropriate choice after puberty corresponds to childhood preference. There is something new to be learned, something old to be given up. Failure to give up the old has been handled in psychoanalytic theory by the concept of *fixation*. In the present connection this word signifies that an early choice has gained preemptive strength, so that it is not relinquished in favor of the choices now considered appropriate. When this concept is treated in systemic terms it is necessary to consider not just the power of a fixation but also the person's freedom and initiative with respect to alternate forms of behavior. It may not be so much the attraction of the old that holds up growth as it is anxiety about the new. Homosexual interest, fantasy, and mutual experimentation are so common in early adolescence that from this alone one might anticipate a widespread fixation; yet the great majority, sensing both social expectations and the superior future possibilities of heterosexual choice, readily make the transition with no more than an occasional flicker of the abandoned interest. But if as a child a person has learned to associate heterosexual relations very strongly with danger, disease, and vicious impulses, it may be difficult to advance out of the seeming innocence and safety of homosexuality. Similarly one might anticipate a substantial tendency to select mates who resemble parents, yet there is much that serves to modify this choice. The wish to reinstate a dependent relation is strongly opposed in adolescence by a desire to achieve independent adulthood and make one's life one's own; this tends to heighten the attractiveness of partners who represent an improvement upon the parents. But young people who feel great anxiety about independence may find it hard to experience sexual interest toward any but parent surrogates. In sexual object choice, in short, there are inducements to progress as well as inducements to repeat, and repetition is favored both by strong gratification in the old and strong anxiety about the new.

---

[21] A detailed exposition, including clinical and literary examples, of the psychoanalytic view of these aspects of development is contained in P. Blos, *On Adolescence: A Psychoanalytic Interpretation* (New York: The Free Press, 1962), esp. Chap. 3.

The Sexual Revolution

That 80 percent of the high school boys studied by Offer gave their approval to eventual premarital intercourse might be considered a significant sign of what has been widely described as the sexual revolution of our time. The change in attitudes toward sex appears most revolutionary if it is set against the publicly proclaimed standards of upper-class and middle-class society three and four generations ago. According to this standard, sexual intercourse outside of marriage was viewed with great disapproval. However, the standard applied strictly to women, for whom a lapse meant permanent disgrace, but not to men, provided their sex outside of marriage was with women of lower status. It will be noticed that this leeway for men presumed the existence of an exploitable lower class having a different outlook on sex. The standard of chastity among "respectable" people may, of course, have had occasional secret violations even when, in the late nineteenth century, it was being most firmly proclaimed. The tremendous impact of the Kinsey reports in 1948 and 1953, based on informants most of whom were born between 1900 and 1930, lay in the revelation that although the old code still had considerable verbal acceptance it was by now being widely disregarded in practice. Premarital intercourse, for instance, was reported by the great majority of men and by more than half of the women interviewed.[22] This led one observer, writing in 1960, to say that the sexual revolution, especially for women, came largely in the 1920s, after which the frequency of premarital intercourse did not greatly change. According to Ira Reiss:

> It was in the iconoclastic environment of the 1920's that the permissive standards took root. The generation of people born between 1900 and 1910 revolutionized our sexual customs. The generations born since that time have somewhat continued these changes, but for the most part they have only consolidated the inroads that this older generation perpetrated. Those born in the 1900–1909 decade vastly increased our former sexual rates in almost all areas when they came to maturity in the 1920's—the decade of the sexual revolution. . . . Women could now choose to accept premarital sexual behavior not as prostitutes or pleasure-seekers but as lovers.[23]

Predicting what would come next, Reiss pictured a further consolidation of the changes that occurred so rapidly in the 1920s. He expected a clarification of sexual attitudes, some further increase of sexual expression, and widening acceptance of female equality and a single standard. He noted, however, that most of the research had been done with a relatively liberal

---

[22] A. C. Kinsey, W. B. Pomeroy, and C. E. Martin, *Sexual Behavior in the Human Male* (Philadelphia: W. B. Saunders Co., 1948); Kinsey, Pomeroy, Martin, and P. H. Gebhard, *Sexual Behavior in the Human Female* (Philadelphia: W. B. Saunders Company, 1953).

[23] I. L. Reiss, *Premarital Sexual Standards in America* (New York: The Free Press, 1960), p. 228.

and talkative segment of the population and that the changes would not go unopposed.[24] Paul Goodman, also writing in 1960, described existing attitudes toward sexuality as "inconsistent and unpredictable" and characterized the sexual revolution as an "interrupted revolution." The greater permissiveness that was clearly guiding many people in practice had not yet influenced the statute books; law enforcement continued to follow the strict codes of the recent past. Conventions about "decency" were still pervasively strong. Public school officials could find themselves in serious trouble if they sponsored innovations that sounded like sex education. Goodman wrote, "It is inconceivable for a publisher to print a sober little juvenile story about, say, playing doctor or the surprising discovery of masturbation. A character in a juvenile (or adult) adventure story may not incidentally get an erection as he may wolf a sandwich or get sleepy." Growing up is not easy when standards are so bewilderingly inconsistent.[25]

What actually took place during the 1960s seems rather more than a consolidation and clarification of an earlier revolution. The movement, of course, was in the same general direction, and the opposition to it continued to take much the same forms. But sexuality became increasingly linked to another sharply rising social trend, the demand of young people for independence and regulation of their own conduct. Sexual behavior provided an appropriate ground on which to fight a battle for self-determination. On this issue both the authority and the confused hypocrisy of the parent generation proved vulnerable to challenge. Allied in this way with a broader cause, freedom of choice in sexual behavior became an explicit value, and the veil of reticence was further pulled aside. College officials who had once worried over the briefest visiting hours of men and women in each other's dormitories were in a short space of time confronted with demands for shared dormitories and complete student autonomy in their management. The changing attitude began to be reflected in more lenient court decisions on such topics as censorship and pornography. Clothes began to fall from actors and actresses on the stage, movie makers began to include sexual intercourse in their films, and the publishers of novels, far from shrinking at mention of erections, began to expect their authors to describe love-making in vivid detail. If this was not a wholly new revolution it was at least a complete new chapter of an old one. It produced a spectacular change in the attitude toward sex of a large segment of the public. But it is still well to remember that cultural change does not occur quickly in a whole population. Taking our culture as a whole, there is still great variation and great inconsistency about sexual behavior.

Codes of Sexual Behavior

Reiss's research was directed not only at the facts of premarital sexual behavior but also at the codes of conduct by which such behavior was governed. He distinguished four main codes. Taken in order of the amount of sexual behavior they permitted, they are (1) the single standard of abstinence

---

[24] *Ibid.*, Chap. 10.

[25] P. Goodman, *Growing Up Absurd* (New York: Random House, Inc., 1960), pp. 119–129.

until marriage, applying alike to both sexes; (2) the double standard, according to which abstinence is required of women but not of men; (3) permissiveness with affection; and (4) permissiveness regardless of affection. As with most typologies, allowance must be made for "mixed" types and intermediate positions. Reiss found many instances, for instance, of a transitional double standard in which premarital intercourse was permissible for women provided it was accompanied by affection, but permissible for men without this proviso. The third and fourth codes in their complete form imply a single standard, applying without discrimination to both sexes.

The code of permissiveness with affection is based on the idea that sexual intercourse is a natural and appropriate expression of strong feelings of love and personal involvement. The women of the Kinsey reports who had engaged in premarital intercourse had done so most commonly with the men to whom they were engaged or at least expected to marry. The code implies that intercourse purely for pleasure, with transient partners who arouse no other important feelings, is not acceptable, being merely a debased form of what can be a highly exciting and moving human experience. Some degree of friendship, some feeling of warmth and closeness, should precede the experience that above all others enhances and expresses warmth and closeness. The most stringent statement of this code might be that intercourse is fine provided the two parties are in love. Being in love, however, is not easily defined, and many who advocate the code would put it simply that the partners must be friends who like and respect one another and want to give further expression to this feeling. The behavior that is disfavored, the implicit "sin" in the code of permissiveness with affection, is the separation of sexual intercourse from the feelings it is so capable of expressing and enriching. Isolated in this way it becomes merely a physical pleasure with an irrelevant partner, and it thus makes a mockery of the implicit human relation.

Permissiveness without the requirement of affection is based on a different conception of the matter. This code has an eloquent advocate, among others, in the British zoologist Alex Comfort, who views sex as a natural, pleasurable activity that should be more widely enjoyed. In human beings, according to Comfort, the perpetual readiness for sexual activity, contrasting with the "seasons" and "heats" of animals, signifies that its real function is no longer primarily reproduction; it is play. As such, sex is natural, sensible, there to be enjoyed. We should not consider it dreadful; neither should we consider it wonderful.

> While it is true that full public discussion and information is essential in this field, it is also true that the task of deflating the emotional currency of sex is equally important. The undermining of an older fake-modesty has unfortunately not yet reduced the tension that exists in the mind of the public or its scientific advisers, and zealots who put forward theories of sex as a *mystique* or a transcendent human activity have already done a great deal to obscure its real place as a single, if important, part of a general pattern of human social activities.[26]

[26] A. Comfort, *Sex in Society* (London: Gerald Duckworth, Ltd., 1963), p. 7.

Elsewhere in his book Comfort makes it plain that he deplores an unfeeling, exploitative use of sex; he even proposes as a new commandment: "Thou shalt not exploit another person's feelings and wantonly expose them to an experience of rejection." But if exploitation is a "sin" under this code, so also is any talk of sex as a transcendent experience, any attempt to inflate it emotionally. Here the code collides head-on with permissiveness with affection, which gives sex precisely the character that Comfort rejects as a "mystique." Let it always be play, he argues, with mutual fun and laughter; let it never be taken too seriously.

The issue that divides the third and fourth codes has to do with how deeply sexual expression should be involved in the personal systems of the two participants. Is intercourse to be considered part of an important relation or is it to be treated as relatively isolated from serious concerns? This is no easy matter to decide. Sexuality is not, of course, wholly divorced from reproduction, and in the marriage relation, playfully as it may be enjoyed, it can hardly be separated from the serious purposes of the institution of marriage, including the lasting care of the children that are produced. Since Freud, the study of personal development has constantly emphasized two points that are not easy to reconcile: sexual freedom and marital stability. All students of the subject have been impressed by the unfortunate consequences of too vigorous a suppression of sexual impulses, consequences that range from a general constriction of emotional life to a whole series of specific disorders including at least part of the neuroses. All students have been equally impressed by the deformations inflicted on the growth of personality in childhood by parental frictions and quarrels and by the breakup of families. These problems seem to call for greater sexual freedom yet also for more successful employment of sex as a means of strengthening and deepening the marriage relation. It is worth remembering that the code of premarital abstinence and of sexual fidelity in marriage embodied an attempt to make the marital relation supremely important and satisfying by reserving to it the rich rewards of sexual gratification. We know now that this plan often went astray, that the restraints on sexuality had to be so severe as to make its enjoyment impossible when it was finally set free, and that the marriage bond might therefore become more a painful yoke than a joyful experience.

What we do not know is the relation between sexual permissiveness and marital happiness. Is a premarital career of frequent sexual experience with many partners compatible with a steadily satisfying and deepening relation with the marriage partner? Is permissiveness with affection the most suitable form of rehearsal for an affectionate relation one hopes will last a lifetime? Is fidelity in marriage most conducive to a strong family life, or would things go better if external erotic adventures by each partner were taken as a matter of course? These questions may sound loaded, but they are not rhetorical; the answers are simply not known. Furthermore, in the light of what we are learning about individual differences, it is possible that they cannot be answered alike for everyone. Can they even be answered alike for men and women?

Sex Differences

Sex differences, like sex behavior, have been the subject of a revolution during the last hundred years. Starting from the position of an inferior caste, legally subordinate to men, women have obtained for themselves the right to vote and to hold office, greater rights in the ownership of property, and entrance into many occupations formerly understood to be strictly masculine. According to Alice Rossi this, too, can be looked upon as an "interrupted revolution": the feminist movement stopped short of securing completely equal rights, and for various reasons women have not pressed as hard as they might for relief from the constrictions of the role of housewife or for full equality in political, occupational, and academic spheres.[27] The legal victories were not followed up with persistent attempts to change the cultural expectations and institutional arrangements through which substantial inequality was maintained. Obviously women have not taken over their proportionate share of important occupational positions. During the late 1960s feminism flared once more into angry life. Spurred on by a general rise of rebelliousness and of demands for reform, the women's liberation movement undertook to set the interrupted revolution once again into forward motion.

It is clearly difficult to arrive at dispassionate judgments when opinions are polarized by revolution. Even in quiet times we find it hard to observe differences without wondering which one is best. "The human mind," wrote C. S. Lewis, "is generally far more eager to praise and dispraise than to describe and define. It wants to make every distinction a distinction of value; hence those fatal critics who can never point out the differing quality of two poets without putting them in an order of preference as if they were candidates for a prize."[28] If we are prone to this trouble with respect to poets, we can hardly expect ourselves to refrain from assigning values and awarding prizes on an issue like sex differences, where nature has put us on one side or the other and where self-respect is likely to be under challenge. But the subject arises inevitably at this point in our study because the most inescapable difference between men and women is in their physical constitution, especially as it relates to sexual intercourse, reproduction, and caring for the young. Perhaps this is not a bad starting point for treating the subject fairly. There can be no doubt about the complementary nature of these differences. "Here Havelock Ellis has spoken the last word," says a recent writer, "in his conception of 'compensatory unlikeness,' which means: however different men and women may be, they have a common task, and are therefore designed for and complementary to each other."[29]

[27] A. S. Rossi, "Equality between the Sexes: An Immodest Proposal," in "The Woman in America," *Daedalus*, **93** (1964), 607–652.

[28] C. S. Lewis, *The Four Loves* (New York: Harcourt Brace Jovanovich, Inc., 1960), p. 27.

[29] O. Schwarz, *The Psychology of Sex* (Baltimore: Penguin Books, Inc., 1949), p. 115.

All thinking about sex differences should start from this biological base. The mammalian scheme of reproduction calls for a division of labor, and this is reflected in body form and function. We are on safest ground when speaking about differences if we relate them in a sensible way to the funda-mental biological design. If we ask whether or not sexuality is a different expe-rience for men and women, involving them with their partners in different ways, having a different relation to other aspects of personality, we are put-ting a question which has clear connections with body form and function, however much learning may enter into the final result. Supposed differences in, for example, logical thinking, in which men have decided they are supe-rior, or intuition, which women have considered to be their secret intellectual weapon, seem at best remotely connected with biological differentiation. Where strictly sexual behavior is not the issue, we may justifiably ask whether a complete explanation of differences can be found in the learning of sex roles under present social conditions, a learning guided by adult expectations about the positions of men and women in the world.

Learning Sex Roles

In a study of seventh grade boys and girls in a lower-middle- to upper-middle-class suburban school, parents were encouraged to talk about their children in whatever way they wanted.[30] Their comments were then ana-lyzed with a view to detecting overall differences in the way sons and daugh-ters were characterized. This group of parents mentioned quite a few qualities that were not sex-typed; these were mentioned equally often for boys and girls, and the same standards were expected of boys and girls. Included among these qualities were the intellectual ones of having a good mind, dis-playing intelligence, being well-read and abreast of the times; the moral ones of working hard, doing one's best, being honest and trustworthy; and certain social qualities like having respect for others, showing a sense of humor, being responsive and spontaneous, and maintaining a neat, well-groomed appearance.

More than half of what the parents had to say about their sons and daughters did fall into categories that were distinctly sex-typed. When talking about sons the parents' conversation was more heavily weighted with re-marks about activity, competitiveness, and achievement. A good deal was said about being energetic, getting things done, showing ambition, exhibiting backbone, trying hard to win, and taking an interest in athletics. Self-assurance and self-sufficiency came into the picture, and parents praised sons for such qualities as having a level head, being stable, taking the lead, and sticking up for one's rights. When talking about daughters the parents were more likely to mention qualities of social interaction. They talked about social poise, politeness, and courtesy, and they spoke with approval about making friends easily, liking people, mingling nicely and possessing charm; success

[30] J. P. Hill, "Parental Determinants of Sex-Typed Behavior." Unpublished Ph.D. Dissertation, Harvard University Library, Cambridge, Mass., 1964.

for a girl was implicitly defined as getting along well with others and being liked by them. Another cluster of traits parents favored for girls centered around doing things for others, being kind, generous, loving, and having a compassionate understanding of other people's difficulties. Parents sometimes mentioned that their daughters had given no trouble and were easy to handle, being eager to please and willing to listen. The relative infrequency of such remarks about sons suggested acceptance of the idea that boys would give trouble and would not be easy to handle.[31]

It is easy to see from this example how pervasive and continuous sex typing is. There is evidence that differential training starts right after birth. Close observers of mothers handling their small babies report a detectable difference in their attitudes, as if they already expected the boys to be more assertive and resistant and the girls to be easier to handle.[32] There is a large body of both research and theory on the subsequent course of the acquisition of sex roles.[33] A vivid description of the process can be derived from a study by Mirra Komarovsky in which college girls were asked to engage in reminiscence about their childhoods. The girls remembered many instances, because they caused wonder or frustration, in which their natural interests were deflected because these were not feminine.[34] A grandmother refused to let a 7-year-old take her favorite toy, a set of tin soldiers, to a party, insisting that she take a doll instead. A girl who asked for a set of tools for Christmas opened the package to find a sewing set. A girl who loved swimming was discouraged by a neighbor on the ground that her muscles might grow unattractively large for a girl. Another was told by her mother, when she came in dirty from play, that unless she learned to play quietly and stay neat no man would ever want to marry her. So effective is this propaganda that the girls themselves learn to enforce it. They may even start to educate their brothers: one laughed her younger brother out of taking a doll to bed and made him take a teddy bear instead. Several girls recalled their frustration at not being allowed to take "shop," which they thought interesting, in school and being obliged instead to take cooking and sewing.

It is evident in all this that a great many of the qualities deemed mas-

[31] The findings of this study are consistent with those of Aberle and Naegele discussed above, Chap. 6, p. 130.

[32] S. K. Escalona, *The Roots of Individuality: Normal Patterns of Development in Infancy* (Chicago: Aldine Publishing Co., 1968).

[33] Contrasting theoretical explanations, with considerable reference to research, will be found in W. Mischel, "A Social-Learning View of Sex Differences in Behavior," and L. Kohlberg, "A Cognitive-Developmental Analysis of Children's Sex-Role Concepts and Attitudes," both in *The Development of Sex Differences*, ed. E. E. Maccoby (Stanford, Calif.: Stanford University Press, 1966), pp. 56–172. See also W. D. Ward, "Process of Sex-Role Development," *Developmental Psychology*, 1 (1969), 163–168.

[34] M. Komarovsky, *Women in the Modern World* (Boston: Little, Brown & Company, 1953), esp. pp. 53–67. Excerpt reprinted in *The Family and the Sexual Revolution: Selected Readings,* ed. E. M. Schur (Bloomington, Ind.: Indiana University Press, 1964), pp. 212–223.

culine and feminine result simply from differential social training. This sort of evidence is entirely compatible with cross-cultural findings such as Margaret Mead's well-known demonstration that practically all the traits considered feminine in one society might rate as masculine in another, and vice versa.[35] Training in sex roles represents the attempt of a culture to fit boys and girls for their prospective roles in society. The traditional and still general expectation in our society is that men will be breadwinners and women homemakers, and virtually every sex-typed quality mentioned by the parents of the seventh graders becomes understandable in this light. The boy must be encouraged to go out and do things, competing confidently with others for scarce resources and thus winning bread and status for his whole household. The girl must be attractive so that she will be "adopted" by a suitable breadwinner, after which she will make the home a sociable and loving place and care well for the children. As with heterosexual object choice the culture does not risk leaving the attainment of such important goals to blind biological pressures. The two-track curriculum starts early and never stops.

Biological Sex Differences

In comparison with the massive accomplishments of learning, the case for biological sex differences may seem small. Reviewing the literature on the part played by sex hormones in development, Hamburg and Lunde show that the connections are looser and more roundabout than had earlier been supposed.[36] But we must remember that no society has yet been found in which the men bear and nurse the babies, and the anatomical differences in the sexual organs can hardly be attributed to social learning. The average man is taller than the average woman, has bigger hands and feet, and is equipped with stronger muscles, especially in the arms and legs. These bodily characteristics are well adapted to going out and doing things, competing if necessary for scarce resources, and it is at least a permissible inference that the presence of such an endowment carries an inclination to use it. At the age of 2 months, according to Harlow, young male monkeys display more "threatening" and sexual behavior than females, and by 6 months they greatly exceed females in the initiation of bodily contact and aggressive play.[37] What holds for monkeys does not necessarily hold for man, but it is suggestive that research with preschool children repeatedly shows greater conflict, quarreling, and aggressive assertiveness among the boys, whereas the girls are more inclined to seek help and approval from others.[39] Given the differences in

[35] M. Mead, *Sex and Temperament in Three Primitive Societies* (New York: William Morrow & Company, Inc., 1935).

[36] D. A. Hamburg and D. T. Lunde, "Sex Hormones in the Development of Sex Differences in Human Behavior," in Maccoby, *The Development of Sex Differences*, pp. 1–24.

[37] H. F. Harlow, "The Heterosexual Affectional System in Monkeys," *American Psychologist*, **17** (1962), 1–9.

[38] For references see the classified summary in Maccoby, *The Development of Sex Differences*, pp. 323–327.

body form and in the parts played in reproduction, are we justified in attributing everything but structure to sex-role learning? Or should we assume that the bodily differences carry with them certain affective differences, certain differences in the nature of sexual experience, and a certain compliance with the roles society is so eager to see played?

The way in which these biological differences have customarily been described is somewhat polluted by prize-giving and value judgments. Men are independent, active, and assertive, women are dependent, passive, and submissive—it is quite clear who is the more important in a competitive industrial society. A lively sketch could be written on the relative importance of the harried housewife, her hair a mess, taking care of the needs and bruises and sorrows of three small children, and her well-groomed husband who by hard competitive work has climbed to a vice presidency, who travels all over the country, magnificent with his expense account, attending trade conventions and holding offices, all in the service of a company that manufactures disposable diapers. But perhaps the mounting social problems of the second half of this century have already undercut the presumed superiority of the male virtues; too many of the world's troubles come directly from competition, assertive aggressiveness, and uncontrolled rivalrous proliferation of technology. If women's supposed traits could be described in positive rather than negative terms they might seem better adapted to preserving civilization.

This view is taken in an essay by Erikson.[39] He writes,

> Maybe if women would only gain the determination to represent as image providers and law givers what they have always stood for privately in evolution and in history (realism of householding, responsibility of upbringing, resourcefulness in peacekeeping, and devotion to healing), they might well be mobilized to add an ethically restraining, because truly supranational, power to politics in the widest sense.

It is interesting to notice the different picture created by the traditional stereotype—dependence, passivity, submissiveness—and the nouns chosen by Erikson—realism, responsibility, resourcefulness, devotion. Male readers may be offended by their implicit demotion, but they will perhaps admit good sense in Erikson's hope that women will assume their share of leadership "in those fateful human affairs which so far have been left entirely in the hands of gifted and driven men, and often of men whose genius of leadership eventually have yielded to ruthless self-aggrandizement. Mankind now obviously depends on new kinds of social inventions and on institutions which guard and cultivate that which nurses and nourishes, cares and tolerates, includes and preserves."[40]

It is a nice question, one that deserves much more detailed consideration than we can give it here, how far the respective male and female qualities

[39] E. H. Erikson, "Inner and Outer Space: Reflections on Womanhood," in "The Woman in America," *Daedalus,* **93**, no. 2 (1964), 582–606.

[40] *Ibid.,* p. 605.

appropriate for reproduction extend into other aspects of personality and slant the course of sex-role learning. But we are concerned at this point with developmental problems that lie close to the reproductive process, especially with matters of sexual experience. Here there is good reason to believe that the biological division of labor with respect to reproduction produces differences of experience that may result in much misunderstanding. The female part in this division consists in producing, one at a time, ova suitable for fertilization. Once fertilized, this valuable creation must be preserved and provided with the necessities for growth within the womb; once the child is born, it must still be provided with nourishment, care, and protection. The male part in this division stops almost at the point where the female's begins. He is responsible for the fertilization, for which purpose he must get around in search of opportunities to release his ever-lavish supply of spermatozoa. He may become attached to the female, but this will be because of the satisfaction of intercourse, not because he is sharing in her cycle of internal growth and care. Sexual intercourse for the male is more nearly than for the female an isolated act, soon over. This difference is represented in the slower decline of female emotional arousal after the climax of intercourse. Many a woman has complained at her husband's rolling over and starting to snore when she would like to go on basking in feelings of tenderness and warmth. There is plausible biological reason behind the common observation that sex in women tends to be more ramified and embedded in personality, more deeply a part of existence, than it is for men.

One consequence of this difference is to give decidedly different meanings to early experiences of intercourse. The boy is likely to construe his first few occasions as a test, and passing the test may effectively obscure the possibilities of the act as an expression of tenderness and intimacy. This set may be so strong that he sees the partner as someone to be conquered, and the number of his victories may be a ground for boasting. The more the sex act is interpreted as an achievement, an expression of virility and social power, the less it is likely to include respect for the partner and any real reciprocity of feeling. Nevertheless, the male role in the sex act requires potency as well as a certain acquirable skill, and novices can hardly avoid feeling that they must prove themselves and learn how to do it. In a personality study a college student, sexually inexperienced but in love and engaged, told of deciding that it would be better not to enter marriage an untried and ignorant virgin. He therefore visited an experienced girl of his acquaintance with a view to correcting this defect. The meeting reached a successful culmination, but he came away quite dissatisfied because it had been necessary for the girl to help him secure sufficient arousal. In a relation as close and inherently mutual as sexual intercourse one might suppose that help would be considered kind and friendly, but in this case it came as a humiliation because the goal had been set at a magnificent solo performance to which the girl would admiringly submit. The student indicated that it would be unbearable to him if anything of this sort happened with the girl he loved; he would have to continue his premarital field studies until he achieved dependable potency. A great many men treasure potency not just for its own value but as a symbol of manhood and personal worth.

Girls' early experiences have a decidedly different character. Intercourse is less a test; the proof that one is lovable and desirable does not require going so far. On the first occasion it may entail pain, and it may continue to be marred by discomfort if the partner is impatient or unskillful in making it fully pleasurable. Furthermore, the danger of pregnancy is not completely controlled by modern technology. For these reasons alone we might expect reluctance to enter upon sexual relations, but there is more. It would be surprising to find a female counterpart of the male student just described. Already the girl is apt to be aware that sexuality is important and involving, so that she wants to experience it with the person she cares for most. It is, of course, possible for a woman to learn to enjoy sex just for its pleasurable properties and for a man to learn to enjoy it as an expression of affection and tenderness. But these are probably modifications of the sex differences provided by nature.

The natural differences assert themselves again in the attitudes taken toward accidental pregnancy. Following such a mishap boys sometimes claim that it was not their fault, but if concerned they are likely to think about abortion as a practical way of solving the problem. The girl may feel pressed to think about abortion, too, but she is likely to have trouble treating pregnancy merely as a practical problem. She may want to take the "impractical" course of having the baby, and if she does not do so she may experience feelings of loss and mourning that bother her for some time. Even more than sexuality, pregnancy is a widely ramified part of her experience, not something that can be coolly put aside.

The differences express themselves again in transitory premarital affairs. From the start the partners are likely to construe the affair differently. The boy may see it as a chance to undertake a mature sexual relation without making a binding decision about marriage, the preservation of his freedom being of real importance. For the girl, it is a chance to give herself fully to a relation that has attracted her, subject to the risk that her involvement will be painfully interrupted. If termination occurs, through either circumstance or agreement, both may find separation difficult, but the boy will more likely be able to turn over and snore, so to speak, or move on to another relation, while the girl will experience nostalgia and have trouble getting her lover out of her mind.

Concluding Comment

It will be recognized that the generalizations made here about biologically determined sex differences are very rough, leaving a lot of room for individual differences. But careful studies of personality, clinical or otherwise, as well as literary treatments of the subject, make it clear that a great many of the frustrations and sorrows that occur in sexual partnerships arise out of failure to understand that the other person's feelings are not always the same as one's own. The partners in a sexual union may experience much that is wonderful together, but this does not guarantee that what they have experienced is the same. The point is especially pertinent with respect to sexual relations, where bodily structures and functions are demonstrably different, but to a degree it can be generalized to all close relations, even those between two people of the same sex. Friendship and intimacy have their troubles, and often enough the reason lies in profound differences perhaps of constitution and temperament, perhaps of personal experience and motive, perhaps in the way the situation is construed, which mean that the two members of the pair are not in full communication with each other. The improvement of human relations depends upon developing an increased awareness of possible differences in the way others feel and experience things.

14 Education and Intellectual Growth

One of the characteristics all intelligent men and women have in common is that they were once illiterate. All alike start life in perfect ignorance of the chief cultural tools for communication and calculation. All things considered, the mastery of reading, writing, and arithmetic and all that goes with them moves forward at a remarkably rapid pace. Even in a lumbering school system the steep ascending path from recognizing the word "cat" to writing a freshman essay on existentialism can be climbed in ten years, from age 7 to age 17. This aspect of learning is often treated as if it were an independent strand in the course of development, as if intellectual growth were one thing and the growth of personality something quite separate. Intellect, however, is part of the personal system, sometimes a highly important part of that system, and its growth cannot be isolated from the whole in which it is embedded. Thinking, behaving, and feeling do not belong in separate compartments. We shall therefore begin this chapter by considering how the business of being educated is construed, what varieties of motivation it enlists, what frustrations it implies and what satisfactions—in short, how schooling fits into the individual's enterprise of living.

Motivation and Scholastic Achievement

Even though educational philosophies differ widely, the meaning of going to school does not seem particularly obscure to adults. It would be a grave handicap in living to have no knowledge of reading, writing, and arithmetic; the first function of the school is to teach those basic skills. A certain amount of information about the world also seems necessary for practical and social living. Agreement is less complete on what this information should be, but if one thinks only of the fundamentals taught in grammar schools—an elementary knowledge of geography, history, civics, and natural science—it is clear that a person innocent of such training would be oddly disoriented amongst his fellow men. Children go to school, their parents might put it, to learn what they need to know in order to communicate with others and to understand what is going on around them. Some such statement seems beyond the realm of dispute.

Meaning of Achievement at School

How does this process look to children during the early years of school? The adult conception of education is decidedly future-oriented, and we can hardly suppose that a child of 6 or 7 will view today's struggle with reading or arithmetic as a useful stepping stone to a future he can scarcely imagine. Yet children at school age are capable of understanding that what they are asked to do is somehow connected with growing up and being admitted to the serious concerns of adult existence. Erikson has drawn attention to this side of the child's appreciation of what is going on, saying, "At no time is the child more ready to learn quickly and avidly." At this age, children really want to be able to do things and make things, to understand and participate in the real world. "Children now also attach themselves to teachers and the parents of other children, and they want to watch and imitate people representing occupations which they can grasp—firemen and policemen, gardeners, plumbers, and garbage men." Fantasy begins to be put aside in favor of realistic action and mastery. No matter how well entertained children may be, they are dissatisfied if they are not able to do things and make things. Erikson calls this a *sense of industry*; it is the school-age version of what has been described in this book as a sense of competence. When all goes relatively well at school, a child can develop this feeling in connection with scholastic accomplishments. "He develops perseverance and adjusts himself to the inorganic laws of the tool world and can become an eager and absorbed unit of a productive situation."[1]

These feelings make it possible for children to become interested fairly early in their own schooling. Now they may add to their sense of competence, receive recognition and praise from teachers, compete successfully with other children, cooperate pleasantly in joint undertakings. But these positive values are far from having a clear field. Whatever else it may mean, attending school is inevitably construed as something that adults require. Parents make you go to school in the first place; once you are there, teachers make you obey rules, sit still, pay attention, and study things that are usually less than utterly fascinating in themselves. Adult requirements and authority are unavoidably present. If they are felt to be largely irksome, they may generate sullen resentment or mischievous rebellion. Furthermore, difficulty with schoolwork can easily produce feelings of incompetence and inferiority, failure in competition,

[1] E. H. Erikson, *Identity: Youth and Crisis* (New York: W. W. Norton & Company, Inc., 1968), pp. 122–124.

and a depressing lack of teachers' recognition and praise. Schools that try to be progressive labor mightily to reduce these hazards, but the average educational system, narrowly sustained by public taxes, is hard pressed to keep them under control. Many children see achievement at school as a distasteful combination of self-control, disagreeable effort, and knuckling under to unappreciative authority.

Dropping Out of School

In recent years great uneasiness has been created by the problem of high school dropouts. Although at present one student in four drops out before finishing high school, it is not this rate in itself that constitutes the problem. As recently as twenty years ago more students dropped out of high school than graduated, and in earlier times the proportion was of course many times larger. The problem lies rather in what happens to those who drop out now. Historical perspective is important. Not many years ago, businessmen often preferred to hire willing high school graduates than to hire college graduates who thought they knew too much already. In this climate of opinion, even an incomplete high school education was not a serious bar to finding employment. By leaving school and getting a job, getting married, or both, one could advance directly into adulthood and spare oneself further boredom and frustration in the classroom. Today, the character of the work market has changed. Technological advances and automation have decreased the proportion of jobs requiring little thought or skill. Correspondingly there is a much greater demand for workers in offices and service occupations, for which education is felt to be a distinct asset. As a result, many employers take a high school diploma as a minimum credential for any but the lowest grades of occupation, and dropping out becomes a serious handicap for any later improvement of one's vocational position. Much more than in earlier times, the dropout puts himself into an economic trap from which there is small chance of future escape. Thus, dropping out has become a serious social problem instead of a reasonable way of life. "The overriding fact is that there are fewer and fewer places in our society for the dropout, and it becomes increasingly clear that he has no future."[2]

Schreiber has ventured to draw a profile of the average dropout.

> The dropout is a child just past his sixteenth birthday who has average or slightly below average intelligence, and is more likely to be a boy than a girl. He is not achieving according to his potential; he is not reading at grade level; and academically he is in the lowest quarter of his class. He is slightly overage for his grade placement, having been held back once in the elementary or junior high school grades. He has not been in trouble with the law although he does take up an inordinate amount of the school administrator's time because of discipline problems. He sel-

[2] D. Schreiber, ed., *Profile of the School Dropout* (New York: Alfred A. Knopf, Inc., Vintage Books, 1968), p. 6.

dom participates in extracurricular activities, feels rejected by the school and his fellow classmates, and in turn rejects them as well as himself. He is insecure in his school status, hostile toward others, and is less respected by his teachers because of his academic inadequacies. His parents were school dropouts as were his older brothers and sisters. His friends are persons outside the school, usually older dropouts. He says that he is quitting school because of lack of interest but that he intends to get a high school diploma in some manner because without it he can't get a job. He strongly resents being called a dropout, knows the pitfalls that await him in the outside world, yet believes that they can't be worse than those that await him were he to remain in school.[3]

This description makes it clear that dropping out has a great deal to do with motivation and feeling. It is the culmination of a long experience of incompetence, inferiority, rejection, and failure to discover bases for self-respect. Scholastic aptitude makes a contribution but not a wholly decisive one; many children with equally moderate scores on intelligence tests pursue their course unfalteringly to graduation day. Characteristic of the dropout is accumulated negative feeling toward a hard, unprofitable experience that makes school bells, lessons, and teachers' didactic voices hateful and that urgently prompts escape as soon as the law permits. A child may dislike school and do poorly but continue because his friends are there and they have good times together. He may continue because parents and siblings went through high school and he does not want to be a family disgrace. But if school has never led to the discovery of what he is good at or to the arousal of intrinsic interest, and if he does not feel at home there socially, it is not surprising that, recognizing the risks, he can no longer endure the life that goes on inside those dreary old brick or shiny new glass walls.

In the chapter on social class status it was mentioned that teachers' appreciation of their pupils was likely to be influenced not just by scholastic aptitude but also by evidence of class position.[4] The status origins and aspirations of teachers and the control of educational systems by the community combine to make public schools represent middle-class values. Children of lower status may regard as foreign values like restraint, politeness, careful language, and neat, orderly ways. But although this type of prejudice on the part of teachers, often unintentional, makes disadvantaged children feel estranged, there is reason to think that low social and economic status starts to be a handicap still earlier. The child of poverty experiences cultural disadvantage even before he enters the school building. In comparison with a middle-class child he has been less impressed with the importance of school, less trained in appropriate language habits, less familiar with the existence of books and periodicals, less accustomed to sitting still and being read to, less experienced in continuous listening. As Martin Deutsch points out, a first grade teacher often talks to a class for ten minutes or so, but a lower-class

[3] *Ibid.*, pp. 5–6.
[4] See above, Chap. 6, pp. 140–141.

child may be quite inexperienced at listening to sustained communication and may find such a flow almost impossible to follow.[5] The experiences that accumulate to produce ultimate dropping out of high school may start in the earliest years and take form in the child's very first exposures to school. It is this insight that has prompted movements such as Head Start, which aim through preschool training to give disadvantaged children the basic attitudes and skills that middle-class children have already acquired at home.

Scholastic Overachievement and Underachievement

Except in cases of severe intellectual limitation, the high school dropout is an example of scholastic underachievement. He is typically bright enough to do the work, but he does not have enough interest to make the effort. Underachievement is defined as a discrepancy between potential and accomplishment, the latter falling short of the former; overachievement is the reverse. For research purposes achievement is measured simply by school grades, potential by scores on intelligence tests. It is important to avoid the fallacy that intelligence tests measure one's innate intellectual endowment. As we shall see presently, they cannot be interpreted in this light. But it is not unreasonable to suppose that intelligence tests devised for use in a given society yield an approximate measure of aptitude for doing the schoolwork devised by that society. When school grades are much lower than intelligence test scores, it is justifiable to assume that a student is not living up to his academic capabilities.

Academic underachievement is not limited to those who are culturally handicapped. Boys and girls from highly advantaged homes, from cultural backgrounds that should be unusually stimulating and encouraging, sometimes fail in school. That this is a problem of motivation, not of ability, is especially clear when after a good record in earlier years a child starts to slow down, or when after a period of underachievement a student suddenly picks up again. Such cases are not the culmination of an unhappy struggle against handicaps. The motivational problem is clearly of a different kind.

In an attempt to investigate this problem Kimball chose as subjects the boys at a prominent private college preparatory school, boys who as a group came from clearly advantageous backgrounds.[6] As a first step, several boys with grades far below intelligence measures were studied in detail through interviews and tests. Some hypotheses were thus formed that could be tried out with the school's population as a whole, using a sentence completion test. This test consists of a series of incomplete sentences, which the subject is asked to complete with the first thoughts that come to his mind. The prof-

---

[5] M. Deutsch, "Early Social Environment: Its Influence on School Adaptation," in Schreiber, *Profile of the School Dropout*, pp. 203–214. See also J. McV. Hunt, *The Challenge of Incompetence and Poverty* (Urbana, Ill.: University of Illinois Press, 1969).

[6] B. Kimball, "The Sentence-Completion Technique in a Study of Scholastic Underachievement," *Journal of Consulting Psychology*, **16** (1952), 353–358; "Case Studies in Educational Failure During Adolescence," *American Journal of Orthopsychiatry*, **23** (1953), 406–415.

fered fragment might be, for instance, "I get angry when . . . ," and the subject's response is obviously chosen from a wide universe of possibilities such as "when my father scolds me," "when my mother won't listen," "when my roommate uses my toothpaste," or "when I fumble a grounder playing baseball." The test has been found useful, though by no means infallible, when information is needed on spontaneous, unedited attitudes—in this case, especially attitudes toward parents, teachers, fellow students, and schoolwork.

The principal hypothesis yielded by the case studies and supported by the sentence completion test was that the underachieving boys differed from the rest of the students in having more severe conflict with their fathers. This conflict took the form not of open battles but of hostile feelings coupled with anxiety and difficulty in expressing the feelings. Thus one student studied in detail was compliant and gentle when interviewed by men, denying any negative feeling toward his father, but when talking to a woman he expressed sharp resentment at his father's dominance. It appeared that his father was given to both confident assertiveness and outbursts of temper, a combination the boy found difficult to resist. As time went on, the father's blind determination to have his son enter his own occupation became increasingly unbearable yet wholly unresponsive to reasoned argument. But there remained one way of blocking the father's purpose: failing to qualify for college. As a conscious policy this would certainly be judged a poor bargain in that it might be hurting the son as much as the father. When one both resents and feels guilty about the resentment, however, a solution that punishes both the object of resentment and the self is appropriate, and in any event, one might easily lose interest in studies without being aware of a concealed aim. Scholastic underachievement in this case, and with variations in the other cases at the school, seemed to be a passive rebellion against paternal dominance and authority.

These findings in a particular setting raise the always important question of generality. Clearly an ambitious, authoritative father is not at the root of the matter in disadvantaged neighborhoods. It might even be that the findings were peculiar to a boys' preparatory school with a largely male faculty. Would the same thing appear in a public high school taught largely by women, in a middle-class setting where, according to sociological studies, the mothers are more likely than the fathers to be the source of ambitious pressures? It might be expected that in such a setting underachieving boys would be carrying on a passive rebellion against their mothers. Silbert chose a public school to maximize this possibility, but her results were in agreement with Kimball's findings.[7] Conflict with fathers and their expectations still came to light most frequently in the underachieving boys.

Scholastic overachievement might be thought a contradiction in terms. However, a certain number of students do get much better grades than their intelligence scores would lead anyone to predict—another bit of evidence

[7] A. R. Silbert, "Achievement and Underachievement." Unpublished Ph.D. Dissertation, Harvard University Library, Cambridge, Mass., 1960.

that intelligence tests cannot be pure measures of inherent potential. If under-achievement works through boredom and inertia on the part of someone who is disgruntled with school work, overachievement can be presumed to occur when there is unusual enthusiasm and zest flowing from a conviction that academic success is the way to all good things. Overachievers put extra effort into studying to please ambitious but accepting parents, to stand high in teachers' esteem, to surpass siblings, to demonstrate superiority among other students, or for combinations of such essentially interpersonal goals.

A Study of Academic Types

Some years ago Ruth Munroe, making personality studies of students in a women's college, described two types of approach to academic work.[8] These two types can be considered fairly extreme instances of the manner in which motivation enters the intellectual process. The *conscientious* or *rigid* type is moved by a strong desire to please and to enjoy the approval of the adult world. These students' behavior is well controlled and reliably guided by adult standards, but at some cost in easy warmth toward peers and with a certain timidity in trusting their own impulses and judgment. This pattern of strivings disposes the student to absorb information passively and to learn according to set rules. The rigid student prefers to amass and arrange infor-mation and is not offended by regurgitating it on examinations as proof to the teacher of how well she has absorbed his wisdom. When asked to write an original paper she may feel helpless and confused, may request definite sug-gestions, and will feel most comfortable if she finds a small, neat problem that can be wrapped up by careful work. The *temperamental* or *scattered* type takes college studies in a different spirit. She hates rules, cannot take notes, deplores filing cards, and starts to read many more books than she finishes. Disciplined work is abhorrent to her, but sometimes writing a paper suddenly produces involvement and excitement. She may then dash off at white heat an essay characterized by eloquence and interesting ideas, but the personal feeling and the generalities prove to rest on a precariously small basis of facts. The intellectual qualities thus displayed reflect a certain personal confusion. Basic needs are unsatisfied, problems go unsolved, and this type of student shows academic involvement only when she hits upon an external topic that is analogous to her personal distress. Thus resentment at her own rejecting parents may issue in a paper on delinquent children whose parents are de-scribed as odiously rejecting and who themselves deserve understanding and loving care; or chronic parental preference for her brother may lead this stu-dent to a burst of interest in oppressed minorities and civil rights. These ex-ternalized interests are unlikely to persist, however, if they do not help with the analogous personal problem. This is what is meant by characterizing these students as scattered.

[8] R. Munroe, *Teaching the Individual* (New York: Columbia University Press, 1942).

As described, neither type produces the best kind of college work. Solution of most intellectual problems, indeed most practical problems having any degree of complexity, requires that relevant facts be carefully brought together. Such solution also requires personal involvement, zest, and a willingness to try one's hand at independent judgment. Munroe's types veer too far in one direction or the other, but her descriptions suggest the combination of attitudes that is most propitious for dealing with intellectual problems.

Sophomore Slump

Dropping out of college should not be considered simply a later version of dropping out of high school. College students are recruited from those who have finished high school, who therefore do not typically carry the burdens that prompt earlier dropping out. Nevertheless, a substantial number of students drop out of college and a good many more experience an inclination to do so. This general phenomenon has been nicknamed *sophomore slump*, in recognition of the college year in which it most frequently occurs, although of course it can happen at any time. Unlike the high school phenomenon, sophomore slump may occur rather suddenly following a fine scholastic performance in school and a correspondingly good first year at college. Essential to understanding it is recognition of the tremendous importance that getting into college has recently assumed in American society. The upgrading of aspirations and of requirements for the better jobs has put a high premium on continuing one's education at least to a college degree. Many students describe admission to college as their greatest triumph and the freshman year as a chance to prove that they were worthy of that triumph. Having proved that point, however, they may suddenly discover themselves wondering whether a college education is something they really want.

The question arises partly because of the nature of college work. The college student can no longer treat studying as a series of daily guided steps; assignments are given for more distant deadlines and may involve choices of topic. However the student may have managed before, this pattern of work requires much more planning, organization, initiative, and decision making. If studies have acquired intrinsic interest for him, he will probably experience no fatal difficulty in operating according to this pattern. But if lessons are still simply a chore and a duty, he will see the effort at organization as painfully irksome if not impossible. The motives that may have been sustaining the student until he was safely in college prove to be no longer adequate. The slumping sophomore does not want to do things any more just to please parents and teachers or to fulfill anyone else's expectations. His education has come home to roost. He must now take it on as his own enterprise, an expression of himself, and if he cannot experience it in this way he will find continued work an insupportable burden.

Sometimes college work suffers from the rival claims of other attractions. Outside interests may beckon, social life may become enjoyably demanding, politics and protest may claim attention, and students may feel a need to investigate new aspects of experience, perhaps to experiment with alcohol and drugs. If these merely interfere with college studies, which would still be interesting enough if one only had time, the result does not qualify as a full-fledged case of sophomore slump. This term should be reserved for a more serious disturbance of one's sense of direction at college. The disturbance manifests itself in an apathy, inertia, and procrastination that is not confined to studies but that invades other aspects of college life. Unable to study, the student is equally unable to join in bull sessions, to take part in college social life, or to engage in college-related extracurricular activities. There are doubtless many reasons for arriving at this kind of blockage, but the main result seems to be that the student regards the whole business of being in college, perhaps of being still a student, as irrelevant to what he needs for personal growth. What he does need, what he really wants to be doing, may be difficult to discern, but the college way of life feels wrong. Often the best solution is to leave college at least temporarily. Testing oneself in a job, in volunteer work, in direct involvement with social or political problems may have the good effect of restoring both a sense of competence and a sense of the relevance of a college education. Some of these dropouts, of course, simply find a good way to live and realize that for them a college education really is irrelevant. Sophomore slump can be a serious personal crisis that should not be taken lightly. It is not always easily resolved. But it is in essence an acute form of a common developmental problem, that of discovering the personal relevance of the education that in the beginning was simply a requirement imposed by adults on children.[9]

Graduate School Dropouts

Dropping out of graduate school is often analogous to sophomore slump. Graduate education is highly specialized. This is clear enough in medical, law, education, business, and theological schools, the entering of which implies that one's occupation is already chosen. Dropping out from these schools signifies that one has found the work uncongenial or too difficult, so that the choice of occupation has to be changed. The situation is often less clear to students entering a graduate school of arts and sciences. Such schools hesitate to consider themselves strictly professional, but the student quickly finds that whatever field he has chosen he is being trained to become a professional member of that field. He is expected to identify himself as a physicist, an historian, a sociologist, or a linguist, and a prospective member of the national association of like specialists. Many students enter graduate school because it is "the thing to do," because they have enjoyed college and found their major subject reasonably entertaining, because they had high grades and can get a scholarship, perhaps even simply because they have not chosen

[9] G. B. Blaine, Jr. and C. C. McArthur, *Emotional Problems of the Student* (New York: Appleton-Century-Crofts, 1961), esp. Chap. 5. See also the discussion of study motivation in P. Madison, *Personality Development in College* (Reading, Mass.: Addison-Wesley Publishing Company, Inc., 1969), Chap. 6.

an occupation and cannot think of anything else to do. If the choice is made on such grounds, graduate school is likely to be a painful experience. Thrust before the student is a huge preoccupation with theory, methodology, and the technical tools of the trade. If he entered with the idea of learning a little more history, for instance, covering areas for which he had not previously had time, he finds himself instead confronted by pressure to become an historian and to concentrate on the technical problems of historical research. His teachers assume that he has chosen their specialized way of life as his own. When his interest was more casual, the discipline of an academic field seemed unbearably remote and abstract.

Thus far in this chapter we have concentrated on the motivational aspects of intellectual growth. We have considered how the process of schooling is construed by the individuals passing through it, what motives become enlisted, what frustrations arise along the way. We have seen that education involves important interpersonal problems, especially those arising from the fact that schooling enters each person's life as an adult requirement rather than a personal need. For a variety of reasons at different levels of schooling, the educational environment may be experienced as unsympathetic, uncongenial, and unclearly related to the main business of personal growth.

There is, however, another significant consideration to which we now turn. If schoolwork arouses intrinsic interest it becomes a source of personal satisfaction and ceases to be simply an imposed task. This interest gives a decidedly different character to the process of being educated.

Intrinsic Interests

Interest is one of those words that has such wide and indiscriminate everyday use that it cannot readily be captured for systematic description. To say of a person that he has a wide range of interests may mean simply that he shows a diffuse scattering of activity without even settling down to the continuous concentration that is the true mark of interest. To say that one is interested in people may similarly signify an enjoyment of social interaction without much attachment to particular individuals or much sustained curiosity about human nature. These diffuse meanings can best be avoided by calling the topic of this section *intrinsic interests*. An object or activity can be said to have intrinsic interest when it is pursued not merely at someone else's behest and not merely to fill time pleasantly but to carry the activity itself continuously forward. This is most clearly seen in the kind of interest we often refer to as passionate. The passionate flower gardener, for instance, does not stop work at the first hint of fatigue, leave the beds half planted, allow weeds and pests to multiply, or let the plants wilt for lack of water or fertilizer. His interest goes beyond the momentary pleasure of gardening to include the work that is necessary to bring the garden to its fulfillment. Friends will say that he has become a slave to his garden. Intrinsic interest involves a certain enslavement to the needs of its object, but it is a willing enslavement. To a passionately interested person, being free of the yoke would mean merely a life of shallow and evanescent satisfactions. The real fun is making the garden grow.

John Dewey, in one of his influential contributions to education, described interest as being always connected with an activity that engaged a person wholeheartedly.

> Interest is not some one thing; it is a name for the fact that a course of action, an occupation, or pursuit absorbs the powers of an individual in a thorough-going way. But an activity cannot go on in a void. It requires material, subject-matter, conditions upon which to operate. On the other hand it requires certain tendencies, habits, powers on the part of the self. Wherever there is a genuine interest, there is an identification of these two things. The person acting finds his own well-being bound up with the development of an object to its own issue. If the activity goes a certain way, then a subject-matter is carried to a certain result, and a person achieves a certain satisfaction.[10]

It is not hard to see what this conception of interest implies for education. Lessons may be learned as a duty or for the sake of social rewards without even a spark of interest in them. Such motivation is vulnerable; if the duty becomes increasingly irksome or if the level of social rewards is not kept high, the student is likely to drop out, at least mentally. But the moment a child becomes involved in discovering how to make a drawing come out, how to carry on a story to its own issue, or how to make arithmetic accomplish its intended end, he finds a new motivation. Perhaps it is the geography book, with its pictures of certain familiar places and certain unfamiliar ones, that turns on a flow of interest. The child begins to wonder how the world is laid out, how one gets from one part of it to another, how other parts look and what products come from them. Wanting to know about the world, wanting to develop a cognitive map, may now prompt reading ahead in the geography book, asking questions, examining maps and globes, and looking for other books. A grumpy teacher and unfriendly classmates may no longer be fatal to satisfaction at school. Intrinsic interest is its own reward.

Interests and Personality

We arrive at the topic of intrinsic interest because of its significance in education and intellectual growth, but its importance for personality is not limited to that sphere. As a long-time investigator of the subject, Anne Roe, expresses it: "Interests, as an aspect of personality, have a place in any significant personality theory and must be subject to the same developmental principles as any other aspect of personality."[11] Already in the first grade it

---

[10] J. Dewey, *Interest and Effort in Education* (Boston: Houghton Mifflin Company, 1913), p. 65.

[11] A. Roe and M. Siegelman, *The Origin of Interests* (Washington, D.C.: APGA Inquiry Studies, no. 1, 1964), p. 4.

is possible to notice individual differences in direction and strength of interests. During childhood and early adolescence, interests may still be transient and diffuse, but in some cases they are stable and highly important, exerting an influence on the course of development and making a marked contribution to feelings of worth and happiness. "As an interest grows," wrote Gordon Allport, "it creates a lasting tensional condition that leads to congruent conduct and also acts as a silent agent for selecting and directing whatever is related to the interest."[12] Having several strong interests, or even a single area of eager absorption, gives structure to personality, provides principles of organization, and solves a good many problems about what to do with one's energies.

The import of these general statements will be clearer if we look at two sharply contrasted examples. These will be hypothetical but not untrue to life, being distilled from numerous studies of personality and vocational choice. We shall endow the first case with two strong interests that, though utterly different, have often enough dwelt side by side in a single personality. Case 1 is an absorbed scientist and also a passionate musician. As a college student he is majoring in biology and spending a good deal more than the required hours doing research in the laboratory. In music he is taking enough courses to constitute a minor, is playing the violin in the college orchestra, and is a member of a student string quartet. Both lines of interest go far back in his history. He can remember being fascinated when very small by watching tadpoles grow and turn into frogs and by observing birds through the cycle of nest building, egg laying, and the hatching and feeding of the young. He can also recall pleasurable excitement in the rhythm band at kindergarten and in learning a little later how to blow a recorder so that it would produce nice tones at intended pitches. By the time he entered junior high school he knew that he liked science, especially the science of living things, and he equally knew that he liked music. He looked forward eagerly to the opportunities afforded by the school to push forward with these interests. The question of social acceptance was not prominent in his mind; he quickly felt at home with the boys and girls who loved nature study and who played music, and he did not think about the others. Biology and music are unquestioned good things in his life, deeply absorbing and richly rewarding. He knows what he is good at and what he likes. One interest will be his vocation, the other his hobby; only later will he have to decide which is which and whether or not one life can be patterned to give scope for both.

To emphasize the contrast we shall put Case 2 in the same neighborhood and school system and make him a fellow student of Case 1 at college. Case 2's memories of early schooling are scattered and neutral. The teachers tried to interest the pupils in taking care of a cageful of hamsters; some kids seemed to think it was fun. He got a prize in drawing but didn't go on with that activity. He dimly recalls being encouraged to play the recorder, but it

[12] G. W. Allport, *Pattern and Growth in Personality* (New York: Holt, Rinehart and Winston, Inc., 1961), p. 237.

was a lot of work and what did you get out of producing all those whistling sounds? In junior high school he was not quite sure where he stood with the other kids and joined two or three clubs in order to find out. Photography proved to be interesting but he has not kept it up in college. Choosing a college major put him into painful indecision; he finally elected social science because his roommates were taking it and the requirements were not too stiff. As the end of college approaches he is again gripped by indecision. He has no idea what he is good for or what he likes. He spends a lot of time talking to his roommates and friends, trying to get their ideas about a good vocational choice. His mild and transient interests provide him with no guidance as to what might make a satisfactory adult life.[13]

Origins of Interests

Most people's experience will probably lie somewhere between the two extremes represented by these examples. It is evident, however, that the emergence of intrinsic interest can be an event of real importance for the development of personality, having consequences for social experience and for the whole pattern of one's life. What are the origins of intrinsic interest? How does it happen that for Case 1 certain experiences catch on and become deeply satisfying, while with Case 2 nothing seems really to get hold of him? On a smaller scale, how does it happen that after a school science class most of the pupils troop noisily out of the room and bolt for the cafeteria, while one or two hang around the desk asking questions about every detail of the demonstration, even to the point of exasperating the teacher, who wants his own lunch? For educators these are highly practical questions, but, as usual, the answers are far from simple. Intrinsic interest implies a relation between a person and an activity. An outsider has only a modest power to bring it about.

Reinforcement theory can make certain contributions toward understanding the origin of interests. In a simple formula, interest means doing certain things, and these responses occur frequently and strongly because they have been rewarded. We have much reason to believe that interests can be killed by ridicule, discouraged by an atmosphere of indifference and rejection, assisted by a climate of appreciation, and strengthened by praise. It is easy in theory, though it may be difficult in practice, to translate this conception into school procedures. The quality of teaching is improved if the teacher is able to create a climate of appreciation and to fan with praise whatever sparks of interest may appear.

These social reinforcements, however, are extrinsic to the activity itself. Giving praise and prizes may encourage children to do certain things, but extrinsic reinforcement is seriously incomplete as an explanation of interest. Every teacher has the experience of paying out the coin of praise without

---

[13] A similar if less dramatic contrast is described in R. W. White, *Lives in Progress*, 2d ed. (New York: Holt, Rinehart and Winston, Inc., 1966), Chap. 2 ("Hartley Hale, Physician and Scientist") and Chap. 5 ("Joseph Kidd, Business Man"); see also the discussion on pp. 390–396.

eliciting any trace of interest. Furthermore, the life histories of distinguished artists and writers, and even sometimes of scientists, repeatedly testify that these people have pursued their talents and developed their gifts in spite of a virtually solid wall of social opposition. Parents, teachers, and peers are more likely to try to stamp out, rather than reward, interests that take a person away from social interaction. If reinforcement is to be used as an explanation of intrinsic interest it must include the idea of intrinsic reward, a satisfaction that is obtained from the activity itself as an expression of one's powers and sensitivities. Extrinsic rewards are not powerless, but they are not sufficient to account for the seemingly self-evident positive value that certain forms of activity have for certain people.

How are we to conceive of intrinsic interest? It can be viewed in different ways, but two of the most pertinent concepts are the related ones of *curiosity* and *competence*. "Curiosity," says Bruner, "is almost a prototype of the intrinsic motive."

> Our attention is attracted to something that is unclear, unfinished, or uncertain. We sustain our attention until the matter in hand becomes clear, finished, or certain. The achievement of clarity or merely the search for it is what satisfies. We would think it preposterous if somebody sought to reward us with praise or profit for having satisfied our curiosity. However pleasant such external reward might be, and however much we might come to depend upon it, the external reward is something added. What activates and satisfies curiosity is something inherent in the cycle of activity by which we express curiosity.[14]

There may be wide individual differences in the force of this urge to achieve cognitive clarity, and its enlistment in schoolwork may be far from equally easy for all pupils, but curiosity is a deeply rooted, survival-relevant tendency some of which must be present in everyone.

The concept of competence also has something to do with intrinsic interest. In Dewey's view, interest meant an identification between a certain material or subject matter that allows for development and certain powers in the self that promote this development. The exercise of powers to produce effects is precisely the thing that yields feelings of efficacy and that builds a sense of competence. It is possible that interest takes hold with the discovery that one is capable of doing something with gratifying results. One is able, for instance, to elicit lovely sounds with one finger on the piano, produce intriguing lines and spots of color on a piece of paper, or make tall constructions with blocks. The desire to feel competent certainly makes a contribution to intrinsic interest; it is difficult to sustain interest in things about which we are helpless. Competence is especially useful in understanding the deepening of an interest when it is pursued over the course of time. A person builds up skill, knowledge, and judgment about the subject of his interest, an accumu-

---

[14] J. S. Bruner, *Toward a Theory of Instruction* (Cambridge, Mass.: The Belknap Press of Harvard University Press, 1966), pp. 114–115.

lated expertness that enables him to solve new problems and advise and teach other people.

Curiosity and competence are grounds for interest over which educators have indirect control. They can, in the first place, avoid killing these motives by a didactic attitude that presents all problems along with ready-made solutions and that invites passive learning. They can, in the second place, aim to make the pupils' experience as real, vivid, and exciting as possible. But the crux of the matter is the activity that takes place in the pupil. Sometimes a teacher may satisfy a child's curiosity simply by giving him information, but the process is far more rewarding if the child is able, as Bruner expresses it, "to put things together for himself, to be his own discoverer."[15] In similar fashion the child can feel efficacious and add to his sense of competence only to the extent that he initiates action and experiences its consequences. To teach by exposition is easier than to teach by activation, but it is far less effective in creating intrinsic interest.

Although these principles are helpful in understanding the origins of interests, they do not do full justice to the more passionate and consuming interests that exert such a powerful steering influence in certain lives. Psychoanalytic theory deals with these preemptive interests by relating them to early childhood experiences involving vital needs. A well-known hypothesis about scientific curiosity, for instance, makes it a continuation of the child's burning and very likely thwarted eagerness to find out about such phenomena as sexual anatomy, childbirth, and sexual intercourse. Similarly, an interest in painting could be derived from the young child's naughty pleasure in smearing feces, a socialized ("sublimated") way of continuing to enjoy that satisfaction when its original form was renounced. In retrospect it appears that Freud overemphasized the force of infantile sexuality and bodily preoccupations, but if the theory is loosened to include a wider range of childhood problems it may well contribute to understanding intrinsic interests. Lasting adult interests may be laid down by chronic happenings in the family circle. Thus it could be that a lawyer's preference for defending clients whose rights had been violated by people in power might have its roots in the injustices he had long suffered as the less favored of two children. Amplified in this way, the hypothesis can be useful that at least some forms of intrinsic interest are continuations, either direct or symbolic, of preoccupying problems of early life.

Yet it seems that all these explanations fall short with respect to certain types of interest. At a concert for children a large part of the audience squirms in the seats, turns around to look and whisper, and is with difficulty restrained from bolting up the aisle, whereas a certain number sit perfectly still, enthralled as if they were receiving a message from heaven. Among the latter would have been Mozart, one of the best authenticated of infant prodigies, and no doubt also the youthful Handel, who was discovered at the

---

[15] J. S. Bruner, *On Knowing: Essays for the Left Hand* (Cambridge, Mass: The Belknap Press of Harvard University Press, 1962), p. 82.

harpsichord in the middle of the night by an irate father who thought he had made the child understand that musicians were nothing but street beggars. Special sensitivities may have to be involved for musical and other artistic interests and perhaps, as we shall presently see, for a large number of individual differences in the use of mind. There are many sides to interest. Much as we would like a simple theory, the phenomena seem resistant to such marshalling.

Changing Conceptions of Intellectual Growth

For the first half of this century the study of intellectual growth was almost completely dominated by intelligence testing. The history of this "movement," as it can quite properly be called, illustrates at once the importance of measurement in advancing our understanding of any given topic and the obstacles created by measurement to taking fresh views of the problem. Intelligence tests have made it possible to study the distribution of a certain kind of ability over wide ranges of the population. They have made it possible to measure by means of the *intelligence quotient* (I.Q.) something that remains relatively stable from year to year. On this basis scholastic achievement could be predicted and children sorted into programs intended to suit their ability, thus adapting educational requirements more nearly to individual differences of aptitude. Furthermore, the analysis of different types of performance called for by intelligence tests has shed light on the components that enter into intellectual operations and promoted research pointing toward qualitative individual differences in the use of mind. All this belongs on the credit side of the ledger, but there are entries also on the debit side. The stability of the I.Q., even though it was something of an artifact, encouraged the idea that intelligence was a fixed thing, a genetic endowment not subject to change, which flowered from within according to its natural strength. Such an interpretation drew attention away from the manner in which intellectual development took place. It did not promote inquiry into how a child learns from year to year to pass more difficult tests. It did not encourage a search for the educational methods and environmental supports that might best contribute to this development, nor did it help to see intelligence in relation to other aspects of personality. Small wonder that school systems, ever pressed for shortcuts, entered the I.Q. on a pupil's record as a final statement of his potential and of his fate.[16]

Intelligence and Experience

There is, of course, a great deal of evidence that individual differences in mental ability have biological roots. Various forms of mental retardation are associated with biochemical abnormalities and with structural peculiari-

---

[16] The history of intelligence testing is conveniently traced in J. McV. Hunt, *Intelligence and Experience* (New York: The Ronald Press Company, 1961), Chaps. 2, 3.

ties of skull and brain tissue. Studies of family lines, though usually not perfect, strongly suggest that intellectual capacity tends to run in families. Studies of twins reared together and apart provide some evidence for unusual similarity even though those reared together are more similar than those reared apart. But it is now widely recognized that we have no direct way of measuring such a thing as innate potential, that intelligence is always judged through performances of some kind, and that performances are never free from the influence of past experience, hence of the environment in which learning took place. Consistently with the conception of the person as a system partly open to the environment, the development of intelligent behavior has to be seen as a transaction between the individual and his surroundings. Intelligence does not just emerge from the personal system; it requires input, stimulation, material from the environment on which to work. According to Hebb, who bases his conclusions on neurological considerations, on animal studies, and on research on human sensory deprivation, adaptive behavior depends heavily on sensory stimulation and the internal assembling of perceptual patterns through experience.[17] According to Piaget, whose source of information is the closely observed behavior of children, intellectual growth requires constant "aliment" in the form of sensory input and feedback on the consequences of action.[18] According to Hunt, the essence of intelligence is the processing of information, and there must be a varied supply of information if good processing strategies are to develop.[19] These ways of thinking have drawn attention back to the environment of learning and to the actual sequences of intellectual growth.

One consequence of the new outlook is a more optimistic approach to educational handicaps. Children from economically disadvantaged areas are now seen as doing poorly in school not because they are inherently stupid but because they have lacked mental stimulation, a handicap that can perhaps be prevented by early intervention. Optimism has likewise increased with respect to improving educational methods so as to provide a maximum challenge to intellectual growth. It is worth mentioning, however, that these hopeful and benign ideas have already begun to suffer commercial exploitation directed at ambitious, competitive parents who want their children to climb to the top. Books are being advertised which explain how to give your child a superior mind, how to turn him into a classroom wizard, how to help him streak ahead in mathematics, how to run up a vocabulary that would stump most college students, how by a few minutes of instruction at home each day he can be made to shine so brightly that the teacher will telephone to ask what has happened. There are legitimate ways in which parents can help children,

[17] D. O. Hebb, *The Organization of Behavior* (New York: John Wiley & Sons, Inc., 1949), is the original milestone in this way of thinking; see also D. W. Fiske and S. A. Maddi, eds., *The Functions of Varied Experience* (Homewood, Ill.: The Dorsey Press, 1961), especially with reference to sensory deprivation.

[18] J. Piaget, *The Psychology of Intelligence*, trans. M. Piercy and D. E. Berlyne (London: Routledge & Kegan Paul, Ltd., 1947).

[19] Hunt, *Intelligence and Experience*, Chap. 4.

but this kind of anxious pressure and intensive coaching runs the danger of re-creating in the child his parents' driven competitiveness. Accenting winning prizes and surpassing others reduces the possibility that the student will find intrinsic interest in schoolwork, and if the overcoached student ever tires of the race he may become a spectacular case of underachievement or sophomore slump.

Developmental Sequences

The new outlook on intelligence encourages a careful study of the course of intellectual development. As previously mentioned, the lead in this undertaking was long held by Piaget, who described in much detail the stages and sequences of intellectual growth from the earliest years onward. Relevant at this point in our study of personality is the evolution in mental outlook that he describes as taking place approximately at the onset of adolescence.[20] Piaget rejects the idea that the change can be attributed to the physical transformations of puberty or that it results directly from the taking of adult roles. There is autonomous growth in thinking, following a sequence of its own, which leads to increased interest in generalization and abstraction. Children are not disposed to build speculative systems or to extend their thinking much beyond concrete realities. The adolescent begins to look beyond the present, contemplate a range of possibilities, and see things in terms of larger principles.[21] An incident that would have angered him a year or two ago simply because it involved unfairness now angers him because it violates principles of social justice and discloses a trend toward oppressive lawlessness. As this power develops, cognition of the world enlarges rapidly, and his wider perspective opens to him, as Hunt puts it, "the role of social reformer." The adolescent begins to see that "the way the world is run is only one out of a great variety of possible ways. He takes delight in conceiving of alternative ways that might be better."[22]

Attaining this power to generalize, think hypothetically, and formulate abstract principles is only the beginning of a further progression. The first stabs at social philosophy owe much to ideas already prevailing in the environment. Even if the newly fledged social thinker takes a rebellious position he will at first fortify himself largely with borrowed ideas. Studies of intellectual growth during the four years of college suggest that the entering student, no longer an early adolescent, is often still far from being an independent thinker. Nevitt Sanford, who made intensive studies of Vassar students during the mid-1950s, noticed in the intellectual outlook of freshmen of that period a certain rigidity and intolerance that he likened to "authoritarianism of a mild sort," and it is this that the course of college education is

---

[20] B. Inhelder and J. Piaget, *The Growth of Logical Thinking from Childhood to Adolescence*, trans. A. Parsons and S. Milgram (New York: Basic Books, Inc., 1958).

[21] *Ibid.*, pp. 339–340.

[22] Hunt, *Intelligence and Experience*, pp. 230–231.

likely to shake in a way that will be "eye-opening and disillusioning—and broadening and maturing."[23]

William Perry has studied the growth sequence during college with Harvard students during the early 1960s. Perry and his associates faced squarely the question that if you want to study how people think you have to make them think, creating conditions favorable for serious, concerned reflection. This requirement ruled out the questionnaire, which, useful as it may be for gathering certain types of information, blocks discriminating thought by providing precast answers with no opportunity to indicate how the question ought to be phrased and the reply qualified. Subjects were asked during the course of each of their college years to sit down with the interviewer and his tape recorder and to talk over informally what they had been thinking about and how things were going in their lives. Indispensable for the success of this method was the interviewer's interest, which caused him to become sympathetically absorbed in what the subject was trying to say. The resulting interviews disclosed a progression that could be agreed upon by independent judges reading the tape recordings.[24]

As Perry describes it, the prevailing position during the freshman year is an *absolute* one, characterized by a basic conception that things are good or bad, right or wrong, true or untrue, and that there is a correct answer to every question. If a lecturer tells about three theories on a given topic the student looks for the right one, the one that he is supposed to learn. "When I came here," said one student in retrospect, "I didn't think any question could have more than one answer." Another reported that at the first lecture he attended, "I believed everything he said, because he was a professor." Fortunately this second student listened to more sophisticated peers who took professional wisdom less for granted. "And I began to—ah—realize," he said, a hopeful sign that he was embarking on what Perry describes as "a longer and more complex journey than he could foresee." The absolute position permits intolerant stereotypes, such as that all poor people are lazy, but it includes also such benignly oriented generalizations as that love conquers all or that debate and compromise will solve all political disagreements. Instruction can be most helpful at this point if it emphasizes specific conditions, calls to mind negotiations that failed and led to strife, asks what the record shows about love conquering alcoholism or delinquency, urges consideration of the particular circumstances under which events take place.

The next stage of the journey is a position of *relativity*. Different people have different values that seem right and true to them; history and anthropology are especially eloquent on the side of this point of view. The students in Perry's study reported that they had sometimes resisted taking this disconcerting step, believing that their teachers put things in this light

---

[23] N. Sanford, *The American College* (New York: John Wiley & Sons, Inc., 1962), pp. 253–261.

[24] W. G. Perry, Jr., *Forms of Intellectual and Ethical Development during the College Years* (New York: Holt, Rinehart and Winston, Inc., 1970).

merely to make them use their own minds in discovering the right answers. But often they welcomed relativity because it helped them criticize and break away from constraining parental values. The uninhibited sexual life of Samoa could serve as a useful image in challenging American middle-class sexual constraints, and the existence of communistic societies made it easier to crack the folklore of American capitalism. A position of complete relativity, however, can create such a wide-open mind that nothing appears better than anything else. The student who listens to three theories on a given topic may now be inclined to write down all three and see each as valid from someone's point of view. Instruction is most helpful at this point if it suggests decision making, asking the student to try to resolve the controversy, consider the weight of evidence, and arrive at an opinion of his own.

The final stage involves *commitment*. "The assumption is established," writes Perry, "that man's knowing and valuing are relative in time and circumstance, and that in such a world the individual is faced with the responsibility for choice and affirmation in his life." College life itself offers more paths than any one person can take. One student, recognizing that "every one of them is a good thing in its own way," saw at the same time that it was impossible to participate in everything. "You kind of focus on the type of career you want, and when you think about that, then if you're going to work toward it, it has its own imperatives. It means that you have to drop certain things and focus more on others." Another student, who had feared that college work might be isolated from the rest of his life, became seriously interested in a girl with whom he talked over basic values and philosophies. "I was frankly amazed," he said, "that I had such firm convictions on many things and was actually able to back up a lot of them with what I consider logical reasoning and sensibility." College education, he concluded, had really become a part of his life: "It really is working."[25] Perry warns against interpreting this kind of thing as a regressive return to the earlier absolute position. Such regressions can occur, but the interviews that exhibit the stage of commitment make it plain that the affirmation of beliefs and the making of decisions is now at a new level. Relativity is recognized, the importance of circumstances is understood, but the student does not shrink from using his own mental powers to decide how he personally stands.

In evaluating the studies of the college years by Sanford and by Perry it is important to keep in mind place, time, and the fact that one is dealing with composite portraits. It is possible that some individuals will have reached the committed stage by the time they enter college and that some will graduate still in the absolute or relative positions. Making due allowance, however, for individual differences, for the specialized samples, and for the time at which the studies were made, there is a residue of evidence for a true intellectual progression from earlier to later stages. Further indication that

[25] Quotations are from Perry, *Forms of Intellectual and Ethical Development during the College Years*, pp. 85, 86, 92, 210, 211.

this occurs is found in a study that compares high school graduates who did and did not go on to college.[26] Continuing to college appeared to be related to continuing growth in flexible, tolerant, open-minded attitudes and in intellectual receptivity. During the same time those who did not attend college became if anything less flexible, less curious, and less interested in new experience.

Individual Differences in the Use of Mind

When due allowance is made for general intelligence, opportunity, environmental support, and type of training, we are still left with the impression that there is more to the story of individual difference in the ways in which we use our minds. This conviction is strongest when observation is directed at people whose opportunities for intellectual growth have been abundant and whose occupations depend upon using their minds to the utmost. When mental development has gone on unimpeded and reached distinctive heights, does a universal way of perceiving, of processing information, and of reasoning emerge that can be accepted as the perfect pattern? Evidently this is not at all what happens. When closely examined, the human minds that seem most fully developed reveal an extraordinary range of individual differences. So great are those differences that mutual understanding can be dangerously impaired. C. P. Snow, a scientist and novelist who felt as if he were crossing an ocean when he passed from one group of colleagues to the other, warned us of the perils to civilization if these "two cultures" diverge further to the point of being wholly out of communication.[27]

Qualitative Differences in Measured Intelligence

As a first line of inquiry into this problem we can ask what qualitative dimensions have made their appearance in the extensive research on intelligence testing. Emphasis on a general intelligence score and an I.Q. has not prevented the study of individual test items to see which items are repeatedly intercorrelated. Using for this purpose the mathematical technique of factor analysis, Thurstone in a historically important study distinguished six factors that "behaved as functional units" and could therefore be tentatively identified as components of overall intelligence.[28] Thurstone's *primary mental abilities* have stood up fairly well in subsequent research, appearing again and again in the factorial analysis of test batteries; the results obtained by

[26] J. W. Trent and L. L. Medsker, *Beyond High School: A Psychosocial Study of 10,000 High School Graduates* (San Francisco: Jossey-Bass, Inc., 1968).

[27] C. P. Snow, *The Two Cultures and the Scientific Revolution* (London: Cambridge University Press, 1959).

[28] L. L. Thurstone, *Primary Mental Abilities* (Chicago: University of Chicago Press, 1938).

other workers differ more in detail than in main outline. These are the factors described by Thurstone:

V   (Verbal Comprehension), exhibited most simply in recognizing the meanings of words in a vocabulary test

W   (Word Fluency), shown in the production of words, as in anagrams or in simply thinking of as many words as possible

S   (Spatial), revealed most clearly in performance tests involving form boards, picture puzzles, and fitting together oddly shaped blocks

N   (Number), displayed in the arithmetic problems included in most tests of intelligence

M   (Memory), shown when previous information or a previous set of instructions have to be kept in mind

I   (Induction), indicated in reasoning tests where a principle of procedure must be discovered

The descriptions, of course, come from simple tasks such as appear even at lower levels of intelligence scales, but it is not hard to imagine how they might contribute to adult uses of mind. The spatial factor seems especially applicable to engineering and architecture, the induction factor to philosophical and scientific endeavors. College students know that scores on scholastic aptitude tests are broken down into a verbal factor (Factors V and W) and a quantitative or mathematical factor (Factor N). Nothing could be clearer than the wide differences between these two aspects of aptitude in the college population. High overall aptitude is consistent with large discrepancies between verbal and quantitative scores.

Using a different method, Vigotsky called attention to contrasting methods of problem solving, which have since been named *conceptual* and *perceptual*. In the test devised by Vigotsky the subject is given a variety of small blocks and asked to group them into four consistent categories. It is soon evident that the more obvious principles do not apply; there are more than four colors, sizes, and shapes. The correct solution is complex enough so that college students typically arrive at it only after a good deal of trial and error and a certain amount of prompting by the examiner. The subject who approaches this problem *perceptually* moves the blocks around freely, without any well-defined idea. The properties of the blocks are constantly invited to declare themselves, and the correct grouping is perceived rather than reasoned out. The *conceptual* approach involves less actual movement of the blocks and more mental experimenting. The subject forms the hypothesis that the principle might be color plus shape; only then does he start to arrange the blocks to confirm or disconfirm the hypothesis. Although the conceptual approach seems to imply a more active mastering of the problem, in the Vigotsky test it is not any more effective than the perceptual mode; in this particular task, seeing the solution is as likely to work as thinking it. The current prestige of science and technology has made us sharply aware of the virtues of explicitly verbalized hypotheses and their testing. In many situations, however, a perceptual approach is both more suitable and more accurate. To keep seeing and hearing what is happening in a group discussion or a social gathering is more effective than the cumbersome process of forming hypotheses about the different participants, hypotheses that there is no time or means to test.[29]

Sex Differences

Most tests of general intelligence have been standardized in such a way as to eliminate sex differences, but certain average differences emerge with respect to the component variables. Girls make a faster start than boys in verbal ability and continue throughout school to do better on tests of grammar, spelling, and word fluency. There seem to be no sex differences in the realm of number ability until high school, when boys move ahead of girls in arithmetical reasoning, a difference that persists in adult years. Boys surpass girls much earlier on spatial tasks and maintain this advantage into adulthood. With respect to "analytic ability," which possibly includes the induction factor and the conceptual approach, boys tend to make a better showing. The findings on creativity, the tests for which will be taken up in the next section, are not conclusive. It seems clear that at school girls get better grades than boys, but men are more likely than women to make notable intellectual achievements.[30]

In case male readers think they have won this round, we should point out that the differences, statistically significant with large numbers of subjects but rather small in net amount, do not call for awarding a particularly handsome prize. There is tremendous overlap in scores. Men make a bad mistake if they assume that their numerical, spatial, and analytic abilities are superior to those of all the women they meet. Women make a similar error if they suppose that verbal, perceptual, and intuitive skills are always feebler in men. The reasons for such sex differences as the tests have established are not easy to disentangle, as we saw in the last chapter. That there might be genetic differences is not out of the question. In view, however, of the early and continuing differences in the way boys and girls are treated—in view of the developmental importance of sex role learning and sex typing—there is reason to believe that training has a good deal to do with it. Even a general expectation that boys will be more assertive and girls more dependent might have effects on manner of intellectual functioning. Specific preconceptions, such as that girls will be more literary and artistic, boys more scientific and technical, are certainly capable of creating a push in those directions.

[29] The Vigotsky test and its uses are fully described by E. Hanfmann and J. Kasanin, "Conceptual Thinking in Schizophrenia," *Nervous and Mental Disease Monographs*, no. 67 (1942).

[30] The literature on sex differences in intellectual functioning is evaluated in a chapter, and summarized in an appendix, in E. E. Maccoby, ed., *The Development of Sex Differences* (Stanford, Calif.: Stanford University Press, 1966), pp. 25–55 and 323–351.

Individual Patterns

Because intelligence has been considered measurable, there has been little effort to make systematic descriptive studies of the growth and qualities of individual minds. Such evidence as we have, however, points to wide differences of pattern in the way mind is used. Occasionally the writer of an autobiography considers his intellectual style worthy of communication, and occasionally shrewd observations have been written down about other people's intellectual peculiarities.

A remarkable field study of his own mind was made by H. G. Wells, author of an influential popular book, *The Outline of History* (1920), as well as novels and early works of science fiction well known in their day. In a book called *Experiment in Autobiography*, Wells introduced his brain as the hero of his life story. Although in his school years he had been precocious, his reflections on the quality of his brain were not flattering. He found it "not a particularly good one," a "poorish instrument," in comparison with those of numerous great people he had met. Its poor quality was displayed in faulty registering of experience, rapid loss of detail, and poor recall. Wells described himself as bad at numbers, cards, chess, new languages, and finding his way around London, all of which called for an alert clear-mindedness that was foreign to him. He felt in himself a lack of "excitable 'Go'." "There is a faint element of inattention in all I do. . . . I am rarely vivid to myself. . . . I am just a little slack, not wholly and continuously interested, prone to be indolent and cold-hearted . . . readily bored." From all this he deduced that his brain must be of "a loose, rather inferior texture," leading to "inexact reception, bad storage and uncertain accessibility."

This inadequate brain, however, was not without assets. Wells found comfortable congeniality in algebra, trigonometry, and drawing. "It seems probable to me," he wrote, "that this relative readiness to grasp form and relation indicates that the general shape and arrangement of my brain is better than the quality of its cells, fibres, and blood vessels. I have a quick sense of form and proportion; I have a brain good for outlines. Most of my story will carry out that suggestion." Wells dramatized his mental style by telling of a conversation with Joseph Conrad as they sat looking out over the sea. Conrad asked Wells how he would "describe how that boat out there sat or rode or danced or quivered on the water." Wells answered that he would describe it in the commonest phrase unless he wanted it to be important, that is, related to a story or thesis which might further be linked up "with my philosophy and my world outlook." Conrad's sensitive perception was outraged that a boat should be seen just as a boat. "He wanted to see it with a definite vividness of his own." Of people who thus feel and hear and see with vivid color and emotionality, Wells wrote:

> Their abundant, luminous impressions were vastly more difficult to subdue to a disciplined and coordinating relationship; thus they tended to lapse into arbitrary, inconsistent, and dramatized ways of thinking and living.

. . . The very coldness and flatness of my perception gave me a readier apprehension of relationships. . . . I was not dealing with glowing impressions. . . . My mind became a mind systematically unified because of a relative defect in brightness of response.[31]

Wells' attribution of his mental qualities to the shape and quality of his brain tissue can be regarded as merely whimsical, but there is enduring value in his delineation of his own preferred pattern of intellectual functioning. His most important work, *The Outline of History*, is written with a good deal of vividness as histories go, and exhibits a quietly persistent dedication to the principle of world government, but its true genius lies in having organized the whole of human history into a coherent story based upon central themes of social development.[32] Scarcely a page escaped the criticism of specialists who complained bitterly about poor registration and loss of detail, but there was wide acclaim for the author's quite exceptional grasp of form and relation.

Very different is Jean Jacques Rousseau's description of the tempestuous workings of his mind. Rousseau's impressions were uncommonly luminous and vivid, his feelings exceptionally strong. Throughout his *Confessions* he describes transports of exhilaration, joy, and love as well as miseries of humiliation and depression, and his story is conspicuous for arbitrary, inconsistent, and dramatized ways of thinking and living. Wells described himself as easy to educate; Rousseau was almost impossible to educate. So great was Rousseau's resistance to disciplined mental activity that he could not listen to a teacher's exposition, remain in a school, or even stay in a promising job that entailed steady application. "My understanding," he wrote, "must take its own time, and cannot submit to that of another." When he eventually decided to educate himself he had to discover his own method. He could read serious works with understanding and interest only a few pages at a time. He found it necessary to keep shifting from one topic to another and to give his power of attention frequent rests by wandering in the garden and in the woods. In view of this spotty method it is surprising that his works on social and political philosophy, so tremendously influential on the French and American Revolutions and for long thereafter, exhibit such a grasp of the relevant problems and proceed in such logical steps. But this order, Rousseau explained, was achieved with incredible difficulty. "Feeling takes possession of my soul more rapidly than a flash of lightning," he wrote; the flash was more blinding than illuminating and the resulting agitation too great to permit any sensible arrangement of ideas.

Hence comes the extreme difficulty which I find in writing. My manuscripts, scratched, smeared, muddled and almost illegible, bear witness

[31] H. G. Wells, *Experiment in Autobiography* (New York: The Macmillan Company, 1934); quotations from pp. 13–20, 528–532.

[32] H. G. Wells, *The Outline of History* (New York: The Macmillan Company, 1920).

to the trouble they have cost me. There is not one of them which I have not been obliged to copy four or five times before I could give it to the printer. I have never been able to produce anything, pen in hand, in front of my table and paper; it is during a walk, in the midst of rocks and forests, at night in my bed while lying awake, that I write in my brain; one may judge how slowly, especially in the case of a man utterly without verbal memory and who has never been able to learn six lines by heart in his life. Many of my periods have been turned and turned again five or six nights in my head before they were fit to be set down on paper.[33]

It is noteworthy that Rousseau, like Wells, complains so much about his mind. The same is true of Freud, who with respect to memory and method of writing provides an extreme contrast to Rousseau. Freud, whose career started in physiological research, disparaged his mind roundly for its stumbling incapacity with mathematical problems and cold logic. Many people would settle gratefully for Rousseau's or Freud's or even Wells' mind, but the original owners of these minds seemed often to find them frustrating. Freud's mind, as disclosed by his biographer Ernest Jones, was characterized by extraordinary powers of memory and organization. At an early congress of psychoanalysts he astonished his colleagues by giving a four-hour case report, full of well-arranged incident and detail and building logically to a brilliant interpretation, without a single note in front of him. In like fashion he delivered a series of lectures, writing them out afterwards with almost perfect memory, which became his most widely read book, *A General Introduction to Psychoanalysis*.[34] Jones reports that as far as is known Freud's scientific papers were written in single drafts that were ready for the printer with few changes. This bespeaks the same capacity for the internal organization of ideas that showed in his noteless lectures.[35]

The value of case studies of the type sketched here is that they rest on extended uses of mind rather than on the short isolated tasks offered by intelligence tests. They reflect how intellect is used not in compliance with a relatively meaningless imposed task but in the service of a person's strong interests. The variables revealed under such circumstances may well be different from those disclosed by the factor analysis of tests. Thurstone's list of primary mental abilities includes a variable of memory, but there is nothing to suggest Wells' variable of vividness and certainly no hint of the organizational patterns in which Wells, Rousseau, and Freud so conspicuously differed. Studies of the individual uses of mind are needed to amplify the restricted picture of intellectual functioning that comes from tests.

[33] J. J. Rousseau, *The Confessions of Jean Jacques Rousseau* (1768) (New York: The Modern Library, p. 117). Rousseau's chief political and social writings are *Discourse on the Sciences and Arts* (1749), *The Origin of Inequality* (1755), and *The Social Contract* (1762).

[34] S. Freud, *A General Introduction to Psychoanalysis* (1917), trans. J. Riviere (New York: Permabooks, 1953).

[35] E. Jones, *The Life and Work of Sigmund Freud*, Vol. 2 (New York: Basic Books, Inc., 1955), Chap. 15.

Relation to Nonintellectual Traits

Little is known about the origins of qualitative differences in the uses of mind. The hypothesis could be offered that such differences are entirely due to learning: intelligence comes to be employed in those ways that have been most importantly rewarded during the course of life. This does not seem plausible, however, in view of what we know about the rewarding of mental performance at home and in school. Recalling Munroe's two types of college student, we could suppose that in most schools there would be clear rewards for the conscientious or rigid type but only disapprobation for the temperamental or scattered type, yet the latter does not fade out. More believable would be an hypothesis that made room for internal rewards. The conscientious student could then be seen as one who stood in strong need of external rewards—the approbation of teachers—whereas the scattered student was more influenced by the solving of internal conflicts through intellectual productions. For this reason it is always important to determine the needs that are being satisfied in intellectual work, including deference, affiliation, autonomy, competition, and aggression, all of which bear on one's relation to other people. The uses of mind cannot be separated from the rest of a person's strivings.

The idea of internal reward, however, goes even deeper. It includes the self-rewarding properties of those forms of action and experience that come to us most easily, that seem most natural and congenial, that go with the grain, not against it. If this is so, we should expect to find relations between intellectual variables and the more broadly conceived *styles of functioning* described in an earlier chapter, styles like activity level, impulsion-deliberation, and sensitivity.[36] Conceptual problem solving, to take an instance, suggests a higher activity level than perceptual problem solving, even though it may not work any better. Is it not probable that if Rousseau, Conrad, Wells, and Freud had been studied as babies they would already have exhibited differences not hard to predict in sensitivity, impulsiveness, and distractibility-persistence? These variables, it will be recalled, were defined by observable features of infant behavior at a time of life when no one could separate intellectual from other behavioral qualities. This would suggest—and it remains a suggestion in the absence of anything like definitive research—that individual differences in the use of mind are deeply built into our constitutional makeup. Possibly Wells' whimsy about his brain, translated into current sophisticated biochemical and neurological concepts, points to certain real and vital roots of intellectual individuality.

Creativity as an Object of Study

Although it is not possible to perceive the whole relation between use of mind and the rest of personality by any method short of extensive individual study, the creative aspect of intelligence has proved to be not altogether

[36] See above, Chap. 7, pp. 171–180.

resistant to measurement. By 1940 the limitations of the ordinary intelligence tests were widely recognized. As predictors of scholastic performance their place seemed secure, but it was not certain that they spoke with equal relevance to the wider uses of intelligence. During World War II the need to select men for unusual and difficult assignments, which often called for imagination and novel improvisations, strengthened the discontent with I.Q. tests and speeded the effort to find ways of measuring these creative qualities. In the subsequent years research has moved steadily forward in finding measures of creativity, testing large numbers of people, and establishing connections between mental originality and other aspects of personal functioning.

Is it not presumptuous to try to capture human creativity with the cumbersome tools of psychological measurement? Does it not suggest looking for a pat formula, an easy technical explanation for the least explicable feature of living beings? It would indeed be both presumptuous and stupid to suppose that short artificial tests of creativity unlocked the secrets of great intellectual achievement or pointed the way to manufacturing future Shakespeares, Beethovens, and Einsteins. This makes it incumbent to stick closely to what is actually done in studies of creativity and to hold interpretation within these limits.

The creativity that can be measured is a quality that shows itself in short mental performances. It can best be described by such words as "fresh, novel, unusual, ingenious, divergent, clever, and apt," to quote from Frank Barron's review of the subject.[37] Tests capable of eliciting such a quality must be rather unstructured, providing freedom of response. When such tests are given to groups of people, they at once disclose wide individual differences. This quality makes it possible to look for correlations between creativity as tested and other variables of personality. It is also possible to find out, by testing people who have already shown themselves conspicuously creative in their life work, whether or not the originality shown in the tests is significantly correlated with creativity in this larger sphere. This modest undertaking has had interesting results that are not without practical application.

Tests of creativity have to be open-ended, permitting a wide range of responses. They can be described as asking for *possible* answers to a broad question rather than the *correct* answer to a precise question. The person being tested may be asked, for instance, to list six uses to which each of several common objects, like bricks or paper clips, can be put (Unusual Uses Test), or to imagine some dramatic change of circumstances, as that all glass is suddenly shattered, and to describe the ensuing consequences (Consequences Test). He may be asked to work on verbal puzzles (e.g., Anagrams), to think up possible titles for given story plots (Plot Titles Test), to make up stories of his own (Thematic Apperception Test), or to tell what he perceives in inkblot shapes (Rorschach Test).[38] There is plenty of room in these

---

[37] F. Barron, "The Psychology of Creativity," in *New Directions in Psychology*, Vol. II (New York: Holt, Rinehart and Winston, Inc., 1965), pp. 1–134.

[38] F. Barron, *Creativity and Psychological Health* (Princeton, N.J.: D. Van Nostrand Company, Inc., 1963), esp. pp. 202–207.

tests for replies that are novel, ingenious, and apt. At the same time it is possible to find ways in the scoring system to exclude the frivolous or absurd. In the Rorschach Test, for instance, an interpretation that is given by fewer than one person out of a hundred is scored O (original), but it is further qualified as O-plus or O-minus depending upon whether or not the examiner, and preferably other judges as well, consider it appropriate now that it is called to attention. Creative replies are thus defined not simply as novel but as aptly novel.

At first glance it might appear that these tests should not be considered separate from general intelligence tests. Is creativity more than an aspect of intelligence? Several studies have shown that there is a correlation of the order of .3 or .4 between intelligence tests and tests of creativity, taking the population as a whole.[39] But this is not true in all circumstances. In a number of studies in which eminent scientists, mathematicians, writers, architects, and other gifted people served as subjects, there was no correlation between intelligence measures and measures of creativity. At this already high level of intelligence, originality acts as if it were an independent dimension. Furthermore, within more average ranges the correlation between creativity as tested and intelligence as tested shrinks from .3 or .4 to a mere .1 by making a change in the way the tests of creativity are given. Wallach and Kogan, arguing that freedom of mental associations is the hallmark of creativity, tested fifth graders individually, without haste or time limits, in the spirit of playing a game for fun. Group testing in a classroom with time limits, no matter how open-ended the tasks, sets an atmosphere of competition and pressure. When these are eliminated as well as possible in favor of playful freedom, creativity again acts as if it were virtually independent of what is measured by intelligence tests.[40] This makes it possible to distinguish individuals whose creativity is greater than their intelligence, others whose intelligence is superior to their creativity. There are also, of course, those who are equally high on both and those who are equally low.

Enough research has been done with people who score well on tests of creativity, or who exhibit creativity in their professional lives, to permit the drawing of a composite portrait. Dellas and Gaier, following a thorough review of the literature, reach the conclusion that "despite differences in age, cultural background, area of operation or eminence, a particular constellation of psychological traits emerges consistently in the creative individual, and forms a recognizable schema of the creative personality."[41] The cognitive aspect of creativity includes the central qualities of ability to produce unusual and appropriate ideas and ability to put together ideas that are remote or

[39] J. P. Guilford, *The Nature of Human Intelligence* (New York: McGraw-Hill, Inc., 1967).

[40] M. A. Wallach and N. Kogan, *Modes of Thinking in Young Children: A Study of the Creativity-Intelligence Distinction* (New York: Holt, Rinehart and Winston, Inc., 1965).

[41] M. Dellas and E. L. Gaier, "Identification of Creativity: The Individual," *Psychological Bulletin,* **73** (1970), 55–73.

disparate. These qualities are supported by keenness of observation and effectiveness of retention, but these are less peculiar to creativity. Characteristic further of the original person is "relative lack of self-defensiveness," an absence of impulse control through repression, and an openness to experience that makes it possible to deal flexibly with complex, inchoate problems. These qualities, taken together, can be called flexibility as opposed to rigidity. Another cluster of qualities has to do with independence of thought and a relatively inner-directed, as contrasted with other-directed, way of life. Creative people are not socially enslaved; they are less preoccupied than most people are with the impression they make on others and are not oversensitive about making mistakes. The evidence seems to show that the reputed connection between genius and madness is a bad case of half-truth. Although creative people are, as Dellas and Gaier put it, "subject to considerable psychic turbulence," there is no correlation with any measure that suggests psychopathology; rather, the evidence indicates "that the creative individual is possessed of superior ego strength and a positive constructive way of reacting to problems."

This is obviously not a portrait that deals only with intellectual characteristics. Creativity is a quality of the whole personality, a finding that fits well with systemic thinking. The composite portrait includes freedom from defensiveness, a quality that applies to many aspects of behavior and feeling. It includes also a pattern of social interactions. Conducive to the production of apt novelty in the realm of ideas, we can conclude, is a kind of inner freedom, self-trust, and fearlessness that shows in many other aspects of a person's life. This relation has often been guessed at in the past by gifted teachers, especially in the arts. A successful sculptor put it this way in his autobiography:

> The most difficult thing, when I had developed a degree of originality in a pupil, was to get him to give real value to his work. Few persons have the moral or intellectual courage to believe in themselves. . . . Most persons could be original if they had the courage.[42]

This is surely an overstatement if one has in mind distinguished sustained accomplishments for which unusual mental aptitudes would appear to be indispensable. But it does call attention to the linkage between originality and other features of the personal system.

A good example of research on this topic is the study of architects made by MacKinnon and his associates at the Institute of Personality Assessment and Research at Berkeley.[43] Subjects for the study were 124 American

[42] D. Edstrom, *The Testament of Caliban* (New York and London: Funk & Wagnalls Company, 1937), p. 252.

[43] D. W. MacKinnon, "Creativity and Images of the Self," in *The Study of Lives*, ed. R. W. White (New York: Atherton Press, 1963), Chap. 11; "The Creativity of Architects," *Widening Horizons in Creativity*, ed. C. W. Taylor (New York: John Wiley & Sons, Inc., 1964).

architects, all in successful practice, representing a fair cross-section of the profession as a whole. They were divided into three groups, which can be roughly designated as most creative, moderately creative, and least creative. This division was the consensus of a large number of judges who were themselves architects, including most of those in the research group, through a procedure of rating their professional colleagues. The architects were given two self-rating procedures designed to elicit their conceptions of themselves. The first of these was an Adjective Check List on which the architect was asked to check those of the 300 given adjectives that he judged to be most descriptive of himself. Sometime later he was asked to check from the same list the adjectives that described the person he would like to be. Simple as this procedure sounds, it is quite successful, when taken seriously, in eliciting a person's image of his real self and of his ideal self. The second procedure employed the Q-Sort method: the subjects were given fifty statements, printed on cards, describing various skills, interests, values, work habits, and points of view of architects. They were asked to sort these statements into five piles, representing statements most characteristic of themselves and those least characteristic, with three intermediate steps. MacKinnon describes as follows the contrasting self-pictures formed in these ways by the most creative and the least creative architects.

> Above all else the creative architect thinks of himself as imaginative; unquestionably committed to creative endeavor; unceasingly striving for creative solutions to the difficult problems he repeatedly sets for himself; satisfied only with solutions which are original and meet his own high standards of architectural excellence; aesthetically sensitive; an independent spirit free from crippling restraints and impoverishing inhibitions; spontaneous; forthright; and self-accepting. He has a sense of destiny about his career as an architect.
>
> The picture which the relatively uncreative architect holds of himself and conveys to others is in striking contrast. Where the creative architect is most impressed by his imagination and inventiveness, the less creative architect sees himself as most saliently conscientious, responsible, and sincere. In his professional role he prides himself on his ability to get along with others and to accept and work over their ideas and concepts. He thinks of himself as most importantly a team man; it is clear that both as an architect and as a person he is strongly oriented to others, emotionally dependent upon them, and overly accepting of the values and judgments of his profession and of society.[44]

Studies made at an earlier stage of development have shed light on the vicissitudes of creativity during the school years. Getzels and Jackson, studying highly gifted adolescent subjects in a private school, made the discovery that teachers preferred pupils whose I.Q.'s exceeded their creativity. These pupils valued the traits that the teachers valued, accepted these quali-

---

[44] MacKinnon, in *The Study of Lives*, p. 276.

ties as leading to success in life, and thus appeared understandable and congenial to the teachers. On the other hand, a group of pupils whose creativity exceeded their I.Q.'s placed a high value on sense of humor, which is a quality especially in adolescents that is unlikely to make the teacher's daily work go smoothly. In their fantasies the first group told conventional stories of success and happiness, whereas the more creative group went in for offbeat, humorous tales with unexpected endings.[45] Wallach and Kogan, whose subjects were fifth graders, also found that creativity did not necessarily make for a happy life at school. Children who scored higher on tests of creativity than on intelligence tests were likely to have difficulty with concentration and steady application, to exhibit disruptive behavior in the classroom, to feel uncertain of themselves, and to be uncomfortable in peer relations. Even those who scored high in both types of test and did well in school seemed to need an occasional disruptive fling that did not sit well with the teachers.[46] If these findings suggest that the influence of teachers falls like a wet blanket on the livelier manifestations of creativity, another study, done by Torrance at the University of Minnesota Bureau of Educational Research, brings out the hostility of peers to these same manifestations. Other children can have a decidedly inhibiting effect upon behavior that is unconventional, diverges from what everyone can understand, and makes a person stick out from the crowd.[47] Being original is hazardous not just in the overcrowded classroom but in many other aspects of social life.

It is an interesting bit of social history that in the 1930s and 1940s social adjustment was a leading value, whereas in the 1950s and 1960s, it is beginning to be seen as in serious conflict with the value of creativity. This represents a move toward a greater cherishing of individuality, toward the fuller development of each person along his own lines. But creativity has become in many quarters such a craze that it is well to remind ourselves of its limitations. Creativity alone, without the backing of other qualities of intellect and personality, can be decidedly ineffectual. Ernst Kris, in his reflections on artistic creativity, distinguished a *phase of inspiration* and a *phase of elaboration*; no real work of art could be produced without both phases. The phase of inspiration, sometimes experienced almost as a rapture, is characterized by a spontaneous flow of thoughts and images that carries no sense of volition; the ideas just well up. The phase of elaboration, in contrast, is one of purposeful organization guided by the intent to solve problems of expression and communication, to work the ideas into shape.[48] We all recognize an attempted work of art that lacks inspiration, but works that lack elaboration either are never finished or are too formless to speak to us.

[45] J. W. Getzels and P. W. Jackson, *Creativity and Intelligence: Explorations with Gifted Students* (New York: John Wiley & Sons, Inc., 1962).

[46] Wallach and Kogan, *Modes of Thinking in Young Children.*

[47] E. P. Torrance, *Guilding Creative Talent* (Englewood Cliffs, N.J.: Prentice-Hall, Inc., 1962).

[48] E. Kris, *Psychoanalytic Explorations in Art* (New York: International Universities Press, Inc., 1952).

The requisite balance between inspiration and work is still more obvious in scholarship and in scientific research. There was inspiration in the idea of studying creativity in successful practicing architects, but a vast amount of careful work went into securing nominations, enlisting willingness to participate, collecting ratings on one another, and gathering and analyzing the data from self-ratings. Concerning the architects themselves, it is instructive to recollect that they typically work for other people, planning buildings that must meet the specific needs of their clients. If one is having a house built for oneself and has ideas about how it should be arranged, the architect's independent spirit, sense of destiny, and insistence upon original solutions might be far less welcome than a little conscientious listening and a socially oriented willingness to incorporate the future owner's ideas. For his best work the creative architect requires a client who is not at all creative; he reaches his peak with a wealthy client who gives him a free hand. Obviously only a part of the profession of architecture is practiced under such conditions, and it is probably fortunate that many architects are better adapted to the cooperative aspects of their work.

Concluding Comment

Education and intellectual growth are to a large extent the province of schools. The study of this aspect of personal development reveals many ways in which schools are not successful in promoting maximal growth. These failings suggest that the educational system stands in need of reform. Such a thought cannot be considered novel: the entire history of education is a story of ideas leaping ahead of practice and of schools as social institutions lumbering far behind what the more creative teachers knew ought to be done. The difficulty of avoiding such a lag is apparent if we glance back over this chapter and consider the variety of things that ought to be done better. The public school teacher, who certainly has not been drawn into her profession by the promise of wealth and fame, has always been asked to see to it that her pupils acquire the basic skills of reading, writing, and arithmetic. She has always been asked to maintain order and relative quiet in a classroom of twenty to forty children; without this the basic skills can hardly be taught. She is now asked to do better with another problem, that of making economically disadvantaged children feel at home. She must express to them her acceptance and she must avoid making them feel inferior even though the handicaps of their background make it hard for them to perform well. She must avoid contributing to the kind of school experience that culminates in dropping out. While doing this she must still manage to recognize and reward superior accomplishment and provide stimulating and nutritious fare for those of her pupils who will otherwise be bored and fall short of realizing their promise. She is asked to moderate her authority, so that she will not stimulate passive resistance in the form of academic underachievement. She must also beware of distributing her rewards in such a way as to encourage the conscientious, rigid pattern of compliance. She must be vigilant for signs of intrinsic interest and arrange things to assist its increase. In addition, she must now put up with the disruptive aspects of her more creative children; the flowering of originality must not be crushed by disapproval. And if a spirited creative pupil, a dimly resentful underachiever, and a sour rejected lower-class child get together in some splendid prank that reduces the class to shrieking hilarity just as the school principal looks through the door, then indeed she must rise to the stature of a superwoman.

These remarks are not intended to imply that improvement in education is impossible. Improvement is possible, but it is not a simple thing that can take place all at once and be equally helpful with respect to all developmental pitfalls. Like children, teachers have distinct personalities, including individual patterns of constitutional predisposition, motivation, cognitive outlook, and preferred strategies of living. In the performance of their work they have their strong and weak points; parts of the teaching role are bound to be more congenial than others. We cannot expect teachers to be all things to all children, and as they are the ultimate channel of educational reform we cannot suppose that institutional innovations and new techniques will transform themselves straightway into perfect performance. There is no reason to counsel despair, but there is every reason to counsel patience.

15 Strategies of Living

Strategy is a term that refers to means rather than ends. As a psychological concept it is designed to take account of behavior that is instrumental to the securing of benefits and the avoidance of harm. For the student of personality, there is value in placing special emphasis on the word "strategy" in describing this aspect of human action. When we talk of behavior we are often thinking of short segments, things that happen quickly in a moment of crisis or in contrived situations where most of the conditions are controlled. This manner of thinking is serviceable for certain purposes. It follows the honored principle of reducing phenomena to simple instances in order to disclose their basic nature. For other purposes, such as gaining familiarity with personality in its natural habitat, this reduction may oversimplify behavior. In the open and continuing situations of real life, benefits and harms are strewn all around us. We must choose and maximize some of the benefits while avoiding or minimizing as many as possible of the harms. The child must choose between the family picnic, with its drawback of whining and temper fits by the younger siblings, and playing in the yard with peers, one of whom has annoying proclivities toward tyranny. The behavior that results may be more or less adaptive, but we are better able to grasp the complexities, the weighings, the compromises that make it adaptive if we see it as strategy. Strategy implies taking a number of things into account, consciously or unconsciously, and is highly characteristic in meeting the problems of living.

One aspect of strategy has already claimed our attention. The defense mechanisms, brought to light largely by Freud and subsequent psychoanalysts, must be counted as instrumental to avoiding anxiety and thus as part of the adaptive process in spite of their questionable long-run effects. Defense mechanisms are primitive and so nearly automatic that we hardly think of them as strategic, yet they serve the purpose of protection against fearsome situations. When defense becomes extended into some lasting form of protective organization, exerting a continuing influence over the course of growth, it more nearly fits the usual concept of strategy. But it is a serious mistake to identify adaptation with defense and to treat the versatile human capacity for dealing with the environment as if it were hardly more than a use of defense mechanisms. Maintaining ourselves intact is not our only problem; we live for satisfactions as well as for security. Strategies of living thus cannot be circumscribed as methods of dealing with anxiety, coping with danger, responding to frustration, or maintaining a secure equilibrium. They must include the ways in which a person learns to maximize benefits, to influence the environment so that it better serves his needs, to discover what is wanted to further his own growth, to increase and enrich the possibilities for enjoyment.

It is difficult to talk about any of the psychological roots of personality —motivation, cognition, action—without using language that seems to imply that everything lies open to awareness. This difficulty besets a term like "strategy" just as it does one like "perceiving." Strategy can be something highly planned and conscious, talked over with others, based on carefully gathered information, as when a high school boy talks over with his parents a detailed educational and financial plan for going through college and graduate school and entering a chosen profession. But just as it is necessary to recognize unconscious motivation and unconscious cognition, so we have to allow that strategies of living may be devised and practiced wholly outside of awareness. Defense mechanisms, character armor, protective organization, style of life—concepts derived originally from psychoanalytic practice—have never been seen as typically conscious; they are discerned only through protracted observation by the analyst and by the patient with the analyst's help. To speak of unwitting strategy may seem an awkward use of terms, but there is no good way to avoid it.

Consider, for example, the paradoxical behavior of a young man repeatedly jailed for burglary and larceny. Outwardly determined to flout authority and take what he wanted, this man had in fact proved himself a failure as a criminal. During the nine years, starting at age 14, in which he had tried to live largely by stealing, he was at liberty for only twenty-two months, in reform school or prison for eighty-six months. At the end of his last previous sentence he had been released to go home on a Saturday morning, only to be arrested again Sunday evening for possession of a stolen car. His crimes were badly planned and carelessly executed, and he made errors of judgment about subsequent concealment. From psychological studies it became evident that he carried a heavy burden of guilt feelings dating from early childhood, that initiative was associated with severe anxiety, and that he yearned for a way of life that was almost perfectly fulfilled in prison: an aura of punishment, no decisions to be made, provision of material necessities. Unconscious motivation is represented in his passive dependence and need for punishment, the opposites of his conscious desires; unconscious cognition in his construing of prison, which he thought he hated, as a place where these needs could be well satisfied; unconscious strategy in his carrying out of crimes in such a way that he was sure to be caught.[1]

The study of strategies is sometimes approached in an optimistic spirit which regards everything as manageable and advocates facing reality squarely and attacking problems head on. But when dangers are real or when information is incomplete it is in no sense adaptive to march boldly forward. In the language of military strategy, situations may call for delay, seeking fresh intelligence, strategic retreat, abandoning untenable positions, regrouping forces, and deploying new weapons. Such steps may be needed in dealing with personal problems. Just by living in the family circle children learn the limitations of frontal assault, the need for a reading of parental moods, the tactic of indirection, and a certain skill in dealing with power relations. Once outside the family, they soon learn that many situations can be met only by compromise or even resignation. Events may require us to give in, relinquish things we would have liked, perhaps change direction or restrict the range of our activities. We may have no recourse but to accept a permanent impoverishment of our lives and try to make the best of it. In addition, strategies tend to be extended over time and to evolve in the course of time. Recovery from personal loss or severe injury both require a long period of readjustment that may not be well served by forceful action or total clarity of perception at the outset. Sometimes adaptation to a severely frustrating reality is possible only if full recognition of the bitter truth is postponed for a long time.

If the study of strategies were confined to animals, we could describe what they accomplish in terms of relatively simple appetites and aversions. Human beings are complicated by self-images and feelings of self-esteem. In ordinary life and in everyday conversation people are not typically exposed to dangers of desertion or destruction, nor must they constantly strive for survival. Yet it is plain that they are often confronted by something that makes them uneasy, some risk of not making a good impression, being belittled, having pride injured, losing in some implicit competition. A great deal of the strategy of everyday life is aimed at maintaining at all costs and raising if possible the level of one's self-esteem.

Representative Studies

We shall begin by examining a number of research studies that have been aimed at the general problem. These are, first, a study of preschool children introduced into situations that were new to them; second, a group of studies of adults in situations of acute stress; third, a study of the transition from high school to college.

---

[1] This case is described more fully in R. W. White, *The Abnormal Personality*, 3d ed. (New York: The Ronald Press Company, 1964), pp. 68–76.

The Topeka Studies of Preschool Children

Strategies in their early stages are well illustrated by Lois Murphy in her study of young children in Topeka.[2] She describes a number of 3-year-olds brought for the first time from their homes to her study center, where the business of the day is to meet a psychologist and engage in some activities that constitute a test of intelligence. In addition to the psychologist, an observer was present at every session whose sole duty was to make a detailed running account of the child's experiments with strategy. The research as a whole included interviews with parents and many other observations of the children, but our interest here is especially in the ways in which the young subjects dealt with a novel situation.

The first two illustrations, boys named Brennie and Donald, present us at once with a striking contrast. Brennie appears to be confidence incarnate. He climbs happily into the car, alertly watches and comments upon the passing scene, charms everyone with his smile, walks into the testing room with perfect poise, accepts each proffered task with eager interest, makes conversation and asks for appropriate help from adults, and finally leaves the scene with a polite expression of thanks. Brennie might be judged a paragon of mental health, and any 3-year-old so easy to deal with is certain to be a psychologist's delight. In contrast, the day of Donald's visit is a taxing one for the staff. The child comes accompanied by his mother, and he utters not a word either on the ride, when entering the building, or for some time in the psychologist's office. Invited to sit down, he stands resolutely beside his mother, his feet spread slightly apart. He will string beads only when his mother has done so first, and once embarked on this operation he refuses to be diverted by the psychologist, who would like to get on with the test. Slowly he warms up enough to dispense with his mother's mediation and deal directly with the psychologist, but the testing still drags because Donald becomes involved in, for instance, building block constructions of his own instead of those required for the test. The session ends with the assessment far from complete.

Donald has displayed anxiety in separating from his mother, dependence upon her, and evasiveness with respect to the tasks set before him. But before we conclude that he is showing poor strategy we should look at the situation from a child's point of view. As adults we know something that Donald does not know: we know that Lois Murphy and her staff, responsible and sensitive investigators, are full of kindness and patience, and that they will go to great lengths to keep discomfort and anxiety at a minimum. Donald can know only that he is being taken to a strange place for a purpose he cannot fathom. Many children by the age of 3 have been to the pediatrician's office, to the barber, and perhaps even to the dentist, and they may well have noticed a credibility gap between parental assurances and the discomforts

[2] L. B. Murphy, *The Widening World of Childhood: Paths toward Mastery* (New York: Basic Books, Inc., 1962).

actually experienced during these visits. Now they are being taken to play games with a nice lady—a likely story indeed! If such conditions existed for Donald, he exhibits commendable common sense in sticking close to his mother, the one familiar object, until he can figure out the nature of the racket. It is his good fortune that his principal observer understands his position, perceives him not as anxiously dependent but as a "sturdy boy," and appreciates his strategy of adaptation. Murphy says:

> Over the years we have seen Donald, this pattern has continued: cautious, deliberate, watchful entrance into a new situation, keeping his distance at first, quietly, firmly maintaining his right to move at his own pace, to make his own choices, to set his own terms, to cooperate when he got ready. These tendencies persisted long after he became able to separate from his mother.[3]

Given time, Donald eventually took full part in the psychological testing. We cannot therefore call his strategy unsuccessful or pin upon him some damaging label such as "neurotic" or "withdrawn." He has approached the new situation with a shortage of information; he cannot really understand its nature. Once present in the testing room with the psychologist, the observer, and a collection of more or less unfamiliar materials, he is suddenly flooded by an input that, because of its newness, he cannot easily put in order. He experiences anxiety that freezes him in one position, and he takes no action. But he is not stuck with this initial reaction. In order to control disruptive anxiety and feel secure he stays close to his mother and performs only acts that she ratifies by performing them first. This step of the strategy is successful: he becomes calm enough to string beads and thus experience a bit of competent action. He now resumes his scrutiny of the situation and discriminates another area, the blocks, with which he sees a possibility of dealing competently. For a while he keeps the initiative in his own hands by building his own designs, but later he can tolerate the challenge to competence implicit in making someone else's designs. Through this sequence of maneuvers he manages to increase relevant information, control and diminish disruptive affect, and extend the range of competent actions, all to the point at which he can take the psychological tests like an old hand, a cautious and deliberate but nevertheless sturdy boy.

What of the perfectly adjusted Brennie? This charming little boy puts one in mind of a genial cocker spaniel who welcomes friend and burglar with equal joy. He seems to trust everyone without discrimination. This is fine as long as he stays in a highly restricted circle consisting of family, nursery school teachers, and sympathetic psychological researchers, who support him lovingly and are considerate of his capacities. But eventually Brennie is going to find out that life is not a rose garden. Before long he will be exposed at school and on the playground to the relatively crude competition and aggression of his peers, some of whom are likely to impose on his good-natured

---

[3] Murphy, *The Widening World of Childhood*, p. 32.

friendliness. He will run into adults who do not respect children and may take advantage of them. In his teens he who has trusted everyone may be urged by his contemporaries to trust no one over thirty. It is easy to imagine his later career, in the competitive adult world with the self-seeking, scandals, and rackets that fill the daily newspapers. By that time Brennie may have been badly burned for his innocent credulity and thus learned to be circumspect, but if we compare him with Donald at the age of 3, we reach the painful conclusion that it is the cautious Donald who is better prepared to meet the average expectable human environment.

The Topeka study provides vivid illustrations of the disruptive effect of anxiety. Certain of the children confronted their first session with the psychologist with a degree of emotion that made it difficult for them to use the available information or to attempt any persistent action. One little girl, for instance, became tearful and inert, as if drained of energy. When able to try the tasks at all, she could scarcely muster enough force to listen, handle objects, or speak above a whisper, and her most characteristic movement was to push the materials gently away. The inhibition vanished magically when she started for home. A normally active boy showed the paralyzing effect of anxiety first by keeping close to his mother, avoiding contact with examiner and test materials, then by tentative work on the tasks, quickly giving up in the face of difficulties. He was able by these tactics to control the anxiety and work up to an active part in the testing. As his uneasiness abated he spoke more loudly, moved more vigorously, explored the materials more boldly, initiated conversation, and became increasingly master of the situation.

Quite different was the behavior of another child, Sheila, not yet 3, who based her strategy on finding openings for competent activity. After looking at the test materials she announced that she did not want to watch them and instead would play with the toys on the floor. She showed no sign of anxiety, and very quickly she involved the examiner in her game with the toys. Momentarily intrigued by a performance test set up before her, Sheila began to play with it, but when gently pressed to follow the examiner's rules rather than her own, she returned to the floor, announcing "I want to do *this*. We don't like the game we had." Lois Murphy comments as follows:

> Here we see a child who in the face of continuing and skillfully applied adult pressures maintained her own autonomy. And it was not merely a matter of refusing and rejecting; it was a matter of doing this without allowing the pressures to depress her mood or to restrict her freedom of movement. Instead, during most of the time, the pressures served to stimulate her to her own best efforts in structuring the situation and obtaining enjoyment from it and from the relationship with the adult.[4]

An important feature of the Topeka study was its extension over time. The examiners did not confine themselves to the children's first encounters with the new experience; observations continued through subsequent sessions,

[4] Murphy, *The Widening World of Childhood*, p. 62.

and contact was maintained with the subjects for several years to come. This made it possible to recognize the real strength and initiative of children like Donald and Sheila, whose initial tactics prevented the psychologist from proceeding with her testing but who in their own good time and in their own way arrived at a thoroughly competent mastery of newness. Strategy is not created on the instant. It develops and is modified over time. To become familiar with the cognitive field, one may first need simply to look it over thoroughly before doing anything at all. This scanning may lead to sharper discrimination of the field, discovery of areas of likely competence and enjoyment, the quieting of disturbing feelings in favor of pleasurable excitement, and a lowering of the premium on immobility. Closer familiarity requires one to test the environment, discovering one's competence to deal with promising portions of it.

Studies of Coping with Stress

In one of the first psychiatric studies of severe life stress, Lindemann described in detail the working through of grief after bereavement.[5] Bereavement disrupts a great many established patterns of conduct both in the present and in the expected future. As Lindemann put it, "The bereaved is surprised to find how large a part of his customary activity was done in some meaningful relationship to the deceased and has now lost its significance." The bereaved must assume burdens, discover new patterns of meaningful conduct; how will he manage all this, and where will he find opportunities? Often, the bereaved person is for some time unequal to contemplating the future, because to do so would only emphasize the magnitude of the loss and increase painful and paralyzing grief. The person cannot maintain organization, think, or act as long as this disruptive emotion remains strong. Equanimity is also challenged by the intrusion of unexpected feelings of guilt. Lindemann noticed how often "the bereaved searches the time before the death for evidence of failure to do right by the lost one; he accuses himself of negligence and exaggerates minor omissions." Thoughts of preserving or opening up some avenue of competent movement present themselves as soon as the immediate crisis has passed. Sometimes a death may be experienced as increasing the survivor's freedom, but typically a widowed spouse, especially if there is a family to bring up, looks into a future that is gravely constricted.

In a more recent paper Hamburg and Adams, reviewing a number of studies of behavior during major life transitions, put a strong emphasis on the seeking and use of information.[6] They perceive the cognitive quest,

[5] E. Lindemann, "Symptomatology and Management of Acute Grief," *American Journal of Psychiatry*, **101** (1944), 141–148. For a review of subsequent work see J. R. Averill, "Grief: Its Nature and Significance," *Psychological Bulletin*, **70** (1968), 721–748.

[6] D. A. Hamburg and J. E. Adams, "A Perspective on Coping Behavior: Seeking and Utilizing Information in Major Transitions," *Archives of General Psychiatry*, **17** (1967), 277–284.

however, in relation to the possibilities for action. Thus in patients with severe injuries that are bound to restrict their future activity, the search for information is seen as serving the following purposes: "keeping distress within manageable limits; maintaining a sense of personal worth; restoring relations with significant other people; enhancing prospects for recovery of bodily functions; and increasing the likelihood of working out a personally valued and socially acceptable situation after maximum physical recovery has been attained." The time dimension proves to be significant in these cases. For a while the depressing impact of the event must be controlled, and one often accomplishes this by extensive denial of the seriousness of the illness. As time goes on, there is an increase of cognitive clarity, but patients usually achieve it at the cost of an increase of depression, which they now can better tolerate. The dismal truth is perceived only as rapidly as one can stand it.

Similar processes of balance are revealed in studies of the parents of children suffering from leukemia. Again one can see delays in taking in the full meaning of the diagnosis, and slow progress toward appreciation of the inevitable outcome. Again one can see the outcropping of guilt and parents' need to be reassured that more attention on their part to the early manifestations of the disease would not have changed the prognosis. Thus, parents could experience grief in advance, and it was noticed that the more they did so, the less they were overwhelmed when the child's death finally occurred.

From High School to College: The Bethesda Studies

The use of strategies of adaptation in advance, in anticipation of problems that lie ahead, is unusually well exemplified in a study by Silber and others of high school seniors in the vicinity of Bethesda getting ready to enter college in the fall.[7] The subjects were chosen because of their high level of competence in the more important aspects of adolescent life; their previous success gave them confidence but did not exempt them from misgivings over the important step soon to be taken. The interviewers became aware of a large repertory of adaptive strategies serving to increase information about college life, dampen anxiety, sustain and improve a sense of adequacy, and provide reassurance that the new life would offer a variety of pathways to self-satisfaction. The students sought information by writing to their college, visiting the campus, and talking with the college students and graduates of their acquaintance. They filtered the information, selecting those aspects of their college that seemed benign, friendly, and supportive. They dealt with anxiety by the thought that worrying was normal, was shared by other prospective students—"Everybody feels this, everybody has to be a freshman once"—and might even have a useful function in preparing for eventuali-

[7] E. Silber, D. A. Hamburg, G. V. Coelho, E. B. Murphy, M. Rosenberg, and L. D. Pearlin, "Adaptive Behavior in Competent Adolescents: Coping with the Anticipation of College," *Archives of General Psychiatry*, **5** (1961), 354–365.

ties. They further reminded themselves of previous analogous situations they had successfully dealt with, such as the transition from junior to senior high schools, identified themselves as part of a group well prepared for college, and lowered their levels of aspiration with respect to academic performance and social prominence during the freshman year. Particularly significant was the building of a sense of competence by a process of role rehearsal during the spring and summer. The students began to read books they thought would be required at college, to exert themselves in courses considered to be on a college level, and to take special pains with term papers, which they understood to be of great importance in college performance. Anticipating their increased independence, some of them began buying their own clothes and practiced more careful budgeting of their time. In their choice of summer jobs they veered away from those associated with adolescent status, like babysitting and mowing lawns, looking instead for work that would put them in competition with adults and would increase their experience in dealing with adults on an equal level. With respect to future action they rehearsed in fantasy the different things they might do to secure help, win popularity, and find avenues for their individual skills and interests. And if worse came to worst, as one of them expressed it, "If I want to go home, I'll be able to."

The strategies of adaptation pursued by these prospective college students accomplished more than could reasonably be implied by the words "defense" and "protection." The men and women who walked on to their respective campuses in September were not quite the same people who received news of their admittance the previous spring. Whatever distortions and defensive operations may have crept into their college-oriented behavior, these were greatly overbalanced by substantial increases in realistic information, in realistic expectations, and in actual competence through role rehearsal and summer jobs. Even before they registered, the high school adolescents of six months before had taken substantial steps toward enlarging their lives.

Main Aspects of Strategy

Dealing with any situation, whether it be simple newness, an acute crisis, or pursuit of long-range plans, usually involves attending to several things at the same time. It will simplify the discussion if we distinguish three main aspects of strategy. What we do is likely to be successful to the extent that (1) *adequate relevant information* can be brought to bear, (2) *affect* can be kept *supportive* rather than disorganizing, and (3) *competent action* can be discerned and attempted. The most successful strategies will therefore be those that increase the securing and processing of relevant information, that enhance positive feelings and control or diminish disruptive ones, and that enlarge the range within which competent action is possible.

Strategy calls in general for pushing all three lines, often simultaneously, but circumstances may require differences of timing and emphasis.

We may feel sure of what ought to be done (adequate information) and strongly desire to do it (adequate motivation and supportive affect) but have no idea how to go about it (lack of avenues for competent action). This is the situation that faces citizens who disagree with national policy but cannot find effective ways to influence the political process. In other circumstances the difficulty may lie in the realm of affect: we may know what should be done and how to do it but be too paralyzed by fright or disorganized by fury to act appropriately. Many times, shortage of information is the chief sticking point, as typified in the physician who is capable of giving treatment and eager to do so if only he can find out what is wrong with the patient. Depending on circumstances, strategy calls for deploying effort where it is most needed while never neglecting the other aspects or failing to keep the overall plan in balance. Strategies of living are not, of course, as conscious and calculated as this sounds, but even when they are wholly unwitting they can be better understood with these three aspects in mind.

Adequate Relevant Information.   Action can be carried on most successfully when the amount of information to be processed is neither too small nor too great. If the channels are underloaded, there will be no way to decide what to do. If the channels are overloaded there will again be no way to decide what to do, this time because the number of possibilities creates confusion. Of course this is not just a quantitative matter; what really counts is the relevance of the information in terms of potential benefits and harms. With this modification, however, it is permissible to use a quantitative metaphor and say that there is a certain rate of information input that is conducive to unconfused, straightforward action, and that both higher rates and lower rates will tend, though for different reasons, to make action difficult. Adaptive behavior requires that the cognitive field contain the right amount of information to serve as a guide to action. Depending on circumstances, then, strategy may take the form either of seeking more information or of trying to cut down on the existing input.

These possibilities can be illustrated by simple examples from animal behavior. When a cat hears a strange noise in a nearby thicket it stops moving, points eyes and ears in the direction of sound, and seems to concentrate its whole being on obtaining cognitive clarity. The exploring cat behaves as if it asked the question, "What is it?" But if the same cat is in the house exposed to the affection and curiosity of several children, it will retire under a sofa to cut down on the overwhelming input and might be imagined to ask, "What is all this, anyway?"

In human experience, as shown in the representative studies we have examined, the problems of adequate relevant information are analogous though often more complicated. Seeking more information was characteristic of the high school students about to enter college and of the parents of seriously sick children. On the other hand the Topeka studies showed that a flood of new impressions could be paralyzing, causing immobility and alert scanning until the subject could make something of it all. A further example might be provided by a college student choosing a field of concentration. At first he is short of information on what is offered in the different fields, and it is good tactics to learn more. But his inquiries may elicit such abundant and confusing advice from the people around him that the only wise course is, like the cat, to escape into solitude and take time to sort out all he has been told.

Supportive Affect.   Feelings and emotions play a part in behavior that we must suppose to be on the whole useful for effectiveness and survival. Fear supports flight, anger strengthens attack, and feelings of well-being and joy assure the continuation of behavior that overcomes obstacles and satisfies needs. Many affects, however, including an excited euphoria, can become disruptive. Even in animals prolonged fear, for instance, debilitates bodily resources and paralyzes action. The vastly expanded cognitive range of human beings, allowing them repeatedly to imagine situations of the past or future, increases the tendency of certain affects to become disruptive. As has already been pointed out, anger can turn into chronic indignation, anxiety can haunt a person when danger is not actually present, and grief over bereavement can paralyze effective action for long periods of time. One of the tasks of adaptive behavior is to avoid or control such disruptive affects and strengthen those that provide support.

Among animals fights are common, but it is noteworthy that except when one creature is another's prey these fights rarely result in death. The animal that begins to experience pain, sustains injury, feels incompetent, or is slowed by fatigue shifts its tactics to flight and lives to fight another day, surrendering whatever advantage was sought on this occasion. An accumulation of negative experiences weakens the animal's behavior until retreat is the only alternative.

An abundance of human illustrations is provided by the representative studies. Some of the Topeka children were at first frozen by anxiety and did not recover the use of their voices or their cognitive and active capacities until this unwelcome affect had subsided. Control of the debilitating affect of grief is one of the serious problems of bereavement. Especially impressive was the management of depression by victims of serious injury, whose prospects for a full life were much reduced. Often it was strategic for them to postpone a vigorous seeking of information until they could bear their prospects without overwhelming despair. To continue the example of the student choosing his major, the day spent in exploration may have produced an accumulation of negative feelings: fatigue at the deluge of advice, fear that he may not find anything he really likes, humiliation and anger because his friends with oppressive honesty have said, "Let's face it, you're no good at ———." Under the sway of these disorganizing affects nothing will seem attractive and no decision possible, but perhaps the next morning, when the student is rested and relatively calm, he can take the important step.

Possibilities for Competent Action.   A person's repertory of competent actions at any given time depends upon innate qualities, stage of development, and types of experience that have provided practice. In a new situation of any kind there is an inverse relation between sense of competence and stress. We are given pause, confused, made to feel helpless, and perhaps frightened to the extent that we are unable to produce relevant and expectably effective actions. This problem is most obvious in situations of great danger, which can, however, be met by those with appropriate training. When a building is on fire the ordinary bystander can often do no more than wring his hands while the fire engine crews proceed swiftly and efficiently with what look like appallingly dangerous maneuvers. There are perhaps few people with the calm collected courage to carry out a space flight, but the astronauts themselves could not do it if they did not have a certain amount of control over the course of events and a set of contingency plans in case of mishap. Even the small difficulties of daily living can be successfully overcome to the extent that one's existing repertory can be applied or that one's confidence is strong enough to permit novel combinations and improvisations. What you can do and what you think you could do are important ingredients of strategy.

Among animals this aspect of adaptation is seen most dramatically in the maintaining of routes of escape. We sometimes marvel at the boldness of a squirrel who sits just out of reach on a branch and scolds us angrily, but the squirrel feels safe with every branch of the tree available as an escape route. The cat investigating a noise in the thicket does not rush in to see what is there only to find itself without ready exits; its approach is cautious, and the seeking of information is balanced against keeping the field open for rapid flight. In human terms it could be said that animals are deft at maintaining contingency plans, avoiding situations which do not allow them alternative competent actions. This aspect of strategy is often overlooked in theoretical discussions, which are apt to be concentrated on the obstacle to be overcome rather than on the further consequences of available actions. We all know, but sometimes forget, that it is possible to jump from the frying pan into the fire.

The human search for avenues of competent action is well illustrated in those of the Topeka children who hung back and stayed near their mothers until they saw among the proffered materials something, like blocks, that they knew how to handle. Parents of sick children likewise sought to take action, and the Bethesda high school students went a step further by actually doing beforehand some things they believed they would be called upon to do at college. Our hypothetical college student choosing a major confronts similar issues with respect to competent action. He may be wise to have a contingency plan for shifting to another field if his first choice proves bad, and he can always drop out if nothing appeals to him. But his strategy will be weak if it does not include an attempt to evaluate, in the light of what he has already studied, his present pattern of competence and interest, together with an attempt to predict the likely enlargement of this competence and interest through more intensive work in the chosen field. Being human, he must also make sure that the choice is consistent with his self-concept and raises rather than lowers his self-esteem. A certain field might be interesting, but if he and most of his friends regard it as unchallenging or irrelevant, pride may forbid him to elect it.

Short-Range Strategies (Tactics)

Sechrest and Wallace have suggested that with respect to adaptive behavior we observe the distinction between strategy and tactics. "Tactics are plans for dealing with relatively immediate and limited problems," whereas "strategies involve longer term plans that are more pervasive."[8] These authors recognize that the distinction is not absolute, but it is useful for descriptive purposes. Tactics are more easily observed than strategies. Nevertheless we must keep in mind that although they may stand alone as occasional, isolated behavior, they may also be instrumental to larger strategies extending over long periods of time.

Presentation of Self

The behavior of people entering a social situation that is new to them provides an opportunity to study tactics. A good deal of the initial behavior discloses what can best be described as a presentation of self, which tends toward maintaining an adequate self-image and preserving, if not increasing, self-esteem. We shall first examine an example from an interview occurring early in the course of a study of personality.

The subject was a Jewish shopkeeper in his early thirties, a recent veteran of World War II, who had been engaged in 1946 to take part in studies focusing on opinions about public events.[9] His history up to this point made it difficult for him to maintain a satisfying self-image. He was in a sense the family's black sheep. His formal education had stopped after a single unsuccessful year at an obscure college; in contrast, his elder brother had graduated from medical school and was embarked on a successful medical career, and his sisters had married professional men. As came out later, he based his self-image on an ideal of simple decent living, free from material ambitions; prominent among his values were cultural self-improvement and alert, informed participation in the democratic process. What he hoped of himself was doubtless pitched all the higher, but at the same time severely threatened, by the fact that he was being interviewed at the university from which his brother had graduated. Early in the interview he was asked in general terms about his philosophy, and he replied that it had changed as a result of his military service. He had seen the war as a crusade against anti-Semitism, but he had met anti-Semitism both in the service and afterwards when the crusade was supposedly won. He veered quickly from this subject to talk about American policies in Europe, but he soon spoke of the tragedy of displaced persons and the follies of British policy in Palestine, topics from which he again veered with signs of embarrassment.

[8] L. Sechrest and J. Wallace, Jr., *Psychology and Human Problems* (Columbus, Ohio: Charles E. Merrill Books, Inc., 1967), pp. 305, 307.

[9] M. B. Smith, J. S. Bruner, and R. W. White, *Opinions and Personality* (New York: John Wiley & Sons, Inc., 1956), esp. pp. 210–218.

These tactics display a self-image of exceptional integrity. He had no reason to fear offending his interviewer, who agreed with his sentiments, but his own ideal of intelligent, judicious citizenship was violated by the disclosure that he could not keep a personal preoccupation with anti-Semitism out of his thinking. Before long he encountered another difficulty. Something he said caused the interviewer to ask if he sometimes experienced a "what the hell" attitude of resignation. This he hotly denied—to him, it was an attitude unworthy of a concerned and committed citizen—but later in the interview, feeling more secure about his listener's sympathy, he said, "It's an almost 'what the hell,' what can you do about it feeling, there aren't enough people interested in this," relaxing his initial sternness to admit that discouragement can sometimes happen. His self-image again came under pressure when the interviewer, trying to follow his leads, asked questions about being well-read, well-informed, and in close touch with the arts. That he was in charge of a business, responsible for its harassing and time-consuming details, was explanation enough for shortcomings in these realms, but he was obviously unhappy in using even the most legitimate excuses for imperfections.

It can be seen from this example that a conversation about values and opinions is not confined entirely to its avowed content, but involves presentation of self. The subject in the interview presents himself as a certain kind of person, and he enhances the image, both to impress the interviewer and to increase his self-evaluation, as much as he feels the situation warrants. In the example described, the subject is not in the least flamboyant about this. He is in fact unusually honest and makes no attempt to deceive. Nevertheless he presents himself as best he can in the image of a wise, impartial, informed, cultured, sophisticated person. The presentation of self in an interview is always a two-way process. The interviewer, closely as he may stick to business, is also to some extent making a presentation, usually one that puts emphasis on warmth, sympathetic understanding, and a capacity to give support. Training may have helped the interviewer to keep his presentation from interfering with the subject's, but he can hardly say a word, or even emit a murmur, without implying, for instance, that he is a person who listens and understands, in contrast to one who might be censorious toward what the subject had said. In this sense, presentation of self is a constant happening in human relations, implicit and inescapable. It occurs even when neither party is consciously dramatizing, and it certainly should not be taken to mean that everyone puts on a big act to convince others that he is something he knows he is not. Imposture is merely the limiting case, the blatant conscious extreme, of a phenomenon widely present in human life.

This phenomenon is the subject of a book by Erving Goffman, who purposely describes it in the language of a theatrical performance, though admitting that the analogy is not perfect.[10] Goffman views self-presentation as part of the process whereby the participants in a social interaction come

[10] E. Goffman, *The Presentation of Self in Everyday Life* (Garden City, N.Y.: Doubleday & Company, Inc., 1959).

to define one another and construe the nature of the situation. The force of this idea becomes clear if we imagine a person entering a room full of strangers and stopping on the threshold to announce his name, age, occupation, marital status, and political opinions, give a brief autobiography, and state in downright terms what the group can expect of him and what he expects of them. One usually does not do this in real life, yet one often arrives at the same ends in more subtle ways. Each member of an interacting group presents himself and his activities to others, trying in this way to control their impressions of him, using what Goffman calls "arts of impression management" such as are "required of a performer for the work of successfully staging a character."[11] The result is by no means inevitably a battle of conflicting presentations. Often enough, Goffman points out, the members unwittingly conspire to support and even protect each other's performances. They may ignore flaws in a performance, as when the actor fluffs a line, drops a brick, or in some other way slips up in the staging of his character. Social interaction goes forward more pleasantly, more constructively, if threats to pride are avoided and each person is allowed a bit of scope to enhance his self-image. Only if a self-presentation is particularly abrasive does it become necessary—preserving the theatrical analogy—for the audience to greet it with hisses.

A Study of Ingratiation

One type of tactics that can be used in relation to other people goes by the general name of ingratiation. Ingratiation refers to behavior that is designed, wittingly or unwittingly, to influence another person in the direction of liking and being attracted by one's personal qualities. This can, of course, be used as a perfectly conscious bit of tactics when one seeks some benefit from another person; historically it was standard practice to use it when asking favors from a reigning monarch or a person in noble estate. It can also be almost entirely unconscious, and when generally employed in the majority of human relations, it can be said to qualify as a trait or as a strategic style. Ingratiation is the subject of a series of studies by Edward E. Jones and a group of workers at Duke University.[12] Jones lists self-presentation as one line of available strategy, but he also speaks of two others: conformity to the opinions and beliefs of the other person, and enhancement of the other's self-image by expressions of appreciation and esteem.

Conformity works according to the proposition that people like those whose values and beliefs are similar to their own, a proposition already well established in the research literature.[13] The ingratiating use of conformity may consist of no more than calling attention to a similarity of opinions that already exists, but it may take the form of actually changing one's opinions

---

[11] *Ibid.*, p. 208.

[12] E. E. Jones, *Ingratiation: A Social Psychological Analysis* (New York: Appleton-Century-Crofts, 1964).

[13] F. Heider, *The Psychology of Interpersonal Relations* (New York: John Wiley & Sons, Inc., 1958), esp. Chap. 7.

in the direction of those held by the person to be impressed, and in more crass instances it may take the form of pretending to do so. Enhancing another person's self-image by expressions of esteem likewise occurs in a wide range of forms. To appreciate and admire another person's good qualities and to communicate these feelings is, of course, an important part of a truly loving relation. Ingratiation begins at the point where such communication is not quite an expression of true feeling but slips over into a tactic, not necessarily conscious or calculated, of attracting the other person's liking. A strongly dependent person may do this simply to avoid the anxiety of loneliness or to feel bolstered by another person's support. But the tactic may be instrumental to securing some ulterior purpose like a job, a sale, a promotion, or a seduction, and again as its crass extreme it can take the form of coolly calculated flattery.

Jones has undertaken to investigate the conditions that affect the use of ingratiating strategies by setting up model situations in the psychological laboratory. He instructed one group of subjects in a contrived social situation to try their best to make themselves attractive to a so-called "target person." What they did could then be compared with the behavior of a control group not so instructed. For the results to be quantified, the situations had to be made rather unnatural, but the subjects seem to have entered into the experiments with good humor and imagination, revealing in their performances several features of ingratiation that are congruent with common observation. Two points emerge that are important for understanding interpersonal tactics.

In the first place, much depends on the status and power of the participants and on their respective feelings of competence. If a candidate is being interviewed for a job in competitive business he is likely to make a strong presentation of his ability and initiative, and he may well fortify his case by evidences of opinion conformity. But if the candidate is a nationally known college football hero, has been speedily hired, and is now meeting his less distinguished co-workers, he will ingratiate himself, if at all, by showing that in spite of his self-evident strengths he is really a nice friendly fellow. Ingratiating tactics are much influenced by the precise character of the interpersonal situation in which they occur.

In the second place, ingratiation can be successful only in so far as the "target person" or the group to be impressed believes that the ingratiator really means it. The strategy becomes a boomerang the moment its credibility is questioned and the recipient suspects that he is being manipulated. Ingratiation therefore contains an element of risk that sets restrictions on its use and may lead to refinement of tactics. Presentation of the self must not be so radiant as to be judged a boastful, shallow performance. Conformity of opinions must not go so fast and so far as to look like an act; indeed, it is more convincing to maintain disagreement on a few minor matters and to allow oneself to be persuaded only reluctantly on major issues, always with the hope that the recipient will not see through these tactical elaborations. Enhancement of the other person's self-image requires equal caution. Praising the "target person" for his obvious strengths or for qualities he knows he does not have are both likely to make him suspect flattery; he will be most susceptible with respect to qualities he desires but is not quite sure he possesses. Credibility is improved by communicating the praise to some third party who is certain to pass it along. But there is always the risk that the person being courted is a genius at intuition, a seasoned student of Machiavelli, or a reader of Jones's book, so that even the most roundabout approaches do not fool him.

If we limit ingratiation, as Jones does, to tactics that are not an expression of true feeling, we must not overlook situations in which one person sincerely admires another and desires friendship. Under these circumstances tactics such as favorable self-presentation, calling attention to conformity of values, and offering expressions of esteem look like sensible steps toward a worthy goal. This active approach compares favorably with shy inhibited silence whereby true feelings are concealed. Strategy of some sort, behavioral implementation of some kind, is necessary to achieve any goal—honest, dishonest, or somewhere in between.

Games People Play

The somewhat military metaphor of tactics is changed to a more playful one in a book by Eric Berne entitled *Games People Play*.[14] Berne was a psychiatrist whose sphere of observation included the doctor-patient relation, the discordant marital relations so often reported by patients, and the interactions that occur during group psychotherapy. The games of which he speaks are not played for fun. They have implicit purposes: self-assertion, securing what one wants, enhancing the self-image, avoiding blame, and controlling other people by bringing them into the game. They can equally well be called short-range strategies or tactics. Berne describes thirty-six games, using such picturesque titles as "Kick me," "See what you made me do," "Look how hard I've tried," "I'm only trying to help you," and "Wooden Leg," the latter being an excuse-making game following the pattern, "What can you expect of a man with a wooden leg?" One of the described games, "Why don't you—yes but," is best exemplified in therapeutic groups. The player appears to ask for suggestions from others with respect to some problem, but rejects each suggestion with a "Yes, but," followed by a statement that it has already been tried and failed or a reason why it would certainly fail. The purpose of this game, says Berne, "is not to get suggestions but to reject them," to prove that no one can make the player surrender by coming up with an idea that is new to him. The player wins the game when everyone gives up and silence reigns. This is what Berne calls the "emotional payoff."

Readers of Berne's book are likely to experience flashes of insight and a sharpened awareness of what may be going on beneath the surface of ordinary conversation. His descriptions of games—glaring examples drawn

---

[14] E. Berne, *Games People Play: The Psychology of Human Relationships* (New York: Grove Press, Inc., 1964).

mostly from neurotic behavior—seem designed to appeal to the cynical side of our natures, providing a remarkable exhibition of human folly. It is therefore chilling when he remarks that because real intimacy is so difficult, "the bulk of the time in serious social life is taken up with playing games." If we are to accept this we must allow that Berne did not describe all possible forms of games. Those that he chose are short-range tactics designed to achieve a hidden, unwitting "payoff" of a rather personal and petty character. In "Why don't you—yes but," for instance, the other players are invited to show helpful interest by offering suggestions, then slapped down to the greater glory of the principal player. These tactics combine manipulation with childish and egotistical motives. Once we see through the game we are more than likely to pity the losers and hold the winner in contempt.

Tactics, however, can take other patterns. When a group of strangers assembles for a common purpose, such as attending a meeting or spending a vacation, one person frequently takes it upon himself to give his name, ask others their names, introduce the now named individuals to one another, make opening remarks to disclose what they may have in common to talk about, and thus set in motion a whole series of social interactions where none had been before. This can be called a game, and following Berne we could give it a title, perhaps "Let's be acquainted and friendly," but there is nothing infantile about the "emotional payoff" that is being sought. The person who has acted as social lubricant is generally viewed as a benefactor who has put everyone more nearly at ease. Similarly beneficent tactics may be employed by a hostess making her guests comfortable, by the chairman of a meeting keeping conflicting opinions from bursting into destructive flames, by a psychologist assuaging a young child's anxiety before starting a psychological test. Tactical games should not be identified with manipulations that are deceptive, selfish, and insincere. They can be all these, but they can also serve general well-being.

Strategic Styles

If strategies of living were always employed in a manner that was perfectly balanced and fully appropriate to the circumstances, we would probably take them for granted as we do the silent workings of our internal organs. But strategies are in fact a showcase for individual differences. Each person's strategies are arrived at in the course of his life and are colored by the problems that are important in his life. To the extent that they are successful, they are not easily modified to meet new problems. Each of us can therefore be said to have one or more preferred strategic styles, colored by the past but in most cases serving passably in the present.

Working out the most commonly used styles of strategy is one of the most pertinent forms of analysis in studying the individual personality. To this end the observer must know a strategy when he sees one, so to speak: he must develop a keen appreciation of what seems to be accomplished by the subject's characteristic behavior in terms of benefits obtained and harms avoided, of effects produced on other people, of self-esteem defended or enhanced. This requires familiarity with considerable samples of the subject's behavior over periods of time. Strategic styles come in such a variety of patterns that it is virtually impossible to capture them in a systematic descriptive scheme that covers all possibilities. What we shall undertake to do here makes no pretense of completeness. We shall take merely a sampling of strategic styles with a view to analyzing how a style works, what purposes it achieves, and what other purposes it is likely to exclude.

Derogatory Style

A person who relies heavily on what we may call a derogatory style may find fault with just about everything and everybody. He seems selectively aware of other people's ineptitudes, deceptions, self-seeking, and corruption. He cannot read an article without discovering that somebody's self-interest is being subtly promoted by it. He cannot see a picture of a proposed new building without thinking of rackets in awarding the contract and of exorbitant rents the owner will charge. His conversation is studded with devastating criticism and with rhetorical questions like "How stupid can you get?" but he will never be heard to ask "Who am I to talk?" To live in a world so perpetually disagreeable might seem incompatible with happiness, but it is hard to divert a person so disposed by suggesting pleasanter topics. Apparently his purposes are well served by the derogatory strategy. He puts himself constantly in the position of a shrewd person who cannot be fooled, and who from some unspecified moral height has the right to judge all men.

The chief accomplishment of the derogatory style is to belittle and blame the outside world while implying that the self is free from faults and maintaining a flattering self-picture of wisdom. In its cognitive aspect this strategy calls for securing a great deal of relevant information; listeners are often impressed by the speaker's detailed knowledge of corruption and folly. The search for information, however, is highly selective: introspection is virtually barred, and instances of what is worthy in the world do not seem to be well retained. On the affective side, the principal service of this strategy seems to be the steady discharge of resentment simultaneously with the enhancement of supportive feelings of self-esteem. It can be inferred that the person is fairly heavily charged with aggression, which he needs to externalize lest it take the form of disruptive self-blame and self-belittlement. On the side of action he may, if he does not confine himself wholly to talk, discover ways of pointing out and dealing with real evils, and his habituated strategic style seems well suited to such roles as prosecutor and reformer. One of the immediate side effects of his style is to intimidate those around him, who cannot help wondering what belittling phrases he will use when describing them to others, and who may be anxiously driven into tactics of ingratiation. This is further conducive to self-esteem, but it is evident that the derogatory style puts up obstacles to affection. It is hard to love a person whose principal output is belittlement.

Lest the reader conclude that this description of the derogatory style is itself an example of that style, it should be added that strategies that seem too slanted to work well in the average environment may be perfectly adapted to certain types of situation. Practitioners of the derogatory style are not likely to become penetrating critics of themselves, nor are they apt to achieve tolerance for the faults of others. They may, however, become penetrating critics of society and develop great skill in exposing human folly and corruption. Carrying a heavy burden of resentment is the natural consequence of living amidst chronic deprivation or prejudice. In these circumstances, blaming the outside world is not necessarily a falsification. The derogatory style may both salvage self-esteem and serve truth.

Indeed, failure to perceive what is wrong with the world would suggest that an opposite strategy was in use, one in which keeping things as they are is the chief concern. Timidity, love of comfort, or desire to maintain a favored status may lead a person to restrict the input of disturbing information, avoid the arousal of feelings like guilt or sympathy for the plight of others, and thus prevent the interruption of a satisfying pattern of existence. This, too, may be more or less appropriate depending on circumstances. It can be simply evasive, a way of maintaining a favorable view of oneself and one's situation. But it can also serve the legitimate purpose of controlling a flood of input that might paralyze action. Individual development, the nurturing of one's intrinsic interests and the discovery of one's particular aptitudes, may require considerable resistance to distraction; we cannot each be everything. We do not expect of people who are wholeheartedly immersed in demanding roles like that of physician or that of performing artist that they also be the ones who take the lead in social criticism and reform. Better for all if they concentrate on doing their own thing well.

Humorous Style

The role of humorist can best be played by a person with a quick perception of the incongruous and verbal fluency in expressing it. If these gifts are used and improved they create for their possessor a position among associates that is likely to be highly rewarding. The humorist makes a large contribution to happiness. There is intrinsic pleasure in seeing incongruity and in laughter, and laughing together can increase a sense of fellowship. Humor can create insight and bring critical tendencies to a focus. Laughter at the expense of an unpopular teacher is the forerunner of what the cartoonist and humorous columnist can later do to an unpopular political administration. Humor injected at the right moment can quickly reduce unpleasant tension, as when tempers are rising or embarrassment is becoming acute. The following incident was reported by a student who had been in military service.

At the desert post where he was stationed a newly developed missile was to be displayed to a large audience of top brass and very important people; speeches preceded and were to follow the demonstration. At the critical moment the missile, instead of rising majestically into the air, sputtered feebly and fell over on its side. There was a silence filled with almost unbearable tension. The student's friend, standing a little behind him, stepped closer to remark "Back she goes to the drawing board!" Inadvertently he moved beside an open microphone so that his voice boomed over the whole field, "*Back she goes to the drawing board!*" The tension broke in a general burst of laughter, and a much-needed public service had been performed.

Because of its substantial contributions to well-being, the strategy of humor is likely to make for social acceptance. The entertainer stands a good chance of becoming a popular character. But there are other consequences of the humorous style. It can be used as a way of taking the center of the stage by a person who has no other claim to that position. If the humor is at all caustic it may give the humorist power over others, who may nervously wonder when their turn will come to be the butt of a joke. Humor can serve protective purposes: When made at one's own expense it can be used as a method of forestalling criticism by others. Little disapproval is likely to rest on a person who has entertained his listeners with a laughable account of his own stupidity. Humor also provides a way of exemption from making up one's mind and taking stands on controversial issues—everyone is expecting a humorous contribution and does not require a serious one. The strategy can go astray in an atmosphere of intensely serious discussion when nobody wants the tension reduced or the flow of ideas interrupted. Thus although the humorist tends to be popular, his strategic style may limit him in other directions: he may ultimately want more firmness in his own opinions, more respect as a serious person, more weight in matters of state than is generally accorded to the court jester.

Cool Intellectual Style

A cool intellectual style is often favored by those who are accustomed to read, study, think, and otherwise give intellect a prominent place in leading their lives. Good logical analysis and scientific observation, as we all know, must be dispassionate. These operations can be well performed only if we manage to detach ourselves from personal preference sufficiently to perceive the phenomena of the world exactly as they are. The way we would like things to be must be set aside, made at least temporarily inoperative, if we are to find out what is actually there. Being dispassionate in this sense is instrumental to accurate cognition, but it is easy to see that it might also have a spurious appeal to a person in whom "passion"—feeling and emotion—was a source of anxiety. Under these circumstances detachment carries the bonus of keeping dangerous feeling out of action. The detached person uses intellectual analysis wherever possible, even in situations where others count it inappropriate. In contrast to people who are afraid to think, the person strongly habituated to a cool intellectual strategy conveys the impression that he is afraid not to think.

Certain features of the educational process tend to encourage and strengthen the use of this style. The ordinary classroom almost inevitably puts a premium on verbal facility and quick response. The upraised hands of the brightest boys and girls in the class are a help to the teacher, and it is hard not to convey the unintended lesson that talking off the top of your head is what really counts. Thus bright children, as they move up the educational ladder, are so continually rewarded for their mastery of words and their fluency with abstract ideas that they are tempted to use this competence as a generalized strategy of living. Even in the intellectual sphere itself, where the strategy is basically appropriate, they may talk comfortably about theories without establishing a firm connection with facts. In considering political issues they may speak of historical backgrounds and conflicting ideologies but give no hint of indignation or of strong commitment. Their comments on an evening of music may take the form of placing the works in the history of composition or criticizing the technique of performance, leaving unspecified whether or not they had been moved by it. They may even come to have a theory about love and describe their own experiences in love so abstractly that no one can tell what emotions were involved. In a study of a small liberal arts college where a program of psychological testing of freshmen had been in force for twenty years, Heath points out a steady increase in the cool intellectual style. Concomitant with rising admission standards the incoming students are increasingly given to a pattern of intellectual control, "playing it cool," absorption in self, lack of social feeling, and a weakness in warm relations with others. At the same time the more recent students report greater amounts of strain, emotional tension, disturbing dreams, and struggles with irrational impulses, all of which suggest that the strategy of intellectual control over affect is not completely successful.[15]

At a simpler level the same strategy takes the form of keeping away from feeling by attending strenuously to the details of objective happenings. This strategy is vividly portrayed in the opening scenes of *The Stranger* by Albert Camus. The narrator, Meursault, having received a telegram that his mother has died, becomes at once involved with a point not specified in the telegram—whether she died today or yesterday. Later he is preoccupied with details of securing time off from his job, of the bus trip, and of the scenes and people at the nursing home where she died. Meursault, we are going to learn in the course of the novel, is a man capable of breaking out in violent passion, including rage to the point of murder, but he describes the whole sequence of his mother's death, wake, and burial as something seen and heard but not felt, something to which he is indeed an emotional stranger.[16]

---

[15] D. H. Heath, *Growing Up in College* (San Francisco: Jossey-Bass, Inc., 1968), Chap. 3.

[16] A. Camus, *The Stranger*, trans. S. Gilbert (New York: Vintage Books, 1946).

Impulsive Style

There is, of course, a style almost opposite to the cool intellectual strategy, one in which the person is close to his feelings and allows them a large part in the direction of behavior. Emotions are welcome provided they are not disruptive or inhibiting; the person attempts to maximize such affects as enthusiasm, joy, excitement, and affection. He expends much less effort on securing and weighing information, and may undertake action with little thought for its consequences. It may seem that the impulsive style amounts to nothing more than being natural, living spontaneously in accord with one's impulses. To live this way, however, has a great many consequences both for oneself and for others, and it is legitimate to speak of a strategy when these consequences, in addition to impulse satisfaction, form part of the desired "emotional payoff."

One of these consequences has already been examined in an earlier chapter on social class environments.[17] People in hopeless economic circumstances, unable to anticipate any rewards from organizing their lives around future goals, keep despair at bay by heavy use of the impulsive style, drowning themselves in the immediate satisfaction of their strongest needs. In this way impulsiveness becomes a strategy for avoiding a perception of oneself and the world that is devoid of hope for a better future. Impulsiveness also has a variety of effects on interaction with others. At best these may be warm and friendly, but acting on whims sometimes becomes a kind of dominance. The impulsive person may sweep up everyone into his plans—for instance, making an enthusiastic call to a friend to drop everything and go skiing, so that friend finds himself dropping things he really did not want to drop. The impulsive style in speech often has a pleasing directness, giving listeners the feeling that they know where they stand, but the speaker may exert insufficient control over remarks that are tactless, callous, and needlessly wounding. Finally, acting on impulse can be used to push irksome responsibilities off upon others. Rarely does impulse produce an eagerness to attack the daily chores, and a common consequence of the style is that these are left to other hands.

These four strategic styles are only a sample, as was pointed out, of the many adaptive patterns of which human beings are capable. To make clearer what is involved, they have been described as if each one constituted a person's entire repertory, being used indiscriminately in season and out of season. Our actual circumstances call for different strategies at different times. It is easy to imagine a fairly close sequence of events, each one of which could best be dealt with by a different tactic. The ideally flexible person would be successively derogatory, humorous, coolly intellectual, impulsive, and several other things as he made a triumphal progress through life. Unfortunately

[17] See above, Chap. 6, pp. 143, 149.

the ideally flexible person is an improbable phenomenon. Most of us can manage some changes of strategy as occasion demands, but we still have our preferred ways of doing things based on our personal histories and aptitudes.

Strategies under Changed Conditions

Strategies that are effective at one period of life may not work at another. It is everyone's fate to find himself confronted by new situations that do not fit his accustomed repertory. At one extreme he may respond with behavior that is perfectly fitted to the new demands. At the other extreme he may repeat an old strategy, unresponsive to the novel circumstances. Most behavior under changed conditions lies somewhere in between.

Strategic Inertia

The idea is familiar that strategies resist change because they have been made rigid by anxiety. When his strategies are protecting him, a person may not feel safe in changing them. But strategies can also become fixed because of their success. Some people may be unsuccessful in a new situation precisely because they apply so faithfully the strategies that have always worked before.

Strategies overlearned through success may easily be illustrated with extreme examples. We are all familiar with those self-appointed experts who confidently tell us how to do everything in terms clearly drawn from their own experience. But it is more to the point to close this chapter by briefly examining the inertia of strategies amid the usual complexities of human living.

College students who were once the jesters of their circle sometimes report that they went through a bad time when they began to want to be taken seriously. This was partly the fault of their associates, who did not want to release them from their valuable service of providing entertainment. In Chapter 11 this situation was used to illustrate the influence exerted on behavior by the expectations of others. Listeners smile in anticipation when the jester starts to speak, and are distinctly disappointed if he does not say something funny. When he tries to offer remarks in all seriousness, which he may not do as proficiently as those who have been trying it longer, he has to cut through this almost palpable atmosphere of disappointment, and he is all too likely to see something incongruous in what he is saying and to end with a joke. Attuned as he is by the previous success of his strategy to perceive the humorous aspect of things, he can hardly stop himself from doing so even when he wants to be serious. A variant form of this strategic inertia arises when the jester wants to express sympathy, indicate understanding of troubles, or make a sincere declaration of affection. The habit of treating things flippantly may be hard to control even in situations where flippancy has no place.

The broad basis for this type of strategic inertia is that each individual confronts a new situation not with universal wisdom and competence but with the personal version of wisdom and competence that he has built up in the course of his life. Much as he may have widened his understanding by reading, study, and observation of others, his own sense of competence—his feeling of what he can do—is always especially influenced by what he himself has done. This sometimes comes out with striking clarity when a successful man is promoted to a higher office having different requirements from any he has hitherto met. What he does can be described in part as searching among his past strategies for those that are most relevant. Finding and applying them is one way, for better or for worse, in which he puts his personal stamp on the office.

This is how it works, according to political scientist James D. Barber, with those who receive the important promotion of being elected president of the United States.[18] As has been long recognized, there are requirements in this office for which no one can be wholly prepared by previous experience. As Barber describes the role, the president is an isolated figure who must share his work with innumerable helpers but must bear responsibility alone. He is required to relate himself to the national audience, typically through speeches. He must work out his personal relations with those around him, policy being significantly influenced by the people who constitute his closest circle and have his ear. He must finally determine policy by making decisions. Each president, Barber points out, distributing his energies differently among these tasks, "shapes his style in a distinctive way." For it is true that "no president is born anew on Inauguration Day: like most people past middle age, a president tries to use his experience; he draws on what has worked for him before in coping with new work." Barber then makes the interesting suggestion that the relevant strategy may not be taken from the most recent experience, cases in point being Hoover as secretary of commerce, Truman as vice president, and Kennedy as senator. As likely as not, a president will draw upon earlier experiences, earlier successful steps in his political career, that may be more analogous to emerging alone at the top. The personal stamp the president puts on his performance in office may have origins anywhere in his life history.

In closing this account of strategies of living it is appropriate to repeat the reminder given at the beginning of the chapter. The most basic image that should underlie one's thinking about personality is that of the living organism, which not only tries to maintain itself intact but also reaches out into the environment in a constant effort toward growth and greater satisfaction. This image keeps us from overlooking the inherently expanding and creative aspect of human life. It is instructive to unearth the strategic inertia in a president's personal style, but a full understanding of presidential behavior must reckon also with what is not inert, with the novel synthesis that is progressively achieved under the influence of new information, daily fresh experience, the desire for yet higher levels of achievement, and the hope of

[18] J. D. Barber, "The Character of Richard Nixon," *Boston Sunday Globe Magazine*, November 9, 1969, pp. 7–14.

going down in history as an admirable president who served his country well. This forward-moving aspect of behavior has been implicitly present throughout the chapter even when the focus was on protective rigidities, repetitive games, and resistances to change. It is implicit in the humorist who does not remain satisfied with his useful and well-rewarded role but wants to enlarge himself into a person who is taken seriously. It is implicit in those who reject game-playing and ingratiation because they aspire to human relations that are wholly honest and deeply felt. It is implicit in those who refuse to settle into comfortable conformities and insist upon exploring the unknowns within them and without. It is implicit in those who do not take the world as it is but work to change it for the better. If part of the time we study strategies that serve defense, protection, and petty advantage, we must be equally ready to study strategies that lead to more abundant living.

On Being One's True Self

Thinking over what has been said about the games people play, ingratiation, and strategic styles, one may well be tempted to ask why all this is necessary. Is it not possible to live honestly and openly, expressing what one feels, being one's true self, forswearing the devices and deceits and hypocrisies that seem only to pollute human relations? In those sections of contemporary culture that have absorbed Freud and are accustomed to putting human nature under close, unflattering scrutiny, being honest with others and with oneself sometimes emerges almost as an ultimate standard of ethics.[19] Can we not speak the truth, go directly to the point, act according to inclinations that spring from within, and thus to our own selves be true?

In the novel *Demian*, Hermann Hesse's principal character, Sinclair, utters the words, "I wanted only to try to live in accord with the promptings which came from my true self." Then he asks the question, "Why was that so very difficult?"[20] If we stick to the case of Sinclair the answer is simple: his "true self" was a mess. The promptings that came from it were inchoate, conflicting, impossible to follow on anything like a steerable course. They welled to the surface in philosophical reflections that drifted off the mark and in dreams and symbolic fantasies almost impossible to understand. Hesse dramatized the theme again in *Steppenwolf*, creating another character who is attracted by, yet alienated from, traditional values and social conformities, and whose search for a "truer self" is anything but a simple matter.

Unfortunately the notion of a "true self" embodying all real goodness is something of a romantic fiction. Childhood cannot be so golden that we pass through it free from compromises with imperfect actualities. If among our own deep-set motives we have some that make for tenderness, love, and care, we have others that make us fearful, that lend themselves to competition,

---

[19] P. Rieff, *Freud: The Mind of the Moralist* (New York: The Viking Press, Inc., 1959), esp. Chap. 9, "The Ethic of Honesty."

[20] H. Hesse, *Demian: The Story of Emil Sinclair's Youth* (1919), trans. M. Roloff and M. Lebeck (New York: Bantam Books, 1966), p. 80.

and that prompt us to resentment and cruelty. Whatever its virtues, our family cannot spare us problems connected with security, acceptance, control, jealousy, and rivalry. The resulting strategies of living—bold, devious, and timid alike—are an integral part of us. Our impulses are channeled into them; they cannot easily be switched off. So if we reach a point of insight at which we become disgustedly aware of how we stage ourselves, play games, and ingratiate others, to say nothing of using defense mechanisms and strategies, and if at this point we want to enrich life by finding honest, deeply felt, loving interactions with others, it is tempting to believe that we can change simply by opening a door and letting out our "true" unsullied impulses. Change is never so simple. What is really involved is not the releasing of a true self but the making of a new self, one that gradually transcends the limitations and pettiness of the old. This can be done only by behaving differently when interacting with other people. New strategies have to be evolved that express the new intentions and encourage others to take their reciprocal part in finer human relations.

16 Self and Ego Identity

One of the prime difficulties in describing personality is to avoid repetition. This trouble is inherent in the fact that the object of study is a system. In a system, quite a few things happen at once and influence one another. It is thus impossible to separate different parts and treat them as if they followed autonomous paths of development. Nowhere is this difficulty more obvious than in a chapter on self and ego identity. These concepts have been in a sense present all along, implicit in much that has been said, cropping up repeatedly in different parts of the account. Can there be anything more to say about them?

There would indeed be volumes more to say if we were to follow the ideas of self and ego through their long difficult tribulations in the history of philosophy. But even in a description of personality we must afford these ideas a place, because these are the two concepts most often used in accounting for organization. They owe their recurrent vitality to the fact that they reflect something central in personal experience: that each of us is one person, the same in certain essential respects from day to day, or, to put it differently, that I continue to be me no matter how swiftly things whirl around me. The phenomenon of selfhood is something that cannot be left out if one elects to take personality as the object of study. In recent years it has become common to express certain kinds of personal bewilderment in the form of the question, "Who am I?" This is a poignant question, the reasons for which we shall presently consider. But it is in a way a figurative rather than a literal use of the words. The literal "Who am I?" is the question asked by the amnesia victim who awakens with no recollection of his name, his circumstances, or his personal past.

Organization, of course, is a relative matter. Human beings are far from perfect specimens of it. When we make three trips to the refrigerator to fetch articles that could have been brought in one, when we return from shopping having forgotten one of the items on a list that seemed too short to write down, we become aware that we are not designed with computer-like precision. We have constant difficulty remembering what we said yesterday, what impressions we tried to make on people the day before, and what we decided to do tomorrow. But what bothers us more than our small confusions is to be so often at odds with ourselves with respect to the important concerns of life. Our perceptions of the world are made inconsistent by moods and by physical states such as fatigue. Our needs keep coming into conflict: we aim, for example, simultaneously to be cared for and to be free and independent, or we are argumentative and try to put others down while at the same time hoping to be loved. We arrive at sensible decisions and then do not act upon them, marveling when we realize later how the same old apathies and distractions have tripped us up. We discover that different roles are crowding each other off the stage; to be the bright scholar, the star athlete, and the social lion is a little too much for our time and skill. We carry on interior conversations in which at least two people seem to be talking within one head, sometimes in violent controversy. A chapter on the organization of personality should not be taken to imply that personality is ever a smoothly organized affair, nor indeed that such an outcome would necessarily be desirable. What has to be taken into account is not that we are well-organized but that we are even as organized as we are. For there are times when we are capable of controlling impulses, resisting distractions, resolving conflicts among needs, achieving commitment, and pursuing in a steadfast manner some distant goal or difficult ideal for which much has to be renounced.

Meaning of Self

William James, writing in a period when introspection enjoyed high favor as a psychological method, addressed himself to describing what seemed to be involved in the consciousness of self.[1] A person's self, he began, is "all that he is tempted to call by the name of *me*," but there is also what he calls *mine*, and the line between the two is difficult to draw.

> We feel and act about certain things that are ours very much as we feel and act about ourselves. Our fame, our children, the work of our hands, may be as dear to us as our bodies are, and arouse the same feelings and the same acts of reprisal if attacked. . . . *In its widest possible sense a man's Self is the sum total of all that he* CAN *call his*, not only his body and his psychic powers, but his clothes and his house, his wife and children, his ancestors and friends, his reputation and works, his lands and horses, and yacht and bank-account. All these things give him the

[1] W. James, *The Principles of Psychology*, Vol. 1 (New York: Henry Holt & Co., 1890), Chap. 10.

same emotions. If they wax and prosper, he feels triumphant; if they dwindle and die away, he feels cast down—not necessarily in the same degree for each thing, but in much the same way for all.

This description of what comes to be called *me* and *mine* makes up what James called the *material self*, having the body as its innermost part and possessions as its outermost. In addition he described the *social self*, and this, too, was something less than a perfect unity.

> Properly speaking, *a man has as many social selves as there are individuals who recognize him* and carry an image of him in their mind. To wound any one of these his images is to wound him. But as the individuals who carry the images fall naturally into classes, we may practically say that he has as many social selves as there are distinct *groups* of persons about whose opinion he cares. He generally shows a different side of himself to each of these different groups. . . . From this there results what practically is a division of the man into several selves; and this may be a discordant splitting, as where one is afraid to let one set of his acquaintances know him as he is elsewhere; or it may be a perfectly harmonious division of labor, as where one tender to his children is stern to the soldiers or prisoners under his command.

James gave recognition here to the interactive nature of personality and also to the governing of behavior by social role expectations. Such opposite traits as tenderness and sternness are not discordant if they are exhibited appropriately in different roles or if they occur in sequence as reactions to different types of behavior on the part of others.

This account of the social selves allows for a great deal of conflict within the personality. James described this conflict in one of his most memorable passages, in which he also indicated the vital selective process whereby conflict can be reduced to a tolerable minimum.

> I am often confronted by the necessity of standing by one of my empirical selves and relinquishing the rest. Not that I would not, if I could, be both handsome and fat and well dressed, and a great athlete, and make a million a year, be a wit, a *bon-vivant*, and a lady-killer, as well as a philosopher; a philanthropist, statesman, warrior, and African explorer, as well as a "tone-poet" and saint. But the thing is simply impossible. The millionaire's work would run counter to the saint's; the *bon-vivant* and the philanthropist would trip each other up; the philosopher and the lady-killer could not well keep house in the same tenement of clay. Such different characters may conceivably at the outset of life be alike possible to a man. But to make any one of them actual, the rest must more or less be suppressed. So the seeker of his truest, strongest, deepest self must review the list carefully, and pick out the one on which to stake his salvation. All other selves thereupon become unreal, but the fortunes of this self are real. Its failures are real failures, its triumphs real triumphs, carrying shame and gladness with them. . . .

I, who for the time have staked my all on being a psychologist, am mortified if others know much more psychology than I. But I am contented to wallow in the grossest ignorance of Greek. My deficiencies there give me no sense of personal humiliation at all. Had I "pretensions" to be a linguist, it would have been just the reverse. So we have the paradox of a man shamed to death because he is only the second pugilist or the second oarsman in the world. That he is able to beat the whole population of the globe minus one is nothing; he has "pitted" himself to beat that one; and as long as he doesn't do that nothing else counts. . . .

Yonder puny fellow, however, whom everyone can beat, suffers no chagrin about it, for he has long ago abandoned the attempt to "carry that line," as the merchants say, of self at all. With no attempt there need be no failure; with no failure, no humiliation. So our self-feeling in this world depends entirely on what we *back* ourselves to be and do.

In this description James included not only the diverse character of different social selves but also the additional element of self-feeling, the range of emotions lying between complacency and dissatisfaction or, in more dramatic terms, between triumph and humiliation. Implicit also are aspects of the experience of self that have to do with its protection and enhancement. James recognized that the experience of activity was of central importance in one's sense of self.[2] In a personal letter he made this clear when he described as the core of a man's personality "the mental or moral attitude in which, when it came upon him, he felt himself most deeply and intensely active and alive. At such moments there is a voice inside him which speaks and says: *'This* is the real me!' " Such moments, he reported, contain "an active element of tension, of holding my own, as it were." A necessary condition is uncertainty about the outcome, so that the feeling includes "a bitter willingness to do or suffer anything"—which, however, is experienced as "a sort of deep enthusiastic bliss."[3]

These descriptions make it apparent that there are several aspects of self. In studying its development it will be helpful to keep constantly in mind at least these three aspects:

1. The self is something about which we know, as an object like other objects in the world of experience. This is its *cognitive* aspect, taking eventually the relatively organized form of self-image or, a little more accurately, of *self-concept*.
2. The self is something that we experience directly, not as "me" and "mine" but as "I." The experience includes a sense of agency, and this can be considered its *active* aspect, which culminates in a *sense of competence*.

[2] Quotations from *The Principles of Psychology* are from pp. 291, 294, 296, 298, 301, 309–310.

[3] *The Letters of William James*, ed. H. James, Vol. 1 (Boston: The Atlantic Monthly Press, 1920), p. 199.

These two aspects of the self correspond to the historical distinction between the self as object and the self as subject.

3. The self is something that we value; this can be called its *affective* aspect. We have an attitude toward ourselves variously compounded of love and hate, pride and belittlement, appreciation and criticism, with an easily arousable urge to enhance the positive valuations. This we shall refer to as *self-esteem*.

Methods of Studying the Self

Before advancing to the problems of development we need to make the topic of the self more immediate by considering the methods used by those who want to find out about other people's selves. The method of introspection has unique virtues but also obvious limitations. It might be interesting simply to ask a person to tell all about himself and then turn the switch that started a tape recorder. Some informants, thus encouraged, would use up a good many reels of tape, but others would feel awkward in replying and puzzled about what was wanted, and in any event it would be unwise to suppose that an account so quickly improvised would yield a searching and unretouched portrait. A variety of sophisticated methods has been devised to approach the topic more circumspectly and give the informant a better chance to disclose his self in its natural habitat.

Best for the purpose, but requiring a great deal of time, is an *intensive personality study* in which the subject participates in a large number of interviews, tests, and experimental situations, being seen by quite a few different examiners. This is the method proposed by Murray in 1938, modified by him and co-workers for use in the selection of personnel during World War II, and embodied in several subsequent research programs including that of the Institute for Personality Assessment and Research at Berkeley.[4] By this method the subject's conception of himself is disclosed gradually in a variety of specific situations and through numerous incidents recollected from the past. Recalling James's views on social selves, it is appropriate that several interviewers differing in age and sex be involved in the proceedings; the subject is likely to show a somewhat different side of himself to each. On the other hand most subjects find it advantageous to have one interviewer who sees them on a number of occasions. If a relation of friendliness and trust develops, it is easier to pass beyond one's immediate repertory of interactions, set aside customary strategies of protection, and talk about more private aspects of one's experience. When subjects are interested in understanding themselves better, and when they have confidence in the good will and respect of the examiners, they will often communicate the information that is needed to form a comprehensive idea of their self-concepts, self-awareness, and self-

[4] H. A. Murray, *Explorations in Personality* (New York: Oxford University Press, 1938); *Assessment of Men* (New York: Holt, Rinehart and Winston, Inc., 1948). See also F. Barron, "The Psychology of Creativity," in *New Directions in Psychology*, Vol. 2 (New York: Holt, Rinehart and Winston, Inc., 1965), pp. 1–134.

esteem. Long and slow as it is, this method is truly basic. Anything less must be accepted as a shortcut, which inevitably misses part of the information.

As an example of the building up of information we can take a procedure that consists simply of an interview on abilities. A specific ability is named, such as mechanical ability, and the subject is asked how good he thinks he is in this respect. He is then asked for specific instances illustrating good performance and others illustrating poor performance. This procedure is directed partly at assessing actual abilities, but the replies almost necessarily include information about the self-concept and sense of competence. One outcome of the procedure is to bring out the importance a subject attaches to different abilities. Harold Merritt, one of the subjects described in Chapter 2, showed in the interview on abilities that he was content to wallow in the grossest ignorance of natural science, even turning it into a virtue—"That's one thing I'm proud of, my scientific ignorance." His low self-rating on physical and athletic ability was a shade more troublesome to him: "I never bothered much with playing sports; preparing for college boards—that may be a slim excuse, I don't really know why." Running through various aspects of economic ability, he characterized himself as having no head for business, disliking shopping, and never arguing with salesmen, but it was clear that this, too, was a line of goods he did not really care about carrying. When it came to qualities such as leading and governing, social ability, entertaining, and understanding other people, as well as intellectual and observational powers, the tenor of his comments was entirely different, even though he did not rate himself especially high. He was backing himself to be an intelligent, alert, poised, confident person who could exert leadership when necessary but who would generally be accepted as likeable, friendly, and kind. He was not afraid to recognize a gap between his *actual* and his *ideal* self-concept; he did not despair of improvement over the course of time. The interview on abilities contributed richly to the understanding of Harold Merritt's self.

The virtue of this sort of leisurely procedure lies in directing the subject's attention to specific happenings. It avoids global and perhaps hasty judgments with respect to abstract qualities. Sometimes an initial statement like "I'm very good at this" or "I'm terrible at that" is modified and even retracted when actual incidents are called to mind. The impression is sometimes strong that real gains are occurring in the informant's understanding of himself. Like everything else, self-judgments can become habituated and automatic. It can be a true educational experience to think systematically about relevant life experiences and to perceive their bearing on an implicit sense of self.

Research would creep forward too slowly, however, if shortcuts in the gathering of data were altogether avoided. For some purposes the saving of time outweighs the loss of information, provided that what is lost is not the real heart of the matter. One can learn something valuable about self-concepts by the use of an *adjective checklist* on which respondents check the qualities they believe to be characteristic of themselves.[5] In itself the method offers

[5] H. G. Gough, *The Adjective Check List* (Palo Alto, Calif: Consulting Psychologists Press, 1961).

little protection against hasty and erroneous self-judgments or against the desire to create a good impression. But if the respondents feel seriously involved in the purposes of the research, and give a moment's reflection to each checkmark, they will provide significant information that can be useful in comparing different groups. Besides the adjective checklist there are various *questionnaires* and *self-rating scales* that can be employed when large numbers of subjects are needed for group comparisons.[6]

A technique that seems matchless in its simplicity is the *Who Am I?* method. In its original form this test asked the informant to write down three answers to the question, "Who are you?"[7] Later the test question was changed to "Who am I?", and the number of answers was enlarged to twenty. A time limit such as twelve minutes is usually set, which keeps the answers brief, gives them a certain immediacy, and precludes extensive revision. Taking the test can be an interesting experience. Many respondents begin with objective facts like name, physical characteristics, and occupation. But it is hard to think of twenty such facts, and before long one is forced to start putting down detailed characteristics. One respondent, for instance, gave as her first five entries: "Clarie M., 5 feet 5 inches tall, a Negro, Catholic, 118 lbs." Then she listed characteristics such as "interested in sports, not conceited, honest with people, one who likes to dance, sometimes easy to get angry, quick to respond to some emotions"—and a portrait of herself began to emerge. Of course, it is necessary to code and score these free responses if the method is to be used with large numbers. A carefully wrought scheme of this kind, tested in several research projects, has been described in detail by Gordon.[8] It includes ascribed characteristics, roles and memberships, interests and activities, and several categories referring specifically to self: sense of moral worth, of self-determination, of unity, and of competence. Based on the sound principle that if you want to know something about somebody the way to find out may well be to ask him, the *Who Am I?* method puts a direct question. After answering it twenty times, most people find that they have said quite a lot.

Self-Esteem

Psychologists eager to affirm their status in the natural sciences have often felt that concepts like the self were too vague and subjective for serious consideration. More recently, however, the self has been honorably readmitted to the psychological laboratory through discovery of the effects

[6] R. Wylie, *The Self Concept: A Critical Survey of Pertinent Research Literature* (Lincoln, Nebr.: University of Nebraska Press, 1963), esp. pp. 69–107.

[7] J. F. T. Bugental and S. L. Zelen, "Investigations into the Self-Concept," *Journal of Personality,* **18** (1950), 483–498.

[8] C. Gordon, "Self-Conceptions: Configurations of Content," in *The Self in Social Interaction,* Vol. 1, ed. C. Gordon and K. J. Gergen (New York: John Wiley & Sons, Inc., 1968), Chap. 11.

of "ego-involving" instructions. Subjects can be given two different types of set with regard to a task they are asked to perform. Instructions that are not ego-involving put emphasis on the casual nature of the requested task. The subject is perhaps told that tests are being tried out to see how long they take and how sensible they seem to be, or it is implied that the information being sought is of an impersonal nature like the mechanics of perception. Ego-involving instructions put emphasis on the personal importance of what is to be done: the task is presented as a test of intelligence, a measure of alertness, an indication of creativity, or an assessment of mental soundness. Subjects perform differently under the two conditions. Ego-involvement tends to evoke a better performance up to a point, but if it calls forth tension and anxiety the performance may be decidedly worse. Many types of performance have been shown experimentally to change in response to the two types of instruction.[9]

What is it that changes when a subject's attitude toward a given task shifts from casual to ego-involved, from "This doesn't really matter" to "This really does matter"? What makes the test matter is that one's self has been drawn into the picture: the subject feels, "I am being tested, my worth is being evaluated in relation to others, I am being called upon to show how good I am, how alert, how on the ball, how able to take it." What is at stake is not simply the cognition of oneself nor the feeling of activity; it is the *value* of the self, one's *worth* as a person in the eyes of others but especially in one's own eyes. The issue is self-esteem.

The maintenance and enhancement of self-esteem has often been classified as a motive. Sometimes it is given the status of the master motive in human life.[10] It might be more accurate to conceive of the self as a nexus of motives, a configuration into which are gathered different kinds of motives now stamped as "me" and "mine." The existence of this larger configuration adds a *superordinate motive* to those already present; satisfaction of a particular need must now be made consistent with being a person who is worthy of respect. This may mean the renunciation of some forms of need satisfaction and the redirecting of others. The dramatic religious conversions in Christian history, like those of St. Augustine and St. Francis of Assisi, represent a turning away from easy hedonism, in spite of its many satisfactions, in order to give one's life lasting meaning on earth and in heaven. The childhood prototype of such reorganization is becoming aware, often with outside prompting, that one is now a big boy or a big girl and that big children do not whine or cry or leave things in a mess the way little ones do. The growing configuration of the self may also require new ventures: it is time now to have a summer job, to earn money, to have sexual experience, to think about marriage, to take on adult responsibilities. To the extent that we accomplish what we back ourselves to be, self-esteem is maintained and enhanced. But

[9] M. Sherif and H. Cantril, *The Psychology of Ego-Involvements* (New York: John Wiley & Sons, Inc., 1947).

[10] F. LeDantec, *L'egoïsme, seule Base de toute Société* (Paris: Flammarion, 1916).

if we fall short, even by being second best where we had rashly backed ourselves to be first, our hearts are likely to be dark with humiliation, shame, and feelings of inferiority.

Daydreaming and Self-Esteem

One way to convince oneself of the importance of self-esteem is to examine the part it plays in the covert thoughts that often accompany our activities and in the daydreams it is our pleasure to manufacture.

A theological student, very successful by external standards, was repeatedly troubled by an intrusion of selfish motives into his work. When he received praise after preaching eloquently, he was aware of basking in it, and he recalled that the anticipation of such a result had influenced the preparation of his sermon. When he visited the sick and tried to bring comfort he would sometimes be conscious of satisfaction in how well he was doing the job. When as a student pastor he reconciled warring factions in the parish he found himself thinking how pleased his teachers would be with his diplomatic prowess. These manifestations of self-love distressed him because he aspired to truly altruistic conduct. His ideal was exceptionally high, but otherwise there is nothing unusual about his experience. Many people are aware, or can easily become aware, that along with the realistic and public reasons for their behavior run wishes of a more private character. Sometimes these wishes can be captured just as they occur, as when in the act of applauding a speaker one thinks of being oneself applauded, very likely more loudly for a success more dramatic. Usually the awareness comes in brief retrospect; a student realizes afterward that when congratulating a friend on a good grade he was also wondering what combination of luck and favoritism had made the grade so much better than his own. This running accompaniment would doubtless be observed with greater regularity if it yielded more unmixed pleasure. Even those who do not aspire to complete altruism find it hard to avoid embarrassment at the vanity, pettiness, and egotism so frequently displayed in these thoughts.

Daydreams seem to be built out of the same material. They differ in being of longer duration and more elaborate construction. Of some daydreams we are fully aware; we may enjoy them to the point of building upon them from occasion to occasion, so that they come to have a permanent character. In a recent study, Singer describes with admirable candor three recurrent daydreams that formed a part of his mental life in childhood and many years later. The first of these dealt with the exploits of a football hero, the second with the distinguished achievements of a great statesman, the third with the triumphs of a great composer of music. These daydreams developed almost like novels, involving a whole series of incidents and characters, and they were always available for enjoyment in times of boredom or fatigue.[11] Rousseau tells in his *Confessions* that upon reaching an age at which he felt

---

[11] J. L. Singer, *Daydreaming: An Introduction to the Experimental Study of Inner Experience* (New York: Random House, Inc., 1966).

there was no longer any chance that his erotic daydreams would have counterparts in reality, he simply gave them their head, so to speak, to evolve as they wanted; the result was his romantic novel, *La Nouvelle Héloïse*.[12] The compensatory possibilities of a conscious fantasy life of this kind are memorably represented in Thurber's sketch, "The Secret Life of Walter Mitty."[13]

Much daydreaming is more fleeting, less structured, and less readily recalled. In an early introspective study Varendonck developed a technical method for recovering these more elusive forms of fantasy. The method was derived from Freud's study of dreams, in which the dreams of each night were written out in full immediately upon waking, before they had a chance to fade from memory. Varendonck developed the habit of watching for bits of daydreams and whenever possible writing them down at once. He was able in this way not only to capture material that would otherwise have been lost but also to reconstruct long chains of free associative thoughts leading up to the item that had caught his attention. The daydreams recaptured by this method showed much egotistical content, but they were not simply wish-fulfillments. Sometimes they were steered by anxiety and were not pleasant. On other occasions they dealt with their author's intellectual work as though continuing the preoccupations of his waking life.[14]

At its best, human motivation is channeled into behavior that is adapted to valuable purposes and responsive to surrounding conditions. The study of daydreams gives us a glimpse of motivation when the inevitable constraints of reality can be laid aside and we can have things exactly as we would like them. Under these circumstances we appear to be rather startlingly interested in personal glory. We want other people to applaud, admire, envy, and perhaps even fear us. We are cruel in our jealousies and resentments, unbounded in our erotic wishes. Daydreams, of course, are not always so embarrassingly self-centered. They sometimes contain generous impulses, the giving of presents, caring for those who stand in need, or attaining an ideal of mutual love. But it is hard to escape the conclusion that when thinking of things exactly as we would like them, we would especially like them to contribute more handsomely to our pride and glory.

Daydreams provide important information about the force and range of our wishes, but they are not highly successful in actually enhancing self-esteem. What they lack is the experience of accomplishment, of bringing about a desired result through effortful influence upon the environment. Thus no matter how brilliantly we imagine the thunderous applause and delirious rapture of a colossal audience utterly overwhelmed by our stupendous performance, the daydream is weak in one respect: we did not actually perform. When we have actually performed in some way, a mild clatter of handclap-

[12] J. J. Rousseau, *The Confessions of Jean-Jacques Rousseau* (New York: The Modern Library, Inc.).

[13] J. Thurber, "The Secret Life of Walter Mitty," in *My Life—and Welcome to It* (New York: Harcourt Brace Jovanovich, Inc., 1942).

[14] J. Varendonck, *The Psychology of Daydreams* (London and New York: The Macmillan Company, 1921).

ping or even a few privately spoken words of appreciation will probably yield a greater satisfaction than the most extravagant daydream. It is important to keep this principle in mind because certain developments in psychiatry have tended to give daydreaming an undeserved bad name. The apparent absorption of schizophrenic patients in fantasy led to the idea that daydreaming satisfied the wishes and stole the energy that ought to be directed toward realistic effort. More likely this proposition should be turned around: daydreams become an exclusive activity only when efforts at realistic behavior are badly frustrated. Many people can remember elaborate daydreams that did not in the least undermine their active living or spoil such satisfactions as came their way. A girl who has imagined princes and heroes does not on that account reject the awkward attentions of the not very attractive first real boy who shows an interest in her. A boy who has pitched and batted his baseball team to glorious victories on the diamond of his fancy does not on that account fail to enjoy being substitute right fielder on a real team that loses most of its games. Self-esteem requires real performance. As a usual thing it cannot settle for imagined substitutes.

Dual Sources of Self-Esteem

Theorizing about self-esteem has often been hampered by a failure to appreciate that it is fed from two different springs. There is an external source, the esteem in which we are held by other people, and an internal source, our own sense of competence in dealing with our surroundings. Sometimes self-esteem is thought of as if the external source were the only one; its level is regulated by the amount of love and attention pumped in by the immediate environment. As Fenichel expressed it, "The small child loses self-esteem when he loses love and attains it when he regains love."[15] Others have expressed doubt about the power of the external source: Silverberg, for example, considered it "always more uncertain" and regarded the inner source as "the steadier and more dependable one." "Unhappy and insecure is the man," he continued, "who, lacking an adequate inner source of self-esteem, must depend for this almost wholly upon external sources. It is the condition seen by the psychotherapist almost universally among his patients."[16]

This contrasting of external and internal sources should not obscure the important interactions that go on between them. The child's self-esteem is certainly much influenced by the evaluations that proceed from others. Their acts and attitudes show how they think of him and thus influence him to think of himself in the same way. A young child's self-esteem can be dramatically buoyed by parental praise and as dramatically crushed by contempt. Writing with reference to the second and third years, Stern pointed out that

[15] O. Fenichel, *The Psychoanalytic Theory of Neurosis* (New York: W. W. Norton & Company, Inc., 1945), p. 41.

[16] W. V. Silverberg, *Childhood Experience and Personal Destiny* (New York: Springer Publishing Co., Inc., 1952), p. 29.

the child "feels a craving not only for sympathy but for applause for his little accomplishments from those around him. No child really flourishes without the sunshine of this praise, with the encouragement it gives to ever-renewed effort."[17] But the child's own behavior certainly has a part in influencing the amount and warmth of the sunshine; he must produce the little accomplishments and make the necessary effort. People do not usually bestow praise whimsically or continuously without reference to what the child has actually done. As Erikson expresses it, children "cannot be fooled by empty praise and condescending encouragement. They may have to accept artificial bolstering of their self-esteem in lieu of something better," but they gain real strength only from "wholehearted and consistent recognition of real accomplishment."[18] If the external source were solely responsible for self-esteem, children could always be fooled by empty praise. They are not fooled because, increasingly in the course of time, they have an internal criterion of the success and value of what they do. If an act falls short of one's intention, if it fails of its purpose even though it may qualify as a "good try," if it brings no feeling of efficacy and adds nothing to one's sense of competence, then praise will be experienced as empty.

A Study of Antecedents

Pertinent to this problem is a study by Coopersmith of the antecedents of individual differences in self-esteem.[19] The subjects were public school boys in the age range from 10 to 12. Their current level of self-esteem was first measured by their self-ratings on an inventory especially prepared for the purpose. This was given to a large number of subjects from whom eighty-five were selected for further study, representing a good range of individual differences. Further information was obtained from ratings by teachers, from a program of psychological tests and an interview, and from a series of experimental situations presumably related to self-esteem. From this considerable amount of information it was possible to make ratings of the subjects' current level of self-esteem. Information on antecedents was derived from three sources: a questionnaire dealing with the parents' child-rearing attitudes and practices, filled out by the mothers; a two-hour interview with each mother; and the child's own responses to questions on parental attitudes and practices.

What makes for high self-esteem? Coopersmith concludes as follows:

> The most general statement about the antecedents of self-esteem can be given in terms of three conditions: total or nearly total *acceptance* of the child by the parents, clearly defined and enforced *limits*, and the

[17] W. Stern, *Psychology of Early Childhood* (1914) (New York: Holt, Rinehart and Winston, Inc., 2d ed., 1930), p. 503.

[18] E. H. Erikson, *Childhood and Society*, 2d ed. (New York: W. W. Norton & Company, Inc., 1963), p. 235.

[19] S. Coopersmith, *The Antecedents of Self-Esteem* (San Francisco: W. H. Freeman and Company, 1967).

respect and latitude for individual action that exist within the defined limits. In effect we can conclude that the parents of children with high self-esteem are concerned and attentive toward their children, that they structure the worlds of their children along lines they believe to be proper and appropriate, and that they permit relatively great freedom within the structures they have established.[20]

It comes as no surprise that parental acceptance should be among the antecedents. We would expect this attitude to build a feeling of being loved and cherished, serving thus as an external source of self-esteem. Hardly more surprising is the presence of "respect and latitude for individual action," which implies giving scope to the initiative and effort that contribute to a sense of competence, then ratifying this inner source by respectful recognition. Perhaps somewhat more unexpected is the association in this connection between respect and clear parental values and limits. "Detailed definitions of standards," Coopersmith writes, "and their consistent presentation and enforcement, presents the child with a wealth of information that he himself can employ to appraise and anticipate the consequences of his actions." In a world thus structured the child has more abundant opportunities to experience competence. When there are no standards of social behavior, the child has a good deal less chance to experience success or failure of his efforts. But we must not overlook the subjects' level of development. They were preadolescent boys, not yet as touchy about independence as they would probably become in a few years' time.

Development of the Self

There need be nothing mysterious about the origin of the self-concept. The human organism is well endowed with powers of observing and knowing. Among the things that enter its cognitive field are the visible surfaces of the body, the sounds of the voice, and the sensations of touch and muscular activity. There is no reason to suppose that these impressions originally carry any special marks of selfhood. Indeed there is a good deal of evidence that young children do not at first discriminate between me and not-me; it is only through experience that one learns such interesting facts as that the shoe comes off but the foot does not. But because the living organism is in fact an integrated system the experiences arising from it tend to occur together. On this basis, to quote Gardner Murphy, "the organism appropriately orders these diverse impressions into an integrated whole and agrees to call it by the name which others have given it, just as it accepts the names that are current for other distinguishable wholes."[21] The same principles of learning can be involved for self-perception as apply to the perception of any

---

[20] *Ibid.*, p. 236.
[21] G. Murphy, *Personality: A Biosocial Approach to Origin and Structure* (New York: Harper & Row, Publishers, 1947), p. 479.

other object. The self, however, does not long remain one among many objects in a republic of equals. It has something special that soon makes it a supremely important object, a treasured possession.

If the body provides the original nexus for a sense of self, another source of unity and continuity is experienced through the action of memory. Gordon Allport described as follows the almost paradoxical persistence through change that springs from this source.[22]

> Today I remember some of my thoughts of yesterday, and tomorrow I shall remember some of my thoughts of both yesterday and today; and I am certain that they are the thoughts of the same person—of myself. Even an oldster of eighty is sure that he is the same "I" as at the age of three, although everything about him—including the cells of his body and his environment—has changed many times over. This sense of self-identity is a striking phenomenon, since change is otherwise the invincible rule of growth. Every experience we have modifies our brain, so it is impossible for the identical experience to occur a second time. For this reason every thought, every act is altered with time. Yet the self-identity continues, even though we know that the rest of our personality has changed.

No doubt this phenomenon should be classed with the broader one of *object constancy*. Similarly at 80 we recognize objects first encountered when we were 3, knowing that this dusty, faded, motheaten cloth cat found in a long-forgotten box is the very one we used to take to bed with us at that earlier time. There is a continuity of configurations even when every detail seems to have changed.

These two characteristics, the constant presence of the body and the succession of interlocking memories, constitute the core of the self as an organized system. With us always, and peculiar to ourselves, are our body and our stream of mental experience. But the self as a system undergoes a large growth and differentiation over the course of time. It is in part a social product, developing in interaction with others; in part an internal product, consisting of an organization of motives, preferences, and capacities. Just as self-esteem has an outer and an inner source, the self as system and concept develops through the dual action of external influences and internal powers.

Self as a Social Product

Developing a self-concept implies perceiving oneself as an object. We are able to do this, according to G. H. Mead, because other people take us as objects and show in their behavior what kinds of objects they think we are. "The self," wrote Mead, "is essentially a social structure. . . . It is impossible to conceive of a self arising outside of social experience."[23] There are, of

---

[22] G. W. Allport, *Pattern and Growth in Personality* (New York: Holt, Rinehart and Winston, Inc., 1961), pp. 114–115.

[23] G. H. Mead, *Mind, Self and Society* (Chicago: University of Chicago Press, 1934).

course, things that we can perceive about ourselves without social mediation, but Mead was calling attention to our considerable dependence upon other people to characterize us and show us how we affect our social environment. A child incorporates in his own repertory the behavior he elicits from others. Scolded for breaking his toys, he may be heard next day scolding himself for starting another piece of destruction; praised for putting the toys neatly away, he may again perform this act to a verbal accompaniment of self-congratulation on being a neat child. Without social judgments, we might have grave difficulty in learning about ourselves as social beings.

Much of this learning through social interaction can go on without coming to a clear focus in awareness. When two adults talk over a child's head it is implied, not stated, that the child is too young to understand, and the child may register merely a dim sense of exclusion and inferiority. But the process can be quite explicit, as Gardner Murphy indicates in the following statement.[24]

> Children are forever classifying one another by the use of good and bad names, applying to one another the nouns and adjectives which they have heard used in such a tone as to make them appropriate for praising or damning. The vocabulary of the self becomes, so to speak, less and less *visual*, and in general less and less *sensory*. It becomes more and more a language of traits. Most of the trait names that are used represent general action tendencies; and as soon as they are applied to oneself, or as soon as one finds himself applying them to others, they stimulate a trait psychology in their user. Consequently, over and above the generalities of behavior which are already there, generalities are evoked by means of labels, and behavior is made to generalize as would any conditioned response; the child lives up to the terms employed. . . . Child psychiatry has empirically confirmed the fact that the appellations which become part of the self work more and more to induce behavior appropriate to them. The child forms general ideas of himself. *In short, the self becomes less and less a pure perceptual object, and more and more a conceptual trait system.*

The development of the self as a conceptual trait system might be taken to imply greater finality and rigidity than is in fact the case. When they fill out self-rating scales every day for a period of weeks, some individuals show only a small amount of change, but others fluctuate greatly from occasion to occasion depending on state of health, mood, and immediately preceding experiences of success and failure.[25] The conceptual trait system is likely to include qualities rated by their possessor along a scale from good to bad. When physical vigor is high or when events go well, the good traits in the spectrum tend to shine with a brighter light, but the fortunes and fatigues of another day can shift the beam toward the bad end. In cases of extreme mood swing the two self-concepts may show almost no overlap, but ordinary

[24] Murphy, *Personality*, pp. 505–506.

[25] See the research, discussed above in Chapter 7, by A. E. Wessman and D. F. Ricks, *Mood and Personality* (New York: Holt, Rinehart and Winston, Inc., 1966).

fluctuations have the character of changes of emphasis in what is a relatively enduring configuration.

Dependence of the self-concept on external sources is illustrated in the already mentioned case of Harold Merritt, who as a college sophomore still often described himself by reporting what others said about him. "I have often been told that I am bashful," he wrote; "I think that those whom I know have a favorable attitude toward me"; "My mother says I talk too much"; "There are members of my family who say that I ought to be success-ful because I have a pleasing personality and can get along with people." Merritt's reliance on what other people said about him demonstrates the importance of this source of information in the forming of a self-concept. It also suggests a certain difficulty in making up his own mind, and this was congruent with the timid, uncertain, anxious character of his strategies of adaptation. He was so disinclined toward assertion that he had in fact a some-what dim perception of himself as an active agent. Ten years later, seasoned by military, vocational, and marital experience, Merritt described himself without constantly resorting to the opinions of outside authorities. His exam-ple points to the importance of the internal aspect of self, the experience of activity and its relation to sense of competence.

As we saw in Chapter 11, a substantial part of what we come to know about the human environment comes from *responding to the expectations of other people*. These expectations contribute also to the construction of the self. Important in this respect are the various roles that we learn to enact through the tutelage, explicit or implicit, of the social environment. These include sex roles, a variety of childhood roles, and in the course of time the roles that are appropriate for vocation and place in adult society. A transi-tional role that is sometimes imposed with great force by ambitious parents is that of bright and well-rounded high school student qualified for admission to a highly rated college. This is vividly shown in the following account, given in retrospect by a college student, of an interview with a college admissions officer. The student had been aware of strong family pressure to be outstanding.

> The interviewer's first words to me were a simple, "Tell me about your-self." Expecting specific questions and being extremely nervous, I was at a loss as to what to say. It dawned on me that I had no "self" to describe, my ego being only a carefully constructed image, an impressive but empty facade formed during my high school years with the increas-ingly conscious purpose of getting myself into college. An embarrassing silence ensued, relieved at last by the interviewer's asking, "Well, what are your interests, for a start?" I began methodically listing the many extracurricular activities I was involved in and the offices I held, but it was painfully apparent to me—and undoubtedly to the interviewer—that I was listing activities, not interests.
>
> This episode marked the beginning of a period of self-examina-tion which is still going on, a period of reassessing values and searching for genuine interests and goals.

What interpretation is to be put on this student's distinction between "activities" and "interests," and upon his search for goals that he would experience as "genuine"? There is certainly a sense in which he must have accepted the parentally inspired goal of "getting myself into college," but we must also account for the fact that he came to realize so clearly what was lacking in it. Once more we are confronted with those interior aspects of a person that make it possible to discriminate between congenial and uncongenial roles, between qualities he wants to copy and those he does not, between social expectations he is glad to meet and those he would experience as crippling, between interests that are momentary and those that are intrinsic. Such discriminations, which would be impossible for a responding machine, turn out to be highly characteristic of human living systems.

Self as an Internal Product

Implicit in the self-concept is what the person feels himself to be capable of doing. The answers written down in the "Who Am I?" procedure often include capabilities and accomplishments. The picture of the self that takes shape during extended interviews is typically supported by events in which the subject took an active part and by indications of his feelings of efficacy, or lack of them, in various directions. Level of confidence is an important aspect of the self-concept, even if the subject takes it somewhat for granted and does not make it central in describing himself. Thus the self as object and the self as subject do not stay separate in a person's conception of himself. What he is like as an object, as if seen through other eyes, cannot be divorced from what he is like as an agent as directly experienced by himself.

The internal contribution to the growth of the self comes from the fact that as living creatures we are active and expansive and that very early we begin to develop preferences in the directions taken by our strivings. Indeed we are born with nascent preferences: biological individuality ensures that each of us begins life with a subtle blend of constitutional and temperamental qualities that make certain modes of functioning more natural and agreeable than others. Each of us then embarks upon life in a unique family, which will further affect our preferences through the encouragements of affection and praise and the discouragements of frustration and anxiety. Meeting a wider social environment, we learn to strike some kind of bargain between its demands and our capacities. In such ways each person develops a whole pattern of personal preferences. The many different things that it is possible to do, the roles it is possible to fill, the expectations that are always a part of the environment come to be colored by different shades of congeniality, and to the extent that the person feels free to act upon his preferences he can select the possibilities he most wants to make his own.

The following illustration presents a contrast to those described in the previous section. A young man whose parents kept a small country store had with great effort worked his way through a teachers' college and taken a position in a local high school. The nature of his preferences had already been exhibited in the role he found for himself as helper in the family store. The customers considered him an asset because he was unfailingly pleasant, helped them find what they needed, and took time to chat with them about things that were going on. Teaching in high school, he found it necessary to behave in a different fashion. He could maintain an acceptable minimum of order and work only by a strictness that put him at a distance from the students. He could play this part, but it was not what he wanted. His natural and acquired preferences called for human interactions that were warmer, more personal, less tinged with the assertion of authority. With further economic sacrifice he returned to school to prepare himself for the position of counselor to students, a role more consistent with being unfailingly pleasant, helping to find what is needed, and taking time to chat.

Sometimes the experience of finding one's niche, discovering the activity that feels right and seems to release all one's powers, can be a highly dramatic event. "This is what I have always wanted," "This is really me," "Now I have found myself"—such are the statements that often express this experience, signifying that harmony has been found between some pattern of living and the pattern of one's inner preferences.

As we saw in Chapter 11, *identification* provides a shortcut to forming new patterns of behavior. This form of imitation can be said to occur when copying a model is generalized beyond specific acts and springs from wanting to be and trying to be like the model with respect to some broad quality such as competence or attractiveness. Identification assuredly has a significant place in the development of the self. If one could recover the complete history of a person's identifications it would tell a great deal about the growth of his personality. But if it were truly complete, so that one also knew the available models that had not been imitated, the history would exhibit a steady process of selection based upon internal preferences. It would also show that identification does not mean copying everything about a model. A boy may imitate his father's gait, the tilt of his head, the sound of his voice, and his language when the power lawn-mower will not start, all in the interest of being a competent male, without being drawn irresistibly into the father's vocation and style of life. Children identify with qualities they perceive and infer in others, but these are simply parts or fragments of the people copied. Identifications with parents sometimes seem to be quite pervasive, but typically children copy certain qualities drawn from a large number of models, each of whom has appealed because of a particular strength. What identification produces, then, is a collection of what might be called self-fragments, and it is at once evident that these have to be put together into some kind of workable pattern. A living system cannot be a museum of copied traits. Selection and synthesis are implicit.

It is not sufficient, however, to let the last sentence stand as if it were a final explanation. We need to come nearer, if possible, to the nature of the happenings that produce selection and synthesis. To this end we shall now examine in some detail a concept that will be given the name *self-dramatization*.

The Concept of Self-Dramatization

The need for an additional concept to account for the development of the self arises from the observation that people are capable of making designs for their own development. The clearest evidence of this capacity is forward planning, which may be realistic, practical, and fully conscious. Planning one's life, however, can be regarded as simply a rational implementing of a broader tendency better described as imagining what one wants to do and be. If we spend a certain amount of time thinking ahead, we probably spend a lot more time imagining ahead, dreaming ahead, creating pictures of ourselves behaving in future situations. However much these imaginings owe for their material to the self-fragments picked up by identification, to the roles adopted from the expectations of other people, and to the capacities and preferences arising from personal experience, what we tend to create is pictures—concrete instances of ourselves in particular situations. The high school teacher disgruntled with discipline pictures himself as a guidance counselor acting as a sympathetic friend to his students. Only after developing this scene in the realm of imagination does he turn to college catalogues, calculate his economic resources, and plan the practical steps that may turn the dream into a reality. Imagining, forming images, is at the heart of self-dramatization. Even when it occurs only momentarily in a specific situation, it implies an organization of behavior according to an image of what one wants to be at that moment. In more enduring manifestations there comes to be a long-range organization of behavior under the guidance of an internally developing conception of the person one would like to become.

Misgivings may be felt at calling such a process self-dramatization and thus introducing the analogy of the stage. The analogy is not wholly welcome. It suggests behavior that is superficial, histrionic, put on for a purpose; it does not sufficiently imply the real self or the true personality, which even a professional actor harbors in his private life. Contemporary sophistication about timid conformities, self-deceptions, putting up a social front, and creating a public image has produced for many people a revulsion against human interactions that are not expressive of how one really feels—that do not meet a strenuous standard of honesty and authenticity. Self-dramatization can indeed produce much that is false and deceptive, done merely to create an impression, the extreme instance being that of the purposeful imposter. But the term is used here in the broader sense of Shakespeare's metaphor in *As You Like It*—"All the world's a stage, / And all the men and women merely players." If the world is a stage, what is played may be entirely appropriate to one's inner state of development. Self-dramatization can produce good consequences as well as bad. To speak of dramatizing is still a metaphor, but it seems a singularly apt one for the events it is intended to describe.

There is always an element of drama in what we imagine for ourselves. In daydreams we typically manufacture dramatic scenes involving ourselves and a cast of other actors in a plot that is likely to be flattering to our self-esteem. We hear ourselves speaking, often rather brilliantly, and we hear others replying, often rather feebly. Furthermore, the idea of social roles, upon which we have leaned in several of the previous chapters and which has become a key concept in social science, is built on an analogy with the theater. A social role can be likened to a script provided by society. The person must play the part, even though there may be scope for individual interpretation. The ubiquity of the theatrical analogy should not be considered surprising. The theater is supposed to represent real life and real human interactions; no wonder that we think of ourselves as players on a stage even when casting ourselves in modest parts. The imagery is natural and spontaneous.

We can assume that a great deal of self-dramatization is only fleetingly if at all conscious. One of the illuminations that sometimes happens as a result of self-examination is the recognition of a totally unwitting bit of drama in oneself. One has been entering rooms like a great actress coming on stage, expecting everyone to look and applaud. One has been speaking in a condescending tone of voice as if one were a great authority explaining things to the ignorant. One has been telling a tale of unremitting hardship and unfairness, hoping to evoke the sympathy that is due a victim. To describe the controlling process in such instances as a part in a drama is not merely metaphorical; it is the only adequate way to account for the effects produced. Even our most honorable ideals can be described as images of a part to be played. If a person seeks a way of life in which open, authentic emotional relations are given the highest priority, his purpose should not be considered demeaned if he describes it as the part he would like to play in an ideal human drama. If he wants to guide his life according to high principles, his aspirations are not cheapened by the dramatic element in his public stands. When Thoreau went to jail rather than pay taxes, when he moved to his cabin on the shore of Walden Pond to demonstrate the practicality and satisfactions of a simplified life, he was standing for principles in a memorable way, the more memorable because he chose such dramatic forms.

It will be recalled that when describing strategies of living in the last chapter we found the theatrical analogy already in use in Goffman's account of presentation of self. It is easy to think of the tactics of ingratiation as a part that is being enacted, and to translate Berne's "games people play" into "dramas people stage." Even the more enduring strategic styles lend themselves to this translation; the derogatory style, for instance, is expressed in lines appropriate to be spoken by a character with unassailable self-confidence, whom nobody can fool. The Bethesda high school students were properly described as rehearsing the kind of parts they believed would be required of them in college. And surely the aspiration to go down in history as a good president fits the imagery of playing a part on the wide stage of public life. We can pursue this theme to further advantage by looking at two very different examples in which self-dramatization had an organizing effect over a long stretch of time.

Sartre on His Childhood

The power of self-dramatization and the struggle, as understanding developed, to make it compatible with both outer and inner conditions, is brilliantly described in Jean-Paul Sartre's story of his childhood.[26] Following his father's early death, Sartre was brought up in a household consisting of his mother and her parents. Because of fancied poor health he was not sent to school until the age of 10, but he had the run of his grandfather's extensive library and spent a great deal of time there. The grandfather, a language teacher and scholar, was given to dramatizing his quiet old age with exaggerated scenes of emotion and affection in which he characterized the little boy as a gift from heaven and as a miracle of intelligence and taste because of his precocious absorption in great works in literature. Jean-Paul's self-image was further inflated by the doting admiration of his mother, who was certain that her son was destined for greatness. The child constantly tried to live up to this billing. However slightly he understood or liked the great books, he continued to exhibit zeal in reading them and in making comments that were treated as pearls of wisdom. The household revolved around him, and he accepted the dramatization that was conferred upon him by the expectations of his mother and grandfather. When he began to write stories, visitors were allowed to peek into his room and see him working at a small desk, but they were not permitted to speak or to disturb the young genius while the creative process was going on.

This state of affairs was not destined to endure. As his understanding grew, Jean-Paul became aware that the household did not wholly revolve around him. The adults had things of their own to talk about and would sometimes exclude him from their conversations. Attempting to construe this frustration, the boy began to sense that there was something false about his grandfather's scenes and his mother's boundless admiration. "I suspected adults of faking," he wrote years later; "the words they spoke to me were candies, but they talked among themselves in quite another tone." Less disposed now to please them, he also suspected himself of faking: "I was an imposter." He discovered, in other words, that his playing up to adult expectancies had not embodied interests of his own other than that of eliciting their praise. Through other channels he had begun to make contact with deeply rooted wishes of another sort. His indulgent mother had allowed him access to a kind of literature much deplored by his grandfather, cheap books of adventure written for boys, and with the help of these stories he had constructed for himself a rich fantasy life of bold action and heroic rescues. These fantasies were absorbing and real to him, and they provided the material for the stories with which he filled many notebooks.

These attainments in self-dramatization, at their height at the age of 8, were also not destined to endure. As cognitive development continued he

---

[26] J.-P. Sartre, *The Words*, trans. B. Frechtman (New York: George Braziller, Inc., 1964).

perceived with increasing sharpness the incongruity between the heroes of his tales and the small, lame, ugly boy he saw in the mirror. He also sensed incongruity between the heroic fantasies that were spun out of his head and the actual deeds of heroism that began to be reported back to Paris from the battlefront of World War I. These challenging difficulties were met by a new effort at self-dramatization, a new imaginative construction in which, as he put it, "I palmed off on the writer the sacred powers of the hero." Continuing to feel himself a gift from heaven (once rooted, this idea is extremely difficult to eradicate) he now pictured himself as a gift to all mankind as a great writer. He perceived on a grandiose scale the service performed by great writers. By putting great thoughts into words they provided mankind with an illumination, a guidance, even a salvation that could come from no other source. No wonder, then, that they called forth passionate gratitude and achieved lasting fame.

Sartre tells us that this self-dramatization, heir to the fantasies of heroic action, took form in his mind when at 9 he was still isolated from influences outside the family. Although he refers to it as a "madness" and a "delirium," measuring it against his adult conception of the limited influence exerted by writers, he makes it clear that this fantasy did not disappear. When he went to school, made friends with other boys, and thus greatly enlarged the scope of his experience, he stopped writing stories; the great writer "gladly consented to remain incognito for a while." Although the self-dramatization receded from awareness, it continued as a forcible influence upon the course of his life. "I stopped seeing it," he wrote; "it shaped me; it exercised its power of attraction on everything. . . . My mandate became my character; my delirium left my head and flowed into my bones." Only when nearly 50 did he begin to realize the subtle continuing presence of this self-dramatization in his life. For the next decade, up until the writing of *The Words*, he was "a man who's been waking up, cured of a long, bittersweet madness." Doubtless we owe to this belated awakening Sartre's extraordinary insight into the origins, history, and power of his 9-year-old self-dramatization. Often enough, it is reasonable to guess, the parts in which we cast ourselves guide our performance without ever being fully exposed to the seasoned cognitions of later years.[27]

The Rise and Decline of a Tennis Star

That a self-dramatization can influence extensive tracts of behavior over a long time is well shown in the case of a girl who at the age of 12 decided to become a tennis star. The circumstances that led to this decision were unusual. The girl, whom we shall call Gloria, had until then showed neither special interest nor remarkable ability in tennis. Her decision resulted quite suddenly from reading an article about a former woman champion. Describing this article some years later, she put especial emphasis on the pictures, which showed the striking suppleness and grace with which the former

[27] The quotations from *The Words* are from pages 83, 85, 167, 230, 253.

champion made her shots. This, Gloria decided, was what she wanted to be: a graceful figure, effective, a champion, the center of attention of an admiring, applauding crowd. When an image of this kind exerts such magnetic power we are entitled to suppose that it suddenly brings to a focus a number of different wants that have not hitherto joined in a single pattern. Be this as it may, the direction of Gloria's life was considerably changed by her reading of the article. Schoolwork and social life, though sketchily maintained, were now subordinated to the goal of learning to play championship tennis.

The pursuit of this goal was arduous. Expert coaching and year-round practice were clearly required. As the family lived in a cold climate, it was necessary during the long winter months to drive every day after school to a city an hour away where there were indoor courts. In summer the program called for intensive coaching at a tennis camp where she went as a boarder. Maximum physical fitness was prerequisite to success, and for Gloria this entailed a strict diet, as she had a tendency to put on more weight than was compatible with a supple and graceful game. Enduring this strenuous regimen was aided by her mother's support. Gloria was the only child and the mother had no job, so she took on her daughter's career as her own main occupation, serving as chauffeur, watchdog, critic, and source of encouragement. At the end of three years Gloria was doing well enough in minor competitions to put it within the bounds of possibility that her dream of championship might someday come true.

As is usual in personality, a number of different processes were involved simultaneously in this aspect of Gloria's life. Her initial decision can be adequately described as an identification; she was going to copy the model who apparently enjoyed so much felicity. But the model was present only in print and could not be directly imitated in detail. Such an elusive model, even though the central image retained its position as a guiding light, had to be continually filled out by ideas and images composed by the subject herself. Gloria was also responding to her mother's expectations, trying to be an ideal daughter, for the mother had quickly formed a powerful self-dramatization as mother of a tennis champion. Again, however, these expectations on the part of a person who had never been a tennis star could hardly define the role in more than a general way. In a very real sense Gloria had to be the author of her script and the director of the production.

For three years Gloria's life was organized mainly by her self-dramatization, but eventually she tired of the show and let it close. The sacrifices were too great to be endured any longer. Her own purpose weakened sooner than her mother's; at the end there was an element of rebellion against maternal expectations, symbolized by her stealing the food that would assuage her appetite but add to her weight. No longer practicing or dieting faithfully, she decided to pass up a match that could have been a stepping-stone toward the top, thus effectively killing her chances of championship. Her interests turned back to schoolwork and social life, and her racquet was put on a shelf. In the cool light of reason—not the warm light of feeling in which self-dramatizations flourish—one can say that it is always a mistake to specify in one's drama such highly improbable achievements as being first, being a champion, winning a Nobel prize, becoming a renowned pianist, being elected president. The sacrifices and disappointments are almost certain to be too great if the activity along the way is not in itself sufficiently rewarding to provide contentment at a lower echelon of performance. Gloria did not enjoy tennis enough to play it without a distant and glittering goal. But possibly Sartre would not have continued through the discouraging early stages of a literary career without his silent self-dramatization as a writer-hero, and that would have been a pity.

Undoubtedly these two examples are more dramatic, lending themselves more readily to the metaphor of the stage, than would generally be the case. Images of what one would like to become can be less vivid, less inclusive, less uncompromising, more open to revision, more accessible to growing knowledge of concrete realities, without altogether losing their significance in the organization of personality. We live our lives in a forward direction, thinking and planning to some degree for the future; this is true even if we choose to look ahead only for a day or an hour. Inseparable from looking ahead is at least some nascent imagining of what we will do and how we will feel—some nascent self-dramatization—which contributes to the ensuing organization of behavior.

Ego Identity

The concept of ego identity has been widely used since its introduction by Erik Erikson in 1950.[28] As we have not in this book made a distinction between self and ego, we might for consistency's sake speak of self-identity, but the alternate form is the one that has become widely known. As a concept, ego identity occupies a somewhat curious position. It overlaps self and ego, being especially reminiscent of the self-concept, but it is not the same; contained in it is a new emphasis on membership in a social system as a source of one's sense of identity. Better than earlier psychoanalytic formulations it honors the principle that personality is a partially open system. One can best grasp its meaning not by attempting a distinguishing definition but by recognizing that Erikson has recast the whole psychoanalytic theory of development and come out with a different way of picturing personality in its mature forms. Erikson's discussion of eight stages in the development of the ego owes much to Freud's account of the so-called psychosexual stages, but the emphasis is different and the scheme is carried further through the course of life. Erikson's way of thinking is more explicitly interactive, emphasizing, for instance, the mutual regulation by mother and child of each other's behavior; this leads him to describe sense of identity as mutually regulated on the one hand by the person's strivings and preferences,

[28] E. H. Erikson, *Childhood and Society* (1950) (New York: W. W. Norton & Company, Inc., 2d ed., 1963).

on the other by the scope and recognition afforded by the social order. Readers will immediately see the pertinence of this idea in our time.

The social reference of the concept becomes clear in the following description.

> It is this identity of something in the individual's core with an essential aspect of a group's inner coherence which is under consideration here: for the young individual must learn to be most himself where he means most to others—those others, to be sure, who have come to mean most to him. The term identity expresses such a mutual relation in that it connotes both a persistent sameness within oneself (self-sameness) and a persistent sharing of some kind of character with others. . . .
>
> It is of great relevance to the young individual's identity formation that he be responded to, and be given function and status as a person whose gradual growth and transformation make sense to those who begin to make sense to him.[29]

This description shows that ego identity is vulnerable on two sides. It can be weak when the individual's history has not built up a reliable sense of self-sameness, and it can be weak when the surrounding society offers no meaningful roles and no firm sense of membership. Fortunate indeed is a person who, surrounded by encouraging and esteem-building influences, early develops a consuming interest in some line of activity that can be turned into a vocation currently in short supply, so that society stands in great need of his services. Vocation is not the whole of identity, but it can form a substantial part.

Strong ego identity, in Erikson's thinking, depends upon negotiating with relative success the childhood stages of development. It is helped by encouraging experiences in the family and in the widening environments of the school years. But in the timetable of growth it reaches its most important crisis at adolescence, which brings to a peak the possibility of what Erikson calls "ego diffusion" and thus puts identity under crucial strain. It is at this time, when identity as a child no longer fits and when all the choices, problems, and unknowns of being an adult loom directly ahead, that the question "Who am I?" may be asked with special urgency. What results may be a despairing sense of *identity confusion*. "For the moment," says Erikson, "we will accept Biff's formulation in Arthur Miller's *Death of a Salesman*: 'I just can't take hold, Mom, I can't take hold of some kind of a life.' "[30] The person may develop an overstrong dependence on other adolescents and a search for immediate membership that imperils individuality, or rather than accept standardized adolescent roles may drop out, run away, and experiment with behavior that borders on delinquency. The frequency and intensity of identity

[29] E. H. Erikson, "Identity and the Life Cycle," *Psychological Issues*, **1**, no. 1 (1959), 102, 111.

[30] E. H. Erikson, *Identity: Youth and Crisis* (New York: W. W. Norton & Company, Inc., 1968), p. 131.

confusion is increased when the social order has moved in directions that leave adolescents with a dearth of meaningful roles. Ego identity is recovered to the extent that the person finds himself able to "take hold of some kind of a life."

One of the vicissitudes in the development of ego identity is a phenomenon described by Erikson as *negative identity*. This is an identity "based on all those identifications and roles which, at critical stages of development, had been presented as most undesirable or dangerous."[31] If the identities favored by family and community are unacceptable, and especially if this unacceptability results from rebellious hostility toward parents, a person may dramatize his defiance by becoming the very character he is not supposed to become. If it is part of family tradition that drunkenness is a disgrace, a young person disgruntled with his family may feel irresistibly drawn to alcohol. If social status is a cherished family possession, downward social mobility and companions who are rated as anything but respectable may prove to be enormously attractive. In such instances something more is going on than the rejection of forms of identity favored by one's environment. Negative identity is better than none. When one cannot bear to be a white sheep it is preferable to be a black sheep than to be no sheep at all. Adopting a negative identity means following a pattern and making a sort of commitment, even if it is largely oppositional in character.

A Sample Study

For use especially in the study of college students, Marcia has described four types of what he calls *identity status*.[32] These types are established on the basis of interviews, and different judges reading the interviews agree fairly well in assigning subjects to the different categories. The information that specifically defines the statuses has to do with (1) the extent of the experience of crisis, and (2) the degree to which the subject is committed to an occupation and a set of beliefs and values. The four types of status are as follows:

> *Identity foreclosure:* the subjects "seem to have experienced no crisis, yet have firm, often parentally determined commitments." They have found the values of home and society sufficiently congenial to be accepted without struggle.
> *Identity diffusion:* the subjects exhibit no apparent commitments, but they also do not seem driven to do very much about it. If they appear to be somewhat adrift, they are not acutely discontented with drifting and are not in a state of crisis.
> *Moratorium:* the subjects are vague in their commitments, but unlike those in the previous category they are "characterized by the presence of struggle and attempts to make commitments." Being in college

---

[31] Erikson, *Identity: Youth and Crisis*, p. 174.
[32] J. E. Marcia, "Development and Validation of Ego Identity Status," *Journal of Personality and Social Psychology*, **3** (1966), 551–559.

allows them a moratorium before making final, binding decisions, but they are actively working toward ultimate commitments.

Identity achievement: the subjects have experienced a period of crisis but have passed through it and arrived at firm commitments to occupations and ideologies.

It is to be noticed, of course, that these statuses are not necessarily permanent characteristics of the subjects. Many students during their college years pass from a comfortable acceptance of family values to an intellectual outlook characterized by relativity, often accompanied by identity diffusion, after which they struggle for and eventually achieve commitment and a firmer sense of identity.[33] But it seems likely that each of these statuses may be the final one for a considerable number of subjects. Early identity foreclosure is presumably the typical way of dealing with values and commitment in societies that are not undergoing rapid change. There is some evidence from another of Marcia's studies that among contemporary college students this status is correlated with relatively rigid, oversimplified ways of thinking.[34] Identity diffusion without a sense of crisis may also be the end point for somewhat impulsive, warm-hearted, sociable people who are comfortable in their social surroundings. It is not unknown for a person to extend the moratorium status throughout life, staying perpetually in search of ultimate meanings and values. Further research is needed to put these impressions on a firmer basis, but it seems likely that susceptibility to identity crisis and variations in the time, manner, and extent of commitment will prove to be matters of wide individual differences.

Contemporary Difficulties

To the extent that ego identity depends on finding an accepted, useful, congenial place in society, it offers to many contemporary young people a problem of special difficulty. Recent trends in economic, political, and social organization have produced a conspicuous amount of alienation. The amount should not be exaggerated: opinion surveys from time to time suggest that a majority of American college students see no insuperable difficulty in finding a place for themselves, even though it be a somewhat critical one, in the social order as they find it. But to others the social order appears to have become fatally inhuman, materialistic, and dangerous. Following World War II there was a rapid increase in the size of business organizations. Critical observers pointed out the resulting enlargement of deadening bureaucracy and the pressure toward becoming a good "organization man." In certain quarters there emerged the somewhat new perception of business

[33] W. G. Perry, Jr., *Forms of Intellectual and Ethical Development in the College Years* (New York: Holt, Rinehart and Winston, Inc., 1970); cf. Chapter 14 above, pp. 345–346.

[34] J. E. Marcia, "Ego Identity Status: Relationship to Change in Self-esteem, 'General Maladjustment,' and Authoritarianism," *Journal of Personality*, **35** (1967), 118–133.

vocations as secure but unchallenging and as stifling to personal development. Furthermore, as corporate organizations grew larger their control of
huge financial resources and their consequent political power became increasingly conspicuous. This power was enhanced by an alliance between
industrial and military interests; the industrial giant, so prodigiously productive, could best be kept in financial health by a continuing output of hugely
expensive instruments of war. In 1960 President Eisenhower, himself a military man, warned of the public danger inherent in too strong an "industrial-
military complex." To the extent that self-interest reigned, the power exerted
by such a group would tend to fall on the side of continuing high armaments
and complicated supporting research at the expense of programs bearing on
health, welfare, education, and social justice. During the next decade the
reality of this public danger was affirmed by a series of publicized incidents
of price-fixing conspiracies among corporations, indifference to public safety,
waste and graft in military procurement, carelessness about fair employment,
and the control of political power through well-financed lobbies. Individual
businessmen and military leaders could protest that they were not unmindful
of human welfare, but the image grew of an industrial juggernaut rolling relentlessly toward a world smothered in wastes, drowned in pollution, top-
heavy with military hardware, and finally blown up in a nuclear explosion.

Those members of the younger generation who alertly watched these
trends have obviously not been inspired by confidence or trust. Theirs is the
generation in which the advertising arm of modern business reached its full
strength, devoting great ingenuity and expense to the creation of favorable
public images of everything from political candidates to soap powders. A
generation raised on television is also raised on television commercials, and
however these may be perceived and disregarded at different ages, they are
scarcely conducive to trust. To thoughtful watchers they disclose a large zone
in which, because it helps business, our society accepts remarkably lax standards of truth and is remarkably permissive about being manipulated. Symbolic of the intrusive nature of advertising was an issue of a weekly news
magazine in 1969 in which the pages of a featured article on the problems
and frustrations of blacks, carefully supported by research, were interlarded
with brightly colored advertisements showing whites enjoying expensive lux-
uries in settings of huge houses, yacht clubs, and plush resorts.

If one is sharply aware of these powerful trends in current society
and does not agree with the implicit values, it is difficult to discern for oneself a meaningful and effective role. Furthermore, the belief that society is
corrupt may rise to such strength as to destroy all sense of intrinsic worth;
everything is somebody's racket. These are the conditions that prevail, as
we saw in the chapter on social status, in the lowest economic class typified
by the urban slum, and they are uncongenial to planning, sustained effort,
serious vocation—to anything but a rather short-range hedonism.[35] A similar outlook is now often found at the opposite end of the economic scale,

[35] See above, Chapter 6, pp. 143, 149.

among relatively affluent youth who construe the social order, though for different reasons, with like pessimism and helplessness. It is not an easy time in history to find the social niche one needs to complete the formation of a solid sense of ego identity.

A Puzzling Instance: Ego Identity in Richard Wright

Rather than deal further with ego identity in general terms, we shall try to illuminate the concept by examining it in the natural setting of an individual life. For this purpose the black American writer Richard Wright (1908–1960) proves to be a valuable informant, not because he used the concept explicitly but because he wrote so honestly and with such keen observation about a life in which everything conspired to make identity an acute problem. In an earlier chapter we drew upon Wright's insight into the effects of chronic frustration and perpetually blocked aggression.[36] With respect to identity he can be regarded as a puzzling case well suited to put the concept to test.

The puzzle manifests itself in the bare overall facts of Wright's life. He was brought up in Mississippi, son of a sharecropper who early deserted the family and left the mother in a perpetual struggle with poverty. Several members of the mother's family were teachers in black schools, but this evidence of middle-class status did not imply either a safe economic margin or an outlook that could include the idea of a black boy becoming a writer. Yet out of such surroundings Wright made his way to Chicago, New York, and finally Paris, where during the last thirteen years of his life, by now a tremendously successful author, he was part of a circle of outstanding literary and artistic celebrities. He had no reason to feel out of place in this sophisticated company after being told by Gertrude Stein: "It is obvious that you and I are the only two geniuses of this era."[37]

The problem was framed by Wright himself in some reflections at the end of *Black Boy*, the autobiography covering his first nineteen years and ending when he headed north for Chicago. He described the motive behind this bold step as one of escaping from the South; he had little conception of what he might find in the North. "I had not had the chance to know who I was," he wrote. Yet he recognized the paradox that this problem with identity had not made him apathetic or confused. "What was it that made me conscious of possibilities?" he asked. "From where in this southern darkness had I caught a sense of freedom?" Furthermore, he immediately described a self-concept that was anything but feeble. "It had never occurred to me that I was in any way an inferior being. And no word that I had ever heard fall from the lips of southern white men ever made me really doubt the worth of

---

[36] See above, Chapter 10, pp. 240–241.

[37] The two chief sources of information used in this account are R. Wright, *Black Boy: A Record of Childhood and Youth* (New York: Harper & Row, Publishers, 1945) (also issued in paperback as Perennial Classic P3056D); and C. Webb, *Richard Wright: A Biography* (New York: G. P. Putnam's Sons, 1968).

my own humanity."[38] Here can be seen side by side a strong sense of himself as a vital human being and a weak sense of what he might aspire to become in the world. His awareness of himself as agent, fighting to live, was strong enough to counteract the adverse judgments of his social environment, but the hostility of his surroundings made it difficult for him to foresee a situation in which any group of people, however small, would recognize his merit and afford him a significant social role. Such a combination appears incongruous, but it happened and we must try to understand it.

As a start we might advance the hypothesis that during his early years Richard Wright received an abundance of love, a goodly measure of respect, and a firm sense of support in his activities. This favorable input from the family circle, we might argue, developed in the boy a basic confidence and self-respect that armored him against the crushing effects of southern white stereotypes about blacks. With this inner strength he could fight his way through the southern darkness and preserve an awareness of better possibilities. This sounds plausible, but the hypothesis proves to be badly at odds with the facts. However much Wright may have selected his material in developing a theme of hardship and oppression, we cannot suppose that the long series of reported incidents constituted exceptions to an otherwise loving and supportive regime. From the moment at the age of 4 when he set fire to the house Richard embarked upon a career as bad child, leaving the role of good child to his younger brother, who sometimes brought Richard's misdeeds to the parents' attention. He soon became accustomed to direful descriptions of his evil nature and violent beatings designed to correct it. After his father's departure the punitive circle expanded to include grandmother, uncles, and aunts. He asked himself, "What on earth was the matter with me, why it was I never seemed to do things as people expected them to be done. Every word and gesture I made seemed to provoke hostility." And he told himself that no matter what he did he would be "wrong somehow as far as my family was concerned."[39] He was tense and active, and they tried to keep him quiet; he was curious, and they told him not to ask questions; he was assertive, and they commanded him to do as he was told. That he preserved these qualities certainly cannot be laid to encouragement and reward on the part of his family.

It sometimes happens that the love and support of a single significant person compensates for the destructive hostility of the rest of the family. There is evidence that Richard's relation to his mother might have had such an effect. He was deeply attached to her, and it appears that she, disappointed in her husband, developed a fierce devotion to her eldest son. "I had always felt a certain warmth with my mother," he wrote, a feeling that was absent from his relations with other family members.[40] There were times when his mother was on his side in family quarrels, and when at last he began attend-

---

[38] *Black Boy*, Perennial edition, pp. 282–284.
[39] *Ibid.*, p. 158.
[40] *Ibid.*, p. 100.

ing school, he writes, she "maintained her interest in me, urging me to study hard and make up for squandered time."[41] When Richard was 12 his mother suffered a paralytic stroke and was bedridden for some time. Witnessing her suffering, he described himself as ceasing to react to her emotionally, saying, "my feelings were frozen." As a consequence "a somberness of spirit" settled upon him and he began to feel that "the meaning of living came only when one was struggling to wring a meaning out of meaningless suffering."[42] His mother recovered partially and kept house for him during the lean years in Chicago, and he did not marry until he had left her for New York. But we should not build too heavily on these evidences of enduring support. The relation was a tortured one. The mother's outlook was limited, her attitude moralistic, and her influence highly restrictive. She had no sympathy for his curiosity or for his energetic independence, and she was responsible for some of his most violent beatings. She expressed contempt for his first published story on the ground that it was not the truth. His life developed along lines of which she largely disapproved. Thus if we attribute to his mother's influence an early conviction of self-worth, we must balance the picture by recognizing how strenuously he had to fight against her in order to develop a coherent sense of himself.

Turning to the influence of peers we again fail to find impressive evidence for social support. There were times when he fought his way to acceptance by other boys and enjoyed the experience of group membership. For a short while he was aware, as he puts it, that "the gang's life was my life," that family injunctions must give way to the demands of the group, and that there was strength in numbers, while "we frantically concealed how dependent we were upon one another."[43] But he seems on the whole to have felt rather isolated from his peers: "The religious home in which I lived, my mush-and-lard-gravy poverty had cut me off from the normal processes of the lives of black boys my own age."[44] As a teen-ager he was already too independent to accept the norms of his contemporaries. Because of his high scholastic standing he was elected valedictorian of his class, but when he rejected tradition by refusing to give the safe speech written for him by the principal and insisted upon delivering a speech of his own, his classmates urged him to be sensible and yield. He gave his own speech, but afterwards marched out of the hall shaking off attempts at congratulation; "I did not want to see any of them again."[45]

Richard Wright's strong sense of himself thus cannot be understood as the consequence of a substantial input of love and respect from the people around him. The youth who set forth for Chicago was following the expectations of no one in his environment, black or white. He was defying everything that Mississippi whites declared to be possible for blacks and that Mississippi

[41] *Ibid.*, p. 135.
[42] *Ibid.*, pp. 111–112.
[43] *Ibid.*, pp. 88, 94.
[44] *Ibid.*, p. 191.
[45] *Ibid.*, p. 197.

blacks believed to be possible for themselves. "My environment," he wrote, "contained nothing more alien than writing."[46] But it was in rebellion that the core of his strength seemed to lie. Quite early he learned to respond to chastisement in an extrapunitive manner, blaming not himself but the others. He learned to fight for his rights in the family long before he had any inkling that a black man's rights would constantly be violated by whites. When in his early teens he was pressured to confess religion he felt that he had in him "a sense of living as deep as that which the church was trying to give"; he "simply could not feel weak and lost in a cosmic manner."[47] He did not, then, feel guilty or inferior; a proud inviolacy stayed with him even when punishments were most savage and social pressures most crushing. This attitude was extremely dangerous for a southern black boy. Carried over into his relations with whites it could easily have resulted in his early death. He was aware of difficulty in learning the expected obsequious black role, and he was often warned by friends, but here his quick perceptiveness served him well and he escaped physical harm. But he lived in a state of boiling anger and latent anxiety, and from this there could be no escape except by leaving the South.

If moving to Chicago was mainly an escape from chronic tension, it was not without a positive goal, even though this was still dimly perceived. Wright answered his own question with regard to what kept him "conscious of possibilities" by pointing to books. His interest in books began dramatically in late childhood when a friendly black school teacher who boarded with his grandmother told him the story of Bluebeard and his seven wives. It was an overwhelming experience. "The tale made the world around me be, throb, live," Wright recalls. "My sense of life deepened and the feel of things was different. . . . My imagination blazed." The story was interrupted by grandmother's arrival and her fury that "Devil stuff" was being talked in her house. But the boy was vowing, "As soon as I was old enough I would buy all the novels there were and read them to feed that thirst for violence that was in me, for intrigue, for plotting, for secrecy, for bloody murders. So profoundly responsive a chord had the tale struck in me that the threats of my mother and grandmother had no effect whatsoever." The teacher's "whispered story of deception and murder had been the first experience in my life that had elicited from me a total emotional response."[48]

From this point on he struggled to read everything he could find, even though at first he could understand only a part of the words. Presently he wrote a story that was published in a black newspaper; everyone but the editor condemned him for it. But a larger meaning of the world of literature dawned upon him in his late teens when he discovered H. L. Mencken and was thereby guided into the rebellious debunking literature of the 1920s. In novels such as those of Sinclair Lewis and Theodore Dreiser, but especially

[46] *Ibid.*, p. 133.
[47] *Ibid.*, pp. 124, 127.
[48] *Ibid.*, pp. 46–48.

in Mencken, he learned that words could be used as weapons in a fight against everything that was wrong with the world. He was not alone in his bitterness; others were fighting, and this gave him "nothing less than a sense of life itself."[49] For the first time he found figures with whom he could identify, who revealed to him a channel through which the thirst for violence that was in him might come to effective expression. The goal was still dim and distant for the almost penniless black boy who was not allowed to use the public library and who secured books only through the good offices of a white Catholic friend who resented Jim Crow segregation. But it is significant that in the tiny apartment he presently found in Chicago, he placed a writing table in a corner reserved to be his study.

That Richard Wright discovered positive identification figures only so far along in his life raises the question of what held him together, so to speak, up to that point. The concept of negative identity is pertinent. Unable to please, the "bad" boy characteristically makes it a business to displease, shock, and outrage, and his self-concept is to this extent shaped by what the family defines as "bad." Most readers of *Black Boy* reverse the values, seeing Richard's rebellion, initiative, and anger as "good" and the surrounding constrictions as "bad," but much of his behavior still looks like negative identity in the system in which he lived. Care must be taken, however, to discriminate the special place occupied by his interest in literature. In his environment this could not be an obvious item for negative identity because nobody even thought of it. This was an original discovery to which his unusual sensitivity, verbal intelligence, and capacity for blazing imagination made contributions as well as his hate and thirst for violence. He was criticized for it and told that it would addle his brains, but this was not something he pursued merely out of defiance or as the realization of a direful expectation. To an extraordinary extent it sprang from within and gathered up his intrinsic aptitudes and energies into a possibly workable way of life.

Could he go it alone, without social support or recognized significance in the social order? The importance of social recognition for ego identity is well shown in what happened in Chicago. Working irregularly in marginal jobs, Wright made the acquaintance of members of the Communist party and gradually convinced himself, overcoming recurrent suspicions, that this political group was free from race prejudice. He brought home some Communist literature and was swept by it; "here at last, in the realm of revolutionary expression, Negro experience could find a home, a functioning value and role." Over a sixth of the earth, he realized, there already existed "an organized search for the truth of the lives of the oppressed and the isolated."[50] His ardor was momentarily damped when his mother glanced at the literature and called it evil, but presently a perception of his own role dawned in sharper outlines. As a writer of stories it would be his contribution to express in simple, concrete form the way oppressed people

---

[49] *Ibid.*, p. 272.
[50] Webb, *op. cit.*, pp. 119–121.

felt and the possibilities that existed for them in the hopeful ideals of communism. In this way he could appeal to people like his mother upon whom Marxist dialectics would be lost, and he could reveal the nature of the black experience even to the benighted white world. He saw his niche and was elated; to a strong sense of active self he now added a strong sense of identity.

It happened that the Communist party of the 1940s wanted him to organize and agitate rather than write fiction. This threatened both his identity and his freedom, and he broke with the party. By this time his books *Uncle Tom's Children* and *Native Son* had won him fame as an author, so that he could find social support in purely literary circles. To the end of his life, however, he retained a sense of mission about his writing. His own special contribution, revealing how black people felt and what white oppression had done both to them and to the whites themselves, was destined, he believed, to bring about a radically changed conception of human nature.[51]

Conclusion

The example of Richard Wright illustrates the variety of ingredients that is likely to enter into the organization called ego identity. His case is unusual in that both his immediate environment and the larger social system in which he grew up provided such meager encouragements and such massive constrictions. It was an environment in which millions accepted the docile role planned for them, and Richard Wright was virtually unique in making his escape. The lack of external support serves to highlight the internal sources of ego identity. It also serves to shift emphasis away from love and trust, calling attention to the power of anger and resentment as central motives in a pattern of life. The assumption should not be made that Wright's identity was ideally secure or that his life was especially happy. No one could pass through such a history without scars. But despite everything he did arrive at an identity that helped him to channel his energies into a highly significant contribution to modern literature.

Ego identity must be regarded as in every instance an individual creation. It is compounded out of ingredients that are never quite the same in any two lives. A significant contribution is made by capacities, illustrated in Wright's case by his verbal virtuosity, his high level of activity, and the force of imagination that made him seize so powerfully on the Bluebeard story and later create his own realms of fiction. Temperamental qualities, sensitivities or the lack of them, traits of skill or awkwardness all have a part

---

[51] Shortly after the publication of *Black Boy*, R. K. White made a systematic quantitative analysis of the values expressed by the author: "*Black Boy*: A Value Analysis," *Journal of Abnormal and Social Psychology*, **42** (1947), 440–461. This analysis gave more weight to physical safety than might have been anticipated; it also supported the idea of a weak identification with peers and the conception of the mother as frustrating yet as a possible source of a certain support and respect.

in the process of discovering what feels natural and congenial. Although Wright was for a time an ardent Communist, he could not fit himself into a life of political activity; he had to be a writer. Identification figures provide a variety of models for one's own identity, but only certain aspects of each chosen model can be literally copied, and the fragments must be united in a workable image and pattern for oneself. All the while there is interaction between the individual and his society, which specifies a variety of roles considered acceptable and socially valuable. Recognition that one has a place in society, even if this be in an esoteric group with values divergent from the mainstream, is a vital aspect of ego identity, and the search for such recognition may go on for a considerable time. Ego identity can thus be seen as a gathering up into patterned form of the many strands out of which the fabric of personality is woven.

17 Finding an Occupation

The enterprise of living is continuous from birth to death. Challenges occur in young adulthood, in middle age, and during old age just as they do in childhood and adolescence. Cognitive maps must be constantly revised and strategies of living continually altered. In a woman's life, the combined impact of the menopause and the growing up of her children may be felt as a crisis of great magnitude, threatening a well-established ego identity. In a man's life, retirement may be similarly experienced as a major dislocation of existence. Advancement in career, obstruction of career, unemployment, political victory or defeat, accidents, injuries, ill health, and the troubles of family and close friends can all create crises that make life seem anything but a smooth pathway. The growth of personality and its crises cover the entire span of life.

The plan of this book does not call for detailed study of later life. But in choosing a stopping point it is important to resist the convention that personality attains its final form at 21. The force of this convention has seriously obscured the continuities between late adolescence and early adulthood. It has led to an image of adult personality as a fixture rather than a continually evolving system. Especially misleading is the idea that adult status, in other than a legal sense, is reached at any one time. However we define it, adulthood is certainly not entered all at once. Each individual edges his way into it one aspect at a time, at his own pace, in his own way, to his own extent. What happens between 21 and 30 is a new chapter in a continuing story, and it is an important chapter for understanding personality.

The chief happenings that mark young adulthood are the finding of an occupation and the establishing of a new family. With these go a variety of developments consequent upon the fact that the person has made commitments intended to last a long time. In an older vocabulary, this period was described as one of settling down, the wild flightiness of youth being tamed by the responsibilities of work and family. Recent changes of social outlook have put this imagery in a questionable light. Young critics of contemporary society accuse their elders of having settled down only too well, constricting their vision to job and home and neighborhood while allowing great social evils to multiply around them. In this view settling down, far from being a virtue, may become a surrender to immediate circumstance and short-sighted tradition, destructive of the innovative spirit and of a true social conscience. Jobs and families do, of course, call for a steady, patient application of one's energies at some expense to physical and mental freedom. Constantly meeting demands of this kind can indeed have a constricting effect with loss of interest in what lies outside the immediate round of existence. But we should not assume that being a reliable worker and a good parent necessarily kills the possibility of seeing the world with broad vision and trying to improve the conditions of life. Filling occupational and family roles need not be incompatible with an innovative spirit; indeed, for many people "settling down" in these ways is a necessary condition for "opening up" in other ways. Young adulthood is a time during which significant developments of a fairly complex nature take place.

The making of lasting commitments has the general effect of concentrating the sphere in which one lives. Entering an occupation usually implies staying in one place, at least for the time being, and pursuing one line of activity. Marriage means bringing a diffuse liking for the other sex to a focus on one representative with whom the daily details of life are shared. Having a family means translating a benign feeling toward the young into loving one or more children for whom one has become responsible. If the quality of life is judged wholly in terms of *breadth*, these trends could be construed as constriction. If it is judged on a dimension of *depth*, they appear as desirable opportunities for growth.

One of the characteristic products of the period between 20 and 30 is an increased understanding of the specifics of everyday living. Even if formal education has done a good job of relating broad visions and abstract ideas to practical realities, which is by no means always the case, there remains a great deal that can be grasped only through relevant personal experience. Much that seemed easy when thought about in the abstract turns out to be slow and laborious in the actual doing. The intention to bring up one's children in the best possible way now faces the test of day-by-day implementation. A whole series of decisions must be made about what to do in specific situations containing elements of the unexpected, and no actual child ever behaves just like "the child" of the psychology books. The hope of reforming education the world over may face its first battle in work for a small new program in the schools of one's home community, where the full force will be encountered of public apathy, conservatism, and dislike of higher taxes. Zeal for humanizing the political and economic systems may lead to frustrating experiences with the cumbersome electoral process or with entrenched interests unwilling to make sacrifices for safety and an improved environment. Adolescent ideals may be badly shaken by such confrontations. It is easy to be discouraged and to deal with this unpleasant feeling either by impatient anger or by giving up on larger issues and constricting the range of one's concern. But dealing with realities can be effective only to the extent that one understands them, and young adulthood is likely to provide conditions favorable for achieving this cognitive enlargement. Out of such experience may come a person who knows what can be done and what cannot be done, and who has lost none of his urge to do what can be done.

Selection of an Occupation

Some societies prescribe with great rigidity the kind of work that is open to a person in a given status or caste. In others there is a strong expectation that sons will follow in their fathers' footsteps. In the United States the idea has long prevailed, though the practice has badly lagged, that anyone should have the chance to enter any occupation, and it rates as a virtue to surpass one's father in prestige. "Thus a man's work is one of the things by which he is judged, and certainly one of the more significant things by which he judges himself." Everett Hughes, the author of these words, continues as follows:

> Many people in our society work in named occupations. The names are a combination of price tag and calling card. One has only to hear casual conversation to sense how important these tags are. Hear a salesman, who has just been asked what he does, reply "I am in sales work" or "I am in promotional work," not "1 sell skillets." Schoolteachers sometimes turn schoolteaching into educational work, and the disciplining of youngsters and chaperoning of parties into personnel work. Teaching Sunday School becomes religious education, and the Y.M.C.A. Secretary is in "group work." Social scientists emphasize the science end of their name. These hedging statements in which people pick the most favorable of several possible names of their work imply an audience. And one of the most important things about any man is his audience, or his choice of the several available audiences to which he may address his claims to be someone of worth.
>
> These remarks should be sufficient to call it to your attention that a man's work is one of the more important parts of his social identity, of his self; indeed, of his fate in the one life he has to live, for there is something almost as irrevocable about choice of an occupation as there is about choice of a mate.[1]

In view of this importance it is disconcerting to realize that occupations must often be chosen under conditions unfavorable to wise selection.

[1] E. C. Hughes, *Men and Their Work* (New York: The Free Press, 1958), pp. 42–43.

Good choice implies a good fit between the person and the occupation.[2] It implies that the person finds congenial the activities and roles required by the occupation. Good choice is thus dependent on self-understanding, or knowledge of what feels congenial and what satisfies one's needs. It depends equally on knowledge about the occupation, on images of the way one's time will be spent, the human relations likely to be encountered, and the possibilities for advancement. But occupational choices are usually made at a time in life when both kinds of knowledge are far from adequate. Images of the occupation may be decidedly unrealistic, and images of the self may still be diffuse. Entering an occupation is thus a venture into the unknown. Even when the young person makes use of expert vocational guidance, which aims to enlarge his information both about jobs and about his own capacities, there remains a large amount of uncertainty.

People often take jobs, of course, simply because they are open. The school dropout has little choice in the matter, and even those with greater educational qualifications must often grab the first thing that offers financial support. If he doesn't like the job, he may nevertheless be unable to escape it. Some people accept work simply as a way of making a living, not looking for personal involvement, and may feel little distress about limited choice. Some hold one simple job throughout life without becoming restive, and others change jobs every few months without feeling distracted. But occupations of a more complex character, which make considerable demands upon their members, cannot be dealt with so easily. The requirements of the professions, especially, cannot be met without a large investment of time and energy that cannot be sustained unless the whole thing feels right. Here the question of congenial fit is crucial, and making the choice is indeed a critical step.

Images of Occupations

In a study made during the late 1950s O'Dowd and Beardslee undertook to find out what images of common occupations existed in the minds of college undergraduates.[3] They developed a set of rating scales whereby the students could rate the members of each occupation with respect to thirty-four characteristics. The scales were filled out by nearly a thousand undergraduates, both men and women, in four different colleges of liberal arts. There was considerable agreement among the students about the characteristics of people in each occupation, enough to warrant speaking of occupational stereotypes. The authors cast their findings in the form of portraits derived from the average ratings on each trait. Liberal arts students in the late 1950s are obviously not a universal sample, but their images doubtless played a part in the vocational decisions they were making.

For these students the *doctor* emerged as something of a culture hero.

---

[2] L. A. Pervin, "Performance and Satisfaction as a Function of Individual-Environment Fit," *Psychological Bulletin,* **69** (1968), 56–68.

[3] D. C. Beardslee and D. D. O'Dowd, "Students and the Occupational World," in *The American College,* ed. N. Sanford (New York: John Wiley & Sons, Inc., 1962), Chap. 18.

They attributed to doctors high status, wealth, success, pretty wives, and happy homes. Doctors were seen as realistic and rational, stable and responsible, confident, oriented to people, and intelligent in a strong masterful sense, and on the average they were rated high on no undesirable traits. The *lawyer* came off pretty well, having many of the same qualities with the added asset of being a power in public affairs, but he was seen as self-assertive, manipulative, and not particularly happy in his home life. The *scientist* appeared as a cool, controlled intellectual, competent in the world of objects, influential and well rewarded by society, but on the other hand disdainful of people, emotionally shallow, living an unsatisfactory home life with a wife who was not pretty. The *schoolteacher* was among those who had to make do with a plain wife, but his home life was believed to be happy. He was seen as low in wealth, status, opportunity, and influence and as lacking in confident, assertive qualities, but he stood well with respect to service and orientation to people. Of all the occupations listed, the *accountant* came nearest to being a cultural antihero. Status, wealth, influence, and success were all denied him, and his traits added up to a wretched picture: limited intelligence, inadequate sensibilities, passivity, weakness, coldness, shallowness, evasiveness. The model in the students' minds, apparently, was "a Victorian bookkeeper, chained to a desk and ledger, from which he has no inclination to depart for traffic with the world or contact with man." The *artist*, on the other hand, though almost the opposite of the doctor, was viewed with more charity than the accountant, perhaps because his profile of traits was not unlike that of a teen-ager in the throes of adolescent problems. To him were attributed high aesthetic sensitivity, violent emotions, impulsive expressiveness, and colorful individuality, along with a lack of interest in people, poor success with them, and a resistance to disciplined and useful work.

As we shall see presently, these images are not an accurate representation of reality. Perhaps in a rough way they correspond to actual differences among occupational groups, but as guides to a personal choice these stereotypes can be seriously misleading. The image of the lawyer's heartlessness, the stereotype of his association with corporations and affluent clients, might serve to steer into another occupation a person who could have become an influential legal champion of victims of social injustice. The drab circumstances associated with schoolteaching might block the choice of this occupation for someone with a remarkable flair for teaching young children or with the qualities likely to make for leadership in educational administration. The prestige surrounding the doctor might attract students whose aptitude for the biochemical sciences was marginal.

There are various ways in which knowledge of occupations can be made more specific prior to final choice. In principle these have already been described in the chapter on strategies of living; the methods were especially well illustrated by the high school students admitted to college who tried to adapt themselves in advance, so to speak, to the new demands.[4] Prior expe-

---

[4] See above, Chapter 15, pp. 368–369.

rience in the form of volunteer activities and summer jobs is often of great assistance in making a choice realistic. Of two friends who volunteer for mental health work, for instance, one may discover that working daily with patients is unexpectedly rewarding whereas another becomes discouraged and upset by it. As a usual thing, however, choices are made with a far from adequate understanding of what is really involved in the selected occupation.

Family Influences

It seems likely that family expectations will influence choice of occupation. In a family in which grandfather, father, and uncles have all been physicians, the expectation may be powerful that at least one son will bend his steps toward medical school. If mother was popular and married young and daughter finds herself popular, her career line is quite strongly indicated. School dropouts are often found to be following the tradition of parents who left school as early as possible in favor of wage-earning. But family expectations can point to something entirely different from what the parents have done. Upward social mobility and a concern that the children should have a better life may produce strong pressures. In extreme cases the parents specify the very occupation they expect the child to enter. The determination to have a son who is a doctor or a professor is not uncommon in intellectually gifted families that have suffered from economic handicaps. An Irish Catholic student in a personality study related that his father, rising economically from a humble background, had assigned specific occupations to his four sons: the first was to be a lawyer, the second a doctor, the third to go into business, and the fourth, still only 12, to enter the priesthood.[5] Even if one feels a lack of interest in the assigned career and questions one's aptitude for it, the influence of such expectations is not always easy to resist.

Family expectations can also exert a negative influence. If a son or daughter feels hostile, rebellious, or alienated, careers will be appealing only if they are widely different from those favored by the parents; perhaps, as part of negative identity, their attraction will depend on outraging parental sensibilities and disappointing parental expectations. In recent years a somewhat different pattern has emerged, as shown in studies of the generation gap. Children reject parental emphasis on success, security, and suburban living in favor of values more reformist and more humanistic; but they also sense that the parents themselves are disappointed by the emptiness of their lives and are not recommending that their children follow in their footsteps. In these circumstances the younger generation can feel that it is espousing values latently held by the elders but crushed by the exigencies of the industrial system.[6]

Although family influence is in a sense extraneous, it should not be

[5] R. W. White, *Lives in Progress*, 2d ed. (New York: Holt, Rinehart and Winston, Inc., 1966), Chap. 5.
[6] K. Keniston, *Young Radicals: Notes on Committed Youth* (New York: Harcourt Brace Jovanovich, Inc., 1968).

seen as automatically producing bad choices. Entering an occupation harmonious with family tradition does not necessarily violate individual interests and aptitudes, and it often means greater familiarity with what is involved and greater environmental support in carrying out career plans. Desire to avoid family tradition, in turn, can lead to a more thorough search for what is personally congenial. But family expectations are not reliable guides, either positive or negative. Internal factors must also be weighed.

Influence of Fantasy

If the choice of occupation is typically made with a shortage of factual information, considerable leeway is left for fantasy. The attraction of a particular line of work may be much affected by a fantasy of what it is like in its more dramatic and spectacular moments. Much material is provided for this kind of imagining by television and motion pictures, newspapers, magazines, and books. The screens especially are unburdened by tedious detail about how things happen in the world. A young man is shown deeply shocked and moved by the sight of chronically sick children in a neglected ghetto hospital; he resolves to do something about this unnecessary suffering; in the twinkling of an eye he appears again with white coat and stethoscope, his medical training and internships completed, his specialty boards passed, ministering to happy, smiling children in an ultramodern health center that has suddenly materialized. With such eloquent assistance from sources of entertainment it is no wonder that fantasy leaps forward to clothe occupations in a garb suitable for splendid self-dramatizations. Who would not like to be the lawyer whose piercing cross-examinations and brilliant summations win the uphill fight for humanity against cold justice? Who would not like to be the school social worker into whose arms the shy, abused, rejected child, at last able to trust and love, throws himself with sobs of relief and comfort? Things like these sometimes happen, but they are not frequent enough to sustain a daily round of occupational duties if these have no intrinsic interest. When an occupation becomes too highly embellished with fantasies of peak moments, reality will seem flat and stale by comparison.

Again, however, it should not be concluded that self-dramatization necessarily produces a poor choice. The opposite procedure, choosing one's occupation by a coolly rational balancing of one's traits against the characteristics of the occupation, can also defeat real congeniality. All the indications from aptitude tests may point toward, for example, promotional work, yet the client may feel not the slightest inclination to do such work. The idea bores him; no agreeable fantasies come to him of a promotional career. A certain amount of agreeable fantasy about a contemplated occupation, even if it departs somewhat from probable realities, suggests personal involvement and intrinsic interest, and these are assets of great importance for a long-term commitment.

Sometimes the congeniality of an occupation is influenced by urges of which the person is largely unaware. These urges can on occasion be inferred from fantasies, though their presence may not at first be clear to the creator of the fantasy. A premedical student with an inclination toward psychiatry had the fantasy of a special room so constructed that he could overhear psychoanalytic treatments without either doctor or patient knowing it. As he thought about this and talked it over with friends he realized that he was motivated by a desire for omniscience. From his special observation post he would learn simultaneously the secrets of the patient's unconscious mind and the way to unlock these secrets through psychoanalytic technique; then he would know all. Obviously this fantasy of omniscience was not destined to be fully satisfied in his later professional life, but the urge to unlock secrets played an energizing part in what proved to be a distinguished career of psychiatric research. Another premedical student aiming toward psychiatry might have preferred fantasies of rescuing swimmers from drowning or of snatching victims from the hands of dangerous enemies. The implicit urge to rescue the helpless could well play a continuously energizing part in the daily practice of psychiatry, but it would be less likely to sustain an interest in the more abstract operations of research.

Latent urges centering around the avoidance of anxiety can also play a part in occupational choice. A vocation may be appealing not only for what it does require but for what it does not. Anxiety connected with assertiveness may exercise a silent veto over any choice that would call for this characteristic and dictate choice of noncompetitive occupations. The reverse picture is seen in those whose latent dread is of passivity and being put down. For them, interest and other considerations are allowed free choice only among occupations that promise a strenuous, embattled life. Fear of people may restrict the choice to vocations in which the main work is done alone, whereas fear of loneliness may dictate a job always performed in the company of others. Constitutional and temperamental qualities may operate also to limit the range of choices. A highly active person will like the sound of work calling for vigor and change and will perhaps hope to become part of the jet set; a less active one will favor jobs that are done in a relaxed atmosphere, sitting in chairs that do not leave the ground. Unwitting anxieties may steer the person away from things he would otherwise be well able to do. Strong constitutional proclivities, on the other hand, can be regarded as a kind of wisdom through which occupations are avoided that would produce continuous strain or frustration. To tell acquired anxiety from native proclivity is apt to be a difficult problem. Sometimes, but not always, the characteristics of fantasy may provide an indication.

Need for Achievement

Another influence on choice of occupation is the extent to which a person is motivated by a need for achievement. This need is directed toward realistic accomplishment, as when a child realizes the intention of making three blocks stand in a tower or, a little later, of constructing a house in a tree or, still later, of building a skyscraper topped by a penthouse. Murray, in his description of this need, emphasizes the element of independent accomplishment with self-appraisal of the results. He uses the following phrases to describe the chief desires and effects:

> To accomplish something difficult. To master, manipulate, or organize physical objects, human beings, or ideas. To do this as rapidly and as independently as possible. To overcome obstacles and attain a high standard. To excel one's self. To rival and surpass others. To increase self-regard by the successful exercise of talent.[7]

This conception was the starting point from which McClelland initiated an important program of research on achievement motivation. McClelland's definition of the goal of the need for achievement—"success in competition with some standard of excellence"[8]—reflects at least an aspect of Murray's idea. His method of measuring the strength of this need consisted of a test in which four pictures, ambiguous in content but lending themselves to a possible achievement interpretation, were shown successively on a screen, and the subjects were asked to write quick stories about them in the spaces provided in a booklet and within strict time limits. The strength of the need for achievement was estimated by counting the instances of achievement imagery in the subject's four stories, the number of times he attributes to the principal characters some striving or idea that qualified as seeking success in competition with a standard of excellence. That the stories really reflected such a need in the storytellers was shown by giving the test under contrasting conditions, one relaxed and informal, another directly following a procedure designed to stimulate ambitious strivings. Under the second condition the average amount of achievement imagery in the stories was significantly greater. Typically the test yields large individual differences in achievement imagery and thus by inference in the strength of the internal need to achieve.

Looking for possible roots of these differences in earlier experience, Winterbottom tested a group of boys 8 to 10 years old and then interviewed their mothers on child training practices.[9] It was clear from the results that the mothers of boys with high need for achievement had expected their sons to meet independence demands earlier in life. The mothers of "highs," for instance, were more likely to have expected the boys before the age of 8 to know their way around the city, to try out new things, to do well in competition, and to make their own friends. It is of interest that this correlation between need for achievement and maternal independence training faded out in the course of time. In a study by Feld the same boys were tested again at 14 to 16 years, and the correlation no longer held.[10] This finding does not

---

[7] H. A. Murray, *Explorations in Personality* (Fairlawn, N.J.: Oxford University Press, 1938), p. 164.

[8] David C. McClelland, J. W. Atkinson, R. A. Clark, and E. A. Lowell, *The Achievement Motive* (New York: Appleton-Century-Crofts, 1953.), pp. 75–81.

[9] *Ibid., The Achievement Motive*, pp. 297–304.

[10] S. C. Feld, "Longitudinal Study of the Origins of Achievement Strivings," *Journal of Personality and Social Psychology*, **7** (1967), 408–414.

negate the initial importance of maternal attitudes in fostering the need for achievement. It is consistent with the supposition that the strength of motivation can be appreciably changed by environmental opportunities in later childhood and by influences outside the family.

Further research has shown that there are distinct sex differences in the patterning of achievement motivation.[11] These differences showed most clearly in the procedures found necessary to stimulate the motive. To arouse it in boys and men there had to be a challenge to intelligence and capacity for leadership. On girls and women this sort of challenge had little effect, but their achievement imagery increased significantly if desires in the direction of social acceptability were stimulated. Perhaps one can express the difference by saying that for men achievement has overtones of single-handed mastery, whereas for women it is more colored by desires for recognition and acceptance by other people.

The strength of the need for achievement has an obvious influence on the attractiveness of different occupations. People in whom this need is strong are likely to give much thought to career prospects, opportunities for expanded action, and chances of working up to higher responsibilities. They will reject paths that look as if they might come to an early dead end.

Intrinsic Interest

The influences thus far described operate with different strengths in different cases. Working all together they might exert an impressive impact. A person can easily be imagined who, let us say, arrives at the decision to become a research biochemist on a combination of the grounds already described. His image of a research scientist includes good pay, security, scope for achievement, an ultimately influential and well-rewarded position, and valued qualities of intellectual competence and emotional control. His position would satisfy a strong parental desire to have a prestigeful "doctor" in the family. His fantasies contain honors for scientific discovery culminating in a Nobel Prize, and he assuages shyness and social anxiety by picturing himself as working for the most part alone. Such a pattern would put a good deal of force behind the choice, even though it might not add up to an accurate picture of what lay ahead. But the explanation does not sound complete. All these specifications could be met equally well by occupations other than biochemical research. We have to account for our subject's choice of just this field of knowledge rather than astronomy or botany or neurology. The missing element is intrinsic interest, a peculiar fascination of biochemistry above all other branches of science.

It is true that many people must choose an occupation without having discovered in themselves any strong or lasting intrinsic interests. They can specify only that they are interested in people, like to travel, or want to do something significant, but none of these vague "likes" points to any particular channel for the exercise of their talents. If not too desperately beset by indecision these people are likely to try whatever comes up within their vaguely

[11] McClelland et al., *The Achievement Motive*, pp. 173–181.

specified zone. They may at least gain specific experience and may even find the job to be a congenial choice. Moreover, we should not assume that a powerful, consuming intrinsic interest lies latent in everyone and is either expressed or strangled. For many persons the wish to work with people, for instance, is about as far as they can ever go in specifying their interest, and they are not at all dissatisfied in later years to recall a long list of jobs they have held, jobs with nothing in common except that they involved people.

In other instances, however, the question of interest is central to job choice. We have already discussed the important part played by intrinsic interests in the educational process.[12] They are capable of occupying a similarly significant position in the choice of a life work. A strong intrinsic interest that has been deepening since childhood may point so directly to an occupation that there is really no experience of choosing. Questioned on why he selected biochemistry, our imaginary subject would probably reply that he had always been interested in it, by which he would not mean that the interest was determined by his genes and flourished while he was still in the womb, but that he remembered having it in childhood and could not recall when and how it started. The study of intrinsic interests is much hampered by this difficulty in recollecting how they began, how they developed, and what constitutes the fascination. To the possessor of a strong intrinsic interest in some particular class of objects the fascination is obvious and its origins are of no concern. Interests are among the good things of life that we are disinclined to question.

A great deal of research has been directed toward detecting differences in the characteristics of people in different occupations. Average differences are usually found, though they are not as large or as dramatic as our stereotypes lead us to expect. In this type of research a wide variety of measuring devices has been used, including standard intelligence tests, aptitude tests, questionnaires on interests, projective methods such as the Rorschach inkblots and Thematic Apperception Test, and when possible extensive interviews intended to build up a picture of personality in the making. When interviews are not possible it is necessary to rely mainly on average scores on tests, which reveal certain general differences that characterize occupational groups but cannot disclose the history of specific interests.

The general findings, of course, are of value in themselves, and their interpretation can present intriguing problems. In a paper on creative physical scientists (physicists and chemists), McClelland, summarizing a number of previous studies, calls attention to eight points on which the members of this group tend to differ from members of other professional groups; he then invites readers to regard these differences as clues and to act as detectives in trying to find their meaning.[13] Physical scientists (1) are almost certain to be

---

[12] See above, Chapter 15, pp. 336–339.

[13] D. C. McClelland, "The Psychodynamics of Creative Physical Scientists," in *Contemporary Approaches to Creative Thinking*, ed. H. E. Gruber, G. Terrill, and M. Wertheimer (New York: Atherton Press, 1962). Reprinted in D. C. McClelland, *The Roots of Consciousness* (Princeton, N.J.: D. Van Nostrand Company, Inc., 1964), Chap. 7.

male, (2) come from strict Protestant backgrounds, though they are not themselves religious, (3) tend to avoid interpersonal contact, (4) work hard to the point of seeming obsessed with their work, (5) avoid and are disturbed by complex emotions, especially aggression, (6) like music but dislike art and poetry, (7) are intensely masculine in their interests, and (8) have had since early life a strong interest in analyzing the structure of things. Different detectives, we may expect, will discover somewhat different plots behind these clues. McClelland calls attention to a possible psychodynamic plot centering on the suppression of aggression under conditions of strict and frustrating upbringing. This could lead to anxiety about emotion in general, avoidance of interpersonal situations that might evoke it, and discovery of a safer outlet in analyzing and conquering the physical environment. But these connections, McClelland cautions, have not been verified by firm observations, and in any event we have to avoid turning statistical tendencies into laws. There are physical scientists who confound generalization by liking art better than music, by being sociable, and by coming from permissive agnostic backgrounds. Their route into science must have been their own.

The part played by intrinsic interest is best revealed in a series of studies by Anne Roe based on extensive interviews with people well established and recognized in their careers. Included in her studies were biologists, physicists, social scientists, and artists.[14] The earliest study was of 20 American painters, ranging in age from 38 to 68, all of high professional standing. To the eyes of a psychologist this group was not a group at all except with respect to vocation. As people, the artists did not differ distinctly from other people; Roe found that "there are no personality or intellectual traits and no constants in their life history which characterize them all and set them off from all other persons." Tests of intellectual qualities and reconstruction of family patterns alike yielded such variety as to defy generalization. The one common trait was an intense interest in painting that had begun in their teens if not earlier and that had flourished in many cases in spite of parental discouragement. The artists themselves described becoming totally absorbed and lost in their work, an experience they found "exquisitely satisfying," sometimes even "ecstatic." To those who have had this experience, Roe comments, it is small wonder that "economic difficulties, lack of recognition, and all the rest are of minor importance." But although in this study she demonstrated the power of intrinsic interest, the artists were not able to give her much idea of how this started and developed in their lives.

The studies of the scientists were somewhat more productive in this respect. Most of them could give a detailed history of the steps in their choice of occupation. Some of them had been fascinated in early childhood with

---

[14] A. Roe, *The Making of a Scientist* (New York: Dodd, Mead & Company, Inc., 1953); in more technical detail, "A Psychological Study of Physical Scientists," *Genetic Psychology Monographs*, **43** (1951), 121–239; "A Study of Eminent Psychologists and Anthropologists, and a Comparison with Biological and Physical Scientists," *Psychological Monographs*, **67**, no. 2 (1953); "Artists and Their Work," *Journal of Personality*, **15** (1946), 1–40.

some aspect of the environment: birds, plants, minerals, mechanical devices. But early fascination was by no means a universal feature, and in any event it is not a necessary precursor of scientific interest; nature appeals to poets as well as to scientists. The true scientific passion centers around doing something with objects: arranging, classifying, but especially coming to understand them by intellectual analysis and experimentation. It was almost universally true that the biologists and physical scientists from the start of their schooling had preferred mathematics and science courses to those that depended on language. One physicist put this preference with startling clarity when he said that in eighth grade, becoming interested in chemistry, he spent his "spare time memorizing the table of elements," but "couldn't see any sense in memorizing grammar." The scientists were thus recruited from those with a characteristic intellectual preference, but beyond this their choice of occupation was greatly influenced by encountering the actual process of research. The importance of this particular experience gave to several of the life stories almost the character of a series of accidents. A starting interest in chemistry might change to a career in physics because a physics teacher encouraged each student to do an independent piece of research. An intended graduate program in psychology might be switched to anthropology because a fellowship turned up that entailed working as collaborator with an anthropology professor. These seeming twists of fate show the importance of action in scientific interest. It is not just that a certain subject matter is fascinating to contemplate; the real joy is to analyze things and find out by experiment how they work.

The social scientists—psychologists and anthropologists in Roe's sample—were largely recruited from those with stronger verbal than mathematical aptitude. On the whole they were likely to have done well in English courses, to have taken part in school activities, and to have been somewhat sociable. Entrance into psychology reflected for some of them a dissatisfaction with what could be learned about human behavior in literary fields and a desire for the more precise analytic tools of experimental science. For others a motive of service seemed uppermost, with social science providing secular tools for what would probably have been a religious vocation in earlier generations of their families. On the whole, intrinsic interest was less sharply defined, though usually strong, in the developmental stories of the social as compared to the physical scientists.

Mutual Effects of Person and Occupational Role

The place of work in personality can be clarified by using the concept of occupational role. As we have already seen, a social role is defined as "the ways of behaving that are expected of any individual who occupies a certain position."[15] When the role in question is an occupational one, it can be

[15] T. M. Newcomb, *Social Psychology* (New York: Holt, Rinehart and Winston, Inc., 1950), p. 280.

defined as the ways of behaving that are expected by society of any individual who occupies a certain occupational position. The expected ways may not be restricted to the vocational sphere. Carl Jung called attention to this possibility in the following words:

> Society expects, and indeed must expect, that every individual should play the role assigned to him as completely as possible. Accordingly, a man who is also a pastor must not only carry out his professional functions objectively but at all times and seasons he must play the role of pastor in a flawless manner. Society demands this as a kind of security. . . . It is therefore not surprising that everyone who wants to be successful has to take these expectations into account.[16]

What Jung chose to illustrate by pastors is easily matched in the experience of American public school teachers, who are often made painfully aware that they are expected not only to perform well in the classroom but also to lead private lives that will serve as a constant model for improving the young. But these two occupations are somewhat exceptional. There is no great pressure of social expectation on the behavior of businessmen outside the office, and even physicians are permitted a somewhat wilder private life so long as it does not interfere with their medical responsibilities. Typically the core of occupational role expectations is the responsible performance of what the job requires, and the spread to other aspects of life may not be large. Vocational role is not all; there are family roles and other roles connected with other groups of people. Multiple roles limit the influence of work roles in personal development, and there are certainly people who compensate comfortably for their occupational restrictions by leading quite different lives the rest of the time.

Effects of Occupational Role on the Person

We can best understand the effects of occupational roles by bearing in mind that they often include a distinct set of valuable privileges. This is especially true of the professions, which are entered through a long course of training designed to equip the candidate with specialized knowledge and skill. Yet even a humble occupation may provide opportunities to do what others cannot do and to know what others cannot know. Hughes has pointed out that janitors, whose main work is humdrum and dirty, often build up a close knowledge of the secret life of their tenants by observing their comings and goings and the character of the trash that emerges from each suite.[17] The lawyer, of course, is privileged to ask people directly about certain phases of their private life, including, if the business at hand is a divorce action, some of the items inferred by the janitor. The psychotherapist has

[16] C. G. Jung, *Two Essays on Analytic Psychology*, trans. H. G. and C. F. Baynes (New York: Dodd, Mead & Company, Inc., 1928), pp. 164–165.
[17] Hughes, *Men and Their Work*, pp. 49–54.

even more extensive license to pry into private life, but not in the spirit of nosey gossip; when he is not treating a patient, any prying on his part would be resented as much as if it came from one's banker or from a neighbor. Occupational roles include specified rights and privileges as well as restrictions and demands for responsible performance. They are not straightjackets; the paths they open may lead to otherwise impossible resources for personal growth and creative contribution.

The role of physician can be taken to illustrate what is meant. In a detailed analysis, Parsons starts from the physician's specific competence, acquired through long training, to understand and alleviate sickness. This task is performed through the application of scientific knowledge, which implies that the physician will work in relatively impersonal fashion, avoiding emotional entanglements with his patients. Included in the role expectations is a strong emphasis on service; the patient's health is given clear priority over the interests and comfort of the doctor. The sharp specification of the role, its understanding alike by physician and patient, is important in controlling a variety of feelings that might otherwise invade medical practice. The doctor has the right to ask highly personal questions and to examine the patient's naked body; to do so could lead to fantasies and personal complications on both sides if it were not an implicit part of the appropriate application of scientific knowledge. Male physicians who seduce female patients, and doctors who use their patients' personal secrets for conversation at cocktail parties, clearly violate role expectations and receive the displeasure not only of their professional colleagues but of society at large.

Parsons draws a contrast between the role of physician and that of businessman. The latter is expected to make a profit for his company, to consider the likelihood of profit in new undertakings, and to avoid poor credit risks; if he disregards these expectations he becomes a dismal failure. A physician would be equally at fault if he considered the possibility of profit when accepting a new patient and refused those whom he judged to be poor credit risks. The medical role, Parsons observes, entails "sharp segregation from the market and price practices of the business world, in ways which for the most part cut off the physician from many immediate opportunities for financial gain which are treated as legitimately open to the business man." The physician who acts like a businessman and the businessman who acts like a physician make themselves targets for the sharpest criticism.[18]

Occupational positions influence those who hold them by providing a pattern of privileges, opportunities, requirements, and restrictions. The result is to extend personal experience in some directions and limit it in others. The lawyer constantly deals with people who are abused, angry, and contentious. The businessman is most regularly exposed to human nature in its aspect of competition for material gain. The doctor lives in a world of sickness. The woman who chooses homemaking as her vocation is selectively exposed to childlike behavior and to adults who are tired after a day's work.

[18] T. Parsons, *The Social System* (New York: The Free Press, 1951), Chap. 10.

It is not surprising that we have difficulty in reaching general agreement about human nature. Each person, made something of a specialist by his occupation, tends to interpret human behavior in the light of his own inevitably biased experience. Occasionally a person incautiously casts himself in the role of sage and delivers pronouncements upon world affairs. Thus an episode in international politics may be described by different sages as essentially a power struggle, essentially an economic conflict, essentially an instance of national paranoia, essentially a conflict of attention-getting behaviors, and essentially a contest between rival ethical systems. No one sage, unless he has given the matter very careful study, is likely to utter the final word, but a judicious examination of all their words may indeed contribute to ultimate sagacity.

The effect of occupational role on personality has been studied by Merton in the special but now common situation of the large bureaucratic organization.[19] It seems likely that a bureaucracy attracts people who already have some of the requisite characteristics, but these qualities can be strengthened by continual performance of bureaucratic roles. We are accustomed today to question the efficiency of large bureaucracies, but it is for efficiency's sake that they are originally designed. In a bureaucracy there is a clear-cut division of activities arranged in a hierarchy of authority. Each activity is governed by abstract, explicit rules, which make it unnecessary to keep issuing directions. The worker is expected to follow the rules applicable to his position, and he is therefore disposed to put individual cases into categories rather than being sensitive to their peculiarities. As Merton expresses it, "Bureaucratic structure exerts a constant pressure upon the official to be methodical, prudent, disciplined. If the bureaucracy is to operate successfully, it must attain a high degree of reliability of behavior, an unusual degree of conformity with prescribed patterns of action." The discipline that infuses the whole system can be effective only if individual workers have "strong sentiments which entail devotion to one's duties, a keen sense of the limitation of one's authority and competence, and methodical performance of routine activities." In return, of course, the official can count on considerable security, automatic promotions, and a safe career in the organization. The resulting need to conform, however, easily leads to a timidly strict adherence to rules that become ends in themselves. There is pressure also toward impersonal relations both within the organization and with the clients. Merton speaks of a "trained incapacity" to function in other than rule-defined, depersonalized ways—an incapacity that comes as no surprise to anyone who has tried to get some bureaucratic error corrected. Trained capacity to perform in certain ways leads to trained incapacity to perform in other, more flexible ways. The bureaucratic traits may become so strengthened that they affect the person's behavior even when he is away from work.

But here we must again remember that work is not all of life. There may be well-organized, efficient, coolly impersonal bureaucrats who leave

[19] R. K. Merton, "Bureaucratic Structure and Personality," *Social Forces*, **18** (1940), 560–568.

their posts at five o'clock to enter a different existence characterized by spontaneity, adventure, wild exuberance, and highly personal relations. If this disparity does not sound probable, it is at least possible, and the possibility emphasizes the fact that we occupy positions and enact roles other than those connected with work.

Effects of Persons on Occupational Roles

Approaching the problem of roles from the opposite side, it is pertinent to ask what influence is exerted upon the character of occupational roles by the individuals who occupy them. Social roles are not usually defined down to the last detail. People must meet certain broad expectations but within these limits there is often room for considerable individuality. If we consider the teachers, lawyers, doctors, and janitors of our acquaintance it is at once evident that they are not rigidly stereotyped by their occupations. Each individual fulfills the general expectations in his own way, with his own personal touches, using whatever freedom there may be in the role specification to carry out his tasks in the fashion that he finds most congenial. The members of an occupational group are alike only in certain respects. Otherwise they are individuals, and they show a wide range of individual differences.

The enacting of roles in a personally congenial fashion, and the relation of this congeniality to experience earlier in life, are well illustrated in a study of problem-solving groups by Moment and Zalesznik.[20] The subjects of this study were drawn from middle-level and upper-level business executives and engineers brought together in small groups for an experiment in problem solving; a total of 52 subjects in four groups was studied. The situation was, of course, artificial, but the hypothetical problem in business management was sufficiently realistic that the subjects took it seriously and became involved in finding a solution. It was assumed that experienced men dealing seriously with a familiar sort of task in an experimental situation would act much as they are accustomed to act in real life. Analyzing the recorded discussions, the investigators paid particular attention to two dimensions of competence, technical and interpersonal. Their subjects, it turned out, could be placed in four categories: the technical specialists, the social specialists, the "stars" who were high in both forms of competence, and those who were low in both. The study included an extensive background questionnaire, which made it possible to relate performance in the problem-solving group to certain features of personal history.

Those whose performance earned them the classification of technical specialists contributed good ideas about which they spoke freely. Their interest was centered on solving the problem through an application of knowledge, and they pursued this goal with little reference to the feelings of others. Their only social contact took the form of joking. They were obtuse to signs that

---

[20] D. Moment and A. Zalesznik, *Role Development and Interpersonal Competence* (Boston: Harvard Business School, Division of Research, 1963).

others would like to speak and paid little attention to ideas offered by other members. In contrast, the social specialists did not contribute outstanding thoughts, but they increased the congeniality of the group, reduced friction, and thus in their own way had a favorable influence on the work at hand. Their attitude toward the others was friendly, attentive, and respectful; they voiced little criticism and welcomed with appreciative comments the ideas presented by the technical experts. There were average differences between the previous life experiences of these two groups. The technical experts, who had pushed their education further and attained success more quickly, tended to have moved upward from the status occupied by their fathers. It seemed a likely inference that they had used their intellectual gifts in a competitive spirit that crowded out affiliative tendencies. The social experts, on the average, had less education and less conspicuous occupational rewards, but they tended to recall family life as pleasantly free from deprivation and full of affectionate warmth. Among them, interestingly enough, there was a relative preponderance of second and later-born children. First-born children from stable families were predominant in the category of "stars," those subjects who contributed both ideas and congeniality to their groups. Relatively free from status anxiety, comfortable in authority relations, these subjects may have been prepared for their managerial roles by a securely favored position among siblings. The unfortunate subjects who contributed neither ideas nor social lubrication appeared to be strongly self-oriented and burdened with conflict and hostility. Their backgrounds showed a greater incidence of broken homes, a cool, rejective attitude toward early family life, much status anxiety, and sharp upward mobility. It seemed possible that self-assertion had been so urgent as to hamper both an intrinsic interest in ideas and an affiliative feeling toward people.

As usual, it is important not to turn average differences into stereotypes. In each group were some individuals whose backgrounds did not fit. Too many factors enter into the process of growth to allow the singling out of simple relations of cause and effect. But the study shows that there are decidedly different ways of enacting the role of business executive, and it suggests that congeniality based on previous life experience, possibly going back as far as early childhood, has an influence on the chosen style of enactment.

The fact that roles are not specified down to the last detail, so that room is left for individuality in their execution, opens the way for creative performances that lead to a change in role expectations. These expectations are not forever frozen. Existing in the minds of men, they can change when conditions change or when someone demonstrates that things can be done in a better way. A lone individual entering upon a well-established occupational role may feel that he is the one who must do all the adapting; he is hemmed in by expectations. But if his career in the role is characterized by inventiveness and initiative, the next occupant of the position may face a greatly changed set of expectations.

An historical example on a national scale is provided by the Supreme Court of the United States. The men who wrote the Constitution, having suffered from the arbitrary power of a monarchy, designed a government in which power was divided among different agencies: executive, legislative, and judicial. These agencies were expected to check and balance one another, thus protecting the people from the crushing effects of a single power. The design worked well with respect to executive and legislative powers; since 1789 the president and Congress, whatever else they may or may not have done, have successfully checked and balanced each other so that neither became the sole seat of power. It was less easy to assure that the Supreme Court would have weight enough to affect the other two powers, and in fact it played a relatively weak part during the early years. From 1801 to 1835, however, the chief justice was John Marshall, who through the opinions he handed down established the Court as the sole interpreter of the Constitution and thus as the guardian of the rights and privileges specified in that document. Since then the Supreme Court has played the part designed for it, but the role of chief justice could easily have continued to be a weak one if no one had come along who could enact it with John Marshall's authority and distinction. Through his occupancy of the position the role became permanently enlarged.

A similar enlargement may be said to have occurred in the role of psychiatrist through Freud's occupancy of this position. The right of a psychiatrist to probe deeply into personal problems, fantasies, dreams, and memories of early life was by no means part of the role until Freud enacted it in this manner and demonstrated that this probing led to an increase of understanding. The various roles currently associated with mental health work have all been influenced by Freud, by Adler, and by later workers who have experimented in different ways with the therapeutic relation.

It need not be supposed that a role can be changed only by a person of outstanding genius or towering stature. Role expectations are constantly evolving. This movement is occasioned by individuals whose enacting of a role adds something to existing expectations; the cumulative effect of their innovations leads eventually to a redefinition of the role. The public school teacher's role, as we have seen, has in recent years been given a number of new dimensions that constitute a marked departure from the way this role was understood fifty years ago. In the beginning John Dewey played a conspicuous part analogous to those of Marshall and Freud, but later the changes were brought about much more by the combined experience of a great many teachers who in one way or another gave an original touch to their manner of doing their job. The influence of persons on occupational roles, it can be surmised, is more likely to be slowly cumulative than dramatically swift.

Enduring Occupational Satisfaction

Living with a job is a different matter from choosing it. The circumstances that produce enduring satisfaction may prove to be quite different from those that made the occupation seem attractive in the first place. Becoming wedded to a job has sometimes been likened to marrying a spouse.

Initial infatuation may fade into dreary endurance of a relation that is not really congenial, or into separation and search for a more suitable line of work. In more fortunate cases the relation may prove to be a growing one in which the person finds in his occupation unexpected sources of interest and contentment. The variables that contribute to lasting occupational satisfaction have been studied in a great many different settings. All that can be done here is to sketch some of the more prominent threads out of which individual patterns are woven.

Pay and Security

Pay and security are unquestionably major variables in job satisfaction. These alone may make a person feel that he holds a good job, provided his personal satisfactions are largely found away from work. These alone can trap a person in a job that becomes intensely boring. In a variety of studies of job satisfaction in industrial and clerical workers, pay is regularly listed near the top, and having securely steady work is generally an important consideration.[21] Pay, in particular, is so obvious an issue that social scientists have shown a tendency to glide over it without comment. In the words of one research team that has resisted this tendency, "Pay is the most important single motivator used in our organized society."[22] Even at professional levels, where it may not be good form to talk about such mundane matters, the threat of a cut in pay or the shortening of an expected term of employment will quickly show that these are not questions of minor importance. Higher wages and greater job security have always been central to the purposes of labor unions. They are likely to be implicitly significant even in occupations that are rich in other forms of satisfaction.

Status and Prestige

Jobs can be ranked according to their status, and people in high and low status agree fairly well on the rankings. Studies of job satisfaction show, as one would expect, a strong correlation between status and contentment. When subjects are asked whether or not they would take a different choice if they had another chance, it is those in occupations of low status who would most like another deal. Frequency of absence from work is possibly a rough index of discontent; there is a positive correlation between the status of the work and regularity of attendance.[23] When pay scales within a company are being revised, one group of workers may protest not because their increase is too small but because another group, previously a notch lower, has been moved up to a position of equality. Their cherished superiority of status has

---

[21] B. M. Bass, *Organizational Psychology* (Boston: Allyn and Bacon, Inc., 1965), Chaps. 2–3.

[22] M. Haire, E. E. Ghiselli, and L. W. Porter, "Psychological Research on Pay: An Overview," *Industrial Relations*, **3** (1963), 1–8.

[23] B. M. Bass, *Organizational Psychology*, pp. 113–116.

been obliterated. The group feels downgraded if its position is no longer publicly recognized.

Many a young person who feels drawn toward work in the mental health fields has found the choice of precise occupation complicated by status considerations. Perhaps the training and subsequent activity of the psychiatric social worker, or of the clinical psychologist, seem to be just what he wants, but in most mental health services the psychiatrist with his medical degree occupies the highest status and gives the final orders. This consideration may overcome a fierce distaste for organic chemistry and motivate a grueling passage through a medical curriculum much of which is experienced as dull and irrelevant to mental health work.

The importance of status and prestige comes clearly to light when we consider how rare it is for a person to refuse promotion, and how common to fight for it. In almost all occupations promotion entails a change of function; the person will now do less of the work that defines the occupation and will do more administration and supervision of others. Promotion is sometimes both a social and a personal disaster. A highly gifted teacher of young children, a veritable genius in the kindergarten or first grade, may be offered the "better" job of school principal and spend much time behind an office desk choosing teachers, directing curriculum, developing financial policies, keeping personnel happy, and never coming face to face with a small child trying to learn. A creative architect who delights in problems of design and whose best work is done alone in deep absorption may be offered an executive vice presidency, in which he is responsible for securing contracts, for company finances, or worse still for problems of personnel, which strike him as endlessly petty and boring as he mourns for his lost drawing board. College presidencies are given to people who discover that they can barely stand the job; they suffer homesickness for the classrooms, seminars, and research for which they no longer have time. Promotion may, of course, lead to the developement of new skills and interests, and the new work may be experienced as more significant and valuable than the old; sometimes a person comes into his own when elevated to the right position. But promotion should be refused more often than it is, and stepping down should be easier than it is, if status and prestige were not in themselves powerful intrinsic rewards. If we take a candid look at our daydreams it will be clear that we like to toy with the idea of being at the top even when we know that in reality being there would cause us unremitting misery. Rarely is there a lack of candidates for prestigeful positions.

Social Interactions

Only recently has the importance of the social interactions that accompany work been recognized. To people with numerous interests and a taste for variety it has always seemed that monotonous, repetitive work, especially that which is done on an assembly line, must be unbearably boring. Yet a great many people do it without going to pieces, and some even accept it without much complaint, The possibility is generally overlooked that although the work itself is dull the accompanying social interactions may be a source of reward. An industrial worker, who had been employed for many years on a work crew engaged in storing raw materials and moving them around the plant as needed, reported great satisfaction in the daily social life of the group. Conversation was more or less continuous; it included a great deal of joking, an ever-flowing stream of banter, and a pleasant outpouring of gripes about the way things were done in the plant and in the world.[24] A similar phenomenon has been studied by Roy in a most unpromising situation: four men in a factory room each working at his own machine.[25] Roy, who became a participant-observer by taking a job at one of the machines, describes a regular daily sequence of pauses or "times" during which food was eaten, conversation took place, and pranks were played. What was done and said during these interruptions was amazingly similar from day to day, having almost the character of a ritual. Yet the breaks provided an opportunity for real if not very novel social interaction that "captured attention and held interest to make the long day pass."

More can be involved, however, than relief from boredom and maintaining a pleasant level of entertainment. Most work situations include a varied pattern of relationships both within the organization and with the people being served. Individual workers may have strong preferences and antipathies with respect to different types of relation. Bass quotes the words of a railroad engineer who said, "I wouldn't last three days in a shop with a foreman breathing down my neck. Here I'm my own boss. When I run the trains, nobody tells me what to do."[26] Some workers strongly desire independence and responsibility; others' strongest social needs may be for acceptance and support. It will be recalled that Harold Merritt, described in Chapter 2, responded well to being sandwiched between a boss who was responsible for all major decisions and a group of workers whom he could treat with consideration so that they tended to like him. The other subject in that chapter, John Chatwell, who was independent and competitive, would have found this social position intolerable.

The amount and variety of social stimulation that goes with a job can have an important, if not always recognized, bearing on satisfaction. The level of stimulation may be too high for some tastes. Those with a deep interest in some topic other than people may find social stimulation annoying and seek conditions behind the doors of laboratories, libraries, or studios wherein they can work with uninterrupted absorption. Stein and associates have described an industrial chemist who throughout childhood had suffered

[24] M. B. Smith, J. S. Bruner, and R. W. White, *Opinions and Personality* (New York: John Wiley & Sons, Inc., 1956), pp. 196–203.

[25] D. F. Roy, " 'Banana Time': Job Satisfaction and Informal Interaction," *Human Organization*, **18** (1960), 158–168; excerpted in *Interpersonal Dynamics: Essays and Reading on Human Interaction*, ed. W. G. Bennis, E. H. Schein, and D. E. Berlew (Homewood, Ill.: The Dorsey Press, 1964), pp. 583–600.

[26] Bass, *Organizational Psychology*, p. 116.

much competition and defeat by an older brother, but who had surpassed the brother by going to graduate school and becoming an expert in research. Continuing this strategy, he avoided arguments and minimized even casual conversation with his associates and spent most of his time hard at work at his own laboratory bench.[27] Even those whose work is by choice with people may find that the level of stimulation sometimes runs too high. With weary relief they see their pupils boarding the school bus to go home, their last patient leaving the office, their final committee meeting of the day being adjourned. On the other hand a high level of social interaction may be essential to happiness. The schoolteacher may experience a feeling of emptiness when the bus moves away on the last day before vacation. Life becomes poorer when there is no surrounding clamor of children, and the teacher waits hungrily for the opening of the new term. One of the sharpest problems of retirement in many cases is being abruptly separated from the group of associates with whom one has been working every day. Sometimes a retired person, after a week or two of enjoying his freedom, drops in at the office just to see what is going on, and thus momentarily restores the input of social stimulation to which he has long been accustomed.

Use of Abilities

Jobs may become unsatisfactory when they no longer challenge one's competence. Not having scope to do all that one feels able to do can become extremely irksome. It is this feeling that lies behind many a request for greater responsibilities and many a search for work in another organization where greater demands can be expected. Although escape from monotony may be involved in steps of this kind, mere change and variety may give only temporary satisfaction. What one wants is to have one's competence more severely taxed, to advance to more complex forms of mastery, and to experience an enlargement of one's effects on the environment. It is not uncommon to hear a person explain his happiness in a job by calling it challenging and by saying that it "keeps him growing."

Valuable light is thrown on this phenomenon in a study by Bidwell of young professional men drafted into the Army.[28] The study was made by participant observation, the author being himself a draftee like the eighty-four subjects whom he eventually persuaded to talk over their experiences. Begun in 1957, it covered a period of continuing cold war when there was no feeling of national crisis or expectation of armed conflict. The subjects therefore regarded their tour of duty as a great hardship, an arbitrary interruption of their civilian careers, and they were especially irked by the thought that peers who had escaped the draft were gaining two years on them in profes-

---

[27] M. I. Stein, J. N. MacKenzie, R. R. Rodgers, and B. Meer, "A Case Study of a Scientist," in *Clinical Studies in Personality*, ed. A. Burton and R. E. Harris (New York: Harper & Row, Publishers, 1955), pp. 726–767.

[28] C. E. Bidwell, "The Young Professional in the Army: A Study of Occupational Identity," *American Sociological Review*, **26** (1961), 360–372.

sional advancement. This unwelcome reflection was not much mitigated by the fact that the subjects were all attached to a headquarters research laboratory, having been selected for this duty because of their special training. They were engaged in research, but in only a few cases were their capabilities and initiative being fully utilized. "Even though these men were assigned to work in areas of special competence, they felt that the level of work was far too low for their training and experience. In no case did statements to the contrary occur." The result was much grumbling and great dissatisfaction.

The subjects were also unhappy on the score of status and prestige. Unlike Army medical personnel, they were obliged to live in barracks under the command of a professional military officer and to take their turns in humble duties such as kitchen work. This they felt to be beneath their dignity, and most of them argued that they should be allowed to live in civilian circumstances rather than on the Army post. In their spare time they showed an unaccustomed proclivity to attend theaters and classical concerts in a nearby city, a preference that one of them explained, oddly in view of their exclusive association with other professionals, as "a chance to get back to your old way of life . . . and spend some times with people of your own kind." The small book space allotted to each man in the barracks was likely to be filled with books about his professional specialty, but he seldom read them, choosing popular books instead. It was evident that these men, young and still insecure in their occupational identity, were made anxious by their temporarily ambiguous status and clung nervously to everything, including highbrow interests and the symbolic books, that affirmed them as highly educated intellectuals.

Significance of Work

It is probably fair to say that a good many workers care little about the larger significance of their work, seeing it simply as a way of earning a living. Others obviously care a great deal; they want their work to have an important influence on others, perhaps even a lasting effect on the stream of history and the progress of civilization. Lest it be thought that such aspirations can exist only at a highly sophisticated educational level, we shall examine instances chosen from well below that level.

In the course of a detailed study of health statistics in Great Britain between the two world wars, Halliday discovered a sharply rising incidence of illness among coal miners.[29] This led him to investigate the British coal industry, where he discovered developments that were injurious in several ways to the miners' sense of significance and worth. The prestige of coal was in rapid decline. Once the main source of power and the heart of British industrial preeminence, it was now yielding to other fuels and sinking to a secondary place in the economy. Added to this drop in significance were

[29] J. L. Halliday, *Psychosocial Medicine: A Study of the Sick Society* (New York: W. W. Norton & Company, Inc., 1948).

technical changes that reduced the individual miner's prestige and use of his skill. Machines had been introduced which did the actual digging, turning the miner into a "mere shoveler" who picked up after the machine and had to adapt himself to its pace. The great dissatisfaction among miners appeared to be the cause of the increased frequency of illness in themselves and in their families.

In an intensive study of opinions about public events made shortly after World War II, Smith and associates were able to trace the significance individuals attached to their work.[30] Alike yet different were the meanings given by two of the subjects, both in modest circumstances, to their occupations. One of these men held a monotonous industrial job tending a machine, but he had branched out into union activities, becoming a shop steward, an officer of his union, and thus a member of the team that did battle with management over wage contracts. His work for the union became the central organizing principle of his life, and he saw it not as a matter of merely local achievement in the company for which he worked but as part of a larger pattern of social progress. He believed that through collective bargaining the capitalist system could be redeemed, the position of workers made strong and secure, and an equitable shape given to the democratic way of life in the United States. The other man was somewhat irregularly employed on small weekly newspapers and on occasional publicity jobs. He used these opportunities to expound his views on communism, which he espoused with great warmth. A firm Marxist, he believed that historical forces assured the ultimate triumph of communism even in the United States, which would thus at last come to embody its democratic ideal. It is noteworthy that neither of these men anticipated much personal gain from the causes they espoused. Both were by this time aware of the slow rate of social change and did not expect much betterment during their lifetimes. But it was highly meaningful to each of them to feel himself part of a historical movement that promised ultimate benefit for the whole nation, perhaps even for the whole world.

The effect of the significance of one's work is illustrated in reverse by those who feel alienated from the larger implications of their occupation. If it is felt that work forms part of an objectionable economic system, if a job seems crassly oriented toward making money or callously injurious to human and environmental welfare, there can be none of the satisfaction experienced by the two men just described. In recent years there have been increasing numbers of late changes in occupation motivated by the desire to find greater significance in work. People in middle life have resigned from well-paid traditional jobs and turned to vocations bearing more directly on contemporary human problems and needs. In doing so they are likely to make sacrifices in salary, security, and accumulated knowledge and skills, but these losses are compensated by the feeling that the new vocation is humanly significant in a way that the old one was not.

[30] Smith, Bruner, and White, *Opinions and Personality*, esp. Chaps. 8 and 9.

Conclusion

In a book that surveys a great deal of research on work, Walter S. Neff reaches conclusions that well summarize the theme of this chapter.[31]

> An individual's ideas about work, his manner of working, and the values that work has for him, appear to be determined by an extremely complex network of factors. Some of these factors relate to events and circumstances within the life history of the individual, while others appear to reflect the history of the entire human species. Similarly, some of the determinants of work behavior appear to be clearly personal—individual styles of feeling, emotion, thought, and action. Other determinants appear to be clearly external—the physical, social, and cultural conditions of work. Inevitably, our search has led us into very diverse fields of knowledge.

[31] W. S. Neff, *Work and Human Behavior* (New York: Atherton Press, 1968), p. 252.

18 Establishing a New Family Circle

At some point during young adulthood almost everyone participates in setting up a new family of his own. This step has become more rather than less popular in recent generations: marriages take place on the average at an earlier age, and there are relatively fewer unmarried adults in the population. As an institution the family continues to undergo a certain amount of change, in some places even a certain amount of radical experimentation; on the whole, however, the family system retains much of its traditional outline. In the United States, where geographical mobility is high, the central core consisting of parents and their children often stands nearly in isolation, separated from place of origin and from relatives. Today's American family tends to be a more isolated, less extended family than those in other cultures and those in our own historical past. But this is only a mild deviation from the human average.

If the American family is thus in its central aspects much like families the world over, the manner of its formation represents an extreme of deviance from the typical human pattern. In no other society is the selection of a marriage partner left so much to individual initiative and attached so closely to the experience of being in love. Speaking cross-culturally, in this respect we are "way out," being the most extreme apostles known to anthropology of romantic love as a condition for marriage. This does not automatically make us wrong; here no more than elsewhere does conformity to a human average guarantee the appropriateness of behavior under a particular set of conditions. We may be "way out," but an engaged couple deeply in love is likely to judge all the world crazy except those who know what it means to be deeply in love. But our attachment to the romantic ideal should not keep us from appreciating other ways of looking at marriage, other aspects of an institution so central to social organization. In some societies the selection of a spouse is placed entirely in the hands of parents, who are deemed old enough and wise enough to make this important decision for their inexperienced young. Rarely has it been mankind's belief that a step so fraught with significance should be left to youthful whim and passion.

Contrasting cultural values on this subject can best be understood through examples. In a novel, *Remember the House*, Santha Rama Rau, who was born in Madras, India but educated in England and the United States, tells the story of a Hindu girl, Baba, with a history much like her own, who returns to India to live and becomes involved with problems of love and marriage.[1] Baba's Western education has accustomed her to the romantic ideal of marriage; furthermore, she is quite close to a newly married American couple whose mutual affection is constantly and unselfconsciously displayed. In a conversation with the American girl Baba admits that she has never been in love. The girl is much concerned—"Oh, how *sad* for you!"—and recalls her own experience of being constantly in love with one boy or another, though not quite in the way it was when she finally met her husband. Answering her friend's questions, Baba says that she will probably marry Hari, a steady man, financially secure, who is considered very suitable by her family. The American girl, whose parents considered her choice highly unsuitable, cannot understand thinking of marriage without being in love, and Baba, too, wishes that she might experience the excitement and happiness she is witnessing. When Hari in a matter-of-fact way proposes to her, she resents the absence of this feeling between them and refuses him. But the novelist does not let Baba remain a stranger to love. Going south to visit her grandmother, she meets a young schoolteacher, Krishnan, who begins calling on her, always with great propriety on the veranda in her grandmother's presence. His interest seems clear and Baba's heart is captured. After one of his visits the girl sits talking with her grandmother, and the dialogue expresses to perfection the gulf between their values.

Baba becomes incensed as the old woman reflects on Krishnan's occupation, security, respectability, and chances of a pension. In a suddenly loud voice she says, "I'm in love with him." This statement confuses her grandmother and causes her to suspect that some shameful relation has occurred. Convinced at last by Baba's tears that the girl really wants marriage, the grandmother offers to make overtures to Krishnan's parents, and another misunderstanding arises: to one mind, the prospective bridegroom's parents must be prompted to make the desired proposal; to the other mind, it would have to come as a personal communication straight from the bridegroom's heart. Grandmother is again bewildered at Baba's violent rejection of her offer of help. The old woman points out that "devotion, children, respect, and honor for a woman" are necessary for a good marriage, but not love. Questioned about her own marriage, she explains that she came to

[1] S. Rama Rau, *Remember the House* (New York: Harper & Row, Publishers, 1956).

experience the "glory of loving" only later, when deep intimacy had been established between her and her husband, whom thereafter she loved more than anything else on earth, even her children. Evidently, she points out, they do not mean the same thing by love. Baba asks if the kind of love she feels for Krishnan is less valuable, less glorious. The old woman replies with serene conviction, "Of course. Just think—what is it, this 'love' of yours? A little excitement, a little impatience, much imagination—is that enough to found your life on?" The novel ends with the disclosure that Krishnan's marriage to another woman has already been arranged for him, and with Baba's decision to take Hari after all. Is this to be considered a tragedy? It depends upon one's cultural outlook.

This story serves as a reminder that establishing a new family circle is not in most cultures left to individual enterprise. It is a step of great importance for the society as a whole, affecting as it does the production, care, and socialization of the next generation, and it is accordingly hedged in by extensive tradition and ceremony. In what follows in this chapter we shall describe the course of development mainly as it occurs in a society devoted to the romantic ideal of marriage. It will be apparent that the desired warm climate of love does not wholly do away with other considerations that surround establishing a family.

Selection of a Marital Partner

The typical course of events that leads eventually to marriage begins far back with casual acquaintances and diffuse dating. When some relation begins to be experienced as possibly durable, the pair may signify this feeling by going steady, a practice that does not necessarily imply permanence. If mutual intentions become more serious, the relation enters the stage of courtship, and if it goes well during this period the decision will follow to make it permanent and legally binding. Though typical, this sequence is not inevitable; there is much individual variation in the amount of time and energy invested in each step, and some steps may be omitted, as when a shy social isolate plunges directly into ardent courtship.

In the recent past generally, and in large segments of the population today, this sequence has been surrounded by a variety of social institutions, customs, and ceremonies. Even when devoted to the romantic ideal, society keeps a thumb on the founding of families. Traditional courtship is a definite social institution with explicit rules and expectations. The same is true of marriage itself, which holds its place as an important ceremony even for those who no longer ascribe to it a religious significance. Even the honeymoon stands as a strongly institutionalized custom. Going to work the morning after the wedding, failing to use the prescribed period of withdrawal from usual surroundings and exclusive devotion to one another, is a deviation from cultural expectations that still awakens a great deal of surprise. Through these conventions society tries to see to it that the whole business is taken seriously and that the impending responsibilities are fully appreciated, even though, paradoxically, it is assumed that the private experience of being in love is the most important thing of all.

Family Influences

It is not surprising that in describing the influences that bear on the choice of a marital partner some of the same headings are appropriate that applied to choosing an occupation. Family influences can certainly be expected to play a part in both types of choice. Family tradition is likely to contain certain specifications, overtly or covertly, as to the sort of person it is desirable to marry. The individual's experience with life in the family of his childhood is also likely to influence his conception of the proper mate.

Family tradition is often expressed as advice to marry someone like yourself, someone who can be considered your own kind. What is meant by "own kind" usually turns out to be a person similar in social status, economic situation, ethnic background, religious affiliation, educational level—some or all of these. It was mentioned in an earlier chapter that disapproval of intermarriage is one of the most sensitive indicators of status differences.[2] When the young George Apley of Marquand's novel, scion of an old Boston business family, loses his heart to a girl who is wrong on every count—she is lower middle class, poor, Irish, a Roman Catholic, and not sufficiently educated—vast family pressure is brought to bear to bring him to his traditional senses.[3] Actual studies of marriage choice repeatedly show that in the majority of marriages there is little social distance between the partners. Such findings, of course, cannot be taken as testimony simply to the force of family tradition. There is the question of propinquity, the tendency for cliques and friendship groups to form in the immediate neighborhood, the simple greater availability of the boy or girl next door. But who lives next door and in the neighborhood is itself much affected by status and ethnic considerations, so that physical propinquity and social suitability generally exert an influence in the same direction. Most children are exposed to a long course of briefing, ranging from the crudely overt to the subtly indirect, that one's marriage partner should not be too far away in social space.

As in the choice of occupation, family expectations influence marital choice in a variety of ways. The young person may simply share them without giving the matter much thought, eventually falling in love with someone nearby in social space. Or he may share them after giving the matter a great deal of thought. Even the most ardent believer that love conquers all may realize that love is given a lot more to conquer when partners differ widely in outlook and values. The young person may see marriage as already requiring enough adjustments without adding the misunderstandings that can arise from differences in social experience, religious outlook, and ethnic member-

---

[2] See above, Chap. 6, p. 122.

[3] J. P. Marquand, *The Late George Apley* (Boston: Little, Brown & Company, 1937).

ship. On the other hand, needs for novelty, variety, and an enlargement of personal experience may lend attractiveness to potential partners whose background is conspicuously different. As a new venture of one's own, marriage can be an expression of movement into a different world from that of one's childhood. Finally, if rebellion is an important theme, the person may choose a marital partner who will shock his family. One of the possible components of a negative identity is to find a mate who is foreign to family tradition. As usual in the study of personality it turns out that one variable does not produce one result. Acting in concert with other variables in the system, it helps produce a whole spectrum of results.

Another type of family influence is related to individual experience in one's family of origin. If the father's role has been generally satisfactory, the daughter will be disposed to look for like potentialities in her prospective husband; similarly the son will be alert to those qualities that made his mother a satisfying character in the domestic scene. Opposite consequences may follow if the parents were a source of woe: a girl accustomed to paternal tyranny may be startlingly attracted to a boy who is considerate and fair, and a maternally overprotected boy may rejoice in the company of a girl who expects him to make his own decisions and lets him catch cold. If one tried to cast in a systematic scheme all influences of this kind, the scheme would become impossibly vast and detailed. Yet in the study of any individual life it would be a serious mistake to overlook the influence of family experience. We are all a little biased by that particular version of the family in which we grew up, and this bias is likely to have an effect on the course of our feelings as we move toward establishing a new family circle.

Influences of Congeniality

Is a person more likely to be attracted by someone with similar personal characteristics, or one whose characteristics are complementary? The basis of personal attraction is, of course, a highly complex affair, which has been the object of a good deal of research in recent years.[4] With respect to the specific problem of mate selection the question was raised in a researchable form by Winch, who collected evidence that seemed to show that *need complementarity* was more important than *need homogamy* in the choice of a marital partner.[5] The evidence, however, has been severely challenged, and other students of the topic are convinced that homogamy—like choosing like —is more characteristic, though complementarity may prevail in certain re-

---

[4] T. M. Newcomb, "The Varieties of Interpersonal Attraction," in *Group Dynamics,* 2d ed., ed. D. Cartwright and A. Zander (New York: Harper & Row, Publishers, 1960); G. Lindzey and D. Byrne, "Measurement of Social Choice and Interpersonal Attractiveness," in *Handbook of Social Psychology,* Vol. 2, 2d ed., ed. G. Lindzey and E. Aronson (Reading, Mass.: Addison-Wesley Publishing Company, Inc., 1968).

[5] R. F. Winch, *Mate Selection: A Study of Complementary Needs* (New York: Harper & Row, Publishers, 1958).

spects.[6] Reviewing the subject in 1970, Barry puts it that "as of now homogamy has a clear hold on the field," though need complementarity is not wholly excluded. He calls attention to a study by Bermann and Miller on roommate choices that "indicates that in stable relationships, need complementarity, at least in regard to certain needs, does prevail whereas it tends not to in unstable relationships."[7]

Readers of this book must by now be tired of hearing that everything is complex, that variables interact, that conditions have to be taken into account, that thinking must be systemic; in short, that any one process in personality depends upon a lot of other processes. But they will realize that it is a bad blunder to phrase the question under discussion as if one had to decide which of two alternatives was right. What needs, what traits, what circumstances is one talking about? Similarity is probably the more popular choice in matters of social background, whereas complementarity is widely preferred when it comes to the structure of the sex organs. If the question is left floating in unmanageably broad terms it is simply not a legitimate scientific query. Even if it is restricted to needs, as Winch undertook to do, there should be no expectation that one can come out with a valid *general* answer. Some needs are inherently complementary, like nurturing and being nurtured; two people trying to nurture one another or two asking each other for succor are not likely to hit it off well. Affiliation, on the other hand, flourishes when it is met by affiliation, and two people alike with respect to this need may find each other unusually congenial. The importance of complementarity depends upon the nature of the needs one has in mind.

The problem of congeniality needs to be recast in such a way as to do justice to *cognition*—the images and expectations with which each individual approaches a relation—and to *motivation*—the several needs that are activated and either satisfied or frustrated in the relation. A useful reminder of the cognitive aspect is provided by Barry, who points out that "in any interpersonal situation, behavior is at least partly determined by the internal reference system of self to others and others to self, which is the product of each one's experience with significant others up to that point in time."[8] This allows for what was described above as bias derived from the particular version of the family in which each of us grew up. We approach new people with expectations derived from the past, and our experience with them—gratifying, frustrating, surprising, intriguing, disappointing—is influenced by what we expected to happen as well as by what we wanted.

On the motivational side it is important to think of congeniality as a developing process rather than a meshing together of fixed needs or traits.

[6] R. G. Tharp, "Psychological Patterning in Marriage," *Psychological Bulletin*, **60** (1963), 97–117.

[7] W. A. Barry, "Marriage Research and Conflict: An Integrative Review," *Psychological Bulletin,* **73** (1970), pp. 41–54; E. Bermann and D. R. Miller, "The Matching of Mates," in *Cognition, Personality, and Clinical Psychology*, ed. R. Jessor and S. Feschbach (San Francisco: Jossey-Bass, 1967).

[8] Barry, "Marriage Research and Conflict," p. 41.

This point can be illustrated from a study by Coombs, who conducted what might be called an experimental dance as a means of observing the ways of congeniality.[9] The experimental aspect of the dance lay in the fact that the participants were drawn from a pool of college students who had previously answered a questionnaire about their values, and they were chosen so that a wide range of values was represented. The experiment also called for a follow-up of the students to see which pairs continued their acquaintance in the weeks following the dance. It turned out that value consensus increased the probability that the relation would continue. But Coombs does not interpret this finding in static terms. Value consensus gets the relation off to a good start because the two individuals share a large number of presuppositions, which makes it easy for them to communicate without misunderstanding, argument, and threats to self-respect. As the relation continues, however, these early facilitating circumstances may come to be of secondary importance. They give place to other grounds for attraction, so that it is not legitimate to ascribe to value consensus more than a contributory part in the events that lead to choice of a marital partner. Congeniality develops in the course of a series of interactions, with different influences becoming important at different times.

The influence of the evolving experience of congeniality on mate selection is another of those topics that involves too many possibilities to be treated in comprehensive form. Here, we will have to be content to indicate a small number of those possibilities.

Anxiety and inferiority feelings may play an important part. Studies of dating have disclosed that certain couples go steady as a defense against the surrounding competitive system. The boy is shy and gentle; the girl, too, is shy and believes herself unattractive. Both seem destined to fail until they find each other, at which point an alliance is formed on the basis of sharing a common plight. This qualifies as an homogamous choice, but anxiety and inferiority feelings can also form one side of a complementary choice. This happens when a shy, insecure individual meets a boldly assertive one who supplies enough confidence for two; dominant leader and deferent follower are both happy in their reciprocal relation. Choices in which relief from anxiety and inferiority play a strong initial part may prove lastingly congenial, but there is the possibility that once security is attained, other needs will emerge that generate conflict. Safe in each other's company, the shy unattractive couple may begin to blossom, and it may turn out that each has a latent need to be first, to dominate, and to hold the center of the stage. If this happens early enough, they may decide against permanent commitment; if they are already committed, they will have work to do on their relation.

Needs for novelty and excitement can play a considerable part in mate selection. Each member of a pair is likely to introduce the other to a new circle of acquaintances, friends, and relatives. Each member is likely

[9] R. H. Coombs, "Value Consensus and Partner Satisfaction among Dating Couples," *Journal of Marriage and the Family*, **28** (1966), 166–173.

to have certain favored interests into which the other is drawn. Perhaps the girl discovers unexpected excitement in watching hockey games, and the boy is surprised to find beauty in chamber music. Each can experience a highly gratifying personal enlargement through being taken into realms hitherto closed. This experience may increase as acquaintance grows, but it may decline. The new realms may prove to be less than lastingly congenial; after hockey games the girl, and after chamber music the boy, comes home irritable with an incipient headache. It is noteworthy that intimacy, as described in a previous chapter, tends not to take the downward course of this rather extreme example. It may be novel and exciting to discover someone with whom a real exchange of personal experience is possible, but these exchanges also have intrinsic value that makes them tend to grow, to gain in depth, and to be constantly renewed as new circumstances arise.[10]

Personal attraction quite easily comes to grief if one or both parties still have strong childlike dependent needs. Especially if the dependence is of a demanding character, such needs cannot be complementary, and anxious clinging by one party is likely to frustrate the other party's need for autonomy. The following extended illustration, which also provides sidelights on the nature of dreaming, shows the vicissitudes of this type of conflict.

An Illustrative Case: Linda's Dreams

That dreams can provide in condensed pictorial form a commentary on what is happening in one's personal life is shown in an autobiographical study by a college junior whom we shall call Linda. Her report was organized around two dreams, which occurred about a month apart and which dealt with the same topic, but with interesting differences of detail and feeling.

> *Dream 1.* I am in a swimming pool. It is fairly cozy because it is an indoor pool and the water is pleasantly warm. I am about to be married. The intended bridegroom is waiting in a room just off the pool, and though his identity is somewhat blurred, the recognizable elements show him to be Steve. Mother is standing by the pool, and when I get out she will help me put on my floor-length white lace sheath dress, veil, and shoes. I feel no anxiety in the dream.
>
> *Dream 2.* I am standing at the back of an outdoor theater with Mother. I am about to be married, and the bridegroom, the rabbi, and the best man are standing on the stage. The identities of the rabbi and best man are unclear, but the bridegroom is a combination of my paternal grandfather and a boy, Jonas, with whom I have had several dates recently. Though there is no one in the seats, there seems to be a vague crowd which I do not see but hear. They are telling me that I should put on a formal white gown to get married. But I am standing in a skirt and sweater complaining to Mother that I don't *want* to get all dressed

---

[10] M. Sarton, in a novel entitled *Kinds of Love* (New York: W. W. Norton & Company, Inc., 1970), beautifully describes the discovery of new depths of intimacy in a long-married couple in their seventies.

up and have a fancy wedding. I just want to wear my nice wool skirt and sweater. Mother says, "Why don't you compromise and wear a beret?" It is a long way down the aisle from where I am standing to where the bridegroom is waiting, and my feeling is mixed: I want to go, but I am not in any hurry, and it doesn't seem as if the actual wedding is to take place very soon. However, I feel no uncomfortable anxiety at the thought of walking down the aisle to be married; rather, the feeling is one of "I can take my time, and when I do walk down there it will be fine."

The dreams are alike in that marriage is about to take place, Mother is helpfully present, and the bridegroom is waiting. But there are differences. The scene of the first dream is a warm, cozy, enclosed place where Mother will dress her and hand her along to the bridegroom. The second dream takes place out of doors, and there is a long aisle to be traversed alone before she reaches the bridegroom. Mother herself is different: in the first dream she stands for formal clothing, but in the second she accedes to her daughter's wish to dress informally, rejecting the conventional voices of the unseen crowd, and even suggests a beret, a symbol of freedom to Linda, who associates it with an acquaintance admired for her independence. The bridegroom has changed: in the first dream it is Steve, an earlier boyfriend who constantly reassured her with expressions of his love and admiration; in the second it is Jonas, a recent acquaintance more taciturn and less expressive, with whom she has been trying to develop a relation unmarred by her usual demanding dependence. And Linda, too, feels differently about things. In the second dream she has a mind of her own about what she will wear, and she feels in control of the situation to the extent of deciding when she will start up the aisle, rather than being handed perforce straight from her mother to the bridegroom.

There is much, of course, that is incongruous in these dreams, testifying to the light grip of everyday reality on the dreaming mind. Yet the differences between the two dreams are not fortuitous; they reflect a highly significant development that was going on in Linda's experience. Not long before the first dream she had become sharply and miserably aware, through a violent scene with one of her boyfriends, of her tendency to spoil all close relations by compulsive demands for expressions of love, esteem, and reassurance. She knew that she must find a way to stop it, and she was struggling to do so, not with complete success. The first dream expresses the wish that she could lay down this burden by finding someone like Steve who would indulge her and excuse her from growing up, in which case everything would be easy, warm, and cozy; there would be no distance to traverse between being Mother's daughter and being Steve's wife. Between then and the second dream two events occurred. One of these was a visit from her mother, during which she became aware that her mother was now treating her like an adult rather than a child, refusing to direct, avoiding moralistic parental judgments, taking the daughter's own inclinations seriously. At one point they had an argument based on a misunderstanding; it was resolved, and new understanding reached, as between two equals. The other event was Jonas himself, about whom she wrote:

> In my brief but pleasant relationship with Jonas I have conducted a kind of test case with myself, and so far it has succeeded. I have not begged for reassurance from him, have not demanded more affection than he was ready to give, and have not fantasized my feelings for him into a love which can replace my love for my parents. . . . Jonas represents, in the dream *and* consciously, my new behavior and my new view of myself.

The changes in herself that were reflected in the second dream were not things of which she was unaware, but it seems likely that by dreaming about them she increased her own insight. Even with their incongruities the dreams must be credited with artistic creativity and an illuminating use of symbolism about the things that really mattered.

Influence of Fantasy

Choice of occupation, as we saw, can be affected by fantasies of what it is like to be a member of the occupation. Choice of a marital partner is even more open to fantasy, especially under the influence of the romantic ideal, which makes it so predominantly a matter of feeling rather than reasoned calculation. Fantasy does not necessarily inject difficulties into the process of choice. Anything involving the future is bound to awaken imagination, and happy images of camping trips together, for instance, create a probblem only if one of the partners is violently opposed to camping trips. But there is the possibility that fantasies, especially if they spring from strong latent needs and enter consciousness only in ambiguous forms, will build expectations so unrealistic as to lead to inevitable disappointment.

One such group of imaginings might be called rescue fantasies. Attraction is felt toward a person in trouble, and it is hoped that love will bring rescue from the trouble. Perhaps the prospective partner is apathetically lazy or deeply depressed, addicted to alcohol or hooked on drugs, chronically irresponsible or wildly reckless; the lover hopes that the beloved will turn over a new leaf through the healing influence of love. It should be noticed that such fantasies contain a nurturing, cherishing element, which under more promising circumstances contributes much to good relations. Nor should it be overlooked that on occasion love has produced remarkable changes. Too often, however, the trouble from which the partner is to be rescued proves deep-seated and resistant to change; love's labor appears lost as behavior continues in its accustomed channels. Undoubtedly rescue fantasies contain a touch of omnipotence as well as nurture. Both are frustrated when their object fails to change.

The most carefully studied influence of fantasy on marital choice has to do with the Oedipus complex. The theoretical basis is that children around the age of 4 or 5, reaching the phallic stage of psychosexual development, form a truly erotic attachment to the parent of opposite sex. This relation, however, has to be renounced, and recollections of it are repressed during the latency period; but when erotic interest bursts forth again at puberty the choice of objects is influenced by residues from the earlier period. Especially when it comes to thinking of a lasting relation, the boy unwittingly prefers someone like his mother and the girl gravitates to someone who reminds her of her father. The influence of these residues may create difficulties. Too strong a dependence, too much of a child's attitude toward a parent, may be reanimated, and because sexuality was suppressed in the earlier relation it may not be free from inhibition in the new one. This, in a very small nutshell, is the way Freud worked it out on the basis of what was communicated to him by neurotic patients undergoing psychoanalytic treatment. A textbook case for Freud's idea would be a young man falling in love with a woman probably older, but in any case maternal in her attitude; becoming jealously demanding, idealizing her purity, and experiencing guilt at the thought of sexual consummation. The evidence is strong that unconscious needs and fantasies can operate in this way, but how often they do so is a question just about impossible to answer.

In an early work on marital happiness Burgess and Cottrell, basing their conclusions on questionnaires filled out by 526 American husbands and wives, showed that close attachment of a child to parents, especially of son to mother and of daughter to father, was highly correlated with subsequent marital happiness.[11] This is not the result one would have predicted if Freud's account had wide applicability; such a history should have led to marital difficulties. Of course the data are of such a different character that it is hardly legitimate to put them into direct confrontation. The findings of Burgess and Cottrell deserve comparison with Toman's research, described in an earlier chapter, which showed that marriages tend to be more stable when the partners have previously occupied analogous positions with siblings; for instance, when the husband was an older brother of a sister and the wife a younger sister of a brother.[12] Toman's findings point to the importance for marital congeniality of previous appropriate practice in the closeness of the family. The results obtained by Burgess and Cottrell can be given the same interpretation: those who have had a close relation with the parent of opposite sex enter marriage well versed in closeness and establish it more easily with the spouse. Probably we are justified in supposing, as a tentative judgment, that relevant social experience in the old family influences performance in the new one. Relations that have been close and reasonably harmonious—whether with parents or with siblings—tend to produce like closeness and harmony in marriage. But when the earlier relations have been fraught with difficulty, when the Oedipal situation has been intense and fol-

[11] E. W. Burgess and L. S. Cottrell, Jr., *Predicting Success or Failure in Marriage* (Englewood Cliffs, N.J.: Prentice-Hall, Inc., 1939).

[12] See above, Chap. 5, pp. 112–115.

lowed by much repression, or when sisters and brothers have fought like cats and dogs, the residues of these experiences will tend to injure the marital relation.

Being in Love

After reading this sketch of a variety of influences on the choice of a marital partner, some readers may be inclined to speak up loudly for the importance of being in love. Even if these factors have a contributory significance, are they not overridden by the superior force of love, by that experience of powerful attraction that seems to defy analysis? Have we not described marital choice without its central component? Readers thus protesting can find support in words by psychologist Harry Harlow, who said, "So far as love or affection is concerned, psychologists have failed in their mission. The little we know about love does not transcend simple observation, and the little we write about it has been written better by poets and novelists."[13] This judgment is rather sweeping, but it is true that the cumbersome tools of scientific research have not come up with one of their resounding triumphs on the subject of romantic love. But the scientific inquirer does not easily give up. A scale for the measurement of romantic love has lately been developed by Rubin.[14] He distinguishes between love and liking, the scales for the two being only moderately correlated. The love scale appears to have three chief components, described as follows:

> 1. *Affiliative and dependent need*—for example, "If I could never be with _____, I would feel miserable"; "It would be hard for me to get along without _____."
> 2. *Predisposition to help*—for example, "If _____ were feeling badly, my first duty would be to cheer him (her) up"; "I would do almost anything for _____."
> 3. *Exclusiveness and absorption*—for example, "I feel very possessive toward _____"; "I feel that I can confide in _____ about virtually everything."

When the scale was given to dating couples, they scored themselves much higher in relation to one another than they did when answering the same questions about their best friends. Those who said they were in love scored higher than those who were uncertain, and higher scores were likewise made by those who predicted that their relation would lead to marriage. Thus a certain validity can be claimed for Rubin's love scale, and it will doubtless be put to use in further research.

Only time can tell how far such research will advance, how much light it is capable of shedding on a powerful affective experience that most people are more disposed to enjoy than to analyze.

[13] H. F. Harlow, "The Nature of Love," *American Psychologist*, **13** (1958), 673–685.
[14] Z. Rubin, "Measurement of Romantic Love," *Journal of Personality and Social Psychology*, **16** (1970), 265–273.

Development of the Marriage Relation

If the choice of a marital partner is seen as a developing process, still more is this true of the relation between the partners after marriage. Conceivably one could make an estimate of a couple's suitability at a given point in time, as on the wedding day, but it would be a mistake to think of this in static terms, as if the pair either fitted or did not fit like the pieces of a picture puzzle. A more pertinent question is how likely these two people are to stay suitable or to become suitable over the course of time. Both are certainly going to change as they grow older, and the character of their relation will likewise change. It is thus important to consider, among other things, the strategies they develop for managing their evolving relation.

The Honeymoon

The honeymoon is a widespread human custom linked with the rituals of marriage. Because one of its aspects is privacy, it has not fallen much under the prying eyes of psychological and social scientists. But it is clear that the honeymoon, like the marriage ceremony itself, is a social institution that contributes to a major transition in which old bonds of relationship must give place to new ones. In a formal marriage ceremony the two families publicly relinquish their children from old ties, the bride in particular being "given away" by her father, and the new social unit is officially brought into existence by an exchange of vows and the ritual of the ring. Up to this point the marriage has been much in the public domain. The institution of the honeymoon provides for the next step, the developing and deepening of the new relation, which is a private matter best handled by a temporary withdrawal from accustomed social ties and external obligations. Thus after the wedding the couple is expected to vanish to an unknown destination; not, in all likelihood, literally unknown, but ceremonially so, as a means of emphasizing detachment from the previous ties. It is bad form to ask the couple where they are going, and good form for them to make a mystery of it.

In a study of honeymoons, based on interviews with young couples shortly before marriage and shortly after their return, the Rapoports distinguish three common American types.[15]

> In the United States the honeymoon takes a variety of forms. There is the *lovers' nest* conception, as exemplified in the convergence of honeymooners in places such as Bermuda, Niagara Falls, and honeymoon camps in the Poconos and Florida. This seems to be a peculiarly North American custom, perhaps reflecting the general cultural trait of "other-directedness," "groupiness," and the fear of intimacy noted by many observers of the American scene. Europeans tend to be astonished by this custom, noting that they would wish to get away from other people at such a time, certainly from others in the same situation.

[15] R. Rapoport and R. N. Rapoport, "New Light on the Honeymoon," *Human Relations,* **17** (1964), 33–56.

Another prominent type of honeymoon in the United States, superficially like that of the European but at a deeper level reflecting some of the same uniquely American traits mentioned above, is the *perpetuum mobile* honeymoon. Here a couple gets into the omnipresent automobile and travels, often without predetermined plans, reservations, schedule, or itinerary, but with a budget and a date for return.

The *vacation type* of honeymoon is also characteristic of American life, and here one finds as many sub-types of honeymoon as there are conceptions of what constitutes an enjoyable vacation. Essentially, the honeymoon is defined as a kind of vacation and the criteria for having a good honeymoon get assimilated with those for having a good vacation. Those who like night life and excitement seek a situation that will provide these diversions for their honeymoon; those who like camping and hiking seek that sort of a setting, and so on.

The vacation-like characteristics of the honeymoon do not obscure the fact that certain special developments are expected to take place, referred to by the Rapoports as *phase-specific tasks*. These are, in essence, (1) moving forward on the development of a mutually satisfactory sexual relationship, and (2) becoming accustomed to living in close contact, sharing the details of everyday existence. The importance and difficulty of these developments depends, of course, on the couple's previous experience. They may already have lived together, celebrating the honeymoon informally before the wedding, but this is hardly a guarantee that the phase-specific tasks are finished. The couple chosen for detailed description in the Rapoports' paper were novices with respect to the two tasks. Symbolic of the uneasiness they felt about sexuality and intimacy was their choice of an inn frequented by honeymooners, their decision to share a table with another couple so as to have someone to talk to at meals, their participation in social activities that often kept them up late, the husband's excessively rational attitude toward sex, and the wife's pain during first attempts at intercourse. Even so, they used the honeymoon period for progress that was almost certainly faster than it would have been if after the wedding they had simply moved into their apartment and continued with their regular occupations.

The Adaptive Process

Obviously the evolution of a satisfactory marriage relation continues long after the honeymoon, indeed throughout marriage. To capture it for observation a little further along in time, Raush, Goodrich, and Campbell made a study of young middle-class couples in their early years of marriage, before the arrival of children.[16] Listing the areas in which mutual adaptation is required, these authors mention those for which the honeymoon is expected to provide a good start: sexual relations and situations of physical intimacy such as nudity, dressing habits, and sleeping and waking habits. But there is

[16] H. L. Raush, W. Goodrich, and J. D. Campbell, "Adaptation to the First Years of Marriage," *Psychiatry*, **26** (1963), 368–380.

also now the establishing and maintaining of a household, with its attendant problems of mealtime rituals, food preferences, and money handling. Furthermore, relationships must be worked out with each other's families, with previous friends, and with new friends; these steps may prove to be far from easy. Plans must be made for the future, and must include future parenthood and the further education and careers of both husband and wife. Finally, the couple must seek harmony between the husband's and the wife's hobbies and political and religious activity, either by drawing closer or by respecting existing differences. This inventory serves as a reminder that adaptation to marriage will not be quickly wrought. There is a lot to do.

The authors of this paper directed their attention especially to the patterns of communication developed by the partners for reaching decisions and resolving conflicts. They approached the problem, in other words, by looking for strategies of adaptation. They illustrate the possibilities of this approach by describing in some detail two couples called the Gerharts and the Vreelands. In an external sense these couples were not conspicuously different. They had adapted successfully enough to the main problems of married life and were relatively happy together. Study of their patterns of communication, however, showed consistent differences, suggesting that in the face of new difficulties the Gerharts would be much less successful than the Vreelands in coming to an adequate solution. The contrast came out sharply even in the first interview. It happened that both Mrs. Gerhart and Mrs. Vreeland in telling about childhood mentioned disturbing problems with their parents, became upset, and in consequence gave somewhat muddled accounts. Mr. Gerhart's comments were to the effect that his wife had gotten him confused, too, and that it all sounded like a soap opera. Mr. Vreeland took a prompting role, quietly mentioning details such as his father-in-law's drunkenness and gambling when he saw that his wife wanted to tell about them but was having difficulty in doing so. The difference could be expressed by saying that Mr. Vreeland took his wife's side, showing sympathy and giving support, whereas Mr. Gerhart distanced himself with criticism and sarcasm as if bent on maintaining his separate identity. In a simple count of pronouns it turned out that the Vreelands used *we* and *us* more often, *I* and *me* less often, than the Gerharts.

Included in the research was an experimental situation in which husband and wife were given hypothetical problems to solve, the ensuing dialogue being recorded. The problems were of an interpersonal nature likely to elicit conflict. Simply in terms of efficiency the Vreelands handled these situations better, taking only half the time needed by the Gerharts. The Vreelands were more successful in sticking to the problem and avoiding digressions. For the Gerharts, the authors comment, "a problem acts as a fuse to inflame a wide range of sensitivities. . . . An issue is not discussed or argued on its own merits, but expands so that it incorporates much more than what is ostensibly involved. . . . The issue is transformed so that it represents threats and counterthreats to the balance of power and affection." Furthermore, the Vreelands' strategies for resolving conflicts involved mutual recognition and respect for each other's feelings, whereas for the Gerharts communication had more to do with manipulation and defense. Failing to recognize or to sympathize with the other's subjective experience, each of the Gerharts could only "assert and reassert his own." The other person's statements were thus often heard "only as threats to be parried or as gaps in the other's defensive line."

It is obvious, of course, that these two couples do not differ simply in strategies of communication. There are important differences in the sphere of motivation. Yet conceivably these differences may not lie in the strength of personal attraction—in the degree to which husband and wife are in love. They may have their principal locus in the realm of anxiety, reflecting mainly a lack of confidence either in others or in oneself. Possibly the Gerharts are much in love, yet so insecure that conflict almost inevitably calls forth defensive operations. Furthermore, although strategies of communication reflect motives, they become habituated and thus acquire a certain independent life of their own. Couples who consult marriage counselors sometimes profit more from learning about their strategies than from having their motives analyzed. They want to get along but do not know how; they have become trapped in unwitting strategies that prevent the resolution of conflict. It may be that they can change their strategies once they see what is going on. If such is the case, the positive motives that connect them may be more fully expressed and progressively strengthened.

One of the points made in the specific comparison of the Gerharts and the Vreelands can be considered to have fairly wide generality. This is the loss of cognitive focus when conflicts touch off substantial amounts of anxiety. In a study of this subject Deutsch makes a distinction between productive and destructive conflicts.[17] In the former, the specific issue is kept in focus, and the partners communicate openly, honestly, with recognition of each other's interests and feelings; this permits flexibility in the search for a solution. Conflict is destructive when the arena is expanded, irrelevant resentments brought in, and tactics used that involve threats, deceptions, and coercions. The probability that disagreements will take a destructive course is greater when the partners are personally insecure. It is also greater when there are deep differences in their basic values, so that the immediate issue readily becomes a symbolic threat to something that is deeply cherished. Boulding calls attention to the conflict-generating power of those core values or images around which a great deal of one's personality is integrated.[18] It is clearly easier to stick to the point in an argument and to settle a question on its merits when there is essential harmony in basic values.

Sharing and Individual Autonomy

As a close and lasting relation, marriage is often described in a language of sharing. But however strongly the partners share common interests they are still two people. The concept of ego identity still applies to each of

---

[17] M. Deutsch, "Conflicts: Productive and Destructive," *Journal of Social Issues*, **25** (1969), 7–41.

[18] K. E. Boulding, *Conflict and Defense: A General Theory* (New York: Harper & Row, Publishers, 1962).

them; if in certain circumstances they think of themselves as the Smiths, one and indivisible, there remain two Smiths, each with an individual identity. One aspect of adaptation in marriage can be described as achieving a balance between becoming one and still being two. In more formal language this is usually expressed as a balance between mutual interdependence and individual autonomy.

At the beginning there may be a strong desire to share everything. This may take an imperceptive form, as in the young geologist who planned to spend the honeymoon near some rock formations of special interest for his research and was surprised that his bride did not enjoy collecting specimens every day. There are many things that can be shared, though in a highly specialized technological society the husband's occupation is not likely to be one of them. There are the home and, later on, the raising of children, in both of which, even with division of labor and differentiation of male and female roles, both partners are importantly involved. There are also common friends and common participations in the community, and shared interests may include such further items as the outdoors, sports, gardens, travel, art, music—innumerable possibilities. When interests overlap in this way, not only do they come to be shared, but the sharing becomes a part of them. If the partnership dissolves, each member may find that the interest loses some of its savor.

It is to be expected, however, that certain aspects of each partner's personality cannot be shared. Each may have strong interests that do not overlap and cannot be pursued in proximity. Each may have a personal style, influenced by constitution as well as previous experience, that makes unbroken sharing virtually impossible. It is easy to say that such differences should be handled by each partner's recognizing and respecting those aspects of the other that require taking his own course. But the attempt to behave in this enlightened fashion may prove to be a strain on feeling. In a literal sense the emotion of jealousy is activated. How can he like puttering around with those old rocks so much better than he likes me? How can she enjoy that women's clacking club so much more than she enjoys taking care of me? A marriage can be entirely successful in which each partner has a sharply etched ego identity, in which domestic life is happily shared but independent ways are happily taken the rest of the time. This solution, however, usually represents an achievement in which both parties have learned to deal with jealousy, possessiveness, excessive dependence, envious comparisons of status, and all the other feelings that can stand in the way of such an outcome. The achievement is all the more difficult when the two partners want different amounts of autonomy. If the couple consists of a dependent husband and an ambitious professional woman, or a dependent wife and a jet-riding practitioner of nationwide promotional work, an acceptable balance cannot easily be reached between sharing and individual autonomy.

Enduring marital happiness depends not only upon reaching balances of this kind but also upon constant work on restoring balances as conditions change. Living happily together changes its meaning radically between the wedding and the golden wedding. Those who manage it successfully have probably done so not just by luck but by creative adaptation.

Early Stages of Parenthood

A major reorganization of the new family occurs with the birth of the first child. Young parents, whose thinking may have been mainly about bringing up a child, now abruptly discover the element of truth in Erikson's observation that the child also brings up the parents. At first this upbringing on the part of the baby takes the crude form of demands for attention and care, which call for a considerable change in parental behavior. If the parents are convinced of the virtue of self-demand schedules for the baby, they will have to accommodate themselves to giving up their own self-demand schedules. It is fortunate for new parents that infants spend a considerable amount of time asleep. Fortunate also is the circumstance that parents, as members of the mammalian order, are more deeply disposed than they may realize to take care of a creature so small and helpless, especially when it is the product of their own bodies. This assist from nature helps to insure that the baby will have some success in bringing up the parents to deliver essential services.

Detailed observations of the effects of having the first child lie widely scattered through the literature of psychology and psychiatry. In a recent publication, Senn and Hartford have assembled observations on eight couples "as each lived through the transition from married couple to family through the birth of the first child." The authors undertake to include "the family climate preceding the firstborn, the 'personality' of the neonate as he enters the family orbit, the action of the environment upon the infant, and the infant's impact on his milieu." The resulting descriptions, though unsystematic, contain a wealth of detail about this important step in the evolution of the family circle.[19]

Psychological Aspects of Having the First Child

In his description of the stages of ego development, Erikson locates an important crisis at the time of life when founding a family typically occurs. He calls this the crisis of *generativity vs. stagnation.* Generativity means "primarily the concern in establishing and guiding the next generation"; it is most literally expressed in having and bringing up children of one's own, though it may also be manifested generally in caring and teaching roles and in promoting the growth of cultural institutions. The inner push in this direction does not have to be manufactured—"mature man needs to be needed"—but if it is obstructed the consequence is likely to be "a pervading sense of stagnation and personal impoverishment."

> Individuals, then, often begin to indulge themselves as if they were their own—or one another's—one and only child; and where conditions favor it, early invalidism, physical or psychological, becomes the vehicle of self-

[19] M. J. E. Senn and C. Hartford, eds., *The Firstborn: Experiences of Eight American Families* (Cambridge, Mass.: Harvard University Press, 1968).

concern. The mere fact of having or even wanting children, however, does not "achieve" generativity. In fact, some young parents suffer, it seems, from the retardation of the ability to develop this stage. The reasons are often to be found in early childhood impressions; in excessive self-love based on a too strenuously self-made personality; and finally in the lack of some faith, some "belief in the species," which would make a child appear to be a welcome trust of the community.[20]

The difficulties of surmounting the crisis of generativity will be illustrated in a moment in connection with having the first child, but an example from outside the family will serve to show the wide scope of this important concept. A brilliant graduate student, his career supported for years by scholarships, finished his degree, held a postdoctoral fellowship for further study, and then took a position as a teacher in a college of only moderate fame. In the middle of the year he resigned from this job on the ground that neither his colleagues nor his students were intellectually stimulating. His stated reason, which he gave as self-evident justification, reflects the step he could not take, the step from being an object of stimulation to being a source of it for those around him. That he was being paid to teach the next generation of students failed to elicit care for their interests or desire to transmit a heritage of knowledge; instead, he construed his job as another fellowship intended for his personal development and felt free to drop out when the nourishment proved inadequate. Some other object, such as the enlargement of knowledge, might later elicit his care, but at this point generativity was still beyond his reach.

It is not surprising that new parents should sometimes stumble in the crisis of generativity in view of the sudden weight of demands on their time and attention. Very likely they were eager for the baby to arrive, proud to have produced a child, and full of aspirations to provide a climate of warmth and love. But the new schedule is exacting. One must be on hand a great deal, day and night, seven days a week, yet the recipient of all this care does not even smile at first and expresses no gratitude for what is being done. The bargain begins to feel one-sided. How can one maintain an even flow of warmth to a creature so little capable of making any overt return? The mother begins to feel like a mere nursemaid and the father like a hired man. Fortunately the baby will soon become more responsive and the bargain will seem less unequal, but generativity is certain to be put through some fairly sharp tests.

Many young parents are surprised at the extent to which having their first child creates a difficult emotional triangle. Jealousies and resentments intrude upon the first happy excitement of having a baby. The husband discovers that he has lost exclusive possession of his wife. If he is strongly dependent, this may feel like having to share his mother. In either event he may find himself prey to feelings of jealousy toward the new rival for his wife's

[20] E. H. Erikson, *Childhood and Society*, 2d ed. (New York: W. W. Norton & Company, Inc., 1963), pp. 266–267.

affections. The wife is distressed if her husband does not rave over the new-comer and shows any signs of indifference. If she is strongly dependent she will feel that he should be carrying a larger part of the burden of care. Troubles with past emotional triangles in their respective families may give an extra push to the feelings elicited by the new one, but the triangular situation is really there; it is not just borrowed from the past. To meet it requires transcending the feelings of dependence, of jealousy, and of self-concern, which to some extent linger in just about everyone.

Another type of experience that is sometimes disquieting to young parents can be described as shocks of recognition. Frustrated one day at the tiring demands of their offspring, they suddenly notice a painful similarity between their feelings and those of cold rejecting parents who, so they have read, can ruin their children's development. Trying to restrain an active child, they hear in their own voices the crisp authoritative tones that used to come so annoyingly from their own parents. And sometimes, finding themselves stumped by a nursery crisis, they will recognize with shock that their indecisive utterances and evasiveness come straight from past occasions when their own parents failed them. Like everyone embarked on a serious undertaking, new parents aspire to do well, very likely to do better than their predecessors; it is therefore painful to recognize those moments in which they fall miserably below their own standards. But shocks of recognition at least sometimes lead to an improvement of insight and a true deepening of empathy. When shouting impatiently at a foot-dragging child precocious in the art of filibuster, a parent may suddenly recall his own early exploits along this line and appreciate the feelings of anger, outrage, and possibly fright that lie behind them. Such lessons are not always pleasant, but they are lessons none the less, and they may favorably alter the ensuing interactions.

Dealing with More than One Child

The birth of a second child produces a new complication. As a rule the parents take this event more calmly than they did the first birth; they have been through it before. But now they have created an emotional quadrangle, and this may call forth a whole new range of feelings not necessarily easy to manage.

It is at this point in their lives that parents, even if they have strongly opposed the idea before, become convinced about innate constitutional differences. The second child is obviously not a replica of the first. The genes have been shuffled for a new deal, and the result is unique. The parents discover that their accumulated wisdom about child rearing must now go into a second edition, with revisions that may be surprisingly large. What worked with the highly active, wiry first-born may prove wholly inappropriate to the plump, placid, serenely smiling character who has somehow emerged from the second genetic mix. Wide differences only add to the difficulty of managing the emotional quadrangle.

The most challenging problem is that of fairness. The parents must rise to new heights in the administration of justice. As we saw in an earlier chapter, they must expect a certain amount of sibling rivalry, possibly a large amount. The only way they can mitigate this rivalry over the course of time is to arbitrate fairly when clashes occur, to avoid favoritism, and to give evidence to both parties of continuing esteem. But the circumstances in which fairness has to be practiced make it extraordinarily difficult to behave judiciously. The children are of different ages, so that different things should properly be expected of them; they cannot quite be treated, as adults should be, as equals before the law. Furthermore, the circumstances in which controversy arises may not have been witnessed by the arbiter, may not be correctly reported, and may thus easily defeat clear judgment. Nor is the parent always able to give the matter undivided attention. A not uncommon sight in a supermarket is a mother with two children, one screaming with empurpled countenance, the other looking smug. Who can blame the mother if, while struggling to get the shopping done and restrain the children from shoplifting, she has failed in some way to hold steady the scales of justice? All very well is the ideal of loving one's children equally and being unfailingly fair, but practicing it effectively is quite another matter.

The administration of justice would be easier if the courts themselves were impartial. It soon dawns on observant parents, however, that they are caught up in the quadrangle. By analogy with legal practice they should disqualify themselves from sitting in judgment where they have so much personal involvement—but the parental role does not permit this abdication. Let us say that the contending parties are an older boy and a younger girl, that the father was an older boy in his own family often plagued by a younger sister, and that the mother was a younger girl who suffered much injustice at the hands of an older brother. Can we expect the court to be impartial in such a case, and can we even look for a unanimous decision on the part of the two magistrates? If something resembling fairness emerges from such an unpromising situation it results from a great deal of observation, work, and correction of prejudices on the part of the parents.

A peculiarly difficult problem in justice is set for some parents by a child who makes himself their foreman and impresses their values on his siblings. Often enough, parents are unthinkingly pleased by this alliance and give their child foreman complete support. Some parents, however, see the foreman's role as an unfortunate one, leading to imperceptive self-righteousness and possibly a harsh dominance over the other children. But this puts them in a curious trap. How can they discourage self-righteousness and soften undue policing on the part of their "good" child without appearing to disbelieve in their own precepts, thus creating a confusing vacuum of values? Taking into account the slow progress of children's moral understanding, as described in an earlier chapter, one must not expect easy and satisfying resolutions of this dilemma.[21] It is one of the built-in hazards of dealing with more than one child.

---

[21] See above, Chapter 11, pp. 266–267.

Parental Sense of Competence

Readers of this book will notice that we have now come full circle from the early chapters. We started with the family circle, looking at it from the child's point of view and considering the effects of parental attitudes on the growth of the child's personality. In the course of the book the child has grown up and become a parent, and in this section we have been considering the effects of having and raising children on the further development of the parent's personality. Recognizing the interactive nature of personality, it is certainly legitimate to reverse the inquiry in this way. There has been, however, less investigation of the question in this form; thus the description is more impressionistic.

Considering all that has been said, the conclusion might be drawn that it is difficult to develop a sense of competence as a parent. Goals of being warm, affectionate, fair, and a worthy model are easy to state but extremely difficult to reach amidst the rapidly moving daily happenings of family life. Many parents soon come to feel that all they can do is stumble along somehow, and when one's behavior is experienced as stumbling, groping, and hastily improvised, it is hard to feel efficacious. The feeling of efficacy is clearest when intentions and results are both sharply defined. These conditions are only rarely approximated in the bringing up of children, and sense of competence as a parent is likely to be a somewhat flickering flame.

That such a sense is important is shown in work with the parents of troubled children. It is now widely recognized that beneficial changes in a child's behavior occur most readily when there is a corresponding change on the part of the parents. One of the methods employed by professional workers is to consult with the parents and suggest, or sometimes even demonstrate, a different way of interacting with their child. It is of great help to parents and to children when these measures are successful, when everyone discovers that an angry or tearful impasse is not the inevitable result of interaction and that understanding is possible. Sometimes a parent who has given the impression of being consumed by anger at a recalcitrant child experiences a rapid change of feeling upon discovering a way to be a more efficacious parent. We are made angry by the frustration of being unable to have any effect; the anger is reduced to the extent that effects are found possible. This applies also, of course, to the child. Typically, the parent becomes more efficacious by giving the child more room to be efficacious. Deadlocked opposition gives place to a certain amount of give and take on both sides, and parent and child alike feel that there is more scope for effective action.

If for most parents the sense of parental competence is destined to flicker, it is well to remember that child rearing is one of the things that can never be perfectly done. Indeed, in a process that is essentially interactive, the idea of perfection is out of place. A parent would be rated unbearably arrogant who said, "I brought up my children perfectly," as if the action were all in one direction and the children had no part in it. A grown-up child would properly be humiliated to say, "I was brought up perfectly," as if none of the credit were his. This is another question about which thinking has to be systematic and interactive, breaking the mold of simple cause and effect. Once this is done we make room for the insight that children are resilient and have a considerable capacity to resist ruin by their parents. Must one be "perfectly" fair? Evidently not, because sometimes unfavored children, victims of injustice in the family circle, manage to transform their suffering into empathy for those who are victims of social injustice, and make a satisfying career out of trying to set things right.

Parenthood and Values

Any study of personality that aims for completeness must take account of values. Because values are sometimes stated and argued about, they can to a certain extent be investigated at an intellectual level, but the concept of value inescapably implies motive and feeling. What we value means what we will live for, work for, fight for, possibly even die for; it guides the making of countless decisions both great and small in the course of life. Motive, affect, knowledge, and judgment are all involved. It is appropriate to look upon values as crystallized outcomes of motivational preferences and of one's experience and knowledge of reality.

The Analysis of Values

To a considerable extent values are learned from others, not generated wholly out of personal experience. This is typical in childhood; the superego, as Freud described it, is at first a collection of precepts picked up directly from the environment long before the child is capable of ethical reflections. Even the values of reflective adults are not wholly wrought from within; prophets and moral philosophers, who sometimes manage to create new values, are a tiny minority of mankind. Most people select their values from those that are available in the environment, the selection being guided, however, by motives and personal experience.

Values are not necessarily conscious or carefully elaborated. A stated ethical system represents the full flowering of a person's values, but this is not the typical form in which they operate. Furthermore, stated values may diverge from real ones and misrepresent them. By *real* ones we mean those that actually steer and affect behavior, regardless of whether or not they are present to awareness. Since Karl Marx and Nietzsche in their different ways wrote so persuasively on the subject, the idea has become familiar that conscious and stated values may be screens for actual values crudely related to self-interest. Freud's version of the same theme was that instinctual urges really shaped our behavior behind a façade of socially acceptable sentiments. This heritage has led to an exaggerated distrust of values publicly expressed, but it is the part of wisdom in studying personality to direct attention to both levels. Such study should involve eliciting the person's stateable values and also judging from his conduct the nature of his effective guiding values. The gap between them may be great or it may be small to the vanishing point, depending on the individual.

The analysis of a person's values, both those stated and those deduced from behavior, usually leads to discerning a value system of some sort, with central or deeper values governing the rest. It then becomes possible to look for relations between this system and the values present in the culture, the family, and membership groups. It may also become possible to establish connections with fundamental motives and anxieties. In subjects who are both reflective and communicative one can often observe a growth of values over the course of time as a result of experience. This latter trend can be called the *humanizing of values*: it is a movement away from absolute received values toward those that are more personally wrought. There are two aspects of this process: (1) the person increasingly discovers the human meaning of values and their relation to the achievement of social purposes, and (2) he increasingly brings to bear his own experiences and his own motives in affirming and promoting a value system.[22] Insights of this kind often come at the point where adult roles are assumed. Thus a girl who takes a job with a family as a mother's helper will have a chance to amplify her values with respect to child rearing, whatever they are, by discovering exactly what happens as a result of each move she makes. Or a student who volunteers for work with mental hospital patients may change his preconceptions about the paying of taxes by observing what is and is not being done in a tax-supported public institution. Even when values retain their basic shape, experience gives them greater meaning, greater specificity, and more discriminating espousal.

At the age at which young adults start having children they are often midway in the process of humanizing their values. Having made lasting commitments, they are learning a great deal, at work and at home, about the specifics of everyday affairs. Their ideals are perhaps being tempered by contact with insistent and complicated realities, and their values may be undergoing revision. But parenthood makes an abrupt new demand. Parents are the transmitters of values. Children must be brought up from the moment they are born, and this implies an immediate application of values even though it will be some time before these are transmitted in words. The parents' value systems, one might say, must now be ready to go, but in fact they may be far from ready. At the present time, moreover, there are special difficulties in becoming a transmitter of values, and it is important to understand these difficulties.

Contemporary Problems in Being a Transmitter of Values

There are two main problems here: (1) uncertainty about values in a world of rapid change, and (2) anxiety about the process of transmission and its consequences. As the household authorities on values, parents do not

[22] R. W. White, *Lives in Progress: A Study of the Natural Growth of Personality*, 2d ed. (New York: Holt, Rinehart and Winston, Inc., 1966), pp. 396–400.

feel sure which to espouse, and they have been made to feel that it is bad to be authoritative about anything.

That the world is in rapid change is not likely to be disputed. The change is, of course, not only in the realms of technology but also in values themselves; there has been accelerated crumbling of long-held conceptions that used to be relied upon for guidance. Thus at a time when there is increased uncertainty about the future shape of the world, beliefs that in the past have helped people to deal with uncertainty have lost some of their force. The bringing up of children has thus in many quarters lost two of its usual guidelines. Parents hesitate to rely upon traditional precepts and attitudes, yet they also, feeling unable to foresee what kinds of lives their children are going to lead, find it hard to form new precepts and attitudes. Both of these circumstances tend to interfere with effectiveness. Especially when parents cannot assume that their children's lives will be like their own, they are hindered in making use of their childhood experience and being guided by what worked well or worked poorly in their own cases. Just when careful observation and research has begun to shed light on child rearing, new darkness has been generated by uncertainty about the goals.

Another difficulty in being a transmitter of values lies in the widening gap between sophisticated adult values and children's capacity for moral understanding. Adults who reflect upon their values are likely to move away from general precepts and dichotomies of right and wrong. As their values become humanized they develop a greater awareness of the complexity of moral judgments, of the large numbers of particulars that affect the moral quality of a given act. Ethical judgments, they may say, should be situational; the underlying principles are simple enough, but their application depends on a full understanding of everything that is involved in a given human situation. The expression of hostility, for example, cannot be stereotyped as wrong, or for that matter as right; everything depends on the situation, and in a struggle against cruel injustice it may seem right to use degrees of force that would be sheer tyranny in any other situation. The expression of sexuality may likewise be judged to depend heavily on circumstances. Even telling the truth cannot survive as an unqualified virtue; statements that are literally lies may sometimes be justified to mitigate friction and to avoid causing unnecessary pain. For many parents this sophisticated relativity is part of the essence of morality, and they see black-and-white moral judgment as leading inevitably to harm. But if we look back to Chapter 11, where the growth of children's moral understanding was described, it will be clear that children must attain considerable maturity before they can frame moral questions in a relative or situational way. If fighting is wrong it is wrong under all circumstances; if sexual curiosity is naughty, it is always naughty; a lie is a wicked lie even if told to spare somebody. Children are often simply confused by attempts to qualify their notions about good and bad, and parents are frustrated at the absolutism they know to be capable of so much harm if it persists into adulthood.

These inherent difficulties are compounded if parents are strongly moved to avoid an authoritarian stance. There are historical and psychological reasons, as we have seen, for associating the authoritarian personality with disastrous social attitudes and with a rigidity that can only be injurious to human interactions. The attempt to swing wide of being an authoritarian parent can easily beget a reluctance to make demands of any kind on children, even to insist on simple rules that would make everyone's life easier. The force of this worry about exerting authority adds greatly to the difficulty of being a transmitter of values. It can lead, as we have already noted, to a permissiveness so indecisive as to deprive children of the minimum of guidance necessary for their sense of security. In any event it tends to impair parental confidence and thus adds to the problems of contemporary parents in fulfilling the requirements of their role.

Does the study of personality suggest ways of improving this situation? A good deal of what has been described in this book bears upon it in one way or another. In raising questions about the future shape of the world, however, and about the kinds of lives today's children are likely to lead, we have touched upon matters of wide import, which challenge whatever insights we may have reached about the nature of personality. What kinds of lives do we want for ourselves? Can we specify values that have meaning regardless of social and technological change? Can we form values for the next generation that are compatible with rapid external change? Once more it is evident that personality cannot be studied as a closed system. The fates of individuals are bound up with the fate of the surrounding world.

19 The Diversity of Life Patterns

The study of personality, however refined and detailed it may ultimately become, has its basis in the observation of people leading their lives over the course of time. Almost inevitably this fact carries one's thinking in an evaluative direction. Are there certain patterns of personality, are there certain life styles and life courses, that are to be considered good, healthy, mature, desirable—that are to be admired and adopted as goals? We could take a sternly naturalistic attitude and say that as scientific observers our whole duty is to describe and interpret the lives of other people in strictly dispassionate terms. Such an attitude is indeed indispensable for building up a body of sound knowledge about personality. Yet we must recognize that few people can honestly keep to it all the time. It is impossible to be neutral when dealing with the people in one's environment or when thinking about one's children; for the most part, interacting with others necessarily implies value judgments. It is impossible to keep from asking what pattern and career one should seek for oneself, what manner of man or woman one should try to become.

To say that the study of personality had found answers to such eternal questions would be indeed presumptuous. But perhaps this study can be of some small assistance in pondering the questions, if only by showing how much has to be considered and how wide are the possibilities for leading life in a worthy fashion. A gain is already made when we change the ancient query from singular to plural, asking not what is a good life but what are the various ways of leading a good life. In this chapter we shall first look at some past and present conceptions of what constitutes an ideal personality. We shall then examine a number of studies directed toward understanding human strengths. This will provide us with a basis for considering the diversity of life patterns, the relation between individual and social requirements of growth, and the manner in which experience becomes creatively transformed in the course of development.

Conceptions of the Ideal Personality

In different times and places there have been widely different ideas on the proper course and goals of human development. When these ideas reach sophisticated forms they may be set down in treatises on ethics, but they are also likely to appear in works on the theory and practice of education. What it is felt necessary to encourage and discourage in children often provides the best clue to beliefs about an ideal developmental outcome.

Some Historical Examples

Most statements of the ideal personality represent an optimum that is not likely to be reached by more than a few individuals. This was true in ancient Athens, the fountainhead of humanism, in which democracy prevailed only within a small group of male citizens whose pattern of life depended upon the labors of women and slaves. Thus supported, it was possible for the Athenian citizen to take seriously Aristotle's statement, in his *Politics*, that "in men, reason and mind are the end toward which nature strives." But reason and mind could never develop fully in a person who was enslaved by his appetites or passions; in childhood, steps had to be taken to bring these under control. For this purpose Aristotle recommended the inculcation of habits, through rewards and punishments, that would steer the appetites into channels conducive to higher development. Furthermore, obligations to the State could by no means be neglected; in order to discharge his duties the citizen must learn to become temperate, brave, magnanimous, and just. In the performance of civic duty reason would curb the passions, but beyond this useful function it had intrinsic properties and satisfactions of its own. Reason enabled a man to lead the life of speculation, to imagine things better than what he knew, to investigate the properties of nature, to enjoy literature and the arts, and thus to raise himself nearer to the level of the gods. Aristotle distinguished between what was useful and what was fine, and the highest happiness was reserved for him who could subordinate the useful to the fine.

The influence of classical Greece on Western thought was powerfully revived during the Renaissance, and from a combination of Greek ideals and Italian political life during the fifteenth and sixteenth centuries came the image of what today we call Renaissance man. This ideal, symbolized by Leonardo da Vinci—astoundingly gifted as artist, scientist, and engineer—put a strong accent on versatility. More oriented to action than speculation, it seemed best embodied in the life of the courtier who took an active part in politics and administration while participating in the elegant life of a princely court. In 1528 a writer by the name of Castiglione published *The Book of the Courtier*, in which he set forth an awesome array of accomplishments necessary for full development. Castiglione's courtier was to be a man of action, skilled in the arts of war, courageous but modest, accomplished in sports, a master of apt speech, having the wit and intelligence of a scholar, well read, skilled in painting and music, exhibiting always the control of passion by reason and the civic virtues described by Aristotle, and, finally possessing the vision of heavenly beauty that comes only through transcendent religious experience. This sounds like a tall order attainable only by a peculiarly favored courtier. "That, in spite of this," wrote a modern historian of education, the book "found a ready welcome throughout Europe and helped to impress the moral and intellectual ideals of the Italian Renaissance on many generations of the ruling classes elsewhere, is only to be explained by the fact that the fundamental attributes of Castiglione's courtier are not the attributes of a single class or of a special social group, but of mankind in all the high possibilities revealed by a great age. His theme is the perfect man."[1]

The Greek conception of the life of reason was a broad one, including the cultivation of the arts, but it has not always been given the priority assigned to it by Aristotle. Of marked significance in Western thought is a set of ideals that had its origin in Jewish history and is reflected especially in the Old Testament books of *Deuteronomy* and *Proverbs*. The good life was one that was constantly guided by the will of God as transmitted to man in the laws of Moses. Wisdom lay in understanding the sacred writings and correctly interpreting the law. Thus reason and learning were instrumental to leading a moral life, and qualities such as those Aristotle listed as necessary for citizenship became the highest values. This priority of moral values— of values pertaining especially to interpersonal behavior—continued into the Christian tradition, where at least during the Middle Ages it subordinated the life of reason to a degree unfavorable to the spirit of inquiry. The same priority was made explicit again in the Protestant Reformation, the educational goals of which were sometimes described as "lettered piety." In the course of time *piety* has acquired a good many unfavorable connotations, but in traditions derived from Calvin's form of Protestantism its practice came to signify not simply religious devotion but a whole way of leading one's worldly life. This way of life was ascetic in the sense that the appetites had to be controlled and frivolous pleasures avoided. It was rational in the sense that all actions and all plans had to be scrutinized to assure their moral character, their fitness to express the divine will. The implicit ideal was an ordered, organized life guided constantly by the enduring purpose of exhibiting God's will and being worthy of salvation.

Today we hear frequent reference to the "Protestant ethic" as a value system strong in the recent past but more lately in decline. This modern

---

[1] W. Boyd, *The History of Western Education*, 3d ed. (London: A. & C. Black, Ltd., 1932), p. 227.

version, however, is almost wholly secular and has only a tenuous connection with past religious forms. A German scholar, Max Weber, pointed out a similarity between the ordered, planful life of pietistic Protestants, sacrificing present pleasure for future salvation, and the ordered, planful procedures of capitalistic business enterprise, sacrificing immediate gain for future profits. Noting that capitalism as a system had developed most strongly in Protestant countries, Weber proposed that the habits of life generated by religious goals produced a type of character peculiarly suited to the economic purposes of capitalism. The ability to sacrifice impulse and pleasure in favor of rationally planned future goals was a decided asset for an entrepreneur trying to establish a business that would grow and prosper in years to come.[2] The current conception of the Protestant ethic, emphasizing work, thrift, and sacrifice, is much less religious than it is economic.

The Influence of Psychiatry

A new note was brought to ideals of personality by modern psychiatry. Trying to treat people with mental disorders and emotional difficulties implied some standard from which they had fallen and to which, if possible, they must be returned. When this standard was made explicit it was usually described as *mental health*, by analogy with physical health. Sometimes the patient's need was described as *adjustment*, which implied striking a more workable bargain between his own characteristics and the requirements of his social environment. In themselves neither being healthy nor being adjusted suggested any specific pattern of excellence. But these terms opened the possibility that by considering the different ways in which patients departed from mental health, one could arrive at an idea of the traits most conducive to health. A positive conception of mental health might correspond in some way to the bounding vitality of people with conspicuously good physical health.[3]

As soon as a serious attempt is made, however, to specify what is meant by positive mental health, it becomes evident that the metaphor of health is a hindrance rather than a help. It is hard to define health as anything more than the absence of disease, hence the mentally healthy person comes to be described as having a long list of traits that are simply the opposites of unhealthy mental symptoms. Because schizophrenics are confused and interact poorly with others, alert extraversion and sociability become part of the mental health specifications; because manic-depressives have excessive mood swings, mood stability becomes an item; because neurotics are in some respects inhibited, freedom from inhibition joins the list of virtues; because delinquents are sometimes impulsive, control of impulses is added to the total pattern. Not being based on the study of healthy people, this method

---

[2] M. Weber, *The Protestant Ethic and the Spirit of Capitalism* (1904), trans. T. Parsons (New York: Charles Scribner's Sons, 1958).

[3] M. Jahoda, *Current Concepts of Positive Mental Health* (New York: Basic Books, Inc., 1958).

simply develops a list of qualities without reference to consistency or to the possibility of their all being embodied in an individual life. The embodiment of perfect mental health emerges as a colorless phantom, a schematic rather than a real person.

Adjustment as an ideal suffers from the same lack of specificity. It is also open to the criticism of playing into the hands of social conformity. Literally this does not follow: to attain an improved condition, patients may have to change their environments as well as their own attitudes. But in practice a psychiatrist, seeing individual patients and having no control over their surroundings, exerts his influence on the patient's attitudes and may seem to neglect what is wrong with the environment. In any event, adjustment as a concept says even less than mental health about the shape of personality.

A little more substance is contained in the psychoanalytic concept of *ego strength*. This concept was of practical importance in selecting patients for a long course of treatment and estimating the chances of a favorable outcome. Hendrick described ego strength in everyday language as "strength of character," "grit," and "a certain capacity for fighting difficulties."[4] In more technical language it meant the capacity to endure frustration, control emotional tension, and keep working toward rationally planned goals. The ego in psychoanalytic theory being the part of personality that is responsible for reality testing and planful activity, its strength would be shown in the predominance of these functions over instinctual urges, anxiety, and irrational pangs of conscience. Fenichel stated schematically that ego strength depended upon how well the ego had managed to avoid using primitive defense mechanisms that continued to sap its energies and weaken its dealing with reality.[5] When free from such hindrances, it would be able to tolerate tension and excitement, to perceive and judge validly, to carry out intentions despite obstacles, to channel instinctual urges appropriately, and to reconcile conflicting tendencies in personality. These expressions contain an implicit ideal, that of a person who leads life effectively in spite of the buffetings of fortune and the treachery of internal weaknesses. As we shall see, studies in which ego strength is the central concept have usually been made with subjects undergoing severe stress.

It is of interest that a similar concept has emerged from the factor analysis of traits of personality. The procedures used for this purpose, consisting of questionnaires and short experiments, seem remote from depth psychology, yet there is a striking convergence of results. In his very extensive work on the measurement of traits, Eysenck has repeatedly found a basic dimension that he calls *neuroticism*, the opposite end being something like will power or self-direction.[6] The same dimension comes out of a factor

<hr>

[4] I. Hendrick, *Facts and Theories of Psychoanalysis* (New York: Alfred A. Knopf, Inc., 1934).

[5] O. Fenichel, "Ego Strength and Ego Weakness," *Collected Papers*, Vol. 2 (New York: W. W. Norton & Company, Inc., 1954), pp. 70–80.

[6] H. J. Eysenck, *The Structure of Human Personality* (London: Methuen & Co., Ltd., 1953).

analysis of *The Minnesota Multiphasic Personality Inventory*, a widely used questionnaire. The authors of the study name the dimension *ego weakness vs. ego strength*; they characterize low scorers as poorly adjusted, anxious, dependent, and prone to psychological disorder, whereas high scorers, free from anxiety and emotional disturbances, exhibit confidence, qualities of leadership, and effective use of abilities.[7] Ego strength in this sense can thus be roughly measured. It need not be considered a wholly elusive variable of personality.[8]

Conceptions of Psychological Maturity

The most substantial derivative of modern thinking in psychiatry and developmental psychology is the concept of psychological maturity. This idea has its analogue in bodily growth and physical maturity, but it is capable of much greater specification than a concept like mental health. To be psychologically mature means to have moved along certain main pathways of learning, outgrowing the limitations of childhood and bringing one's potentialities to full development. "The maturity concept," according to Overstreet, "is central to our whole enterprise of living. This is what our past wisdoms have been leading up to."[9] The second sentence is perhaps too strong. Maturity hardly provides us with a key to unlock the ethical secrets for which past ages have searched in vain. But there is much to be gained by considering at least some of what we value in personality in terms of being fully developed, fully grown up.

This plan is followed in an influential book by Saul entitled *Emotional Maturity*.[10] Saul enumerates eight lines of development along which the natural ineptitudes of childhood give place to qualities necessary for adult life. (1) One of these paths leads from the parasitic dependence of fetus and newborn baby to substantial independence from parents. Dependent longings, to be sure, are never wholly stilled and remain legitimate in certain situations, but adult functioning is much impaired in a person who remains under his parents' wings. (2) Closely related is a shift in the balance between getting and giving, between receptive needs and productive activity. A reversal of role must be accomplished from being a child to being a parent. (3) "A third characteristic of maturity is relative freedom from the well-known constellation of inferiority feelings, egotism, and competitiveness," the constellation so sharply pointed out by Alfred Adler. (4) "Another aspect of maturity consists in the conditioning and training necessary for socialization

[7] G. G. Kassenbaum, A. S. Couch, and P. E. Slater, "The Factorial Dimensions of the MMPI," *Journal of Consulting Psychology*, **23** (1959), 226–236.

[8] The scale for ego strength in the MMPI was first devised by Barron. Cf. F. Barron, *Creativity and Psychological Health* (Princeton, N.J.: D. Van Nostrand Company, Inc., 1963), Chaps. 9, 10.

[9] H. A. Overstreet, *The Mature Mind* (New York: W. W. Norton & Company, Inc., 1949), p. 14.

[10] L. J. Saul, *Emotional Maturity*, 2nd ed. (Philadelphia: J. B. Lippincott Company, 1962).

and domestication." The amount of conformity to be expected in adolescence and adult life is obviously a controversial matter, but adults who were not housebroken, who could not dress themselves, and who grabbed everything they wanted would operate under a considerable handicap. (5) Sexual development should take a course from the small child's preoccupation with self-stimulated bodily pleasure to what Freud called the "genital level," which implies valuing and loving the objects of sexual interest. (6) "Hostile aggressiveness, using the term to include all sorts of anger, hate, cruelty and belligerency," is "symptomatic of a childishness which has not been outgrown. . . . The mature adult is parental and creative and is not destructive toward himself or others." Saul closes the list with two attributes that are centered in the cognitive sphere, (7) "a firm sense of reality," and (8) "flexibility and adaptability." As we have seen, childish ways of thinking differ decidedly from adult ways, and the path between them can be traversed only by learning through experience.

Being grown up, even when we can define eight aspects of it, is still rather less specific as an ideal of personality than such historic ideas as the life of reason or the practice of piety. But we can justly regard the concept of maturity as a necessary foundation, calling attention as it does to the real character and limitations of human nature and the conditions under which development takes place. The idea has caught on to the extent that even in junior high school, if not earlier, children accuse each other of being immature and urge one another to act their age. Commenting especially on the influence of Freud on the contemporary outlook, Rieff proposes that a new ideal, a new character type, has lately come into existence.[11] In contrast to such past ideals as political man, religious man, and economic man, he calls this new type *psychological man* and describes him as living "by the ideal of insight—practical, experimental insight leading to the mastery of his own personality." This results in an "ethic of honesty," which dictates continuing self-examination in order to detect and eliminate whatever is childish, defensive, and hence immature in one's nature. We do not know how widely this conception is held, but it seems to represent a new variant among ideals of personality.

Sample Studies of Human Strengths

We can best sharpen our understanding of human strengths by examining a sample of studies directed toward elucidating their nature. Compared to the vast flood of research on abnormality, the study of human strengths has the appearance of a modest brook just starting to be larger than a trickle. It leads us, however, in the direction of more discriminating ideas about the character of human potentialities.

[11] P. Rieff, *Freud: The Mind of the Moralist* (New York: The Viking Press, Inc., 1959), esp. Chaps. 9 and 10.

Grinker's Study of Psychiatric Soundness

The first study to be considered here developed almost by accident out of research on psychosomatic medicine. Looking for a comparison sample of normal young men, the investigators tested and interviewed a large group of students from a nearby college. The interviewer, psychiatrist Roy R. Grinker, candidly reports that the impact of these interviews was "startling."

> Here was a type of young man I had not met before in my role as a psychiatrist and rarely in my personal life. On the surface they were free from psychotic, neurotic, or disabling personality traits. It seemed that I had encountered some mentally "healthy" men who presented a unique opportunity for study.

The accidental discovery turned into a formal research on sixty-five subjects, using extensive interviews, tests, and questionnaires.[12]

The college from which the subjects were recruited, George Williams College in Chicago, was founded and mainly supported by the Young Men's Christian Association. When the study was made in 1959 it received most of its students from Y.M.C.A. sources and sent them out into Y.M.C.A. work, trained to be leaders in group work, recreation, and physical education. In the value system of the college the accent was upon an active life of human service, intellectual development being considered instrumental to this end. The students, drawn almost wholly from the nearby Midwest, were outstanding neither in intellectual gifts nor in sophistication of background; they came mainly from lower-middle-class homes and had an average tested I.Q. of 110. Impressed by these facts as well as their conspicuous freedom from psychological troubles, Grinker referred to his group as *homoclites*, those who are close to the common rule, the contrasting word being *heteroclites*, those who deviate from the common rule. These terms, however, have not come into general use.

The subjects are described as having self-images that are fair and realistic, free from large illusions and achieved with little evidence of identity crisis. As a group they exhibited fairly strong impulse control. They went in for little premarital sexual experimentation, but those who were married reported generally satisfactory sexual experiences. Anxiety, depression, and anger appeared to the interviewers to be evoked by real external situations and to be of no more than appropriate strength. The most common sources of worry were school grades and performance in athletic contests. Frustrations were met chiefly by strategies of active counteraction, and there was little brooding over failure; depressed feelings were dissipated by muscular activity (sports, games, a long walk), by denial ("it does not matter"), by concentrating on music or some other interest, or by taking a nap, none of these devices being typically carried to excess. From the subjects' reports the interviewers deduced that they had a strong social interest and a good

[12] R. R. Grinker, " 'Mentally Healthy' Young Males (Homoclites): A Study," *Archives of General Psychiatry*, 6 (1962), 405–453.

capacity for human relations. They were not given to introspection or internal communication with themselves, and they rated low on tests of creativity and fantasy.

These were the qualities shown by this sample of young men conspicuous for mental health. The life histories indicated that the subjects had typically received strict early religious training, mostly Protestant, that they felt parental discipline to be firm, fair, and consistent, that they had grown up well informed about the boundaries of permitted behavior, that ideas about ethics and morality were prominent in their lives, and that early work experience had trained them in persistent and serious endeavor. Grinker described the subjects' ambitions in the phrases, "to do well, to do good, and to be liked," goals that could be achieved by relatively quiet and simple but comfortable patterns of life.

Grinker does not conceal his admiration for these men who live their lives with so much confident serenity, good sense, and freedom from emotional turmoil. He tells of describing the findings to professional groups of "driving social upward-mobile or prestige-seeking people, who, although outwardly serene, were consumed with never-satisfied ambitions. The invariable comment was, 'those boys are sick, they have no ambition.'" This observation serves as a forceful reminder of the difficulty we all experience in keeping our own favorite values under control when trying to study other people. These young men came from backgrounds, espoused values, and planned lives for themselves that can touch off in people differently circumstanced a large number of negative reactions. The subjects are religiously oriented, Christian, lower middle class; they are not especially intellectual, sensitive, or creative; they have very moderate ambitions and do not plan to go to a leading graduate school; they have been strictly brought up, are more controlled than spontaneous, have not partaken of the new sexual freedom, and seem decidedly "square"; they have not rebelled and are not in the forefront of social protest. To observers who see any or all of these qualities as faults and limitations, it may be an affront that the subjects are said to possess good mental health. For mental health rates as a virtue or strength, and we prefer to think that no pattern of life better exemplifies it than our own. Grinker properly limits his admiration to the subjects' mental health, defined as absence of pathology, and to the specific traits that contribute to this end. He does not argue that theirs is the supreme way to live or that mental health as defined is the highest goal of living. Thus the study serves as a sharp reminder that in thinking about ideal personalities and life patterns we must discriminate carefully among concepts and not assume that everything called a virtue is bound to be ours.

Studies of Maturity in College Students

Shifting the scene to different college environments, we turn attention next to a study of the ideal Vassar College student.[13] The judges in

[13] D. Brown, "Personality, College Environments, and Academic Productivity," in *The American College*, ed. N. Sanford (New York: John Wiley & Sons, Inc., 1962), Chap. 16.

this case were the members of the faculty, who were asked to nominate those senior students well known to them who best answered the description, "the kind of young woman we want at Vassar." At the time of the study, in 1957 and 1958, the classes in question had been the object of a large-scale personality research, and it was thus possible to determine the characteristics of the nominated ideal students in comparison with those of their classmates. Faculty members of a liberal arts college would be expected to favor intellectual qualities, but it turned out that they preferred to find these associated with certain personal traits as well.

> Faculty see "ideal" students as having a high degree of intellectual power which is directed toward objects of intellectual interest in an independent manner and disciplined along integrative, penetrating, and analytic lines. It is important, however, that the cognitive, intellectual aspect of the student's development not be one-sided, so that qualities of friendliness, helpfulness, and cooperativeness are lost, or the moral qualities are slighted. . . . It appears, then, that the faculty admires high ability but prefers to find it housed in a well-integrated, developing, pleasant, purposeful young person.

It should be remembered that in a study of this kind one is dealing not with an ideal of personality in the abstract but with an ideal in the particular situation of being a college student. Furthermore, what is judged ideal by the faculty may diverge widely from what the students would consider most valuable in themselves and each other. Interaction with teachers is only one of the spheres in which development at college goes forward. In a study of maturing at Haverford College, Heath spread the nomination of most mature and least mature subjects more widely by including fellow students, athletic coaches, and other acquaintances as well as teachers in the panel of judges.[14] In making his comparisons he is careful to state that he is describing the Haverford mature and immature person rather than patterns that can be taken as universal.

The Haverford students nominated as being most mature presented a picture of effectiveness in all aspects of college life.

> He was a highly determined, conscientious, energetic, purposeful, and ambitious person fully in command of his talents. . . . He fulfilled his potential as an excellent college student, a responsible leader actively involved in numerous student activities and athletic teams. Such heavy involvement was not at the expense of his physical health. Nor were his efficiency and effectiveness bought at the price of consideration, fair-mindedness, personal integrity, or empathy for others—if we are to believe his peers' personality ratings of him. Self-report and impressionistic evidence tend to confirm his peers' ratings, for the mature person (in poignant contrast to the immature men) was deeply involved emotionally in the lives of his close friends—both men and women. . . .

[14] D. H. Heath, *Explorations of Maturity: Studies of Mature and Immature College Men* (New York: Appleton-Century-Crofts, 1965).

The immature person was just that—to others and to himself. His peers and the faculty saw him as erratic, disordered, scattered, illogical, and purposeless. Although the faculty sensed that some of the immature men had the potential for gifted and creative expression, the consensus of all the judges was that their gifts remained frustratingly, to both the faculty and the immature men themselves, unrealized. Except for an occasional gifted athlete, actor, or musician, the immature man achieved little of distinction during his four years at the college. He was seldom elected or appointed to a responsible office. He just never seemed to get caught up in the academic pulse or the extracurricular and social rhythm of the Haverford community.[15]

These sharply contrasting sketches are based on relatively small numbers of men selected because they were extreme: the most and the least mature. It would be ungenerous to deny the described big men on campus their bigness, which shows in so many directions, but such all-around effectiveness must be reserved for rather few individuals; no college society would survive if everyone were an outstanding leader. The picture drawn by Heath is clearly, as he recognizes, a portrait of the best and the poorest functioning in the quite special situation of a small, highly selective liberal arts college with a strongly ethical tradition. The mature students are those for whom this environment was just right, so that they did indeed grow up in it. The students called immature found the environment uncongenial and failed to flourish. Of course there were differences between the groups when they entered, but it is important to recognize that maturing is partly a function of environment. "In the words of one perceptive student," Heath remarks, "at Haverford the mature become more mature, the immature more immature. Resumed growth for some of our immature youths probably awaited a more responsive environment."[16]

Studies of Exceptional Ego Strength

If the topic of an investigation is ego strength rather than mental health or maturity, subjects are likely to be chosen on the ground that they have mastered severe stress. The concept of ego strength as it emerged from psychoanalytic theory was not supposed to be restricted to the mastery of stress, but this is an aspect that lends itself to observation.

As an illustration of ego strength, Hanfmann has presented the case of Boris, a former Soviet citizen displaced during World War II and studied in Germany in 1950.[17] The example was chosen not as typical of people similarly displaced but for this subject's conspicuous "ability to function adaptively, and without breaking down, under extreme and chronic stress." Life became highly stressful for Boris in 1929 when Stalin announced a pol-

---

[15] *Ibid.*, pp. 167, 171.

[16] *Ibid.*, p. 173.

[17] E. Hanfmann, "Boris: A Displaced Person," in *Clinical Studies of Personality*, ed. A. Burton and R. E. Harris (New York: Harper & Row, Publishers, 1955), Chap. 29.

icy of liquidating the well-to-do peasants (kulaks) as a class, a policy that was first carried out by confiscation, harassment, and threats of arrest, later by methods that caused several million peasant households to disappear. Before he was 20 Boris, because his father was a kulak, was obliged to live as a member of an alien sector of the population without civil rights or defense against discrimination. Because he was skillful with machines he could always find work, but he had to keep moving from place to place to keep ahead of persecution and imprisonment. The cumbersome processes of Soviet bureaucracy helped him maintain this nimble existence: when a new person arrived in a community, it took two years for the officials to look up his political background.

Boris not only survived this strenuous way of life but did so with a sturdiness and solid self-respect that indicated highly effective strategies of adaptation. There were certain assets, such as a strongly supportive early family life, his competence as a worker, and his happy marriage. But the qualities whereby he met constant crises and lived in perpetual danger were not the automatic consequence of these background sources of strength. Hanfmann shows, for instance, that Boris was extraordinarily alert to what was going on around him, sensing dangers and changes in the administrative climate in time to initiate evasive action. He was sharply realistic, keeping his desires out of his judgments, learning through experience, admitting mistakes when they happened. "The first element in his essentially sound approach to life is his ability to see things as they are, without systematically perverting them or persisting in misinterpretation in the face of proof to the contrary. . . . He makes only a minimal use of those means of defense which result in distortion, such as projection, displacement, reaction formation, or rationalization." Another aspect of his successful living is described as an "essential interrelatedness with others . . . a matter-of-fact readiness to participate in the general give-and-take." This was easier for him because, in spite of living so often by his wits and initiative, he did not suppress his dependent feelings, showing "a nice balance between mobilizing his own efforts and approaching others for help." Yet another characteristic was his equanimity, his "complete control of his impulses and emotions," which in the Soviet Union "must have guarded him from any dangerously impulsive actions which often proved the undoing of others." This control, Hanfmann points out, was not without cost; it "leaves him without vividness or sparkle and gives him a quality of sobriety." He must also restrict ambition and be content with a modest way of life. Hanfmann summarizes as follows:

> The case of Boris has been presented as a demonstration of how self-limitation can result in a personality structure which is both firm and flexible and which enables a person to withstand a great deal of stress. . . . Since directing one's life always involves making choices and giving up alternatives incompatible with that chosen, self-limitation is a part of any successful adjustment. In the case of Boris this process was quite central and extensive, and it enabled him to attain genuine self-realization under conditions of scarcity, insecurity, and danger. The ways he had

developed for dealing with inner threats through vigilance, cautious retreat, and realistic self-limitation proved to be the optimal ones for coping with his real external environment.[18]

The control of disruptive emotions is a prominent consideration in studies by Korchin and Ruff of the Mercury astronauts.[19] These seven men, the first Americans to make flights into space, were selected from sixty-nine jet test pilots who volunteered; this group, of course, was already highly selected for success in dealing with danger. Astronauts have to have an exceptional power to control anxiety, to maintain efficiency and cool judgment when any wrong move would be fatal. In these seven men this capacity was not associated with lack of emotion or sluggish arousal. They had strong feelings, including fear, but their power of conscious control was even stronger. Apparently a certain amount of tension improved the men's performance: on standard measures of efficiency they scored better just before a test flight than they did after coming down. Rational control in time of crisis was well described by one of the astronauts who said, "Get your mind busy thinking and not worrying," and by another who reported that "in tight situations you have to stop, take stock, decide what you are going to do, and go ahead and do it." Many readers will admit that such tactics elude them even in situations far less tight than sailing through space.

The studies by Korchin and Ruff included the astronauts' backgrounds and life histories. All came from small towns or farms, from middle-class Protestant homes in relatively comfortable circumstances, from stable families and communities where they had enjoyed outdoor living and sports, often shared with their competent fathers. All had been educated in public schools and had majored in engineering at college; their I.Q.'s ranged from 130 to 141, putting them close to the top in the population as a whole. All were married and had children. They were on the whole oriented to action rather than thought or feeling, preferred facts to speculation, and were little given to fantasy and introspection. Though socially competent and getting along well with others, they were not highly involved in human relations. Their conspicuous capacity for teamwork was based on respect for the expertness of the other members rather than a more personal feeling; basically they were strongly independent men with confidence in their own powers of mastery.

There appears to be some generality in this picture of unusual ego strength. In a study of 105 outstanding jet pilots, for instance, Reinhardt found unusual father-son closeness during childhood, and characterized the men as self-confident, eager for challenge and success, not introspective, and

---

[18] Quotations are from Hanfmann, "Boris: A Displaced Person," pp. 652, 659, 664–665.

[19] S. J. Korchin and G. E. Ruff, "Personality Characteristics of the Mercury Astronauts," in *The Threat of Impending Disaster,* ed. G. H. Grosser, H. Wechsler, and M. Greenblatt (Cambridge, Mass.: Massachusetts Institute of Technology Press, 1964), pp. 197–207; G. E. Ruff and S. J. Korchin, "Psychological Responses of the Mercury Astronauts to Stress," *Ibid.,* pp. 208–220.

tending toward interpersonal and emotional distance.[20] He also noted a marked predominance of first-born children, a finding confirmed by studies he cites of successful men in other branches of military service. It is possible to believe that the background factors found in these studies, including family stability, father-identification, and school success, are favorable to the development of ego strength, but we certainly cannot conclude that they uniquely produce it. Thinking back to a much earlier chapter on constitutional differences, recalling such variables as physical constitution, extraversion-introversion, activity level, impulsion-deliberation, and sensitivity, differences all of which can be detected in quite young children, there is at least a possibility that genetic endowment has a hand in the matter. Then there is the whole concatenation of influences operating during the course of life, and it would be necessary to study samples in widely different circumstances to discover everything that might influence ego strength. Studies centered on the mastery of stress give us at present only hints about the sources of ego strength.

In the studies thus far described we have been looking at very different varieties of human excellence. Because terms have been used that sound like all-encompassing virtues—mental health, ego strength, maturity—it is easy to misread the results as if they contained an implicit prescription on how to live, a guide to ideal personality. Such a claim could be counteracted by saying that there are many ways of being mentally healthy, strong, and mature, but it is more to the point to look past these value-overloaded terms with two considerations in mind: Precisely what aspects of personality have been described, and in precisely what situations are they related to excellence? As regards situations, it is evident that a machinist living as a virtual social outcast, a person of ordinary talents preparing for a life of service, a military engineer specializing in space flight, and an intellectually gifted student attending a distinguished college will need quite different qualities to perform well. Boris and the astronauts can survive in their environments only if they achieve a masterful control over disruptive emotions, an amazing level of equanimity and rationality under stress. For the college students other qualities are more relevant. Intellectual inquiry, suspended judgments, a rich imagination, and creative ability have a lot to do with excellence in this situation, and sensitive feeling is not out of place. Natural as it is to want to be a twentieth-century Renaissance Man, nobody can seriously expect to house all possible virtues within one skin. This is not only a question of time and opportunity; the studies suggest that strengths have their cost and may be incompatible with other strengths. Having the power to keep one's head on a space flight may not be congruent with sensitive creative imagination or with spontaneous warmth toward other people. Qualities we are likely to admire are ideal for certain purposes, in certain situations, and their relative importance depends heavily upon the kind of life that is being led.

[20] R. F. Reinhardt, "The Outstanding Jet Pilot," *American Journal of Psychiatry*, **127** (1970), 32–36.

Maslow's Study of Self-Actualizing People

We take up finally a study that was designed to recognize the many-sided nature of development. Maslow used the term *self-actualization* as more suitable than *health* or *maturity* to express the active character of growth. His influential study was in fact a highly informal one consisting of his own personal observation, over a long period of time, of certain individuals with whom he was well acquainted, together with study of the biographies of selected outstanding men and women.[21] It becomes evident at the outset that Maslow had in mind an extremely high standard of development. Among the historic cases he listed Thomas Jefferson, Lincoln in his last years, Spinoza, Einstein, William James, Jane Addams, and Eleanor Roosevelt as sure or highly probable instances of self-actualization, but he placed in another category, partial cases who in some respects fell short, the names of Beethoven, Whitman, Thoreau, Franklin Roosevelt, and Freud, and there was a still lower echelon occupied among others by Goethe. This way of dealing with the historic cases suggests that to be a truly self-actualizing person is a rare and difficult accomplishment reached only now and then by a most unusual person. But Maslow's study rested more heavily on those friends and acquaintances whose lives he observed at first hand; to be self-actualizing did not imply being prominent or historically important. It is permissible, though not exactly what Maslow intended, to think of self-actualizing less as a rare total accomplishment and more as a composite dimension of growth along which people move, with wide individual differences in how far they go. When revising his book Maslow introduced an important clarification.[22] The people he described in whom human potentialities had been most fully actualized were necessarily older people who had had time to profit by long experience. Their strengths were not necessarily the same as those appropriate to youth. When young people are the objects of study Maslow preferred to use the term "good-growth-toward-self-actualization," a concept which he felt could be translated into acceptable research terms.

One group of qualities attributed by Maslow to self-actualizing people of mature years lies somewhat in the cognitive sphere. Compared to others, these people have a "more efficient perception of reality and more comfortable relations with it." They see what is there, they judge correctly, and their perceptions are not distorted by desires, anxieties, or rigidified habits. They are "strongly focussed on problems outside themselves— problem-centered rather than ego-centered." Furthermore, they discriminate successfully between means and ends, keep worthwhile ends in mind, and do not become distracted by immediate problems of means. "This impression of being above small things, of having a larger horizon, a wider breadth of

---

[21] A. H. Maslow, *Motivation and Personality* (New York: Harper & Row, Publishers, 1954). The study is described in Chaps. 12 and 13.

[22] A. H. Maslow, *Motivation and Personality*, 2d ed. (New York: Harper & Row, Publishers, 1970).

vision, of living in the widest frame of reference . . . is of the utmost social and interpersonal importance; it seems to impart a certain serenity and lack of worry over immediate concerns that makes life easier not only for themselves but for all who are associated with them." Possibly the two expressions *effective intelligence* and *largeness of outlook* summarize what Maslow described.

Another group of qualities seems best gathered under the heading of *spontaneity*. "Self-actualizing people can all be described as relatively spontaneous in behavior and far more spontaneous than that in their inner life, thoughts, impulses, etc." In behavior they are simple and natural, never artificial or straining for effect. Sometimes this makes them unconventional, but they are quite willing to conform and avoid friction over conventions that are not of major importance. In matters of intense interest, however, they can be guided wholly from within and at such times will be anything but conforming. Going with these qualities is a continued "freshness of appreciation," a capacity to enjoy good and beautiful things and to keep experience from becoming stale or automatic. Openness and spontaneity prevail also with respect to mystical or "oceanic" feelings; these are received gladly, found valuable and transforming, and not weighed down with improbable interpretations. Self-actualizing people, in short, are friendly alike to their inner impulses and outer experiences, and find these a source of enduring enjoyment.

A third group of qualities is more specifically *interpersonal*. Maslow found in his self-actualizing subjects the kind of social interest that Adler described, an identification and sympathy with other people, indeed with the human race as a whole despite its follies and imperfections—a "basic underlying kinship" and a genuine desire to help. The subjects were high in acceptance both of themselves and of others. Their interpersonal relations were unusually deep, and on this account the circle of their friends was likely to be small; they had not time for many real friends. They all exhibited a democratic as contrasted with an authoritarian character structure. They also exhibited a "philosophical, unhostile sense of humor," as often as not at their own expense, a trait earlier mentioned by Allport as a sign of mature self-acceptance.[23] But the self-actualizing subjects steered a middle course between social participation and solitude. They cared little for trivial social interactions, often enjoying and needing privacy. In no sense socially enslaved, they could detach themselves from others, when they wanted to, without anxiety.

The last group of qualities runs like a theme through the whole description and is given two specific headings: "*autonomy, independence of culture and environment*," and "*resistance to enculturation*." Self-actualizing people, according to Maslow, come to depend less on external sources of satisfaction and more on "their own potentialities and latent resources." This

---

[23] G. W. Allport, *Personality: A Psychological Interpretation* (New York: Holt, Rinehart and Winston, Inc., 1937), Chap. 8.

gives them a certain serenity in the face of misfortune and frustration. This growth trend is probably common; it has been described elsewhere as a progressive stabilization of ego identity.[24] But Maslow made the further point that his self-actualizing subjects "resist enculturation and maintain a certain inner detachment from the culture in which they are immersed." This is not intended to imply a constant fight with minor cultural expectations or an activist policy of rebellion; the subjects accept the slowness of change and respect the contribution they are making through their own particular careers. It means that they are able to "stand off" from their culture "as if they did not quite belong to it." They are "ruled by the laws of their own character rather than by the rules of society." In this sense they feel themselves to be "not merely Americans, but also, to a greater degree than others, members at large of the human species."

Maslow's study was too informal and too little protected from its author's predilections to be taken with any degree of finality. The ideas behind it, however, which contain much that was implicit in other studies but also include a number of newly discriminated variables, are of great value in thinking about directions of growth in personality. The emphasis on spontaneity, freedom from inhibition, healthy enjoyment of instinctual urges, and general openness to experience puts this line of thinking directly in the Freudian tradition. Part of the specification is to be free from the convoluted neurotic inhibitions typically brought to light in an extended psychoanalysis. More was added, but it is possible that the idea of resistance to enculturation was overstated because of what Freud had shown about the roots of neurosis. At all events the relative claims of society and self in personal growth, often swamped in polemics, deserve another look.

Self-Actualization and Social Purpose

Self-actualization, including resistance to enculturation, is an appealing concept, especially in an historical period when the defects of American culture have become increasingly glaring. It speaks compellingly to those who have accepted the idea, like Rousseau in eighteenth-century Paris, that the effect of civilization is to crush and distort an inherently noble human nature. But it must be remembered that this feeling of an opposition between becoming socialized and actualizing oneself is totally at variance with another not ignoble belief that man is human only to the extent that he interacts with his fellows and becomes part of the human community, finding the "basic underlying kinship" that Maslow claimed to be also characteristic of his self-actualizing people. How much of oneself can be actualized, we might ask, outside of a civilized society? Maslow's self-actualizing subjects, well-educated, intellectually trained, aesthetically developed, in comfortable eco-

---

[24] R. W. White, *Lives in Progress*, 2d ed. (New York: Holt, Rinehart and Winston, Inc., 1966), Chap. 9.

nomic circumstances, engaged in satisfying occupations, were in constant debt to a whole array of beneficent social and cultural institutions that made their way of life possible. Like the minority of Athenians called citizens, like the aristocrats of later times, their opportunity for full self-development required the support of a whole educational and social system. That they resisted enculturation could hardly be counted a strength if it meant that they denied what they owed to society and felt obligations only to themselves.

The difficulty here is not so much with Maslow's picture of full development as it is with his chosen term *self-actualization*. This term is easily seized upon as an ideal by young people in a stage of growth at which the main current task is to establish autonomy and discover identity. It does not express equally well an ideal for later life, when, as Erikson points out, *generativity* becomes a more central issue—when children's full development and the actualization of worthy social and cultural institutions become major objects of concern. It is hard to imagine that Maslow's surest historical examples—Jefferson, Lincoln, Spinoza, Einstein, William James, Jane Addams, and Eleanor Roosevelt—would have thought it appropriate to measure their own worth in terms of self-actualization. They all cared that what they did, thought, and wrote should be of value to mankind. Maslow characterized his subjects as "strongly focussed on problems outside themselves" and as having "some mission in life, some task to fulfill . . . which enlists much of their energies." It is just this quality, the quality of being dedicated to something outside oneself, that the term *self-actualization* does not properly imply. As an expression it is compatible with unbounded preoccupation with oneself and a snobbish rejection of common interests and common people. If it is used as an ideal of personal development it should be combined with *generativity*, in recognition that no human self can be fully actualized without some measure of commitment to the interests of others.

In a provocative foray into recent cultural history, Philip Rieff describes the long decline of the religious symbols which served to affirm the individual's place in a communal order and thus control the panic and emptiness to which we are otherwise disposed. He then puts the question "whether our culture can be so reconstructed that faith—some compelling symbol of self-integrating communal purpose—need no longer superintend the organization of personality."[25]

> From Plato and Aristotle, through Burke and de Tocqueville, the therapeutic implication of social theory is remarkably consistent: an individual can exercise his gifts and powers fully only by participating in the common life. This is the classical ideal. The healthy man is in fact the good citizen.

But with the advance of rational enlightenment from Voltaire and Rousseau to Freud all settled convictions and symbols have been mercilessly analyzed

---

[25] P. Rieff, *The Triumph of the Therapeutic: Uses of Faith after Freud* (New York: Harper & Row, Publishers, 1966).

and attributed to various kinds of immaturity and self-deception. The idea has grown that socialization can warp and constrict personal growth, that self-actualization and social membership can indeed be at odds. This opposition, we have seen throughout this book, is a real phenomenon and a critical problem in the growth of personality, even though social embeddedness is a vital part of the human condition. But if we talk only of the opposition and forget the embeddedness, Rieff points out, we lose all sense that there can be "salvation" in community. A man so disposed is likely to be indifferent to ancient questions of value "so long as the powers that be preserve social order and manage an economy of abundance," for it is clear that "a high standard of living, in our post-ascetic culture, is considered the permitting condition for attaining a higher quality of life."[26] What remains as the meaning of living is a sense of personal well-being. Even this is subject to technical manipulation by the doctor's pills and by psychotherapy. In a study of high school students Friedenberg has shown how widely, indeed almost automatically, these young people think in what might be called therapeutic terms. If a fellow student violates group mores, behaves eccentrically, or gets himself into repeated trouble, they want him referred to the school counselor and if necessary to a psychiatrist.[27] This attitude compares favorably with the conformist cruelties of the past. It does suggest, however, a growing faith in what Rieff calls a "manipulatable sense of well-being."

Doubt that such a bland conception of life can yield real satisfaction is the theme of Saul Bellow's novel, *Mr. Sammler's Planet.*[28] The chief character, an elderly man who was mildly distinguished between the two world wars and who narrowly escaped death in a concentration camp, now lives in New York in a circle of younger relatives who for the most part are unfulfilled, restless, and somewhat frantic. Mr. Sammler, although he is no foe of individuality, feels that he is witnessing griefs and miseries that arise from too great a preoccupation with being an individual. His younger but now middle-aged relatives and their friends, with abundant liberty and leisure, appear to him to be suffering from emptiness and boredom. To his eyes they exhibit a craving for an interesting life, but this is channeled into hectic attempts at self-presentation as an interesting individual, into compulsive impulse expression, and into an indiscriminate search for religious and philosophical novelties. There can be no path in these directions, thinks Mr. Sammler in his older vocabulary, for the real growth of the human spirit, which flourishes only when it is immersed in occupation, in parenthood, in the common life, in interests lastingly pursued—in objectives outside and larger than the self. The cultivation of the self, taken as an ideal, offers no protection against stagnation and despair.

The issue raised and variously handled by psychologist Maslow, psy-

---

[26] Quotations from Rieff, *The Triumph of the Therapeutic*, are from pp. 5, 26, 68, and 243.

[27] E. Z. Friedenberg, *Coming of Age in America: Growth and Acquiescence* (New York: Random House, Inc., 1965).

[28] S. Bellow, *Mr. Sammler's Planet* (New York: The Viking Press, Inc., 1970).

choanalyst Erikson, sociologist Rieff, and novelist Bellow does not lend itself to easy adjudication. Self-actualization and social purpose are deeply intertwined. The pattern varies from one life to another; each person's ideal mix has to be his own. Whatever is said on such an eternal topic should be read not as an emanation of pure wisdom but as a personal statement. The important thing is to stay aware that such problems exist, have a history, and demand a place in one's thinking about ideals of personality.

Individual Life Pattern and Historical Opportunity

A serious difficulty in considering ideal patterns of personality arises from the fact that we have only one life to lead. This life occurs at a specific moment of history, amidst a specific set of circumstances, with a specific range of opportunities. It is exposed, as Hamlet said, to "the slings and arrows of outrageous fortune" and to "the heartache and the thousand natural shocks that flesh is heir to." It entails a series of choices, and each of these means restricting some possible line of growth in order to develop another line more fully. It involves luck, for it is often impossible to foresee the future course of events when making a present choice. During a person's lifetime, for instance, his occupation may come to be of declining importance so that in his later years he finds himself phasing out an obsolescent institution; on the other hand it may boom expansively and sweep him upward to unexpected success and prominence. The typical human being, essentially a versatile creature, is conceivably capable of living quite a few kinds of lives, but there is time and opportunity for only one. To dream of complete self-actualization is indeed to dream; we can actualize only those aspects of ourselves that can fit into one life. This does not imply that our one life has to be pinched and mean. We can be rich and full, but not everything.

None of this is likely to be disputed, but what does it mean in practice? We can profit most at this point by illustration. Two examples will first be described from the realm of public affairs, two men who became outstanding leaders in their time, whose ideas were wholly incompatible, and who intensely disliked each other. Sir Winston Churchill (1874–1965) and Mahatma Gandhi (1869–1948) disagreed violently about the relations between their native lands. Yet each became a hero not only in his own nation but to large numbers of people elsewhere in the world. When we consider how each man dealt with the main task put in his way by the course of historical events there is nothing inconsistent in conceding to each his heroic stature.

Winston Churchill

Churchill's supreme accomplishment was that of turning back the tide of Nazi military success and saving the Western world from Hitler's tyranny. Becoming prime minister of Great Britain in 1940, when the Nazi military machine in lightning blows had occupied the whole European Atlantic coast from Norway to the Spanish border and the situation appeared utterly hopeless, he rallied his countrymen to desperate resistance, staved off an invasion, and kept morale high until the added resources of Russia and the United States tipped the scales of military power the other way.

> The man and the moment matched one another to perfection. The unparalleled danger of 1940 was to discover in the Prime Minister qualities of heart and mind and speech such as he himself could hardly have realized that he possessed. As the world well knows, Churchill now rose to heights of courage and resolution, of eloquence and inspiration, which no past occasion in his life had ever been able to call forth. . . . Now every resource at his command was compressed into a single moral quality—the will to victory. The plenitude of power, which for the first time in his life he now wielded, gave him the opportunity to reveal on a grand scale his extraordinary powers of organization, as well as the capacity to coordinate large masses of detail. His vitality was never more intense, his resilience never more pronounced.[29]

Churchill's rising to this occasion is the more remarkable because he was 66 years old, an age now customarily associated with retirement and diminishing vigor. But he seemed to have every quality in great abundance that was needed for the next five critical years. He was a rare master of the English language and could thus in his speeches and broadcasts communicate his messages with memorable eloquence. His pugnacity, his truculence, his determination and supreme confidence inspired his countrymen through long months of disaster and privation. His astonishing practical intelligence and store of relevant information enabled him to run effectively the huge enterprise of a wartime national government. He himself reported that he was never happier than during these five momentous years when everything was in his hands, when his whole self was at its top level of performance.

The student of personality need not cease to admire this accomplishment in order to look behind it for further enlightenment on Churchill's career. Had he died at 65 Churchill would have been known in history as rather a failure in public life. Up to then he had never been prime minister, though he aspired to that office, and his choice of policies had often seemed opportunistic. In cabinet posts he was vigorous and effective but so arrogant that he made more enemies than friends. He tended to believe what he wanted to believe, and certain of his decisions, headstrong and bellicose, produced disastrous consequences. His outlook, including his determination that India should remain a subjugated part of the British Empire, was in some respects late Victorian rather than contemporary. As prime minister he treated his cabinet and military advisers outrageously, insulting them as if they were stupid servants; only the grim emergency kept them working together.

---

[29] G. Costigan, *Makers of Modern England: The Force of Individual Genius in History* (New York: The Macmillan Company, 1967), pp. 284–285.

Sir Winston Churchill's faults loom as massive as his virtues, and it would be a poor compliment to him to pretend that they did not exist. Perhaps the most discerning tribute one can pay him is to admit that only some extraordinary, perhaps unique quality of personal greatness could have endeared to his fellow countrymen a character in many ways so forbidding—insensitive, egotistical, arrogant, aggressive—and a mind in many respects so limited and so often lacking in sympathy with the problems, aspirations, and sufferings of all who found themselves outside the particular class in which he himself happened to be born. To have transcended such limitations, to have put democracy so notably in his debt, and to have become for millions the most cherished symbol of their lives—this suggests something of the unusual depth and many-sided nature of his personality.[30]

Taken altogether, it is obvious that Churchill did not achieve his ultimate eminence because he was an ideal personality. On a scale of maturity he would receive quite a few low marks. While he can be said to have actualized a great many aspects of himself, he did so often at considerable expense to those around him, and he corresponds very little to the sensitive self-actualizing people of Maslow's study. But let us suppose that the growth of his personality had taken place amidst highly humanizing surroundings so that he learned to be more flexible, more tolerant, more sympathetic, more modest, and in better control of aggression—would this have cost the Western world its freedom and made Hitler its master? For Churchill's greatness in a specific historical situation may well have been inseparable from his faults. He had the bulldog tenacity, the single-minded will to victory, and the ego strength required to meet the emergency; could he have mobilized such uncommon strengths if he had been otherwise a less arrogant and dogmatic person? As we saw, those excellent qualities called mental health, equanimity, and ego strength have been found in people not conspicuous for such other virtues as imagination, intellectual creativity, and self-knowledge. Thoughts about ideals of personal development must always be qualified by asking, "Ideal for what?" Churchill's personality, numerous as were its shortcomings, was ideal for the Battle of Britain.

Mahatma Gandhi

At the height of his career Mohandas K. Gandhi came to be assigned by his countrymen the reverential title of Mahatma ("Great Soul"). This was partly in recognition of his leading the struggle for Indian independence from British rule. More than that, however, it was because he had invented a method of opposing oppression and bringing about social change, the method of nonviolent resistance.

Gandhi showed that non-violent resistance was at least as powerful as guns; and he opened the way for more enduring conquests. Through him

[30] *Ibid.*, p. 244.

men have learned that no government, even the most tyrannical, is immune from non-violent resistance in the hands of determined and fearless men. No power on earth can resist the aroused consciences of men once they are disciplined and prepared to die for their beliefs. Gandhi was prepared to die: this was his most powerful weapon. . . . He had a mind of great originality and daring, and perhaps never before on so grand a scale has any man succeeded in shaping the course of history while using only the weapons of peace.[31]

It is necessary, of course, to recognize a paradoxical quality in Gandhi's method: though nonviolent, it was nevertheless militant, and it entailed an application of force to make one's convictions prevail against an opposition. There is nothing incongruous, therefore, in seeing Gandhi as a fighter, as a man who once said that he loved storms and who appeared to enjoy nothing more than being in the midst of a battle. Known for his spiritual principles, his fasts, and his experiments in disciplined communal living, he is sometimes stereotyped as a withdrawn saint. This is a bad mistake. When Gandhi fasted he was playing his ace in a power struggle, confronting the opposition with the alternative of giving in or enduring the public consequences of letting the Mahatma die. This slender wiry man was frail only in his last years. His life was tremendously active, his travels up and down India were enormously energetic, and his power to lead and inspire bespoke that quality of personal magnetism that is always difficult to analyze.

The practice of militant nonviolence calls for extraordinary organization. The effectiveness of an event like the strike of industrial workers at Ahmedabad, which Erikson makes the focus of his study of Gandhi, requires leadership, resources, and a constant struggle to maintain the morale of people who are risking their livelihood for the sake of the cause.[32] When the government is being resisted, the nonviolent fighters must be ready to go peaceably to jail and to endure with rare fortitude the indignities and violence of police action. Gandhi's last years were darkened by several episodes in which desperation broke down this type of organization, leading to uncontrolled riots with a high death toll. Militant nonviolence uses the methods of peace but has the objectives of war and revolution. It requires a degree of organization suitable to such objectives.

If we think of Gandhi as an organizer of force and a builder of morale it is not surprising that some of his qualities were like those of Churchill. His outlook, of course, was vastly different. He sided with those who were oppressed, including in India the bottom class of Untouchables. He believed in living with the greatest simplicity, tried to obliterate marks of status, and attached great importance to the virtue of humility. But when it came to exercising personal influence and rallying the spirits of his countrymen he had very

[31] R. Payne, *The Life and Death of Mahatma Gandhi* (New York: E. P. Dutton & Co., Inc., 1969), pp. 14, 16.

[32] E. H. Erikson, *Gandhi's Truth: On the Origins of Militant Nonviolence* (New York: W. W. Norton & Company, Inc., 1969).

much the same effect on his environment that Churchill had during the Battle of Britain. Perhaps because he looked so much less like a bulldog than Churchill, Gandhi is not usually described as having bulldog tenacity, but the powers of holding on and persisting that are suggested by this expression were certainly his in uncommon measure.

Have we here, then, an ideal personality? A great man and a great life, undoubtedly, but does it follow that Gandhi can serve in all respects as an object of admiration and imitation? Closer acquaintance discloses qualities that are not likely to elicit applause from a contemporary audience. Gandhi's attitude toward sex, for instance, seems excessively puritanical, involving as it did both personal renunciation and a considerable attempt to control this impulse in the young members of his communes. Erikson takes him to task for adopting celibacy in early middle life regardless of what his wife might have wanted, and for his punitive spirit in imposing the idea of chastity on others.[33] In present terms Gandhi would be rated an authoritarian father, though in his time and culture this was an expected aspect of the role. The story of his treatment of his eldest son, given in detail by Payne, sadly illustrates excessive paternal control, anger at signs of independence, declarations of suffering, and self-righteous statements that everything was being done out of love and consideration for the son.[34] Gandhi's use of the fast, once he had discovered its power, was not always limited to great public issues; this conspicuous form of suffering served him on occasion to bring his immediate following into line on a domestic problem. It was not easy to exist with any freedom in the Mahatma's entourage.

In both Churchill and Gandhi great powers of assertive leadership spilled over into petty tyrannies and cruelties. Both had serious shortcomings in self-insight. Does this mean that these strengths and faults are inseparably linked? The question is not rhetorical. We do not know from sufficient studies of sufficient numbers of people whether or not it is possible to separate the different aspects of one's development so as to be both a great public leader and a kindly, considerate person in more intimate relations. We know only that this often does not happen, and there is considerable opinion to the effect that power has a corrupting effect on personality as a whole. Considering how each of these two men met his historical opportunity, it would seem unduly demanding to ask that they be good at everything else.

Virtually a contemporary of Churchill and Gandhi was Eleanor Roosevelt (1884–1962), whose life pattern merits examination not only in its own right but also because she was one of the few historical figures rated by Maslow as unquestionably self-actualizing. Historical opportunity again played a conspicuous part in her ultimate influence, but the ability to seize it came only from a substantial transformation of her somewhat unpromising early life.

---

[33] *Ibid.*, Part III, Chap. 1.
[34] Payne, *The Life and Death of Mahatma Gandhi*, esp. pp. 241–247, 468–477.

Eleanor Roosevelt

Eleanor Roosevelt was the plain little daughter of a handsome, charming father and a mother who had been a great belle. According to a study of her life by Joan Erikson, the mother was put off by the child's lack of beauty and grace, favored the two younger brothers, and nagged her daughter in a way that made for constant feelings of shame and estrangement.[35] The father, on the other hand, made something of a pet of her, but he was presently banished from the household because of chronic heavy drinking. When Eleanor was 9 her mother, and shortly thereafter one of her brothers, suddenly died, leaving her in her grandmother's care. For a year her lonely life centered around the occasional brief visits of her father, but then he, too, died, and she was left with nothing more than her memories of him. The grandmother's regime seemed to consist mostly of deprivations, and Eleanor was kept from the company of other children. She led a lonely life of reading, walking, and daydreaming. At 15 she was sent to England for three years of schooling under a gifted headmistress who challenged her thinking powers and awakened her interest in public events. But she then returned to the traditional intensive social life of an upper-class young lady, which revived all her feelings of inferiority and brought her close to a "state of nervous collapse."

> Eleanor Roosevelt's account of her early life highlights a lesson often lost in the study of biographies. This record of her childhood experiences could, if it were offered as a case history, account for a total failure to accept the challenge of participation in an active and productive life. Such documentation could be used trauma for trauma to "explain" failure. Yet Eleanor Roosevelt "succeeded," in many ways triumphantly, in other ways not without tragic overtones.[36]

That she soon married a future president of the United States may seem to some readers a reversal of fortune that might account for a lot of this success. But for the first fifteen years of married life, living under the shadow of her possessive mother-in-law, afraid of the nurses hired to take care of her children, she was by no means yet capable of using the opporunities provided by her husband's growing career. It is likely, furthermore, that Franklin would not have become president after being crippled by infantile paralysis without Eleanor's extraordinarily effective support. With unexpected firmness she overruled her mother-in-law, who wanted to keep him in a life of permanent invalidism, nursed him back to relative health, and encouraged him to return to public life. Possibly she feared that he would fade out as her father had faded out, and she had only to continue her usual

---

[35] J. M. Erikson, "Notes on the Life of Eleanor Roosevelt," *Daedalus*, **93** (1964), 781–801.

[36] *Ibid.*, p. 792.

deferent behavior to let this happen. Instead, her behavior was transformed into the very image of purposeful persistence and determination. One of her favorite quotations was "Back of tranquillity lies always conquered unhappiness." At this point in her life the unhappiness of her lonely childhood and of her subjugated early married years steeled her for a new kind of behavior designed to change things for the better.

Another example of transformation occurred as she turned her personal experience of unhappiness into concern for the unhappiness of others. This change is described by Joan Erikson as follows:

> She seems to have settled her account with her unlucky childhood by a determined rebalancing of the scales and by projecting this shift onto an almost global screen. Once deeply ashamed of her own unattractiveness, she spent her entire life developing her capacity for empathizing with people. She listened with compassion. Her response to any demonstrable need was immediate and generous to a fault. Indignation was by no means foreign to her, but she transformed it into strong feelings in the service of causes. Such empathizing requires the capacity to be self-effacing. Having set her own needs aside, as it were, her relationships with others could be immediate and warm. She became one of the most attractive and charming women in public life.[37]

Through this transformation the once unhappy rich girl became the champion of the poor and the oppressed; ultimately she became chairman of the committee which drew up the United Nations Declaration of Human Rights.

It is true that the scope of Eleanor Roosevelt's influence was much enlarged by her husband's position as president. This enabled her eventually to carry on her activities on a worldwide scale. But there again her achievement was partly her own; she made use of an opportunity that had not before been seized in any such way. In her early years as First Lady she was roundly criticized for meddling in public life and was compared unfavorably with the wives of previous presidents who had construed their role in the White House in more housewifely fashion. In this respect Mrs. Roosevelt illustrates a process discussed earlier in this book, that of the enlargement of a preexisting social role through the manner in which an innovative individual enacts it.[38] It is doubtful that anyone who knew the awkward, unhappy, socially inept child would have predicted that she would become on such a scale a role innovator.

Epilogue: The Enterprise of Living

The study of personality yields as its largest lesson a knowledge of the diverse and powerful ways in which individual lives are shaped by the influences surrounding growth. To understand the contours of a given personality

[37] *Ibid.*, p. 793.
[38] See above, Chapter 17, pp. 439–441.

we need a vast amount of information about these shaping influences. There is the family, where the young child forms his earliest experience of the nature of the world and of human interactions. There is the surrounding larger culture and the more immediate subculture represented by social class and ethnic group. There is individual genetic makeup, which exerts a selective influence on what will be most intensely experienced. There is the pressure of motives and the tendency of patterns learned early in life to dominate behavior in new situations. Finally, we need to know about the whole sequential course of development, the series of situations, problems, and crises through which the person has passed in the process of growing up. A large part of the description of personality is an account of the cumulative impress left on the individual by the influences amidst which he has lived. Sometimes it seems appropriate to conclude that we are lived by our lives and have no real hand in steering the course.

In spite of all this, however, the title of this book proposes that living is an enterprise. This follows from the premise that the object of our study, the human living system interacting with its environment, is indeed alive, and that being alive necessarily implies active agency in all transactions. The living system, with its properties of self-maintenance and its inherent movement toward enlargement, is itself a center of force capable of exerting an influence upon its environment. We live our lives as well as being lived by them. Our scope to influence surroundings and steer our own course may not be large, but it is still of crucial importance. Large transformations of personality may be rare, but there is a touch of creation in almost everything we do. New situations are always a little different from those that have gone before, so that there is room for initiative and innovation in every event. Actual living is at least to some extent a venture into the unknown, and it is thus inherently an enterprise.

Bibliography

Aberle, D. F., and K. D. Naegele. "Middle Class Fathers' Occupational Role and Attitudes toward Children." *American Journal of Orthopsychiatry,* **22** (1952), 366–378.

Abraham, K. "The First Pregenital Stage of the Libido (1916)." In *Selected Papers on Psychoanalysis.* London: Hogarth Press, Ltd., 1927.

Ackerman, N. W. "Family Psychotherapy Today: Some Areas of Controversy." *Comprehensive Psychiatry,* **7** (1966), 375–388.

———. *The Psychodynamics of Family Life.* New York: Basic Books, Inc., 1958.

———. *Treating the Troubled Family.* New York: Basic Books, Inc., 1966.

Adler, A. *Understanding Human Nature.* New York: Greenberg, Publisher, Inc., 1927.

Adorno, T. W., E. Frenkel-Brunswik, D. J. Levinson, and R. N. Sanford. *The Authoritarian Personality.* New York: Harper & Row, Publishers, 1950.

Aichhorn, A. *Wayward Youth.* New York: The Viking Press, Inc., 1935.

Ainsworth, M. D., et al. *Deprivation of Maternal Care: A Reassessment of Its Effects.* Public Health Papers. Geneva: World Health Organization, 1966.

Allee, W. C. *The Social Life of Animals,* rev. ed. Boston: The Beacon Press, 1958.

Allport, G. W. *Letters from Jenny.* New York: Harcourt Brace Jovanovich, Inc., 1965.

———. *Pattern and Growth in Personality.* New York: Holt, Rinehart and Winston, Inc., 1961.

———. *Personality: A Psychological Interpretation.* New York: Holt, Rinehart and Winston, Inc., 1937.

Altus, W. D. "Birth Order and Its Sequelae." *International Journal of Psychiatry,* **3** (1967), 23–32.

"Ambivalence in First Reactions to a Sibling." *Journal of Abnormal and Social Psychology,* **44** (1949), 541–548.

Anastasi, A. "Heredity, Environment, and the Question 'How?' " *Psychological Review,* **65** (1958), 197–208.

Apple, D. "The Social Structure of Grandparenthood." *American Anthropologist,* **58** (1956), 56–63.

Averill, J. R. "Grief: Its Nature and Significance." *Psychological Bulletin,* **70** (1968), 721–748.

Azrin, N. H., and O. R. Lindsley. "The Reinforcement of Cooperation between

Children." *Journal of Abnormal and Social Psychology,* **52** (1956), 100–102.

Baldwin, A. L. *Behavior and Development in Childhood.* New York: Holt, Rinehart and Winston, Inc., 1955.

————. "Socialization and the Parent-Child Relationship." *Child Development,* **19** (1948), 127–136.

————, J. Kalhorn, and F. H. Breese. "Patterns of Parent Behavior." *Psychological Monographs,* **58,** no. 268 (1945).

Baldwin, J. *Nobody Knows My Name.* New York: Dell Publishing Company, 1962.

————. *Notes of a Native Son.* Boston: The Beacon Press, 1955.

Baltzell, E. D. *An American Business Aristocracy.* New York: The Free Press, 1958.

Bandura, A., and R. H. Walters. *Adolescent Aggression.* New York: The Ronald Press Company, 1959.

————. *Social Learning and Personality Development.* New York: Holt, Rinehart and Winston, Inc., 1965.

Barber, J. D. "The Character of Richard Nixon." *Boston Sunday Globe Magazine,* November 9, 1969, pp. 7–14.

Barron, F. *Creativity and Psychological Health.* Princeton, N.J.: D. Van Nostrand Company, Inc., 1963.

————. "The Psychology of Creativity." In *New Directions in Psychology,* Vol. 2. New York: Holt, Rinehart and Winston, Inc., 1965.

Barry, W. A. "Marriage Research and Conflict: An Integrative Review." *Psychological Bulletin,* **73** (1970), 41–54.

Bartemeier, L. "The Contribution of the Father to the Mental Health of the Family." *American Journal of Psychiatry,* **110** (1953), 277–280.

Baruch, D. W., and H. Miller. *Sex in Marriage.* New York: Hart Publishing Company, Inc., 1962.

Bass, B. M. *Organizational Psychology.* Boston: Allyn and Bacon, Inc., 1965.

Bateson, G., D. D. Jackson, J. Haley, and J. H. Weakland. "Toward a Theory of of Schizophrenia." *Behavioral Science,* **1** (1956), 251–264.

Baumrind, D. "Child Care Practices Anteceding Three Patterns of Preschool Behavior." *Genetic Psychology Monographs,* **75** (1967), 43–88.

Bayer, A. E. "Birth Order and the Attainment of the Doctorate: A Test of Economic Hypotheses." *American Journal of Sociology,* **72** (1967), 540–550.

Bayley, N., and R. Tuddenham. "Adolescent Changes in Body Build." In *43rd Yearbook.* New York: National Society for the Study of Education, 1944.

Beardslee, D. C., and D. D. O'Dowd. "Students and the Occupational World." In *The American College,* ed. N. Sanford. New York: John Wiley & Sons, Inc., 1962.

Becker, J., and C. H. Nichols. "Communality of Manic-Depressive and 'Mild' Cyclothymic Characteristics." *Journal of Abnormal and Social Psychology,* **69** (1964), 531–538.

Becker, W. C. "Consequences of Different Kinds of Parental Discipline." In *Review of Child Development Research,* Vol. 1, ed. M. L. Hoffman and L. W. Hoffman. New York: Russell Sage Foundation, 1964.

Bell, A. P. "Role Modelship and Interaction in Adolescence and Young Adulthood." *Developmental Psychology,* **2** (1970), 123–128.

Bell, D. "National Character Revisited: A Proposal for Renegotiating the Concept." In *The Study of Personality: An Interdisciplinary Appraisal,* ed. E. Norbeck, D. Price-Williams, and W. M. McCord. New York: Holt, Rinehart and Winston, Inc., 1968.

Bell, N. W. "Extended Family Relations of Disturbed and Well Families." *Family Process,* 1 (1962), 175–193.

Bellow, S. *Mr. Sammler's Planet.* New York: The Viking Press, Inc., 1970.

Bennis, W. G., E. H. Schein, and D. E. Berlew, eds. *Interpersonal Dynamics: Essays and Reading on Human Interaction.* Homewood, Ill.: The Dorsey Press, 1964.

Bergman, P., and S. K. Escalona. "Unusual Sensitivities in Very Young Children." *Psychoanalytic Study of the Child,* 3–4 (1949), 333–352.

Berlyne, D. E. *Conflict, Arousal and Curiosity.* New York: McGraw-Hill, Inc., 1960.

Bermann, E., and D. R. Miller. "The Matching of Mates." In *Cognition, Personality, and Clinical Psychology*, ed. R. Jessor and S. Feschbach. San Francisco: Jossey-Bass, 1967.

Berne, E. *Games People Play: The Psychology of Human Relationships.* New York: Grove Press, Inc., 1964.

Bettelheim, B. *The Children of the Dream.* New York: The Macmillan Company, 1969.

———. "Individual and Mass Behavior in Extreme Situations." *Journal of Abnormal and Social Psychology,* 38 (1943), 417–452.

Biber, B., L. B. Murphy, L. Woodcock, and I. Black. *Life and Ways of the Seven-to-Eight Year Old.* New York: Basic Books, Inc., 1952.

Bidwell, C. E. "The Young Professional in the Army: A Study of Occupational Identity." *American Sociological Review,* 26 (1961), 360–372.

Birmingham, S. *Our Crowd: The Great Jewish Families of New York.* New York: Harper & Row, Publishers, 1967.

Birns, B. "Individual Differences in Human Neonates' Responses to Stimulation." *Child Development,* 36 (1965), 249–256.

Blaine, G. B., Jr., and C. C. McArthur. *Emotional Problems of the Student.* New York: Appleton-Century-Crofts, 1961.

Blanchard, W. H. *Rousseau and the Spirit of Revolt: A Psychological Study.* Ann Arbor: University of Michigan Press, 1967.

Blenkner, M. "Social Work and Family Relationships in Later Life." In *Social Structure and the Family: Generational Relations,* ed. E. Shanas and G. F. Streib. Englewood Cliffs, N.J.: Prentice-Hall, Inc., 1965.

Blos, P. *On Adolescence: A Psychoanalytic Interpretation.* New York: The Free Press, 1962.

Bossard, J. H. S., and E. S. Boll. *The Large Family System.* Philadelphia: University of Pennsylvania Press, 1956.

Boulding, K. E. *Conflict and Defense: A General Theory.* New York: Harper & Row, Publishers, 1962.

Bowlby, J. "Forty-four Juvenile Thieves." *International Journal of Psychoanalysis,* 25 (1944), 1–57.

———. *Maternal Care and Mental Health,* Monograph Series, no. 2. Geneva: World Health Organization, 1951.

———. "The Nature of the Child's Tie to His Mother." *International Journal of Psychoanalysis,* 39 (1958), 350–369.

Boyd, W. *The History of Western Education*, 3d ed. London: A & C. Black, Ltd., 1932.

Bradley, R. W. "Birth Order and School-Related Behavior: A Heuristic Review." *Psychological Bulletin,* **70** (1968), 45–51.

Brazelton, T. B. *Infants and Mothers: Differences in Development*. New York: Delacorte Press, 1970.

Bronfenbrenner, U. "Freudian Theories of Identification and Their Derivatives." *Child Development.* **31** (1960), 15–40.

————. "Socialization and Social Class through Time and Space." In *Readings in Social Psychology*, 3d ed., ed. E. Maccoby, T. Newcomb, and E. Hartley. New York: Holt, Rinehart and Winston, Inc., 1958.

Brown, C. *Manchild in the Promised Land*. New York: The Macmillan Company, 1965.

Brown, D. "Personality, College Environments, and Academic Productivity." In *The American College*, ed. N. Sanford. New York: John Wiley & Sons, Inc., 1962.

Brown, R. *Social Psychology*. New York: The Free Press, 1965.

Bruner, J. S. *On Knowing: Essays for the Left Hand*. Cambridge, Mass.: The Belknap Press of Harvard University Press, 1962.

————. *Toward a Theory of Instruction*. Cambridge, Mass.: The Belknap Press of Harvard University Press, 1966.

Bryan, J. H., and P. London. "Altruistic Behavior by Children." *Psychological Bulletin,* **73** (1970), 200–211.

Bugental, J. F. T., and S. L. Zelen. "Investigations into the Self-Concept." *Journal of Personality,* **18** (1950), 483–498.

Bühler, C. "The Social Behavior of Children." In *A Handbook of Child Psychology,* 2d ed., ed. C. Murchison. Worcester, Mass.: Clark University Press, 1933.

Bühler, K. *Mental Development of the Child*. New York: Harcourt Brace Jovanovich, Inc., 1931.

Burgess, E. W., and L. S. Cottrell, Jr. *Predicting Success or Failure in Marriage*. Englewood Cliffs, N.J.: Prentice-Hall, Inc., 1939.

Buss, A. H. *The Psychology of Aggression*. New York: John Wiley & Sons, Inc., 1961.

Byrne, D. "Parental Antecedents of Authoritarianism." *Journal of Personality and Social Psychology,* **1** (1965), 369–373.

Caldwell, B. M. "The Effects of Infant Care." In *Review of Child Development Research,* Vol. 1, ed. M. L. Hoffman and L. W. Hoffman. New York: Russell Sage Foundation, 1964.

Camus, A. *The Stranger*, trans. Stuart Gilbert. New York: Vintage Books, 1946.

Canfield, D. *The Home-maker*. New York: Harcourt Brace Jovanovich, Inc., 1924.

Cannon, W. B. *Bodily Changes in Pain, Hunger, Fear and Rage,* 2d ed. New York: Appleton-Century-Crofts, 1929.

Caplan, G. "Clinical Observations on the Emotional Life of Children in the Communal Settlements in Israel." In *Problems of Infancy and Childhood,* ed. M. J. E. Senn. New York: Josiah Macy Jr. Foundation, 1950. Reprinted in C. F. Reed, I. E. Alexander, and S. S. Tomkins, eds., *Psychopathology: A Source Book*. Cambridge, Mass.: Harvard University Press, 1958.

Cartwright, D., ed. *Studies in Social Power*. Ann Arbor: University of Michigan Press, 1959.

Cattell, J. M. "Statistical Study of American Men of Science." *Science*, n.s., **24** (1906), 658–665, 699–707, 732–742.

Cattell, R. B. *Personality and Motivation: Structure and Measurement*. New York: Harcourt Brace Jovanovich, Inc., 1957.

Cattell, R. B., and J. R. Beloff. "Research Origins and Construction of the IPAT Junior Personality Quiz." *Journal of Consulting Psychology*, **17** (1953), 436–442.

Chess, S., A. Thomas, and H. G. Birch. *Your Child Is a Person*. New York: The Viking Press, Inc., 1965.

Clausen, J. A. "Family Structure, Socialization, and Personality." In *Review of Child Development Research*, Vol. 2, ed. L. W. Hoffman and M. L. Hoffman. New York: Russell Sage Foundation, 1966.

Cohen, A. K. *Delinquent Boys: The Culture of the Gang*. New York: The Free Press, 1955. ·

Coleman, J. S. *The Adolescent Society: The Social Life of the Teenager and Its Impact on Education*. New York: The Free Press, 1961.

Coleman, R. P., and B. L. Neugarten. *Social Status in the City*. San Francisco: Jossey-Bass, Inc., 1971.

Coles, R. *Children of Crisis: A Study of Courage and Fear*. Boston: Little, Brown & Company, 1967.

Collins, P. A. W. *James Boswell*. London: Longmans, Green & Co., Ltd., 1956.

Comfort, A. *Sex in Society*. London: Gerald Duckworth, Ltd., 1963.

Coombs, R. H. "Value Consensus and Partner Satisfaction among Dating Couples." *Journal of Marriage and the Family*, **28** (1966), 166–173.

Coopersmith, S. *The Antecedents of Self-Esteem*. San Francisco: W. H. Freeman and Company, 1967.

Costigan, G. *Makers of Modern England: The Force of Individual Genius in History*. New York: The Macmillan Company, 1967.

Davis, A. "American Status Systems and the Socialization of the Child." *American Sociological Review*, **6** (1941), 345–354.

Davis, A., and J. Dollard. *Children of Bondage*. New York: American Council on Education, 1940.

Davis, A., B. B. Gardner, and M. R. Gardner. *Deep South: A Social and Anthropological Study of Caste and Class*. Chicago: University of Chicago Press, 1941.

Davis, A., and R. J. Havighurst. "Social Class and Color Differences in Child-Rearing." In *Personality in Nature, Society and Culture*, 2d ed., ed. C. Kluckhohn, H. A. Murray, and D. Schneider. New York: Alfred A. Knopf, Inc., 1953.

Dellas, M., and E. L. Gaier. "Identification of Creativity: The Individual." *Psychological Bulletin*, **73** (1970), 55–73.

Deutsch, H. *The Psychology of Women: A Psychoanalytic Interpretation*, Vol. 1. New York: Grune & Stratton, Inc., 1944.

Deutsch, M. "Conflicts: Productive and Destructive." *Journal of Social Issues*, **25** (1969), 7–41.

———. "Early Social Environment: Its Influence on School Adaptation." In *Profile of the School Dropout*, ed. D. Schreiber. New York: Alfred A. Knopf, Inc., 1968.

508   Bibliography

Dewey, J. *Interest and Effort in Education.* Boston: Houghton Mifflin Company, 1913.
Diamond, S. *Personality and Temperament.* New York: Harper & Row, Publishers, 1957.
Dollard, J., L. W. Doob, N. E. Miller, O. H. Mowrer, and R. R. Sears. *Frustration and Aggression.* New Haven: Yale University Press, 1939.
Dollard, J., and N. E. Miller. *Personality and Psychotherapy.* New York: McGraw-Hill, Inc., 1950.
Drake, St. C., and H. R. Cayton. *Black Metropolis.* New York: Harcourt Brace Jovanovich, Inc., 1945.
Durbin, E. F. M., and J. Bowlby. "Personal Aggressiveness and War." In *War and Democracy: Essays on the Causes and Prevention of War*, ed. E. F. M. Durbin and J. Catlin. London: Routledge & Kegan Paul Ltd., 1938.
Edstrom, D. *The Testament of Caliban.* New York: Funk & Wagnalls Company, 1937.
Eisenberg, L. "School Phobia: A Study in the Communication of Anxiety." *American Journal of Psychiatry,* **114** (1958), 712–718.
Elder, G. H., Jr. "Family Structure and Educational Attainment." *American Sociological Review,* **30** (1965), 81–96.
Ellis, H. *A Study of British Genius.* London: Hurst and Blackett, 1904.
Emmerich, W. "Family Role Concepts of Children Ages Six to Ten." *Child Development,* **32** (1961), 609–624.
Emmerich, W. "Young Children's Discrimination of Parent and Child Roles." *Child Development,* **31** (1960), 315–328.
Erikson, E. H. *Childhood and Society* (1950), 2d ed. New York: W. W. Norton & Company, Inc., 1963.
———. *Gandhi's Truth: On the Origins of Militant Nonviolence.* New York: W. W. Norton & Company, Inc., 1969.
———. "Identity and the Life Cycle." *Psychological Issues,* **1** (1959), 1–171.
———. *Identity: Youth and Crisis.* New York: W. W. Norton & Company, Inc., 1968.
———. "Inner and Outer Space: Reflections on Womanhood." In "The Woman in America." *Daedalus,* **93** (1964), 582–606.
Erikson, J. M. "Notes on the Life of Eleanor Roosevelt." *Daedalus,* **93** (1964), 781–801.
Escalona, S. K. *The Roots of Individuality: Normal Patterns of Development in Infancy.* Chicago: Aldine Publishing Company, 1968.
Escalona, S. K., and G. Heider. *Prediction and Outcome.* New York: Basic Books, Inc., 1959.
Eysenck, H. J. *The Structure of Human Personality*, 3d ed. London: Methuen & Company, Ltd., 1970.
Faigin, H. "Social Behavior of Young Children in the Kibbutz." *Journal of Abnormal and Social Psychology,* **56** (1958), 117–129.
Feld, S. C. "Longitudinal Study of the Origins of Achievement Strivings." *Journal of Personality and Social Psychology,* **7** (1967), 408–414.
Fenichel, O. "Ego Strength and Ego Weakness." In *Collected Papers,* Vol. 2. New York: W. W. Norton & Company, Inc., 1954.
———. *The Psychoanalytic Theory of Neurosis.* New York: W. W. Norton & Company, Inc., 1945.
Fiske, D. W., and S. A. Maddi, eds. *The Functions of Varied Experience.* Homewood, Ill.: The Dorsey Press, 1961.

Flapan, D. *Children's Understanding of Social Interaction.* New York: Teachers College Press, 1968.

Flavell, J. H. *The Developmental Psychology of Jean Piaget.* Princeton, N.J.: D. Van Nostrand Company, 1963.

Frank, A. *The Diary of a Young Girl,* trans. by B. M. Mooyaart-Doubleday. Garden City, N.Y.: Doubleday & Company, Inc., 1952.

Franklin, B. *Autobiography* (first published in 1791), Everyman's Library Edition, No. 316. London: J. M. Dent & Sons, Ltd., 1908.

Freeman, D. "Human Aggression in Anthropological Perspective." In *The Natural History of Aggression,* ed. J. D. Carthy and F. J. Elbing. New York: Academic Press, Inc., 1964.

Freud, A. "The Bearing of the Psychoanalytic Theory of Instinctual Drives on Certain Aspects of Human Behavior." In *Drives, Affects, Behavior,* ed. R. M. Loewenstein. New York: International Universities Press, Inc., 1953.

————. *The Ego and the Mechanisms of Defence.* London: Hogarth Press, Ltd., 1937.

Freud, A., and D. Burlingham. *Infants without Families.* New York: International Universities Press, Inc., 1944.

Freud, A., and S. Dann. "An Experiment in Group Upbringing." *Psychoanalytic Study of the Child,* **6** (1951), 127–168.

Freud, S. "Analysis of a Phobia in a Five-Year-Old Boy" (1909). Reprinted in *Collected Papers,* Vol. 3. New York: Basic Books, Inc., 1959.

————. *Civilization and Its Discontents.* London: Hogarth Press, Ltd., 1930.

————. *The Ego and the Id.* London: Hogarth Press, Ltd., 1927.

————. *A General Introduction to Psychoanalysis* (1917), trans. J. Riviere. New York: Permabooks, 1953.

————. *Group Psychology and the Analysis of the Ego.* London: Hogarth Press, Ltd., 1922.

————. *New Introductory Lectures in Psychoanalysis,* trans. W. J. H. Sprott. New York: W. W. Norton & Company, Inc., 1933.

————. "Three Contributions to the Theory of Sex (1905). In *The Basic Writings of Sigmund Freud.* New York: The Modern Library, 1938.

Friedenberg, E. Z. *Coming of Age in America: Growth and Acquiescence.* New York: Random House, Inc., 1965.

————. *The Vanishing Adolescent.* Boston: The Beacon Press, 1959.

Fries, M. E. "Psychosomatic Relationships between Mother and Infant." *Psychosomatic Medicine,* **6** (1944), 159–162.

Fries, M. E., and P. J. Woolf. "Some Hypotheses on the Role of the Congenital Activity Types in Personality Development." *Psychoanalytic Study of the Child,* **8** (1953), 48–62.

Fromm, E. *Man for Himself: An Inquiry into the Psychology of Ethics.* New York: Holt, Rinehart and Winston, Inc., 1947.

Funkenstein, D. H., S. H. King, and M. E. Drolette. *Mastery of Stress.* Cambridge, Mass.: Harvard University Press, 1957.

Gesell, A., and F. L. Ilg. *The Child from Five to Ten.* New York: Harper & Row, Publishers, 1946.

————. *Infant and Child in the Culture of Today.* New York: Harper & Row, Publishers, 1943.

Getzels, J. W., and P. W. Jackson. *Creativity and Intelligence: Explorations with Gifted Students.* New York: John Wiley & Sons, Inc., 1962.

Gilbreth, F. B., Jr., and E. G. Carey. *Cheaper by the Dozen.* New York: Thomas Y. Crowell Company, 1948.

Ginsburg, H., and S. Opper. *Piaget's Theory of Intellectual Development: An Introduction.* Englewood Cliffs, N.J.: Prentice-Hall, Inc., 1969.

Glueck, S., and E. Glueck. *Delinquents and Non-Delinquents in Perspective.* Cambridge, Mass.: Harvard University Press, 1968.

————. *Unraveling Juvenile Delinquency.* New York: The Commonwealth Fund, 1950.

Goffman, E. *The Presentation of Self in Everyday Life.* Garden City, N.Y.: Doubleday & Company, Inc., 1959.

Goldfarb, W. "Emotional and Intellectual Consequences of Psychologic Deprivation in Infancy: A Revaluation." In *Psychopathology of Childhood,* ed. P. H. Hoch, and J. Zubin. New York: Grune & Stratton, Inc., 1955.

Goldin, P. C. "A Review of Children's Reports of Parent Behaviors." *Psychological Bulletin,* **71** (1969), 222–236.

Golding, W. *Lord of the Flies.* New York: Coward-McCann, Inc., 1954.

Goodman, P. *Growing Up Absurd.* New York: Random House, Inc., 1960.

Gordon, C. "Self-Conceptions: Configurations of Content." In *The Self in Social Interaction,* Vol. 1, ed. C. Gordon and K. J. Gergen. New York: John Wiley & Sons, Inc., 1968.

Gordon, C. W. *The Social System of the High School.* New York: The Free Press, 1957.

Gough, H. G. *The Adjective Check List.* Palo Alto, Calif.: Consulting Psychologists Press, 1961.

Greenspoon, J. "The Reinforcing Effect of Two Spoken Sounds on the Frequency of Two Responses." *American Journal of Psychology,* **68** (1955), 409–416.

Grier, W. H., and P. M. Cobbs. *Black Rage.* New York: Basic Books, Inc., 1968.

Grinker, R. R. " 'Mentally Healthy' Young Males (Homoclites): A Study." *Archives of General Psychiatry,* **6** (1962), 405–453.

Groos, K. *The Play of Man,* trans. E. L. Baldwin. New York: D. Appleton, 1901.

Guilford, J. P. *The Nature of Human Intelligence.* New York: McGraw-Hill, Inc., 1967.

Haire, M., E. E. Ghiselli, and L. W. Porter. "Psychological Research on Pay: An Overview." *Industrial Relations,* **3** (1963), 1–8.

Hall, C. S., and G. Lindzey. *Theories of Personality,* 2d ed. New York: John Wiley & Sons, Inc., 1968.

Halliday, J. L. *Psychosocial Medicine: A Study of the Sick Society.* New York: W. W. Norton & Company, Inc., 1948.

Hamburg, D. A., and J. E. Adams. "A Perspective on Coping Behavior: Seeking and Utilizing Information in Major Transitions." *Archives of General Psychiatry,* **17** (1967), 277–284.

Hamburg, D. A., and D. T. Lunde. "Sex Hormones in the Development of Sex Differences in Human Behavior." In *The Development of Sex Differences,* ed. E. E. Maccoby. Stanford, Calif.: Stanford University Press, 1966.

Handel, G., ed. *The Psychosocial Interior of the Family.* Chicago: Aldine Publishing Company, 1967.

Hanfmann, E. "Boris: A Displaced Person." In *Clinical Studies of Personality,* ed. A. Burton and R. E. Harris. New York: Harper & Row, Publishers, 1955.

Hanfmann, E., and J. Kasanin. "Conceptual Thinking in Schiozphrenia." Washington, D.C.: *Nervous and Mental Disease Monographs,* no. 67, 1942.

Harlow, H. F. "The Heterosexual Affectional System in Monkeys." *American Psychologist,* **17** (1962), 1–9.

———. "The Nature of Love." *American Psychologist,* **13** (1958), 673–685.

Hathaway, K. B. *The Little Locksmith.* New York: Coward-McCann, Inc., 1943.

Hawkes, G. R., L. Burchinal, and B. Gardner. "Size of Family and Adjustment of Children." *Marriage and Family Living,* **20** (1958), 65–68.

Heath, D. H. *Explorations of Maturity: Studies of Mature and Immature College Men.* New York: Appleton-Century-Crofts, 1965.

———. *Growing Up in College.* San Francisco: Jossey-Bass, Inc., 1968.

Hebb, D. A. *The Organization of Behavior.* New York: John Wiley & Sons, Inc., 1949.

Heider, F. *The Psychology of Interpersonal Relations.* New York: John Wiley & Sons, Inc., 1958.

Heinstein, M. I. "Behavioral Correlates of Breast-Bottle Regimes under Varying Parent-Infant Relationships." *Monographs of the Society for Research in Child Development,* **28,** no. 4 (1963).

Hendrick, I. *Facts and Theories of Psychoanalysis.* New York: Alfred A. Knopf, Inc., 1934.

Henry, J., and S. Warson. "Family Structure and Psychic Development." *American Journal of Orthopsychiatry,* **21** (1951), 59–73.

Hess, R. D., and G. Handel. *Family Worlds: A Psychosocial Approach to Family Life.* Chicago: University of Chicago Press, 1959.

Hesse, H. *Demian: The Story of Emil Sinclair's Youth* (1919), trans. M. Roloff and M. Lebeck. New York: Bantam Books, 1966.

Hill, G. B., ed. *Boswell's Life of Johnson,* Vol. 4. Oxford: Clarendon Press, 1887.

Hill, J. P. "Parental Determinants of Sex-Typed Behavior." Unpublished Ph.D. Dissertation, Harvard University, 1964.

Hodge, R. W., and D. J. Treiman. "Social Participation and Social Status." *American Sociological Review,* **33** (1968), 722–740.

Hollingshead, A. B. *Elmtown's Youth: The Impact of Social Classes on Adolescents.* New York: John Wiley & Sons, Inc., 1949.

Hollingshead, A. B., and F. C. Redlich. *Social Class and Mental Illness: A Community Study.* New York: John Wiley & Sons, Inc., 1958.

Homans, G. C. "Social Behavior as Exchange." *American Journal of Sociology,* **63** (1958), 597–606.

Horney, K. *The Neurotic Personality of Our Time.* New York: W. W. Norton & Company, Inc., 1937.

———. *New Ways in Psychoanalysis.* New York: W. W. Norton & Company, Inc., 1939.

———. *Our Inner Conflicts: A Constructive Theory of Neurosis.* New York: W. W. Norton & Company, Inc., 1945.

———. *Self-Analysis.* New York: W. W. Norton & Company, Inc., 1942.

Hughes, E. C. *Men and Their Work.* New York: The Free Press, 1958.

Hunt, J. McV. *The Challenge of Incompetence and Poverty.* Urbana, Ill.: University of Illinois Press, 1969.

———. *Intelligence and Experience.* New York: The Ronald Press Company, 1961.

———. "Intrinsic Motivation and Its Role in Psychological Development." In

Nebraska Symposium on Motivation, ed. D. Levine. Lincoln, Neb.: University of Nebraska Press, 1965.

Hunt, W. A., and C. Landis. "The Overt Behavior Pattern in Startle." *Journal of Experimental Psychology,* **19** (1936), 312–320.

Inhelder, B., and J. Piaget. *The Growth of Logical Thinking from Childhood to Adolescence,* trans. A. Parsons and S. Milgram. New York: Basic Books, Inc., 1958.

Inkeles, A., and D. J. Levinson. "National Character: A Study of Modal Personality and Sociocultural Systems." In *Handbook of Social Psychology,* 2d ed., Vol. 2, ed. G. Lindzey and E. Aronson. Reading, Mass.: Addison-Wesley Publishing Company, Inc., 1968.

Jahoda, M. *Current Concepts of Positive Mental Health.* New York: Basic Books, Inc., 1958.

James, H., ed. *The Letters of William James,* Vol. 1. Boston: The Atlantic Monthly Press, 1920.

James, W. *Pragmatism: A New Name for Some Old Ways of Thinking.* New York: Longmans, Green & Co., Ltd., 1907.

———. *The Principles of Psychology,* Vol. 1. New York: Henry Holt and Company, 1890.

Jones, E. *The Life and Work of Sigmund Freud,* Vol. 2. New York: Basic Books, Inc., 1955.

Jones, E. E. *Ingratiation: A Social Psychological Analysis.* New York: Appleton-Century-Crofts, 1964.

Jones, M. C. "The Later Careers of Boys Who Were Early- or Late-Maturing." *Child Development,* **28** (1957), 113–128.

Jones, M. C. and N. Bayley. "Physical Maturity among Boys as Related to Behavior." *Journal of Educational Psychology,* **41** (1950), 129–148.

Josselyn, I. M. "Cultural Forces, Motherliness and Fatherliness." *American Journal of Orthopsychiatry,* **26** (1956), 264–271.

Jung, C. G. *Psychological Types, or the Psychology of Individuation* (1920), trans. H. G. Baynes. New York: Harcourt Brace Jovanovich, Inc., 1924.

———. *Two Essays on Analytic Psychology,* trans. H. G., and C. F. Baynes. New York: Dodd, Mead & Company, Inc., 1928.

Kagan, J. "The Concept of Identification." *Psychological Review,* **65** (1958), 296–305.

———. "Information Processing in the Child." *Readings in Child Development and Personality,* ed. P. H. Mussen, J. J. Conger, and J. Kagan. New York: Harper & Row, Publishers, 1965.

Kagan, J., B. Hosken, and S. Watson, "The Child's Symbolic Conceptualization of Parents." *Child Development,* **32** (1961), 625–636.

Kagan, J., and J. Lemkin. "The Child's Differential Perception of Parental Attributes." *Journal of Abnormal and Social Psychology,* **61** (1960), 440–447.

Kagan, J., and H. A. Moss. *Birth to Maturity.* New York: John Wiley & Sons, Inc., 1962.

Kahl, J. A. *The American Class Structure.* New York: Holt, Rinehart and Winston, Inc., 1957.

———. "Educational and Occupational Aspirations of 'Common Man' Boys." *Harvard Educational Review,* **23** (1953), 188.

Kanfer, F. H. "Vicarious Human Reinforcement: A Glimpse into the Black Box." In *Research in Behavior Modification: New Developments and Implica-*

tions, ed. Leonard Krasner, and Leonard P. Ullmann. New York: Holt, Rinehart and Winston, Inc., 1965.

Kassenbaum, G. G., A. S. Couch, and P. E. Slater. "The Factorial Dimensions of the MMPI." *Journal of Consulting Psychology*, **23** (1959), 226–236.

Kaufman, H. *Aggression and Altruism.* New York: Holt, Rinehart and Winston, Inc., 1970.

Kelly, G. A. *The Psychology of Personal Constructs: A Theory of Personality,* Vol. 1. New York: W. W. Norton & Company, Inc., 1955.

Keniston, K. *Young Radicals: Notes on Committed Youth.* New York: Harcourt Brace Jovanovich, Inc., 1968.

Kimball, B. "Case Studies in Educational Failure during Adolescence." *American Journal of Orthopsychiatry*, **23** (1953), 406–415.

———. "The Sentence-Completion Technique in a Study of Scholastic Under-achievement." *Journal of Consulting Psychology*, **16** (1952), 353–358.

Kinsey, A. C., W. B. Pomeroy, and C. E. Martin. *Sexual Behavior in the Human Male.* Philadelphia: W. B. Saunders Company, 1948.

Kinsey, A. C., W. B. Pomeroy, C. E. Martin, and P. H. Gebhard. *Sexual Behavior in the Human Female.* Philadelphia: W. B. Saunders Company, 1953.

Klein, G. S. "Freud's Two Theories of Sexuality." In *Clinical-Cognitive Psychology: Models and Integrations,* ed. L. Breger. Englewood Cliffs, N.J.: Prentice-Hall, Inc., 1971.

Koestler, A. *Arrow in the Blue: An Autobiography.* New York: The Macmillan Company, 1952.

Kohlberg, L. "A Cognitive-Developmental Analysis of Children's Sex-Role Concepts and Attitudes." In *The Development of Sex Differences,* ed. E. E. Maccoby. Stanford, Calif.: Stanford University Press, 1966.

———. "Development of Moral Character and Moral Ideology." In *Review of Child Development Research,* Vol. 1, ed. M. L. Hoffman and L. W. Hoffman. New York: Russell Sage Foundation, 1964.

Köhler, W. *The Mentality of Apes,* trans. E. Winter. New York: Harcourt Brace Jovanovich, Inc., 1922.

Kohn, M. L. "Social Class and Parent-Child Relationships: An Interpretation." *American Journal of Sociology*, **68** (1963), 471–480.

Komarovsky, M. *Women in the Modern World.* Boston: Little, Brown & Company, 1953.

Korchin, S. J., and G. E. Ruff. "Personality Characteristics of the Mercury Astronauts." In *The Threat of Impending Disaster,* ed. G. H. Grosser, H. Wechsler, and M. Greenblatt. Cambridge, Mass.: Massachusetts Institute of Technology Press, 1964.

Krasner, L. and L. P. Ullmann. *Research in Behavior Modification: New Developments and Implications.* New York: Holt, Rinehart and Winston, Inc., 1965.

Kris, E. *Psychoanalytic Exploration in Art.* New York: International Universities Press, Inc., 1952.

Kroeber, T. C. "The Coping Functions of the Ego Mechanisms." In *The Study of Lives,* ed. R. W. White. New York: Atherton Press, 1964.

Landreth, C. *Education of the Young Child.* New York: John Wiley & Sons, Inc., 1942.

———. *The Psychology of Early Childhood.* New York: Alfred A. Knopf, Inc., 1958.

Lasko, J. K. "Parent Behavior toward First and Second Children." *Genetic Psychology Monographs,* **49** (1954), 97–137.

Lawrence, D. H. *Sons and Lovers.* New York: The Modern Library, 1913.

Le Dantec, F. *L'egoïsme, seule Base de toute Société.* Paris: Flammarion, 1916.

Leeper, R. W. "A Motivational Theory of Emotion to Replace 'Emotion as Disorganized Response.' " *Psychological Review,* **55** (1948), 5–21.

Lefcourt, H. M. "Internal vs. External Control of Reinforcement: A Review." *Psychological Bulletin,* **65** (1966), 206–220.

Lenrow, P. B. "Studies of Sympathy." In *Affect, Cognition and Personality: Empirical Studies,* ed. S. S. Tomkins and C. E. Izard. New York: Springer Publishing Company, Inc., 1965.

Lerner, E. "The Problem of Perspective in Moral Reasoning." *American Journal of Sociology,* **43** (1937), 249–269.

Levinson, D. J. "Role, Personality, and Social Structure in the Organizational Setting." *Journal of Abnormal and Social Psychology,* **58** (1959), 170–180.

Levy, D. M. "Experiments on the Sucking Reflex and Social Behavior in Dogs." *American Journal of Orthopsychiatry,* **4** (1934), 203–224.

———. "Hostility Patterns in Sibling Rivalry Experiments." *American Journal of Orthopsychiatry,* **6** (1936), 183–257.

———. *Maternal Overprotection.* New York: Columbia University Press, 1943.

———. "Oppositional Syndromes and Oppositional Behavior." In *Psychopathology of Childhood,* ed. P. H. Hoch and J. Zubin. New York: Grune & Stratton, Inc., 1955.

———. "Release Therapy." *American Journal of Orthopsychiatry,* **9** (1939), 713–736.

Lewis, C. S. *The Four Loves.* New York: Harcourt Brace Jovanovich, Inc., 1960.

———. *Surprised by Joy.* New York: Harcourt Brace Jovanovich, Inc., 1955.

Lewis, O. *The Children of Sanchez: Autobiography of a Mexican Family.* New York: Random House, Inc., 1961.

Lidz, T., et al. *Schizophrenia and the Family.* New York: International Universities Press, Inc., 1965.

Lindemann, E. "Symptomatology and Management of Acute Grief." *American Journal of Psychiatry,* **101** (1944), 141–148.

Lindzey, G., and D. Byrne. "Measurement of Social Choice and Interpersonal Attractiveness." In *Handbook of Social Psychology,* Vol. 2, 2d ed., ed. G. Lindzey and E. Aronson. Reading, Mass.: Addison-Wesley Publishing Company, Inc., 1968.

Lippitt, R., N. Polansky, and S. Rosen. "The Dynamics of Power." *Human Relations,* **5** (1952), 37–64.

Lorenz, K. *On Aggression,* trans. M. K. Wilson. New York: Harcourt Brace Jovanovich, Inc., 1963.

Macaulay, J. R., and J. Berkowitz, eds. *Altruism and Helping Behavior.* New York: Academic Press, Inc., 1970.

Maccoby, E. E., ed. *The Development of Sex Differences.* Stanford, Calif.: Stanford University Press, 1966.

MacFarlane, J. W. "Perspectives on Personal Consistency and Change: The Guidance Study." *Vita Humana,* **7** (1964), 115–126.

Machiavelli, N. *The Prince,* trans. N. H. Hill, 3d ed. Oxford: The Clarendon Press, 1913.

MacKinnon, D. W. "The Creativity of Architects." In *Widening Horizons in Creativity*, ed. C. W. Taylor. New York: John Wiley & Sons, Inc., 1964.

———. "Creativity and Images of the Self." In *The Study of Lines*, ed. R. W. White. New York: Atherton Press, 1963.

Madison, P. *Personality Development in College*. Reading, Mass.: Addison-Wesley Publishing Company, Inc., 1969.

Malcolm X. *The Autobiography of Malcolm X*. New York: Grove Press, Inc., 1965.

Mann, T. *Stories of Three Decades*, trans. H. T. Lowe-Porter. New York: Alfred A. Knopf, Inc., 1936.

Marcia, J. E. "Development and Validation of Ego Identity Status." *Journal of Personality and Social Psychology*, **3** (1966), 551–559.

———. "Ego Identity Status: Relationship to Change in Self-esteem, 'General Maladjustment,' and Authoritarianism." *Journal of Personality*, **35** (1967), 118–133.

Marquand, J. P. *The Late George Apley*. Boston: Little, Brown & Company, 1937.

Martin, W. E., and C. B. Stendler, eds. *Readings in Child Development*. New York: Harcourt Brace Jovanovich, Inc., 1954.

Maslow, A. H. *Motivation and Personality*. New York: Harper & Row, Publishers, 1954; 2d ed., 1970.

McArthur, C. C. "Personality Differences between Middle and Upper Classes." *Journal of Abnormal and Social Psychology,* **50** (1955), 247–254.

———. "Personalities of First and Second Children." *Psychiatry*, **19** (1956), 47–54.

McClelland, D. C. "The Psychodynamics of Creative Physical Scientists." In *Contemporary Approaches to Creative Thinking,* ed. H. E. Gruber, G. Terrill, and M. Wertheimer. New York: Atherton Press, 1962.

———. *The Roots of Consciousness*. Princeton, N.J.: D. Van Nostrand Company, Inc., 1964.

McClelland, D. C., J. W. Atkinson, R. A. Clark, and E. A. Lowell. *The Achievement Motive*. New York: Appleton-Century-Crofts, 1954.

McCurdy, H. G. *The Personal World*. New York: Harcourt Brace Jovanovich, Inc., 1961.

McDougall, W. *An Introduction to Social Psychology* (1908), 16th ed. Boston: John W. Luce and Company, 1923.

Mead, G. H. *Mind, Self and Society*. Chicago: University of Chicago Press, 1934.

Mead, M. *Sex and Temperament in Three Primitive Societies*. New York: William Morrow & Company, Inc., 1935.

Meers, D. R., and A. E. Marans. "Group Care of Infants in Other Countries." In *Early Child Care: The New Perspectives,* ed. L. L. Dittman. New York: Atherton Press, 1968.

Merton, R. K. "Bureaucratic Structure and Personality." *Social Forces,* **18** (1940), 560–568.

Mill, J. S. *Autobiography* (1873). New York: Columbia University Press, 1924.

Miller, W. B. "Lower Class Culture as a Generating Milieu of Gang Delinquency." *Journal of Social Issues,* **14** (1958), 5–19.

Mira, E. *Psychiatry in War*. New York: W. W. Norton & Company, Inc., 1943.

Mischel, W. "A Social-Learning View of Sex Differences in Behavior." In *The Development of Sex Differences,* ed. E. E. Maccoby. Stanford, Calif.: Stanford University Press, 1966.

Mishler, E. J., and N. E. Waxler. "Family Interaction Processes and Schizophrenia: A Review of Current Theories." *The Merrill-Palmer Quarterly,* **11** (1965), 269–315. Reprinted in *The Psychosocial Interior of the Family,* ed. G. Handel. Chicago: Aldine Publishing Company, 1967.

Mittelmann, B. "Motility in Infants, Children, and Adults." *Psychoanalytic Study of the Child,* **9** (1954), 142–177.

Moment, D., and A. Zaleznik. *Role Development and Interpersonal Competence.* Boston: Harvard Business School, Division of Research, 1963.

Morgan, C. D., and H. A. Murray. "A Method for Investigating Fantasies." *Archives of Neurology and Psychiatry,* **34** (1935), 289–306.

Munroe, R. *Teaching the Individual.* New York: Columbia University Press, 1942.

Murphy, E. B., E. Silber, G. V. Coelho, and D. A. Hamburg. "Development of Autonomy and Parent-Child Interaction in Late Adolescence." *American Journal of Orthopsychiatry,* **33** (1952), 643–652.

Murphy, G. "Psychological Views of Personality and Contributions to Its Study." In *The Study of Personality: An Interdisciplinary Appraisal,* ed. E. Norbeck, D. Price-Williams, and W. M. McCord. New York: Holt, Rinehart and Winston, Inc., 1968, Chap. 1.

———. *Personality: A Biosocial Approach to Origin and Structure.* New York: Harper & Row, Publishers, 1947.

Murphy, L. B. *Social Behavior and Child Personality.* New York: Columbia University Press, 1937.

———. *The Widening World of Childhood: Paths toward Mastery.* New York: Basic Books, Inc., 1962.

Murray, H. A. *Assessment of Men.* New York: Holt, Rinehart and Winston, Inc., 1948.

———. *Explorations in Personality.* London: Oxford University Press, 1938.

Mussen, P. H. "Some Antecedents and Consequents of Masculine Sex-Typing in Adolescent Boys." *Psychological Monographs,* **75,** no. 2 (whole no. 506) (1961).

Mussen, P. H., and L. Distler. "Masculinity, Identification, and Father-Son Relationships." *Journal of Abnormal and Social Psychology,* **59** (1959), 352–356.

Mussen, P. H., and M. C. Jones. "Self-Conceptions, Motivations, and Interpersonal Attitudes of Late- and Early-Maturing Boys." *Child Development,* **28** (1957), 243–256.

Nash, J. "The Father in Contemporary Culture and Current Psychological Literature." *Child Development,* **36** (1965), 261–297.

Neff, W. S. *Work and Human Behavior.* New York: Atherton Press, 1968.

Neill, A. S. *Freedom—Not License!* New York: Hart Publishing Company, 1966.

———. *Summerhill: A Radical Approach to Child Rearing.* New York: Hart Publishing Company, 1960.

Newcomb, T. M. *Social Psychology.* New York: Holt, Rinehart and Winston, Inc., 1950.

———. "The Varieties of Interpersonal Attraction." In *Group Dynamics,* 2d ed., ed. D. Cartwright and A. Zander. New York: Harper & Row, Publishers, 1960.

Nietzsche, F. *The Will to Power: An Attempted Transvaluation of All Values,* trans. A. M. Ludovici. London: T. N. Foulis, 1914.

Offer, D. *The Psychological World of the Teenager.* New York: Basic Books, Inc., 1969.

Overstreet, H. A. *The Mature Mind.* New York: W. W. Norton & Company, Inc., 1949.

Parsons, T. *The Social System.* New York: The Free Press, 1951.

Parsons, T., and R. F. Bales. *Family, Socialization and Interaction Process.* New York: The Free Press, 1955.

Parten, M. B. "Leadership among Preschool Children." *Journal of Abnormal and Social Psychology,* **27** (1933), 430–440.

Pavlov, I. P. *Conditioned Reflexes and Psychiatry,* trans. W. H. Gantt. New York: International Publishers, 1941.

Payne, R. *The Life and Death of Mahatma Gandhi.* New York: E. P. Dutton & Company, Inc., 1969.

Pedersen, F. A., and P. H. Wender. "Early Social Correlates of Cognitive Functioning in Six-Year-Old Boys." *Child Development,* **37** (1968), 185–194.

Perry, W. G., Jr. *Forms of Intellectual and Ethical Development during the College Years.* New York: Holt, Rinehart and Winston, Inc., 1970.

Pervin, L. A. "Performance and Satisfaction as a Function of Individual-Environment Fit." *Psychological Bulletin,* **69** (1968), 56–68.

Peterson, D. R. *The Clinical Study of Social Behavior.* New York: Appleton-Century-Crofts, 1968.

Pettigrew, T. F. *A Profile of the Negro American.* Princeton, N.J.: D. Van Nostrand Company, Inc., 1964.

Piaget, J. *The Construction of Reality by the Child,* trans. M. Cook. New York: Basic Books, Inc., 1954.

———. *The Judgment and Reasoning of the Child.* New York: Harcourt Brace Jovanovich, Inc., 1928.

———. *The Language and Thought of the Child,* trans. M. Warden. New York: Harcourt Brace Jovanovich, Inc., 1926.

———. *The Moral Judgment of the Child.* New York: Harcourt Brace Jovanovich, Inc., 1932.

———. *The Origins of Intelligence in Children,* trans. M. Cook. New York: International Universities Press, Inc., 1952.

———. *The Psychology of Intelligence,* trans. M. Piercy and D. E. Berlyne. London: Routledge & Kegan Paul Ltd., 1947.

Plant, J. S. *Personality and the Cultural Pattern.* New York: The Commonwealth Fund, 1937.

Rabin, A. I. *Growing Up in the Kibbutz.* New York: Springer Publishing Company, Inc., 1965.

Rainwater, L. "Crucible of Identity: The Negro Lower Class Family." *Daedalus,* **95** (1966), 172–216. Reprinted in *The Psychosocial Interior of the Family,* ed. G. Handel. Chicago: Aldine Publishing Company, 1967.

Rapoport, R., and R. N. Rapoport. "New Light on the Honeymoon." *Human Relations,* **17** (1964), 33–56.

Rau, S. Rama. *Remember the House.* New York: Harper & Row, Publishers, 1956.

Rausch, H. L., W. Goodrich, and J. D. Campbell. "Adaptation to the First Years of Marriage." *Psychiatry,* **26** (1963), 368–380.

Rausch, H. L., and B. Sweet. "The Preadolescent Ego: Some Observations of Normal Children." *Psychiatry,* **24** (1961), 122–132.

Reich, W. *Character-Analysis,* 3d ed., trans. T. P. Wolfe. New York: Orgone Institute Press, 1949.

Reinhardt, R. F. "The Outstanding Jet Pilot." *American Journal of Psychiatry,*
    127 (1970), 32–36.
Reiss, I. L. *Premarital Sexual Standards in America.* New York: The Free Press,
    1960.
Reppucci, N. D. "Individual Differences in the Consideration of Information among
    Two-Year-Old Children." *Developmental Psychology,* **2** (1970), 240–246.
Ribble, M. A. *The Rights of Infants.* New York: Columbia University Press, 1943.
Rieff, P. *The Triumph of the Therapeutic: Uses of Faith after Freud.* New York:
    Harper & Row, Publishers, 1966.
———. *Freud: The Mind of the Moralist.* New York: The Viking Press, Inc.,
    1959.
Riesman, D. *The Lonely Crowd: A Study of the Changing American Character.*
    New Haven, Conn.: Yale University Press, 1950.
Robertson, J., ed. *Hospitals and Children.* New York: International Universities
    Press, Inc., 1968.
Roe, A. "Artists and Their Work." *Journal of Personality,* **15** (1946), 1–40.
———. *The Making of a Scientist.* New York: Dodd, Mead & Company, Inc.,
    1953.
———. "A Psychological Study of Physical Scientists." *Genetic Psychology Mono-
    graphs,* **43** (1951), 121–239.
———. "A Study of Eminent Psychologists and Anthropologists, and a Com-
    parison with Biological and Physical Scientists." *Psychological Mono-
    graphs,* **67,** no. 2 (1953).
Roe, A., and M. Siegelman. *The Origin of Interests.* Washington, D.C.: APGA
    Inquiry Studies, no. 1, 1964.
Rosen, B. C. "Social Class and the Child's Perception of the Parent." *Child Devel-
    opment,* **35** (1964), 1147–1153.
Rosenfeld, H. M., and D. M. Baer. "Unnoticed Verbal Conditioning of an Aware
    Experimenter by a More Aware Subject: The Double-Agent Effect."
    Psychological Review, **76** (1969), 425–432.
Rosenzweig, S. "Types of Reaction to Frustration." *Journal of Abnormal and
    Social Psychology,* **29** (1934), 298–300.
Rossi, A. S. "Equality between the Sexes: An Immodest Proposal," in "The Woman
    in America." *Daedalus,* **93** (1964), 607–652.
Rousseau, J. J. *The Confessions of Jean Jacques Rousseau* (1768). New York:
    The Modern Library.
———. *The New Héloise* (1760). New York: The Modern Library.
Roy, D. F. " 'Banana Time': Job Satisfaction and Informal Interaction." *Human
    Organization,* **18** (1960), 158–168.
Rubin, Z. "Measurment of Romantic Love." *Journal of Personality and Social
    Psychology,* **16** (1970), 265–273.
Ruff, G. E., and S. J. Korchin. "Psychological Responses of the Mercury Astro-
    nauts to Stress." In *The Threat of Impending Disaster,* ed. G. H. Grosser,
    H. Wechsler, and M. Greenblatt. Cambridge, Mass.: Massachusetts
    Institute of Technology Press, 1964.
Sanford, F. H. "Speech and Personality: A Comparative Case Study." *Character
    and Personality,* **10** (1942), 169–198.
Sanford, N. *The American College.* New York: John Wiley & Sons, Inc., 1962.
———. "The Dynamics of Identification." *Psychological Review,* **62** (1955),
    106–118.

Sarton, M. *Kinds of Love*. New York: W. W. Norton & Company, Inc., 1970.

Sartre, J.-P. *The Words*, trans. B. Frechtman. New York: George Braziller, Inc., 1964.

Saul, L. J. *Emotional Maturity*, 2nd ed. Philadelphia: J. B. Lippincott Company, 1947.

Schachter, S. "Birth Order, Eminence and Higher Education." *American Sociological Review,* **28** (1963), 757–768.

Schaefer, E. W. "A Circumplex Model for Maternal Behavior." *Journal of Abnormal and Social Psychology,* **59** (1959), 226–235.

Schnabel, E. *Anne Frank: A Portrait in Courage,* trans. R. and C. Winston. New York: Harcourt Brace Jovanovich, Inc., 1958.

Schreiber, D., ed. *Profile of the School Dropout*. New York: Alfred A. Knopf, Inc., 1968.

Schur, E. M., ed. *The Family and the Sexual Revolution: Selected Readings*. Bloomington, Ind.: Indiana University Press, 1964.

Schwarz, O. *The Psychology of Sex*. Baltimore: Penguin Books, 1949.

Scott, J. P. *Aggression*. Chicago: University of Chicago Press, 1958.

Sears, R. R. "Ordinal Position in the Family as a Psychological Variable." *American Sociological Review,* **15** (1950), 397–401.

Sears, R. R., E. Maccoby, and H. Levin. *Patterns of Child Rearing*. New York: Harper & Row, Publishers, 1957.

Sechrest, L., and J. Wallace, Jr. *Psychology and Human Problems*. Columbus, Ohio: Charles E. Merrill Books, Inc., 1967.

Senn, M., J. E., and C. Hartford, eds. *The Firstborn: Experiences of Eight American Families*. Cambridge, Mass.: Harvard University Press, 1968.

Sewall, M. "Two Studies of Sibling Rivalry, I. Some Causes of Jealousy in Young Children." *Smith College Studies in Social Work,* **1** (1930), 6–32.

Sheldon, W. H., and S. S. Stevens. *The Varieties of Temperament*. New York: Harper & Row, Publishers, 1942.

Sheldon, W. H., S. S. Stevens, and W. B. Tucker. *The Varieties of Human Physique*. New York: Harper & Row, Publishers, 1940.

Sherif, M., and H. Cantril. *The Psychology of Ego-Involvements*. New York: John Wiley & Sons, Inc., 1947.

Sherif, M., O. J. Harvey, B. J. White, W. R. Hood, and C. W. Sherif. *Intergroup Conflict and Cooperation: The Robbers Cave Experiment*. Norman, Okla.: Institute of Group Relations, University of Oklahoma, 1961.

Silber, E., D. A. Hamburg, G. V. Coelho, E. B. Murphy, M. Rosenberg, and L. D. Pearlin. "Adaptive Behavior in Competent Adolescents: Coping with the Anticipation of College." *Archives of General Psychiatry,* **5** (1961), 354–365.

Silbert, A. R. "Achievement and Underachievement." Unpublished Ph.D. Dissertation, Harvard University, 1960.

Silverberg, W. V. *Childhood Experience and Personal Destiny*. New York: Springer Publishing Company, Inc., 1952.

Singer, J. L. *Daydreaming: An Introduction to the Experimental Study of Inner Experience*. New York: Random House, Inc., 1966.

Skinner, B. F. *Science and Human Behavior*. New York: The Macmillan Company, 1953.

Smith, M. B., J. S. Bruner, and R. W. White. *Opinions and Personality*. New York: John Wiley & Sons, Inc., 1956.

Snow, C. P. *The Two Cultures and the Scientific Revolution.* London: Cambridge University Press, 1959.

Solomon, R. L., and L. C. Wynne. "Traumatic Avoidance Learning: The Principles of Anxiety Conservation and Partial Irreversibility." *Psychological Review,* **61** (1954), 353–385.

Spiegel, J. P. "The Resolution of Role Conflict within the Family." *Psychiatry,* **20** (1957), 1–16.

Spitz, R. A. "Hospitalism: An Inquiry into the Genesis of Psychiatric Conditions in Early Childhood." *Psychoanalytic Study of the Child,* **1** (1945), 53–74.

———. "Anaclitic Depression." *Psychoanalytic Study of the Child,* **2** (1946), 313–342.

Stein, M. I., J. N. MacKenzie, R. R. Rodgers, and B. Meer. "A Case Study of a Scientist." In *Clinical Studies in Personality,* ed. A. Burton and R. E. Harris. New York: Harper & Row, Publishers, 1955.

Stern, W. *Psychology of Early Childhood* (1914), 2d English ed., trans. A. Barwell. New York: Holt, Rinehart and Winston, Inc., 1930.

Sullivan, H. S. *The Interpersonal Theory of Psychiatry.* New York: W. W. Norton & Company, Inc., 1953.

Tasch, R. J. "The Role of the Father in the Family." *Journal of Experimental Education,* **20** (1952), 319–361.

Terman, L. M. "Genetic Studies of Genius." In *The Mental and Physical Traits of a Thousand Gifted Children,* Vol. 1. Stanford, Calif.: Stanford University Press, 1925.

Tharp, R. G. "Psychological Patterning in Marriage." *Psychological Bulletin,* **60** (1963), 97–117.

Thomas, A., S. Chess, H. G. Birch, M. E. Hertzig, and S. Korn. *Behavioral Individuality in Early Childhood.* New York: New York University Press, 1963.

Thurber, J. "The Secret Life of Walter Mitty." In *My Life—and Welcome to It.* New York: Harcourt Brace Jovanovich, Inc., 1942.

Thurstone, L. L. *Primary Mental Abilities.* Chicago: University of Chicago Press, 1938.

Toman, W. *Family Constellation: Its Effects on Personality and Social Behavior,* 2nd ed. New York: Springer Publishing Company, 1969.

Torrance, E. P. *Guiding Creative Talent.* Englewood Cliffs, N.J.: Prentice-Hall, Inc., 1962.

Trent, J. W., and L. L. Medsker. *Beyond High School: A Psychological Study of 10,000 High School Graduates.* San Francisco: Jossey-Bass, Inc., 1968.

Tumin, M. M. *Social Stratification: The Forms and Functions of Inequality.* Englewood Cliffs, N.J.: Prentice-Hall, Inc., 1967.

Varendonck, J. *The Psychology of Daydreams.* London: The Macmillan Company, 1921.

Venable, V. *Human Nature: The Marxian View.* New York: Alfred A. Knopf, Inc., 1945.

Vogel, E. F., and N. W. Bell. "The Emotionally Disturbed Child as a Family Scapegoat." In *A Modern Introduction to the Family,* ed. E. F. Vogel and N. W. Bell. New York: The Free Press, 1960.

Wallach, M. A., and N. Kogan. *Modes of Thinking in Young Children: A Study of the Creativity-Intelligence Distinction.* New York: Holt, Rinehart and Winston, Inc., 1965.

Ward, W. D. "Process of Sex-Role Development." *Developmental Psychology,* **1** (1969), 163–168.

Warner, W. L. et al. *Democracy in Jonesville: A Study in Quality and Inequality.* New York: Harper & Row, Publishers, 1949.

Warren, J. R. "Birth Order and Social Behavior." *Psychological Bulletin,* **65** (1966), 38–49.

Washburn, R. W. "A Study of the Smiling and Laughing of Infants in the First Year of Life." *Genetic Psychology Monographs,* **6** (1929), pp. 397–537.

Watson, J. B. *Psychology from the Standpoint of a Behaviorist.* Philadelphia: J. B. Lippincott Company, 1919.

Weatherley, D. "Self-perceived Rate of Physical Maturation and Personality in Late Adolescence." *Child Development,* **35** (1964), 1197–1210.

Webb, Charles. *The Graduate.* Philadelphia: J. B. Lippincott Company, 1963.

Webb, Constance. *Richard Wright: A Biography.* New York: G. P. Putnam's Sons, 1968.

Weber, M. *The Protestant Ethic and the Spirit of Capitalism* (1904), trans. T. Parsons. New York: Charles Scribner's Sons, 1958.

Welker, W. I. "Some Determinants of Play and Exploration in Young Chimpanzees." *Journal of Comparative and Physiological Psychology,* **49** (1956), 84–89.

Wells, H. G. *Experiment in Autobiography.* New York: The Macmillan Company, 1934.

——. *The Outline of History.* New York: The Macmillan Company, 1920.

Wenar, C. *Personality Development from Infancy to Adolescence.* Boston: Houghton Mifflin Company, 1971.

Wessman, A. E., and D. F. Ricks. *Mood and Personality.* New York: Holt, Rinehart and Winston, Inc., 1966.

Wessman, A. E., D. F. Ricks, and Mary McI. Tyl. "Characteristics and Concomitants of Mood Fluctuation in College Women." *Journal of Abnormal and Social Psychology,* **60** (1960), 117–126.

Westley, W. A., and N. B. Epstein. *The Silent Majority.* San Francisco: Jossey-Bass, Inc., 1970.

White, B. L. "An Experimental Approach to the Effects of Experience on Early Human Behavior." In *Minnesota Symposium on Child Psychology,* Vol. 1, ed. J. P. Hill. Minneapolis: University of Minnesota Press, 1967.

White, R. K. "*Black Boy:* A Value Analysis." *Journal of Abnormal and Social Psychology,* **42** (1947), 440–461.

White, R. W. *The Abnormal Personality,* 3d ed. New York: The Ronald Press Company, 1964.

——. "Competence and the Psychosexual Stages of Development." In *Nebraska Symposium on Motivation,* ed. M. R. Jones. Lincoln, Neb.: University of Nebraska Press, 1960.

——. "Ego and Reality in Psychoanalytic Theory." *Psychological Issues,* **3,** no. 3 (Monograph 11) (1963).

——. *Lives in Progress: A Study of the Natural Growth of Personality,* 2d ed. New York: Holt, Rinehart and Winston, Inc., 1966.

——. "Motivation Reconsidered: The Concept of Competence." *Psychological Review,* **66** (1959), 297–333.

——, ed. *The Study of Lives.* New York: Atherton Press, 1963.

Whiting, J. W. M., and B. B. Whiting. "Contributions of Anthropology to the

Methods of Studying Child Rearing." In *Handbook of Research Methods in Child Development*, ed. P. H. Mussen. New York: John Wiley & Sons, Inc., 1960.

Whyte, W. H., Jr. *The Organization Man.* New York: Simon and Schuster, Inc., 1956.

Winch, R. F. *Mate Selection: A Study of Complementary Needs.* New York: Harper & Row, Publishers, 1958.

Wolfe, T. *Look Homeward, Angel.* New York: Charles Scribner's Sons, 1929.

Wolfenstein, M. "Trends in Infant Care." *American Journal of Orthopsychiatry,* **23** (1953), 120–130.

Wood, A. B. "Another Psychologist Analyzed." *Journal of Abnormal and Social Psychology,* **36** (1941), 87–90.

Worchel, P. "Catharsis and the Relief of Hostility." *Journal of Abnormal and Social Psychology,* **55** (1957), 238–243.

Wright, R. *Black Boy: A Record of Childhood and Youth.* New York: Harper & Row, Publishers, 1945.

————. *Native Son.* New York: Harper & Row, Publishers, 1940.

Wylie, R. *The Self Concept: A Critical Survey of Pertinent Research Literature.* Lincoln, Neb.: University of Nebraska Press, 1963.

Wynne, L., I. Ryckoff, J. Day, and S. Hirsch. "Pseudo-mutuality in the Family Relations of Schizophrenics." *Psychiatry,* **21** (1958), 205–220.

Yarrow, L. J. "Separation from Parents during Early Childhood." In *Review of Child Development Research,* Vol. 1, ed. M. L. Hoffman and L. W. Hoffman. New York: Russell Sage Foundation, 1964.

Yates, E. *Is There a Doctor in the Barn?* New York: E. P. Dutton & Company, 1966.

Young, M., and P. Willmott. *Family and Kinship in East London.* London: Routledge & Kegan Paul Ltd., 1957.

Zachry, C. B. *Emotion and Conduct in Adolescence.* New York: Appleton-Century-Crofts, 1940.

Author Index

Subject Index